Africans in Colonial Louisiana

GWENDOLYN MIDLO HALL

Africans in Colonial Louisiana

The Development of Afro-Creole Culture in the Eighteenth Century

LOUISIANA STATE UNIVERSITY PRESS   Baton Rouge

Published by Louisiana State University Press
Copyright © 1992 by Louisiana State University Press
All rights reserved
Manufactured in the United States of America

Designer: Amanda McDonald Key
Typeface: Palatino
Typesetter: G & S Typesetters, Inc.

Library of Congress Cataloging in Publication Data

Hall, Gwendolyn Midlo.
    Africans in colonial Louisiana : the development of Afro-Creole
culture in the eighteenth century / Gwendolyn Midlo Hall.
      p.   cm.
    Includes bibliographical references and index.
    ISBN 0-8071-1686-6 (cloth)
    ISBN 0-8071-1999-7 (paper)
    1. Afro-Americans—Louisiana—History—18th century. 2. Creoles—
Louisiana—History—18th century. 3. Slavery—Louisiana—
History—18th century. 4. Louisiana—History—To 1803. I. Title.
II. Title: Afro-Creole culture in the eighteenth century.
E185.93.L6H16 1992   91-46648
976.3'00496073—dc20   CIP

Louisiana Paperback Edition, 1995
15   14   13   12   11   10   09   08   07   06
11   10   9   8   7

To the memory of my late husband, Harry Haywood (Haywood Hall), 1898–1985, son of slaves, a self-educated and brilliant theoretician and a fighter for the freedom of African-Americans and for all the exploited and oppressed throughout the world, and to our two children, Dr. Haywood Hall, Jr., and Rebecca L. Hall, Esq.

Contents

Contents

Illustrations

Figures and Tables

Figures and Tables

Preface

Southern history has long played the role of myth reinforcing racism. While a great deal of progress has been made since World War II in rewriting the history of the Chesapeake and the Carolinas, the history, especially the colonial history, of Louisiana has been badly neglected. This neglect stems partially from the Anglophone orientation of American historians. All the documentation for colonial Louisiana is in French and Spanish. Both languages are necessary to study the Spanish, as well as the French, period. The manuscripts are scattered about in France, Spain, and Louisiana. Furthermore, Louisiana history, especially the history of race relations, cannot be fit into neat, rigid categories. In colonial Louisiana, there was more chaos than order. The study of any one historical question taken out of context leads to serious distortions. Colonial Louisiana was a complex, changing society that responded to a great extent to international pressures. "National" history must be transcended, and colonial history treated within a global context.

In Louisiana, it is especially important to avoid treating the formation of slave culture in isolation, as if it were sealed off from the rest of society and the world. Culture is a dynamic process. The definition of *culture* as socially acquired knowledge, as, according to Goodenough, "what people have to learn as distinct from their biological heritage . . . whatever it is one has to know or believe in order to operate in a manner acceptable to its members"[1] is far too static. Eric R. Wolf's redefinition of *culture* as "a series of processes that construct, reconstruct, and dismantle cultural materials, in response to identifiable determinants," is closer to the mark.[2] In the Americas, new cultures were formed through intense, and often violent, contacts among peoples of varied nations, races, classes, languages, and traditions. The Europeans in this equation were far from omnipotent.

1. W. H. Goodenough, "Cultural Anthropology and Linguistics," in *Report on the Seventh Annual Round Table Meeting on Linguistics and Language,* ed. P. L. Garvin (Washington, D.C., 1957), quoted in R. A. Hudson, *Sociolinguistics* (Cambridge, Eng., 1980, 74.
2. Eric R. Wolf, *Europe and the People Without History* (Berkeley, 1982), 387.

It is wrong to assume that there was an all-powerful, static, national culture and society brought over by the European colonizers into which non-Europeans were more or less socialized and acculturated.[3] Cultural influences intensely interpenetrated the extremely varied population of the Americas. Like the Indians and the Africans, Europeans were acculturated by the peoples, and by the world, they encountered.

Patterns of behavior and response among newcomers, whether European or African, were molded by the situation they encountered when they arrived. The cultural assumptions they brought with them were often useless and had to be modified or discarded. In French Louisiana, there was a long period of chaos and violence. These conditions selected the most plastic, open, flexible elements from among the distinct cultures of the red, white, and black peoples who met and mingled. Almost-constant warfare and frequent famine subjected acquired beliefs and standards of behavior to enormous stress. The shift from French to Spanish and then to American rule did not allow for a stable model of behavior and belief that could be enforced by the larger social structure.

The Louisiana experience calls into question the assumption that African slaves could not regroup themselves in language and social communities derived partly from the sending cultures. This study focuses to some extent on the changing patterns of introduction of Africans of specific ethnic groups, ages, and genders and the conditions they encountered that allowed them to adapt and reinterpret elements of the cultures they brought with them. It firmly embraces a dynamic, developmental approach to culture formation and explicitly rejects a structuralist approach, avoiding a masculine vision of power and control, which assumes that culture is a static thing passed on and enforced from the top of the social hierarchy. Culture is a creation of the folk and is passed on to a great extent by parents, especially by biological mothers and women who played the role of mothers for whites as well as for Afro-Creoles. Cultural materials were more or less functional in a dynamic world and were preserved or discarded mainly in response to their usefulness to the agonizing process of survival while a new world was being created. Culturally, all Americans owe a deep debt to Africa.

Colonial Louisiana left behind a heritage and tradition of offi-

3. For an influential contrary view, see Louis Hartz, *The Founding of New Societies: Studies in the History of the United States, Latin America, South Africa and Australia* (New York, 1964).

cial corruption, defiance of authority by the poor of all races, and violence, as well as a brutal, racist tradition that was viewed by its ruling groups as the only means of containing its competent, well-organized, self-confident, and defiant Afro-Creole population. But it also left behind a tradition of racial openness that could never be entirely repressed.

I wish to acknowledge the help of colleagues who were kind enough to read chapters and drafts of this manuscript, giving much-needed help and encouragement. Among my colleagues at Rutgers University, my obligations to Robert A. Rosenberg of the Edison Papers run deep for his enthused, generous attention to my early problems with the database. Rudolph M. Bell, Paul G. E. Clemens, Tilden G. Edelstein, Gerald N. Grob, Allen M. Howard, the late Warren Susman, and Trian Staionavitch, all of the History Department, and Andres Perez y Mena of the Department of Puerto Rican and Hispanic Caribbean Studies have all read portions of earlier versions of the manuscript. Colleagues throughout the profession have been extremely generous with their time and attention. Stanley Engerman read an early draft chapter by chapter, sending prompt and detailed comments. Michael Craton, David Geggus, Arnold Hirsch, John Holm, Morris F. Goodman, Joseph Logsdon, Patrick Manning, Ann Pérotin Dumon, Paul Lachance, Richard Price, John Singler, Ibrahim K. Sundiatta, Emilia Viotti da Costa, and Eric R. Wolf all read portions of an early draft. John H. Clarke allowed me to read to him the chapter on Senegambia and gave helpful suggestions. I am deeply indebted to Ira Berlin for a careful reading of a recent draft, giving frank and extremely useful comments and suggestions. Eugene D. Genovese worked graciously within the framework of my short press deadline, sending his insightful comments upon the final version of the manuscript. David Hackett Fischer sent encouraging words about the importance of the book.

I wish to thank the Rutgers Research Council, the Rutgers Faculty Academic Studies program, the Rutgers President's Coordinating Council on International Programs, the United States Fulbright Commission, the National Endowment for the Humanities Travel to Collections program, and the Program for Cooperation Between the Ministry of Culture of Spain and United States Universities for making it possible for me to travel to Europe and work in archives in France and Spain. I also wish to thank the Louisiana Endowment for the Humanities for financial assistance toward preparing the illustrations. Paul Estrade of the Institut des Etudes Hispaniques et Hispano-

Américaines of the University of Paris VIII and the Equipe de Recherches Histoire des Antilles Hispaniques was kind enough to invite me to spend a most stimulating year working with him and his colleagues. Enriqueta Vila Vilar of the Escuela de Estudios Hispano-Americanos and Justina Sarabia Viejo of the University of Seville were most gracious and helpful to me during my research in Seville. Hernan de Granda of the Departimiento de Filología, Universidad de Valladolid in Spain, extended his department's hospitality to me during my research at the Archivo de Simancas. Jean-Pierre Paute of the University of Dakar was most kind and helpful to me in polishing my oral French during my lecture tour of Francophone Africa, and Mohamed m'Bodj of the History Department, University of Dakar, gave me the privilege of intellectual exchange with him and with his graduate students.

I wish to acknowledge my obligations to the following persons and archives: above all, the Archives Nationales in Paris and its wonderful staff, who bent all the rules for me while I spent several months studying some very difficult documents; the Archive du Port de Lorient; the Archivo General de Indias in Seville; the Archivo de Simancas; the Archivo Histórico Nacional in Madrid; the Amistad Collection at Tulane University, where I was most effectively assisted by Ulysses S. Ricard, Jr.; the Historic New Orleans Collection, where Dr. Alfred E. Lemmon guided me around the microfilm collection of Spanish documents; Steven G. Reinhardt at the Louisiana Historical Center of the Louisiana State Museum; the New Orleans Public Library, where I was generously assisted by Colin Hamer; Sally Reeves of the Notarial Archives, Orleans Parish Civil Court; Una Daigre of the Catholic Life Center of the Archdiocese of Baton Rouge; and the Family History Center of the East Brunswick, New Jersey, branch of the Mormon Genealogy Library, which allowed me to consult invaluable microfilm copies of documents from Pointe Coupee Parish, and where Helen J. Rogers extended every courtesy to me, squeezing me in with busy, dedicated genealogists.

Several women outside the profession have given me invaluable help. Vilma Perez, Secretary of the Department of Puerto Rican and Hispanic Caribbean Studies, Rutgers University, gave me her good-natured support. Lois Katz Brown has been consistently enthusiastic and supportive. Janine Netter, friend of my youth in Paris, gave me her hospitality and enthusiastic interest in my work when I returned to Paris after thirty-two years. My sister, Razele Lehmann, took care of my affairs while I was abroad and has always been there for me. My son, Leo Yuspeh, has been enthusiastic and supportive of my work during the times when parts of him came back. I wish to acknowledge my debt to my father, the late Herman L. Midlo, for shared interests and the example he set, and to my mother, Ethel Midlo, a strong and independent-minded woman whose help was never lacking, even when she did not approve.

Abbreviations and Short Titles

Acts	Acts and Deliberations of the Cabildo of New Orleans, Spanish Transcription, 5 volumes, in Louisiana Collection, New Orleans Public Library
AN	Archives Nationales, Paris
ANC	Section Coloniales, Archives Nationales, Paris
ANM	Section Marine, Archives Nationales, Paris
APL	Archives du Port de Lorient, France
DB Free	Databases created by the writer from Original Acts, Pointe
DB Inventories	Coupee Parish, Pointe Coupee Parish Courthouse, New Roads, Louisiana, microfilm edition by the Mormon Genealogy Society, consulted at the Family History Center in East Brunswick, New Jersey
GM, AS	Sección Guerra Moderna, Archivo de Simancas, Spain
LH	*Louisiana History*
LHQ	*Louisiana Historical Quarterly*
Mina, OAPC	Testimonio del Proceso criminal de los Negros rebueltos de este Puesto contra los blancos de dicho Puesto, June, 1792, Doc. 1758. Spanish transcription by Ulysses S. Ricard, Jr., in Ricard Family Papers, the Amistad Research Center, Tulane University, New Orleans
Mina, AGI	Papeles de Cuba, Legajo 168A, fols. 354–501 (399–546), Archivo General de Indios, Seville, March 26, 1792, through April 8, 1794. Spanish transcription by Ulysses S. Ricard, Jr., in Ricard Family Papers, the Amistad Research Center, Tulane University, New Orleans
MPA	Dunbar Rowland and A. G. Sanders, eds. and trans., *Mississippi Provincial Archives: French Dominion* (3 vols.; Jackson, Miss., 1919–1932), Vols. I–III. Patricia Kay Galloway, ed., and Dunbar Rowland and A. G. Sanders, eds. and trans. *Mississippi Provincial Archives: French Dominion* (2 vols.; Baton Rouge, 1984), Vols. IV–V
OAOP	Original Acts, Orleans Parish, in Notarial Archives, Civil Courts Building, New Orleans

OAPC	Original Acts, Pointe Coupee Parish, Pointe Coupee Parish Courthouse, New Roads, Louisiana
PC, AGI	Papeles Procedentes de Cuba, Archivo General de Indias, Seville
RSC, LHC	Records of the Superior Council of Louisiana, manuscripts housed at the Louisiana Historical Center of the Louisiana State Museum, New Orleans
RSC, *LHQ*	Heloise H. Cruzat, trans., "Records of the Superior Council of Louisiana," *Louisiana Historical Quarterly*, Vols. II–XXII
SD, AGI	Papeles de Santo Domingo, Archivo General de Indias, Seville
SHA	Service Historique de l'Armée, Chateau de Vincennes, France
SJR, LHC	Spanish Judicial Records, manuscripts housed at the Louisiana Historical Center, Louisiana State Museum, New Orleans
SJR, *LHQ*	Laura L. Porteous, trans., "Index to Spanish Judicial Records," *Louisiana Historical Quarterly*, Vols. VI–XXV
Trial, OAPC	Procès contre les esclaves du Poste de Pointe Coupée, May 4–29, 1795, fols. 1–265, Original Acts, Pointe Coupee Parish, Pointe Coupee Parish Courthouse, New Roads, Louisiana

Africans in Colonial Louisiana

CHAPTER 1

Settlers, Soldiers, Indians, and Officials
The Chaos of French Rule

Capon vive longtemps.

The coward lives a long time.
—from Lafcadio Hearn, *Gombo Zhèbes: Little Dictionary of Creole Proverbs*

The colonization of the Americas was the earliest stage of the internationalization of the world. New cultures were formed through the encounter of peoples from Europe, Africa, and the Americas. Varying social and cultural patterns emerged, determined to a great extent by the economy, labor demands and necessary skills, the physical environment, the priorities of the colonizing power, the racial, national, gender, and age structure of the population, and the level of peace, security, and stability prevailing in the various colonies.[1] Louisiana, first colonized by France, was a strategic colony, where military considerations outweighed economic concerns. French control was extremely fragile. French Louisiana was a chaotic world where the cultural materials brought by Africans often turned out to be the most adaptive.

The founding of French Louisiana must be understood within the context of the French empire in North America. France's primary concern was to prevent England from gaining control of the mouth of the Mississippi River.[2] By colonizing the Mississippi Valley, France intended to outflank and surround the British mainland colonies along the Atlantic coast. With control of Canada, the St. Lawrence waterway, and the Mississippi Valley, France could dominate the continent. At the end of the seventeenth century, France, Britain, and Spain rushed to claim the strategic Mississippi River Valley.[3] France explored down the Mississippi River from her Canadian settlements and staked her claim, establishing a beachhead at Biloxi, in 1699, on what is now the Mississippi coast of the Gulf of Mexico.

France was ill equipped to begin this ambitious undertaking. The country was exhausted by the wars of Louis XIV. The War of the Spanish Succession began in 1702, shortly after Louisiana was founded, and raged for more than a decade. France's population had

1. For a discussion of some of these factors in the formation of slave culture in Anglo North America, see Ira Berlin, "Time, Space, and the Evolution of Afro-American Society on British Mainland North America," *American Historical Review*, LXXXV (1980), 44–78.

2. For an excellent, recent study of French colonial policy and its impact upon Louisiana, see Mathé Allain, *"Not Worth a Straw": French Colonial Policy and the Early Years of Louisiana* (Lafayette, La., 1988).

3. W. J. Eccles, *France in America* (New York, 1972), 158; Verner W. Crane, *The Southern Frontier, 1670–1732* (1928; rpr. New York, 1981), 47–70.

been drained and reduced to dire poverty and its treasury bank-
rupted by protracted warfare. An ambitious continental power with
no natural boundaries to protect its frontiers, France was reluctant to
allow the departure of its "useful" population. This vast colony,
which included the entire Mississippi Valley, was therefore thinly
populated by whites, many of whom were the rejects of French society—the defiant ones, both civilians and soldiers, who challenged
and threatened the brutal and exploitative social structure of prerevolutionary France. Others were Canadian *courreurs du bois*, fur
traders who lived in Indian villages and often took Indian women for
wives. Many French settlements of lower Louisiana began in Indian
villages.[4]

The first census of Biloxi, dating from December, 1699, lists 5 officers, at least 2 of whom were Canadians, 5 petty officers, 4 sailors, 19
Canadians, 13 pirates from the Caribbean, 10 laborers, 6 cabin boys,
and 20 soldiers. With this motley crew, France established her claim
to the entire Mississippi Valley and the coast of the Gulf of Mexico
between the Spanish colonies of Florida and New Spain (Mexico). The
colony developed slowly. According to a census taken on August 1,
1706, Louisiana had a total of 85 French and Canadian inhabitants, 48
of whom were in the pay of the king. On August 12, 1708, there were,
in all of Louisiana, 278 persons in French settlements, including 80
Indian slaves of both sexes, 14 major officers, 76 soldiers, including 4
army officers, 13 sailors, including 4 marine officers, 3 Canadians, one
of whom served as interpreter for the Chickasaw language, 1 valet, 3
priests, 6 workers, and 6 cabin boys (*mousses*) who had been brought
in to learn Indian languages, as well as to serve on sea and land. The
garrison totaled 120 men. Aside from Indian slaves and military per-
sonnel, there were only 24 male settlers, 28 women, and 25 children,
none of whom had been assigned land. The Canadian *courreurs du
bois* were the best-adapted colonizers, but they were not considered
legitimate settlers. The 1708 census mentions "over 60 wandering Canadians who are in the Indian villages situated along the Mississippi
River without the permission of any governor and who destroy by
their bad and libertine conduct with the Indian women all that the
missionaries and others teach the savages about the divine mysteries
of the Christian Religion."[5]

4. Marcel Giraud, "France and Louisiana in the Early Eighteenth Century," *Mississippi Valley Historical Review*, XXXVI (1949–50), 657–74.
5. Charles R. Maduell, Jr., *The Census Tables for the French Colony of Louisiana from*

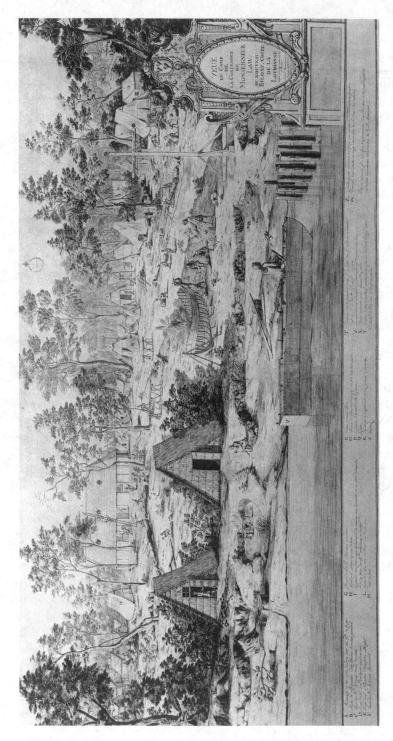

View of the camp of John Law at Biloxi. The original print dates from December, 1720.
Courtesy The Historic New Orleans Collection, Museum/Research Center, Acc. No. 1974.25.10.168.

When Antoine Crozat turned Louisiana over to John Law's Company of the West in 1717, the French population, including men, women, and children, totaled only about 400.[6] The Company of the West was a private company that issued and sold shares. It was granted a monopoly of Louisiana's trade for twenty-five years and of the Canadian beaver trade in perpetuity, and it was given ownership of lands and mines as well as the right to build fortifications and to nominate company directors and colonial officials. The king assumed the responsibility for manning and maintaining the forts and garrisons and for furnishing Indian presents. The Company of the West was expanded to include the Company of Senegal in December, 1718, the Company of China and the East Indian Company in 1719, and the Company of St. Domingue and the Company of Guinea in September, 1720. This conglomerate was then renamed the Company of the Indies.[7]

The advent of John Law and the Company of the West opened the way for the true colonization of Louisiana and its transformation from simply a weak military garrison. Permanent settlers were brought from France in significant numbers. But it was hard to find voluntary colonists in France, and there was, moreover, a great reluctance to allow useful subjects to leave the country. Louis XIV had resisted the notion of populating his colonies by forcing indigent subjects to go to America. But these qualms died with him, and when the Company of the Indies began to colonize Louisiana, a new philosophy prevailed. The French colonization of Louisiana became to a great extent a penal colonization. During 1717 and 1718, the sentences of prisoners who had been condemned to the galleys were commuted, and these prisoners were sent to Louisiana to work for three years. Thereafter, they were to be given part of the land they had cleared and cultivated. The prisoners were brought to the ports under heavy guard and chained aboard the ships. Also during this period, soldiers who had deserted, vagabonds, and persons without means were placed upon lists of those to be deported to Louisiana. Some had been arrested for acts of violence, murders, debauchery, and drunkenness,

---

1699 Through 1732 (Baltimore, 1972), 1–3, 10; Recensement de la colonie de la Louisiane, garnison, habitants, bestiaux, Fort Louis, August 12, 1708, in Ser. C13A 2, fol. 225, ANC (all translations from unpublished French and Spanish documents throughout this volume are by the author).

6. Crozat was granted proprietary rights over Louisiana for fifteen years in 1712, but he abandoned them five years later.

7. Allain, "Not Worth a Straw," 66, 67.

but they were mostly beggars and vagabonds from Paris and all the provinces of France. By 1719, deportation to Louisiana had become a convenient way to get rid of troublesome neighbors or family members. Some families asked for deportation of incorrigible sons, daughters, and nephews. Persons from all social milieux were denounced for their conduct, and police inquiries were held. Comments found in police files included "Here is a true subject for Louisiana" and "A very bad subject who deserves . . . to be among those who are destined for the new colonies."[8]

During 1719, 416 men accompanied by 30 women and children were deported from France to Louisiana. During the same year, 134 more women were deported. Many other women had escaped while being forced toward the ports. Some of the women had been removed from dungeons. One had been accused of fifteen murders. Most of these women were in their thirties and had been accused of theft, debauchery (sometimes with married men), prostitution, repeated lies, blasphemy, irreligion, and assassination. Some were put on the deportation list at the request of their families. The superior of Salpetrière asked that a number of women be deported because of their rebellion in prison. The sister superior asked to "deliver *l'hôpital* and the public from a number of seditious women." By July, 1719, there were more than 220 women on the deportation list.[9]

A special police force received a head tax for each person apprehended for possible deportation. Members of the force roamed around Paris and the provinces grabbing people for profit, their actions often based upon false accusations. Bloody collisions took place in Paris between these police brigades and the population. Kidnapping occurred; fights between police and potential deportees, as well as full-scale riots, erupted in the streets. There were also riots among prisoners in Paris awaiting deportation to Louisiana. On January 1, 1720, the prison of St. Martin-des-Champs held 107 prisoners destined for Louisiana. Fifty men and women forced the doors, wounded 2 guards, and fled. In order to restore public peace in France, the king, on May 9, 1720, forbade further forced deportations to Louisiana.[10]

In French Louisiana, usefulness was the overriding virtue for im-

8. Eccles, *France in America*, 148; Marcel Giraud, *Histoire de la Louisiane française* (4 vols.; Paris, 1953–74), III, 252–76.

9. See the list of women sent to Louisiana by order of the king, dated October 6, 1719, on *la Mutine*, December 17, 1719. Fiche de désarmenent, June 24, 1720, in Sec. 2P 20, fol. 2, No. 4, APL.

10. Giraud, *Histoire de la Louisiane*, III, 252–76.

Table 1. French Colonists Sent to Louisiana Between 1717 and 1721

Officers	122
Soldiers	977
Employees	43
Workers of the Company of the Indies	302
Holders of land concessions	119
Their indentured servants (*engagés*)	2,462
Salt smugglers and other exiles	1,278
Women	1,215
Children	502
TOTAL	7,020

SOURCE: Mémoire sur l'etat actuel ou est la colonie de la Louisiane, n.d. [after 1721], in Ser. C13C 1, fol. 329, ANC.

migrants, transcending race, nation, humanity, and any other consideration. The deportees were not considered *utils* by officials in Louisiana. A report of June, 1720, referring to colonists sent by the squadron led by de Saujon and by the ship *les Deux Frères*, commented:

> Without wishing to criticize the conduct of the Directors, I dare say that one should not be deluded into believing that it is possible to establish the colony with persons who were incapable of discipline in France, especially since it is noted that a man who was an excellent subject becomes a mediocre subject in America and a mediocre subject becomes very bad. We do not know the reason for this deterioration. Some attribute it to the food which does not have the same substance as in Europe, to a greater dissipation of the mind, or to other causes. Regardless of the reason, the fact is certain. What can one expect from a bunch of vagabonds and wrongdoers in a country where it is harder to repress licentiousness than in Europe?[11]

Between October 25, 1717, and May, 1721, the Company of the Indies sent 43 ships, which in addition to de Saujon's squadron, embarked 7,020 colonists. Table 1 gives a breakdown of the colonists.

According to a report written sometime after 1721, about 2,000 whites died during the crossing because of mistreatment by the cap-

11. Etat de la Louisiane au mois de juin 1720, in Ser. A1 2592, fol. 95, SHA.

tains, or they deserted or returned to France. From this information, one could estimate that about 5,420 whites should remain in the colony. However, a census dated January 1, 1726—the first complete census of the entire colony—lists 1,952 French citizens, including Germans, and 276 indentured servants. This drastic drop in population was due largely to an extremely high mortality rate among these white immigrants, both voluntary and forced.[12]

In 1729, the Natchez Indians and their allies revolted against the French settlers, destroying one-tenth of the white population. The Company of the Indies gave up the colony to the French crown in 1731. Many white settlers left, and practically no new colonists came. The dangerous Indian frontier, poverty, famine, anarchy, and chaos depleted the population and discouraged new immigration. Louisiana was viewed as an expensive, burdensome military outpost, and its colonization with permanent settlers was practically abandoned by France. Diron d'Artaguette, writing from Mobile, described conditions prevailing in 1733: "Our planters and merchants here are dying of hunger, and those at New Orleans are in no better situation. Some are clamoring to return to France; others secretly run away to the Spaniards at Pensacola. The colony is on the verge of being depopulated."[13]

In 1738, Edme Gatien de Salmon, *commissaire ordonnateur*, wrote to the Ministry of Colonies that many settlers had left during the past few years, none at all had entered the colony, the numbers of settlers was decreasing every day, and there had been a heavy mortality among children that year. By about 1740, the white population had been reduced to less than 1,200, including troops as well as settlers, and they were all dispersed. A report from about that time stated: "If it is left in this situation without increasing the population, a catastrophe will happen. It is too extensive to be held on to. . . . Little by little, the colony is destroying itself."[14]

In 1740, Salmon wrote a communique to the colonial ministry, stating that he hoped for some salt smugglers (*faux sauniers*) on the next vessel of the king, because the colony was being depopulated. These

12. Mémoire sur l'état actuel ou est la colonie de la Louisiane, n.d. [after 1721], in Ser. C13C 1, fol. 329, ANC; Maduell, *Census Tables*, 26. For mortality reports for lower Louisiana between 1720 and 1725, see Sec. 1P 274B, No. 9, Dossier 1, APL.

13. Charles Gayarré, *History of Louisiana* (4 vols.; 1854–66; rpr. Baton Rouge, 1974), I, 457–58.

14. Salmon to the Ministry of the Colonies, November 25, 1738, in Ser. C13A 23, fol. 136, ANC; Mémoire sur la colonie de la Louisiane, n.d. [*ca.* 1740], in Ser. C13C 1, fol. 384, ANC.

convicts were needed to replace the *voyageurs* who had been killed during the various defeats suffered by their traders in the Illinois country.[15]

There were no systematic censuses taken by the French authorities in Louisiana after 1731. In 1746, during King George's War between England and France (1744 to 1748), the white population was estimated to be 3,200, and the black population 4,730.[16] Louisiana was thoroughly Africanized during the early years of colonization, and slaves were still a majority in the French settlements when France abandoned the colony to Spain in 1763 (see Figure 1).

Lower Louisiana was not the place to come to establish production of commodities for export. French Louisiana was very poor. Unlike French Canada, where the fishing industry and the beaver trade with the Indians provided a firm economic basis for colonization even though the French population remained small, Louisiana was never a colony of economic exploitation. The furs of lower Louisiana were far inferior to those of Canada, and they often rotted in the humid climate while awaiting a ship. French Louisiana cannot be accurately described as a plantation society. It never really developed a viable, self-sustaining economy. Unlike the French West Indies and the tidewater region of the British continental colonies, Louisiana was not a prosperous slave plantation society producing valuable export staples. It was viewed as the least valuable of France's colonies, one whose economic development might threaten not only France but also the more important French West Indies.

The ruling elite of French Louisiana was a military-bureaucratic clique whose wealth derived mainly from commerce, often smuggling, and sometimes piracy. Access to trade goods and commercial ties with France were crucial. The Indian fur trade, control of desperately needed supplies, the smuggling of French goods into Spanish Pensacola, Mexico, and Cuba, as well as some piracy, enriched the elite.[17] Naval stores and tobacco were exported, but the quality was

---

15. Salmon to the Ministry of the Colonies, June 28, 1740, in Ser. C13A 25, fol. 185, ANC.

16. Mémoire sur l'état de la Colonie de la Louisiane en 1746, in C13A 30, fols. 244–57, ANC. For summary of population settlement by settlement, see fol. 256. King George's War was known in Europe as the War of the Austrian Succession, beginning in 1740.

17. For a discussion of the centrality of the Indian fur trade in colonial Louisiana, see Daniel H. Usner, Jr., "Frontier Exchange in the Lower Mississippi Valley: Race Relations and Economic Life in Colonial Louisiana, 1699–1783" (Ph.D. dissertation, Duke University, 1981), 213–55.

Africans in Colonial Louisiana

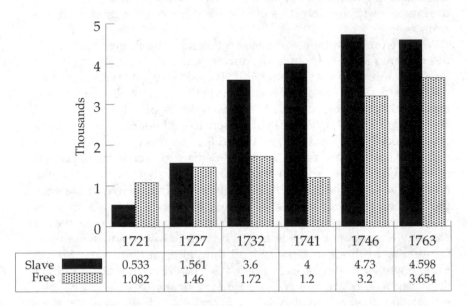

	1721	1727	1732	1741	1746	1763
Slave ■	0.533	1.561	3.6	4	4.73	4.598
Free ▨	1.082	1.46	1.72	1.2	3.2	3.654

Figure 1.   Slave and Free Population of French Louisiana, 1721–1763

SOURCES: Figures for 1721, 1727, and 1732 calculated from Charles R. Maduell, *The Census Tables for the French Colony of Louisiana from 1699 Through 1732* (Baltimore, 1972). Figures for 1741 calculated from Mémoire sur la colonie de la Louisiane, n.d. [*ca.* 1740], in Ser. C13C 1, fol. 384, ANC. Figures for 1746 calculated from Mémoire sur l'état de la Colonie de la Louisiane en 1746, in Ser. C13A 30, fols. 244–57, ANC. Figures for 1763 calculated from Antonio Acosta Rodríguez, *La población de la Luisiana española (1763–1803)* (Madrid, 1979), 31, 110.

NOTE: The 1763 census covers the area from the mouth of the Mississippi River through Pointe Coupee only.

often poor, and the cost of production, shipping, and transport was prohibitive unless heavily subsidized. Reliance upon the Indian nations to furnish corn quickly wore thin as Indians were encouraged to hunt for pelts and engage in warfare for the benefit of France. French officials often had to feed hungry Indian nations. The first two slave ships from Africa, which arrived in 1719, brought several barrels of rice seed and African slaves who knew how to produce the crop. Rice became the only reliable food crop for local consumption in Louisiana; little was exported. Cotton was grown, but the problem of separating the seed from the lint was never adequately solved. The major agricultural export crops, tobacco and indigo, were normally not competitive in the world market. There were short-lived indigo booms when crops failed in Central America and the French West Indies, floods and insects mercifully spared the Louisiana crop, and a lull in warfare and piracy allowed for shipping. There was little direct trade with France, and trade with the French West Indies was limited during the 1730s and 1740s. During a brief peace between England and France during the early 1750s, small ships brought goods, with a high markup, from France via the islands, taking a return cargo of cypress. But these ships were too small to carry much lumber. Trade and monetary restrictions intended to protect the French West Indies from competition from Louisiana strangled this budding economic development. Additionally, there was a chronic labor shortage. Only one African slave-trade ship arrived in Louisiana after 1731, and the export of slaves from the French islands was prohibited—except for a few the West Indian planters were trying to get rid of—sharply limiting the possibilities of economic growth. The sugar industry also could not develop because of lack of labor and fear of competition with the French islands.[18]

In truth, Louisiana had little to offer. The colony was poor, unhealthy, dangerous, and uninviting. Communication with the outside world was difficult. Far removed from normal trade routes, its few harbors, as well as the several mouths of the Mississippi River, were shallow and often blocked by ever-shifting sandbars. Ships often broke up on these sandbars in and near the river. The voyage to Louisiana through pirate-infested waters was long and dangerous. The damp climate was unhealthy, the long summers very hot, the winters sometimes quite cold. The mortality rate was high. Hurricanes and floods regularly decimated settlements and fortifications. Land had to be ditched and drained, and flooding of the Mississippi River had to be controlled with dikes called *levées*, now *levees* in English. Because the inferior skins and hides bought from the Indians often rotted while awaiting a ship, troop ships arriving from France often found no return cargo. It was also difficult to get food for the return voyage in a land often gripped by famine. The early colony had little to offer

18. Nancy N. Miller Surrey, *The Commerce of Louisiana During the French Regime, 1699–1763* (1916; rpr. New York, 1968); Thomas Marc Fiehrer, "The African Presence in Colonial Louisiana: An Essay on the Continuity of Caribbean Culture," in *Louisiana's Black Heritage*, ed. Robert R. Macdonald, John R. Kemp, and Edward F. Haas (New Orleans, 1979), 32–62; De Villars Dubreuil to the Ministry of the Colonies, New Orleans, September 30, 1752, in Henry P. Dart, "The Career of Dubreuil in French Louisiana," *LHQ*, XVIII (1935), 287–88 (letter translated by G. Lugano); Hurson to the ministry, Martinique, September, 1752, in Collection Moreau de St.-Méry, Ser. F3 90, fols. 70–71, AN.

except for a few deerskins, buffalo hides, and some poor-quality pitch.[19]

Two streams of previous French colonization in North America merged in Louisiana. One component comprised pirates from the Caribbean, who were experienced in enriching themselves through raiding settlements, seizing ships, goods, and slaves, selling the booty, and holding wealthy citizens for ransom. The pirates moved toward legitimization through smuggling and commerce. The other component was the Canadian *courreurs du bois*, experienced in living and trading with Indian peoples. Both components were essential to the survival of early Louisiana. Neither was interested in producing wealth.

These two components merged in the careers of the Canadian founders, the brothers Pierre Le Moyne, Sieur d'Iberville, Jean Baptiste Le Moyne, Sieur de Bienville, and the less famous Chateaugue de Serigny. Iberville and Bienville led the first successful colonizing expedition. Bienville dominated the politics of the colony for decades. While the first colonists of Louisiana were racked by hunger and disease when the outbreak of the War of the Spanish Succession (May, 1702) cut them off from supplies by sea, the Le Moyne brothers were busy lining their pockets at the expense of the colonists, of France, and of any victims they might encounter. Their profiteering was many faceted and was carried out with great ingenuity and determination. Profiteering and malfeasance began with the outfitting of the naval squadron that Iberville commanded during the War of the Spanish Succession. Iberville took funds from the navy to stock the ships and instead filled them with merchandise for illicit sale for the benefit of himself, his officers, and some merchant associates. The ships ran out of supplies and had to stop to make purchases along their route at much higher prices than in France. Iberville simply added these charges to the navy's bill, raising the total cost of the expedition. He sold contraband iron and various merchandise in Havana and in St. Domingue. He carried out piratical raids at Nevis, holding prominent citizens for ransom. He seized booty, including 1,309 slaves who were sold for Iberville's profit by a merchant in St. Domingue. Other booty seized during the campaign was sold at St. Domingue and Martinique for the benefit of the officers, mainly of Bienville. Serigny's malfeasance was most serious for the starving, infant colony. He left France in command of the *Coventry* with instructions to sail to the Mississippi to resupply the colony. After the

19. Eccles, *France in America*, 160, 163.

Nevis expedition, he took his ship to Veracruz instead, where he sold merchandise, slaves, and the booty from a Portuguese ship that he had taken at St. Christopher, returning with a cargo of tobacco. He charged the navy for the unauthorized trip to Veracruz and made 60,000 piastres in profit. This detour compromised the resupplying of the colony partially because Serigny substituted a ship of lesser tonnage, *l'Aigle*, for the trip to Louisiana. *L'Aigle* could not carry all the supplies sent, and some had to be left at Havana. Losses were also incurred through negligence in reloading. Of the supplies that actually arrived, some of the munitions were stolen or "lost" in transportation from Massacre Island to Fort Louis.[20]

Bienville was accused of employing His Majesty's crews and boats to transport his own goods and those of his clique to Veracruz and to France and of treating the king's merchandise in the warehouse as his own, appropriating whatever he pleased, and then selling it at an exorbitant price to the desperate settlers, making an enormous profit. When he did not appropriate the king's goods outright, Bienville bought them at a markup of 25 percent and resold them at a profit of 400 percent. Father Raphael complained that the military grabbed up the few products brought to market and that soldiers took items sent to individual settlers and forced them to buy them back at three or four times their original price.[21]

Could the colony have survived without the Le Moyne brothers' swashbuckling talents in accumulating illegitimate wealth for themselves and their clique in the absence of more legitimate sources of wealth? The answer is probably no. It seems that they knew how to make the colonization of Louisiana worthwhile, at least for themselves and their followers. Crozat's attempt to establish Louisiana as a proprietary colony based upon the development of agriculture and mining was a costly failure. Law's Company of the West gave Louisiana back to the French crown in 1731 after investing 20 million livres in the colony at a substantial loss. Bienville was brought back to Louisiana in triumph, to rule as governor. By midcentury, Louisiana was costing France 800,000 livres a year.[22]

It has been claimed that France had a particular gift for understanding and conciliating the Indians and that, unlike the English colonists

20. Giraud, *Histoire de la Louisiane*, I, 95–120; King Louis XIV to d'Artaguette, June 30, 1707, in *MPA*, II, 62, 63.

21. Pontchartrain to Bienville, June 30, 1707, *ibid.*, 67, 68; Pontchartrain to La Salle, June 30, 1707, *ibid.*, 70; Father Raphael to Abbe Raguet, September 15, 1725, *ibid.*, 511, 512.

22. Eccles, *France in America*, 161–66.

on the North American continent, the French were more interested in the fur trade and military alliances with the Indians than in taking over their land. The French therefore aimed to preserve the Indians, while the English aimed to displace them.[23] The English Atlantic colonies were comparatively thickly populated by whites, had developed a productive, self-sustaining economy, and could therefore afford an attitude of racial exclusiveness toward Indian nations. But religious and cultural differences between the French and Canadian colonists of Louisiana and the English colonists were significant factors in how each group treated the Indians. Although the missionary zeal that characterized Canadian colonization had waned by the time Louisiana was founded, missionaries played a vital role in the exploration and early French colonization of the Mississippi Valley, contributing to a degree of racial openness and fluidity. The greatest strength of the Canadian and French settlers of Louisiana was their openness to peoples of other races and cultures. Surely, it was the main reason for their survival in this dangerous and inhospitable land.

During the first years of Louisiana's colonization, Bienville forged an alliance with the Choctaw to help protect them against slave raiders from South Carolina and their Indian allies. But France had comparatively little to offer besides protection from these groups and from the expansion of the English colonies into the Mississippi Valley. If the ability to develop rapport with the Indians was a talent of the French and Canadian settlers of Louisiana, it was also a precondition for their survival. The British colonies on the Atlantic coast of North America, France's great rival, kept up constant pressure on France's sparsely settled colony through their Chickasaw allies and, often, through the successful infiltration of France's great ally, the Choctaw. The supply of French trade goods was unreliable, and they were not competitive with British goods in either price or quality.[24] In spite of these severe disadvantages, France usually managed to retain the loyalty of the most important Indian nations of lower Louisiana.

The Indians of Louisiana taught the white colonists a great deal about the flora and fauna, the topography of the land, the building of boats, the navigation of the rich network of treacherous waterways that allowed communications among French settlements, hunting, fishing, warfare, agriculture, techniques of building houses, clothing

23. *Ibid.*, 8, 17n.
24. Gary B. Nash, *Red, White, and Black: The Peoples of Early America* (Englewood Cliffs, N.J., 1974); Patricia Dillon Woods, *French-Indian Relations on the Southern Frontier, 1699–1762* (Ann Arbor, 1980).

and dress, preparation and preservation of food, and herbal medicine. The delta country to the south and west of New Orleans had been occupied by the Chitimacha, whose population was estimated to be four thousand during the early period of French colonization. They relied mainly upon shellfish and seafood for their diet. Their religion and social organization were complex—an elite class had emerged—their villages were composed of sturdy, wooden houses, and their crafts were sophisticated.[25] The economy of the swamp and of the tidal wetlands in and around New Orleans was built up from Chitimacha beginnings. Techniques of cultivating corn, squash, potatoes, tobacco, and other indigenous crops were surely learned from the Indians.

Many of the early French settlements of lower Louisiana began in Indian villages. During the frequent famines that gripped the colony, French soldiers were sent to live with Indian tribes so they would not starve to death. French and Canadian settlers were acculturated by the Indians. Soldiers and sailors were sent to live in Indian villages to learn their languages and act as interpreters. Soldiers serving at frontier posts became well acquainted with Indian nations and often sought, and received, their protection. The early settlers consolidated their relationships with Indian nations by marrying Indian women. The Illinois Indians, for example, reiterated their loyalty to the French by referring to the "alliances which many of that Nation had contracted with them, in espousing their daughters." A Missouri Indian woman named Françoise married Dubois, a French military officer stationed in Missouri. He died and left several children by her. Thereafter, she married another Frenchman living in Illinois, had several children by him, and predeceased him. Her son-in-law by a daughter from her first marriage sued her widower for property belonging to the community of the first marriage. Intermarriage between French Canadians and Indians was common in lower Louisiana as well. *Ordonnateur* Salmon complained that with the lack of French wives, the missionaries had ignored the government's prohibition against interracial marriage. Charles Hegron executed a will before Father Dagobert, Capuchin priest of New Orleans, leaving half his estate to his Indian wife, Françoise, and the other half to their two legitimate children. A tutor was appointed to administer the estate on the grounds that, as an Indian, the widow was incompetent. Bernard Wig had a

25. Light Townsend Cummins, "Toward Unknown Destinies: Native Peoples and European Explorations," in *Louisiana: A History,* ed. Bennett H. Wall (2nd ed.; Arlington Heights, Ill., 1990), 7.

wife named Fewounica. There was, of course, evidence of more informal relationships as well. For example, the will of a French settler at Natchitoches provided for a cash bequest and freedom for an Osage woman slave. The French settler Jean Huet freed Marie, a Fox Indian woman, and her daughter Jeannette under his will. François Noyon, another French settler, willed three thousand livres to Marie, provided her daughter or her daughter's posterity survived.[26]

The Indian frontier was never remote during the period of French rule in Louisiana. It was ever present, dangerous, and complex. Indian neighbors were essential to the colony. The French authorities relied heavily upon the warriors of their Indian allies. But French control was always weak. White settlers, traders, soldiers, and missionaries were killed by Indians, sometimes after slow torture. When they were not mercifully tomahawked and scalped at once, they were sometimes tied to wooden frames and slowly burned to death. If France's alliances with Indian nations held up at all, it was because the Indians feared the English colonists more than they did the French.[27] But the French-Indian alliances were always brittle. The French settlers were in a constant state of insecurity in a world where they were too few to do without the Indians and too weak to control them. The French were exposed to attack by Indians considered their allies, as well as by those Indians who were openly hostile. British traders were active in undermining Choctaw loyalty to the French, especially during the many periods of open British-French warfare. The revolt against the French carried out by the Natchez nation and their allies in 1729 nearly destroyed the colony. The French wars against the Chickasaw during the 1730s and early 1740s were long, costly, and indecisive. These campaigns nearly emptied the colony of permanent settlers and decimated the African slave population. During the Chickasaw Wars, the Choctaw were divided into the Western Choctaw, a pro-British faction led by Red Shoe, and the Eastern

26. J. Zitomerski, "Urbanization in French Colonial Louisiana, 1706–1766," *Annales de Demographie Historique* (1974), 263–77; James T. McGowan, "Planters Without Slaves: Origins of a New World Labor System," *Southern Studies*, XVI (1977), 5–26; Reuben Gold Thwaites, ed., *The Jesuit Relations and Allied Documents: Travels and Explorations of the Jesuit Missionaries in New France, 1610–1719* (73 vols.; Cleveland, 1896–1901), LXVII, 203; February 24, 1746, in RSC, *LHQ*, XV (1932), 146–51; Salmon to the Ministry of the Colonies, July 17, 1732, in Ser. C13A 15, fol. 166, ANC; Will dated March 18, 1745, Petition dated May 7, 1745, Order dated May 8, 1745, all in RSC, *LHQ*, XIV (1931), 111–12; July 6, 1736, in RSC, *LHQ*, VIII (1925), 299–300; October 22, 1719, in RSC, *LHQ*, IV (1921), 355; December 26, 1744, in RSC, *LHQ*, XIII (1930), 329–30.

27. For an excellent discussion of Indian strategy and tactics during the eighteenth century, see Nash, *Red, White, and Black.*

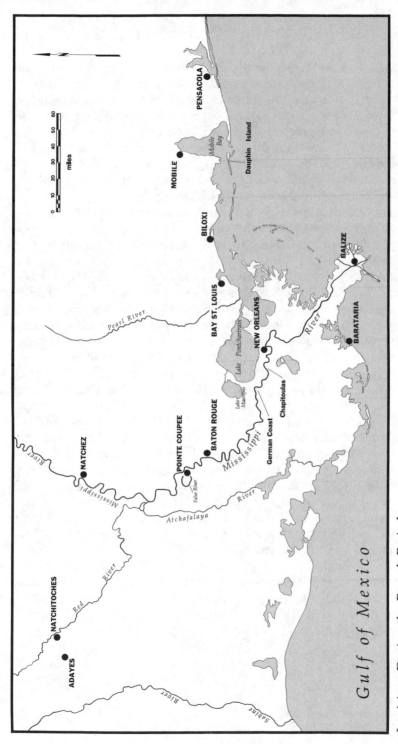

Louisiana During the French Period

Map by John Snead

Choctaw, who were helped by, and who remained loyal to, the French. Red Shoe introduced British traders and large amounts of British trade goods into the villages of the Western Choctaw. During King George's War, attacks against French traders and settlers by the Western Choctaw increased. Governor Vaudreuil considered the Eastern Choctaw no match for them.[28] Although the French managed to have Red Shoe tomahawked by his own nation on June 8, 1747, the Western Choctaw continued to assault French soldiers and settlers near New Orleans and Mobile and at Natchez.

In 1748, the Western Choctaw raided a farm on the Côte d'Allemagne (German Coast) only a few miles north of New Orleans. They killed the husband, scalped the wife, and took the daughter and a black slave prisoner. Germans had been brought to Louisiana by John Law. They suffered high mortality rates while awaiting ships in France, on the barren, sandy beaches along the coast of the Gulf of Mexico, and thereafter in their settlements along the Arkansas River. The remnants of these Germans became a significant and stable element of the white population near New Orleans. By 1724, sixty households of Germans were established at the Côte d'Allemagne. They grew cattle and garden crops that were essential to the food supply of the capital. Soldiers were sent to pursue the Choctaw who had raided the German farm. The soldiers were fired upon by a small band of Choctaw and some runaway black and Indian slaves who had taken refuge among them. One Swiss soldier was killed and two others were wounded, and the troops withdrew, creating further panic on the German Coast and in New Orleans. Governor Vaudreuil blamed the colonists' lack of vigilance for this raid. He complained that instead of organizing to defend themselves against an enemy from whom, according to Vaudreuil, they had nothing to fear if they remained on their guard, the colonists had abandoned their farms and almost all of them had run off to New Orleans. After the governor threatened them and promised a fairly large military detachment for their protection, the Germans returned home. But as soon as the detachment left, they moved to the west bank of the Mississippi River and abandoned their houses, leaving their cultivated and seeded lands to their cattle. Vaudreuil commented, "This is the effect produced in this colony by the least incursions made by the Indians, and this near New Orleans where one has least to fear than anywhere else."[29]

28. *MPA*, IV, 317–21, V, 216.
29. *Ibid*.

But the Germans did not remain in their settlements. Five years after the Choctaw attack, Governor Kerlérec reported: "The settlers are withdrawing from it, to the extent that they are diminishing every day. It was, however, a definite resource for the comforts of life of the capital and of the voyagers, and at the same time an addition to the land in cultivation and to the colonists for the state."[30]

The Indian nations in the Mississippi Valley were powerful in numbers as well as in economic and military importance. The Indian fur trade was vital to the economy of French Louisiana.[31] By 1740, the Choctaw were still a populous nation of 15,000 to 20,000 people, including 5,000 warriors. The Chickasaw, allies of the English, had only about 500 warriors. Indian allies of the French, including Cherokee, Choctaw, and Alabama, still counted 12,000 warriors by mid-century. By 1758, Kerlérec estimated the Choctaw warriors at 3,500 to 4,000. The Alabama also included the Talapoosa and the Abihka, and they could raise 1,000 warriors. The Kawita, allies of the French about 30 leagues from the Alabama, had 2,000 "good and brave warriors." The Tunica, close allies of the French, had been reduced to only 60 warriors. The Apalachee, situated east of Mobile Bay, had been reduced to 30 warriors because of the effects of the alcohol traded to them. The Houma, located 22 leagues from New Orleans, had 60 warriors; the Arkansas, about 250 leagues from New Orleans, included 160 men. These were the only nations of lower Louisiana listed as reliable French allies. The Cherokee had been lost by the French, though they shifted their loyalty back to France when it became clear that the English were about to drive the French out of the Mississippi Valley. Without counting the Cherokee, there were in lower Louisiana alone still about 8,000 reliable and effective Indian warriors who were French allies during the closing years of French rule.[32]

French reliance upon Indian warriors was particularly great because the French troops sent to Louisiana were considered notoriously unreliable, disloyal, treacherous, cowardly, and ready to desert to the enemy at every opportunity. As early as 1712 there were complaints that the French troops were deserting to the Indians and then going to Carolina. They no longer feared being burned alive by the

30. Kerlérec to Rouillé, August 20, 1753, in *MPA*, V, 136.
31. See Usner, "Frontier Exchange."
32. W. Stitt Robinson, *The Southern Colonial Frontier, 1607–1763* (Albuquerque, 1979), 192; Eccles, *France in America*, 169; Memoir on Indians by Kerlérec, New Orleans, December 12, 1758, in *MPA*, V, 203–27.

Indians, because the Carolina colonists had instructed their Indian allies not to harm them.[33]

It is not surprising that French troops often deserted, seeking refuge among the Indians. They were miserably treated. It was reported that during the Spanish siege of Pensacola in 1719, the commander, Bienville's brother Serigny, looked first to his personal property. He used the garrison to move his slaves, silverware, and belongings to Dauphin Island, taking enough time to fold his linens. Serigny and the garrison were absent during the siege; then Serigny surrendered. Several French soldiers who had gone over to the Spanish during the siege were recaptured during the invasion of Mobile. All were shot without trial. Thirty-five more were recaptured on Spanish ships. They were tried; twelve were sentenced to be hanged, and the rest, to work for life on the galleys of France. Bienville's explanation for the desertion of these fifty French soldiers was echoed in various forms by all the governors and commanders who ruled in French Louisiana: "it is exceedingly painful for an officer, who is entrusted with the destinies of a colony, to have nothing better to defend her than a band of deserters, of smugglers, and of rogues, who are ever ready, not only to abandon their flag, but to turn their arms against their country." Bienville claimed that his troops deserted because they had been sent to Louisiana against their will, and asked that only voluntary troops be sent.[34]

However unwillingly the French troops came to Louisiana, their desertion cannot be explained without considering the conditions they found there: the all-pervading corruption, exploitation, and brutality that kept them in desperate want and that made them willing to take any risk to try to escape. Caught between the possibilities of being burned alive or scalped by the Indians or being shot by their superiors, the troops and even the officers often lived under atrocious conditions. D'Artaguette wrote: "It is pitiful to see them as they are all naked and most often living on crushed and boiled Indian corn with a piece of meat. . . . Besides these said soldiers are not paid at all so they can only be very dissatisfied."[35]

The officers were no better off. Their rent cost half their pay. They were reduced to eating beans, when they could get any. They had to

33. Memoir of d'Artaguette to Pontchartrain on Present Condition of Louisiana, May 12, 1712, in *MPA*, II, 60, 61.

34. La Chaise to the Directors of the Company of the Indies, October 18, 1723, *ibid.*, 368–70; Gayarré, *History of Louisiana*, I, 244–48.

35. Memoir of d'Artaguette to Pontchartrain on Present Condition of Louisiana, May 12, 1712, in *MPA*, I, 60, 61.

engage in trade to make a living, but Bienville sold trade goods only to his favorites. There were constant mutinies. Drouot de Valdeterre, who had commanded at Dauphin Island and at Biloxi, wrote about conditions in the colony in 1726. The troops had no arms or ammunition, had no clothing most of the time, and often had to seek food among the Indian tribes. There were no forts for their protection in case of attack. Warehouses were without roofs, and the guns and ammunition were ruined:

> The company as well as the colonists are plundered without mercy and restraint; revolts and desertions among the troops are authorized and sanctioned; incendiaries who, for the purpose of pillage, commit to the flames whole camps, posts, settlements, and warehouses, remain unpunished; prisoners of war are forced to become sailors in the service of the company, and by culpable negligence or connivance they are allowed to run away with ships loaded with merchandise; other vessels are willfully stranded or wrecked, and their cargoes are lost to their owners; forgers, robbers, and murderers are secure of impunity. In short, this is a country which, to the shame of France be it said, is without religion, without justice, without discipline, without order, and without police.[36]

The life of a soldier had no value. In 1745, a thirty-six-year-old French soldier refused to eat the munition bread served at the barracks because, he said, it was not fit for a dog. He was jailed, tried and convicted of sedition, mutiny, and revolt, and condemned "to be hung and strangled until death doth ensue." At Kaskaskia, in the Illinois country, Jean Ducoudray, a French soldier who had been branded with a V (for *voleur*, thief) in France, was accused of burglary. He confessed that he had stolen eight chickens, brought them to the barracks, and put them in a pot to boil. He had no accomplices; he only wanted so many chickens in order to divide them with the other soldiers. Ducoudray was sentenced to be hanged and strangled until death or, if there was no executioner, to be shot down.[37]

Vaudreuil and *Ordonnateur* Michel wrote that few of the soldiers sent to Louisiana were suited to marry, settle down, and cultivate the land. They described them as "men scraped together and very often bandits," and many desertions, legal executions, and homicides occurred among them.

> The diseases occasioned by the licentious life that they have led and by the excess of drink have caused many to perish. . . . They have mutinied

---

36. La Chaise to the Directors of the Company of the Indies, September 6, 1723, in *MPA*, II, 317–19; Gayarré, *History of Louisiana*, I, 375, 376.
37. July 12–14, 1745, in RSC, *LHQ*, XIV (1931), 263–67; July 13, 1752, in RSC, LHC.

in all the fortresses where they have been posted to await embarkation [for Louisiana]. Scarcely have the officers who have conducted them on the different vessels on which they have been sent been able to restrain them, and such violent affairs have occurred that it has been necessary on their arrival to put some of them to death in order to chastise the past and to give examples for the future. They breathe here nothing but desertion and revolt.[38]

Michel soon became convinced that desertion among the soldiers was caused by the misappropriation of the troops' food and supplies by Vaudreuil and "his Canadian creatures and his kinsmen and allies of himself or of his wife who are occupying all the posts." He accused Vaudreuil, his wife, family, and clique of Canadian favorites of stifling the economy and compromising the defense of the colony by selling the supplies intended for the troops to the highest bidder, empty-ing the king's warehouse, and monopolizing and selling scarce goods at a high price. The governor's wife operated a bazaar in her home and forced merchants throughout the colony to sell her goods at the prices she fixed. Troops were mutinying and deserting because they were hungry and naked, Michel claimed. Vaudreuil and his clique helped themselves to the goods from the king's warehouse; they sold the flour intended for the soldiers to the Indians and fed the soldiers corn. One of eight soldiers who deserted from the French fort at Tom-becbè left a note saying that they had left "to pay for the flour." The deserters were arrested by the Choctaw, and a group of about fifty Choctaw chiefs, honored men, and warriors brought them back. Ali-bamon Mingo, one of the chiefs, said:

> I know well that these Frenchmen have done wrong, but that will show the red men so much the more clearly that M. de Vaudreuil, their father, has consideration for their requests. He can easily imagine the infinite pain that it would give the Choctaws to see shed the blood of people who every day bring them the things they need, and that with great difficulty. Fur-thermore are not these Frenchmen, so to speak, our brothers; do we not dwell, as it were, in the same cabin?[39]

Vaudreuil pointed out that these soldiers were guilty but that there was danger of worse consequences if they were not pardoned. The Choctaw might, in the future, refuse to arrest deserters and might even help them, making it difficult to maintain French military posts in the territory. The governor's proposed solution was to offer the

38. Vaudreuil and Michel to Rouillé, May 20, 1751, in MPA, V, 81–84.
39. Michel to Rouillé, July 20, 1751, *ibid.*, 97–105; Dupumeux to [Beauchamp], June 18, 1751, *ibid.*, 89, 90.

Indians a price for the scalps of French deserters equal to the price they paid for the scalps of Chickasaw Indians. So much for racial and national solidarity and fellow-feeling on the Louisiana frontier. The deserters were held in a dungeon at Mobile. It was only when the Choctaw chiefs declared to the French officials, in the presence of French sentinels and soldiers, that they would no longer return deserters but would furnish them guides to facilitate their escape that the officials produced the deserters and pardoned them. Otherwise, they concluded, they "would no longer be able to retain one soldier." The Choctaw agreed to return all future deserters. Several years later, several French deserters were pardoned at the request of the Arkansas nations after two Arkansas chiefs made formal and public promises that all future French deserters would be returned unconditionally.[40]

Kerlérec was governor during the French and Indian War (1754 to 1761), which cost France her empire on the North American continent. He wrote that he had complained in several dispatches that the troops sent to Louisiana by the king were vicious professional deserters who did more harm than good. Some deserted, others succumbed to the most extreme horrors of drink, debauchery, and licentiousness, and the rest, a small number, were more dangerous for the colony than the enemy himself. Kerlérec cited the example of Jean Baptiste Baudreau. He had been pardoned after being condemned to ten years on the galleys, and had escaped from New Orleans and taken refuge among the Indians.[41] His pardon was requested because of "the damage he could do to the colony if he were pushed into siding with the English and the Indians, about whom he knows more than all the other French on the continent." He was subsequently accused of stealing the effects of a shipwrecked Spanish ship and instigating his fellow soldiers to murder their commander and desert to the English. One of his companions, François Vions, was found not guilty because he had been forced to desert at gunpoint. Baudreau and Joseph François Bazille were condemned to be broken live on the wheel, their bodies cut into quarters and thrown into the street. Their sentence was carried out by the troops three hours after it was pronounced.[42]

40. Vaudreuil to the Ministry of the Colonies, January 28, 1752, in Ser. C13A 36, fols. 55–58, ANC; Minutes of a Council of War at Mobile, June 11, 1753, in *MPA*, V, 125–27; Note sur les graces accordées par Kerlérec a la prière des chefs des nations Arkansas a divers soldats déserteurs, June 20, 1756, in Ser. C13A 39, fols. 175–76, ANC.

41. See Vaudreuil to Maurepas, June 6, 1748, in *MPA*, IV, 321–22.

42. Vaudreuil to the Ministry of the Colonies, December 29, 1745, in Ser. C13A 29, fols. 95–99, ANC; Kerlérec to the Ministry of the Colonies, New Orleans, October 20,

One of the Swiss soldiers was sawed in half, the French army's customary form of execution for Swiss soldiers. A Swiss corporal stabbed himself with a knife that he wore around his neck Indian style to avoid such an execution.

Jean-Bernard Bossu, a French soldier who served at various frontier posts in Louisiana between 1751 and 1757 and from 1757 to 1762, claimed that Baudreau had been kept in chains for a long time because he refused to share with the officer the goods he salvaged from the Spanish shipwreck. Bossu wrote that the soldiers on Cat Island revolted because their commander, Duroux, made them grow crops and make lime out of seashells and charcoal for his profit without paying them. Those who refused were tied naked to trees to be stung by mosquitoes. Bossu wrote, "The type of punishment meted out by this officer to the soldiers of his garrison is beneath the dignity of savages." Duroux made them eat flour salvaged from a Spanish shipwreck while he sold the flour provided for them for his own profit. The soldiers went to Kerlérec to lodge complaints and to show him the bad bread they received, but he sent them back to be dealt with by their commander. The next commander at Cat Island appointed by Kerlérec managed to steal and conceal the entire cargo of a Spanish ship set adrift after its crew mutinied. Bossu's informed and convincing book about conditions in Louisiana, though approved by the French censors before publication, landed him in the Bastille for six weeks because of his criticisms of Kerlérec.[43]

With the outbreak of the French and Indian War in 1754, the British established a fixed cruiser blockade at Cape San Antonio at the western end of Cuba, turning the Gulf of Mexico into a British lake. British privateers harassed French traders along the north coast all the way to the approaches to Balize, the fort at the mouth of the Mississippi River. Indians were raising their tomahawks against French traders among them because they were not receiving their customary presents. Kerlérec wrote, "In short we are in want of everything, and the dissatisfaction of the Indians leaves everything to be feared."[44]

In 1758, William Perry, an American seaman held prisoner in New Orleans, reported that he saw "numbers of Indians in town, fifty or sixty in a Gang, and he was told that the French who go out of Town

---

1757, in Ser. C13A 39, fols. 268, 273, *ibid.*; Jean-Bernard Bossu, *Travels in the Interior of North America, 1751–1762*, trans. Seymour Feiler (Norman, Okla., 1962).

43. Bossu, *Travels in North America*, ix–xii, 178–83.

44. Kerlérec to Peirène de Moras, New Orleans, August 23, 1758, in *MPA*, V, 192–93; Kerlérec to Peirène de Moras, New Orleans, October 21, 1757, *ibid.*, 189.

anywhere into the Country are frequently scalped." During January, a message was sent to the "Governor of New Orleans from their friendly Indians, that if they did not send them a Supply of Claothing and Ammunition, they would come and destroy them, on which they mustered their Forces, expecting the Indians to come." Perry reported that a vessel carrying troops from France to New Orleans was taken and that all but one of the sixteen French ships carrying provisions and ammunition to New Orleans were captured by the English.[45]

Kerlérec had a solution. He allowed British ships coming from Jamaica to dock at New Orleans, ostensibly under a flag of truce to exchange prisoners. These ships sold slaves as well as merchandise. In December, 1759, an English trade ship came from Rhode Island loaded with dry goods and without any prisoners. Kerlérec helped guide the ship up the Mississippi River past the vessels of the king and helped hide it near New Orleans. A public sale was held in the capital, announced by drummers marching through the streets. The English were allowed to see the fortifications being built. Kerlérec had convoked the chiefs of France's Indian allies—the Alabama, Talapoosa, Abihkas, and Kawita—to the capital. When they arrived in New Orleans, they were astonished to find English traders there.[46]

As the French colonization of Louisiana approached its end, the French crown reviewed its policy for populating Louisiana. A memorandum of the king dating from 1760 stated that

> populating Louisiana has been absolutely neglected since France has taken possession of the colony. Men and women who were criminals and prostitutes whom one wished to get rid of in Paris and throughout the kingdom were sent at various times, but the little care taken of them upon their arrival as well as their laziness and licentiousness resulted in their destruction, and there are practically none of them left today. It can be regarded as fortunate for this colony that such a bad race was wiped out at its beginning and did not give birth to a vicious people with corrupt blood.

The memorandum called for populating the colony with the rejects of French society who could perhaps nevertheless become functional in Louisiana. Since France had already lost too many inhabitants to permit free citizens to depart, they were to search out those who had been "excluded from society by misfortunes which do not render them unworthy to reenter society . . . without depriving the King-

---

45. Henry P. Dart, ed., "New Orleans in 1758," *LHQ*, V (1922), 56.
46. *Ibid.*; D'Erneville to Berryer, March 15, 1760, in *MPA*, V, 242–50.

dom of its citizens." *Faux sauniers* were suggested, or others who had been condemned to the galleys for the crime of selling products that were a commercial monopoly of the king:

> Regardless of how necessary it is to punish smugglers to assure the revenues of His Majesty, it seems nevertheless that one would achieve the same goal by deporting the guilty ones. Their exile would serve as an example of punishment on the one hand, and on the other, one would reap a benefit from this portion of the population which is dead civilly and subject to a painful and ignominious labor. One might even dare to say that there would be justice in thus using them instead of condemning those caught with a little bit of salt, tobacco, or cloth to the same penalty as forgers, thieves, murderers and other enemies of society and the state.[47]

The memorandum also suggested that soldiers condemned to death or to the galleys for desertion could instead be sent to Louisiana as settlers. While such harsh punishments were necessary to discourage desertions, it continued, "it is nevertheless upsetting to see that since the beginning of the century, more than 60,000 have been shot, most of whom could have become very good citizens if pardoned." In Louisiana, these soldiers could be laborers and form a militia; they could marry honest girls sent from the houses of charity in France and taught to work by the Ursuline nuns in New Orleans. They would provide Louisiana with "useful inhabitants and a healthy population which one could never find among the vagabonds and conscripts whom one could send." The memorandum recommended that all pardonable deserters and smugglers be sent to Louisiana under the condition that they not return to France for twenty years.[48]

But these plans were too late for French Louisiana. When Quebec fell to the British in 1759, it was clear that France had lost Canada to England, and her interest in holding on to her expensive Louisiana colony evaporated. The Treaty of Paris of 1763 ceded Canada and East and West Florida to England. The remnants of French Louisiana were ceded to Spain.

French Louisiana was a dangerous and unstable world. Warfare continued throughout most of the years of French colonization. The colony was often cut off from supplies, and famine was frequent. The French regime was cold, brutal, and corrupt. Officials appointed to rule the colony quickly established cliques of followers who exploited and exercised tyrannical power over an isolated population. They profited by seizing available supplies, monopolizing them, and sell-

---

47. Feuille au roi, Versailles, July 1, 1760, in Ser. C13A 42, fols. 168–74, ANC.
48. *Ibid.*

ing them at a high price to desperate settlers. Most of the soldiers, and many of the settlers, were the rejects of French society whose lives had no value as far as Louisiana's officials were concerned. The French authorities looked to Africa for useful workers.

CHAPTER 2

Senegambia During the French Slave Trade to Louisiana

Dé tit zozos-yé té assis,
Dé tit zozos si la barrier,
Dé tit zozos, qui zabotté,
Qui ça yé di mo pas conné.

Manzeur-poulet vini simin,
Croupé si yé et croqué yé,
Personn pli tend yé zabotté,
Dé tit zozos si la barrier.

Two little birds were sitting,
Two little birds were sitting on the fence,
Two little birds were chattering,
What they were saying I do not know.

A chicken hawk came along the road,
Pounced on them and ate them up,
No one hears them chattering any more,
The two little birds on the fence.

—Louisiana Creole song from George Washington
    Cable, *The Grandissimes*
    translation by G. M. Hall

Two-thirds of the slaves brought to Louisiana by the French slave trade came from Senegambia. While Senegambia means, geographically, the region between the Senegal and the Gambia rivers, it is much more than a geographical area. According to Philip D. Curtin, it is "a region of homogeneous culture and a common style of history." Three of its principal languages, Sereer, Wolof, and Pulaar, are closely related. The fourth language, Malinke, is a mutually intelligible language spoken by the Mande peoples to the east. The peoples of the Senegambia region have lived as neighbors for many centuries, and there has been a steady interchange of people among them.[1] The great medieval empires of Ghana, Mali, and Songhai were founded in the Senegambian region. The Islamic Almoravides empire, which overthrew the Ghana empire and united Spain, North Africa, and Senegambia under its political dominance, was founded during the eleventh century on an island in the Senegal River. The trans-Sahara trade featuring gold from sub-Sahara Africa linked the West African, Iberian, and Mediterranean worlds of medieval Islam.

The Senegal concession of the Company of the Indies included Upper Guinea as well as Senegambia. Some of the slaves embarked for Louisiana were brought to Gorée from the *captiverie* at Bissau on the Upper Guinea coast. But there was a heavy Mande overlay to the culture of Upper Guinea due to the influence of waves of conquerors, immigrants, and refugees displaced from the north. The Mandinga, founders of the Mali empire, were well established on the Upper Guinea coast when the Portuguese arrived during the mid-fifteenth century. All of Upper Guinea had long exhibited a lamina of Mande civilization. For centuries, Mande descendants of the Mali empire had drifted down from the western Sudan to Upper Guinea. One of the most significant of these population movements was the series of Mane invasions between 1545 and 1606, initiated and led by Macarico, a noblewoman from Mandimansa who was forced out because she had offended the emperor. Her friends, relatives, and dependents were transformed into a conquering army that overran vast territories and many nations of Upper Guinea. The entire Senegal concession of the Company of the Indies was a significantly homogeneous culture area. Walter Rodney wrote that knowledge of the

---

1. Philip D. Curtin, *Economic Change in Precolonial Africa: Senegambia in the Era of the Slave Trade* (2 vols.; Madison, Wis., 1975), I, 6.

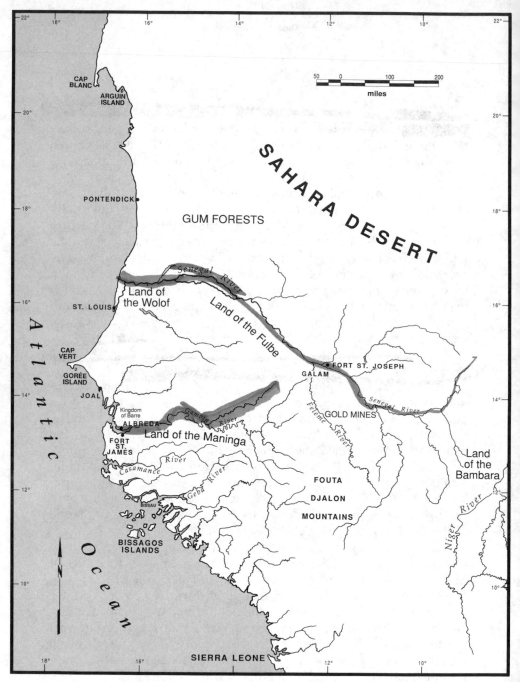

The Senegal Concession of the Company of the Indies

Map by John Snead

proportions of particular African nations in different regions in the Americas "at least opens the way for an enquiry into the dynamics of New World slave culture and the way in which African elements were incorporated," but added that the cultural impact of these African nations was partially a reflection of conditions in Africa and was not necessarily determined by the proportions of particular African nations within the slave population.[2] In view of the close ties between Senegal and Louisiana during the French slave trade, Rodney's emphasis upon looking at both sides of the Atlantic is especially important. Both the proportions of particular African nations present in early Louisiana and the conditions in Africa, as well as in Louisiana, molded the formation of Afro-Creole culture.

Senegambia had been the main source of the Atlantic slave trade during the mid-sixteenth century, but after 1640, it probably never furnished more than 10 percent of the trade. While Senegambia became marginal to the growing African slave trade as a whole during the eighteenth century, its role in providing slaves for Louisiana was an exception.[3] Senegambia remained an important source of the slaves brought to Louisiana throughout the eighteenth century.

This aberrant pattern can be explained by the historical and administrative relationship between Senegal and Louisiana. The slave trade to Louisiana was organized by the Company of the Indies, a private company licensed by the king of France that controlled, administered, and held an exclusive trade monopoly in both Senegal and Louisiana during the years of the African slave trade to the latter colony. Its port was Lorient, and almost all the slave-trade voyages to Louisiana originated from and returned to that port. Ties between Senegal and Louisiana were quite close. Officials of the Company of the Indies in Senegal and in Louisiana were well informed about developments in both concessions. News and dispatches from the two concessions were carried back to France by way of the slave-trade ships returning to Lorient. Passengers, soldiers, and officials for Louisiana embarked on slave-trade ships stopping off in Senegal. Governor Etienne de Périer's brother, Périer de Salvert, commanded military campaigns along the Senegalese coast, as well as in Louisiana, including the seizure of Arguin Island from the Dutch. He was in Louisiana during the war against the Natchez Indians and their allies

2. Walter Rodney, *A History of the Upper Guinea Coast, 1545–1800* (Oxford, Eng., 1970), 1–38, 44; Walter Rodney, "Upper Guinea and the Significance of the Origins of Africans Enslaved in the New World," *Journal of Negro History*, LIV (1969), 336–37.

3. Curtin, *Economic Change*, I, 102.

and returned to France in 1731 to report on the progress of this war.[4]

The Company of the Indies' Senegal concession stretched from Arguin Island southward to Sierra Leone. Fort St. Louis, the headquarters of the Company of the Indies in Africa, was located on an island near the mouth of the Senegal River. Ships had to dock offshore because a sandbar prevented them from entering the river. Lacking a port, the trading post of St. Louis was relatively secure from bombardment by ships but not very convenient for loading and unloading. The Company of the Indies maintained a strategic trading post, Fort St. Joseph, in Galam (Gajaaga) on the upper reaches of the Senegal River near the present boundary of Senegal and Mali. French boats went upriver in the spring at high water and descended the river in the winter. The post at Galam was intended to serve two purposes. The first was to outflank the British post near the mouth of the Gambia River and the interlopers trading there by purchasing slave caravans (*chemins de nègres*) as they descended the Senegal River. Practically all these *chemins de nègres* came from east of Senegambia in Mandinga country and followed the Senegal River and the Feleme River, crossing over to the Gambia River. The Company of the Indies hoped to purchase all the slaves as they descended the Senegal, drying up the supply of slaves in the Gambia River, where rival European slave traders and interlopers operated. Curtin estimates that two-thirds of the slaves shipped from Senegambia during the eighteenth century came from east of the headwaters of navigation. Among these, about one-third came through Galam and two-thirds through the Gambia. Another objective of the post at Galam was to find the fabled gold deposits of Timbuktu, which the Company of the Indies believed to be the richest in the world. Large deposits of gold were reputed to be lying on the ground, only needing to be washed. Gold and slaves were purchased at Galam.[5]

The island of Gorée, near the present city of Dakar, was the best port in the Senegal concession. It was the main "warehouse" of the slave "merchandise." Slaves were brought to Gorée from all the trading posts of the Senegal concession to await ships departing for America. A small trading post, Joual, was located on the coast south

4. Instruction pour le S. Nicolas Despres de St. Robert, Directeur Général à la concession du Sénégal de la Cie. des Indes, Paris, October 14, 1720, in Ser. C6 6, ANC; St. Robert to the Co[mpany], Senegal, May 24, 1721, Art. 3, *ibid.*; Beauchamp to Maurepas, November 5, 1731, in *MPA*, IV, 79.

5. Mémoire sur le Commerce du Sénégal (draft), March 23, 1723, in Ser. C6 7, ANC; Curtin, *Economic Change*, I, 187.

of Gorée. Another post was at Bissau on the Upper Guinea coast. The slaves were called *captifs* (captives). They were not referred to as slaves until they were sold in America: probably a legalistic fiction justifying their enslavement as captives of war, though many slaves shipped from Senegambia during the eighteenth century were indeed war captives.[6] The pens that held the *captifs* until a slave ship came for them were called *captiveries* and were located at Fort St. Joseph at Galam, at Fort St. Louis, and at the trading posts at Bissau and Gorée.

When the African slave trade to Louisiana began, the Company of the Indies' control over its Senegal concession was weak and was challenged by African nations as well as by its European rivals. During the early and mid-1720s, the French and the Dutch fought over Arguin Island, the center of the trade in Arabic gum collected in the forests of Morocco. The gum trade was considered far more profitable than the trade in slaves. The Moors sided with the Dutch. The English had a trading post at Fort James in the Gambia River and were quite active there. The Portuguese had a long tradition of control at Bissau, and the Company of the Indies' trading post there was under great pressure. In June, 1720, M. Marcon, the company's agent at Bissau, complained about the king and the people of the country "who not only make him pay avarices under the least pretext, but steal from him, abuse him verbally, and force him to pay the price according to their whim for what they present him to purchase. And when he does not have the merchandise they ask for, he cannot prevent them from taking twice what is due them, soiling everywhere around the storehouse. They even force him to open his storage chests." Marcon wrote that he would be spared these insults if he were well supplied with good merchandise with which to satisfy them and if the trading post were fortified. He asked to be relieved until the company carried out these suggestions.[7]

The Rois Saratiques of the Kingdom of the Fulbe (Fouls) controlled traffic on the middle reaches of the Senegal River. Their cooperation was purchased at a high price. For 1721, an impressive assortment of goods valued at 4,285 livres was presented to the king, the king's

6. Mémoire sur le Commerce du Sénégal (draft), March 23, 1723, in Ser. C6 7, ANC; Curtin, *Economic Change*, I, 154.

7. Mémoire sur le Commerce du Sénégal (draft), March 23, 1723, in Ser. C6 7, ANC; André Delcourt, *La France et les établissements français en Sénégal entre 1713 et 1763*, Mémoires de l'Institut Français d'Afrique Noire, XVII (Dakar, 1952), 94. For a discussion of Portuguese influence in Upper Guinea, see Rodney, *Upper Guinea Coast* and "Upper Guinea"; St. Robert to the Co[mpany], Senegal, March 28, 1721, in Ser. C6 6, ANC.

wives, and the king's marshals in formal ceremonies called Bon Jour du Roy and Grand Bon Jour.[8]

The French presence was well established in Senegambia long before the African slave trade to Louisiana began. French traders had asserted their right to a monopoly of trade in Senegambia in 1664. French trading posts had long been established at Gorée, at St. Louis at the mouth of the Senegal River, and far up the Senegal River at Galam. The reason the Company of the Indies concentrated upon Senegal for the slave trade during the 1720s is quite clear: The Senegal concession was the only place on the African coast where it held exclusive trading rights. Elsewhere, the company sold private permits to engage in the slave trade. The English had taken Cabinda; and since the entire coast of Angola was dominated by the English and the Portuguese, the French had little hope of trading in that country, except with great difficulty. Although the Company of the Indies had a trading post at Juda (Whydah, on the Gulf of Benin), it competed there with all the nations of Europe. The Portuguese were taking the upper hand at Juda. The kings of Ardres (Allada or Porto Novo) were hostile to the Europeans and interrupted trade. The slave trade at Juda was becoming uncertain and unprofitable.[9]

Between 1726 and 1731, almost all the slave-trade voyages organized by the Company of the Indies went to Louisiana. Thirteen slave ships landed in Louisiana during these years; all but one of them left from Senegambia. Over half the slaves brought to French Louisiana, 3,250 out of 5,987, arrived from Senegambia during this five-year period. The last ship, arriving in 1743, also came from Senegambia.

It is relevant, therefore, to look to Senegambia for the African roots of Louisiana's Afro-Creole culture. During the early eighteenth century, the Senegal Valley was described as rich and productive: a huge area, well integrated, with excellent soil made extremely fertile by the flooding of the river. French observers compared it with the Valley of the Nile. All the major crops of eighteenth-century Louisiana were

8. Facture des Marchandises, Vivres es Ustancils chargés du Magasin du Sénégal sur la Barque l'Union Commandée par M. Lambert pour faire le voiage de Galam es payer en passant la Coutume au Roy Brack pour la presente année. Affaires Financières, Senegal, June 26, 1721, in Sec. IP 274A, No. 15, Dossier 5, APL.

9. Robert Louis Stein, *The French Slave Trade in the Eighteenth Century: An Old Regime Business* (Madison, Wis., 1979), 77; Pierre Pluchon, *La route des esclaves: Négriers et bois d'ébène au XVIIIième siècle* (Paris, 1980), 24; Pierre Verger, *Flux et reflux de la traite des nègres entre le Golfe de Bénin et Bahia de Todos os Santos du 17ième au 19ième siècles* (Paris, 1968), 693; Mémoire sur le Sénégal, approuvé par St. R[obert], October 16, 1723, in Ser. C6 10, ANC.

Senegambia During the French Slave Trade

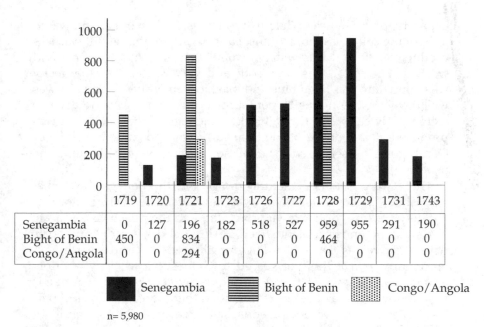

	1719	1720	1721	1723	1726	1727	1728	1729	1731	1743
Senegambia	0	127	196	182	518	527	959	955	291	190
Bight of Benin	450	0	834	0	0	0	464	0	0	0
Congo/Angola	0	0	294	0	0	0	0	0	0	0

Senegambia   Bight of Benin   Congo/Angola

n= 5,980

Figure 2. Slaves Landed in Louisiana by French Slave Trade:
Numbers and Origins
SOURCE: Calculated from Jean Mettas, *Autres Ports* (Paris, 1984), Vol. II of Mettas, *Répertoire des expéditions négrières françaises au XVIIIième siècle.*, ed. Serge and Michelle Daget.
NOTE: See Appendix A for a complete listing of slave voyages.

grown in this area. Rice was domesticated independently along the middle Niger about 3,500 years ago, well before the arrival of Asian rice. Corn was widely cultivated. According to Père Jean Baptiste Labat, "That which one calls *Mil* in Senegal is called *Mahis* in America, *bled de Turquie* in France, *grand Turc* in Italy. There are two kinds, *gros* and *petit*." Both kinds of corn were cultivated in the Senegal Valley; rice was cultivated in several places, as well as several varieties of peas. A great deal of excellent tobacco was grown. Huge fields were planted. Indigo grew "more than one would wish." Cotton was abundant and, according to Labat, grew almost without cultivation.[10]

Indigo grew wild in great quantity all along the rivers of Senegam-

10. Roland Portères, "Primary Cradles of Agriculture in the African Continent," in *Papers in African Prehistory*, ed. J. D. Fage and R. A. Oliver (Cambridge, Eng., 1970), 46–47; Père Jean Baptiste Labat, *Nouvelle rélation de l'Afrique occidentale contenant une description exacte du Sénégal et des Pais situés entre le Cap Blanc et la Riviere de Serrelione, qusqu'a plus de 300 lieues en avant dans les Terres. L'histoire naturelle de ces Pais les differentes Nations qui y sont répandues, leurs Religions et leurs moeurs, etc.* (5 vols.; Paris, 1728).

bia and Upper Guinea. While it was less productive than cultivated indigo, the color was more intense; and it did not matter if it was less productive, since it was widely available. It only had to be cut and worked. The cotton was long, soft, and very white. It was perfectly well spun, and was dyed blue and black or left white. Paddy rice was well developed along the Upper Guinea coast. Both wet and dry rice were widely cultivated throughout the Senegal Concession. Salt was produced at the mouth of the Senegal River and traded far inland. Ocean-going vessels used for deep-sea fishing were built along the Senegal.[11]

There were islands of natural prairies in the Senegal River that nourished "a prodigious quantity of animals. The beef are not big, but they are sturdy, strong, vigorous, fat, and their flesh very delicate in taste. One finds excellent sheep during the dry season, and goats with a marvelous flavor. . . . Fowl of all kinds cover the earth. . . . Since corn [petit mil] is not spared to domestic fowl, they multiply infinitely and are very fat, and consequently very tender. Hunting is very abundant, and one sees regiments rather than companies of partridges, guinea fowl, wood pigeons, sea birds and migratory birds."[12]

The fields in which the farmers planted corn, rice, peas, melons, and other vegetables were called lougans. André Brüe, director of the Senegal concession, described field gangs working in the nude, wielding lightweight, crescent-shaped spades with handles long enough that the workers could avoid bending over while cultivating the earth. The lord who supervised workers toiling in his field went ahead of them, accompanied by his griots singing loudly and beating their drums with all their might. The lord, armed as if going into battle with a sword at his side and a whip in his hand, seconded his griots as much as he could with his voice and with gestures. The soil, though light and sandy, remained inconceivably fertile. According to Labat, the workers barely scratched the earth, contenting themselves with pulling up the grass and some of the roots. Labat attributed to laziness these careful methods of farming, which were actually the response to a delicate environment: "To see them, nevertheless, one would think that they were performing the hardest labor, because they behave like they are possessed, making movements and contortions more or less extreme in accordance with how vehement was the

11. Labat, *Afrique occidentale*, II, 74–75, 165, 186–88, 304, IV, 85; Rodney, *Upper Guinea Coast*, 16, 17, 20–22.

12. Labat, *Afrique occidentale*, II, 189–90, IV, 185.

song of the *griots*." Labat commented that they would surely be too rich if they knew what their land was worth and how they could profit from it. Brüe increased the pace of labor by giving alcohol to the workers and the *griots*.[13]

The metalworkers were highly skilled and multitalented. They were goldsmiths, silversmiths, armsmakers, blacksmiths, horseshoe-makers, and coppersmiths. "In a word, they unite in one single person all the workers who use hammer and anvil." They worked with iron as well as with gold and silver. They made knives, hatchets, axes, and blades for cutting iron that, according to Labat, they tempered at least as well as the Europeans could. European iron was brought in bars and served as real or ideal money in the markets. These craftsmen had neither forge nor shop, but worked in front of their houses under a tree and carried their tools with them to wherever they found work. "One must not believe that this caused them much trouble. Their tools only consist of a very small anvil, a goatskin bellows, a few hammers, tongs, and two or three files." They worked in a relaxed, informal manner, making of labor a social and ceremonial occasion. "They are always sitting down, constantly talking or smoking, putting their anvil on the ground or on the sand, and since it is thin and fragile, it sinks as soon as they strike it with a few blows of the hammer, and they spend most of their time raising it and putting it back into place. There are never less than three of them working together. . . . They strike the material gently, as if they were afraid of damaging it. They never tire of making fairly delicate works of gold or silver." The metalworkers made sword handles and plaques for decorating ovens, "and other similar things which demonstrate their intelligence and their dexterity, and they would be perfectly good workers if they were taught and were a little less lazy." They made very thin jewelry of various shapes called *menilles*. The women decorated their hair and made necklaces and bracelets with it.[14]

According to Labat, laziness prevented their weavers from profiting from the abundance of cotton growing in their lands—an abundance that would have allowed them to produce more cloth than they could consume and to deprive the Europeans of the prodigious sales and considerable profits they made on their fabrics: "They lack neither the intelligence to increase their skills and make their cloth a convenient length, nor the industry to dye them and give them

13. *Ibid.*, II, 307–309.
14. *Ibid.*, II, 304–307.

variety and a pleasing appearance. That which they do not have at all and which to all appearances they never will have is a little emulation."[15]

If we can judge by the decimated appearance of the Senegal Valley today, emulation of European technology and world view, in which the traditional African reverence for all forms of life was replaced by the European drive to maximize production and conquer nature, did not serve the land and its people well. During the early eighteenth century, the Senegal Valley was heavily wooded. Great stands of palms, coming in four varieties, dotted the landscape. One island located only half a lieu from Isle St. Louis was covered with trees, and the French went there to cut all they needed. The French renamed it Isle aux Bois.[16]

By the early eighteenth century, Islam had long been ascendant in Senegambia. The blacks living on both sides of the Senegal River and in the lands to the east and south were Muslims. Those of the Mandinga kingdom were the most zealous and were described as the "missionaries of Mohamedanism," traversing these vast countries to make converts. The rest of the blacks who lived between the Gambia River and Guinea and with whom the Europeans traded were described as idolaters "except for the Seraires and a few others who one regards as savages among whom one remarks no kind of religion." But the Islamic religion established among the blacks was considered distorted because of the "ignorance of those who first introduced it . . . and the nature of those who embraced it." Nevertheless, Labat wrote that the Mandinga followed the law of Mohammed. Most of them drank no wine or liquor. They fasted for Ramadan. They worked hard, their land was well cultivated, they had an abundance of beef, sheep, goats, and fowl, but kept no pigs. They liked commerce and long voyages. They loved and willingly helped each other and never captured each other. The only captives among them were those enslaved as punishment for a crime. They were polite, fine, witty, and clairvoyant. Almost all of them could read and write. They had public schools where the Marabout taught the children to read and write the Arab language, and they used the Arabic characters to write the Mandinga language. These schools were in session only for several hours before dawn. The Marabout made their living by teaching the children and by making *grisgris* (charms). They were hard on

15. *Ibid.*
16. *Ibid.*, II, 189–90.

their women, considering them like cattle. They practiced female circumcision (clitoridectomy) in an effort to promote their fidelity.[17]

According to Labat, all the women of Senegambia worked hard. It was their job to thresh the rice, the corn (*le Mahis ou gros Mil*), and the millet. They made the couscous and the sanglet, prepared the food and the drinks, spun the cotton, made the clothes, dyed the thread and the cloth (*pagnes*), cultivated the tobacco and the grains, cleaned the huts, cared for the animals, collected the wood, and brought the water. "In a word, they are charged with all the work of the house, and when their husbands are holding conversations, they must chase away the mosquitoes which annoy them, and present their pipes and tobacco to them." In spite of all this hard work, they were extremely fertile and gave birth with a surprising facility. Only very young women needed the assistance of other women. They made it a point of honor not to cry out when they were experiencing the strongest birth pains, nor even to make the least complaint, or let escape the least sigh. These hard-working, stoic women were not submissive, wrote Labat. Although their husbands had a right to repudiate their wives and drive them out when they failed to please, "they never tire of departing from their duty," especially when they were princesses and found themselves backed up by their relatives. The Fulbe queens knew very well how to sustain their rank. They were too proud to turn their heads. It was necessary to place in front of them what one wanted them to see. When their heads itched, they scratched with a large gold needle. The kings and the lords who could afford several houses established their wives in separate households to avoid conflict among them. According to Labat, those polygamous husbands who could not afford separate households for their wives had to struggle to avoid conflicts among them.[18]

Labat wrote that the Isle du Sénégal, or Isle St. Louis, and the territory near the mouth of the Senegal River and to the south was known as the Kingdom of the Wolofs (Royaume des Jalofes). It was the generic name of all the peoples who took the particular names of the places where they lived, "approximately as we see in the Kingdoms of France, Spain, England, where the peoples take the names of particular provinces where they live under the general title of French, Spanish, English."[19]

17. *Ibid.*, II, 189–91, 304–309, 271. See Curtin, *Economic Change*, I, 183, for the religious prohibition against enslavement of fellow Muslims.
18. Labat, *Afrique Occidentale*, II, 301–302, 208–209.
19. *Ibid.*, II, 153.

French men stationed at St. Louis were particularly attracted to Wolof women because of their dark skin. According to Labat, the Fulbe women did not have the beautiful, lustrous black skin (*beau noir lustré*) of the Wolof women who lived south of the river. "It is claimed that this results from their alliances with the Moors, who imbued them with the reveries of the Koran and at the same time, ruined their beautiful black color by passing on to them their brown color [*couleur de bistre*]."[20]

When Brüe assumed his employment as director of the Company of the Indies in Senegal, he was astonished to find all of the employees of the company lodged outside the fort in straw huts, where each one had a *négresse* who, under the pretext of cooking their meals and caring for their household, "served them more probably for usages prohibited by the Law of God." He began his duties by chasing away all of these "creatures" and forcing the workers to take their meals at the fort and attend prayers morning and night, under penalty of being deprived of their liquor, which was distributed on the spot to those attending the prayer meetings. It was not explained if this enforced choice between women and alcohol was a success, but it was evidently normal several decades later for French workers and sailors to seek wives among mulatto women. In 1724, the director recommended that young girls be brought from Paris to Galam to marry French workers and sailors who, discouraged by the shortage of mulatto girls to marry at the post, wanted to return to France.[21] The attraction of French men to the Wolof, partially because of what they considered to be "their pure blood" and their "beautiful, black, lustrous skin" calls into question theories positing a revulsion among peoples who least resemble each other in color and appearance in early contact situations.

Although few Wolof slaves were normally shipped from Senegambia during the 1720s, Wolof were brought to Louisiana, where they were called "Senegal" by the French colonists, though they continued to be called Wolof (Djolaufs) among themselves. Le Page du Pratz, who had been director of the Company of the Indies in Louisiana, expressed the same preference for Wolofs as did Labat. Du Pratz claimed that the lighter-skinned slaves smelled bad, that the Wolof were the darkest and of the purest blood, and that he had never known them to have an odor. He recommended that only Wolof

20. *Ibid.*, II, 209.
21. *Ibid.*, II, 232–33; Julien Dubellay to the Company of the Indies, Senegal, May 25, 1724, in Ser. C6 8, Art. 11, ANC.

slaves, male and female, young and old, be selected for any service in the home. They were not as robust as the other slaves, possessed less resistance to great heat, and proved less apt for tilling the soil. But they were the most faithful, their minds were more penetrating than the others, and consequently they were more apt at learning a skill and how to serve. Du Pratz wrote: "They are very appreciative, and when one knows how to attach them to oneself, one sees them sacrifice their own friends in order to serve their masters. They are good commanders of other *nègres*, because of their faithfulness and appreciativeness as well as because they seem to be born to command. Since they are proud, they can easily be encouraged to learn a trade or to serve in the home by the distinction they acquire over the other *nègres*, and the advantage their status allows them in acquiring clothes."[22]

The most important kingdoms of Senegambia maintained a tight control over which peoples could be enslaved and sold to the Europeans. It seems that during the 1720s, neither the Fulbe nor the Mandinga sold their own people or allowed others to sell them. The Bambara (Bamana) enjoyed no such protection during the 1720s. Bambarana, the land of the Bambara, was located on the upper reaches of the Senegal River beyond Galam, near the Niger River. Evidently, no Frenchman had entered Bambara country during the 1720s. Labat called the Bambara kingdoms above Galam "Bambara Cana" and described the region as extremely fertile, heavily populated, and strong militarily, where all the Bambara were slaves of the king and the lords. Labat was no doubt referring to the kingdom of Mamari Kulubali, founder of the Bambara kingdom of Segu. He wrote: "That is just about all one can say for now. Perhaps in the future some employee of the Company will be found who is curious enough to make a voyage to that country and give us a description."[23]

Bambara slaves were brought to Louisiana in large numbers and played a preponderant role in the formation of the colony's Afro-Creole culture. Both Mandinga and Bambara were Mande peoples claiming descent from the Mali empire established by Sundiatta during the thirteenth century, but there were strong religious differences between them. While the Mandinga were the proselytizers of Islam, the struggle against Islam was an important component of Bambara identity until the late nineteenth century. While the Mandinga did not

---

22. Curtin, *Economic Change*, I, 183; Le Page du Pratz, *Histoire de la Louisiane* (3 vols.; Paris, 1758), I, 342, 343n, 344–45.

23. Curtin, *Economic Change*, I, 183; Labat, *Afrique occidentale*, III, 334.

enslave and sell their own people, they were the major slave traders, and they concentrated upon selling the Bambara captured while they fought among and enslaved each other. During his voyage to Galam in 1723, Brüe wrote, "The trade with the Mandinga can only furnish Bambara blacks. But . . . these captives are the best men of all Africa for labor. They are robust, good natured, intelligent. . . . The labor attached to servitude does not bother them at all. They love their masters, are obedient, and are never subject to flight, to revolt, or to despair as are those coming from the Mina Coast and several other places." Brüe esteemed the Bambara highly and kept some of them for labor in the Senegal concession. He wrote in 1720, "I have removed the shackles from 650 Bambara *captifs*, who serve me better than all the blacks of the country. They never refuse to work, provided their stomach is full." [24]

The Bambara played a special role in the Senegal concession. They were used as domestics at the trading posts of St. Louis and Gorée and at the forts of Galam and Arguin. The French used the Bambara to man the boats they operated on the Senegal River and as guides and interpreters. Bambara served as reinforcements for detachments of European troops, and *Bambara* became a generic name for slave soldier. They were considered brave and loyal, and skillful combatants. They had twice destroyed Moroccan armies much larger than their own, using only bows, arrows, and swords. Nicolas Depres de St. Robert, who replaced Brüe as director of the Senegal concession, was less enthused about them. In 1725 he wrote, "If it is true . . . that you are sending the Bambara to Juda only because the blacks serving at that trading post are all thieves, you can be sure that the cure is worse than the disease, because there are no greater thieves in the world than the Bambara." [25]

There is little doubt that the Bambara brought to Louisiana were truly ethnic Bambara. They constituted a language community. Louisiana officials reported that four hundred Bambara slaves speaking the same language were involved in the conspiracy of 1731. There was a Bambara court interpreter in Louisiana. Slaves testifying in court identified their own nations. The influential quotation cited by Gabriel Debien indicating a variety of peoples labeled Bambara who

24. Richard L. Roberts, *Warriors, Merchants, and Slaves: The State and the Economy in the Middle Niger Valley, 1700–1914* (Stanford, 1987), 8; Labat, *Afrique occidentale*, IV, 85; St. Robert to the Co[mpany], Senegal, March 28, 1721, in Ser. C6 6, p. 14; Brüe to Violaine, Senegal, April 30, 1720, copy, *ibid*.

25. Delcourt, *Établissements français en Senegal*, 49, 118*n*, 130, 154, 172–73; St. Robert to the Co[mpany] of the Indies, Senegal, July 18, 1725, in Ser. C6 9, pp. 6, 7, ANC.

were not truly Bambara dates from 1789. By that time—sixty to seventy years after the French slave trade to Louisiana—the term *Bambara* had taken on a generic meaning and was widely applied to peoples coming through St. Louis from the interior of the continent. Many distinct ethnic communities had by then been incorporated into the Bambara warrior group, and Bambara identity had long been ascendant.[26]

The Bambara brought to Louisiana during the 1720s had been captured during warfare among Bambara kingdoms at the early stage of the formation of the Segu empire under Mamari Kulubali, who ruled from 1712 to 1755. The export of Bambara slaves peaked during warfare in Bambarana. In contrast, when peace reigned, the slave trade from Galam to St. Louis was badly disrupted. In 1721, Galam sent few slaves, and those had been of poor quality, even though the trading post had received good and adequate trade merchandise. St. Robert explained that "no slave caravans arrived . . . the Bambara who are almost always at war among themselves . . . were all obliged to unite to protect their country against the Moors of Morocco whom they chased out of their country after having defeated them twice. The said Moors, upon withdrawing, boasted that they would soon come back with an army big enough to destroy the Bambara entirely. This obliges the countries of Bambarana to live in harmony and join forces to oppose the Moroccans whom they expect."[27]

Between 1727 and 1729, when almost all the slave-trade voyages organized by the Company of the Indies went to Louisiana, the trading post at Galam was sending about one thousand *captifs* down the Senegal River to St. Louis each year. Other Bambara slaves were coming from the French post near the mouth of the Gambia River. High mortality in the *captiveries*, aboard the ships, and after landing would indicate that the slaves embarked during this period came from some distance inland. It seems clear that Bambara slaves arrived in Louisiana in large numbers and they were truly Bambara.

The spurt in the trade in Bambara slaves coincided with the rise of Mamari Kulubali. Described as "brutal and energetic," he revolutionized traditional Bambara society by systematically destroying the familial ties of his subjects, both free and slave, and converting them

26. Lamiral, *L'Affrique et le Peuple Afriquain considérés sous leurs rapports* (Paris, 1789), 184, cited in Gabriel Debien, "Les origines des esclaves aux Antilles," *Bulletin de l'Institut Français d'Afrique Noir*, Series B, XXIII (1961), 376; Roberts, *Warriors, Merchants, and Slaves,* 7.

27. Curtin, *Economic Change*, I, 181; St. Robert to the Co[mpany], Senegal, March 28, 1721, Ser. C6 6, p. 3, ANC.

into his close, personal dependents who became the foundation of his army—an army that has been called a slave force. When a criminal had to pay a fine, Mamari Kulubali paid it for him. If he was condemned to death, Mamari Kulubali pardoned him. When a subject could not pay his tax, Mamari Kulubali forgave the debt on condition that he or one of his sons was placed at the disposition of the king. He assured his peoples' personal loyalty by attaching them to cults of which he was the leader and by creating a brotherhood of which he was both political and religious head. Traditional Bambara society was based upon the grain-producing agricultural commune controlled by the elders. Agriculture was their principal labor, and all worthy and noble persons were expected to cultivate the land. Rain-fed millet and sorghum were the major crops. Fishing and hunting supplemented the food supply. Hunters were respected and feared. The Segu empire undermined the traditional gerontocracy that controlled cereal-producing, agrarian corporate communities. The elders' control of access to food, to wives, and to both practical and spiritual knowledge was challenged by the militarization of the young men who found an alternative to submission to their elders in warfare, plunder, and slave raiding—the crucial economic foundations of the Segu Bambara state. Nevertheless, the Bambara agricultural commune managed to survive the disruptions of the Segu Bambara state, the Umarian state, and French colonial rule, and it lives on to the present day.[28]

Warfare and enslavement became the foundations of state power in the Segu Bambara empire. Slave raiding in Bambarana was well organized and institutionalized. The *tó* was an association of hunters who became slave raiders and formed the basis for a standing army. In formal warfare, the booty, including enslaved people, became the collective property of the *tó*. Booty captured in banditry, called *tegereya*, was the private property of the individual raider. The greatest number of slaves were captured by state warriors, *kelakela*, who would take whole villages or groups of villages.[29]

Captured and enslaved Bambara did not all go to the Atlantic. Some went to the desert or to interior markets, and some were retained locally. Many among the enslaved women were sold to the trans-Sahara trade to fill the harems of North Africa and the Middle East. While all slaves captured and owned by warriors could be sold,

28. Louis Tauxier, *Histoire des Bambara* (Paris, 1942), 29; Viviana Paques, *Les Bambara* (Paris, 1954), 47; Roberts, *Warriors, Merchants, and Slaves*, 7, 25, 31.
29. Curtin, *Economic Change*, I, 181.

the king first claimed one-half to two-thirds of the booty captured in formal military campaigns and less formal cavalry raids. Only some of the king's slaves could be sold. Many were instead incorporated into the elite guard and cavalry troops. Some of the king's slaves worked the state's fields near Segu.[30]

Who were the Bambara brought to Louisiana? We know quite a bit about the Bambara during the early eighteenth century without relying entirely upon Eurocentric sources and/or projecting backward in time. The Bambara are a Mande people with a strong tradition of oral history. They trace their ancestry to the great thirteenth-century Mali empire in the region where the upper Niger River intersects Mali and Guinea. The modern Mande peoples are, besides the Bambara, the Mandinka, Maninka, Malinke, Mandinga, Manya, Dyula, Duranko, and Wangara. Their dispersal throughout the West African savannah, mainly because of the imperialistic campaigns of the ancient Mali empire, led to their developing mechanisms for retaining their cultural focus in spite of their geographical displacement. They all speak mutually intelligible dialects of Mandekan and share values defining kinship, politics, and economy. More than recognition of common ancestry, their system of beliefs united them into a "philosophy, ideology, or cosmology—which defines appropriate behavior for individual actors and allows in turn the interpretation of the behavior of others."[31]

The Mande have a strong tradition of oral history communicated by the *jeli*, or bards, and presented in the form of myth and legend. Since the breakup of the Mali empire, Mande culture has been adapted for survival in the face of its population's dispersal. Mande peoples traditionally have had, and still have, strong mechanisms for retaining the cultural focus of their civilization while at the same time providing for necessary innovation among their widely scattered members. Oral tradition plays a major role in preserving their cultural focus. The collective wisdom of the Bambara is passed on by the frequent citing of proverbs in ordinary conversation. According to Moussa Travélé (Traore), a Bambara cannot speak two or three sentences without saying a proverb. Robert Farris Thompson wrote:

30. David Geggus, "Sex Ratio, Age, and Ethnicity in the Atlantic Slave Trade: Data From French Shipping and Plantation Records," *Journal of African History*, XXX (1989), 37; Patrick Manning, *Slavery and African Life: Occidental, Oriental, and African Slave Trades* (Cambridge, Eng., 1990); Roberts, *Warriors, Merchants, and Slaves*, 38.

31. Charles S. Bird and Martha B. Kendall, "The Mande Hero," in *Explorations in African Systems of Thought*, ed. Ivan Karp and Charles S. Bird (Bloomington, Ind., 1980), 13–26.

"Mande partly resolved the tension between tradition and innovation through their rich and extensive oral literature: animal stories, hunting songs, and, especially, the literature of the courts, sung by professional bards. . . . The primary Mande aesthetic value is the search for simplicity, for the elegance of science. Thus the Mandekan word *woron* 'to get to the kernel' also means to master speech, music, song, any aesthetic endeavor."[32]

While the casted *griot* was protected from enslavement and was therefore unlikely to have been sent across the Atlantic, folk-story tellers were legion, and each family, each neighborhood had its favorite. One of the most important sources for information about the establishment of the Mali empire during the thirteenth century is a long legend about the life of Sundiatta, its founder. Richard L. Roberts has collected, studied, and interpreted Bambara myths and legends to reconstruct the history of the founding and development of the Segu Bambara state during the eighteenth century.[33]

Because the Bambara resisted the inroads of Islam, traditional Mande beliefs were no doubt more powerful among them than among the Mandinga. French historians and anthropologists have studied Bambara myths, cosmology, religion, and social organization. Although these studies were made during the twentieth century, they involve customs and beliefs that tend to be conservative and therefore likely to have existed far enough in the past to have influenced the world view of the Bambara brought to Louisiana.

Our understanding of Bambara cosmology as a coherent system is fairly recent.[34] The ethical content of Bambara origin myths and cosmology escaped the more purely descriptive, and often racially prejudiced, anthropologists of earlier times. Bambara religion is based upon fundamental principles known only by priests, heads of families, and the old of both sexes versed in "the science of things of the creation." Their knowledge is acquired slowly, through a series of

32. Moussa Travélé, *Proverbes et contes Bambara, accompagnés d'une traduction française et précédés d'un abrégé de droit coutumier Bambara et Malinke* (1923; rpr. Paris, 1977), 35; Robert Farris Thompson, *Flash of the Spirit: African and Afro-American Art and Philosophy* (New York, 1983), 196.

33. Charles S. Bird, "The Development of Mandekan (Manding): A Study of the Role of Extra-linguistic Factors in Linguistic Change," in *Language and History in Africa*, ed. David Dalby (New York, 1970), 155; Djibril Tamsei Niane, *Sundiata: An Epic of Old Mali*, trans. G. D. Pickett (Atlantic Highlands, N.J., 1979); Roberts, *Warriors, Merchants, and Slaves*, 27–36.

34. The following discussion of Bambara creation myths and world view is based on Germaine Dieterlen, *Essai sur la religion Bambara* (Paris, 1951), xvi–xviii, 17–19, 53–55, 65–68, 109, 152, 227, 230.

initiations and through instruction given at times through rites. The Bambara expression for this knowledge is *doniya duna* or *kuru doniya*, meaning "profound knowledge," differentiated from superficial knowledge, *doni fyêma*, meaning literally "knowledge that has wind." The fear that Bambara traditional society was being destroyed by modernization might have been what inspired the Bambara transmitters of profound knowledge to overcome their great aversion to confiding in strangers, especially in whites, and to entrust a team of French anthropologists working in French West Africa before and after World War II with the task of preserving this knowledge, just as Richard Price was entrusted with this same task by the maroons of Suriname.[35]

The Bambara explain that the creation of the universe was an extremely complex process in which the world emerged from an original void in motion that gradually took on voice and vibration, created all the elements of the universe, and gave birth to sound, light, all creatures, all actions, and all sentiments, as well as to human consciousness. Pemba, the wood spirit, reigned first and spent his first seven years on earth as a whirlwind. He created Moussa Koroni, the first woman, who gave birth to all living creatures, including lower animals and vegetables. Thus, all living creatures, both animal and vegetable, are descended from the first woman and are thus blood relatives of humans. Reverence for all forms of life is therefore central to Bambara beliefs.

The value of androgyny is also a fundamental theme. The conflict between the sexes, symbolized by the corporal separation of Pemba and Moussa Koroni, their conflicts and quarrels, became the source of cosmic discord, which was combated by the harmony established by the androgynous water spirit, Faro. Pemba, the first man, became promiscuous and abandoned Moussa Koroni, the first woman. In order to avoid starving, she created agriculture and taught its techniques. Pemba's desertion drove Moussa Koroni mad. In her madness, called *wanzo*, she traveled in all directions, spreading impurity wherever she went. Pemba pursued her in vain, finally seeking help from Faro. Faro found her, vanquished her, and tried to get her to submit, but she refused, declaring herself free and thus bringing evil, disorder, and death into the universe. Faro then established supremacy over Pemba, establishing the principle of androgyny, the vibration of duality that brings order to the universe. The androgynous

35. Richard Price, *First Time: The Historical Vision of an Afro-American People* (Baltimore, 1983).

CÉRÉMONIE DE LA CIRCONCISION DES NÈGRES.

Circumcision ceremony in Senegambia, 1720s. The original print appeared in Labat, *Afrique occidentale* (Paris, 1728).
Courtesy The New York Academy of Medicine Library.

water spirit's triumph over the promiscuous male wood spirit represents the triumph of reason and moderation over blind force. Faro is the light, the master of the word, builder of the seven heavens, the representative of will and wisdom that control the demands of the sexual impulse.

This creation myth has a Freudian focus, pinpointing uncontrolled sexuality and gender conflict as the source of disorder and madness. In the rites of circumcision and excision, the young person who is about to enter adulthood is symbolically relieved of *wanzo*, representing disorder, which resides in the foreskin of the male and the clitoris of the female. Unlike male circumcision, clitoridectomy is a form of sexual mutilation that is common among Sudanic lands influenced by Islam.[36] It is unclear whether this practice was introduced after the Bambara became Islamized or if it existed among them during the eighteenth century. Labat claimed that the Mandinga used clitoridec-

36. For a recent study of clitoral excision and other forms of sexual mutilation of women in Africa, see Hanny Lightfoot-Klein, *Prisoners of Ritual: An Odyssey into Female Genital Circumcision in Africa* (Binghamton, N.Y., 1990).

tomy as a means of trying to ensure fidelity among their women.[37] Symbolically, at least, the Bambara viewed male and female circumcision as a ritual intended to control the sexual impulse of both sexes through reason, moderation, and wisdom, allowing for the triumph of androgyny over the conflict between male and female. But the women got the worst of it, by far.

Bambara creation myths demonstrate a flexible approach to life: the ability to be comfortable with duality and seeming contradiction. Profound knowledge is the preserve of the few. But knowledge of the mythology upon which the ethical foundation of the culture is built is universal. Knowledge of, and capacity to perform, religious rites and rituals is universal. Religious knowledge and power is in the hands of the many. This knowledge was easily transportable.

The symbolism of Bambara cosmology transcends religious life and ceremonies and penetrates all of secular life and daily conduct. Cultivation of the soil is a religious act: Each blow of the hoe is a wound made upon the earth, a punishment for its impurity, an act of purification. Faro looks after the soul and vital force of grains. Only Faro can give the rain necessary for their germination. Rain contains the *ni*, part of the soul, of the cereals.[38] Germaine Dieterlen wrote, "The Bambara as well as many other Blacks, make of man a universe and of the universe a system where all has its place and role, from the stars to the objects of everyday use, from the mind to garbage." Indeed, the only observable monuments consist of furniture, utensils, and musical instruments, whose forms and ornamentation transmit metaphysical principles upon which Bambara thought is based. Thus, each artisan creates a religious object. Each color, each band of cloth, each design and pattern of textile, each article of clothing, each ornament, each number has religious significance. There is, thus, no separation between artisanship, artistic creation, and religious observance. Cowrie shells, used both as money and as decoration, are sacred because they come from deep water and from the bed of Faro. The number 3 represents the male, for the two testicles and the penis; the number 4 represents the female, for the four lips. Males are scarified with three lines on the face, females with four. The number 7 is the perfect number, representing the androgynous unity of the male-female duality.

The parts of the body have religious significance. Hair contains an important part of the soul, *ni*. The ear is decorated because of its func-

37. Labat, *Afrique occidentale,* II, 300–301.
38. Viviana Paques, *Les Bambara* (Paris, 1954), 107.

tion. Men wear three rings of copper on the right ear and four on the left, representing the complete, androgynous person. Women wear four bobs on each ear. But the symbolism goes deeper. The wind spirit, Téliko, created by Faro, is the master of wind and sound and hears what is said to everyone. Ornaments of copper, the preferred metal of Faro, attract sound and send it to Téliko and Faro, who thus judge the words and acts of people. Perception and speech have transcendent significance. The bearer of false news and bad words is heard and judged by Faro and Téliko. Amiable and constructive words profit the one to whom they are addressed. Téliko changes the air sent by the speaker into favorable *nyama* (spiritual power), and the person to whom good words are addressed should open the eyes wide and look at the person speaking in order to receive them, and close the ears so as not to lose the words' effect. But bad words and insults injure both the hearer and the speaker. Sight has the same transcendent effect as hearing and speech. If an object belonging to a person is seen and desired by another, the owner cannot refuse it to him. Sight alone establishes a bond between the object and the viewer that is stronger than the right of property.

Musical performance is a religious activity; each musical performance is a prayer. The harp, through its rhythms and tones, restores order to all that is troubled in the universe. Before beginning to play, the harpist places his mouth to the opening of the case and whispers to Faro, "Now it is your turn; organize the world." Thus, everyday activities have a ceremonial, religious significance that is—and was—easily transportable.

The Bambara belief in the transmigration of souls was a powerful source of cultural continuity. The souls of the deceased are not lost to the family. One person replaces another, and the same spiritual forces are reused indefinitely. Life is transmitted intact. There are two forms of soul: the *dya*, double or shadow, and the *ni*, which, unless captured at death and kept in the family altar, takes the form of malevolent *nyama*. When a person dies, Faro keeps the *dya* in the water, where it is refreshed and purified; the *ni* is likewise rejuvenated while being kept in the family altar. The first member of the family who is born after a death, regardless of sex, receives the *ni* and *dya* of the deceased. The sex of the *dya* is changed if necessary so that the *dya* is always of the opposite sex, carrying out once again the principle of androgyny.[39]

The Mande became mobile peoples after the breakup of the Mali

39. Dieterlen, *Religion Bambara*, 73.

empire and developed techniques for founding new spiritual communities. New *nyama boli* (charms) were fabricated, and sometimes sold, to be used as the spiritual foundation of newly created *komo* (men's association) as groups of Bambara migrated to new areas. These techniques were undoubtedly known by individual Bambara slaves brought to Louisiana. *Zinzin*, an amulet of support or power in Louisiana Creole, has the same name and meaning in Bambara.[40] *Grisgris*, meaning a harmful charm, comes from the Mande word *ger-regerys.*" DuPratz described the slaves of early Louisiana as "very superstitious and attached to their prejudices and to charms which they call *gris-gris*." Charms are created to protect the wearer. Although animal sacrifice is involved in making these charms, they express, ironically, a respect and reverence for life. The Bambara, for example, believe that every person is vulnerable to the presence of *nyama* because everyone destroys plants, crushes insects, and wounds other living creatures. Not only is one subject to attack from the displaced souls of creatures once alive, but these malevolent forces are transmitted to others through touch. Charms, however, protect the person from the effects of *nyama* from creatures killed unwillingly or out of necessity. But even the charms do not protect the wearer from the consequences of deliberate, useless destruction of life.[41]

In Mande culture, blacksmiths, bards, and leatherworkers are *nyama-kala*, inheriting protection against *nyama* through marriage restricted to their own castes. But hunters are not *nyama-kala* and must manipulate *nyama* through ritual and sacrifice. The *nyama* of a wild animal, *nyama baka*, leaves the animal's corpse and pursues the hunter, who uses "*nyama* laden parts of the kill—skins, horns, teeth, claws, feathers—in fetishes, talismans, and clothes. These serve to control the *nyama* released by each kill, protect him from potential destruction, empower him to perform greater deeds." The Bambara hunter carries a sacred bag suspended from his shoulder in which to capture the soul force of the animal at the moment of its death.[42]

40. *Ibid.*, 85, 145–47, 213; Paques, *Les Bambara*, 85, 94; Marcus Bruce Christian, "For a Black History of Louisiana" (Typescript in Archives and Manuscripts Department, Earl K. Long Library, University of New Orleans); William A. Read, *Louisiana-French* (Baton Rouge, 1931), 127. Christian defines *zinzin* as a charm or fetish, though Read believed it was a Louisiana Creole adaptation of a Bantu word for bird, fowl, or insect.

41. G. Thimans and N. I. de Moraes, "Dencha Fourt souverain du Baol," *Bulletin de l'Institut français d'Afrique Noir*, XXXVI (1974), 695, cited in Oumar Kane, "Le Fuuta-Taoro des satigi au Almaami (1512–1807)" (3 vols.; Ph.D. dissertation, Pantheon-Sorbonne, 1986); Du Pratz, *Histoire de la Louisiane*, I, 334; Dieterlen, *Religion Bambara*, 64n.

42. Bird and Kendall, "Mande Hero"; Dieterlen, *Religion Bambara*, 63.

Magic protects and supports as well as harms. The Bambara believe that all animals and plants have souls—a belief that probably derives from their descent from Moussa Koroni, the first woman, who gave birth to all forms of life. Herbal medicine obtains its strength from the soul force of plants, captured through sacrifice. Certain lineages have taboos against using certain animals or plants for food. There is always a story or legend to explain how the animal or plant rendered a service to an ancestor, such as saving his life, or vice versa, or how, following grave events, the ancestor was transformed into a plant or animal. These tabooed living creatures are viewed as blood relatives who cannot be harmed. The swallow is the messenger of Faro, and it participates in the human fertilization process by collecting the juice of the sacred tomato, which the aspiring parents spread on the water as an offering to Faro.[43] Skills in herbal medicine, as well as reverence for, and identification with, all forms of life, have evolved from these beliefs. In this world facing destruction by the "progress" and the "productiveness" of Western civilization, there is no more appropriate spirit to worship than the androgynous water spirit, nor a more functional belief than the sacredness of all forms of life.

The Bambara came to Louisiana equipped with a concept of sovereignty that was based upon control of people rather than of territory; with experience in creating new spiritual and legal communities; and with extensive experience in self-governing organizations. Bambara social organization had flexible strength, and it traveled well. Traditional Bambara societies did not consist of vast, centralized, hierarchical, despotic institutions. They did not resemble European kingdoms. Viviana Paques wrote, "That which one calls an empire we can only translate as the attraction exercised by a family because of its prestige or its power over groups which accepted its hegemony . . . a family attempted to dominate over groupings of people and not over extended territory."[44]

Although Bambara social organization is rigidly hierarchical and a sense of equality is absent, it is segmented and its members enjoy a high level of participatory democracy. Individual Bambara have a strong sense of justice. They participate in organized groups from early childhood, divided according to age and gender. The first group is for children between the ages of six and nine; the next group com-

43. Dieterlen, *Religion Bambara*, 81.
44. Paques, *Les Bambara*, 59.

prises youth from age ten to about age fifteen, when groups of adolescents are circumcised and admitted into adult societies. Each group has a leader, *ton-tigi* for the boys and *musso-tigi* for the girls. Each has an assistant or leader called *syere*, a treasurer, and a *tondyeli* or *griot*. The leadership is elected by the members. Women have their own powerful hierarchical societies of which less is known because Bambara women are more traditional and closed-mouth than the men. Women's role in practice is more active and autonomous than their status under traditional law would indicate. A woman can inherit all the goods of the head of the family, even a chief, in the absence of a male heir. The Mali empire once had a Keïta woman at its head, daughter of Naré, fa Maghan.[45]

Slavery was not associated with powerlessness; slaves were not pariahs. Prestigious members of society could be enslaved through capture. While slave raiding and sale of slaves became the economic foundation of the Segu Bambara state, slavery was also a means of gradually amalgamating alien, captured people into the community. Hegemony could be achieved through the military use of slaves. Bambara became slaves through capture in warfare, for punishment of a crime, or by birth. Criminals condemned to slavery were sold outside the country. If a slave woman was fertilized by a free man, she and her child became free. Where there were large numbers of slaves, they were organized into age groups. The *wolo-so,* leader of the oldest age group of slaves, became chief of the *dyon-kuru,* the assembly of slaves, and could play an important role in society. In Segu, for example, he became the spokesman for all the complaints of slaves; and he was often a respected adviser of the *fama* (king), at whose death he confirmed or denied the power of his successor by assuring or denying the submission of all the captives. The *fama* arranged the marriage of the *wolo-so,* established him materially, admitted him to his cult, and meted out important tasks to him. The *fama* sometimes married the *wolo-so*'s daughter and united with him through blood brotherhood and oath. The children of the *wolo-so* were often circumcised with those of the master, establishing a powerful age-group bond. He bore the name of his master and could own slaves. The third generation of the *wolo-so* became free. As in any society that relies heavily on slaves for military purposes, the slaves' condition was moderated, and their sense of their own power enhanced, by the

45. *Ibid.,* 55, 56; Travélé, *Proverbes et contes Bambara,* 9–22; Dieterlen, *Religion Bambara,* 74, 75.

essential service they performed and by their access to weapons and military training.[46]

The Bambara have a world view and concept of social organization that is resilient, functional, and designed to travel well. Territorial expansion could take place through the settlement of unoccupied territory, and the first occupant became the chief of the land. If other families wished to settle there, they had to ask his permission. Although there were general principles of traditional law, no codified law such as the Koran or the biblical commandments existed. The creation and administration of law was segmented. Justice was rendered in accordance with rules transmitted from generation to generation within each community, and sanctified by appeals to the heritage of the ancestors. The *fama* and his council could promulgate new laws, but first they had to consult the *komo*, the organization to which all male circumcised men belonged. Each swore on the shrine of the ancestors to obey the law, which thus became sacred.[47]

While the segmentation of Bambara society gave it flexibility, its tradition of alliances gave it strength. These alliances allowed the Bambara to realize their concept of empire through control of people, rather than of territory. Alliances were created by marriages systematically reinforced through the custom of exchanging women between two peoples. Alliances could also be created through *dyonge,* a pact of fraternity symbolically sealed when the parties involved in the pact mixed several drops of blood from their forearms with goat's milk, announced the conditions of alliance, and swore on the ancestors. Each party then drank part of the beverage. Such an alliance committed all their descendants to mutual assistance. The *sénankuya* is a particular form of alliance that can be both inter- and intratribal. It serves, among other purposes, to mitigate inequalities in the society and control any tendencies of the powerful to abuse their power. The *sénanku* can stop quarrels and oppose acts of anger and violence by the one of whom he is *sénanku* regardless of his status or however important is the decision to be made. The *sénanku* of a *fama* can prevent the declaration of war or the execution of one of his subjects.[48]

Mande reasoning is not linear. Rationality is an understanding of balance, duality, and the unity of opposites. This type of reasoning applies to the social order. The Mande provide an honored place for both the conformist and the innovator. The Bambara language

46. Paques, *Les Bambara,* 59–61, 71.
47. *Ibid.,* 55, 56.
48. *Ibid.*

has words for both principles. The term *badenya*—literally, "mother-childness"—which is also the term for the family compound, represents the principle of order, stability, and social conformity centered around obligations to home, village, and kinsmen. However, the community recognizes that it cannot survive without the innovator, the individual who breaks the social bonds. The principle of innovation is called *fadenya*—literally, "father-childness." Mande youth learn that their culture lavishes esteem and adulation on its rebels. Heroic poems are sung continually in the Mande world. The praise song of Sundiatta, the organizer and leader of the great thirteenth-century Mali empire, is heard daily over the radio in contemporary Mali. The innovator operates on the *fadenya* principle rather than on the *baadenya* principle. Innovation involves breaking with the traditions of the family and the village and traveling to foreign lands to win special powers and rewards that are eventually brought back for the benefit of the village. Much socialization is focused upon *fadenya* behavior. "They know that they depend upon the individual who resists the pull of the established social order, just as they depend upon the individuals who do not resist: they know that they require the individual who will change things, even if these changes are potentially destructive. Their ambivalence toward the *fadenya* actor . . . is reflected in a . . . proverb: . . . 'The hero is but welcome on troubled days.'"[49]

During the late 1720s, when large numbers of Bambara were loaded aboard slave ships destined for Louisiana, the Bambara heroic tradition, the *fadenya* principle, validated above all in troubled times, asserted itself. They revolted at sea. After arriving in Louisiana, the Bambara maintained an organized language community, formed alliances with the Indian nations who were in revolt against the French, and conspired to take over the colony.

49. Bird and Kendall, "Mande Hero."

Death and Revolt: The French Slave Trade to Louisiana

Michié Mazureau
Ki dan so bireau,
Li semblé crapo
Ki dan baille dolo.

Mr. Mazureau
Is in his office,
He looks like a frog
In a tub of water.

—Louisiana Creole slave song from Marcus Bruce
Christian, "For a Black History of Louisiana"

[Etienne Mazureau was an attorney whose office faced the New Orleans slave auction. He drew up documents transferring ownership of slaves.]

Although interest in the African slave trade was keen from the first year of French colonization of Louisiana, few blacks were there before the first two slave-trade ships landed from Africa in 1719. In 1699, Iberville asked permission to go to Guinea in a vessel of the king to buy slaves. In 1709, Nicolas de la Salle asked the king to send to Louisiana each year two hundred blacks of both sexes so that they could do without Indian slaves, "who only cause us trouble and from whom we receive very little service since they are not appropriate for hard labor like the blacks."[1]

Bienville proposed to exchange with the inhabitants of the French Caribbean islands two Indian slaves for one African slave. He wrote that a little French boat from St. Domingue had arrived to open up a trade in Indian slaves. He allowed them to purchase fifteen and proposed that they bring black slaves to Louisiana, exchanging two Indian slaves for each black. Bienville expressed hope that the colonial ministry would approve this trade, which he believed would do the colonists much good. Bienville's proposition was forcefully rejected by the ministry on the grounds that "the inhabitants of America in general, French as well as English, do not part with their blacks unless they know them to be bad and vicious. . . . If one wishes to follow what is practiced among the English, French ships must bring blacks to Louisiana [from Africa] and the settlers of this colony must be able to pay for them either in kind or in money."[2]

No blacks, either slave or free, were listed in the 1708 census. It appears that Bienville managed to get some black slaves for himself in 1709. Governor Antoine de Lamothe, Sieur de Cadillac reported that Bienville and D'Artaguette sent a ship to St. Domingue for their own benefit, and at the expense of the king. The ship, *la Vierge du Grace*, stopped over in Havana, under the pretext of looking for powder, and embarked several slaves. This is the first documentary evi-

1. Résumé de diverses demandes d'Iberville (1699), and Demands diverses, n.d., both in Ser. C13A 1, fols. 91, 93, ANC; La Salle to the Ministry of the Colonies, Fort Louis, August 20, 1709, in Ser. C13A 2, fols. 400–401, *ibid.*

2. Résumé annoté par le ministre des lettres de Bienville, July 28, 1706, in Ser. C13A 1, fol. 514, ANC; Bienville to the Ministry of the Colonies, Fort Louis, October 12, 1708, in Ser. C13A 2, fol. 177, *ibid.*; Résumé d'une lettre de Robert, November 26, 1708, *ibid.*, fol. 359.

dence of the entrance of black slaves into Louisiana.[3] While it is likely that Bienville and others smuggled in black slaves, the number involved was probably not great. By 1712, there were only 10 blacks in all of Louisiana.[4] Although seven slave-trade ships had already arrived from Africa by 1721, the census dated November 24, 1721, counted 680 blacks in the New Orleans and Mobile areas. According to this census, Bienville owned 27 of them.[5]

Almost all of the black slaves brought to French Louisiana came directly from Africa and arrived within about a decade. Only one African slave-trade ship came to Louisiana after 1731: a privately financed ship that arrived from Senegal in 1743. There were few blacks in Louisiana before the African slave trade began, and few slaves could have come from the French West Indies. French slave-trade ships en route from Africa to Louisiana normally stopped off in the French islands to take on wood, water, and supplies and to allow their "cargo" and crew to recover from the transatlantic journey. However, the colonists in the French West Indies were so desperate for slaves themselves that they grabbed "cargoes" destined for Louisiana. The slave ship *le Phillipe* had orders to stop off for water in St. Domingue on its way to Louisiana. The settlers of St. Domingue, complaining that they did not receive enough slaves, forced the captain to sell them the "cargo." The Company of the Indies then sent *l'Aurore* and *la Mutine* to Louisiana with slaves from Senegal, and with instructions to take enough supplies to go directly from Senegal to Louisiana because "it would be dangerous for them to stop off at St. Domingue or Martinique where the settlers might retain them under the pretext that they did not have enough blacks." When *l'Afriquain* and *le Duc du Maine* stopped off in Grenada for food, it was reported that M. Pradine, lieutenant of the king in Grenada, forced them to exchange their best blacks for those who were old or sick. Otherwise he refused to sell them food.[6] Several other ships stopping

3. Governor Antoine de Lamothe Cadillac to the ministry, Fort Louis, October 26, 1713, in Ser. C13A (3), fol. 65, ANC.

4. Nancy M. Miller Surrey, *The Commerce of Louisiana During the French Regime, 1699–1763* (1916; rpr. New York, 1968), 231, 232, mistakenly concluded that the African slave trade to Louisiana began in 1721. However, before 1721, four slave-trade ships had already landed 759 slaves. See Appendix A.

5. Charles R. Maduell, Jr., *The Census Tables for the French Colony of Louisiana from 1699 Through 1732* (Baltimore, 1972), 16, 17. See Table 2 for information on the arrival of slave-trade ships.

6. The directors of the Co[mpany] of the Indies [to the Senegal bureau], Paris, May 20, 1725, in Ser. C6 9, ANC; Bienville and Delorme to [?], April 25, 1721, in Ser. A1 2592, SHA.

at Grenada were forced to sell slaves as a condition for obtaining supplies.[7]

These African slaves arrived at a crucial period in the development of French Louisiana. New Orleans was founded in 1718. By January, 1731, twenty-two out of the twenty-three slave-trading ships that came from Africa while France ruled Louisiana had already arrived. Between June, 1719, and January, 1731, sixteen slave-trading ships arrived in Louisiana from the Senegal concession of the Company of the Indies. During the same period, six came from Juda and one from Cabinda (Angola, Central Africa). Five out of the six ships from Juda and the lone ship from Angola had arrived by June, 1721, as shown in Table 2.

The French slave trade to Louisiana is well documented in France, in Africa, aboard ship, and in Louisiana, giving an unusually complete picture of various stages of the trade and throwing light upon questions that strictly quantitative data cannot always convincingly answer.[8]

Although the Company of the Indies made early, sustained efforts to supply Louisiana with slaves from its Senegal concession, most of the early voyages went to Juda. The first two voyages were organized by the Company of the West before it was incorporated into the Company of the Indies. *L'Aurore* and *le Duc du Maine* left St. Malo together during the summer of 1718 and picked up their "cargo" at Juda. They were given nearly identical, detailed instructions that reveal the concerns and priorities of the slave traders. The captains were instructed to try to purchase several blacks who knew how to cultivate rice and three or four barrels of rice for seeding, which they were to give to the directors of the company upon their arrival in Louisiana.[9] Subsequently, rice became an important food staple in French Louisiana and was at times exported.

The captains were instructed to try to purchase two hundred or three hundred pounds of Brazilian tobacco from a Portuguese ship and to give some of the tobacco to the slaves and the rest to the directors of the company in Louisiana. It is possible that the directors wanted samples of Portuguese tobacco to grow in Louisiana in an

---

7. See records for *le Courrier de Bourbon* and *la Mutine* in Appendix A.

8. Joseph C. Miller, "Mortality in the Atlantic Slave Trade: Statistical Evidence on Causality," *Journal of Interdisciplinary History*, XI (1981), 385–423.

9. Instructions pour le S. Herpin Commandant du Vaisseau l'Aurore destiné pour la Traite des Nègres à la Coste de Guynee, July 4, 1718, in Ser. B42B, fols. 201–204, ANM. References in subsequent paragraphs to instructions for *l'Aurore* and *le Duc du Maine* come from this source.

Table 2. French Slave-Trade Ships from Africa to Louisiana

Ships and Their Origin	Year Landed	Number of Slaves Landed
Juda (Whydah)		
l'Aurore	1719	200
le Duc du Maine	1719	250
l'Afriquain	1721	182
le Duc du Maine	1721	349
le Fortuné	1721	303
la Diane	1728	464
TOTAL FROM JUDA (WHYDAH)		1,748
Cabinda (Angola)		
la Néréide	1721	294
TOTAL FROM CABINDA (ANGOLA)		294
Senegal Concession		
le Ruby	1720	127
le Maréchal d'Estrées	1721	196
l'Expédition	1723	91
le Courrier de Bourbon	1723	87
la Mutine	1726	213
l'Aurore	1726	290
l'Annibal	1727	244[1]
le Prince de Conti	1727	266
le Duc de Noaille	1728	262
la Vénus	1728	341
la Flore	1728	356
la Galathée	1729	273
la Vénus	1729	363
le Duc de Bourbon	1729	319
le St. Louis	1731	291
le St. Ursin	1743	190
TOTAL FROM THE SENEGAL CONCESSION		3,909
GRAND TOTAL, FRENCH SLAVE TRADE		5,951

Source: Calculated from Jean Mettas, *Autres Ports* (Paris, 1984), Vol. II of *Répertoire des éxpeditions négrières françaises au XVIIIième siècle*, ed. Serge and Michelle Daget.

1. Since no information exists about the number of slaves embarked on, or landed from, *l'Annibal*, the numbers of slaves embarked on all voyages from the Senegal concession were averaged to arrive at this figure.

Fiche de désarmement of the first two African slave-trade ships to Louisiana, *le Duc du Maine* and *l'Aurore*, dated at Port de Lorient on October 4, 1719.

Courtesy the Archives du Port de Lorient.

effort to compete with the third-grade tobacco of Bahia that was the basis for the direct trade between Bahia and the Gulf of Benin in which tobacco was exchanged for slaves.[10]

The captains were ordered to make their first stop between Cap de Monte and Cap Mesurade, where they were to take on enough water and wood for the voyage to America. They were to try to obtain more water at Juda and corn to feed the slaves. Along their way to Juda, they could stop off at Cap Lahou, Jacques Lahou, and Jacques Jacquet at Cape St. Appoline to trade several blacks and some rice, but they were not to stay more than two or three days at each place. After leaving Cape St. Appoline, they were to avoid the coast until they arrived at Juda, where they could stay ten to twelve days and trade as many blacks as possible. Upon their arrival at Juda, they were to give the normal presents to the king. *L'Aurore* was estimated to be big enough and supplied with enough merchandise to trade four hundred slaves; *le Duc du Maine,* five hundred to six hundred. On arriving in Louisiana, they were to dock at Dauphin Island.

The instructions pay a great deal of attention to minimizing mortality. The captains were to complete their trade as soon as possible, since the health of the blacks and the success of the voyage depended upon the time the slaves remained aboard the ship. To avoid prolonging their voyage and exposing the slaves and the crew to disease, the captains were ordered to make no stops in Africa or America after leaving Juda except at the island of Grenada in the West Indies, where they could take on wood, water, and whatever refreshments they needed. They were to remain at Grenada for as short a time as possible. The captain, the officers, and the surgeon were instructed to take good care of the health of the blacks, to prevent the black women from being debauched by the black men and the crew, and to clean and scrape the slave quarters every day to avoid rot. They were to avoid purchasing slaves who were more than thirty years old or less than eight years old. They were to do their best to avoid pirates.

When *l'Aurore* arrived at Juda on October 18, 1718, there were three English, four Portuguese, and three French ships in the harbor. There were two French, one English, and one Portuguese ship at nearby Jaquin. Three more English ships belonging to the South Sea Company and a Dutch ship were expected. This large number of ships seeking slaves was causing a sharp rise in their price. Slaves were becoming so rare that the director of the French trading post

10. Pierre Verger, *Flux et reflux de la traite des nègres entre le Golfe de Benin et Bahia de Todos os Santos du 17ième au 19ième siècles* (Paris, 1968), 10.

feared that their ships would have to leave with only half their "cargo." The Portuguese, bloated with the gold of Brazil, offered the stiffest competition. They were trying to monopolize the trade from Juda by offering exorbitant prices in gold. In 1721, the Portuguese built the fortress of Whydah, consolidating their predominance at the Gulf of Benin. Before *l'Aurore* left Juda, the nearby trading post at Jaquin had become impractical for Europeans because of the hostility of the king of Ardres. Therefore, all the European ships stopped at Juda, aggravating the shortage of slave "merchandise." *L'Aurore* left Juda on November 30, 1718, with 201 slaves, half the number the company expected her to carry. Although the voyage from Juda to Louisiana took about six months, only 1 slave died, a very low loss in transit for such a long voyage. The "cargo" was rushed to Pensacola to work on fortifications during the siege by Spain. Many of these slaves were reportedly lost when the Spanish took Pensacola. After a voyage of three months from Africa to Louisiana, *le Duc du Maine,* estimated to be able to carry 500 to 600 slaves, landed 250 in Louisiana.[11]

The sale of these slaves posed a problem that was to become chronic in Louisiana. As much as the colonists clamored for slaves, they could not pay for them in hard currency. After two and a half months, not one colonist had come forward to make an offer. To avoid letting the "merchandise" deteriorate on Dauphin Island, the company agreed to accept payment in paper money issued by the new company (the Company of the West) as well as by Crozat, provided that if this paper money was not honored, the purchasers would pay for the slaves in kind or return them to the company. Meanwhile, the colonists would assume all risks for them.[12]

During 1720 and 1721, three voyages organized by the new Company of the Indies picked up their "cargo" for Louisiana from Juda, despite the severe shortage of "merchandise" there. *L'Afriquain* landed

11. S. Bouchel, Arrivé de l'Aurore de la Cie. d'Occident, Juda, October, 1718, in Ser. B1 42, fol. 190, ANM; Verger, *Flux et reflux,* 72, 73; communication from S. Bouchel to the Ministry of the Marine, Juda, November 30, 1718, in Ser. B1 42, fol. 194, ANM; Daniel H. Usner, Jr., "From African Captivity to American Slavery: The Introduction of Black Laborers to Colonial Louisiana," *LH,* XX (1979), 25–48; Jean Mettas, *Autres Ports* (Paris, 1984), Voyage No. 3116, pp. 684–85, Vol. II of *Répertoire des expéditions négrières françaises au XVIIIième siècle,* ed. Serge and Michelle Daget.

12. Procès-verbal du conseil de commerce tenu a l'Isle Dauphine, September 5, 1719, in Ser. C13A 5, fol. 333, ANC. Stemming from her initial error assuming that the first slave-trade ships arrived from Africa in 1721, not 1719, Surrey misinterpreted this document, assuming that the slaves referred to were left over from the time of Crozat. Surrey, *Commerce of Louisiana,* 231.

182 slaves, and *le Duc du Maine,* on its second voyage to Louisiana, landed 349. Both ships arrived in March, 1721. Bienville and Delorme complained that the company was badly served by the captains of these two ships, both in the quantity and the quality of slaves purchased in Guinea. Most of the adults were old and sick. Furthermore, the ships' officers had been forced to exchange their best slaves at Grenada in order to obtain food from the officer in charge there. Bienville claimed that Captain Roseau of *le Duc du Maine* exchanged 10 good blacks for blacks who were habitual maroons, old, or sick.[13] The captain of *la Néréide,* coming from Cabinda, was praised for the quality of his "cargo," and it was noted that he refused to trade his slaves for supplies, making do with what he had. The cargo was considered "among the best, the best assorted." But the slaves arrived in a weakened condition because he had had to feed them biscuit. Twenty-eight of them died after landing, and the rest were sick. There was no corn in Louisiana, and the slaves could not tolerate beans. To prevent further mortality among these slaves, Bienville sent a boat to St. Domingue to purchase six hundred barrels of corn.[14] *La Néréide* was the only slave ship which came from Central Africa (Congo/Angola) during French rule.

The slaves from *l'Afriquain* and *le Duc du Maine* were distributed to the colonists and concessionaires in groups consisting of two men, two women, a boy, and a girl. There were not enough slaves to satisfy all those who had asked for them. However, when *la Néréide* arrived the following month, the concessionaires took few slaves because they had nothing with which to feed them. Of the 825 slaves who arrived on *l'Afriquain, le Duc du Maine,* and *la Néréide,* 537 were sold to individuals and 35 died after landing, leaving 253 slaves. Forty of the remaining slaves were kept to work on boats going up the Mississippi River to the Illinois country. The *négrillons* (boys) were sent to New Orleans to be sold to those who wanted them, and several *"nègres pièce d'Inde"* (adult males) were to be kept for public works and to provide for their subsistence. *Le Fortuné,* the final ship from Juda before the trade focused almost entirely upon Senegal, arrived two months later. It brought 303 "fairly well assorted" slaves: 205 men,

13. Bienville and Delorme to the directors, Biloxi, April 25, 1721, in Sec. IP 274B, No. 20, APL; Bienville and Delorme to [?], April 25, 1721, in A1 2592, SHA. For *le Duc du Maine*'s second voyage, see Désarmement 1721, La Touche, April 22, 1729, in Ser. B3 330, fol. 294, ANM.

14. Bienville and Delorme to [?], April 25, 1721, in Ser. A1 2592, fols. 106–107, 197, SHA.

64 women, 23 boys, and 11 girls. The "cargo" was to be distributed to the colonists, but some slaves were to be kept for the company.[15]

If the slave trade from Senegal to Louisiana got a late start, it was not for lack of trying. As soon as the Company of the Indies took control of Louisiana, it devoted serious attention to supplying the colony with slaves from the Senegal concession. In October, 1720, its directors informed Senegal that it had sent *le Comte de Toulouse* with well-assorted trade goods, principally to strengthen Galam and stimulate trade there. *Le Comte de Toulouse* was to be sent quickly to Louisiana with a "cargo" of slaves. *Le Maréchal d'Estrées* had picked up its cargo of wine, liquor, and foods at Bordeaux, and this vessel was also to be sent to Louisiana with slaves. Any ship seized from interlopers was to be likewise sent to Louisiana with slaves and its papers sent to France for confiscation proceedings. After retaking Fort d'Arguin, the French were to enslave any Moors taken prisoner, send them to Senegal, keep them in shackles, and transport them to Louisiana on the first available ship. Aside from the four ships sent to Juda during 1720, three ships were reportedly sent to Madagascar in June of the same year to load slaves for Louisiana.[16]

Few of these projects materialized. There is no record of any interloper seized and sent to Louisiana with slaves. There is no evidence that any ships from Madagascar arrived in Louisiana. The Moors taken at Fort d'Arguin were not deported and enslaved: They were needed there to cut wood and to make salt. The French were afraid of antagonizing all the Moors if they enslaved those who had turned Arguin Island over to the Dutch. The Moors (called *"cette Morvaille"*) still had not forgotten the affair of M. Ducas, who had taken Moorish captives to the French islands. Instead of enslaving Moorish captives, the French decided to try to win over that nation with kindness. In order to attract and control the Moors, it was proposed to hire Boaly, a great Marabout (Muslim holy man) and an interpreter at Portendic.[17]

Le Ruby was the first slave-trade ship that arrived in Louisiana from the Senegal concession. It left Le Havre in December, 1719, and Gorée in May, 1720, with 130 slaves, arriving in Louisiana in July, 1720, with

---

15. Bienville and Delorme to [?], Biloxi, May 4, 1721, in Ser. A1 2592, fols. 109–10, SHA; Bienville and Delorme to [?], Biloxi, June 24, 1721, in Ser. A1 2592, fol. 111, *ibid.*

16. Instruction pour le S. Nicolas Despres de St. Robert, Directeur Général à la concession du Sénégal de la Cie. des Indes, Paris, October 14, 1720, in Ser. C6 6, ANC; Mémoire sur l'état actuel ou est la colonie de la Louisiane, n.d. [after 1721], in Ser. C13C 1, fol. 329, *ibid.*

17. St. Robert to the Co[mpany], Senegal, May 24, 1721, in Ser. C6 6, Art. 55, *ibid.*

127 slaves. *Le Ruby* would have carried 50 more slaves, but the Senegal concession did not have enough food available to embark them.[18] Between November, 1720, and September, 1721, the Company of the Indies sent several ships to Senegal to bring slaves to Louisiana. *Le Maréchal d'Estrées* left Le Havre for Senegal on December 15, 1720, loaded with most of the trade goods needed by several ships to buy slaves. She was taken by the Algerians, who seized all her cargo, valued at 202,171 livres. As a result, it was anticipated that most of the projected slave-trade voyages to Louisiana would have to be abandoned. The Algerians returned *le Maréchal d'Estrées* to Senegal, where she loaded 200 slaves and arrived in Louisiana with 196 slaves, valued at 117,600 livres. In November, 1720, the Company of the Indies ordered *l'Expédition* to bring 100 slaves, *le Duc d'Orléans* 300, and *le Comte de Toulouse* 200, for a total, with those on *le Maréchal d'Estrées*, of 800 slaves from Senegal to Louisiana. Only *le Maréchal d'Estrées* arrived. Evidently, there was effective pressure from the French islands to send slave ships there instead. *Le Duc d'Orléans* went to Martinique; *le Comte de Toulouse* was subsequently ordered to St. Domingue instead of to Louisiana. Although *l'Expédition* left Senegal on May 7, 1721, with 100 slaves for Louisiana, it was evidently diverted, because the ship did not get to Louisiana until its next voyage, from 1722 to 1723.[19]

No slave ships arrived in Louisiana in 1722, and only two small ships, *l'Expédition* and *le Courrier de Bourbon*, landed a total of 182 slaves in 1723.[20] The slaves from these ships came from Gambia, Gorée, and Bissau. *L'Expédition* left Gorée with 100 "*beaux captifs ou captives*" on June 13, 1723, while *le Courrier de Bourbon* left for Gambia

18. Le vaisseau Ruby capitaine Grenier party du Havre le 13 décembre 1719 pour le Sénégal, in Nouvelles Acquisitions Françaises, Vol. 9340, fol. 78, art. 6, Bibliotheque Nationale, Paris; St. Robert to the Company, Senegal, March 20, 1721, in Ser. C6 6, fol. 15, ANC. The voyage was nevertheless profitable. The slaves sold for 76,000 livres. The cargo sent to Senegal cost 27,153 livres, and the expenses of the voyage were 31,563 livres, for a net profit of 17,284 livres. See Le vaisseau Ruby, in Nouvelles Acquisitions Françaises, Vol. 9340, fol. 78, art. 6, Bibliotheque Nationale, Paris.

19. Le vaisseau le Maréchal d'Estrées capt. Prudhomme party du Havre pour le Senegal le 15 decembre 1720, in Nouvelles Acquisitions Françaises, Vol. 9340, fol. 79, art. 14, Bibliotheque Nationale, Paris; Mémoire sur l'état actuel ou est la colonie de la Louisiane, n.d. [after 1721], in Ser. C13C 1, fol. 329, ANC; St. Robert to the Co[mpany], Senegal, May 24, 1721, in Ser. C6 6, Arts. 11, 12, 28, 43, 79, 85, No. 2, ANC; Duverger and Delorme to [?], August 20, 1721, in Ser. A1 2592, fol. 1154, SHA; Julien Dubellay to the Ministry of the Colonies, St. Louis, March 28, 1721, in Ser. C6 7, ANC; Julien Dubellay to the Ministry of the Colonies, May 3, 1722, in Ser. C6 7, ANC. See Appendix A for details of the voyages.

20. See Appendix A.

with trade goods and food and orders to bring back dry merchandise and *captifs* to Gorée. When *l'Expedition* landed 95 *captifs* at Biloxi in October, 1723, there was general famine. Bienville had gone off to fight the Natchez Indians. Only 15 slaves were sold to the colonists because few had Spanish piastres, which were required for payment. The officials were satisfied not to sell the slaves, because the company needed hard labor for its construction projects. The officials, however, appropriated these slaves and their labor for their personal use. Chevalier de Loubeoy, the king's lieutenant at New Orleans, falsely claimed that all the slaves were sick from scurvy. Actually, only about 7 or 8 of them were sick; the rest were *"beaux Nègres, grands, bien faits."* These slaves were so *beaux* that the members of the Superior Council of Louisiana could not keep their hands off them. Each member took one to grow food and cut wood. They gave several to their friends. They swapped these *"beaux nègres"* for their own, less valuable slaves. Bienville had swapped a little girl for a full-grown woman. Bienville had about 50 slaves on two plantations, only 37 of whom he had purchased from the Company of the Indies. It was suspected that the rest came from the cargo of *l'Aurore*, which was supposed to have been lost at Pensacola. Jacques de La Chaise, *commissaire ordonnateur*, was sent to investigate conditions in the colony. He described Bienville, his relatives, and his Canadian favorites living in luxury in fancy houses, with many slaves obtained with ill-gotten gain, while most of the white population literally went hungry and naked.[21] But fortunately for the slaves, Bienville and his friends were interested in seizing and displaying wealth, not in creating it.

Throughout the first half of the 1720s, there was a shortage of slaves to embark from the Senegambian concession. Although St. Robert had been optimistic in 1722, reporting to the company that he expected to be able to supply 2,000 *captifs* a year without much trouble on the part of the Company of the Indies, by June of 1723, the company was discouraged from sending more ships because it was uncertain how many slaves Galam would be able to supply that year. St. Robert thought he would have 600 *captifs* beyond those needed for the "cargo" of *le Maréchal d'Estrées*, but the "merchandise" got "shopworn." Officials of the Senegal concession had expected ships and

21. Julien Dubellay to the Co[mpany], Senegal, May 25, 1724, in Ser. C6 8, ANC; Dubellay to the Co[mpany], July 1, 1723, in Ser. C6 7, Arts. 1, 13, *ibid.;* Le Blond de la Tour to the Co[mpany], New Orleans, October 18, 1723, in Ser. C13 7, fol. 221, *ibid.;* La Chaise to the commissioners of the Company, October 18, 1723, in Ser. C13 7, fols. 51, 59, 59 bis, 60, 60 bis, *ibid.;* La Chaise to the commissioners of the Company, September 6, 1723, in Ser. C13 7, fol. 7, *ibid.*

had collected more than 900 *captifs,* but long detention in irons caused illnesses among them. "Regardless of the care we gave them, more than 100 died, and 15 deserted at Gorée, Joual and Gambia," wrote St. Robert. The service ordered him to retain 50 Bambara and to leave 20 other Bambara at Gorée, 20 at Arguin, and 5 at Bissau. He only had 750 *captifs* left for ships going to Cap François and Louisiana. Nor could he furnish corn for the ships, since he had only enough to provide for the subsistence of the inhabitants of the Senegal concession. The *captiverie* in Galam was at times so overcrowded that in hot weather, many slaves died.[22]

The "merchandise" did not always die quietly. On October 18, 1724, at four o'clock in the afternoon, the 55 *captifs* stored in the *captiverie* at Gorée were in the courtyard, where they were normally brought for fresh air. They revolted, armed themselves with pieces of wood and with several knives, and stabbed the French storehouse guard. They removed their shackles with two axes they found. Hearing the screams of the warehouse guard, the rest of the French came running to help him, but it was too late. He was found all bloody, his intestines cut and hanging out of the wound. He died the next day. The French fired on the *captifs,* killing 2 and wounding 12. The *captifs* took refuge inside the *captiverie* and organized themselves. The French sealed off the door to the *captiverie* and remained on alert all night, making fires in the courtyard and on the ramparts. At eight o'clock the next morning, they informed the *captifs* that if they did not surrender, they would be burned alive. The *captifs* asked the French to open the doors, which they did at once. They made the *captifs* come out two by two, followed by three guards. After all of the rebels were brought out, the French found out who the leaders of the revolt were, tied one of them on two pieces of wood and cut him in four quarters, and shot 2 others, to serve as an example.[23]

During 1724, only 369 slaves descended from Galam. The director of the concession insisted that a slaver who had docked his ship at Gorée go to Juda, not Bissau, for his slaves, in spite of generalized

22. Co[mpany] to St. Robert, director of the Senegal [concession], Paris, February, 1723, and Reply to letters of July 16, 25, August 8, and 27, 1722, both in Ser. C6 7, *ibid.;* Julien Dubellay to the Co[mpany], June 1, 1723, *ibid.;* St. Robert to the Co[mpany], Senegal, May 24, 1721, in Ser. C6 6, Arts. 14, 18, *ibid.;* Mémoire sur le Commerce du Sénégal (draft), March 23, 1723, in Ser. C6 7, *ibid.*

23. La Fore to Julien Dubellay, Gorée, October 22, 1724, copy, in Ser. C6 8, *ibid.;* Procès Verbale de la Révolte des Captifs arrivée à Gorée le 19 octubre 1724, A Ft. St. François de l'Isle de Gorée, sousigniés Simon LaFore, Gouverneur des forts et Isle de Gorée et 10 autres personnes, copy, in Ser. C6 8, *ibid.*

illness among his crew. There were barely enough slaves to load onto the ships already in Senegal. Warfare against the British in Gambia and the Dutch at Arguin Island preoccupied the Senegal concession.[24]

Resistance aboard the slave-trade ships to Louisiana is well documented. The first conspiracy recorded in a pilot's log took place aboard *le Courrier de Bourbon*, a ship of 130 tons, which left Lorient on April 8, 1723. It arrived at Senegal on May 1—a quick voyage—and left Senegal for Gorée on May 9. From there, it went to Joual and then to the Gambia River, where it docked before the French trading post on May 30. Thus far, there had been no illnesses or deaths among the crew, an unusual situation in the *"haute saison."* On June 28, the pilot wrote, "We have embarked our blacks this afternoon to the number of 44 men, 11 women, and two nursing babies."[25]

They returned to Gorée. On July 5, their baker died. On July 27, the captain was forced to load forty blacks who had arrived from Bissau the day before; he wanted to keep the blacks they had brought from Gambia. The pilot commented: "The governor and the warehouse guard have made a choice of the worst blacks to give us . . . most of them are sick and the rest extremely worn out [*extenués*]. It would be better to give these blacks to *le Maréchal d'Estrées* which is going to Martinique and whose journey is nice and short."

Le Courrier de Bourbon embarked sixty males and forty females, adults as well as children, and four or five nursing babies. On July 28, the ship passed Gorée. The voyage did not go smoothly. On July 30, a black tried to jump overboard and drag another black with him. The captain had him tied to the cannon and lashed with two hundred strokes of the *garcette* (a whip made of braided rope)—a punishment that, according to the pilot, "he deserved." On August 6, smallpox began to break out among the blacks, and on August 11 the pilot wrote, "Here it is such a short time since we left Gorée and 15 or 16 blacks, male as well as female, are already sick with smallpox. We fear regrettable consequences." Twelve blacks died of smallpox during the voyage: four in July, four in August, three in September, and one in October. Another black died of scurvy in November.

On September 16, *le Courrier de Bourbon* arrived in Grenada, and its

24. Julien Dubellay to Pierre Oasaunau, Senegal, October 29, 1724, in Ser. C6 8, *ibid.;* Julien Dubellay to the Ministry of the Colonies, Senegal, December 18, 1724, *ibid.,* fols. 12, 15, 17, 19.

25. Soit commencé le voyage de France au Sénégalle pour y prandre des Noirs et les Porter au Misicipy dans le Vaissaux Le Courrier de Bourbon, in Ser. 4JJ 15, fol. 21 bis, ANM. Entries from the log are listed under the dates given here and in subsequent paragraphs.

crew had to submit to the usual blackmail by the French lieutenant in charge there. They sold a black man and a black woman with her nursing baby in exchange for food. Five members of the crew deserted in Grenada. As they were leaving Grenada on October 4, a conspiracy among the slaves was uncovered. A young *nègre* tried to indicate through gestures to the ship's officers that a revolt was planned. The officers could not understand clearly what this *nègre* was saying. They sent for two women slaves, one from Senegal and the other from Gorée, to interpret for them. Both of the women claimed they could not understand the young *nègre*. They were tied to a cannon to be lashed, but the women still said nothing. After several other blacks in shackles were lashed, the woman from Senegal declared that a *nègre* aged about forty-five "was the sorcerer who raised their vain hopes [*était le sorcier qui les abusait de vaine espérance*]" and that the woman from Gorée knew this as well but did not want to admit it right away. They started lashing the woman from Gorée the same as the other blacks, and she affirmed the woman from Senegal's declaration, pointing out the same *nègre* as leader of the conspiracy to slit the throats of the whites. The pilot wrote, "In the interests of the Company as well as the safety of the crew, which is a small number because of desertions and illnesses, we decided to make a necessary example for such cargoes and to hoist him to the top of the main mast and fire upon him with rifles until death ensued."

Le Courrier de Bourbon arrived at Balize, the fort at the mouth of the Mississippi River, on November 1, 1723, with 87 blacks, a total that probably included nursing babies. The survival rate was remarkable for a voyage marked by smallpox, attempted suicide, and conspiracy to revolt, and considering that some slaves had been sold in Grenada to obtain food. *Le Courrier de Bourbon* was lightly packed. The instructions from Paris indicated that the ship could carry 150 *captifs*, "but use your judgment about what this ship can carry without overcrowding her too much. We recommend that you give her only *nègres* who can tolerate the voyage and not give her defective or sick *captifs*." [26]

In late 1724, *le Philippe* and *la Prothée* were loaded with slaves in Senegal and sent to Louisiana. The "cargo" of *le Philippe* was seized in St. Domingue by planters ravenous for slaves, and *la Prothée* was lost at sea. No slaves landed in Louisiana in 1724 or 1725. In 1725, the

---

26. Directors of the Co[mpany] to St. Robert, Director of the Senegal [concession], Paris, February, 1723, in Ser. C6 7, ANC. See also Le Courrier de Bourbon, Armé 8 avril 1723, Désarmé 26 mars 1724. Sommes non reclamées 1724 et 1725, in Ser. B3 322, fol. 299, ANM.

officials of Louisiana reported that the entire colony was impatient for blacks to arrive. The small settlers especially were in great need of blacks. Several colonists who had returned to France could have been kept in the colony if only they had been supplied with slaves, the officials told the Company of the Indies. Threats alternated with promises. "Lack of blacks disgust the colonies, who all ask to return to France. Blacks must be sent if one wishes to keep them in the colony. The country will produce indigo and tobacco provided there is labor with which to do so. The colonists only ask to be put in condition to work. The harvest is abundant in local foodstuffs . . . blacks are needed to establish cultivation and manufacture of tobacco at Natchez."[27]

If the French could not compete with the Brazilians for the popularity of that country's tobacco, they did well with wine. The slave trade in Senegal picked up with the arrival of *la Mutine*, which left Lorient on May 30, 1725, with instructions to bring *captifs* from Senegal to Louisiana. The vessel brought 1,000 bottles of Bordeaux wine, a valuable and welcome commodity that could be exchanged for many *captifs* in Senegal. St. Robert sent his "very humble thanks." Three hundred bottles went to Galam, 150 to Gorée, and another 150 to Bissau. St. Robert also had a case of 60 bottles of liquor that had been confiscated from *le Maure*. *La Mutine* left Bissau on November 26, 1725, with 237 blacks: 95 men, 94 women, 46 boys, and 2 girls. Two men and 2 women were sold in Grenada. Eighteen slaves died at sea, 13 of whom were women. The mortality rate at sea during the French slave trade to Louisiana appeared to be higher among women than among men. *La Mutine* landed 91 men, 79 women, and 43 boys and girls, and several nursing babies in Louisiana on February 26, 1726.[28]

L'Aurore left Lorient on April 2, 1725, and arrived in Senegal thirty-six days later, but it was held up in Senegal because of the pressing need for ships at the concession. *Le St. Jacques* had been lost, and the governor of Arguin was in desperate need of a ship to supply that island. *L'Aurore* was also needed in Gambia. The king of La Barre had

27. The directors of the Co[mpany] of the Indies [to the Senegal bureau], Paris, May 20, 1725, in Ser. C6 9, ANC; The Superior Council to the directors of the Co[mpany], New Orleans, February 27, 1725, in Ser. C13A 9, fol. 54, *ibid.*; Extrait des lettres du Conseil de la Louisiane, August 28, 1725, *ibid.*, fol. 239. Appendix A shows that no slaves were brought to the colony in 1724 and 1725.

28. St. Robert to the directors of the Co[mpany], Senegal, July 21, 1725, in Ser. C6 9, fol. 14, art. 11, *ibid.* For another example of higher mortality among women than among men, see voyage of *la Venus*, 1728, in Appendix A. Details of the voyage of *la Mutine* are included in Appendix A.

invited the Company of the Indies to establish a trading post on his territory at the mouth of the Gambia River. He assured St. Robert that they could trade more than 200 *captifs* there in less than six weeks. St. Robert had planned to send *l'Aurore* to Gambia with a director and supplies for this new trading post, and to pick up the 200 *captifs* whom they expected to trade when the Yancas brought their "*chemins de Nègres*" from the upper Gambia to Couos, their *entrepôt* where they kept their *captifs* while awaiting customers near the mouth of the Gambia River. Having to choose between supplying Arguin Island and pressing their advantages in Gambia, he chose Arguin.[29] After remaining several months in Africa to fulfill the urgent needs of the Senegal concession, *l'Aurore* left Gorée on December 16, 1725, with 350 blacks. It stopped off in Grenada, and arrived in Louisiana on March 29, 1726, with only 290 survivors.

Pauger, chief engineer of the Louisiana concession, wrote that while the arrival of the blacks from *la Mutine* and *l'Aurore* "pleased the colony infinitely, it is a small number compared to the pressing need one has of them to prevent the colonists, mainly the best of them, from returning to France, disgusted because they have had to wait so long for them, and because of the disgraceful rule of this colony." Some of these slaves were kept by the company to engage in public works projects, including the construction of a large, permanent levee to protect New Orleans from flooding and cutting down trees in the city to let air to reach the windmill and to allow for tilling the soil. These ambitious projects required many of these long-awaited slaves. Disputes erupted among private citizens over who would get the rest of them.[30]

The early phase of the slave trade to Louisiana got off to a slow start. The slaves came from several parts of Africa: from Juda as well as from the Senegal concession. One ship came from Cabinda. There was competition among the European powers and a shortage of slaves, and we can assume that those available were quickly embarked. The trade in Bambara coming down from Galam on the Senegal River to St. Louis was not especially fruitful, and it is possible that the slaves sent during this early phase of the trade had not traveled far to arrive at the coast and did not remain there long awaiting a ship. There was great concern about avoiding high mortality at sea,

29. St. Robert to the directors of the Co[mpany] of the Indies, Senegal, April 18, 1725, in Ser. C6 9, No. 64, Art. 30, ANC; St. Robert to the directors of the Company of the Indies, Senegal, June 18, 1725, fol. 71, art. 67, *ibid.*

30. Pauger to the directors of the Co[mpany], New Orleans, March 19, April 3, 1726, in Ser. C13A 9, fols. 374 and 358–59, respectively, *ibid.*

Table 3. Number of Slaves Embarked in Africa and Landed in Louisiana Between 1718 and 1723

Year	Ship	Embarked	Landed
1718–19	l'Aurore	201	200
1719–20	le Ruby	130	127
1720–21	le Maréchal d'Estrées	200	196
1722–23	l'Expédition	100	91
1723	le Courrier de Bourbon	100	87[1]

SOURCE: See source for Table 1.

1. Two slaves were sold at Grenada.

which was viewed as a costly spoilage of the "cargo." Instructions called for preventing overcrowding, providing adequate food, maintaining cleanliness, and avoiding long stays in port and prolonged voyages at sea. Before 1725, the slave trade to Louisiana was characterized by a comparatively low mortality rate at sea and after arrival in Louisiana. The survival rate on voyages before 1725 was relatively high, as shown in Table 3.

Between 1719 and 1723, ten slave ships landed 2,083 slaves in Louisiana. Although the "cargo" of l'Aurore was landed at Pensacola during its siege by Spain and the slaves were reported as lost when Spain retook Pensacola from France, the 1726 census of Louisiana lists 1,540 black slaves. Blacks survived during these years much better than did whites. Many whites died of hunger, thirst, disease, and lack of medical supplies. Two weeks after la Néréide arrived from Cabinda in the spring of 1721, Bienville and Delorme wrote, "Death and disease are disrupting and suspending all operations, and if the famine does not end, all is lost. The best workers are dead." When the slaves from l'Expédition arrived from Senegal in October, 1723, an official wrote, "We are here in a state of general famine. The colony is in the final stages of misery due to lack of food, drink, merchandise as well as medicines, and as a result, most of our convalescents relapse and die."[31]

How can we explain the relatively high survival rate among Afri-

31. Bienville and Delorme to [?], Biloxi, May 4, 1721, in Ser. A1 2592, fols. 109–10, SHA; Le Blond de la Tour to the Ministry of the Colonies, New Orleans, October 18, 1723, in Ser. C13A, fol. 221, ANC.

cans between 1719 and 1726 in spite of famine in the colony? There are several reasons we can consider. The Africans were probably better adapted to the climate than were the French and German settlers. They were resistant to malaria, which no doubt prevailed in this mosquito-ridden climate, and were skilled at feeding themselves through hunting, fishing, and cultivating rice, corn, melons, and other food crops. The market at Galam was not very productive during these years, so fewer of the slaves embarked had been weakened by a long voyage from the interior. Because of fierce competition among Europeans to purchase slaves in a relatively open market, the slaves were not generally held for long periods of time in *captiveries* along the coast of Africa and were therefore stronger during the Atlantic crossing and when they arrived in Louisiana.

Another reason for the survival of the Africans could be the uses to which they were put, before the Company of the Indies replaced Bienville with Périer in August, 1726. Bienville had operated in the predatory tradition of the Caribbean, seizing, displaying, and consuming wealth rather than creating it. His rule was replaced by that of ambitious, hard-driving officials of the Company of the Indies who were determined to enforce their monopoly of trade throughout their far-flung concessions and to turn a profit for their stockholders. They operated under the illusion that the Indians of Louisiana and Africans on both sides of the Atlantic were instruments for creating wealth, not human beings capable of defending themselves. This was their fatal mistake. The Company of the Indies' plans for Louisiana were destroyed in 1729 by indigenous peoples of Africa and America. Africans on both sides of the Atlantic and on slave ships at sea played the major role in ending the Company of the Indies' control of Louisiana and, along with it, the African slave trade to that colony.

The founding of the new, ambitious Company of the Indies had inspired great optimism among its officials. In 1720, Brüe, then director of its Senegal concession, wrote that the company was given a monopoly of trade in Senegal, Louisiana, Cap Nègre, the East Indies, and China, and of shipping in the South Sea, and had made "plans and arrangements which are so beautiful, so solid, and so approved that it has become the strongest and most powerful company in the world." [32] The Company of the Indies and its officials had reckoned without their victims.

By early 1727, peace reigned among the European powers in the

32. Brüe to Violaine, commander of Fort St. Joseph in Galam, Senegal, April 30, 1720, in Ser. C6 6, ANC.

Senegal concession. On January 17, 1727, the Company of the Indies and the Dutch West Indies Company signed a treaty in which the Dutch company recognized the French company's exclusive trade monopoly over the entire Senegal concession from Cap Blanc to the Sierra Leone River, and specifically renounced its claims to Arguin Island in return for an indemnity of 30,000 florins. On February 19, 1727, a peace treaty was signed with the English recognizing the Company of the Indies' right to establish a slave-trading post in the Gambia River at Albreda or Bintani. The English of Fort St. James agreed to cooperate "on occasions when life and the property of the Company of the Indies was at stake," as well as in expelling interlopers.[33]

Peace and stability arrived in Senegal just as Juda went up in flames. The Dada of Dahomey overthrew the Kingdom of Juda. On March 3, 1727, Captain Raingrard of *le Marie* wrote a detailed eyewitness account of the warfare, which totally disrupted commerce in the region. On February 12, 1729, the captain of the slave ship *la Méduse* wrote from Juda, "There are no more inhabitants, and the country is deserted. You can image how hard it is to find captives."[34]

The Company of the Indies was at last in a position to enforce its exclusive right to trade in the Senegal concession. Between 1727 and 1729, practically every slave-trade voyage organized by the Company of the Indies from its port of Lorient was intended to carry slaves to Louisiana. In November, 1728, Louisiana officials noted the arrival of *la Flore. Le Prince de Conti* arrived fifteen days later, and *la Diane* the following month, and they were expecting *la Galathée* at any moment. They wrote, "We will do our best to make known the good intentions you have for this colony, and the colonists on their part are too encouraged by the help they receive from you to frustrate the hopes that you have given them for the success of their efforts."[35]

The slave-trade voyages to Louisiana through 1723 had a loss in transit of only 3.6 percent—an unusually low rate for the African slave trade of the times, especially considering that the voyage to Louisiana required considerably more time at sea than did the voyages to the Caribbean. During 1724 and 1725, no slave ships landed. The Af-

33. Traité ou convention avec les Etats Généraux, January 13, 1727, in Ser. C6 10, ANC; Traités et conventions en presence de M. De la Forte Maison, Capitaine et Commandante du Vaisseau Le Prince de Conti, February 19, 1727, *ibid.*

34. Rélation de la Guerre de Juda par M. Raingrard, Capitaine du Marie, March 3, 1727, *ibid.*; Mettas, *Autres Ports*, Voyage No. 2906.

35. Mettas, *Autres Ports*, Voyages No. 2900–2913; Périer and La Chaise to the Ministry of the Colonies, New Orleans, November 3, 1728, in Ser. C13A 11, fol. 134, ANC.

rican slave trade to Louisiana resumed on a large scale in 1727. In sharp contrast with the early years, the loss in transit during this last, and most active, period of the African slave trade to Louisiana was high. The best explanation for this difference is the poor condition of the slaves embarked in Africa as a result of the ability of the Company of the Indies to enforce its trade monopoly in Senegal, and the success of the trading post at Galam, which began, at last, to send substantial numbers of *captifs* down the Senegal River to Fort Louis. After enduring a stay in the *captiverie* at Galam following a long journey downriver, *captifs* sickened and died in the *captiveries* along the Atlantic coast while awaiting long-delayed ships belonging to the Company of the Indies. By the time these tardy ships arrived, many of the surviving slaves were in no condition to withstand the transatlantic crossing. Documents from France, from Senegal, and from Louisiana all recognize that the long stay in the *captiveries* was the principal cause for high mortality at sea and after landing. The African slave trade to French Louisiana confirms Joseph C. Miller's conclusion that "the experience of enslavement in Africa exercised a major influence over the levels of mortality at sea." [36]

If, during the early 1720s, there were not enough slaves to fill the slave ships, the opposite problem existed after peace reigned in the Senegal concession: There were not enough ships to embark the slaves. A steady stream of *captifs* filled the *captiveries* while the Company of the Indies struggled to refit its ships in Lorient and send them back quickly to Senegal to load them. The *captifs* died en masse in the *captiveries*, and the survivors were so weakened that many of them died aboard ship. The loss in transit on most of the slave ships landing after 1726 was devastating (see Table 4). When these ships arrived in Louisiana, they had to enter the Mississippi River at Balize in the face of contrary winds and tides and ever-shifting sandbars that blocked the channels. Sick and dying, exhausted, short of food and water, often without clothing even in midwinter, the *captifs* waited for days for flatboats and pirogues to take them up the Mississippi River to New Orleans, where they often encountered food shortages. Many of them died on their way to New Orleans or shortly after their arrival.

Many *captifs* from *le Prince de Conti* developed two illnesses: dys-

36. Miller, "Mortality in the Atlantic Slave Trade," 388. For a conclusive discussion of the pre-embarkation experience of slaves in Africa as a primary determinant of levels of mortality at sea, see Joseph C. Miller, *Way of Death: Merchant Capitalism and the Angolan Slave Trade, 1730–1830* (Madison, Wis., 1988), 399–401, 437–42.

Table 4. Mortality Aboard Slave Ships Landing Between 1726 and 1731

Ship	Year	Embarked	Landed
la Mutine	1726	235	228
l'Aurore	1726	350	290
l'Annibal	1727	—	—
le Prince de Conti	1727	300	266
le Duc de Noaille	1728	347	262
la Vénus	1728	350	341
la Diane	1728	516	464
la Flore	1728	400	356
la Galathée	1729	400	273
la Vénus	1729	450	363
le Duc de Bourbon	1729	400	319
le St. Louis	1731	350	291[1]

SOURCE: See source for Table 1.

1. This number includes the remains of the *captifs* of *la Néréide* picked up in St. Domingue. See Appendix A.

entery and an inflammation of the eyes that left many of them sight-less in one eye or totally blind. Officials at the Company of the Indies auctioned off the sick slaves, getting as much as they could for them, and those left unsold were placed with colonists with one month's guaranty.[37]

The voyage of *le Duc de Noaille* is a good example of the toll of mortality during these last French slave-trade voyages to Louisiana. This 250-ton ship left Lorient on May 5, 1727, to collect *captifs* for Louisiana in Senegal, under Captain Dupuis and with a crew of 63 men and with 16 cannons mounted. It arrived in Senegal on June 6 and was in Gorée between July 27 and October 15. It stopped at the Rade of Senegal between October 21 and November 15 while small boats loaded it with 86 *captifs* from the *captiverie* in Fort St. Louis. It left Senegal on November 15 with 347 captifs. The death toll began before the ship left Senegal. The pilot's log kept an unusually com-plete account of mortality.

37. Périer and La Chaise to the Ministry of the Colonies, New Orleans, November 2, 1727, in Ser. C13A 10, fol. 185, ANC.

[At Gorée:]
10/15   Our cook. Sick for 8 days. Died in bed.
                    [Between Gorée and Senegal:]
10/20   *Un négrillon*
                    [At Senegal:]
10/29   *Nègre*
10/31   *Nègre*
11/4   A cooper, from Lorient
11/6   *Nègre*
11/14   *Nègre*
                    [Between Senegal and St. Domingue:]
11/20   A nursing baby boy
11/21   *Négrillon*
11/24   Two *nègres*, one aged 24
11/28   *Négritte*, 9½, and a nursing baby boy
11/29   Three *nègres*
11/30   *Nègre*, aged between 26 and 30
12/1   *Nègre*, sudden death [*mort subite*]
12/2   *Négre*, aged between 24 and 26
12/4   A nursing male baby
12/4   Our master carpenter, a Canadian
12/5   *Négrillon*, and a baptized male nursing infant[38]
12/6   *Nègre*, aged 20, *négrillon*, another *nègre*, aged 30
12/8   *Nègre*, aged 26
12/9   *Nègre*, aged 26, another *nègre*, aged 24
12/11   *Nègre*
12/13   *Négresse*
12/15   *Nègre*, aged 24, *nègre*, aged 20, a baptized male nursing infant,
        nègre, aged 23, *nègre*, aged 18
12/17   *Nègre*, aged 22
12/18   *Nègre*, aged 26–28
12/19   *Négresse*, aged 30
12/22   *Nègre*, aged 25
12/23   A nursing baby, sex undetermined, and a *négresse*
12/24   Two *nègres*, one aged 22–24
        [At Caye St. Louis in St. Domingue, arrived Christmas Day:]
12/25   Two *nègres* and a *négresse*
12/26   A baptized male nursing baby. Twenty *nègres*, as well as some
        sailors, were put on land, all of them sick with scurvy.
12/30   Two *nègres* and a *négresse*
1/1/28 A *nègre*, a *négrillon*, and a *négritte* died on shore.

38. The death of baptized slaves was recognized by a cross in the margin of the log;
the death of nonbaptized slaves with lines around a blank circle.

1/2/28   A *nègre* and a nursing baby boy. Put 61 sick *nègres piéces d'Indes* ashore.
1/4   *Nègre*, on shore
1/5   Four *nègres*, a *négresse*, and a *négrillon*, aged 13–14. Put 25 *nègres* and *négresses* and one *négrillon*, aged 13–14, ashore.
1/7   *Nègre*, aged 22
1/8   *Négrillon* and 3 *négrittes*, all sick, sent to the hospital ashore
1/9   Put 3 sick *nègres* ashore.
1/10   A passenger picked up at Senegal died of fever.
1/10   *Nègre* died on shore.

In spite of their own problems, they sent ten *nègres* aboard *le Cour-rier d'Orléans* on January 19 to help it maneuver because it did not have enough crew members. *Le Courrier d'Orléans* was to accompany *le Duc de Noaille* to Louisiana.

On January 21, *le Duc de Noaille* left Caye St. Louis for Louisiana, leaving behind eighteen sick *captifs* in St. Domingue. Between St. Domingue and Louisiana, the death toll continued.

1/24   *Nègre*, aged 26–27; another *nègre*
1/31   *Négrillon*
2/2   *Nègre*
2/4   *Négresse*
2/6   *Négrillon*, aged 8; *négresse*, of sudden death
2/9   *Négritte*, and a baptized nursing male baby
2/10   *Négresse*
        [At Balize. Arrived February 12 with 262 blacks:[39]]
2/12   *Nègre*, and *négritte*, aged 12
2/12   A soldier
2/13   *Négresse*
2/14   *Nègre*
2/17   *Négresse*, aged 25, another *négresse*, and a *nègre*
2/18   *Négre*, *négritte*, and *négrillon*
2/19   *Négritte*
2/20   *Négresse* and *nègre*
2/21   Two *nègres*
        [At New Orleans:]
3/9   A sailor, embarked sick at Balize
3/25   A sailor who fell into the sea[40]

Le Duc de Noaille waited at Balize from February 12 until February 19, when two pirogues arrived to take its blacks to New Orleans.

39. See Ser. C2 19, fols. 97–98, 114–15, and July 28, 1729, in Ser. C6 10, ANC.
40. For a list of the crew during this voyage, see Ser. C6 961, fol. 172, ANM.

On February 21, the flute *la Loire* embarked all the sick blacks and sailors.[41]

Between Balize and New Orleans, twenty more *captifs* died. The entire "cargo" arrived sick with scurvy and dysentery. It seems that the "cargo," for sanitary and security reasons, was kept practically nude on French slavers. But the climate of Louisiana in winter was not the climate of the French islands. Shirts and cloaks were supposed to have been issued to the *captifs* in St. Domingue; since this did not happen, La Chaise sent shirts and cloaks to Balize for them. They embarked two-thirds of the *captifs* on *la Loire* so they would be warmer, but it was too late: They were thoroughly chilled. Périer and La Chaise complained, "If this vessel had found cloaks at St. Domingue upon its arrival, as it should have, we could very well have saved many of them. Only 242 arrived here. We put the sickest, numbering 110, into the hospital, separating those suffering from scurvy from those suffering from dysentery, but little by little, all of them got dysentery. At least another 25 died." The company was assured that these deaths did not result from neglect. The sick *captifs* had been well taken care of. They were given fresh meat mixed with bread every day. Some of those who were less sick were distributed to the colonists, including to those who could only purchase them on credit, on condition that they promise to furnish a slave for thirty days for public works. Many of these slaves were returned to the hospital the same day or the day after they were purchased. On its way back to France, *le Duc de Noaille* was pursued by pirates in the Bahamas Straits near the Martyrs Crossing.[42]

These officials reported that the *captifs* of *le Duc de Noaille* suffered the same fate as those of *l'Annibal*, a slave ship that arrived in Louisiana in 1727. No information is available on the number of slaves it embarked or landed. However, we do know that *l'Annibal* loaded Bambara in St. Louis. They had come from a great distance inland and were held at the *captiverie* in Galam and then in St. Louis for an undeterminable length of time.[43]

41. Journal du Bord du Duc de Noailles, au Sénégal, Gaure, Cais St. Louis Coste de St. Domingue et ensuite au Mississippi et en France, in Ser. 4JJ 70, Nos. 21, 22, ANM.

42. Pierre Pluchon, *La route des esclaves: Négriers et bois d'ébène a XVIIIième siècle* (Paris, 1980), 197; Périer and La Chaise to the Ministry of the Colonies, New Orleans, April 9, 1728, in Ser. C13A 11, fols. 27–29, ANC; Le Duc de Noaille. Port Louis. Marine de Ponam. M. de Voluire, Port Louis, August 2, 1728, in Ser. B3 322, fol. 171, ANM; Lassebrianne Devincelle to the Ministry of the Marine, Port Louis, June 24, 1729, in Ser. B3 330, fol. 58, ANM.

43. Périer and La Chaise to the Ministry of the Colonies, New Orleans, April 9,

Pilot's log of the slave ship *le Duc de Noaille* en route from Senegal to Louisiana. Entries for December, 1727, show a cross in the margin, recording the death of a nursing baby who had been baptized. Crosses with no centers record the death of unbaptized slaves.

Journaux du Bord, in Ser. 4JJ 70, Doc. 21, ANM.

The voyage of *la Galathée* was deadly for the crew as well as for the *captifs*.[44] This 300-ton ship was supposed to arrive in Senegal the end of May by the latest, but it did not leave Lorient until May 27.[45] It arrived in Senegal a month later. On August 31, the vessel picked up a "cargo" of 131 women and children in the Rade of Senegal for the *captiverie* at Gorée. After making several trips between Senegal and Gorée, it left Gorée on October 21 with 400 *captifs*, men, women, and children.

La Galathée had spent the entire summer, the most dangerous season for the crew, on the coast of Senegal. During the transatlantic crossing, three *négresses* drowned. It is not clear whether these deaths were accidents or suicides.[46] When the ship arrived in Caye St. Louis in St. Domingue on November 29, all the *captifs* and the entire crew were sick from scurvy. They put forty-five sick *nègres* and ten sick crew members ashore and then reembarked those who were doing better. The ship left Caye St. Louis on December 13.

On January 7, 1729, the captain hanged a "*naigre*," described as a thief found in the storeroom that night. He gave "*la calle*" to four other "*naigres*." "*La cale*," or "*estrapade marine*," was a legal punishment normally meted out to sailors found guilty of theft, swearing, or rebellion. The punishment consisted of placing the victim on a platform below the main mast, seating him on a board placed between his legs, and attaching the board to a pulley suspended from the top of the mast. Three or four sailors hoisted the victim to the top of the mast while the victim pulled on the rope to relieve himself as much as possible. The rope was suddenly released, catapulting the victim into the sea. Most often, to make the fall more rapid, a cannonball was attached to his feet. The sailors pulled him up and catapulted him down again as many times as the sentence required, usually not more than five. For the dry *cale*, the victim was attached to a shorter

---

1728, in Ser. C13A 11, fols. 27–29, ANC; [B. Tinimet] to the directors of the Co[mpany], July 7, 1726, in Ser. C6 10, Articles 9, 31, *ibid*.

44. La Galathée. Voyage du Sénégal et de la Louisiane, et de St. Domingue Isle de La Merique, in Ser. 4JJ 16, fol. 13, ANM. Unless otherwise indicated, all information from the discussion of this voyage of *la Galathée* can be found in this Journal du Bord under the entry dates cited in the text.

45. Correspondance de la Cie. avec M. de Fayet au sujet du Radoub et de l'armement de la Galatée pour le Sénégal, February 20, March 10, May 28, 1728, in Ser. C2 19, fols. 197–98, ANC.

46. *La Galathée*, entries for October 30, October 31, and November 18–19, 1728.

rope that prevented him from being catapulted into the sea, instead suspending him five or six feet above the water. The *cale* was described as a rude punishment that tended to twist the arms. The Dutch had their own version of the *cale*, more like keelhauling. The victim was catapulted under the ship, which tended to be, in effect, capital punishment. The *cale* was removed from the maritime penal code by decree of the Provisional Republican Government of France on March 12, 1848.[47]

La Galathée arrived at Balize on January 18, 1729, with 260 slaves remaining from the 400 embarked at Gorée. Forty-five sick slaves had been left at St. Domingue. About 93 slaves died during the voyage; 25 or 30 died of scurvy shortly after their arrival. The *chaloupes* (small boats) brought 90 slaves up to New Orleans, where they were to be auctioned off within three days to minimize mortality among them. The entire crew was sick with scurvy. Eleven of 56 crew members had died and two had deserted during the voyage. Two had died in Senegal and five at sea before *la Galathée* arrived in Louisiana. Nine sick sailors and an officer were left behind in St. Domingue. Their chaplain died there. *La Galathée* was ordered to enter the Mississippi and come to New Orleans so the crew could be cared for. Captain Préville Quinette claimed that his crew was "nothing but children incapable of rendering the least service." On March 22, 1729, Captain Butler of *la Flore* was given command of *la Galathée*, since Captain Quinette and his officers were all too sick to continue their voyage.[48]

In 1723, a memorandum had urged the Company of the Indies not to have ships on the African coast between May 15 and September 15:

> The merchants of the Kingdom have feared this season, but the hunger for profit has often prevailed. Some [ships] have been sent to Guinea in all seasons. It is the mortality among the crew resulting from this type of trade which no doubt contributes towards making sailors so rare today. The loss of sailors is almost irreparable. The Company should consider these interests of State as important as that of her commerce. The one can be reconciled with the other by only allowing her ships to leave between the first of August and the first of February.[49]

47. A. Jal, *Glossaire Nautique: Répertoire polyglotte de Termes de Marine anciens et Modernes* (Paris, 1848), definition of *la cale*.

48. Périer and La Chaise to the Ministry of the Colonies, New Orleans, January 30, 1729, in Ser. C13A 11, fol. 315, ANC; Raport de Laisne party en second sur la Flore de l'Orient, Capt M. de Butlair et revenu sur La Galatée par luy commandé en place M. de Préville Quinette estant tombé malade a la Louisiane, in Ser. B3 337, fol. 23, ANM.

49. This undated memorandum discusses a ship scheduled to depart on August 1, 1723. See C6 10, ANC.

Most of the sailors were born in the ports from which the ships embarked. Their rations were meager. They worked double shifts every day. They had to provide their own clothes and beds. Comte de Maurepas, secretary of the Ministry of the Marine, wrote in 1726, "It is certain that the desertions among the sailors result partly from the harshness with which they are treated and the poor rations which are given to them." According to Pierre Pluchon and many other scholars, the average mortality among whites on French slave ships was higher than among blacks. In port, the sailors got no rest. Bienville wrote, in 1721, that the sailors had to cut wood when they arrived: "This work is very difficult above all because the sailors get no rest from the time they arrive until the day they leave, being occupied in unloading the effects of their cargo; furthermore the crews of those ships which have arrived up till now have all been sick."[50]

Why did these sailors sign up for voyages from which so few returned? Clearly, desperate poverty was the reason. In the ports of France, workers were often not paid. In Brest, people literally starved to death. The wives of shipyard guards were obliged to go begging in the streets. Many of these sailors and cabin boys signed up for the three months' advance pay, which they left with their families.[51]

Some slave-trade ships arriving in Louisiana after 1726 had relatively low mortality during the voyage, but illness broke out after landing. *La Venus* made a rapid trip from Lorient to Senegal and then to Louisiana, with no stops in the French islands. The entire voyage took only four months and six days. Mortality among the *captifs* during the journey was relatively light: only one *nègre*, five *négresses*, and fourteen nursing babies died. The "cargo" arrived in seemingly good condition, but scurvy broke out three or four days after their arrival. Governor Périer wrote:

> We would have pleased a lot of people, but almost all the cargo was attacked [with scurvy]. We made a first distribution . . . of those who were not sick, but within the next day or two most of the private individuals who had bought them returned them to the hospital suffering with this illness. We were obliged, to avoid losses, to get these colonists to take them back and treat them at their homes, guarantying them for a month.

50. Pluchon, *Route des esclaves*, 57–60, 253; Bienville and Delorme to the directors, Biloxi, April 25, 1721, in Sec. IP 274B, No. 20, APL.

51. André Delcourt, *La France et les établissements français en Sénégal entre 1713 et 1763*, Mémoires de l'Institut Français d'Afrique Noire, XVII (Dakar, 1952), 192–94. For examples of men signing up to receive advance pay, see Armement du Prince de Conti, 1726, in Ser. C6 961, fol. 158, ANM.

They accepted, and we branded them with the mark of the Company so others could not be substituted in their place. We did this because we thought that a colonist who only has one or two blacks would take much better care of them than a hospital where there are already almost 200 suffering from this disease.

These officials found it surprising that those who had seemed in good condition upon their arrival and had not suffered from scurvy for a month thereafter nevertheless came down with the illness. The captain of *la Venus* claimed that the slaves became ill because they had been kept in the *captiverie* at Gorée for five months awaiting a ship, had been fed only one meal a day, and had been given only brackish water to drink. This was, according to him, the only explanation, because the voyage had been short and they were well fed aboard the ship.[52]

Many of these deaths resulted, no doubt, from ignorance. As late as 1848, there was no clear understanding of the causes of scurvy. An old dictionary of nautical terms, known as "Le Jal," gives this definition of scurvy: "A grave illness which, according to writers, develops from long sea voyages, living constantly aboard a ship where the air is often contaminated by the presence of many men, and the habitual uncleanliness, the humidity of the ship and of clothing, homesickness, unhealthy food, etc., etc. The true causes and treatment of scurvy are still unknown."[53]

Scorbut, mal de terre, mal de langues, all names for scurvy, punctuate pilots' logs of the slave-trade ships to Louisiana.[54] While there was some vague consciousness that lime juice was perhaps useful in preventing scurvy, it is certain that there was no systematic use of vitamin C aboard these ships.[55] Captains, officers, sailors, and *captifs* died of scurvy in large numbers.

52. *La Venus,* 1728, in Ser. 4JJ 63, ANM; Périer and La Chaise to the Ministry of the Colonies, New Orleans, July 31, 1728, in Ser. C13A 11, fols. 51, 52, ANC.

53. Jal, *Glossaire Nautique,* definition of *scorbut.*

54. See, for one example among many, *le St. Louis,* voyage of 1729–1731, entry for December 25, 1729: "Put 4 *malades* ashore, all suffering from *mal de terre*" (Ser. 4JJ 16, ANM). See Jal, *Glossaire Nautique,* definition of *mal de terre:* "comme on appelait autrefois le Scorbut."

55. Pluchon, *Route des esclaves,* 197. Since Pluchon does not cite specific documentary sources in this otherwise impressive book, we have no idea of the date of the instructions quoted: "Faire laver tous les matins la bouche à tous les captifs avec de l'eau fraîche à laquelle on mélera du jus de citron tant qu'on en aura, prescrit le règlement. Il est même bon de faire avaler de temps en temps quelques gouttes d'eau citronnée à ceux qui paraîtraient avoir quelque disposition au scorbut."

The colonists of Louisiana were so desperate for slaves that they bid up to one thousand livres for slaves suffering from scurvy and other illnesses. In 1729, officials complained:

> We have seen during this last auction as well as the preceding ones, slaves dying 15 minutes after they were sold, and in large numbers. Others died before they left New Orleans, and still others only lasted two days . . . there are settlers all of whose slaves died in less than a week. . . . We believe that you should fix the price of sick blacks below the price of those who are in good health, in order to prevent the total ruin of settlers, because there are some . . . who will never be able to pay for them regardless of how good their intentions may be, unless another slave is given to them [to replace those who die].[56]

By 1729, the slave trade to French Louisiana was drawing to a close. The plans that Director Brüe had described as "so beautiful, so solid, and so approved that it has become the strongest and most powerful company in the world" collapsed in the face of revolts along the Atlantic coast of the Senegal concession and along the Senegal River, revolts of the *captifs* aboard the slave ships, and a devastating revolt of the Natchez Indians, who acted in cooperation with recently arrived slaves from Africa. The Natchez Revolt wiped out the company's ambitious tobacco settlement and about one-tenth of the French population of Louisiana. Many of the surviving colonists left, and those who remained were in desperate straits. In January, 1731, the Company of the Indies formally returned its Louisiana concession to the crown of France.

One of the last ships to go to the Natchez concession before it was destroyed was *la Flore*. It had left Lorient on March 18, 1728, and stopped at Arguin Island on April 12, where the crew blew up Fort d'Arguin with mines, demolished the two cisterns, and took the artillery and the garrison to Senegal, arriving on May 10. On June 18, *la Flore* embarked 400 *captifs* for Louisiana from Gorée.[57] They were attacked on August 12 by a pirate ship off the south coast of Cuba and did battle between 9:00 P.M. and 11:30 P.M. They arrived at Balize on September 4 with 356 *captifs*, 90 of whom were quite sick

---

56. Périer and La Chaise to the Ministry of the Colonies, New Orleans, August 26, 1729, in Ser. C13A 11, fols. 359–60, ANC.

57. Raport de Laisne party en second sur la Flore de l'Orient, Capt M. de Butlair et revenu sur La Galatée par luy commandé en place M. de Préville Quinette estant tombé malade a la Louisiane, in Ser. B3 337, fol. 23, ANM; Voyage du vaisseau La Flore comandé par M. Butler, parti de France pour les còtes d'Affrique et l'Amérique pendant l'année 1728. Entries for dates cited in text in Ser. 4JJ 63, No. 28, *ibid.*

and were taken at once to New Orleans by pirogue. On October 5, *la Flore* left for New Orleans with the cargo of *l'Aurore*. Four sailors from *la Flore* died in New Orleans, one from drowning.

In April, 1729, *la Flore* left Louisiana for France with 66,983 livres of tobacco. In order to pick up the cargo at Natchez, the vessel had gone several hundred miles up the Mississippi River, but it could not get all the way to Natchez because the current was too swift. Flatboats were sent to pick up the tobacco. The officials of the company tried to explain this costly voyage: "We wanted to make an experiment and see if a ship could go up the Mississippi River to Natchez but she was obliged to stop at Three Channels which is six lieus away and send for her cargo of tobacco, which has turned out to be a little expensive for you. And unfortunately, she was not fully loaded because it has been a bad year. We expect to send the *demy Galère* to pick up the next harvest."[58]

There was no next harvest. On November 28, 1729, the French settlers there were massacred by the Natchez Indians in cooperation with the African slaves who had been imported to work on the tobacco plantations. The Natchez settlement was never reestablished under French rule.

The Company of the Indies had great difficulty refitting its ships at Lorient, recruiting sailors, and getting its ships back to Senegal on time. The consequences of these delays were drastic. This was no free market. Many of the *captifs*, especially the Bambara, had made a long voyage from the upper Senegal and were already weakened (*extenués*, as the documents called it) before being held for months in the *captiveries* until a ship belonging to the Company of the Indies was available to take them to Louisiana. The company's ships were not in good condition, and there was a shortage of desperate lads from Lorient to man them. Not that the lads were less desperate: Many of them were already dead. The lucky ones had deserted in the Caribbean and had perhaps joined the buccaneers, that international, interracial confederation of pirates. Blacks died by the hundreds in the *captiveries* as ships scheduled to carry them to Louisiana arrived months late. The survivors were often so weakened that they could not tolerate the voyage. Others revolted aboard ship.

All these problems are well illustrated by the voyages of *la Venus* and *l'Annibal*, companion ships that left Lorient on February 4, 1729,

---

58. *La Flore*, entries for January 25, 26, 29, and March 9, 1729, in Ser. 4JJ 63, No. 28, *ibid.*; Périer and La Chaise to Ministry of the Colonies, New Orleans, April 5, 1729, in Ser. C13A 11, fol. 340, ANC.

to bring *captifs* from Senegal to Louisiana. In May, 1728, *l'Annibal* had been substituted for *le Duc de Bourbon* because this vessel required extensive refitting and it was expected that *l'Annibal* could depart sooner. On September 29, it was reported that the refitting of *l'Annibal* would soon be finished. On November 6, the company's Senegal bureau wrote to Lorient: "We implore you to have the work done on *La Venus* with the greatest possible diligence. We must inform you that there are presently 1,000 blacks in the *captiveries* of Fort St. Louis and Gorée and thus there is nothing more urgent." [59]

On November 17, Lorient reported that bad weather was holding up the work. On December 3, Lorient promised that *la Venus* and *l'Annibal* would leave together: "I only await sailors to begin loading them." On January 7, 1729, it was reported that *la Venus* was ready to leave, barring bad weather. On January 12, 1729, the Paris office of the company wrote to Lorient, "The Company sees with great anguish that the season prevents you from going forward with the loading of *l'Annibal* and *la Venus* whose expeditions are nevertheless very important. We beg of you to do everything in your power to get these vessels off, and this is of extreme urgency." On January 17, a final review of the two ships was ordered so they could leave at once if the winds allowed for their departure. They did not leave until February 4, 1729. [60]

La Venus arrived in Senegal on February 26, and *l'Annibal* two days later. *L'Annibal* left Senegal for Gorée on April 12 with 172 *captifs* and *captives* and with orders to give them to *la Venus* if it did not have a complete cargo. While *la Venus* was loading its cargo at Gorée, a fire started in the chapel at the fort there and the powder magazine blew up. Several whites were wounded and several blacks killed or wounded. On April 16, *la Venus* left Gorée for Louisiana with 450

59. Lettres de M. de Fayet à la Cie. re le Duc de Bourbon, Lorient, May 31, 1728, in Ser. C2 19, fols. 195–96, ANC; Correspondance de la Cie. avec M. de Fayet au sujet du Radoub et de l'armement de l'Annibal pour le Sénégal, Lorient, June 5, 1728, in Ser. C2 18, fol. 198, *ibid.*; Lettres de M. de Fayet à la Cie. re l'Annibal, Lorient, September 29, 1728, in Ser. C2 19, fol. 195, *ibid.*; Correspondance de la Cie. Bureau du Sénégal avec M. de Fayet au sujet du Radoub et de l'armement de la Venus pour le Sénégal, Paris, November 6, 1728, in Ser. C2 19, fols. 199–200, *ibid.*

60. Correspondance de la Cie. avec M. de Fayet au sujet du Radoub et de l'armement de l'Annibal pour le Sénégal, Lorient, November 17, 1728, in Ser. C2 19, fols. 195–96, *ibid.*; Correspondance de la Cie. Bureau du Sénégal avec M. de Fayet au sujet du Radoub et de l'armement de la Venus pour le Sénégal, Lorient, December 3, 1728, and Paris, January 7, 1729, both *ibid.*, fols. 199–200; Correspondance de la Cie. avec M. de Fayet au sujet du Radoub et de l'armement de l'Annibal pour le Sénégal, Lorient, January 12, 17, 1729, and February 4, 1729, both *ibid.*, fols. 195–96.

blacks, and on April 23, *l'Annibal* left Gorée for Gambia with 204 blacks. *L'Annibal* had to go to Gambia for the rest of its "cargo" because more than 300 blacks had died in the *captiveries* since December. They had been held for more than seven months awaiting the arrival of ships. After a month at sea, there was collective suicide aboard *la Venus*: "At 3:30 in the afternoon after the blacks had eaten, five of them threw themselves into the sea. They were all Wolofs. There were others who wanted to do likewise, but we stopped them. . . . We lowered the boat to try to save the said blacks but could not save any of them. They all drowned, although we threw them several poles and other things. They did not at all wish to save themselves."[61]

La Venus arrived at Balize on June 17 but could not land. The vessel was obliged to go to Dauphin Island and then return to Balize on July 2. Again it could not enter the river because of contrary winds, but had to drop anchor five lieus from Balize. Luckily, *la Venus* had been sighted the first time it tried to land, because it had run out of water. Boats were sent to bring water and to pick up its blacks. During July 6 and 7, they debarked the blacks, keeping 40 aboard to help unload the ship. Out of the 450 *captifs* embarked at Gorée, 363 arrived at Balize. Another 43 died at Balize or on their way up the Mississippi River to New Orleans. Only 320 blacks arrived in New Orleans, all of them so sick with scurvy that more than two-thirds of those sold at auction died. They managed to send only 30 blacks from *la Venus* to Natchez. Commenting on the death of over 300 *captifs* in the *captiveries* of Gorée, the Louisiana officials advised, "You must try, Monsieurs, not to leave them there for such a long time, because most of the time they only have one meal and drink nothing but brackish water." Almost the entire crew of *la Venus* came down with scurvy, one after the other. They were brought to the hospital in New Orleans and returned to their ship on August 5. On August 26, the Louisiana officials wrote, "We still have no news of *l'Annibal* . . . she was right behind *la Venus* although she was obliged to go to Gambia to look for the rest of her cargo. We expect her any day."[62]

61. *La Venus,* entry for April 14, 1728, in Ser. 4JJ 63, No. 32, ANM; Extrait de la cargaison de la fregatte de la Cie. des Indes La Venus, in Ser. B3 330, fol. 95, *ibid.; L'Annibal,* voyage of 1729–30, entries for April 11, 14, 16, 23, 1729, in Ser. 4JJ 63, No. 32, *ibid.;* Périer and La Chaise to the Ministry of the Colonies, New Orleans, August 26, 1729, C13A 11, fol. 353, ANC; *La Venus,* voyage of 1729, entry for May 17, 1729, in Ser. 4JJ 63, No. 32, ANM.

62. *La Venus,* voyage of 1729, entries for July 1, 5, 6, 7, August 5, 1729, 4JJ 63, No. 32, ANM; Périer and La Chaise, to the Ministry of the Colonies, New Orleans, August 26, 1729, C13A 11, fol. 351, ANC.

L'Annibal never made it to Louisiana. After picking up 200 blacks at Gorée, it arrived in Gambia on April 28. The "cargo," especially the women and children, were in poor condition. The first woman died the day the ship arrived in Gambia. They put the women ashore during their stay in Gambia, but nevertheless two other women, a boy, a girl, and three nursing babies died there. On May 22, they reembarked the women and the rest of their "cargo," amounting to 300 *captifs* in all.[63]

On May 26, 1729, *l'Annibal* was waiting at the mouth of the Gambia River for a change of tide to take it out to sea. At 2 A.M., the blacks revolted. They killed two sentinels who cried out "To arms!" when the revolt started. The crew fired several rifle shots to intimidate them, but the blacks remained in formation, armed themselves with whatever they could find, and attacked the crew. The pilot wrote, "We were forced to fire upon them and seize them in order to save our lives and the Company's vessel."[64]

The blacks forced their way into the carpenter's and the caulker's storerooms and took hatchets, arms, scissors, and hammers with which they broke into the front and rear bulkheads from the food storage rooms to the powder room. Then they came through the women's compartment under the deck and broke into the gunsmith's bench, taking blades and hammers with which to remove their shackles. They found two pairs of pistols. They had taken several horns of powder from the powder room. They armed themselves with pikes and lances that were hanging from the beams below the main deck. They fired at the crew from behind the *cailboties*, which were lattice-like walls that allowed light and air to enter the ship's compartments. The *captifs* used the *cailboties* as shields and fired through their square holes, killing another crewmember. Several barrels of wine had been opened. The crew got the upper hand after mortally wounding the leader of the revolt. The remaining rebels were forced to retreat behind the anchor cables. The crew forced them out and put the shackles back on them. It was 10 A.M. before the crew got the ship entirely under control. They made a count and found forty-five black men missing, including those who had been killed and several others who had jumped out of the windows and into the sea. One had taken a lifeboat. Three women and two nursing babies had been killed. Forty-seven blacks were wounded, including four or five of the main

63. *L'Annibal*, voyage of 1729–30, entries for April 28, May 7, 11, 12, and 14, 1729, 4JJ 63, No. 33, ANM.

64. *Ibid.*, entry for May 26, 1729.

leaders of the revolt. The leaders, mortally wounded, were hanged from the top of the mast to serve as an example. Four members of the crew had been killed, another seriously wounded, and four others less seriously.[65]

That evening, a British ship entered the river, and its captain was invited to board l'Annibal. He said that the crews of five ships had been slaughtered at this same spot. One of the ships had been his. Only he and one sailor had managed to escape. A few days after the massacre, he found out that the blacks had landed his ship on the coast.[66]

On May 29, the crew of l'Annibal put 23 blacks ashore who were too badly wounded to be reembarked and took 20 captifs still remaining at the French trading post. Since there were no captifs at the English post, they had to leave with only 249. Between Gambia and Caye St. Louis in St. Domingue, two nursing babies, a mother and her nursing baby, two men, and a little girl died. On the morning of July 9, the day they arrived at Caye St. Louis, the quartermaster warned that the other blacks threatened to slit his throat if he did not agree to join a revolt against the whites. At nine o'clock on the evening of July 13,

a flock of our négresses burst into the main bedroom and punched M. Bart, sublieutenant of the ship. Being suddenly awakened, he believed that it was the nègres [that is, men, not women] who had come to murder him. He jumped out of his window into the sea [and then climbed back on deck]. This tumult had caused great alarm. We ran to arms and fired several rifle shots. Seeing that they were trying to come on deck in a crowd, and believing that it was the nègres, the gunfire had alarmed the entire port. Several boatloads of armed men came on board, one from the fort with a detachment of soldiers. We pacified them at once, seeing that their intention was to see if they could catch us off guard, and hearing, furthermore, their constant complaints that we kept them on board in order to eat them.[67]

On July 16, a port official came on board to release six nègres who had been arrested for the security of the vessel and the crew. He advised that it would be more appropriate for them to sell their slaves in St. Domingue and return to France with a load of sugar, in view of the constant mutiny among their blacks. L'Annibal sold her trouble-

65. Ibid.; Jal, Glossaire Nautique, definition of cailbotie.
66. Journal du Bord, l'Annibal, voyage of 1729–30, entry for May 26, 1729.
67. L'Annibal, voyage of 1729–30, entries for May 29, June 16, 19, 25, July 1, 3, 9, 13, 1729, 4JJ 63, No. 33, ANM.

some "cargo" in Caye St. Louis. Before leaving St. Domingue, the crew heard the news from a ship coming from Louisiana that "the *sauvages* [Indians] have made carnage in that place, and have killed 200 whites."[68]

The year 1729 was hard for the Company of the Indies in Africa as well as in Louisiana and at sea. Widespread revolts against the French broke out along the Atlantic coast of Senegal and along the Senegal River. In May of 1729, reports reached Lorient that there had been a "kind of sedition" at Gorée: the commander had been killed and several other Frenchmen imprisoned. A more complete report followed. The governor of Gorée and most of the troops and settlers of that island made a raid at Joual twenty lieus south of Gorée on the coast. The purpose of this raid was to avenge the constant insults that the blacks of that district carried out against the French. Finding no resistance when they landed, they burned all the houses of the blacks and then marched back toward their ship. The raiding party did not notice that several groups of blacks were waiting in ambush along the shore. Observing that the French returned in disorder and with a great sense of security, the blacks came out of their shelters and attacked the French with firearms and arrows. They killed several Frenchmen, including the governor of Gorée. The survivors were captured, and King Barbesin of Joual demanded that the Company of the Indies pay a large ransom for these prisoners and replace the powder and balls the attackers had used.[69]

By 1726, Galam had begun to supply *captifs* on a regular basis, and they expected to send more than one thousand to St. Louis by boat. *L'Annibal*, during her 1726 voyage to Louisiana, was to get its slave "cargo" from the *captifs* descending from Galam. But these productive years came to an abrupt end. *Le Duc d'Orléans* left Senegal on July 18, 1729, loaded with gum. The captain reported that a full-scale war had broken out with "a king called Bracque" (Braque, king of the Fulbe), who controlled the lower reaches of the Senegal River. The boats that went up the Senegal to Galam were scheduled to leave at the end of July. It remained to be seen if they could descend the river or if they had been able to trade. The pilot's log of *le St. Louis* recorded, on October 23, 1729, that the boats had descended from Galam with no slaves because the French commander had burned down a village after a dispute, and they had to send to Gambia for

---

68. *Ibid.*, entries for July 16, 1729, February 3, 4, 1730.
69. Voluire to the Ministry of the Marine, May 6, 1729, in Ser. B3 330, fol. 45, ANM; Voluire to the Ministry of the Marine, May 23, 1729, *ibid.*, fols. 51–52.

slaves. The six hundred to eight hundred slaves normally coming from Galam each year were lost to them. In March, 1730, *l'Annibal* returned to Lorient with the news that a second revolt had taken place in Galam.[70]

No slave ships arrived in Louisiana during 1730. The ships sent to Senegal were too busy putting out fires there. *Le St. Louis* left Lorient on July 10, 1729, armed for warfare and with twelve cannons mounted, to go to Senegal and Louisiana, bringing eighteen soldiers and two passengers for Senegal. There had been a ten-month delay in the ship's departure from Lorient because it had required extensive refitting. It arrived in Senegal on August 28 and remained there for fourteen months, fighting against British interlopers challenging the Company of the Indies' monopoly of the gum trade along the coast of Mauritania. The French had great difficulties with the Moors along the coast. The pilot of *le St. Louis* wrote, "The Moors there behave very badly, and we can never land without risking several attacks by this bunch of Moors who are without pity when they can take advantage of us, whom they hate more than the other nations." Before *le St. Louis* left Senegal, war had broken out in Galam with King Braque and had extended all along the Senegal River. *Le St. Louis* and its companion ship, *la Néréide*, which left Lorient on November 8, 1729, with instructions to bring slaves from Senegal to Louisiana, remained in Senegal until late 1730. On January 1, 1730, a riot erupted aboard *la Néréide*, and one of its officers boarded *le St. Louis* to ask for help. Captain Brebant of *le St. Louis* sent a small boat with some of his crew to restore order. They spent the night aboard *la Néréide*. The officers and the sailors of both ships were decimated by scurvy and fevers. *Le St. Louis'* pilot wrote:

> 9/24/29 The first lieutenant died, after an illness which lasted 10 days. He was buried at sea. His nude corpse floated to the surface. We sent a boat to tie more stones to his corpse.
> 11/19 Father David Dubourg, aged 33, has died of *maladie de langues*. We have given him the waves for his tomb.
> 12/25 We put 4 crew members ashore, all sick from scurvy [*mal de terre*].

By August 15, 1730, Captain D'Antally and four crew members, all of *la Néréide*, had died and several were critically ill from a fever they

70. [B. Tinimet] to the directors of the Co[mpany], July 7, 1726, in Ser. C6 10, Arts. 9, 31, ANC; Fayet to the Ministry of the Marine, September 11, 1730, in Ser. B3 337, fol. 209, ANM; *Le St. Louis*, entry for October 23, 1729, in Ser. 4JJ 144A, No. 3, ANM; Voluire to the Ministry of the Marine, Port Louis, March 24, 1730, in Ser. B3 337, fol. 26, ANM.

had caught in Gambia. On August 21, *le St. Louis* put four crew members ashore, violently attacked by scurvy.[71]

Le St. Louis left Gorée on September 14, 1730, with 350 blacks and 11 nursing babies. Their cauldron broke and they had to stop at Martinique and at Caye St. Louis. Between Gorée and Martinique, 22 *captifs* died; 2 more died at Martinique. Between Martinique and St. Domingue, 3 more *captifs* died. At St. Domingue, they put 45 *captifs* and several crew members ashore, all stricken with scurvy. Between St. Domingue and Louisiana, 12 more *captifs* died, and another *captif* died upon their arrival.[72]

La Néréide never made it to Louisiana. The vessel picked up 200 *captifs* in Gambia in July during the height of the fever season. The captain and 6 sailors died from fevers contracted in Gambia. During the Atlantic crossing, the ship lost 5 more sailors and the chaplain. Before leaving Senegal, 25 *captifs* who were already stricken with scurvy were returned to the *captiverie*. By the time *la Néréide* docked in St. Domingue, all its sailors and the first lieutenant were sent ashore, all very sick. They decided to leave 50 *captifs*, who were too sick to continue the voyage, in St. Domingue and to bring the rest of their *captifs* to Louisiana as soon as the crew recovered. On December 5, 1730, they gave the rest of the "cargo" to *le St. Louis* to take to Louisiana, and *la Néréide* returned to France. *Le St. Louis* arrived in Louisiana on January 21, 1731, and landed a total of 291 *captifs*—the remains of its own "cargo" and that of *la Néréide*. The "cargoes" of both ships comprised 561 slaves, about 100 of whom had been left in St. Domingue too sick to continue the voyage. *Le St. Louis* returned to France carrying the officers, crew, and passengers of *le Prince de Conti*, which had broken up on a sandbar at the mouth of the Mississippi River.[73]

71. *Le St. Louis,* entry for July 10, 1729, in Ser. 4JJ 144A, No. 3, ANM; Lettres de M. de Fayet, February 29, November 17, 1728, in Ser. C2 18, fol. 198, ANC; *Le St. Louis,* entry for September 21, 1729, in Ser. 4JJ 144A, No. 3, ANM; Le St. Louis. Extrait de la Campagne du Vaisseau de la Compagnie des Indes par Le Sr. Brébant venant du Mississippy, in Ser. B3 344, fol. 108, ANM; *La Néréide,* entry for November 8, 1729, in Ser. 4JJ 63, No. 36, ANM; *Le St. Louis,* entries for September 24, November 19, December 25, 1729, August 15, 21, 1730, in Ser. 4JJ 144A, No. 3, ANM.

72. *Le St. Louis,* entries for September 14, January 1, December 3, 1730, January 19, 21, 1731, in Ser. 4JJ 144A, No. 3, ANM; *Le St. Louis.* Extrait de la Campagne du Vaisseau de la Compagnie des Indes par Le Sr. Brébant venant du Mississippy, in Ser. B3 344, fol. 108, *ibid.*

73. *La Néréide,* entries for August 8, 22–24, October 5, 9, November 5, 17, 18, 20, 22, 23, 29, December 2, 1730, 4JJ 63, No. 36, ANM; *Le St. Louis,* entries for September 14, 1730, January 21, 1731, in Ser. 4JJ 144A, No. 3, *ibid.; La Néréide,* entry for October 13, 1730, in Ser. 4JJ 63, No. 36, *ibid.;* Le St. Louis. Extrait de la Campagne du

Death and Revolt

Thus ended the African slave trade to Louisiana sponsored by the Company of the Indies. Its ambitious plans were destroyed by a convergence of revolts of Africans in Senegambia, at sea, and in Louisiana, where Africans, allied with Indian nations, cooperated in conspiracies and revolts to take over the colony.

Vaisseau de la Compagnie des Indes par Le Sr. Brébant venant du Mississipy, in Ser. B3 344, fol. 108, *ibid*.

The Bambara in Louisiana: From The Natchez Uprising to the Samba Bambara Conspiracy

Bouki fait gombo, lapin mangé li.

Hyena makes the gombo; rabbit eats it.

—Louisiana Creole proverb from Lafcadio Hearn,
Gombo Zhèbes: A Little Dictionary of Creole Proverbs

[Although Hearn translated *bouki* as he-goat, *bouki* is a term, widely used in African folklore, meaning hyena. It represents a loud, stupid animal. *Gombo* means okra in many African languages.]

The Bambara, arriving in Louisiana in large numbers after 1726, first encountered Indians as their fellow slaves. The first slaves in French Louisiana, held from the earliest years of colonization, were Indians. Iberville had strongly opposed Indian slavery, attacking the British traders for inciting wars to obtain Indian slaves, but his younger brother and successor, Bienville, was less scrupulous. While proclaiming that they protected the Indians from British-fomented slave-raiding, the French bought, sold, and even exported Indian captives from Louisiana to the French West Indies. As we have seen, Bienville was eager to develop a slave trade with the French West Indies, exchanging two Indian slaves for one African. Although the metropolitan authorities prohibited such a trade, some Indian slaves were exported from Louisiana to the islands. The export of Indian or African slaves from Louisiana was specifically outlawed in 1726, but the export of Indian slaves from Louisiana to the French islands continued on a small scale.[1]

Encounters between African slaves, many of them recent war captives, and Indian slaves, who knew the land and had ties with Indian nations in lower Louisiana, severely undermined discipline among slaves of both races. After New Orleans was founded, escaped Indian slaves remained in and around the city, killing and eating cattle belonging to the settlers. Within a few years, the incursions of the Indian slaves became more organized and dangerous. In 1726, the attorney general complained: "For a long time large bands of Indian slaves have joined together and deserted and hang out around the city well armed. These desertions are always accompanied by thefts from their masters, who are thus deprived of their arms as well as their slaves, putting their lives at risk. Since they have a good supply of powder and balls . . . we are convinced that they are planning a severe blow against us."[2]

As increasing numbers of Africans arrived during the 1720s, African and Indian slaves, sometimes owned by the same masters and

1. Charles Edward O'Neill, *Church and State in French Colonial Louisiana: Policy and Politics to 1732* (New Haven, 1966), 30, 288; Resumé d'une lettre de Robert, November 26, 1708, in Ser. C13A 2, fol. 359, ANC; Baron to the Ministry of the Colonies, Amsterdam, October 7, 1715, in Ser. C13B 1, fol. 60, ANC; Mémoire sur la Louisiane, 1726, in Ser. C13A 10, fol. 156, ANC; Nancy M. Miller Surrey, *The Commerce of Louisiana During the French Regime, 1699–1763* (1916, rpr. New York, 1968), 230.

2. May 24, 1723, in RSC, *LHQ*, I (1917), 109; August 17, 1726, in RSC, LHC.

SAVAGES OF SEVERAL NATIONS, (1735) by Alexandre de Batz.

This 1735 drawing by Alexandre de Batz shows a black slave among Indians of several nations.

From the Smithsonian Miscellaneous Collection, Vol. 80, No. 5, 1928. Courtesy The Historic New Orleans Collection, Museum/Research Center, Acc. No. 1974.25.10.98.

sharing the same fate, ran off together, stealing food, supplies, arms, and ammunition from their masters. They often were well armed and raided the settlers for more supplies. An Indian slave who had escaped and been recaptured revealed the existence of a settlement, named des Natanapallé, where there were fifteen other fugitive slaves, both African and Indian. They were armed with eleven muskets and ammunition with which they expected to defend themselves if attacked. The next month, another fugitive Indian slave was interrogated. He had left two years earlier with a group of slaves belonging to Sieur Tisserant. He had convinced a female Indian slave to leave with him, and she had robbed her mistress before departing. They joined a party of fugitives across Lake Pontchartrain but later left them. When he was captured, he had only potatoes and fish left to eat.[3]

By 1728, Governor Périer complained that the search for runaway

3. April 9, 1727, in RSC, LHC.

slaves had been neglected and that these runaways were assembling in the city. He pointed out that once the runaways had a place of refuge, the colonists could no longer keep them, and the colony would be lost. A tax of 30 pounds per slave was levied upon the masters and converted into merchandise to present to whomever brought back a runaway slave. The Indian nations all the way to Natchez were asked to arrest all runaway slaves, whether Indians or blacks, and were advised that those who gave refuge to the blacks or helped them to escape from the French settlements would be considered enemies of the French, and that those who arrested the runaways and returned them to the French would be considered their friends. French officials offered an attractive reward in goods, valued at 160 pounds, that included two muskets, four lengths of Limbourd cloth, two blankets, twenty pounds of balls, four shirts, a pound of vermillion, mirrors, knives, and musket stones for each slave returned. Périer believed that these rewards to the Indians and the punishment of the runaway slaves would produce two important results. First, the Indians would not allow any blacks to escape, and the blacks would no longer dare run away. And even more important, the French would no longer have to fear any understanding between these two peoples—understandings that would be harmful to the colony. On the contrary, if the Indians attacked the French, they would have no better defenders than the blacks. So, the French reasoned, in using the Indians to keep the blacks in submission, they would have nothing to fear from the Indians. The highest priority of French policy was to sow misunderstandings between blacks and Indians, making their differences forever irreconcilable. With this objective in mind, they forbad Frenchmen living among the Indians to have black slaves, and forbad French trading among the Indians to bring blacks along with them.[4]

Périer came out strongly against Indian slavery for a number of cogent reasons. First, he argued, the Indian nations often went to war in order to take captives to sell to the French. And though it could be argued that wars among the Indians helped the French maintain control of the colony, they also offered an opportunity for the English to penetrate the closest Indian allies of the French. Furthermore, he argued, Indian slaves were useless except for hunting and fishing and were impossible to use for skilled trades or for cultivating the land. They rendered little service and ran away to their nations or to other,

4. Périer and La Chaise, Réponse article par article à la lettre de la Cie en date du 27 octubre 1727, New Orleans, March 30, 1728, in Ser. C13A 11, fols. 97–100, ANC.

neighboring nations, bringing black slaves along with them and developing ties with the blacks that could be harmful to the colony when there were more blacks.[5] Périer's worst fears were realized in short order.

There was a long history of conflict between the colonists and the Natchez Indians. In 1723, Bienville fought against and defeated the Natchez to take revenge against them for killing some French settlers. There was already at that time a free black among the Natchez who had been instigating them against the French and joining them in raids against the Indian allies of the French. According to the peace treaty between Bienville and the Natchez, the Natchez were to bring in dead or alive that free black who had taken refuge among them for a long time, had made seditious speeches against the French, and had fought alongside the Natchez against the Tunica and Tamira. The Natchez reported that they could not bring him in alive; he had been hiding in the canes since the French arrived, they said, and when any of them approached him, he resisted. The Natchez chief Stung Serpent brought in his head on November 26, 1723.[6]

When the slave trade from Senegal intensified between 1726 and 1729, the Company of the Indies was pushing to establish a prosperous tobacco colony at its Natchez settlement, the present site of Natchez, Mississippi.[7] Many of the newly arrived Africans, many of them no doubt Bambara, were sent to Natchez. These African slaves played a prominent role in the devastating massacre of the French settlement at Natchez on November 28, 1729. At the time of the massacre, the settlement consisted of 200 French men, 82 French women, 150 French children, and 280 black slaves. Before beginning this massacre, the Natchez assured themselves of the support of several blacks, including those of the White Earth concession and two of their *commandeurs* (slave foremen), who told the other blacks that they would be free if they supported the Natchez. Those slaves who refused to support the Natchez were threatened with being sold to the Chickasaw along with the French women and children. Contrary to the historical myth that the Natchez intended to incorporate the French women and children into their tribe, Périer reported, based

5. Périer to [Abbe Raquet], New Orleans, May 12, 1728, in Ser. C13A 11, fols. 7, 8, ANC.

6. Rélation Punition des Natchez en 1723, in Ser. F3 24, fols. 153, 154, AN.

7. For an interesting study of the economic aspects of the Natchez Revolt of 1729, see James T. McGowan, "Creation of a Slave Society: Louisiana Plantations in the Eighteenth Century" (Ph.D. dissertation, University of Rochester, 1976), 43–96.

on eyewitness accounts, that the Natchez held these women and children in order to sell them.[8]

Assured of the cooperation of the vast majority of the African slaves, Natchez hunting parties simultaneously visited the homes of all the white settlers, asking to borrow guns for hunting and offering to repay the settlers with corn, fowl, and deer meat. The French settlers gave up all their weapons in return for a promise of food. They were thus totally and peacefully disarmed by the Natchez, who attacked them with their own arms. When the massacre began, the Natchez outnumbered the French two to one in every French household. A Natchez party entered the house of Chepart, the commander of the settlement, with chickens to trade. His officers decided to put them out, but the officers made the mistake of bending down to pick up the chickens before throwing out their unwanted guests. This last gesture of greed—or hunger—put the finishing touches on the Natchez settlement. As the officers bent down to pick up the chickens, the Natchez chief gave orders to fire.[9]

Some of the blacks at Natchez supported the French. Aside from the 145 French men, 36 French women, and 56 French children killed during the massacre, Madame, a *commandeur* of the blacks at White Earth, was also killed, perhaps because he was considered dangerous and unreliable by the conspirators. Three blacks escaped from Natchez and arrived in New Orleans on December 3, 1729. They informed Périer that they had seen the heads of the French officers and employees lined up opposite the heads of the French settlers. It was reported that the Natchez spared as many French women as possible during the massacre, and the surviving French women and children had several black men and women with them, perhaps loyal domestics. They were all kept in two houses, where they were carefully watched.[10]

The French military position was desperate. French settlers, *voya-*

---

8. Diron d'Artaguette to [?] March 20, 1730, in Ser. F3 24, fols. 188–89, AN; Périer, Rélation du Massacre des Natchez arrivé le 28 novembre 1729, New Orleans, March 18, 1730, *ibid.*, fols. 170–72.

9. Périer, Rélation du Massacre, *ibid.*, fols. 170–72.

10. P. Philibert, missionaire capucin, Etat des personnes du poste des Natchez qui ont été massacrées le 28 novembre 1729, par les Sauvages voisins dont le dit poste porte le nom. Aboard *le Duc du Bourbon*, June 9, 1730, in Ser. C13A 12, fol. 366, ANC; Périer to the Ministry of the Colonies, New Orleans, March 18, 1730, *ibid.*, fol. 41; Diron d'Artaguette to the Ministry of the Colonies, Mobile, February 9, 1730, *ibid.*, fols. 362–65.

geurs, and priests were being killed throughout the colony. Governor Périer wrote, "Since December 2nd [1729], each news is worse than the other. The French are being killed everywhere without being able to help each other, because we are in as much danger and have as much to fear by assembling together as by remaining at our posts." On December 15, he sent a pirogue armed with twenty men, including six blacks, to bring powder to the Illinois country and to pick up all the *voyageurs* found along the Mississippi River. Panic seized the French settlers of New Orleans:

> The Chaouchas, a nation of 30 men below New Orleans, caused our settlers to tremble. This made me decide to have them destroyed by our blacks, which was carried out promptly and secretly. These examples made by our blacks had held the other little nations below the river in respect. If I wanted to use our blacks I would have destroyed all the little nations who are not at all useful to us and who can, on the contrary, push our blacks to revolt, as we have seen from the example of the Natchez.

Hesitating to arm more blacks, Périer resorted to arming the few French he had in the city.[11]

The French and the Choctaw attacked the Natchez settlement on January 27, 1730. Fifty to one hundred blacks and fifty-four French women were recaptured by the Choctaw.[12] Those blacks who were not captured fought alongside the Natchez, preventing the Choctaw from taking their powder and giving the Natchez enough time to enter the two forts. The blacks' role was decisive in preventing the total defeat of the Natchez. The French and their Choctaw allies had not expected to have to fight the blacks as well as the Natchez.[13]

Delahaye, militia commander of forty volunteers, mostly from Pointe Coupee, reported that the French troops behaved as if they were "going to a fair and not to war. These savages defended themselves desperately and our troops attacked only with great timidity. They came out of their trench past the post I occupied and ran away after having abandoned their arms in order to run faster." The captain of the port of Lorient expressed the most reasonable and objective

11. Périer to the Ministry of the Colonies, New Orleans, March 18, 1730, *ibid.,* fols. 37–41.

12. Périer reported one hundred blacks and fifty-four French women retaken, one hundred Natchez killed and fifteen to twenty taken prisoner (*ibid.*). D'Artaguette reported about fifty blacks retaken in the same battle (Diron d'Artaguette to the Ministry of the Colonies, Mobile, February 9, 1730, *ibid.,* fols. 362–65).

13. Périer to the Ministry of the Colonies, New Orleans, March 18, 1730, *ibid.,* fol. 43.

appraisal of the performance of the French troops in Louisiana: "It seems to me that these soldiers are good only for guarding military posts and are not used to warfare in the woods. All the grenadiers of Europe would make few conquests given the size of this concession. The only means to assure it is to incite other Indian nations against the Natchez, our enemies, encouraging them to declare war and by this means work towards their destruction. This game is general and known by everyone for this remote country."[14]

Some blacks fought on the side of the French, thereby winning their freedom and laying the basis for an institutionalized black militia. The fifteen blacks who were armed by the French and accompanied their expedition against the Natchez "behaved with surprising valor," wrote Périer. "If these soldiers were not so expensive and so necessary to the colony, it would be better to use them than our soldiers who seem made especially for Louisiana, they are so bad." Attorney General Fleuriau, moved by the massacre at Natchez, urged recourse to every corrective measure and endorsed the plan of freeing those blacks who by report of the officers in charge proved loyally useful to the upper French posts. He proposed a militia company organized among selected blacks for instant call against the Indians as necessary. Freedom had already been promised certain black volunteers in the wake of the Natchez affair. Fleuriau ordered that the promise be fulfilled, subject to relevant clauses of the Code Noir, evidently those referring to emancipation for service to the state. He attached a list of names of candidates for emancipation.[15]

In 1731, a year and a half after the Natchez Indians and their African and Indian allies rose up against the French settlers, Périer wrote: "The greatest misfortune which could befall the colony and which would inevitably lead to its total loss would be a union between the Indian nations and the black slaves, but happily there has always been a great aversion between them which has been much increased by the war, and we take great care to maintain it." To this end, three

14. Lettre en forme de relation du Deslayes au sujet du massacre des françois fait par des sauvages le 28 novembre 1729, New Orleans, March 15, 1730 (received in Balize, April 16, 1731), in Ser. C13C 4, fols. 179–80, ANC; Fayet, Captain of the port of Lorient, to the Ministry of the Marine, December 23, 1730, in Ser. B3 337, fol. 210, ANM.

15. Périer to the Ministry of the Colonies, New Orleans, March 18, 1730, in Ser. C13A 12, fol. 45, ANC; May 13, 1730, in RSC, *LHQ,* IV (1921), 524. Fleuriau became *procureur au conseil supérieur* in 1722. His son was a lieutenant who left Louisiana for France in 1752. See Marie-Antoinette Menier, Etienne Taillemite, and Gilberte de Forges, *Correspondance à l'arrivée en provenance de la Louisiane* (2 vols.; Paris, 1976, 1983), II, 738.

of the most active black leaders who sided with the Natchez had been turned over to the Choctaw and "burned alive with a degree of cruelty which has inspired all the Negroes with a new horror of the Savages, but which will have a beneficial effect in securing the safety of the Colony."[16]

When the French, the Choctaw, the Tunica, and a contingent of fifteen African slaves recaptured the Natchez settlement, some of the Africans fled with the Natchez and others were captured by the Choctaw. Alibamon Mingo, the Choctaw chief, drove a hard bargain for the return of some fifty black slaves they had recaptured from the Natchez. In March of 1731, a French officer went to a Choctaw settlement and met with three of these blacks, who claimed that they would like nothing better than to return with him to Mobile but that they did not wish to be brought there by the Indians. When the officer asked why, they replied that the Indians had made them carry heavy loads, had badly mistreated them, and had taken all their belongings, even their deerskin shirts. One of these three blacks had a tomahawk wound on his head. The French officer was informed that there were still thirty-two blacks held by the Choctaw, including six black women who belonged to the Company of the Indies and eighteen other slaves who were privately owned. Four slaves belonging to the company and three privately owned slaves had died. This same slave informed the officer that he was at the Great Village when the Chickasaw chief arrived and urged the blacks there assembled to go to the Chickasaw, saying that they would be better off with the English than with the French. The Chickasaw chief offered to accompany them to the English. The blacks refused to go, and the Chickasaw chief left very discontented. When asked why they ran away when they saw the French coming for them, the blacks replied that the Indians told them constantly that all those blacks who were retaken by the French were burned alive when they arrived in New Orleans, and they were afraid. They suggested that if the French were to bring with them a slave they had recaptured, to convince the other blacks that they would not be burned alive, they would return gladly.[17]

When the Natchez acknowledged their defeat at Red River in 1731, they raised a white flag and sent an Indian who spoke a little French

16. Mouvements des Sauvages de la Louisiane depuis la prise du fort des Natchez par M. de Périer sur la fin de janvier 1731, July 21, 28, 1731, in Ser. C13A 13, fol. 87, ANC; Reuben Gold Thwaites, ed., *The Jesuit Relations and Allied Documents: Travels and Explorations of the Jesuit Missionaries in New France, 1610–1719* (73 vols.; Cleveland, 1896–1901), LXVII, 199.

17. Régis du Roulet to Périer, March 16, 1731, in Ser. C13A 13, fols. 189–90, ANC.

to negotiate. The French informed the Natchez that before discussing anything else, they had to send them all the blacks who were in the fort, which they did at once. They sent nineteen black men and one black woman. The Natchez claimed that six other blacks were out hunting with several Indians and that the rest had been killed. St. Denis, commander at Natchitoches, retook six blacks when he defeated the Natchez. Three of them gave themselves up, saying they had no master except the Company of the Indies. He distributed the other three among settlers at the post until they could be returned to their masters. One of them claimed he belonged to Champineul and another to Quioit, both of whom had been killed at the Natchez massacre and had left no heir. The third had been paid for in full. St. Denis claimed this slave for himself as war booty. He sent the few slaves, evidently Indians whom the Indians gave to him, as a present to the Spanish in order to remove them from the area and from the French colony.[18]

The black slaves who sided with the Natchez, as well as those taken and held by the Choctaw, greatly complicated French efforts to drive a wedge between Africans and Indians. Périer urged that they rid themselves entirely of the "blacks who had lived for a long time among the Natchez who had taken them from the French and among the Choctaw who retook them from the Natchez. They were not at all badly treated by the one or the other, and they have returned with a spirit of laziness, independence and insolence." The comptroller for the Company of the Indies complained that the Choctaw had held the company's blacks for eighteen months after they recaptured them from the Natchez, and that the governor had made a big mistake by putting these returned slaves among those of the company. The returned slaves let the other blacks know about the freedom that they enjoyed among the Indians, going hunting and cultivating the land only when they felt like it.[19]

Africans who had lived among the Natchez and the Choctaw did in fact maintain ties with Indian nations wishing to drive out the French. Many of these slaves were Bambara belonging to the Company of the Indies, and upon their return, they plotted with the

18. Rélation de la défaite des Natchez par M. de Périer, commandeur général de la Louisiane, Red River, 1731, in Ser. F3 24, AN; St. Denis to Salmon, Natchitoches, November 2, 1731, in Ser. C13A 13, fol. 165, ANC.

19. Mouvements des Sauvages de la Louisiane sur la fin de janvier 1731, July 21, 28, 1731, in Ser. C13A 13, fol. 87, ANC; Mémoire de Raymond Amyalt, Sieur d'Auseville, conseilleur au Conseil Supérieur de la Louisiane, commissaire aux comptes de la Compagnie des Indes, New Orleans, January 20, 1732, in Ser. C13A 14, fol. 273, ibid.

Natchez, the Chickasaw, the Illinois, the Arkansas, and part of the Miami to coordinate an uprising among African slaves in all the French settlements with attacks upon the French by these Indian nations.

During the winter of 1730 to 1731, Périer ordered a French officer living with the Choctaw to organize a party of three hundred men to cut a wedge between the Natchez and the Chickasaw, but this maneuver failed. Then he ordered the officer to enlist the Choctaw to declare war against the Chickasaw to help them hold out until more aid from France arrived. But his plans were foiled when the Natchez and the Chickasaw made overtures to the Illinois, the Arkansas, and part of the Miami, as well as to the black slaves in the French settlements. The Indians sent to New Orleans one of the blacks they had with them to tell the blacks there that they would be free and that they would have everything they could wish for with the English, who would take good care of them. "This black was a Bambara of a nation which the others do not understand. He recruited all the blacks of his nation." [20]

The uprising was scheduled to take place on June 24, 1731, but the conspirators were not yet ready, and it was put off until June 29. During this delay, the plan was uncovered by the French: All the whites from Pointe Coupee to Balize were to be massacred. All the Bambara had joined together to free themselves and take possession of the country by this revolt. The other blacks in the colony who were not of the Bambara nation were to serve them as slaves. It was reported that four hundred Bambara slaves were involved in this conspiracy. French officials did not wish to deepen the investigation because of the damages that would be caused to private individuals if they lost their slaves. [21]

Périer questioned a black domestic slave in New Orleans who had entered into the conspiracy. She had been told that the conspirators had agreed to take the church when everyone was at the parish mass and to set fire to several houses in the city to disperse those who had not been taken in the church. According to Périer, the conspiracy was proven. French officials killed several of the conspirators by breaking them on the wheel and hanged one woman involved in the affair. The

20. Périer to the Ministry of the Colonies, December 10, 1731, in Ser. C13A 13, fols. 63–64, *ibid.*

21. Beauchamp, major from Mobile, to the Ministry of the Colonies, Fort Conde, Mobile, November 5, 1731, *ibid.*, fol. 200; Diron d'Artaguette to [?], Mobile, June 24, 1731, in Ser. F3 24, fols. 427–28, AN; Diron d'Artaguette to the comptroller general, Fort Conde, Mobile, August 20, 1731, in Ser. C13A 13, fol. 155, ANC.

owners of the executed slaves sought to be compensated by receiving a slave from those belonging to the Company of the Indies.[22]

Périer later expressed some doubts about the reality of the conspiracy; but he stated that if it was indeed real, it could be explained by the revolt of the Indians, whom the blacks saw massacring the French every day, and by the small number of troops they knew to be in the country. The comptroller for the Company of the Indies believed that the slaves belonging to the company had plotted to revolt and assassinate the French because of the influence of the contingent of blacks who had stayed for eighteen months among the Choctaw after they had been recaptured from the Natchez. The revolt would have succeeded if the affair had not been revealed by an indiscreet black woman who told her friend that she would be named Madame Périer and by a black who in anger threatened to make war against the French. All the principal leaders of the conspiracy were to have taken the places—and even the names—of the commanders, majors, captains, officers, and storehouse guards. The leaders were tried and found guilty. In order to carry out the execution of the principal leaders and the woman, all the settlers had to be armed.[23]

The version of this conspiracy published by Le Page du Pratz, director of the Company of the Indies in Louisiana, is a bit flattering to him and his role in uncovering it. None of the existing documents mentions him at all. His report appears to be a composite version of several events and places him in the center of developments. But it is more concrete and graphic than some of the drier, documentary accounts and perhaps not too much less authentic.[24] According to Du Pratz, in 1730 (it was actually June, 1731) a weary African slave who wanted to eat her lunch returned to the headquarters of the Company of the Indies in New Orleans from the brick foundry where she worked. A French soldier needed wood for his fire and demanded that she go get it. She said she was tired and refused to go. The soldier gave her a brutal slap in the face. In anger and defiance, she shouted that the French soldiers would not slap blacks much longer.

22. Périer to the Ministry of the Colonies, December 10, 1731, in Ser. C13A 13, fols. 63–64, ANC; Salmon to the Ministry of the Colonies, New Orleans, January 19, 1732, in Ser. C13A 15, fol. 29, *ibid.* The number of slaves reported executed varies in these documents between five and twelve.

23. Mouvements des Sauvages de la Louisiane sur la fin de janvier 1731, July 21, 28, 1731, in Ser. C13A 13, fol. 87, *ibid.*; Mémoire de Raymond Amyalt, January 20, 1732, in Ser. C13A 14, fol. 273, *ibid.*

24. Le Page du Pratz, *Histoire de la Louisiane* (3 vols.; Paris, 1758), III, 304–17. Du Pratz's account in the following paragraphs is taken from this source.

Several French bystanders seized her and had her brought to the governor, who ordered her imprisoned and interrogated. She insisted that she spoke only in anger, that there was no conspiracy. Du Pratz claimed he told the governor, "Monsieur, I feel that a man who is drunk and a woman in anger are more likely to tell the truth than in any other circumstances." He went to the slave quarters of the plantation of the king when the slaves were normally asleep and brought with him a young *nègre* who belonged to the colony's surgeon, probably to interpret from Bambara. They found one hut lighted up, and listening outside, they heard a voice say, "We must not involve others until two or three days before the coup, because they might betray us."

"I spoke," said another voice, "to so-and-so upon whom we can count for sure."

Du Pratz was extremely shocked to discover that it was Samba, his first *commandeur*, who spoke. After arriving in Louisiana as a slave, Samba had won the confidence of Du Pratz and had become *commandeur* of the slaves of the Company of the Indies and interpreter before the Superior Council in cases involving Bambara slaves. Du Pratz was further dismayed to hear next the voice of his second *commandeur* saying, "I spoke this morning to so-and-so, of whom I am very confident, and he told me that we should not speak so soon to the others."

Du Pratz described this plot as "a betrayal from people of whom one had no distrust whatsoever. The *nègres* planned to get rid of all the French and establish themselves in their place, taking over the Capital and all we owned."

The two other slaves present said that all eight of them should say nothing until the return of those who had gone to the Illinois, where there were *nègres* who had many relatives and friends whom they could perhaps recruit, thereby winning over many others. They agreed to return the next night at the same time. Du Pratz could identify six of the conspirators, but he wanted to identify the other two before making his move. They returned the next night after 10 P.M. Both *commandeurs* were there. Du Pratz recognized the voices of two others. One of the slaves, who had been absent the night before, said that they should keep their number at eight until harvest time, and then they could win over many others. Du Pratz isolated the conspirators, sending each on different work detachments. He then sent for them one by one and had them put in shackles. While the rest of the slaves were eating lunch, Samba was sent on an errand that took him past the prison, where the soldiers grabbed him and put him in irons.

The next day the prisoners were tortured by burning to force them to confess their crime, their plans, and their accomplices, but they refused to talk or confess. Samba and his alleged accomplices were tortured again, to no avail.

Samba Bambara had been an interpreter (*maître de langue*) at Galam along the Senegal River, traveling between Galam and the French trading post of St. Louis at its mouth. He was evidently on good terms with his employers. On January 3, 1720, 50 pounds was advanced to one Niobo against a balance of 126 pounds owed to their interpreter, Samba Bambara. At the same time, Samba Bambara asked permission to visit his family in Senegal and then return to Galam. The director of the company asked that permission be granted, if the director in Galam could do without him for a while. By 1722, Samba had established a home in St. Louis, where his wife lived. But she turned out to be fickle, and Samba sought the help of the Company of the Indies to force her to respect her marriage vows. In October, 1722, Samba asked his director to write to his superior demanding that he stop the marriage of Samba's wife, Yeran Galen, to a merchant. Samba wanted her and a captive woman she owned chased out of St. Louis if she persisted in her infidelity. He sent his oldest son to St. Louis to make sure his request was attended to. According to Bambara customary law, a husband can repudiate a wife, but a wife can never repudiate a husband, and he has a right to force her to return to the conjugal domicile.[25] Resuming his role as interpreter after he arrived in Louisiana, he apparently helped obtain mitigated sentences by interpreting what was most favorable to the accused.

Du Pratz employed spies and did research on Samba's background. He claimed that Samba had been the leader of the revolt in Senegal that had cost the French Fort d'Arguin, and that when M. Périer de Salvert retook the fort, one of the principal articles of the peace treaty was that Samba be sent to the French colonies in the Americas as a slave. He was, according to Du Pratz, sent on *l'Annibal*, where he plotted to cut the throats of the vessel's crew and take over the ship, but the officers were warned in time and had him and all the male slaves put in irons until they reached Louisiana. None of these allegations against Samba Bambara finds documentary confirmation. De-

25. Brüe to Violaine, commander of Fort St. Joseph in Galam, Senegal, April 30, 1720, in Ser. C6 6, p. 3, ANC; André Delcourt, *La France et les établissements français en Sénégal entre 1713 et 1763*, Mémoires de l'Institut Français d'Afrique Noire, XVII (Dakar, 1952), listing for Samba Bambara in Index; Moussa Travélé, *Proverbes et contes Bambara, accompagnés d'une traduction française et précédés d'un abrégé de droit coutumier Bambara et Malinke* (1923; rpr. Paris, 1977), 15.

tailed reports of the loss of Fort d'Arguin do not implicate Samba Bambara. There was a revolt of the Moors, who turned the island over to the Dutch. Some of the Bambara defenders of the fort finally saved themselves by climbing over the wall. The garrison, reduced to twenty men, lacking food and water, and most of them suffering from scurvy, surrendered to the Dutch. The records for the slave-trade voyage of l'Annibal in 1726 are the most scanty for any slave-trade voyage to Louisiana (see Appendix A). The treaties with the Dutch were not signed until 1727, and if Samba Bambara did come to Louisiana on l'Annibal, he had already arrived when the treaties were signed. There is no mention of Samba Bambara in these treaties.[26] He did, however, obviously get into some kind of difficulties in Senegal, because he was in fact enslaved and sent to Louisiana.

The alleged conspirators still refused to talk, in spite of their great suffering. They only said they never thought of doing any harm to the French. Du Pratz wrote a memoir about Samba's past and gave it to the judge. The judge sent for Samba, threatening to burn him again if he did not confess, but Samba still refused. The judge read the memoir to Samba, saying, "You see that I know your whole life, which has always been that of a seditious one. You have always sought to do harm and to incite others to do harm."

Samba asked, "Who told you that?" (in Louisiana Creole, "Qui cila qui dire cila á toi?").

"What does it matter who told me that?" the judge replied. "Isn't it true?"

Samba continued to insist that the judge name the person who told him that. Finally the judge said that it was Le Page du Pratz.

"Ah!" said Samba, "Monsieur Le Page is a devil who knows everything" (in Louisiana Creole, "M. le Page li diable li sabai tout").

The other accused conspirators were sent for and they confessed, though apparently they did not implicate anyone else. The woman was hanged in the presence of the condemned men. All eight of the men were broken on the wheel.

Another plot by the black slaves was reported a few months later. Scheduled to take place during the midnight mass on Christmas of 1731, it was to be simultaneous with a revolt at Balize. The plot was discovered by Tizel Pilott. He had been sitting down smoking behind

---

26. Déclaration de M. Jean de Booth Nicolas, Chef de la Traitte de la Gomme a Portendic pour la Cie. des Indes en la Concession du Sénégal et Coste d'Affrique, January 30, 1722, in Ser. C6 7, ANC; Traité ou convention avec les Etats Généraux, January 13, 1727, in Ser. C6 10, ibid.

the slave cabins when he heard the black *commandeur* going from cabin to cabin telling the blacks not to sleep and to be ready when the clock struck. This *commandeur* was arrested and brought to New Orleans.[27]

Ordonnateur Salmon, who took control of the colony from the Company of the Indies in the name of the king, expressed doubt about the reality of this conspiracy of Christmas, 1731: "We paid no attention to these rumors which did not appear to be true, because the blacks are disarmed and the estates are so far apart from each that they could not make the smallest assembly without being noticed. Nevertheless, the riffraff of this city are alarmed to the point where all the little settlers are on guard and go to midnight mass armed like Don Quixote." He wrote Périer that the exaggerated fears of the population could encourage the Indians and the blacks to make such attempts. The citizens were demanding to be armed and organized into a militia, but Salmon remained unimpressed: "I think it is the greatest indication they can give of their cowardice, because if they see 4 blacks armed with sticks, they would flee before them, and I suppose that the weak garrison we have here would behave about the same, even though as we indicated . . . there are only about 80 to 100 Natchez left, and we have nothing to fear from them." He added, however, that he had in fact underestimated the strength of the Natchez. People living in the upper posts reported that there were still 250 to 300 Natchez who had united with the Chickasaw.[28]

The governor and the *ordonnateur* would be motivated to deny slave conspiracies, since the existence of such plots would imply negligence and their own inability to control the situation. Even more important, these officials tried hard not to alarm the settlers, who were already leaving the colony in large numbers. Officials were often quite cold-blooded, denying dangers in order to avoid panic among the colonists, while the fears of the colonists were often quite realistic. Colonists were denounced for cowardice when armed detachments of troops were themselves afraid.

It is clear that there was a large Bambara contingent among the Africans that constituted a language community and that was truly Bambara. A group of Bambara cooperated with the Natchez massacre of the French settlement. The Africans' refusal to go along with the Chickasaw chief who tried to convince them to seek refuge among

27. Mémoire de Raymond Amyalt, January 20, 1732, in Ser. C13A 14, fol. 273, *ibid*.
28. Salmon to the Ministry of the Colonies, New Orleans, January 18, 1732, in Ser. C13A 15, fols. 25–26, *ibid*.

the English indicates that they maintained their own agenda, even after the French and their allies recaptured the Natchez settlement. Building upon their tradition of alliances, the Bambara maintained ties with the Indian nations opposed to the French, even after they were retaken from the Natchez and the Choctaw. In view of their experience with slave raiding in Bambarana, the Bambara quite possibly did plan to enslave the other African nations after they defeated the French. If the pattern of the Segu Bambara kingdoms were followed, many of their slave captives would become soldiers to expand their power and control. On the other hand, the French officials pursued a conscious and deliberate policy of sowing enmity among their potential enemies and could very well have spread a false rumor to create antagonisms between Bambara and non-Bambara Africans.

The Bambara slaves remained particularly defiant during the French colonial period. If we accept Périer's estimate that all the Bambara slaves were involved in the Samba Bambara conspiracy and that they numbered about four hundred, then about 15 percent of the adult African slaves in Louisiana in 1731 were Bambara. But among twenty-seven slaves accused of crimes whose African nation was identified in judicial records during the French period, eighteen were Bambara. In these cases, the slaves often identified their own nations. The sampling shown in Table 5 is small but well distributed in time.[29]

Some of these court cases illustrate the defiant attitude among the Bambara brought to Louisiana. Biron, a Bambara slave who arrived on l'Aurore, had run away several times. When he ran away again, his master fired several shots into the air, then aimed his gun at him and threatened to shoot him. Biron grabbed the gun while his master was trying to have him shackled. The gun broke during the struggle. Biron was brought before the court, and Attorney General Fleuriau charged that his acts were a rebellion against his master, "all the more punishable from the fact that the number of blacks is increasing in this colony, and that one would not be in safety on the distant plantations." Samba Bambara was appointed interpreter in Biron's case and reported that the accused stated he was only trying to prevent his master from shooting him and did not intend to attack his master with the gun. Biron was sentenced to be whipped at the foot of the gallows by the public executioner, warned not to run away again under threat of greater punishment, and returned to his master. The settler Trudeau, living near New Orleans, complained in September 1729, that his Bambara slave Malama threatened to kill him and that

29. For details about all these cases, see Appendix B.

Table 5. African Nations of Slaves Accused of Crimes in Records of Superior Council of Louisiana

Year	African Nation						
	Bambara	Biefada	Fon	Fulbe	Samba	Sango	Wolof
1729	6						
1737							
1738	1						
1739	1						
1741	2	1			3		
1742						1	
1743	2		1				1
1744							1
1746	1						
1748	4			1			
1752	1						
TOTAL	18	1	1	1	3	1	2

SOURCE: See Appendix B.

several times he thought Malama would kill his wife without anyone being able to stop him. Trudeau believed that Malama could very well carry out his threats. The Bambara David ran away in 1729 because his master broke his finger. He admitted that he helped kill a heifer. In 1752, a Bambara named Thomas was walking down a street in New Orleans with a white Cholet linen handkerchief on his head. He was stopped by a French woman who took the handkerchief, claiming that it came from a bundle of clothes that had been stolen from her. She brought him before the authorities, and under interrogation he stated, in good French, "No, sir, I have bought it from some unknown runaway *nègre*." He claimed that he had bought it in the street for six escalins (seventy-five cents), outbidding a Canadian.[30]

Two Bambara, Mamourou and Bayou, both in their forties and neither baptized, ran away from M. de Gruis, an officer in Illinois, be-

30. Heloise H. Cruzat, trans., "Trial and Sentence of Biron, Runaway Negro Slave, Before the Superior Council of Louisiana, 1728," *LHQ*, VIII (1925), 23–27; September 27, 1729, in RSC, LHC; November 16, 1729, in RSC, *LHQ*, IV (1921), 357; March 26, 1752, in RSC, LHC.

cause he beat them a great deal and did not feed them. They testified that their master made them work every day, even Sundays and feast days, gave them neither food nor clothes nor time to sleep during the night, and mistreated them for no reason. When Mamourou was asked if he did not know that a slave was obliged to do what his master ordered, he answered that he knew it, but that when the hoop of a pail got loose and it fell into the well, he was given so many blows on his back with a spade that he had not yet recovered. They had left the Illinois country about a month earlier. They took only corn, a cauldron, and an ax from their master. They had never run away before, nor did they steal. They ate only the provisions they had taken from their master. The man who arrested them saw that they had only a little corn in their pirogue; they had no arms. The boat they came in, which belonged to an Indian, they had found on the bank. After they left Fort Assumption, Indians on the bank of the river called to them to land, but they refused to do so and continued their voyage. They were arrested between Houma and Bayou Goula, taken to Pointe Coupee, and turned over to M. de Pontalba. They were headed for New Orleans to ask Madame Aufrère, their master's mother-in-law, to have them sold because their complaints were not listened to. They were ordered to be sent to Madame Aufrère and then to their master so he could administer "such correction as he should judge proper."[31]

Pierrot, a 45-year-old Bambara herdsman, was questioned about the murder of a French soldier in 1748, though he was never accused of the crime. Charlot dit Kakaracou, a young creole, had implicated Pierrot to put off his own execution for the murder. Although Pierrot testified that he did not speak French very well, he expressed himself quite clearly in his confrontation with Kakaracou: "That's not good. If you have to die, you must die alone, and you should not make people die who had nothing to do with you" ("*Cela n'est pas Bon, s'y toy mourir, mourir seuls et n'y a pas faire mourir monde qui n'y a rien faire avec toy*"). Pierrot said he had belonged to Belleisle for many years, since the time of the Natchez War. He never ate during the day, only in the evening, which, though he did not so testify, was the custom of his country. He never left the cattle alone, because his master would punish him with the four stakes if he did.[32] His only difficulty in the past had been when he was flogged for not stopping a cow from straying

---

31. June 9, 1748, in RSC, *LHQ,* XIX (1936), 1094–96.
32. This was a common punishment for slaves in Louisiana. Their four limbs were tied to stakes driven in the ground, and they were flogged.

onto a neighbor's property. The cow had eaten the neighbor's rice. Pierrot had slaughtered the cow and shared the meat with his fellow slaves. His master, finding the meat in Pierrot's kettle, had flogged him again. Pierrot testified that he and Kakaracou had never visited each other in their cabins, that he was not "a comrade of the creoles." He had given a meal to Kakaracou's sister when she had run away from her master, but he denied that he had hidden her in his cabin. Kakaracou testified that Pierrot's word could not be trusted because he was a Bambara and "the Bambara always lie."[33] This testimony clearly reflects tensions between Bambaras and creoles—at least creoles who were not children of Bambara.

Indian slavery continued in Louisiana, though on a small scale. Matings between Africans and Indians took place both on and off the estates throughout the eighteenth century. Africans and Indians continued to run away together. Documents surviving from the 1730s and 1740s record the departure of Indian and African slaves, who often left together to seek refuge among Indian tribes. A plantation inventory lists an African slave named Thomas who ran away to the Choctaw. An Indian named Chicacha (Chickasaw) enticed away two adolescent African slave girls.[34]

A network led by African-Indian couples that encouraged slaves to escape and that led them to the Choctaw surfaced during King George's War. The Western Choctaw, under the leadership of Red Shoe, sided with the British, introducing British trade goods and traders into their tribes. Like Mamari Kulubali, Red Shoe was an outsider relying upon his status as warrior to challenge the gerontocratic, official nobility among the Choctaw. The lower-river settlements had become a haven for maroon raiders: fugitives from estates ranging from Pointe Coupee to below New Orleans. Settlers had been complaining of the theft of their cattle, provisions, and poultry. Governor Vaudreuil dispatched a detachment of French troops under Tisserant to disperse them. The Choctaw fired on the French detachment as it followed the Tchefuncte River, searching for fugitive slaves. One Swiss soldier was killed and two others were wounded. Tisserant told the Choctaw that their shots had not killed or wounded any of the French troops and that they were hunting not

33. Investigation of the Murder of Pierre Olivy, from January 4, 1748, Confrontation between Charlot and Pierrot, Interrogation of Pierrot, January 10–12, 1748, in RSC, LHC.

34. Inventory of January 24, 1738, in Heloise H. Cruzat, trans., "Documents Concerning Slaves of Chaouachas Plantation, 1737–38," *LHQ,* VIII (1925), 594–646; October 1, 1745, in RSC, LHC.

Choctaw but fugitive red and black slaves. The Choctaw chief whom they had seen fire on the French first replied that he had nine fugitive slaves with him, three red and six black, who had crossed Lake Pontchartrain in pirogues and had sought him out. He would gladly return them if he was paid for them. He denied that either he or his men fired on the French, claiming that it was the three red fugitive slaves who fired. They were afraid of being taken by the French and had defended themselves. He said he was mortified by the contempt for the French that these fugitive slaves displayed, and he invited the officer to cross the river to speak to him. But the officer did not trust him and refused to go or to meet him at a tar factory where the chief promised to bring the fugitive slaves. Tisserant withdrew his troops, which further alarmed the settlers and inspired criticism of cowardice from Vaudreuil.[35]

Several of the fugitive slaves were finally captured and interrogated. They testified that they had been led to the pro-British faction of the Choctaw and welcomed as potential allies against the French. Cocomina, an Indian slave of the Fox nation who belonged to M. Duparc, had led his fellow escaped slaves to the Choctaw. Cocomina had a gun, two pistols, a sack of powder, a coat and a blanket, a little rice and salt, and an old sheet with which he intended to make a *ber* (a sleeping frame covered by mosquito netting). Cocomina boasted that when he aimed at a Frenchman he would not miss unless his gun misfired, and that if the Choctaw came to attack the French, he would come with them.[36]

Cézard, a black slave of Joseph Dubreuil, and his companion, Angelique, an Indian slave of Goudeau, had actively led escaped slaves to the Choctaw. Cézard had a supply of balls and a pirogue he had taken from Dubreuil. They went to Lake Pontchartrain and took another pirogue at Carrière's dock. They passed the Tchefuncte River and on the other side went to the tar factory of M. Aufrère. Cézard, who knew the woods, had the slaves wait there three days for the Choctaw to arrive. The Choctaw finally saw their tracks, came after them, and encouraged them to join them in attacking the French. The recaptured slaves testified that their Choctaw hosts were well sup-

35. See Richard White, "Red Shoe: Warrior and Diplomat," in *Struggle and Survival in Colonial America,* ed. David G. Sweet and Gary B. Nash (Berkeley, 1981), 49–68; Vaudreuil to the Ministry of the Colonies, June 4, 1748, in Ser. C13A 32, fol. 86; *MPA,* IV, 317–21, and V, 216.

36. Testimony from the fugitive slaves in this and subsequent paragraphs is taken from Interrogation of Joseph, François, and their Negro and Indian accomplices, slaves, defendants and accused, May 18–26, 1748, in RSC, *LHQ,* XIX (1936), 768–71.

plied with British trade goods, and described the shirts, blankets, arms, and munitions these Choctaw had. Only one was armed just with arrows. The Choctaw told them that they had been promised all they asked for in return for French scalps. These escaped slaves were with the Choctaw when the detachment of French troops arrived. The French troops tried to assure the Choctaw that they were not at war, that they were only searching for runaway slaves. The Choctaw planned to wait until night when the French troops slept to surprise them. The slaves testified that the Choctaw intended to attack the settlers at the German Coast, where there were fewer men.

Two of the runaways, Joseph, a 25-year-old Chickasaw, and François, an 18-year-old creole *nègre*, claimed that they ran away from the Choctaw and hid together after encountering each other in the woods. Joseph had a horn and a half of powder, some balls, and two pistols that he had taken from M. de Mandeville. This Chickasaw slave had run away with a *négresse* who had brought a pot full of rice with her. They hunted deer and teal ducks before crossing the lake. Joseph wanted to travel toward the setting sun to go to the Chickasaw nation. He claimed that Cocomina had gotten him drunk and induced him to run away. They went toward Bayou St. Jean, where they took a pirogue. They then went to the plantation of a Frenchman who had a canal that ran into the bayou that led to the lake. Joseph testified that he had only his gun, his blanket, and a small iron pot. He claimed that the Choctaw tried to induce him to kill Frenchmen, but he always pleaded that he was sick. He could not warn the French because he was closely watched.

François, the creole *nègre*, testified that he ran away from his master because he had been sold to another master and did not want to go to him. He remained behind his master's plantation, and when the *nègres* were at work, he went into their cabins to take provisions. He got milk from the cows in the pasture. He denied that he had killed any cattle, claiming that he had no gun. Five days earlier, he had met five other runaway *nègres*, three of them from Pointe Coupee, one owned by Dubreuil, and he did not know to whom the others belonged. They were armed with guns and hatchets, and he could see that they lived well and killed many animals. They had stolen sheep and chickens at the German Coast. They told him they came from M. Le Breton's plantation, where they fired on a cow, but they were discovered by an Indian and ran away. François informed his interrogators that many slaves wished to desert to go to the English or elsewhere. He had been told that it was the Choctaw, not runaway slaves, who had attacked the German Coast. This testimony reveals an underground railway involving the Western Choctaw, allies of the English, who were recruiting runaway slaves to fight against the French. In this one group of nine runaways there were two African/Indian couples: one Indian man and a black woman, another black man and an Indian woman.

Formal alliances between African and Indian leaders ended by the early 1730s after attempts to destroy French rule failed. Indian leaders became increasingly dependent upon the colonial state for protection from British and then American encroachments as the eighteenth century advanced. Nevertheless, ties between blacks and Indians remained strong. Family ties among Africans and Indians radiated from the capital, the plantations, the woodlands, and the swamps into Indian villages. As late as 1800, a fugitive slave named María ran away with the Indian Gabriel.[37] Black-Indian mixtures, designated *grif* in Louisiana, emerged as a distinctive, self-conscious group among slaves.

37. Derek Noel Kerr, "Petty Felony, Slave Defiance and Frontier Villainy: Crime and Criminal Justice in Spanish Louisiana, 1770–1803" (Ph.D. dissertation, Tulane University, 1983), 373.

CHAPTER 5

French New Orleans: Technology, Skills, Labor, Escape, Treatment

Misère qui mène nèg-là dans bois,
Dis mo maître que mo mouri dans bois.

Misery led this black to the woods,
Tell my master that I died in the woods.
—Collected from a one-hundred-year-old former
slave, 1934, Crowley, Louisiana.
In Irène Thérèse Whitfield, *Louisiana French Folk
Songs*

New Orleans, the capital of colonial Louisiana, was founded in 1718. Its location was chosen for strategic reasons. It is about 125 miles from the mouth of the winding Mississippi River between the river and Lake Pontchartrain, a shallow lake that leads into Lake Borgne and thence into the Gulf of Mexico. At English Turn, several miles south of New Orleans, the Mississippi River swings eastward, leaving a narrow track of mostly tidal wetlands between the river and Lake Borgne. New Orleans was retrieved from the swamps, and the swamps remained all-pervading in and around the capital throughout the eighteenth century. An enormous amount of labor was required to rescue the capital from the swamps and to try to keep the waters of the Mississippi River at bay. Crops and buildings were often destroyed by flooding. Ships arriving at Balize at the mouth of the Mississippi River had to be unloaded so they could pass the sandbars and then reloaded to continue their voyage to New Orleans. Docks, warehouses, watercraft, public buildings, churches, homes, barns, storage sheds, slave quarters, rice paddies, and indigo sheds and equipment had to be built, maintained, and rebuilt after they were destroyed by floods and hurricanes.

The French settlements of lower Louisiana stretched in a narrow belt along the Mississippi River and the major bayous leading into it. The masters' homes and storehouses and the slave quarters were located near the river and the major bayous. Crops were planted in the rich alluvial soil. Land was distributed in arpents, about 183 linear feet, measured in front footage along the waterways. Property lines went back vague distances, trailing off indeterminately into cypress swamps and woodlands. Each plantation had its dock for loading, unloading, and transporting goods and supplies along the waterways. Boats had to be rowed all the way to the Illinois country up the Mississippi River against its powerful and treacherous currents, avoiding sandbars, whirlpools, driftwood, and hostile Indians. These boats brought soldiers, supplies, Indian trade goods, arms, and ammunition and came back with cargoes of flour, pelts, and returning soldiers.

All kinds of labor, especially skilled labor, was at a premium. While the Company of the Indies sent skilled workers from France, few of them survived. In the spring of 1721, Bienville and Delorme wrote, "Death and disease are disrupting and suspending all operations, and if the famine does not end, all is lost. The best workers are dead."

A 1764 map of the entrance to the Mississippi River documents the hazards faced by ships in this stretch of water.

Courtesy The Historic New Orleans Collection, Museum/Research Center, Acc. No. 1980.172.

It has been claimed that the French settlers wiped out by the Natchez Indians in 1729 were "far above the usual run of immigrants of that period. Among these people were artisans and agriculturists of a class sadly needed then in Louisiana."[1]

The survival of French Louisiana was due not only to African labor but also to African technology. The introduction from Africa of rice seeds and of slaves who knew how to cultivate rice assured the only reliable food crop that could be grown in the swamplands in and around New Orleans. Converting swamps and tidal wetlands into rice paddies involved complex technology. *Oryza glaberrima*, a species of wet rice, was first domesticated along the middle Niger probably

1. Bienville and Delorme to [?], Biloxi, May 4, 1721, in Ser. A1 2592, fols. 109–10, SHA; Henry P. Dart, "A Great Louisiana Plantation of the French Colonial Period, 1737–1738," *LHQ,* VII (1925), 591.

during the second millennium B.C., independently of Asian rice. There was a secondary region of domestication that intensified its productivity. It was located between the Sine-Salum and the Casamance River, which empties into the Atlantic between the Senegal and Gambia rivers. By the sixteenth century, residents along the Gambia grew rice in the alluvial soil, using a system of dikes that harnessed the tides. By 1685, every house had a rice nursery nearby, and the riverbanks had been transformed into causeways with rice appearing above flooded fields. This wet, or swamp, rice had a much higher yield than did dry rice. A large supply could be grown in a small area. The transformation of swamps into rice fields required a great deal of knowledge and skill as well as labor. Large dams made of earth and wood were built along the riverbanks. Their height depended upon the tides in particular areas. Valves, made of tree trunks narrowed into a cone at one end, were fitted into the dikes. These valves allowed water to drain outward only. The valves closed against seawater on the outside and drained excess rainwater from the paddies when the water reached the height of the drain. In tidal wetlands, the rice paddies were left fallow for the first few years to allow the accumulated rainwater to reduce the salinity of the soil.[2]

There has been considerable speculation about the influence of African technology and African slaves upon the introduction, cultivation, and processing of rice in South Carolina. The case for introduction, from Africa into Louisiana, of rice and its techniques of cultivation and processing is much stronger. The captains of the first two ships that brought African slaves to Louisiana in 1719 were instructed to try to purchase three or four barrels of rice for seeding and several blacks who knew how to cultivate rice, which they were to give to the directors of the company upon their arrival in Louisiana. By 1720, rice was growing in great abundance all along the Mississippi River; within a few years, rice was exported to the French West Indies. By 1721, the Kolly concession on the Chapitoulas coast just north of New Orleans produced six hundred quarters of rice from fourteen quarters that had been sown. This concession had forty-six black slaves and two Indian slaves. The production of rice quickly expanded. An advertisement for a lease for the Pailhoux plantation provided that the lessee was to leave six barrels of rice in culture and sixteen barrels of rice or corn for victuals. Settlers near New Orleans

2. Walter Rodney, *A History of the Upper Guinea Coast, 1545–1800* (Oxford, Eng., 1970), 20–22.

contracted to furnish one hundred barrels of rice in straw to the king's warehouse for four francs two sous a barrel.[3]

In French Louisiana, there was always rice. It was cultivated in and around the capital. Heavy rains and floods that destroyed corn and other crops often spared the rice. When Indian warfare forced settlers to flee the countryside, when maritime shipping was cut off, when flour did not arrive from the Illinois country because of ice blockages or warfare along the Mississippi River, there was rice. William Perry, an English sailor held in New Orleans in 1758, reported that English ships had taken a troop ship from France and all but one of sixteen store ships laden with provisions and ammunition heading for New Orleans. There was a "great scarcity of provisions, and Flower, and every other Sort but Rice, of which there is plenty."[4] Rice was sometimes exported to the French islands and to Spanish Pensacola.

But this did not mean that the slaves and poor settlers always got rice. After a storm destroyed some stored rice, there was a shortage, and officials stockpiled rice in the warehouses to keep the price up. The hoarding of food and other merchandise by several directors of the company, who then sold the goods for exorbitant prices in the town, was leading to a mass exodus from the colony. Salmon concluded, "A large number of small settlers and workers are asking us for passage to return to France. If I had agreed to their demands the colony would be deserted." Salmon reported that famine had led to several thefts by blacks, including two committed by the slaves of former governor Périer. These two slaves had broken into the storehouse of the king during the night and were caught with sacks filled with rice that the king had bought from the Company of the Indies. Although it was said that under the Code Noir they deserved death, the Superior Council of Louisiana concluded that "if we hang all the blacks who steal, not one will be saved from the gallows because they are all more or less thieves. And on the other hand, they declared

3. Peter H. Wood, *Black Majority: Negroes in Colonial South Carolina from 1670 Through the Stono Rebellion* (New York, 1974); Daniel C. Littlefield, *Rice and Slaves: Ethnicity and the Slave Trade in Colonial South Carolina* (Baton Rouge, 1981); Instructions pour le S. Herpin Commandant du Vaisseau l'Aurore destiné pour la Traite des Nègres à la Coste de Guynee, July 4, 1718, in Ser. B42B, fols. 201–204, ANM; Nancy M. Miller Surrey, *The Commerce of Louisiana During the French Regime, 1699–1763* (1916; rpr. New York, 1968), 268, 373; Jay K. Ditchy, trans., "Early Census Tables of Louisiana," *LHQ*, XIII (1930), 219, 223; January 21, 1727, in RSC, *LHQ*, III (1920), 430; January 20, 1736, in RSC, *LHQ*, V (1922), 377.

4. Henry P. Dart, ed., "New Orleans in 1758," *LHQ*, V (1922), 56.

that they only stole so they would not die of hunger." Périer's man-ager was blamed for these thefts because he did not feed the slaves. Rice was selling for 180 livres per quarter, which was expensive even for the poor white colonists. The Superior Council, the colony's gov-erning body, self-righteously proclaimed that this was no excuse for letting the blacks die of hunger. The two slaves were condemned to the lash and to be marked with the fleur-de-lys.[5]

Indigo grew wild along the rivers of Senegambia, where it was processed into a vivid, blue dye with which cotton cloth was colored. Indigo grew wild in Louisiana as well. In 1712, a settler noted the existence of wild indigo in Louisiana but stated that neither the few Frenchmen settled there nor the Indians understood its preparation. While it has been claimed that techniques for producing indigo were first introduced by the Jesuits in 1727, this date is too late. Experi-ments in processing wild indigo began in 1721, two years after the arrival of the first slave ships from Africa. It is reasonable to conclude that African slaves with long experience in processing indigo in Africa first introduced and applied this technology in Louisiana. It was not the cultivation but the processing of indigo that required knowledge and skill. The plant grew two and a half feet high and was harvested twice a year. It was cut and brought to a twenty-foot-high, open shed and was processed through three vats arranged to allow water to run from one to the other. Water and indigo leaves were allowed to rot in the highest vat, which was frequently inspected, and the indigo maker had to choose the precise time to open the spout and let the water run into the second vat. If it remained too long in the first vat, the water would turn black. The indigo was beaten in the second vat until the indigo maker, through long experience, knew when to stop. The water was then allowed to settle, and the indigo formed a sedi-ment at the bottom of the vat. As the liquid became clear, it was run off in gradual stages through spouts placed one beneath the other. The indigo was then removed from the vat and placed in cloth sacks. The remaining liquid seeped through the cloth, which was then dried on boards and cut into little squares, packed into barrels, and shipped to the French islands and thence to France. By midcentury, a culti-vated variety of indigo, imported from the French West Indies, was in use. While there were up to four crops a year in the French Carib-bean, there were no more than three in Louisiana, and the indigo was

5. Salmon to the Ministry of the Colonies, December 14, 1731, in Ser. C13A 15, ANC; Salmon to the Ministry of the Colonies, July 18, 1733, in Ser. C13A 17, fol. 152, ibid.

INDIGOTERIE.

1. Figuier d'Inde. 2. Genipa. 3. Rocou, et les Negres qui le pilent. 4. Cierge Cispineux. 5. Bois de Trompette. 6. Bassin. 7. la Trempoire. 8. La Baterie. 9. le Reposoir. 10. Chauffac ou Segoute l'Indigo. 12. Plante d'Indigo. 13. Negres portant l'Indigo aux caissons pour le Secher. 14. Negres coupants et portants l'Indigo.

A seventeenth-century indigoterie in the French West Indies illustrates the indigo-making process also used in Louisiana.

From La Société d'Histoire de la Guadeloupe.

of inferior quality. But it was one of the few export staples of eighteenth-century Louisiana. One of the skills regularly listed on slave inventories was that of indigo maker (*indigotier*). Although twenty tobacco workers were brought from France in 1718 on *le Comte de Toulouse*, mortality was high among skilled workers brought from France, and Africans no doubt also contributed their knowledge of cultivation and processing of tobacco.[6]

Slaves were commonly used as medical doctors and surgeons in eighteenth-century Louisiana. They were skilled in herbal medicine and were often better therapists than the French doctors, who were always described as surgeons. Du Pratz wrote that a slave doctor belonging to the plantation of the king in New Orleans had taught him to "cure all illnesses to which women are subject, because these black women are no more exempt than white women." This slave doctor had an effective cure for scurvy before 1734, the year Du Pratz left Louisiana. First he treated the pain. Then he made a paste from iron rust soaked in lemon juice and herbs, which he placed on the patient's gums at all times except when the patient ate. Every day the patient drank two pints of tea made with lemon juice and herbs. He recommended against dieting. The patient was to eat good food often, but in small quantities. Evidently, this cure was ignored in Louisiana, where it would have been easy to administer: There were so many oranges growing there that the settlers allowed them to rot on the trees. As late as 1779, scurvy among the newly settled Canary Islanders was attributed to eating salt meat.[7]

Although some of the newly arrived Africans ran off to the Indians, most of them worked to build the new colony. When the eagerly awaited African slaves debarked, they were put to work as soon as possible. They cleared, ditched, drained, and cultivated the lands of their masters, built their levees, buildings, and fences, cut trees and trimmed wood, and, in their copious spare time, engaged in public-works projects in New Orleans and elsewhere, clearing land, building and restoring the levees, digging drainage ditches and canals, and constructing docks and public buildings. Since the slaves could not

6. Jack D. L. Holmes, "Indigo in Colonial Louisiana and the Floridas," *LH*, VIII (1967), 330; Ditchy, trans., "Early Census Tables," 225; Jean-Bernard Bossu, *Travels in the Interior of North America, 1751–1762*, trans. Seymour Feiler (Norman, Okla., 1962), 205–206; Albert Laplace Dart, trans., "Ship Lists of Passengers Leaving France for Louisiana, 1718–1724," *LHQ*, XIV (1931), 518.

7. Le Page du Pratz, *Histoire de la Louisiane* (3 vols.; Paris, 1758), I, 336–38; Bossu, *Travels in North America*, 194; Gilbert C. Din, *The Canary Islanders of Louisiana* (Baton Rouge, 1988), 33.

cultivate the land for four or five months out of the year, it was suggested that they be employed cutting trees and trimming wood to export to the French islands and to France. The Company of the Indies was asked to facilitate this trade with the French West Indies.[8]

The masters were urged not to make their newly arrived slaves work for several months. However, the Company of the Indies demanded thirty days of *corvée* (labor on public works) for each slave purchased by private individuals. By 1728, the slaves were clearing land at both ends of New Orleans from the Mississippi River to Bayou St. Jean, removing trees and underbrush to allow air to reach the town and the windmill there and to create pasture for cattle. They dug a canal from the windmill to Bayou St. Jean. The Louisiana officials had to defend themselves against charges of onerous exactions upon the labor of newly arrived slaves. Périer explained that they never meant to demand thirty days of labor from the slaves as soon as they arrived: They always had intended to make demands for labor only in pressing circumstances and during times when the settlers had no more work to do. He explained that when he demanded labor during the first month of the slave's arrival in the colony, he meant that the master should furnish the labor of a slave who had already been in the colony for a while, not that of the newly arrived slave. In 1730, a privately owned slave, whose owner stated that he was in good health when drafted to dig a ditch around the company's ramparts, collapsed while working, was brought to the hospital, and died. His owner asked for restitution.[9] It is clear that the slaves got no rest.

Aside from being overworked, the slaves were underfed. The masters expected the company to feed their slaves while they were engaged in public works, but the officials of the company refused to do so, ordering the masters to feed them until a ruling on this matter was received. The slaves belonging to the company were fed inadequate, and tainted, food. In 1725, it was recognized that one pound of corn a day was not enough for the *nègres* of the company to eat. The Superior Council decided to improve the nourishment of these slaves in order to make them work harder. They increased their ration to one

8. Extrait des lettres du Conseil de la Louisiane, August 28, 1725, in Ser. C13A 9, fol. 239, ANC.

9. Périer and La Chaise to the Ministry of the Colonies, November 24, 1727, in Ser. C13A 10, fol. 207, ANC; Périer and La Chaise to the Ministry of the Colonies, New Orleans, November 3, 1728, in Ser. C13A 11, fol. 134, *ibid.*; Périer and La Chaise to the Ministry of the Colonies, August 18, 1728, in Ser. C13A 11, fols. 63–64, *ibid.*; April 15, 1730, in RSC, *LHQ*, IV (1921), 519.

and a half pounds of corn in addition to a half pound of lard, which they gave the slaves because it was tainted and neither the settlers nor the troops would eat it. By giving this tainted lard to the slaves, the council reasoned, it would not go to waste.[10]

The Africans arrived in an extremely fluid society where a socioracial hierarchy was ill defined and hard to enforce. French Louisiana was a cold, brutal world where contempt for the poor that characterized prerevolutionary France was aggravated by the dangers and deprivations of frontier life. In prerevolutionary France, the poor, and all women, had few rights.[11] Many of the French soldiers and settlers were the rejects of French society: some of them because they would not accept their place in society, others because of chronic drunkenness and other destructive and self-destructive habits. In French Louisiana, the most brutal tortures were inflicted by the state upon whites as well as upon blacks. A slave in Africa probably had more rights than a poor white in France, and certainly more rights than a poor white in French Louisiana. Slaves in French Louisiana, including those who accepted their status, had a strong sense of justice and demanded their rights within the framework of slavery. Recaptured runaways consistently explained that they left because they were overworked, underfed, threatened, assaulted, and maimed by their masters. Some of them demonstrated sophisticated knowledge of their rights under the Code Noir.

Evidence from New Orleans during the 1720s indicates two instances of interracial marriages: a white man married to a black woman, and another white man to a mulatto woman. One document from 1723 mentions that a French locksmith and his black wife were suspects in a theft. Other records show that a French gunsmith named Pinet was deported from Senegal to Louisiana for an unspecified crime. His wife, an African *mulâtresse*, along with her three slaves, followed him to Louisiana as a passenger aboard the slave ship *la Galathée*. They embarked at Gorée. All of them survived the voyage.[12] There are hints of less formal relationships. A black woman,

10. Périer and La Chaise to the Ministry of the Colonies, November 24, 1727, in Ser. C13A 10, fol. 207, and November 3, 1728, in Ser. C13A 11, fol. 134, both in ANC; Extrait des délibérations du Conseil Supérieur de la Louisiane, October 17, 1725, in Ser. C13A 9, fol. 234, *ibid.*

11. Mathé Allain, *"Not Worth a Straw": French Colonial Policy and the Early Years of Louisiana* (Lafayette, La., 1988), 80, 81.

12. July 13, 1723, in RSC, *LHQ*, I (1917), 111; La Galathée. Voyage du Sénégal et de la Louisiane, et de St. Domingue Isle de La Merique, entry for October 21, 1727, in Ser. 4JJ 16, fol. 13, ANM; Délibérations de l'Assemblée des Directeurs de la Cie., Paris, June 3–4, 1729, in Ser. C13A 11, fol. 349, ANC.

Marie Angelique dit Isabelle, was freed by Chavannes. He had bought her from the Company of the Indies and paid cash for her. She owned a desirable lot on Royal Street, which she sold to Joseph Dubreuil in 1739 for six hundred livres cash. François Deserboy, whose family lived in Brittany, willed all his personal belongings and any wages owed him to a black woman belonging to Larou, for her faithful care of him during his illness. In 1737, François Trudeau, a member of the Superior Council, asked to be allowed to free a black woman named Jeanneton for her zeal and fidelity in his service, provided she continued to serve him until he died. Joseph Meunier freed a black slave girl, named Marie, whom he had raised. She was eleven or twelve years old. Meunier, who was about to leave for the Chickasaw Wars, explained that he granted her freedom "in recognition of her affection and her services, not knowing if he will ever return."[13]

A free population of African descent emerged quite early in New Orleans. The earliest record encountered of a free black in New Orleans dates from 1722. Laroze was sentenced to flogging and incarceration for six years for stealing from the warehouse of the Company of the Indies. He was not reenslaved. But Jean Baptiste, a free black, was reenslaved for stealing shirts. There are several cases of free black men who married black women slaves and paid for their freedom through years of labor. John Mingo, an English free black from Carolina, married Thérèse, a slave on an estate managed by Darby. The marriage license was issued with Darby's permission. Mingo contracted to pay as much as he could manage each year toward her price of 1,500 livres. Darby was to supply her rice, corn, beans, and sweet potatoes, as well as her clothing. Any children born to the couple would be free. When her total price was paid, she would also be free. Two years later, in 1729, Mingo and Thérèse signed a contract for him to oversee slaves in the cultivation of tobacco, cotton, and other crops. Thérèse was to engage in "women's work." Mingo was to receive 300 francs per year plus 8 percent of the produce, except for the increase of blacks and cattle. Thérèse was to receive 200 francs a year payable to Darby until Mingo's contract to purchase her was discharged. Mingo supplied Darby with supplies and construction services, which Darby refused to acknowledge, and Darby evidently seized Thérèse. The dispute was settled, and Thérèse was returned to her husband. François Tioucou, a free black of the Senegal (Wolof)

13. September 5, October 4, 1732, both in RSC, *LHQ*, IX (1926), 722; March 20, 1739, *ibid.*, VI (1923), 310; July 13, 1727, *ibid.*, IV (1921), 222; July 11, 1737, *ibid.*, V (1922), 403; March 28, 1736, *ibid.*, VIII (1925), 287–88.

nation who had been emancipated for his services in the Natchez War, agreed in 1737 to work for Charity Hospital for six years in return for the freedom of his wife, Marie Aran, a slave belonging to the hospital. He claimed a credit of 450 francs, the back wages owed to him by the St. Julien estate, to be applied to the price of his wife. Jean Baptiste Marly, a free black, agreed to serve an infantry officer at Pointe Coupee for three years as a cook in return for the freedom of Marly's wife, Venus.[14]

The Superior Council confirmed freedom granted by Cazeneuve and his wife to two of their slaves, provided they served Roussin and his wife for two years. Bienville freed his black slaves Jorge and Marie, Jorge's wife, in recognition of their good and faithful service for twenty-six years. They were evidently among the first group of slaves that Bienville brought to Louisiana from Havana. Jorge died shortly after Bienville agreed to free them. In 1739, a family of six slaves—husband, wife, and four children—were freed under the will of their master. Their emancipation was confirmed by Governor Bienville. A New Orleans free black named Scipion signed a contract with François Trudeau for one year, hiring himself to go to Illinois in Madama Labuissoniere's boat as rower, or in any other capacity as needed. On return from this trip he was to serve Trudeau until the year had expired. He was paid 200 livres. Three years later, Scipion contracted to take charge of Rene Petit's barge going to Illinois and to unload the cargo there. He was paid 50 livres in advance and 200 livres upon arrival.[15]

In early New Orleans, then, being black did not necessarily mean being a slave. Nor was whiteness associated with prestige and power. The first African slaves arrived simultaneously with the rejects of French society, who had been deported to Louisiana. These whites were socially despised and mistreated. When Fazende, a member of the Superior Council of Louisiana, purchased a black woman named Margot for 1,000 pounds to serve as a cook, he explained that it was "impossible to use white men or women because of their laziness as well as their licentiousness." The first African slaves arrived when France and Spain were fighting over Mobile and Pensacola. There

14. September 13, 1722, *ibid.*, VII (1924), 678; September 14, 1743, *ibid.*, XII (1929), 147; November 28, 1727, *ibid.*, IV (1921), 236; October 21, 1729, *ibid.*, 355; November 21, 25, 1730, both *ibid.*, V (1922), 102, 103; July 15, 1737, *ibid.*, IV (1921), 366; June 28, 1737, *ibid.*, V (1922), 401; November 9, 1745, *ibid.*, XIV (1931), 594.

15. July 21, 1729, *ibid.*, VII (1924), 688; October 1, 1733, June 4, 1735, both *ibid.*, V (1922), 250, 265; March 6, 1739, *ibid.*, VI (1923), 304; August 20, 1736, *ibid.*, VIII (1925), 489; March 10, 1739, *ibid.*, VI (1923), 306.

were mass desertions among French and Swiss soldiers. Desperation transcended race and even, to some extent, status, leading to cooperation among diverse peoples in their efforts to escape the settlement. Louisiana was a colony of deserters. Indian and African slaves, deportees from France, including women sent against their will, Swiss as well as French soldiers, and indentured workers fled in all directions, grasping at straws to get away. In 1720, fifteen people were accused of plotting to go beyond the Choctaw and desert to the English in a conspiracy of the damned that included people of various races, genders, ages, and nationalities. The accused included an eighteen-year-old Indian slave, a fifteen-year-old runaway African slave, a French sergeant of the troops, a twenty-eight-year-old Swiss soldier, and a twenty-seven-year-old French woman who had been sent to Louisiana by force and married against her will.[16]

Whites were publicly punished by blacks. In 1720, a French soldier convicted of robbery was sentenced to be whipped by a black for three days and to serve three years as a convict. By 1725, the Superior Council was obliged to engage a regular executioner, or *bourreau*, euphemistically called the *"exécuteur des hautes oeuvres."* It was a messy job, one that required strength and fortitude. The council had great difficulty finding someone willing to break one Coussot on the wheel, and there was another prisoner awaiting the death penalty. "We will have to start over again every day if we are not assured of a man who is always ready to carry out the decrees of the Council. Fear of punishment is the only thing which can control the evil ones. We must always hold up the sword of justice, even more in this colony than anywhere else because of the quality of the people who have been sent by force to work. One cannot hope that they can change enough for all of them to behave." They found the right man for the job: Louis Congo, a slave who had evidently come over on *la Néréide*, the only ship that came from Congo/Angola. He belonged to the Company of the Indies and was described as strong and robust. He had proved his talent for the job by carrying out the last execution "fairly well." But Louis Congo drove a hard bargain. He demanded freedom for himself and his wife, who also belonged to the Company of the Indies, and a complete ration of wines and drinks for himself alone. He also demanded a plot of land apart from the settlers where he would live with his wife and work for his own benefit. Attorney General Fleuriau found his price high, especially the emancipation of two

16. Attribution d'une négresse à Fazende, November 4, 1724, in Ser. C13A 8, fol. 139, ANC; May 31, 1720, in RSC, LHC.

Table 6.   Compensation Paid to Louis Congo, Executioner

Punishment Inflicted	Compensation
Breaking on the wheel or burning alive	40 pounds
Hanging	30 pounds
Flogging or the Fleur de Lys	10 pounds
Le Carcan (iron collar)	5 pounds

SOURCE: Copie des délibérations du Conseil Supérieur de la Louisiane, October 24, November 21, 1725, in Ser. C13A 9, fols. 267–68, ANC.

slaves, but concluded that they might not be able to find anyone else. They were in a hurry, and this Congo had already carried out his "chef d'oeuvre." Fleuriau suggested that they accept his conditions and locate him near the city so he could be available at all times to perform his duties. The council agreed to all of Louis Congo's conditions, but his wife was not formally freed. However, she was allowed to live with him, and the company agreed to make no demands on her time.[17] Table 6 shows the prices affixed to his services.

Louis Congo's life was unenviable. He was attacked during his tenure by Indians as well as by his fellow blacks. In 1726, he complained to the attorney general that during the night, he thought he would be assassinated in his home by three *sauvage* (Indian) deserters, one belonging to the company and two others to Noyan and Raquet. Louis Congo was still in office a decade later when he complained that he was assaulted by two blacks near the king's plantation. One of the men was a runaway slave owned by Augustin Langlois. They left behind a torn blanket and an old coat. Louis Congo stated that his life would not be secure if such assassins were tolerated and asked that an investigation be made and his attackers dealt with according to law. Louis Congo knew how to write and signed his name—a talent that was unusual in those days for inhabitants of Louisiana.[18]

The Company of the Indies could not keep the African slaves at the bottom of a rigid, hierarchical society. Louisiana was primarily a strategic colony. Transportation and the construction and mainte-

17. February 23, 1720, in RSC, *LHQ,* I (1917), 106; Copie des déliberations du Conseil Supérieur de la Louisiane, October 24, November 21, 1725, in Ser. C13A 9, fols. 267–68, ANC.
18. August 17, 1726, in RSC, LHC; January 24, 1737, in RSC, LHC.

nance of fortifications were its primary activities. Most of the skilled workers brought from France quickly died. Those who survived charged very high fees. In 1720, the *conseil de commerce* of Mobile purchased a blacksmith from Bienville because of the "enormous sums charged by private individuals for this trade." Many of the Africans brought to Louisiana had a long tradition of metalworking, shipbuilding, and river transport. In its initial instructions to Périer, the commander appointed in 1726, the Company of the Indies pointed out that it required the services of seventy sailors to load ships and to serve on boats for navigating the river, "which causes a great expense in wages and in rations, which we can spare ourselves by substituting blacks in the place of most of these sailors." Forty young, vigorous blacks were to be placed on the plantation of the company near New Orleans to serve on ships and boats. Whites were to work with the blacks until the blacks became good sailors. Périer was instructed to increase their number, when they were able to teach other blacks, and to decrease the number of whites until all the whites were eliminated. Blacks were also to work with ships' carpenters and caulkers in order to learn how to build and refit ships and boats. The slaves on the plantation of the Company of the Indies were to grow food for these workers so their nourishment would cost nothing, and to supply all the needs of ships docking in the colony. A slave belonging to the Company of the Indies was apprenticed to a French locksmith, who was paid four hundred francs for teaching him. A second slave coming on the next slave ship was to be apprenticed for the benefit of the locksmith, but the company reserved the right to claim the second slave instead of the first if he proved to be better skilled.[19]

When the Company of the Indies turned Louisiana over to the king of France in 1731, the king's officials in Louisiana wanted to make sure that the king retained ownership and control of the slaves who had belonged to the company. They explained that if these slaves were sold to private individuals, the colony could not survive. Although the plantation of the Company of the Indies was not included in the retrocession of the belongings of the company to the crown, the king's officials argued that the company's slaves were not part of the company's plantation because the land was not cultivated, except for a small plot. "The company can argue that the blacks on their planta-

19. Procès-verbal du conseil de commerce tenu a l'Isle Dauphine, January 30, 1720, in Ser. C13A 5, fol. 355, art. 5, ANC; Mémoire de la Compagnie des Indes servant d'instructions à Périer, nouvellement pourvu du commandement général de la Louisiane, Paris, September 30, 1726, in Ser. C13B 1, fols. 87–88, *ibid.*; October 5, 1727, in RSC, *LHQ*, IV (1921), 230.

tion are not part of its donation to the King, but one can reply that these same blacks do not work on the plantation cultivating the land. On the contrary, most of them have skilled trades and work on fortifications. Others are sailors. . . . Not one is attached to the plantation cultivating the land."[20]

These officials went on to explain in detail the occupations of these slaves. Some of them worked with the corps of soldiers guarding New Orleans. Others had been stationed for a long time at Balize. They had always worked on fortifications, and they also went up the river to get fresh water for the garrison. They served on the pirogues and the rowboats that came and went between Balize and New Orleans, bringing food and other supplies to the garrison. Some of them served at the fort at Natchez and some at Mobile. Ten of them were sent to live aboard *le St. Louis* for maritime service, in addition to those who were detached from the company to serve as sailors on the same ship to help bring her back to Louisiana. "The voyages to the military posts are made exclusively by water, mostly up river. Sailors are necessary. Most of these blacks are used in this trade. . . . If the Company . . . is permitted to sell them to settlers, all work will cease . . . and there will be no more navigation."

The king's officials opposed giving up any of these slaves, even those not needed for fortifications and navigation. The rest could cultivate the land to furnish food for themselves as well as for those occupied in skilled trades. They could cut wood for shipbuilding and for the construction and repair of the storehouses and other buildings belonging to the king, and firewood for the barracks and guardhouses. They could be used to raise cattle and to make salt meat for the garrison. Some of them could make boats, and the women could raise food crops and grind rice.

The Louisiana officials insisted that if the slaves of the Company of the Indies were indeed found to belong to the company and not to the king, then the king must purchase them. An inventory of these slaves was sent. There were 148 men, 68 women, 18 boys and girls, and several nursing infants. Almost all of the black men were involved in skilled trades. If purchased by the king, these slaves would pay for themselves within four or five years and, at the same time,

20. Arguments made, in following paragraphs, by the king's officials in Louisiana can be found in Périer and Salmon to the Ministry of the Colonies, December 5, 1732, in Ser. C13A 14, fols. 30–33, ANC, and January 16, 1732, in Ser. C13A 15, fols. 13–14, *ibid.*

would save a substantial amount of money over the cost of compara-
ble paid labor. They could, in the future, teach young boys the skills
of blacksmith, locksmith, carpenter, mason, and other useful trades,
lessening the expenditures officials would be forced to make for the
wages of such skilled workers.

The king did, indeed, purchase these slaves from the Company of
the Indies and established them on the plantation of the king. In 1739,
Bienville tried to dissolve the king's plantation and sell off the slaves,
reportedly to his nephew and to a major stationed at Mobile, because,
he argued, the plantation was not very productive. *Ordonnateur* Salmon argued strongly against this move: "It is true that the King does
not get much use from the land except for firewood which several
black men and women collect when they are not making voyages, and
for some corn which the black women plant for their subsistence . . .
which only reduces the amount of money spent on these items [be-
cause] we are obliged, in addition, to purchase firewood and food."
But he went on to explain that these slaves were engaged in more
important work: making voyages that were more or less long. They
sometimes had to remain in Illinois over the winter and were absent
eight months. The thirty-five slaves serving in New Orleans worked
at the general storehouse, the hospital, and the marine headquarters,
transported firewood, cleaned out and squared drainage ditches in
the streets around the kings' buildings, cured latrines, dug wells, and
performed other vital services. They and their wives took turns bringing wood to the hospital, sweeping, and washing dishes. The twenty
slaves at Balize made voyages to serve the needs of the post, cutting
wood, going fifteen to twenty lieus up the river during seven months
out of the year to get provisions for the garrison. They also served the
pilot when the sandbars were sounded—an activity they were
obliged to repeat because these bars changed almost every year.
When not otherwise employed, they transported soil from the river
to raise the level of the fort. They were useful in unloading and reloading ships to allow them to pass the sandbars. There were twelve
blacks at Mobile who, with their wives, had served this same purpose
for a long time. Some slaves of the king were carpenters, caulkers,
gardeners, surgeons, nurses, and other skilled workers. "If these
services were performed by whites at the lowest possible price, supposing that one could find white workers, it would cost at least 900
pounds for each one, which would amount to 25,000 pounds, not
including the voyages. Furthermore, we know from experience that
we do not obtain from a white half the service which we obtain from

a black, aside from the fact that the whites are sick half the time and we would have to bring them from France," wrote Salmon.[21]

Who, then, would cut and haul firewood for the posts, bring water to Balize, make voyages, and carry out other labors that the whites would refuse to do, if indeed enough whites could be found to do the work? Regardless of any economies made, paying others to do the work performed by slaves would cost the king at least 50,000 pounds. Salmon went on to explain what a good bargain the king had made by purchasing these slaves. He had bought 225 blacks of all sexes and ages, paying 700 pounds for each of them, or a total of 157,500 pounds. The best blacks had been distributed to the military posts according to their skills and talents. They sold those he considered a surplus for 42,000 pounds at once, and thereafter realized another 21,070 from the sale of slaves, amounting to 63,070 pounds, which subtracted from 157,500, left 94,430 pounds—the net cost to the king of the remaining 79 slaves. The parents of these slaves were not creoles, wrote Salmon, and he did not know their exact age, but they were approximately thirty or thirty-five to fifty years old. "I can assure you that those who remain are the elite. Only the lazy ones and the runaways were sold. I even sent them to Illinois to be sold, being unable to get rid of them here." Salmon concluded that Bienville was advising the king to sell these slaves because he and his friends wanted to get their hands on them. "Monsieur having entrusted me with the interests of the Colony, I never thought that M. de Bienville would have offered this advice. He knows as well as I do that the Service cannot be carried out (without them), even supposing that one is in a position to employ whites, which would be a serious setback."[22]

Twelve years later, Governor Vaudreuil wrote that while most of the blacks of the king, especially the men, were quite old and sick, they were "very useful, and are never absent." These "useful" old blacks were distributed to all the military posts, serving as laborers at the storehouses. They could only spare one black to place in each boat on all the convoys to relieve the owners on their difficult voyages, evidently to give advice about navigating the treacherous waters. It was the soldiers, up to twenty-four on each boat, who rowed. The soldiers were given a little bonus in accordance with the distance they had to row. The blacks served all year round at the storehouses in

21. Salmon to the Ministry of the Colonies (extract), September 3, 1739, in Ser. C13A 24, fols. 158–60, *ibid.*
22. *Ibid.*

New Orleans and Mobile. They unloaded the ships of the king. "In a word, they are constantly occupied with service. They are caulkers and carpenters whom M. Michel has placed in the workshops as well as a few young people who are being taught useful trades. The women are also employed in the posts unloading vessels and other ships, cleaning the storehouse, and cultivating a little rice or garden crops for their own use, patrolling the King's warehouse and other buildings, and performing all other labor useful to the service." But they were too few, and too old. Instead of selling them, Vaudreuil recommended, His Majesty should renew them little by little with young people so that this work gang, which was indispensable to the king, could be sustained and strengthened. The king's slaves saved the colony at least 100,000 livres, which they would have had to pay otherwise to skilled workers and day laborers, who were very expensive. It was not until 1760, as France was preparing to abandon Louisiana, that these slaves of the king were sold.[23]

But it was not only the slaves of the king who were skilled workers. Joseph Dubreuil de Villars, a pivotal figure in developing the economy of French Louisiana, was the richest man in the colony. There is evidence that his success was due to a great extent to his ability to tap the African slaves' technological knowledge—how to dam and control the waters of the rivers and bayous, create rice paddies, cultivate and process rice, and process indigo—as well as their skills in working metals, in order to develop machinery and inventions useful to the colony. Dubreuil, a native of Dijon, left from La Rochelle for Louisiana in 1718, accompanied by his wife and two children, some carpenters, coopers, joiners, a tailor, a shoemaker, and some laborers. Evidently most of these French workers quickly died, because by 1721, aside from his wife and children, his household comprised 43 black slaves, 2 Indian slaves, and only 2 French servants. He was quite young when he arrived; he was only thirty years old in 1727. Dubreuil received a land concession on the Chapitoulas coast just north of New Orleans. He was credited with making the first levees to protect his land from flooding and the first deep ditches and canals to drain the waters of the swamps. In 1724, a judgment ordered him to furnish 20 of his *nègres* to correct the flooding of his neighbors' lands that resulted when he closed a bayou on his own land. Dubreuil claimed to be the first to cultivate and produce indigo

23. Vaudreuil and Michel to the Ministry of the Colonies, May 10, 1751, in Ser. C13A 35, fols. 10–11, *ibid.*; Kerlérec to the Ministry of the Colonies, August 15, 1760, in Ser. C13A 42, fols. 64–65, *ibid.*

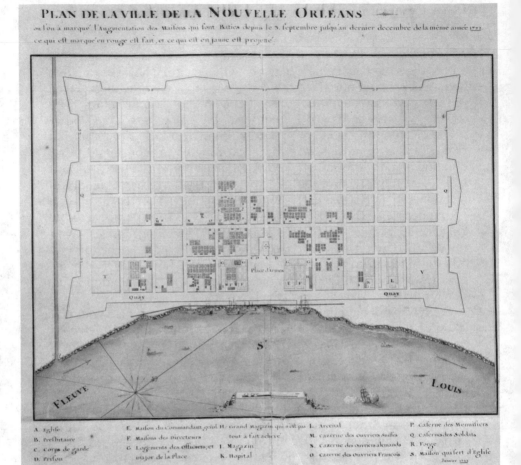

"Anonymous manuscript plan of New Orleans, 1723."
Courtesy Ayer Collection, The Newberry Library.

in Louisiana. As early as 1724, he did indeed receive 1,311 livres from the Company of the Indies for his indigo. It is quite possible that he learned techniques for processing indigo from his African slaves. He invented an early cotton gin. He claimed that he produced the best wax for candles.[24]

Dubreuil played a major role in the early sugar industry. In this case, there is documentation of the introduction of the crop from the French West Indies. The Jesuits introduced sugarcane from St. Domingue in 1751 when a troop ship stopped off there on its way to Louisiana. They shipped to their brethren in Louisiana a quantity of cane and a number of blacks acquainted with the culture and manufacture of sugar. The first sugarcane was planted on the Jesuit estate north of New Orleans, but it was Dubreuil who experimented with the adaptation of sugarcane to Louisiana. He developed the technique of covering the cane so that it would not freeze over the winter, and he established the first sugar mill. Although Etienne de Boré has been credited with commercializing sugar production in Louisiana in 1795, as early as 1763 Boré contracted with one Baudon to remain on his estate for three years to operate his sugar mill and distillery and to teach two of Boré's slaves how to do so.[25]

But Dubreuil's primary occupation was building contractor. By 1734, he was describing himself as "Contractor of Public Works for the King." In 1740, he rebuilt Balize, which had been destroyed by hurricanes. He built a canal connecting Barataria with the Mississippi River to facilitate the extraction of cypress logs.[26]

It was Dubreuil and his partner, Dalcourt, who organized the last slave-trade expedition to Africa. As we have seen, the African slave trade had ended with the arrival of *le St. Louis* in January, 1731. Before the Dubreuil/Dalcourt slave-trade voyage, many schemes were hatched to bring slaves from Africa. In 1738, officials and colonists organized their own company to import African slaves, explaining, "The various means which you have been good enough to attempt to introduce blacks into this colony have not at all succeeded due to obstacles placed by the merchants of France. We are determined to make an effort to procure for ourselves through our own means the help of the blacks whom we need by forming a company among our-

24. Ditchy, trans., "Early Census Tables," 219; Henry P. Dart, "The Career of Dubreuil in French Louisiana," *LHQ*, XVIII (1935), 267–331; July 20, 1724, in Ser. C13A 8, fol. 298, ANC.

25. Dart, "Career of Dubreuil," 276–77; September 26, 1763, in RSC, *LHQ*, XXV (1942), 1165–66.

26. Dart, "Career of Dubreuil," 283–84.

selves." But the Dubreuil/Dalcourt voyage was the only one that materialized. In 1741, *Ordonnateur* Salmon, reviewing the failure of previous plans to introduce blacks into Louisiana, wrote that the colonists of Louisiana see "with regret that their blacks are getting old and die every day, and for 12 years none have been introduced into the colony. . . . [T]his depletion of blacks has engaged M. Dubreuil, contractor of the King's public works, and M. Dalcourt to petition your Grandure to support their initiatives with the Company of the Indies for their proposal to introduce 300 blacks."[27]

Dubreuil and Dalcourt purchased *le St. Ursin*, an eighty-ton ship that left La Rochelle on March 2, 1743. By this time, the trade from Galam down the Senegal River to Fort St. Louis at its mouth was well organized. During 1742, 1,500 *captifs* descended from Fort St. Joseph in Galam, and 2,000 were anticipated during 1743. But the toll of mortality in the *captiveries* remained devastating: "In September the first blacks from Galam descend from Fort St. Joseph and they continue to arrive until about the first days of December. [They must be constantly removed] because 200 or 300 hundred of them die during a stay of two to three months at Fort St. Louis."[28]

Le St. Ursin left Gorée on June 5, before the *captifs* descended from Galam. Part of its "cargo" came from Gambia. The pilot wrote, "We had to await the trade from Gambia in order to be in condition to supply her this number of blacks, because, unlike normal conditions, we found ourselves with many women and few men." *Le St. Ursin* embarked 220 *captifs* and paid for them with 2,189 livres of tobacco, which the Senegal concession needed for its blacks. The ship arrived in Louisiana on August 25, with 190 blacks remaining of the 220 it had embarked.[29]

This last slave-trade voyage to Louisiana under French rule was discouraging for its sponsors. The colonists could not pay for the slaves in piastres. They had sent their currency to France, and their harvest was not yet in. Only 23 slaves could be sold when the ship arrived. Dubreuil and Dalcourt complained that they had to keep the slaves until the next harvest, assuming all the risks of theft and fire. They had trouble collecting on those who were sold. For example,

27. Surrey, *Commerce of Louisiana*, 236–45; Bienville and Salmon to the Ministry of the Colonies, February 20, 1738, in Ser. C13A 24, fols. 120–31, ANC; Salmon to the Ministry of the Colonies, April 25, 1741, in Ser. C13A 26, fols. 138–39, ANC.
28. David to the Company of the Indies, April 20, 1743, in Ser. C6 12, ANC.
29. Brüe to the members of the Co[mpany], Senegal, July 15, 1743, in Ser. C6 12, pp. 1, 2, ANC; Vaudreuil to the Ministry of the Colonies, August 25, 1743, in Ser. C13A 28, fol. 85, *ibid*.

Bobe Descloseaux could not make a 29,260-livre payment for slaves bought from Dubreuil and Dalcourt at auction in September, 1743, because of depreciation of the currency.[30]

Evidently, Dubreuil kept many of these slaves for himself, training them in a wide range of skills. In 1743, Bienville reported that Dubreuil had trained blacks in all kinds of trades and employed few French workmen. In the 1746 estimated census, Dubreuil was listed as the richest settler, "owning 500 blacks, men, women, and children, whom he employs mainly on the public works of the King." Dubreuil had established plantations that were industrial as well as agricultural units, achieving near self-sufficiency. In 1748, three of his slaves were arrested and imprisoned on an accusation of theft. One of them, an eighteen-year-old creole named Louis, when asked his trade under interrogation, replied that he was a surgeon, that his master had him learn surgery, that he went to the king's hospital to be instructed. Another accused slave was Joseph, aged about thirty. He testified that he was of the Bambara nation. He was likely brought over on *le St. Ursin* in 1743, picked up at Gambia. When asked about another Dubreuil slave who was imprisoned, he said that his name was Sary, that he was his comrade, though they were of different countries. Dubreuil complained bitterly in a petition to the council that his sawmill and his blacksmith shop were closed, suspending his cabinetmaking, and he was much in need of his surgeon to dress the wounds and take care of the sick. He insisted that his slaves were innocent and demanded their immediate return. They were released to him pending further investigation.[31]

Dubreuil's estate was sold after his death in 1758. Aside from large amounts of machinery, tools, construction equipment, building supplies, and cabinet-making tools, there were 188 slaves listed: 93 men, 73 women, 21 children, and 1 infant. There were 31 couples, some sold with their children, and 8 mothers sold without husbands but with children. One three-generation family was sold together. About one-third of these slaves were listed under African names—at least fifteen years after many of them had been brought from Africa. The skills of these slaves were not listed, probably because this information was well known to their purchasers. It is clear that many of the

30. Vaudreuil and Salmon to the Ministry, July 24, 1743, in Ser. F3 24, fol. 413, AN; October 19, 1745, in RSC, *LHQ*, XIV (1931), 586–87.

31. Bienville to Maurepas, February 4, 1743, in *MPA*, III, 779; Mémoire sur l'état de la Colonie de la Louisiane en 1746, in Ser. C13A 30, fols. 246–48, ANC; John G. Clark, *New Orleans 1718–1812: An Economic History* (Baton Rouge, 1970), 52; June 9, 1748, in RSC, *LHQ*, XIX (1936), 1091–94.

skilled workers on this estate, which had been re-Africanized from Senegambia in 1743, were Africans who reenforced the nations of the original contingent of slaves. Dubreuil's six grandchildren were reduced to poverty after his death, and their mother reported that they had gone "into the forest where they share the life of savages in order to escape from the shame of their wretched state."[32]

Moluron! Hé! Moluron! Hé!	Moluron! Hé! Moluron! Hé!
C'est pas 'jordi mo dans moune.	It's not today I'm in the world.
Si yé fait ben avec moin, mo resté.	If you treat me well, I'll stay.
Si yé fait mo mal, m'a-chap-pé.	If you treat me bad, I'll escape.
	—Irène Thérèse Whitfield, *Louisiana French Folk Songs*

Moluron was a Louisiana Afro-Creole folk hero, a *nègre maron* (fugitive slave) who feared nothing. He ran away many times, though he was always caught and brought back to his master. "Moluron" was frequently sung openly toward the end of the Civil War, when the slaves were sure of their freedom. Among Creole speakers to this day, someone who runs off is called a *parti maron*.[33]

If Moluron had lived during the eighteenth century, it is quite likely that he would not have been caught. Marronage in and around New Orleans was an especially serious problem for the masters. Except during the coldest winters, the runaways could subsist fairly easily in the tidal wetlands near the Gulf of Mexico. The area was rich in fish, shellfish, and game. The runaways' cash needs, and needs for arms and ammunition, were satisfied through fishing, selling squared cypress logs to sawmill owners, and manufacturing and selling craft products. Runaway slaves from as far north as Pointe Coupee often headed for New Orleans.

Runaway slaves, when asked why they left, almost invariably cited unjustified and excessive punishment, overwork, and inadequate food, and indignantly denied theft except for a little food they took along to survive and, sometimes, a gun and powder to kill game. They occasionally killed cattle for food. A slave testified that he ran away because he was put in irons and wrongly accused of stealing. He and a fellow runaway slave lived on wild cats and wood rats.[34]

32. Succession Sale of the Estate of Dubreuil, in Dart, "Career of Dubreuil," 291–331; Memorial of Madame Dubreuil to the French Government Presented in 1778, *ibid.*, 289–90. For a listing of African names of slaves on the Dubreuil estate, see Appendix D.

33. Whitfield, *Louisiana French Folk Songs*, 140–42; Ulysses S. Ricard, Jr., conversation with author, May, 1989.

34. January 16, 1741, in RSC, LHC.

Runaways were usually well supplied with firearms and ammunition—an extension of conditions that existed among slaves on the estates. Hunting was a vital source of food in this famine-ridden colony, and slaves were often used for defense against Indian raiders. When food was scarce, the slaves sometimes "hunted" the cattle of the masters. Masters were ordered to confiscate the guns, ammunition, and swords of their slaves, including the slave hunters, because "complaints have been brought . . . that in spite of the ordinance heretofore promulgated, their cattle are killed daily, not only in the woods, but even in their pastures and there is reason to believe that these thefts are committed by slave hunters or others from neighboring plantations who have arms at their disposal." A sale was held of a maroon cache of arms in the fields of M. Duparc on the first German Coast.[35]

The Code Noir provided specific penalties for runaway slaves, including branding with a fleur-de-lys and cropping the ears. But masters were reluctant to reduce the value of their slaves by making it obvious that they had tendencies to run away. Two runaway slaves belonging to Périer were so maimed, but this was to some extent a vindictive act against their deposed and despised master. Runaway slaves were difficult to catch even when they remained in the area, when their whereabouts were known, and when they were easily identified. One runaway slave, who had been gone for a year, was frequently seen around New Orleans, but no one apprehended him. Sieur Lange, administrator of Périer's plantation, reported in 1736 that a *nègre* named Pierrot had run away from the plantation about four years earlier. He had Périer's brand on his right breast. Sieur Jacques Roquigny reported in 1736 that five years earlier he had owned a *nègre* named Rencontre who had lost the little toe of one of his feet but that he had not heard of Rencontre for four years. Sieur Jean Prat, physician of the king, reported the theft of a gun and several other articles by a runaway *nègre* owned by Madame Douville, midwife of the city, and asked that she pay for what the runaway stole.[36]

Should the master be lucky enough to recover an escaped slave,

35. June 1, 1753, in RSC, *LHQ*, III (1920), 89; Registry of the sale of a maroon cache of arms in the fields of M. Duparc, September 9, 1776, listed in Derek Noel Kerr, "Petty Felony, Slave Defiance and Frontier Villainy: Crime and Criminal Justice in Spanish Louisiana, 1770–1803" (Ph.D. dissertation, Tulane University, 1983), 368.

36. Salmon to the Ministry of the Colonies, February 10, 1737, in Ser. C13A 22, fols. 124–25, ANC; January 16, 1741, March 15, 1745, both in RSC, LHC; September 2, 1736, in RSC, *LHQ*, VIII (1925), 494; August 29, 1736, in RSC, *LHQ*, VIII (1925), 493.

the story sometimes did not end there. Some slaves cultivated the art of escaping from fetters. Pierrot, slave of Sieur Livet, was captured by another slave named Rafael. His captor agreed to loosen the cord around his elbows, which allowed Pierrot to escape again, "and since then has been continually stealing from said Livet's plantation." In 1746, the planter Joseph Chaperon reported that his forty-year-old slave Manuel ran away with another slave. He was brought back and chained in his cabin, "but he left during the night with the chain and block." Chaperon complained that Manuel had performed this same feat several times. Jacques Judice reported that his slave Manuel had run away and been brought back to him. He chained Manuel in his cabin, but he too left during the night with the chain and block, and Judice prayed that he be retaken "as this has happened several times." He informed the council he heard that several *nègres* were plotting to escape to Cat Island. As late as 1773, an inventory of an indigo plantation lists two *nègres,* Jasmin and Guillaume, who had been fugitives for fifteen months in New Orleans. They were included on the record but were estimated as having no value.[37]

Pursuing fugitive slaves could be dangerous as well as frustrating. Throughout the eighteenth century, the fugitives were usually well armed. The planter Deslandes lost a cow, and he thought he could find her because he suspected a runaway slave of the theft. He and an Indian went to look for the runaway. They found *nègres* armed with guns and hatchets smoking meat in the rear of his plantation. Deslandes and the Indian returned with ten *nègres* to surround them. He ordered the Indian to fire on them, and one was badly wounded. The wounded man was captured and imprisoned, but the rest escaped.[38]

There was no organized slave patrol until late June, 1764. Instead, the slave owner had to rely upon his own resources to recapture runaways, or upon Indian tribes to return them for a reward. The Code Noir prohibited the master from punishing his slave with more than twenty-five blows with a soft implement. According to Carl A. Brasseaux, "In the unlikely event that a fugitive was captured, the slave owner was faced with the choice of chastising the slave himself, in violation of the black Code, or of abandoning his slave 'to public justice' through which the slave owner became liable for the articles

37. August 30, 1736, in RSC, *LHQ,* VIII (1925), 493; August 3, 1746, *ibid.,* XVI (1933), 505; Henry P. Dart, "A Louisiana Indigo Plantation on Bayou Teche, 1773," *LHQ,* IX (1926), 573.
38. June 6, 1748, in RSC, *LHQ,* XIX (1936), 1087–88.

stolen by his bondsman. Therefore, most slave holders opted for the first choice. This opportunity, however, presented itself all too infrequently."[39]

Not much changed after Spain took over Louisiana. Masters were reluctant to abandon their slaves to public justice because of the costs of incarceration and punishment, which were charged to the master, to say nothing of the loss of the service of incarcerated slaves. The Spanish regime was no more charitable to owners of slaves accused of crimes than the French had been. Madame Le Breton was presented with a bill by the jailer not only for the maintenance of her slaves while they were waiting to be judged and hanged and for the articles they stole but also for the cartload of firewood with which they were tortured (*la carreta de leña empleada por el tormento de los negros réos*). The Cabildo of New Orleans believed that masters were reluctant to report slaves who had committed even capital crimes for fear of losing them, and this reluctance resulted in the "insubordination of the slaves and the crimes which they commit daily without fear of punishment because no one denounces them, or rather, because the master is poor, he does not dare to bring him to justice for fear of losing him entirely." Although a voluntary plan evolved during the 1770s for slave owners to contribute to a fund to compensate masters for their runaway slaves killed while being apprehended or for those sentenced to death, the fund was constantly on the edge of bankruptcy, and in any case, it paid only two hundred pesos, which was less than the value of a slave.[40]

Flight from slavery was often a family affair. Going off together and setting up a household in the woods and swamps was sometimes a ritual of courtship. Established families left together, or wives and children followed husbands. Women slaves ran away, sometimes with male slaves, sometimes on their own, sometimes taking their children with them. Sieur Pierre de Manadé, chief surgeon in New Orleans, reported that a *négresse* named Jeanneton whom he rented had run away and was absent from his house for nine days. Pierre Garçon reported that he had imprisoned his slave Jeanneton because she continuously threatened to run away and finally carried out her

39. Carl A. Brasseaux, "The Administration of Slave Regulations in French Louisiana, 1724–1766," *LH*, XXI (1980), 139–58.

40. February 28, 1772, in Acts, Vol. I, 73; August 6, 1773, *ibid.*, 109. For the evolution of the compensation plan, see August 6, 1773 p. 109, February 25, 1774, pp. 151–52, June 9, 1774, pp. 163–64, May 17, 1775, pp. 173–74, November 24, 1775, p. 197, May 10, 1776, p. 206, October 10, 31, 1777, p. 232, May 6, 22, 1778, pp. 244, 249, all *ibid.*

threat and was gone for eight days. She claimed to be six weeks pregnant by him and demanded that she be confiscated, in accordance with the Code Noir. Her master asked to be allowed to leave her in prison until he left for the Illinois country.[41]

There were some cases of whites involved in the flight of black women. Junon and her two small children were working at the Melisan farm about seventeen leagues from Mobile. Loubeoy, an official, had exchanged them for another slave, but definitive ownership was in litigation. L'Eveillé, one of Loubeoy's slaves, went to the Melisan slave quarters late at night, broke through a fence, and carried off Junon's two-year-old son. An officer, a soldier, and another Loubeoy slave came and got Junon and her nine-month-old son. Loubeoy explained that the baby had been injured in the foot from mistreatment by Madame Melisan, and Junon had threatened to drown herself and her child if she and her two children were to remain subject to her master's abuse. They were returned to Melisan, but Loubeoy warned that he would have to answer for all accidents, costs, indemnity, and interest if they were injured.[42]

O Zenéral Florido!	Oh General Fleuriau!
C'est vrai yé pas ca-pab' pren moin!	It's true they cannot catch me!
Yen a ein counan si la mer.	There is a schooner out at sea.
C'est vrai yé pas ca-pab' pren moin!	It's true they cannot catch me!
	—Music and lyrics collected by George Washington Cable during the late nineteenth century from creole former slaves

As the song indicates, slaves escaped by sea. Havana was a favorite destination. Quimper dit La Pigeonnière, a soldier, had been deported to Louisiana. In October, 1739, he and three other soldiers guarding the entrance to Lake Pontchartrain from Bayou St. Jean deserted while the corporal in charge was asleep. They seized a boat that was used to transport naval stores. The captain and six blacks—four men and two women whom they found on the boat—were forced to accompany them. The boat and the six slaves belonged to Tixerant, officer of marine troops in New Orleans, and his partner Aufrère. Tixerant was away at the time fighting in the Chickasaw Wars. Six soldiers and several settlers pursued them, but in vain. They found the boat abandoned and the captain's corpse nearby, half-eaten by alligators. The Spanish posts were alerted, and the Spanish

41. November 20, 1736, in RSC, *LHQ*, VIII (1925), 683; June 29, 1737, *ibid.*, IX (1926), 299.
42. May 20, 1745, *ibid.*, XIV (1931), 108.

officials promised that if these fugitives appeared, they would be shackled and they would inform the Louisiana officials. Nothing more was learned about them, and the Louisiana officials concluded that they had all perished in a storm.[43]

The successful "abduction" of these slaves turned out to be, not a theft of valuable "property," but, more likely, military cooperation between slaves and soldiers to escape from the colony. Almost a decade later, two fugitive *nègres* brought back from Havana supplied the first news of these blacks. The slaves, or former slaves, seemed to be well established in Havana. No master was mentioned. One of these "abducted" slaves, named Suquoy, lived in a cabin near the port in a place called Mouraille. He was a vendor, perhaps a shopkeeper. Suquoy had been married in the church in Mobile to a woman named Susanna and had a daughter in New Orleans. But he had two more wives in Havana, one named Catherine, who lived with him, and another named Juana, who was his neighbor. Another of these "abducted" slaves was the *nègresse* Marie, a creole of Mobile. She was married in Havana and had given birth to two children there, though she was already married to a man named François who still lived in New Orleans. Another *nègresse*, named Babet, was married to a carpenter named André, and they lived on Campeche Street. These witnesses identified other slaves "abducted" from Bayou St. Jean in 1739 who were alive, well, and apparently free in Havana.[44]

The same witnesses identified slaves living in Havana belonging to Chaperon. Two months after the escape from Bayou St. Jean, Chaperon reported that his Bambara *nègre* Antoine, Antoine's wife, Fauchon, of the Senegal nation, his Bambara slave Vulcain, who had been hamstrung, and a Spanish mulatto took off in a longboat belonging to Gonzalez, the Spanish mulatto's master. They stole an uncertain quantity of goods, including a rudderless dugout. One of these slaves was seen five years later in Havana. Chaperon employed the

---

43. Salmon to the Ministry of the Colonies, and Louboey to the Ministry of the Colonies, October 12, 1739, in Ser. C13A 24, fols. 174 and 205–206, respectively, ANC; Bienville and Salmon to the Ministry of the Colonies, June 29, 1740, in Ser. C13A 25, fol. 31, *ibid.*; Louboey to the Ministry of the Colonies, January 6, 1740, in Ser. C13A, fol. 214, *ibid.*; October 16, 1739, in RSC, *LHQ*, VII (1924), 497. See also Aufrère to Le Normand, Paris, August 29, 1749, in Ser. C13B 1, fol. 218, ANC, for protest over late, and inadequate, indemnification for this loss.

44. Declaration by fugitive Negroes Manuel and Juan belonging to M. de Benac, March 22, 1748, in RSC, *LHQ*, XIX (1936), 503.

planter Destrehan to try to recover him. The governor of Havana arrested a slave who had deserted from Louisiana, had him sold, and sent his price to his master.[45]

There was one case of a slave abducted from Louisiana and sold as a slave in Havana, and evidence that there was a regular traffic in escaped or abducted slaves. De Lisle Dupart, a seventeen-year-old native of Louisiana, reported a rumor he heard in Havana that the crew of a ship commanded by Captain Auvray had carried off black slaves from New Orleans. He met a cadet of Auvray's crew in the house of a woman named Balthasar. She had sent her slave, who it was rumored had been abducted from M. de Benac, to her plantation outside Havana. The cadet claimed that he had purchased, not abducted, the slave. A year later, Manuel and Juan, fugitive slaves belonging to M. de Benac, were brought back from Havana in the king's frigate *la Mégère* and returned to their master. These slaves identified several slaves of various masters who had disappeared from Louisiana and who were then living as free persons in Havana.[46]

Slaves escaping from New Orleans sometimes headed up the Mississippi River into the Red River and thence to Natchitoches, a French military post near Spanish territory. Natchitoches to Adayes, a Spanish military post on the Red River in what is now Texas, was an established escape route. Governor Kerlérec complained that he had written to the Spanish captain general several times asking for the return of some fugitive slaves who had taken refuge at Adayes after having "committed crimes which deserve the most exemplary punishment, and this very day, the commander of Adayes refuses to return one of them to me who fits this case." Kerlérec asked that a jail be built for the exchange of deserters and fugitive slaves between these French and Spanish military posts. Escape into Texas (then part of New Spain) did not end when Spain took over Louisiana. Mariana, a slave from New Orleans, and a small child had been in flight for eight months. She met another escaped slave, named Louis, who had been in flight for two years. He took Mariana, the child, and another woman to the woods, where they lived until they were captured in a dairy at Natchitoches.[47]

45. November 7, 1739, *ibid.*, VII (1924), 506; September 1, 1744, *ibid.*, XIII (1930), 156; Vaudreuil to the Ministry of the Colonies, August 28, 1749, in Ser. C13A 33, fol. 65, ANC.

46. March 10, 1747, in RSC, *LHQ*, XVII (1934), 560–61; Declaration by fugitive Negroes Manuel and Juan, March 22, 1748, *ibid.*, XIX (1936), 503.

47. Kerlérec to the Ministry of the Colonies, October 22, 1757, in Ser. C13A 39, fols. 284–85, ANC; July 29, 1772, in SJR, *LHQ*, VIII (1925), 527.

Threats and assaults by slaves against their masters and other whites appear regularly in the judicial records. Bernard Wig and his wife, Fewounica, reported that one of his black slaves attacked and stabbed him and his son-in-law. A mutinous black from the Desfeld plantation was condemned to flogging. A black who stabbed his master to death was condemned to have his hand cut off and to be broken on the wheel. A cabinetmaker complained that a black named Raphael and his wife, Fauchon, had attacked and insulted him without cause, and had him followed and pelted by their children. He asked for protection from the Superior Council, since he often had to work near them. A settler complained to the Superior Council that an African belonging to a French settler assaulted him and tried to kill him. He appealed for protection because he heard that his life was in danger. A master complained that one of his slaves threatened him with an ax.[48]

Jasmin, a twenty-five-year-old slave of the Sango nation, was accused of attacking and seriously injuring a French soldier at Natchez. Jasmin had belonged to the settler Brunet, who sold him to Madame l'Epine of Arkansas because he nearly drove his master crazy. Jasmin ran away from his mistress and hid along the river for a month. He had a gun and powder, but he ran out of food. He stayed in the woods and went to the slave cabins at night, where he was sometimes fed. He was finally found by the soldiers in an Indian cabin, faint with hunger. They brought him to the fort at Natchez. The soldiers fed him, and he remained there until it became known that Madame l'Epine had offered fifty pounds to whoever arrested him. Jasmin found a French soldier waiting for him in the barracks where he slept. Believing the soldier intended to capture him to collect the reward, Jasmin picked up a piece of iron and threw it at him, breaking his jaw, his teeth, almost blinding him, and nearly killing him. Jasmin was first sentenced to be hanged, but after assessing his value, officials changed his sentence. He was to be flogged every day at the crossroads of the city, his right ear was to be cut off, and a six-pound weight was to be attached to his foot for the rest of his life.[49]

This leniency, at least by the standards of the times, can be explained by considering that it was only a soldier whom he had injured and that the state and the masters were reluctant to execute slaves

48. July 6, 1736, in RSC, *LHQ,* VIII (1925), 299; Salmon to the Ministry of the Colonies, February 10, 1737, C13A 22, fols. 124–25, ANC; January 28, 1745, in RSC, *LHQ,* XIII (1930), 506; February 9, 1746, in RSC, *LHQ,* XV (1932), 142; July 29, 1756, in RSC, LHC.

49. January 4, 1742, in RSC, *LHQ,* XI (1928), 288–92.

because they were so valuable. The state would have to pay compensation to the masters. Slaves accused of running away, stealing, or killing cattle were most often flogged, marked with the fleur-de-lys, had their ears cut off, or had their legs mutilated to make it harder for them to run, and then they were returned to their masters. Masters often defended their slaves, even physically dangerous slaves who were accused of crimes. French and Swiss soldiers were tortured and executed for the most trivial reasons, including the theft of small amounts of food. The state tended to sell chronic runaways and physically dangerous slaves outside the colony so some money could be realized from them and so the owners would not have to be compensated for executed slaves. Chronic runaways from lower Louisiana were sold in the Illinois country, where their reputations were not known. This practice was generalized throughout the Caribbean: Dangerous slaves and chronic runaways were foisted off on masters in remote colonies.

Most of the violence surfacing in the documents was white on black. It is not possible to paint an accurate picture of the treatment of slaves based upon the particular cases that appear in the documents. Murder and maiming of slaves by whites became a legal matter when individuals killed or damaged slaves who did not belong to them. Some of these cases involved overseers. Captain de Merveilleux, commander at Natchez, had to leave his post in order to obtain medical treatment at New Orleans. He ordered his substitute, Gaulas, to refer all discipline of unruly slaves to Cazeneuve, and he was not to punish them himself, "not knowing him to be apt and fit in this matter." Contrary to this injunction, Gaulas ruined one of his most valuable blacks by "so strangulating his wrists that mortification of both hands ensued, with loss of three fingers on the right hand and two on the left." The slave's hands were bound for five hours while more than six hundred rawhide lashes were inflicted. Gaulas had been trying to evade restitution by diverting his, and some of de Merveilleux', tobacco from the premises.[50]

One of the most shocking examples of systematic abuse of slaves encountered in surviving documents anywhere in the Americas was perpetrated by Jacques Charpentier dit Le Roy. In December, 1727, Charpentier signed a three-year contract with Raymond Dauseville to manage his farm and ten slaves. Charpentier was to receive two thousand livres per year and was to construct three buildings and a dove-

50. September 24, 1727, in RSC, LHC; September 2, 4, 1727, both in RSC, *LHQ*, IV (1921), 226.

house. Dauseville, fearing that Charpentier might kill his slaves through overwork, agreed to give him one-third of the profits as well. Charpentier, seeking larger profits, convinced Dauseville to purchase another farm, along with its ten slaves and twenty-four head of cattle, promising to clear the farm and make it productive. Evidently, the contract did not make Charpentier responsible for the death of the slaves. Charpentier quickly lost interest in developing the property after he went into business with a settler named Martin to extract lumber and make pilings. Charpentier used Dauseville's slaves and cattle for this purpose. When Dauseville asked him why he was not being supplied with pigeons, poultry, eggs, pigs, milk, and meat in accordance with the contract, Charpentier replied that this was women's work. Since there had been no domestic servant on the property for two years, Charpentier agreed to hire Aimée Courdres, widow of Julien Chartier. She testified that the cattle were not allowed to graze, that the slaves were being fed only one meal a day consisting of a few rotten beans, and that they were not allowed to eat during the day, only late at night. They were awakened several hours before dawn, worked until late at night, even in heavy rain, and then had to thresh grain. The Dauseville slaves were all weak and emaciated. Illness was only recognized when the slaves would not get up after being flogged. A woman slave who was nursing her own baby, as well as an orphan, had been bleeding for nine or ten months. By the time she was sent to the hospital, her womb was rotten and she died. The slaves were not given Sundays off in accordance with the Code Noir, nor Saturdays to grow their own provisions, as was the custom. Pregnant women were not allowed to stop work two hours before sunset, as was the custom, but instead were worked as hard as the men. Their pitiful diet was not supplemented. Courdres said she managed to give them a few potatoes on the sly. She reported that one woman gave birth to a stillborn child whose head had been crushed. Charpentier ran Courdres off because of her complaints about his mistreatment of the slaves and the cattle.[51]

Charpentier had managed to carry out his worst crimes when Courdres was not there, avoiding prosecution because there was no eyewitness to his crimes except for slaves, who could not testify against whites. Dauseville became aware of the depth of Charpentier's depravity when one of his slaves, Brune, complained to him.

---

51. Raymond Dauseville to Jacques Charpentier dit Le Roy, April 29, 1730, and Dauseville to Superior Council, Testimony and Medical Reports, September 5, 18, 1730, all in RSC, LHC.

Charpentier had taken away Brune's suckling pig and forced him to cook it and serve it to him and his friends. Brune told Dauseville that Charpentier had been forcing his sexual attentions upon the slave women, mistreating those who resisted him, raping them in the open fields in the presence of other slaves. He had beaten four slave women who were pregnant with his children, causing them to abort. One of them had aborted three times during the past two years. He had beaten the pregnant wife of another slave. After complaining to his master, Brune was sent to the hospital and died three days later. A slave belonging to a neighbor asked Dauseville if a postmortem examination of Brune had taken place, since Charpentier had beaten him in the chest with a piling in the presence of the other slaves, threatening to kill them if they told. He warned Dauseville that he soon would have no slaves left. A postmortem revealed that Brune's chest was mangled by a wound the size of a large hand and that blood had flowed profusely. One slave threw himself into the river and was rescued by Terrebonne, a neighbor. The slaves asked to be killed rather than subjected to unjust flogging. One of them neither ate nor drank and cried all the time. The surgeon Manadé refused to return to the farm because Charpentier had beaten slaves to death. Dauseville petitioned for the cancellation of Charpentier's lease and for civil damages.[52]

Those two cases were civil matters, involving damage of valuable property that belonged to another person. When soldiers and other poor whites attacked and injured slaves, they were prosecuted as criminals. A young man "without means and a libertine" tried to take a pirogue away from a black man and a black woman, firing two shots at them. The black man was shot in the arm, which had to be amputated, and the woman was hit in the thigh. He was condemned to three years on the galleys and a five hundred pound fine.[53] Pochinet, a drunken soldier, brutally attacked two slave women, Louison and Babet, mortally wounding them with his bayonet. The women belonged to the hospital of the Ursuline nuns. Babet was too ill to answer questions. Louison told the police that they had been working on the riverbank in front of the convent when the soldier approached, stopped, and talked to Babet. Louison could not hear the conversa-

52. *Ibid.*
53. Salmon to the Ministry of the Colonies, February 10, 1737, C13A 22, fols. 124–25, ANC.

tion. Suddenly, he struck Babet in the stomach with a bayonet. When Louison rushed bare-handed to Babet's assistance, Pochinet attacked her. She tried to escape, but she fell down. Pochinet struck her repeatedly with the bayonet, cutting her on her arms and her body. Pochinet ordered her to her knees to beg his pardon. She did, but he continued to attack her with the bayonet. The other blacks went for help. The attack was stopped only by the arrival of Baptiste, Louison's husband, who grappled with the soldier for his bayonet. Baptiste was cut in the hand, and the bayonet was bent during the struggle. Baptiste and several other persons, slave and free, black and white, grabbed Pochinet and brought him to the hospital "where he carried on terribly, screaming and cursing until he was put into the yard and then taken away by the police."[54]

A number of other creole slaves testified that a soldier, perhaps the same soldier, had been trying to rob and terrorize them, but without much success. François, a creole slave, was returning from the waterfront with a purchase of plums. A soldier asked him for some. François told him that if he wanted some plums he could buy them where they were sold, whereupon the soldier knocked the plums out of his hands and slapped him. The soldier drew a bayonet from under his arm, unsheathed it, and tried to strike François with it but failed. François was able to escape and go in search of a policeman. The soldier made off in the direction of the king's warehouse. Manon Négresse testified that about eight days earlier, she and two other *négresses* had been washing clothes on the riverbank opposite the barracks on the side of the intendant's house. A soldier, who appeared to be quite drunk, came up and asked them to wash a handkerchief. They refused because it was raining and they did not have time. He drew a bayonet from under his arm and chased all of them. They escaped into the river, whereupon he trampled all the clothes lying on the bank, then ran off toward the king's warehouse. Pochinet told the police that he was dead drunk when he was arrested and did not remember anything before his arrest. The reverend mothers Xavier and Magdeleine refused to press charges against Pochinet, saying that "quite to the contrary, they would like to save his life and that they would prefer to lose their négresses rather than do anything against charity toward their fellowmen." The colonial officials were less charitable and sentenced Pochinet to forced labor on the galleys, commenting upon "the excesses with which Guildive is distributed at

54. June 12, 1752, in RSC, LHC (WPA summary in English).

the taverns here: a drink which ruins the soldier entirely and throws him into a rage."[55]

It is clear why these two cases were treated as criminal, not civil, matters. The criminals were a penniless vagabond and a soldier whose status in society was at or near the bottom and who could not make restitution. When a master brutalized, maimed, or murdered his own slave, he was immune from prosecution or even from condemnation by his fellow masters. The existence of such brutes was used by more humane masters to keep their own slaves in line. This writer has not encountered any cases in French Louisiana of investigation or prosecution of masters for mistreating their own slaves, or for violating the Code Noir's regulations protecting slaves. The French officer Jean-Bernard Bossu, a reliable witness, saw the planter Chaperon roasting one of his slaves to death in a hot oven. Seeing that his victim's jawbones were drawn back, Chaperon remarked, "I think that he is still laughing." Chaperon then picked up the poker and stirred the fire. Evidently, Bossu did not feel called upon to stop this act. There is no evidence that Chaperon was prosecuted. Masters threatened to sell their slaves to Chaperon to enforce discipline. Chaperon was, in fact, a respected member of the community. He regularly witnessed notarial documents. He was appointed tutor of the widow and minor children of the deceased Larche and was entrusted with the slaves belonging to the estate. Although it became quite clear that Chaperon was neglecting and abusing the slaves belonging to the Larche minors, nothing was done to stop him. Most of the Larche slaves had been rented to the Jesuits, but Maria, her mistress, and her mistress's child were living at Chaperon's. Her duties were to take care of her mistress's child. Maria ran away, and Madame Chaperon discovered that she had gone to Sieur Jacques Larche, brother of Maria's deceased master, who, according to Madame Chaperon, influenced her to desert her post. Maria testified that if she returned to Chaperon she would die. She did nothing but cook for the *nègres*, and she was cruelly treated without cause. Before going to Larche, she had gone to the Jesuit fathers who had hired the slaves of the estate of her late master, but they would not take her in without telling Chaperon, and fearing his wrath, she came to her master's brother asking him to hire her to another to prove that she was not ill disposed and would give satisfaction. Jacques Larche filed a statement with the court pointing out the dangers of mistreatment

55. *Ibid.*; Michel to the Ministry of the Colonies, September 20, 1752, in Ser. C13A 36, fol. 267, ANC.

of slaves by those who were not their owners. A *négresse* died from the treatment she was subjected to at Sieur St. Julien's tar factory. A year later, Chaperon called a doctor to attend to a fifteen-month-old black child from the Larche estate whose mother was hired as a wet nurse to a white child. The black child was unable to stand, was slightly swollen, and had been suffering with diarrhea for three weeks. Her condition was brought on by bad food and neglect.[56]

Chaperon owned forty-one slaves when his plantation was sold in 1760. It is not surprising that the slaves on his estate had a child/ woman ratio of 0.375, the lowest for any estate calculated for French Louisiana, reflecting a low birthrate and a low rate of infant survivals.[57] Chaperon slaves regularly appeared among the runaways. Chaperon was, no doubt, an extreme example of a brutal master. But the fact that his behavior was tolerated—indeed, functional—within the society demonstrates an acceptance of excessive brutality toward slaves.

French New Orleans was a brutal, violent place. But it cannot be understood by projecting contemporary attitudes toward race backward in time. There is no evidence of the racial exclusiveness and contempt that characterizes more recent times. While contempt toward poor whites, especially soldiers, is omnipresent in the documents, there is little indication of contempt toward blacks, nor evidence that white settlers and French officials considered the Africans and their descendants uncivilized people who needed to be taught the French language, culture, or even the religion. It is not unusual to find slaves in the documents who were not baptized. Mere survival was on the line, and notions of racial and/or cultural and national superiority were a luxury beyond the means of the colonists. In French Louisiana, Africans and their descendants were competent, desperately needed, and far from powerless.

56. Bossu, *Travels in North America*, 18; September 18, 29, 1736, in RSC, *LHQ*, VIII (1925), 497; September 8, 1737, in RSC, *LHQ*, IX (1926), 514.

57. Plantation of Joseph Chaperon, October 20, 1760, in Doc. 10, Sales, 1737–1768, OAOP. The child/woman ratio is calculated by dividing the number of children under age five by the number of women aged fifteen to forty-five.

The Creole Slaves: Origin, Family, Language, Folklore

Ça mo di, li ben di.

What I have said is well said.

—Louisiana Creole proverb from Alcée Fortier, "Bits of Louisiana Folklore"

Di moin si to gagnin nhomme,
Mo va fé ounga pouli,
Mo fé tourné fantôme,
Si to vlé me to mari.

Tell me if you have a man,
I'll go make a wanga for him,
I'll turn him into a phantom,
If you want me for your husband.

—Louisiana Creole song in Marcus Bruce Christian, "For a Black History of Louisiana"

Chère mo lem-mé toi,
Oui, mo lem-mé toi,
Avec tou mo couer,
Mo lem-mé toi chère,
Comme tit co-chon lem-mé la boul.

Dear, I love you so,
Yes, I love you so,
With all my heart,
I love you dear,
Like a little pig loves mud.

—from Camille Lucie Nickerson, "Afro-Creole Music in Louisiana: A Thesis on the Plantation Songs Created by the Creole Negroes of Louisiana"

As we move away from a Eurocentric interpretation of American culture and begin to explore the African roots of all Americans, it is important to understand Louisiana creole culture. It is the most significant source of Africanization of the entire culture of the United States. Normally in the United States, the word *creole* refers exclusively to the people and culture of lower Louisiana. But it has a broader meaning throughout the Americas. It derives from the Portuguese word *crioulo*, meaning a slave of African descent born in the New World. Thereafter, it was extended to include Europeans born in the Americas, now the only meaning of the word in Portugal. In eighteenth-century Louisiana, the term *creole* referred to locally born people of at least partial African descent, slave and free, and was used to distinguish American-born slaves from African-born slaves when they were listed on slave inventories. They were identified simply as creoles if they were locally born, or as creoles of another region or colony if they had been born elsewhere in the Americas. In the English Atlantic colonies, the term *country born* had the same meaning as *creole*. The most precise current definition of a creole is a person of non-American ancestry, whether African or European, who was born in the Americas. However, because of the racial and cultural complexity of colonial Louisiana, native Americans who were born into slavery were sometimes described as "creoles" or "born in the country."[1] After the United States took over Louisiana, creole cultural identification became a means of distinguishing that which was truly native to Louisiana from that which was Anglo. *Creole* has come to mean the language and the folk culture that was native to the southern part of Louisiana where African, French, and Spanish influence was most deeply rooted historically and culturally.

In Louisiana, as well as throughout the Americas, the word *creole* has been redefined over time in response to changes in the social and racial climate. With the rise of the independence movements in Latin America, it came to mean people of exclusively European descent born in the Americas. The native-born elite of Latin America was considered incapable of self-rule partially because of its racially mixed heritage. As a defense, the term *creole* took on a racially exclusive

---

1. John Holm, *Pidgins and Creoles: Theory and Structure* (2 vols.; Cambridge, Eng., 1988), I, 9; Stephen Webre, "The Problem of Indian Slavery in Spanish Louisiana, 1769–1803," *LH*, XXV (1984), 118.

connotation and came to mean a person born in the Americas of European parentage. This same redefinition took place in Louisiana with the rise of "scientific" racism during the nineteenth century. Louisiana whites of French and/or Spanish descent rejected the racial openness of Louisiana's past, as well as, in some cases, their own racially mixed heritage, and redefined *creole* to mean exclusively white. By the turn of the century, George Washington Cable, a white Louisianian driven out of his home state because of his liberal views on race, wrote that the term *creole* came early to "include any native, of French or Spanish descent by either parent, whose non-alliance with the slave race entitled him to social rank. . . . [T]here seems to be no more serviceable definition of the Creoles of Louisiana than this: that they are the French-speaking, native portion of the ruling class."[2]

Charles Barthelemy Roussève, the Afro-Creole historian writing in 1937, devoted considerable attention to disproving the claim of white scholars that the word *creole* in its noun form was used only to designate whites of pure French and Spanish ancestry born in lower Louisiana.[3]

By the nineteenth century, the mixed-blood creoles of Louisiana who acknowledged their African descent emphasized and took greatest pride in their French ancestry. They defined *creole* to mean racially mixed, enforced endogamous marriage among their own group, and distinguished themselves from and looked down upon blacks and Anglo-Afroamericans, though their disdain stemmed from cultural as well as racial distinctions. A recent study indicates that in New Orleans during the 1970s, the designations "black" and "creole" were irreconcilable. These young Afro–New Orleaneans embraced a definition of *creole* that is racially rather than culturally defined, as well as being a-historical.[4]

Edward Brathwaite, writing about Jamaica, defined *creolization* as a sociocultural continuum radiating outward from the slave community and affecting the entire culture in varying degrees. This definition is relevant for the United States as well as for the Caribbean.[5] It is especially significant for Louisiana, where the slave culture was early

2. George Washington Cable, *The Creoles of Louisiana* (New York, 1910), 41–42.

3. Charles Barthelemy Roussève, *The Negro in Louisiana: Aspects of His History and His Literature* (New Orleans, 1937), 22–24.

4. Gary B. Mills, *The Forgotten People: Cane River's Creoles of Color* (Baton Rouge, 1977); Virginia R. Domínguez, *White by Definition: Social Classification in Creole Louisiana* (New Brunswick, N.J., 1986).

5. Edward Brathwaite, *The Development of Creole Society in Jamaica* (Oxford, Eng., 1971), 309–11.

and thoroughly Africanized and the first generation of creole slaves grew up in stable, nuclear families composed of African mothers and fathers and creole siblings. We have seen that almost all the black slaves either arrived directly from Africa between June, 1719, and January, 1731, or were the descendants of these first slaves. Two-thirds of these Africans came from Senegambia from a limited number of nations living in a relatively homogeneous culture area. The fragmentation of language and culture communities associated with the African slave trade and slavery in the Americas was limited among slaves in Louisiana. It appears that throughout the eighteenth century, under Spanish rule as well as French, Senegambia remained a more important source of slaves in Louisiana than did Central Africa (see Figure 10). The Louisiana experience calls into question the common assumption that African slaves could not regroup themselves in language and social communities derived from the sending cultures.[6]

Conditions prevailing during the earliest stage of colonization molded a creole or Afro-American slave culture through a process of blending and adaptation of cultural materials brought by the slaves who were first introduced. The founding contingent played a strategic role, since newcomers must adjust to a great extent to the culture and language they encounter.[7] In Louisiana, the impact of the founding African ethnic groups was especially great because of the pattern of introduction of slaves. Before the founding of New Orleans in 1718, French Louisiana was no more than a weak military outpost. With the founding of New Orleans and the sustained efforts of the Company of the Indies to populate and develop the colony and introduce African slaves, the true colonization of Louisiana began. Almost all the black slaves brought to Louisiana under French rule came directly from Africa within a twelve-year period and quickly became a substantial majority of the population. The proportion of blacks to whites in the French settlements rose sharply after 1721. The high mortality in the African slave trade to French Louisiana, especially after 1726, did not result in fragmentation and demoralization but instead facilitated the emergence of a particularly coherent, functional, well integrated, autonomous, and self-confident slave community. The close bonds between survivors coming over on the same

6. See, for example, Sidney W. Mintz, *Caribbean Transformations* (Chicago, 1974), 11, 12, 27, 28.

7. Richard Price, commentary on Monica Schuler's *Afro-American Slave Culture,* in *Roots and Branches: Current Directions in Slave Studies,* ed. Michael Craton (Toronto, 1979), 141–49.

slave-trade ship has been noted throughout the Americas and has been explained as a reinterpreted form of kinship. There were relatively few slave-trade voyages. The ship the slave came off of was often identified when slaves appeared in the Records of the Superior Council. Networks of solidarity among the survivors of these voyages must have been a thickly woven web.

The last systematic census under French rule was taken in 1731 to 1732. Africans outnumbered whites in lower Louisiana by more than two to one. During the 1730s, the white population rapidly dwindled because of high mortality, outmigration, and low birth rate. There were few new slaves introduced before France formally abandoned the colony in 1763. The only French slave-trade ship to Louisiana after 1731 arrived in 1743 and reinforced the existing African ethnic groups brought in during the formative period. Thus, the focus of Louisiana creole slave culture was neither diverted nor diminished by newcomers. It was not until 1758 that another slave ship arrived: a British ship coming from the coast of Africa that had been seized by a French convoy. It left two thirds of its cargo in Grenada and brought the rest, 120 slaves, to New Orleans, where they were sold. During these final years of French rule, some British ships operating under a flag of truce, ostensibly to exchange prisoners, also introduced slaves, probably several hundred of them.[8] But they were introduced late, in relatively small numbers, long after Louisiana's creole language and folk culture had been formed.

The cultural impact of the formative contingent of slaves brought to Louisiana was much more than a simple result of timing and numbers. French Louisiana was not a stable society controlled by a culturally and socially cohesive white elite ruling a dominated, immobilized, fractionalized, and culturally obliterated slave population. The chaotic conditions prevailing in the colony, the knowledge and skills of the African population, the size and importance of the Indian population throughout the eighteenth century, and the geography of lower Louisiana, which allowed for easy mobility along its waterways as well as escape and survival in the nearby, pervasive swamps, all contributed to an unusually cohesive and heavily Africanized culture

8. For information on low fertility among white women during the 1720s, see Mathé Allain, "Not Worth a Straw": French Colonial Policy and the Early Years of Louisiana (Lafayette, La., 1988), 87; Jean-Bernard Bossu, Travels in the Interior of North America, 1751–1762, trans. Seymour Feiler (Norman, Okla., 1962), 124–25; Procès verbaux d'adjudications de nègres, September 27, October 22, 1758, in Ser. C13A 40, fols. 189–98, ANC; Rochemore to the Ministry of the Colonies, January 5, 1759, in Ser. C13A 41, fol. 173, ANC; Henry P. Dart, ed., "New Orleans in 1758," LHQ, V (1922), 56.

in lower Louisiana; clearly, the most Africanized slave culture in the United States.

The pattern of introduction of black slaves into French Louisiana contrasts sharply with that of the English colonies that became part of the United States. The early contingent of slaves introduced into the Chesapeake and Carolina came from the British West Indies and constituted a relatively small minority. They were one or more generations removed from Africa and spoke English or a creolized version of English when they arrived. They spoke a more standard English than those who came after them, constituted a small minority, and interacted fairly freely with their masters, as well as with the English servants. Therefore, "the base upon which African survivals could rest [was reduced], not simply in speech, but other elements of culture. . . . [T]he African folk tales of Anansi, the spider, which are frequent in the West Indies, are rare in the South."[9]

The Gullah dialect, an English-based creole language, survived only on the isolated Sea Islands off the coast of South Carolina and Georgia and was probably never widely spoken on the mainland by blacks or by whites. The Anglo-American society into which Africans were introduced, when they began to arrive in significant numbers, was much more stable than the society in French Louisiana. Thus, the culture of the United States was most heavily Africanized from Louisiana after 1803, when the slave plantation system spread west, when New Orleans was the major entrepôt for new slaves, and when the largest slave plantations of the antebellum South were established in the state. The massive post-Reconstruction migration of African-Americans up the Mississippi Valley spread a partially anglicized Afro-Creole folk culture throughout the United States.

In early Louisiana, the uneven distribution of the newly arrived Africans facilitated their cultural autonomy. There were large concentrations of slaves in the hands of a few members of the military-bureaucratic elite that ruled the colony. Most of the white colonists owned either no slaves or very few. When *Ordonnateur* Salmon took over administration of the colony for the king, he complained that large numbers of slaves had been distributed to concession holders, most of whom did not use them effectively. He wrote that it would have been better to distribute a few slaves to the small settlers and to

9. Allan Kulikoff, *Tobacco and Slaves: The Development of Southern Cultures in the Chesapeake, 1680–1800* (Chapel Hill, 1986), 319; Peter H. Wood, *Black Majority: Negroes in Colonial South Carolina from 1670 Through the Stono Rebellion* (New York, 1974), 20, 21, 21*n*, 175.

the soldiers who established themselves in the colony. The uneven distribution of blacks led to discontent among settlers, most of whom were asking to abandon the colony. This concentration of Africans, many of them from the same ethnic group, on relatively few estates facilitated the preservation and adaptation of African cultural patterns. It is, furthermore, clear that Africans could not be confined to their masters' estates and isolated from contact with other Africans belonging to the same language community. We have seen that four hundred Bambara slaves living throughout lower Louisiana allied themselves with Indians to overthrow the French regime and take control of the colony. Twelve years later, a group of slaves belonging to several different masters met to judge and sentence Corbin, the master of one of these slaves. Corbin had threatened to shoot his slave for running away; and his brother had indeed shot the slave with a gun loaded with a charge of salt. A group of slaves met and "a service was sung in the style and language of the *nègres.*" They evidently sentenced Corbin to death and eventually carried out his execution. A slave who belonged to Corbin's neighbor shot at Corbin and ran away. Remarkably, this slave thereafter returned to his master, and his master pardoned him. We can only conclude that the master was so dependent upon the slave that he had to take the risk. But the slave did not stay long. When his master sent him for provisions, he went into another neighbor's barn, took a horse, and ran away again. Two months after the "service" was held, Corbin went to hunt near his house, saying he would return shortly. He was never seen again, nor was his body found. Thereafter, a slave named Jeannot mutinied against and abused his master, threatening to set fire to his cabin and taunting him by saying he knew who killed Corbin.[10]

African religious beliefs, including knowledge of herbs, poisons, and the creation of charms and amulets of support or power, came to Louisiana with the earliest contingents of slaves. All adult Bambara males knew how to make charms. There are examples of slaves accused of being poisoners during the 1720s. Bonnaud confirmed through a postmortem examination that his *commandeur* had been poisoned. Petit, another *nègre* of Bonnaud, was suspected of the crime because he had threatened several times to kill the *commandeur* through magical means, since the *commandeur* had flogged him under orders of their master. Since Petit Nègre "came from a tribe reputed

10. La Chaise to the commissioners of the Company, September 6, 1723, in Ser. C13 7, fol. 7, ANC; Salmon to the Ministry of the Colonies, December 14, 1731, in Ser. C13A 15, *ibid.;* September 9, 1743, in RSC, LHC.

to be adept at poisoning, it was feared that many more persons would become his victim," according to the Superior Council. The council concluded that while it "does not admit the existence of sorcerers, it does punish poisoners, and perhaps it is poisons which do all the damage attributed to sorcery."[11]

This document from the Superior Council does not identify the tribe "reputed to be adept at poisoning," but if the tribe had been Bambara, the reputation would probably have been well deserved. During the 1950s, Germaine Dieterlen described techniques of poisoning during certain rites of the *komo* that were intended to kill the guilty or the undesirable. One technique was the use of a mask with two arms, at the end of which were talons. The right talon was dipped in mud, ground copper, and snake venom, and even a small wound from it would kill. The musicians at the ceremony took antidotes to avoid being poisoned from breathing the venomous powder. Recent pharmacological and psychiatric investigations in Haiti (formerly, St. Domingue) have confirmed the use of animal and vegetable poisons administered both cutaneously and through inhalation. These poisons are ground into a lethal powder, a technique used in eighteenth-century Louisiana as well.[12]

Du Pratz, who left Louisiana in 1734, wrote of the slaves, "They are very superstitious and attached to their prejudices and to charms which they call *gris-gris*." Reference to *gri-gri* is found in New Orleans court records in 1773. Charms ritually fabricated and worn for protection, as well as charms intended to harm others, have kept their African names to the present day. *Zinzin*, an amulet of support or power in Louisiana Creole, has the same name and meaning in Bambara. *Gris-gris*, a harmful charm, comes from the Mande word *gerregerys*. The words *wanga* and *grisgris* are still widely used in New Orleans by speakers of English as well as by creoles. Although *wanga* may have been an apport, that is, a word borrowed well after the establishment of a creole language, *grisgris* and *zinzin*, Mande terms, were most likely introduced into Louisiana by the earliest contingent of slaves.[13]

11. October 21, 25, 1729, in RSC, *LHQ,* IV (1921), 354–55; Judgment of Superior Council, October 25, 1729, in RSC, LHC.

12. Germaine Dieterlen, *Essai sur la religion Bambara* (Paris, 1951), 151–52; E. Wade Davis, "On the Pharmacology of Black Magic," and Bernard Diederich, "On the Nature of Zombie Existence," *Caribbean Review,* XII (Summer, 1983).

13. Le Page du Pratz, *Histoire de la Louisiane* (3 vols.; Paris, 1758), I, 334; Laura L. Porteus, "The Gri-Gri Case: A Criminal Trial in Louisiana During the Spanish Regime, 1773," *LHQ,* XVII (1934), 60; Viviana Paques, *Les Bambara* (Paris, 1954), 94; Marcus Bruce Christian, "For a Black History of Louisiana" (Typescript in Archives and Manu-

Wanga could have been introduced during the formative period of Louisiana Creole by slaves from the one slave ship coming from Cabinda, by slaves brought from Central Africa during the re-Africanization of the slave population under Spanish rule, or by slaves from any place in West Africa where charms named wanga were diffused.

Detailed knowledge of how the wanga, a harmful charm, was manufactured and used is available to us through documents produced during the investigation of the Mackandal conspiracy in St. Domingue. Mackandal was a maroon leader who had many followers throughout the colony. He was charged with plotting to kill all the whites and take over the colony by poisoning the water supply. He was burned alive in 1758. His life and death inspired the Haitian Revolution (1791–1804), which abolished slavery and established Haiti as the second independent nation in the Americas. These documents discussed various types of charms, their names, their powers, and how they were made. There were charms that gave power and protection to the bearer in the form of strength in combat, luck in gambling, or success in running away. Charms were used for protection against the master. They were tied to the foot of the bed where the master slept or to the table upon which the master worked, protecting the slave from being beaten by the master, blinding the master to his slave's faults, making the master's heart "soft as water." The document also mentions the term *Gry* from the language identified as Mennade (probably Mande) as another term for "what we call at Le Cap the *garde corps* or Mackandal."[14]

It was explained that only sorcerers of the first order created these charms, which were given various names. The charm named *ouanga* was specifically a poison used against an enemy or a rival. "To harm him in his body, one must, according to their expression, approach him, that is to say, make him take *ouanga* or poison."[15]

One of the poisonous substances in the *ouanga* was the ground-up roots of the *figuier maudit* tree, which was evidently brought over

scripts Department, Earl K. Long Library, University of New Orleans); William A. Read, *Louisiana-French* (Baton Rouge, 1931), 127; G. Thimans and N. I. de Moraes, "Dencha Fourt souverain du Baol," *Bulletin de l'Institut français d'Afrique Noir*, XXXVI (1974), 695, cited in Oumar Kane, "Le Fuuta-Taoro des satigi au Almaami (1512–1807)" (3 vols.; Ph.D. dissertation, Pantheon-Sorbonne, 1986); Holm, *Pidgins and Creoles*, I, 81.

14. Mémoire pour servir à l'information des procès contre les nègres devenu sorcier, et empoisonneur, 1758, in Ser. F3 88, AN.

15. *Ibid*.

from Africa and which still grows throughout the French West Indies. These *ouanga* packets also contained bones from a cemetery, preferably those of baptized children, nails, ground-up roots of the banana tree, holy water, holy candles, holy incense, holy bread, and crucifixes. The sorcerer pronounced the words *Alla Alla* several times, invoking protection of the Islamic God, then invoked the Christian God and our Lord Jesus Christ, and finally pronounced, "God gives me what I do" and "God gives them that which they ask" (*"Bon dieu donné qui ça moi faire"* and *"Bon dieu baie yeuse ça qui yeuse demandé vous"*). Mackandal himself reported these magic words that were incanted during the process of making charms. The manufacture of these charms illustrates the openness of African religious beliefs brought to the Americas: the willingness to invoke the protection of both Islamic and Christian gods and to add them to traditional African beliefs. The charms had to be boiled in a covered iron pot (*marmite*) called a *groton de Chaudière* and fed each time they were used. The *nègres* believed that the charms made their heads move involuntarily. The charms were consulted like oracles by the sorcerer as he made his hat move backwards on his head, chanting:

> Ouaie, ouaie,
> Mayangangue,
> Zamis moi mourir
> Moi aller mourir,
> Ouaie, ouaie,
> Mayangangue.

Ouaie was described in the documents as a mysterious word whose meaning was known only by the greatest sorcerers. Five years after Mackandal was burned alive, the Superior Council of Louisiana outlawed the importation of *nègres* from St. Domingue, under penalty of fines, to avoid introducing poisoners into the colony.[16]

Lafcadio Hearn, and others who wrote about voodoo in the late nineteenth century, said, "We cannot share the opinion of many that (voodooism) is a mere 'absurd superstition.' We believe it to be, or at least to have been a serious and horrible reality; and we know of most intelligent families among our French-speaking population who share this opinion."[17]

16. *Ibid.*; Arrêt du Conseil supérior de la Nouvelle-Orléans, July 9, 1763, in Ser. C13A 43, fols. 304, 308, ANC.

17. Lafcadio Hearn, *Creole Sketches* (Boston, 1924), 122; George Washington Cable, *The Grandissimes* (New York, 1980); Robert Tallant, *Voodoo in New Orleans* (New York, 1946).

Names have a great symbolic meaning touching the most profound levels of feelings of identity. Alex Haley's popular book, *Roots*, made widely known through film and television, has received a great deal of attention throughout the world. One of his most memorable stories was about Kunta Kinte, the slave brought from Africa who was forced to give up his African name and take an English name, Toby. If he had been brought to French Louisiana, he would not have faced this problem. The slaves of French Louisiana often kept their African names, many of which were Islamic. Some slaves with French names had Baraca, an Islamic religious title, as a second name. African names abound in the slave lists and in judicial records. Those old Africans who survived into the 1760s and 1770s still had African names, and some of their children born in Louisiana also had African names. During the Spanish period, many newcomers, especially those from Senegambia, kept African names as well. Unlike in South Carolina, these were not reinterpreted names. Some of the same names listed for slaves in the *captiveries* at Gorée and Bissau are found throughout colonial documents in Louisiana. Furthermore, many slaves who were listed in documents under French names actually used African names, which were sometimes listed in court records as second names. When slaves testified in court, their fellow slaves sometimes could not identify them under their French names and used their African names for clarity. For example, Joseph, a Bambara slave of Dubreuil, testified about a slave whose real name was Feriment but whom the court had referred to as Joseph. When asked about another Dubreuil slave, Joseph said that this other slave's name was Sary (or Jarry), though his French name was Claude; that he was his comrade, though they were of different countries. When Jarry testified, he said that his name was Jarry dit (said to be) Claude. Baraca, a Fulbe slave of the king, was referred to throughout his trial by his African name, though he himself testified that his name was François dit Baraca.[18] Thus, we see an often successful resistance to socialization through rejection of French names.

Patterns of family formation and kinship networks are vital to the creation of slave culture. As Herbert Gutman so eloquently stated, "We know now that inter-generational slave kin and quasi-kin linkages served as *passageways through time*, connecting changing structures, and allowing the historian to compare slave belief and behavior

18. June 9, 1748, in RSC, *LHQ*, XIX (1936), 1091–94; Trial of Baraca, slave of the king, for murdering his wife, Tacó, February 9, May 4, 1748, in RSC, LHC. See Appendix D for lists of slave names.

Facture Des Captifs & Captiven
Embarqueés du Magasin de Gorée par ordre
de Mons.r Moüis Gouverneur des forts le
lre Jud.t Leiu, Sur le Navire Le Pouchartrean
Cap.ne M.r Lefsure Pour Porter à Léoganne
& les vendre auproffit de la Comp.e des
Juder.   Scavoir

Captifs Masles

Noms		Ages	Deffauts
1:	Basnin	26 ans	Borgne
2:	Dmiba	26	
3:	Sara	24	
4:	Samesa	22	
5:	Molo	22	
6:	Samesa	24	
7:	Many	24	
8:	queüe	28	Couliounde Cheval
9:	quié	28	
10:	Molo	24	
11:	Guz	20	
12:	Habana	22	
13:	Marba	22	
14:	Izay	25	
15:	Bagnioue	24	
16:	Nafa	28	
17:	Niamar	28	
18:	Naupa	22	
19:	Namefa	22	
20:	Samba	28	
21:	quiacoura	26	Idem
22:	Guz	22	
23:	Malalle	20	
24:	Kié	22	
25:	Doüo	26	
26:	Namuz	24	

Fragment of the first page of a list of slaves embarked at Gorée on October 4, 1722,
showing sex, age, name, and "defects."
From Section Coloniales, Archives Nationales, Paris

over time." In French Louisiana, creole slave children grew up in tightly knit, nuclear families headed by both African parents. The slave family was scrupulously protected in practice as well as in law. Mother, father, husband, wife, and children under the age of fourteen were not sold separately. The role of parents, and of parenting, was even more crucial than in contemporary times. Socialization took place mainly in the home and by the family in a society where educational institutions were practically absent, literacy was rare, and religious institutions weak. The devotion of slave parents to their children was poignantly demonstrated when an eighteen-year-old slave named Joseph was accidentally drowned in the Mississippi River. Both of his parents jumped into the river trying to drown themselves as well. They had to be guarded by the entire workshop to stop them from committing suicide.[19]

During the same period that the slave family in French Louisiana was being scrupulously protected, St. Domingue, a French colony operating under a nearly identical slave code, neglected the slave family and did not pursue a pronatality policy. St. Domingue was a prosperous colony producing valuable exports and regularly importing large numbers of new slaves from Africa. Since Louisiana was to a great extent an abandoned colony after 1731 and few new slaves were brought in either from Africa or from elsewhere in the Americas, the slave population had to survive almost entirely through births. In order to encourage procreation among slaves, the authorities scrupulously implemented a strong profamily policy.

Du Pratz wrote that since it was the blacks who performed all agricultural work, especially in lower Louisiana, it was important to give to each man a wife to prevent libertinage and its bad consequences. Additionally, nothing attached the blacks to an estate more than having children. "Above all, do not allow them to leave their wives when they have chosen one in our presence. Forbid assaults against women under penalty of flogging, and thus the women will give birth very often."[20]

Slave families, including both parents, were inventoried together, and one price was set for the family group. Individual families, sometimes large families, were sold together. A family of eight slaves—father, mother, and their six children—was sold as a unit. Another

---

19. Herbert G. Gutman, "Slave Family and its Legacies," in *Roots and Branches: Current Directions in Slave Studies,* ed. Michael Craton (Toronto, 1979), 198; August 10, 1752, in RSC, *LHQ,* XXI (1938), 892–93.

20. Du Pratz, *Histoire de Louisiane,* I, 350–51.

family, consisting of mother, father, and two children, was exchanged for a black woman and a billiard outfit, with the consent of the slaves involved. A master who was leaving for Pointe Coupee obtained permission to sell his slave Beller so he would not be separated from his wife.[21]

The creation and evolution of the slave family can be traced from available inventories of slaves when entire estates were being sold and when estates were inventoried and sold after the death of the master. These inventories can give us only impressionistic information about overall vital rates among slaves of French Louisiana, but they do show the extent of marriage and natality, and often the age structure, for the slaves on the individual estates inventoried. In the absence of real census counts in French Louisiana after 1732, these inventories are of considerable interest. From detailed knowledge about the French slave trade combined with the census estimates in 1741 and 1746, impressions of the numbers of slaves imported during the last few years of French rule, and a real census taken in 1763 as Spain took over the colony, we can obtain a reasonably valid impression of the origins and evolution of the creole slave population.

The earliest inventory, following the death of Claude Trepagnier, dates from 1724. It shows 3 black children, all boys, all about one year old, 1 adult black man who was in the hospital near death, and an Indian woman slave. The next extant inventory dates from 1730. It does not group the slaves into families, but there were 27 black men, 21 black women, and 27 black children from nursing infants to children aged six or seven. The estate of Claude Trepagnier's widow was inventoried in 1739. The slaves were listed in family groups. The child/woman ratio was 1.000. Two of the estate's 32 slaves were off to the Chickasaw Wars. There were three husband-wife couples, a single mother inventoried with her 2 children, and a black man whose hand had been cut off and who was inventoried with his mother and a three-year-old boy. All 7 children were aged eight or younger and were grouped in families. In the case of an adult man who was inventoried separately, it was explained that he had "neither wife nor child." There was a fourteen-year-old girl inventoried separately. This was the cut-off age under the Code Noir for selling children apart from their mothers and fathers. There were 7 single men and no single women. The d'Hauterive estate, containing 48 slaves, was inventoried the same year. It clearly bracketed the families together. All

---

21. January 2, 1745, in RSC, *LHQ*, XIII (1930), 323; June 3, 1744, *ibid.*, 136; February 28, 1738, *ibid.*, V (1922), 588.

A page from the inventory of the d'Hauterive estate, sold to Bobe Descloseau on September 21, 1739, clearly shows slaves bracketed together in family groups.
Photograph by Jan White Brantley. Courtesy the Historical Center Collection of the Louisiana State Museum.

of the women were married. Among 11 couples, there were 16 children, aged between eighteen months and eight years. The child/woman ratio was 0.800. There were 10 single men. Four of the men (Arada, François, Cyrlon, and Doumany), including a husband and father, had gone off to the Chickasaw Wars. Another estate inventoried together a couple and their 6 children, aged two through twelve, another couple with 1 child, 2 couples without children, 1 unmarried man, and no unmarried women. The Chaouachas estate located at English Turn belonged to the Marquis d'Asfeld. It was a large estate containing 161 slaves and had a child/woman ratio of 0.531.[22] The child/woman ratio in these early inventories showed a reasonable level of fertility for women, especially on the medium-sized estates that were probably owner-managed. These figures are for women who were, no doubt, overwhelmingly African.

The seven French slave-trade voyages to Louisiana from which sex ratios can be determined reveal a ratio of 2.2, which means that 2.2 males arrived for each female. Mortality among women on the slave ships to Louisiana, on the two voyages where these figures are available, was higher than among men.[23] Indian women surely made up the deficit among African women introduced into Louisiana. The extent of Indian-African race mixture is now being studied by calculating the numbers of slaves referred to as *grif* on slave inventories dating from the Spanish and early American periods.

The slave population in Louisiana developed unevenly. Periods of high mortality alternated with periods of stability. After 1726, the mortality rate was quite high among the newly arrived Africans. The Chickasaw Wars took a heavy toll upon the adult male slave population, the vast majority of whom were Africans. Slaves who remained on the estates suffered deprivation as well. There were fewer men to work, and scarce supplies were hoarded by Louisiana's officials.

White men outnumbered white women substantially throughout the eighteenth century, and black women were sexual targets of white

22. Succession of Claude Trepagnier, December 9, 1724, in RSC, LHC; James T. McGowan, "Creation of a Slave Society: Louisiana Plantations in the Eighteenth Century" (Ph.D. dissertation, University of Rochester, 1976), 127; Succession of Dame Elizabeth Burel, former widow of Claude Trepagnier, wife of Lassus Marsilly, August 6, 1739, in RSC, LHC; Inventory of Slaves, Sale of d'Hauterive estate to Bobe Descloseaux, September 21, 1739, in RSC, LHC; Succession of Zeringue (Jacques Michel), September 4, 1738, in Doc. 18, Successions, fols. 72712–13, OAOP; Caouachas estate figures calculated from Heloise H. Cruzat, trans., "Documents Concerning Sale of Caouachas Plantation in Louisiana, 1737–38," *LHQ*, VIII (1925), 628–31.

23. See *la Mutine* and the first voyage of *la Venus* in Appendix A.

Table 7. Male-Female Ratio on Slave-Trade Voyages
to Louisiana

Ship	Men	Women	Girls	Boys	Total
l'Afriquain					
Slaves embarked					
Slaves landed	65	53	35	29	182
le Duc du Maine[1]					
Slaves embarked					
Slaves landed	181	121	37	37	349
la Néréide					
Slaves embarked					
Slaves landed	116	66	26	86	294
le Fortuné					
Slaves embarked					
Slaves landed	205	64	11	23	303
l'Expédition					
Slaves embarked					100
Slaves landed	67	20	1		91[2]
la Mutine					
Slaves embarked	95	94	2	46	235
Slaves landed	91	79		43	213[3]
la Flore					
Slaves embarked	350	40		10	
Slaves landed					356

SOURCE: See source for Table 2.

1. Figures are for the second voyage of *le Duc du Maine*.
2. The total landed included three nursing infants, sex not designated in records.
3. Figures vary for total slaves landed.

and Indian, as well as black, men. Many of the crimes committed by
slaves involved struggles over women or were thefts to obtain clothing to please women. The authorities tried to limit such crimes by
outlawing the sale of alcoholic beverages to slaves without the permission of their masters. The slave Jupiter dit Gamelle, convicted of
breaking and entering and of burglary, was sentenced to ordinary
torture and hanging. His motive was to give clothing to a *négresse*. A
white couple was fined for selling liquor to him without a permit.
Jealousy over women led to assaults and murders in the slave quar-

ters. Chaperon's *commandeur* brought a slave woman to a neighboring plantation in his boat. When he landed, he was attacked and nearly killed by a *nègre*. Quarrels over women extended to the emancipated population. A free black named Gros complained that he could no longer live with his wife because another free black, Matha, had instigated his wife against him, was constantly threatening him, and had killed one of his turkey-cocks.[24]

Some reports of domestic violence among slaves surfaced in the documents when wives were murdered. The government was reluctant to execute slaves because it had to compensate the owners, but a capital sentence was carried out in 1723 in the case of a slave who murdered his wife. In 1745, a black slave named Papa killed his wife with a blow of an ax on her head, then disappeared. Baraca, a baptized Fulbe slave, murdered his wife and then ran away. They were both slaves of the king. Baraca was caught a few months later and interrogated. He explained that he had come back from working in town and asked his wife for food. She went on babbling and smoking her pipe. He hit her on the head with a log and then ran away. Some Indians helped him cross the river. His defense was that his wife had a stick between her legs and he was afraid she would hit him with it. Baraca was sentenced to be hanged on the public square in town. His body was to remain hanging there for twenty-four hours to serve as an example.[25]

Warfare took its toll upon the slave population, especially the adult males. Bienville's disastrous war against the Chickasaw Indians was costly in slave lives. Aside from those used as cannon fodder, many were conscripted to load and unload ships, to row the troops up river, and to build fortifications in remote, frontier areas. In April, 1736, 140 Africans, both slave and free, were enlisted for service in this war. Slaves were promised freedom for risking their lives. During the same month, another company of 45 armed blacks led by free black officers was formed. By 1739, Bienville was commanding 270 blacks, including 50 *nègres libres*.[26]

Despite the heavy toll that the war took on adult male slaves, *Ordonnateur* Salmon complained that his advice that more white colo-

24. June 5, 1729, in RSC, *LHQ*, IV (1921), 489; March 21, 1744, *ibid.*, XIII (1930), 120–23; March 15, 1745, *ibid.*, XIV (1931), 97; May 17, 1745, *ibid.*, 113.

25. Capital Sentence for Murder, New Orleans, October 1, 1723, *ibid.*, I (1917), 115; April 1, 1745, *ibid.*, XIV (1931), 99; Trial of Baraca, February 9, May 4, 1748, in RSC, LHC.

26. Roland C. McConnell, *Negro Troops of Antebellum Louisiana: A History of the Battalion of Free Men of Color* (Baton Rouge, 1968), 11–13.

nists should be sent to the front, sparing the blacks who were more valuable, was not followed. The military decided that they would get more service from blacks than from the white settlers. Bienville ordered thirty-five of the king's slaves to accompany the troops of the garrisons to help construct a fort on the St. Francis River. Salmon wrote, "They conscripted one-fifth of the colonists' *nègres*, which not only caused a great loss to the settlers, but can also be very costly to the King. There is no reason to doubt that some of these blacks will perish. I am convinced that they will be held until the end of the expedition, although M. de Bienville had promised that they would be returned as soon as the boats arrived at the entrepôt." [27]

The conscripted black laborers suffered heavy mortality because of overwork, mistreatment, and neglect. Those who survived were reportedly "greatly reduced in value because of fatigue." François Trepagnier reported that one slave returned in such poor condition that he had to be brought to the King's Hospital. One slave who was drafted into the army was kept in the city loading vessels, exposed to all prevalent diseases. He was then sent to Pointe Coupee, where he died without receiving medical attention. The surgeon reached him a few moments after his death. Another slave drafted for service in the Chickasaw Wars died and was buried at Pointe Coupee on his way back from the front. A slave of Dalcourt arrived at his master's estate hardly able to stand and died shortly thereafter of dysentery contracted at Fort St. François. Three more Dalcourt slaves died during the expedition, and another died at Natchez. Chaperon reported that his two *nègres* who had returned from the Chickasaw campaign were both ill with inflammation of the lungs. One of them was not expected to survive the twofold consequences of bad food and exhaustive floggings by the troops with whom he served. [28]

Some slaves were rented by private contractors to row up the Mississippi River to the Illinois country. The work was backbreaking and dangerous. When slaves were rented to go to the Illinois country to get flour, the master assumed responsibility for natural death only. [29]

27. Salmon to the Ministry of the Colonies, October 10, 1739, in Ser. C13A 24, fols. 168–69, ANC; Salmon to the Ministry of the Colonies (extract), September 3, 1739, *ibid.*, fol. 160.

28. Bienville and Salmon to the Ministry of the Colonies, June 24, 1740, in Ser. C13A 25, fol. 9, *ibid.*; RSC, *LHQ*, VII (1924), 515; August 15, 1739, RSC, *LHQ*, VII (1924), 359; December 3, 1739, RSC, *LHQ*, VII (1924), 514; October 19, 1739, RSC, *LHQ*, VII (1924), 359; April 13, 1740, RSC, *LHQ*, X (1927), 276; December 4, 1739, RSC, *LHQ*, VII (1924), 514; December 21, 1739, RSC, *LHQ*, VII (1924), 519–20.

29. See, for example, August 21, 1736, RSC, *LHQ*, VIII (1925), 490.

A slave named Jacob, hired to Bienvenu and Mathurin for a trip to Illinois, was abducted by the Indians. Mathurin was killed, but Bienvenu completed his trip.[30]

The birth rate among the slaves seems to have remained consistently high. In 1741, Salmon wrote that no new slaves had been introduced into the colony for the past twelve years and that the colonists saw with regret that their slaves were beginning to get old and were dying every day. He wrote: "This species survives almost entirely by procreation which has taken place. In effect, among the approximately 4,000 blacks of all types and ages, two-thirds are Creole. That is the difference between this country and the French West Indies islands where there is very little natural reproduction among slaves. It is certain that if a cargo of 250 black adult men and women would come here every year, little by little the result would be a very considerable quantity of slaves in few years."[31]

If we accept Salmon's figures, the slave population had increased from 3,600 to 4,000 between 1732 and 1741. But only 1,320 African slaves remained from the 5,790 Africans imported between 1719 and 1731. The slave population had fallen to 3,600 by 1732, a decline of 63 percent during the thirteen years since the trade began. But while the overall slave population increased between 1732 and 1741, there was a 37 percent decline among Africans during the same period. This population loss was surely due overwhelmingly to mortality, though an undeterminable number of Africans ran away and were not recaptured, and some slaves were freed. Few African slaves could have been exported from Louisiana. Aside from the fact that the export of slaves was illegal, the demand for slaves in the colony could best be described as desperate.

However, by 1741, 2,680 slaves were creoles: a young population, born in and acclimated to Louisiana, with an even sex ratio. By 1746, it was estimated that there were 4,730 black slaves in all of Louisiana. If we subtract the 190 slaves brought from Senegambia by Dubreuil and Dalcourt, we find a natural increase of 540 slaves. This is a credible figure, since these five years were exceptionally peaceful, encompassing the end of the Chickasaw Wars and the beginning of King George's War. Mortality was probably relatively low, and births relatively high. Although the white population had substantially increased by 1746, French settlements throughout Louisiana were esti-

30. December 26, 1739, *ibid.*, VII (1924), 520.
31. Salmon to the Ministry of the Colonies, New Orleans, April 25, 1741, in Ser. C13A 26, fols. 138–39, ANC.

mated to be predominantly black. New Orleans was overwhelmingly black.[32] Aside from the approximately 900 troops stationed in the colony and about 20 convict laborers at Balize, the population of the various settlements was estimated at 4,730 blacks and 3,200 whites. Table 8 shows a breakdown of the population at the individual settlements.

There are no censuses, not even estimated censuses, for the balance of French rule. Renewed warfare took its toll, once again, on the slave population. In 1748, as King George's War came to an end, Governor Vaudreuil reported that more than 300 blacks had died during the previous two years because of lack of woolen cloth and covers to protect them in bad weather.[33]

The stresses put on Louisiana's population by this war are revealed in a murder investigated by the Superior Council. In early 1748, as King George's War was coming to a close, a French soldier was murdered by a young slave in his early twenties. Under interrogation, the accused slave stated that he was named Charlot by Raquet, his master, and Kakaracou by his parents and the other blacks. Although he was a creole, he was not baptized, and he identified his nation as the Coneda. Both his parents were Raquet slaves. His father, Baptiste, squared lumber at the mill, and his mother, Marie, worked at the Raquet estate. He had six siblings—four sisters and two brothers—and all but two had been sold to neighboring planters by Raquet. One of his sisters had her ears cut for running away. Kakaracou was not liked by the other slaves because he was touchy. The least thing anyone said to him threw him into a rage, though he had never committed a crime before.[34]

It is clear from the testimony that this murder involved a struggle over food and hunting rights. The slaves had little to eat. Their lunch consisted of potatoes, which they roasted (*boucanner*) over a fire. The murdered soldier was known by the young slaves belonging to Dubreuil as Petit Fléchy ("little arrow"), and he hunted and fished every day to feed his mother. Fléchy met his end by hunting in the wrong place. The Raquet slaves had traps in the woods for catching starlings, which they stoned as they flew under the traps. Fléchy came into the Raquet woodlands and started shooting the birds in the traps. He had

32. Mémoire sur l'état de la Colonie de la Louisiane en 1746, in Ser. C13A 30, fols. 244–57, *ibid*. For a summary of population settlements, see fol. 256.

33. Vaudreuil to the Ministry of the Colonies, New Orleans, March 20, 1748, in Ser. C13A 32, fol. 32, *ibid*.

34. Investigation of the murder of Pierre Olivy dit Bonnevie, Testimony of Charlot dit Kakaracou, January 4, 8, 1748, in RCS, LHC.

Table 8. Population of French Settlements in Louisiana in 1746

Settlement	Number of Settlers[1]	Number of Blacks[2]
Balize	—	30
New Orleans	800	3,000
Des Allemands	100	200
Natchitoches	60	200
Natchez	8	15
Pointe Coupee	200	400
Arkansas	12	10
Illinois	300	600
Missouri	20	10
Petits Ouyas	40	5
Pascagoulas	10	60
Mobile	150	200
TOTAL	1,700	4,730

SOURCE: Mémoire sur l'etat de la Colonie de la Louisiane en 1746, in Ser. C13A 30, fols. 244–57. For a summary of population settlement by settlement, see fol. 256.

1. *Settlers* meant males only. French women and children throughout the settlements were estimated at 1500.
2. Men, women, and children were included in these figures.

recruited two young Dubreuil slaves to help him pick up the starlings. François dit Cupidon, a Raquet slave, yelled at him twice, saying, "Hey you, leave our traps alone. Why are you firing under our traps?" (*"Vu! laisser la notre trapes. Pourqoui tirer vois sous notre trapes?"*) The soldier replied, "Is it that they belong to you, not to M. Raquet?" (*"Ce que pour esta a toy ne ree pas a M. Raquet?"*) and continued to fire under their traps. The slaves went to lunch, and when they returned, they found the French soldier fatally wounded by stab wounds in several parts of his body. He asked them for water, but his mouth was so badly cut that he could not hold it. The slaves were afraid to touch him, and they called Baschemin, a white neighbor, to assist Fléchy. Baschemin testified that the slaves refused to help move him before the authorities arrived, "under the pretext, according to them, that these men must come see him first." Baschemin helped carry him on a door "for fear he might fall." Although the soldier said he was attacked by a young *nègre* whom he knew well, he expired before he could identify his assassin. Nevertheless, a knife was found at the scene of the crime that Laurent, Raquet's *commandeur*, identified as belonging to Kakaracou. The authorities found Kakaracou's bloody shirt and cloak, and he had wounds on his body. Kakaracou claimed that the blood came from animals he had caught and denied that the knife belonged to him, saying that neither he nor the other slaves ever owned knives (*"qu'il a pas encore gagner couteau depuis qu'il est dans le monde"*). But all the other slaves identified the knife as Kakaracou's.[35]

Although Kakaracou claimed that he had roasted potatoes in Pluton's cabin during lunch, Pluton had another story to tell. He said that Kakaracou had not dined with him and that Kakaracou's mother, who had cooked rice for him, kept calling him to come eat, but he was not there. Kakaracou arrived just as they were ready to return to the fields. Pluton said to him, "Where did you go while we were eating?" (*"Ou toy courir Charlot pendants que nous diner?"*). Charlot answered, "I was in the woods to see if there were any starlings taken from my traps." Noticing that Charlot's clothes were full of mud, Pluton asked him whom he had killed (*"Qui toy tuer, Charlot?"*). Charlot answered that he had not killed anyone (*"Moy na rien tué"*). Kakaracou's mother, noticing that he wore his shirt inside out, said to him, "Hey, fellow, why do you turn your shirt that way?" (*"Comment, Bougre, pourquoy tourner ton chemise comme ça?"*). Kakaracou did not answer.[36]

After they returned to the fields to plant peas, they found the dying Frenchman. Charlot did not go see him but turned his head from side to side and did not even make four strokes of the pickax at a time. Pluton told him several times, "What are you doing, work, then!" (*"Et quelle manière est cela, travaille donc!"*).[37]

Kakaracou finally confessed that it was he who killed the French soldier. He had several traps in the woods for wild cats and wood rats, which he evidently skinned and sold for cash. He went to see about his traps in the woods and encountered the Frenchman, whom he described as quite drunk. The Frenchman asked him to pick up the starlings with him. He refused, saying he was going to check on

35. Interrogation of Joseph, eighteen-year-old slave of Raquet, January 6, 1748, *ibid.*; Interrogation of Joseph, aged ten, and Claude, aged eleven, slaves of Dubrueil, January 4, 1748, *ibid.*; Interrogation of Baschemin Corbin, January 4, 1748, *ibid.*

36. Interrogation of Pluton, slave of Raquet, about fifty years old, of Devon nation, January 4, 1748, *ibid.*

37. *Ibid.*

his traps, and the Frenchman said to him, "OK, then go to hell!" He replied, "Why do you swear at me like that, sir." The little Frenchman answered, roughly translated, "Go to hell, you guy" ("*Va-ten foutu Bougre!*"). He moved against Kakaracou with his bayonet, cutting him under his left arm and saying, "You guy, if I see you again I'll shoot you with my gun" ("*Bougre, s'y je te revois je le tireray un Coup de fusil*"). Kakaracou replied, "Am I not on my land of my master?" ("*Est-ce je ne suis pas sur moy terrain à mon maître?*"). The Frenchman aimed his loaded musket at Kakaracou, who jumped on him, stabbing him. At the first blow, he dropped the gun. Kakaracou claimed that he acted in self-defense, but he clearly intended to kill his victim. He cut him in the stomach, on the left side, and on the throat. When the Frenchman bit Kakaracou's finger, Kakaracou said, "Will you let go of my finger, you are cutting my finger!" The Frenchman replied, "No, I will not let go, *bougre!*" And to make him let go, Kakaracou cut him in the face; to stop him from screaming, he cut him in the face again, leaving him for dead, though he was still moaning. Kakaracou was sentenced to have his arms and legs broken on the wheel in the public square of New Orleans and left facing the sun until he died. His body was to remain there for twenty-four hours. However, after receiving all the blows while living, it was ordered that he be secretly strangled.[38]

It is clear that the Raquet slaves had a strong sense of property, protecting their hunting grounds and their traps, which were located, as Kakaracou put it, "on my land of my master." Clearly, hunting was an essential means of supplementing their meager diet. But they also hunted to obtain cash for buying clothes and other goods. They operated in a money economy, and some of them accumulated significant amounts of property. A theft in the slave cabins of Jean Pugel, who lived opposite Cannes Bruslées near New Orleans, revealed that forty livres in treasury notes, oxhides, a mosquito screen made of coarse linen, shirts, a new cap, and a loincloth made of Limburg cloth were stolen.[39]

Despite overwork, exposure, and inadequate food, the slaves of French Louisiana managed to survive because they could supplement their food with hunting and fishing, and because the slave women of French Louisiana were quite fertile. Few slaves were imported after 1731. Slaves were never introduced into French Louisiana from the

38. Interrogation of Pierrot, Bambara slave of Belleisle, aged forty-five, January 12, 1748, *ibid.*; Interrogation of Charlot dit Kakaracou, January 8, 1748, *ibid.*; Sentence of Charlot dit Kakaracou, January 10, 1748, *ibid.* The version of this case in RSC, *LHQ,* XIX (1936), 211–28, and XX (1937), 486–90, is inadequate and inaccurate in places.

39. December 26, 1744, RSC, *LHQ,* XIII (1930), 329.

French West Indies in significant numbers. When the Company of the Indies ruled Louisiana, most ships came directly from France. We have seen that slave-trade ships from Africa to Louisiana stopped off in the islands for refreshment, but the demand for slaves there was so desperate that one "cargo" destined for Louisiana was seized and sold in the islands, and captains were forced to sell individual slaves in order to obtain supplies. While there was some trade in the 1720s between Louisiana and the French islands, mostly involving small craft, there were never any plans to import slaves from these islands. During the wars against the Natchez and the Chickasaw, the crown sent troop and supply ships directly from France to Louisiana. These ships stopped off in the French West Indies to pick up their return cargo to France, since few export staples could be found in Louisiana. A few small craft sailed between Louisiana and the French West Indies during the 1730s, but this traffic was fraught with difficulties. In 1735, Bienville and Salmon explained that Louisiana was not in condition to undertake trade voyages with the islands. The few trade voyages organized from Louisiana had poor results. There were few sailors (*gens de mer*) in Louisiana. Officials in St. Domingue had been informed that there was little hope that trade voyages to Louisiana would be organized from that island. There were few ships and little money, and the prices for sailors and for food supplies were high. The risks of the sea and the possibility of being seized by Spanish pirates also discouraged such voyages. In 1737, the king encouraged this trade by exempting goods carried between Louisiana and the French islands from customs duties for ten years. The same year, Bienville and Salmon reported that they feared that the inhabitants of the islands would abandon their trade with Louisiana in disgust, because the ship from Martinique heading for Mobile had been taken near Havana, and a ship from St. Domingue broke up on the coast of Louisiana at the Chandeleur Islands during its second voyage to Louisiana. The brigantine *la Heureuse Etoile* was carrying a cargo of mules, rice, and four Indian slaves, three females and one male, from Louisiana to Cap François in St. Domingue. It was seized by a Spanish coast guard ship and taken to Spanish Santo Domingo, where the ship and its cargo were confiscated. Dubreuil did, however, import two slaves from the French West Indies in 1739.[40]

40. Nancy M. Miller Surrey, *The Commerce of Louisiana During the French Regime, 1699–1763* (1916; rpr. New York, 1968), 371–73; Analyse d'une lettre de Bienville et Salmon au ministre, New Orleans, August 16, 1735, in Ser. C13A 20, fols. 53–54, ANC; Ministry to N. de Campigny and d'Orgeville, Versailles, March 25, 1737, in Ser. F3 24,

Serious obstacles were placed in the path of anyone wishing either to export slaves from the French islands to Louisiana or to emigrate from the French islands to Louisiana with their slaves. In 1741, Bienville and Salmon sent several enthused reports about two brothers-in-law from Martinique, Mercier and Tatin, who had come to Louisiana with nine or ten of their slaves. They bought a plantation, and one of them returned to Martinique to get their families and the rest of their slaves. They assured the Louisiana officials that over fifteen hundred small slave owners of Martinique who were being squeezed off their land would follow them. Two years later, Mercier and Tatin embarked for France to personally solicit the right to emigrate to Louisiana. In 1743, officials of Martinique allowed them to bring their families to Louisiana, but not their slaves. They ruled that no other Martinicans would be allowed to emigrate to Louisiana and that whatever efforts made to contribute to the establishment of Louisiana should not be at the expense of the French islands.[41]

Even in peacetime, when trade with the French islands increased, export of slaves from the French West Indies to Louisiana was, in practice, prohibited, except for individual slaves who were considered uncontrollable. In 1752, Louisiana officials were still trying to get permission for Martinicans to immigrate to Louisiana with their slaves. In reply to this initiative, an official at Martinique explained just where the shoe pinched. He absolutely opposed the export of slaves from Martinique and asked for a specific order prohibiting their export to Louisiana to back up what he was in fact practicing. However, he made an interesting exception to this ban:

> Allow me to observe that there is no inconvenience in permitting the sending of one or two slaves in each ship when permission is obtained. We have here many blacks who are bad characters: poisoners, flagrant maroons. We punish them as best we can but they are often incorrigible, and even more often, there is not enough proof to sentence them to death. Our prisons are full of this type of black who stays there for years and who serves no purpose except to spoil the others. . . . In Mississippi, the

---

fol. 298, AN; Bienville and Salmon to the Ministry of the Colonies, New Orleans, June 1, 1737, in Ser. C13A 22, fol. 39, ANC; Vaudreuil to the Ministry, February 1, 1752, in Ser. F3 24, fol. 464, AN; March 3, 1739, in RSC, *LHQ*, VI (1923), 302.

41. Bienville and Salmon to the Ministry of the Colonies, September 27, 1741, in Ser. C13A 26, fols. 29–30, ANC; Salmon to the Ministry of the Colonies, September 29, 1741, *ibid.*, fol. 168; Vaudreuil and Salmon to the Ministry of the Colonies, August 24, 1743, in Ser. C13A 28, fol. 28, *ibid.*; Vaudreuil and Le Normand to the Ministry of the Colonies, January 4, 1745, in Ser. C13A 29, fols. 5–10, *ibid.*

blacks are better controlled by their masters, and even more by their fear of the Indians and often correct themselves when they are removed from their country. It would be sad to forbid this recourse to the inhabitants of these islands.[42]

When the minister of the marine wrote, in 1708, that inhabitants of America in general, French as well as English, do not part with their blacks unless they know them to be "bad and vicious," he knew very well what he was talking about. Chronically ill slaves from the French islands were also sold in Louisiana. A Louisiana settler bought four slaves coming from the French islands. Two became ill at once, were nursed back to health, and were taken back by the vendor. One died of a lung disease, and before he died, he explained that his malady affected his entire nation and that he had been sold out of Martinique because of his illness. The settler complained that "the inhabitants of St. Domingue and Martinique . . . detach from the *nègres* and the workships but these to send them to be sold in this Colony. . . . Thus several small plantations have been ruined by buying several *nègres* who die shortly afterwards or become invalids and are but a burden. It is necessary to pass a ruling to prevent frequent surprises by the inhabitants of St. Domingue and Martinique on the *nègres* sent here." Furthermore, the settler had paid 3,300 livres, which in letters of exchange was worth 4,950 livres in Martinique.[43]

Although substantial numbers of new slaves came neither from Africa nor from the French islands, the slave population along the lower Mississippi River settlements from the mouth of the Mississippi River to Pointe Coupee increased nevertheless, from 3,630 in 1746 to 4,598 in 1763.[44] There was probably natural increase between 1748, when King George's War ended, and 1756, when the French and Indian War began to affect lower Louisiana. Thereafter, there was probably natural decline due to the hardships and shortages of war, compensated for by the introduction of new slaves by British traders during the last few years of French rule. But because of the poverty-stricken condition of many slave owners during these years, it is probably unlikely that more that a few hundred slaves were introduced by the British before 1763. Aside from the 190 slaves brought

42. Michel to the Ministry of the Colonies, September 23, 1752, in Ser. C13A 36, fols. 269–75, *ibid.*; Hurson to the Ministry, Martinique, September, 1752, in Collection Moreau de St.-Méry, Ser. F3 90, fols. 70–71, AN.

43. Résumé d'une lettre de Robert, November 26, 1708, in Ser. C13A 2, fol. 359, ANC; December 28–30, 1752, in RSC, *LHQ*, XXI (1938), 1251–52.

44. Antonio Acosta Rodríguez, *La población de la Luisiana española (1763–1803)* (Madrid, 1979), 31, 110.

from Senegambia in 1743, the small contingents of slaves brought in from the French West Indies mainly between 1748 and 1756, and several hundred slaves, almost surely Africans, brought in by British traders during the last years of the French and Indian War, the slave population survived because of the fertility of the women. The sexual imbalance must have evened out because of high mortality among male slaves during the Chickasaw Wars and because of the coming of age of the first generation creoles.

The fertility rate among slave women in French Louisiana was reasonably high. It is instructive to compare the child/woman ratios during the French period with child/woman ratios among African and creole slave women during the Spanish period. At the Pointe Coupee post between 1771 and 1802, African women had a child/woman ratio of 0.313, though it must be kept in mind that some of these women had recently arrived from Africa, where they were separated from their small children. However, the child/woman ratios on available inventories of most estates of French Louisiana compare favorably with the child/woman ratio of 0.665 among creole slave women of Pointe Coupee during the Spanish period.[45] Apparently, fertility was higher among slave women in French Louisiana than in Spanish Louisiana, despite the deprivations of frequent warfare and famine, and despite the fact that during the early decades, the mothers were overwhelmingly Africans. This contrast must be attributed to the scrupulous protection of the slave family during the French period and to the deterioration of the protection of the slave family under Spanish rule when the African slave trade revived.

During the last years of French rule, warfare and insecurity put pressure on the slave population. Nicolas Chauvin de Lafrenière, attorney general of Louisiana, was an elite creole and one of the most vehement opponents of the transfer to Spanish rule. He was accused of being one of the two major conspirators involved in the expulsion of the first Spanish governor, Antonio de Ulloa. Lafrenière was convicted and shot by a firing squad on October 25, 1769. On March 18, 1769, probably to prevent confiscation of the property, the Lafrenière estate, an indigo plantation at Chapitoulas, was sold to another Lafrenière, probably the accused's brother, for the modest sum of 10,000 livres. The sale included land, buildings, improvements, thirty-one slaves, and cattle. Further details of the inventory reflect a slave population under stress, despite an even sex ratio and a high birth rate. Both deaths and sales of slaves during the previous ten years were

45. Calculated from DB Inventories.

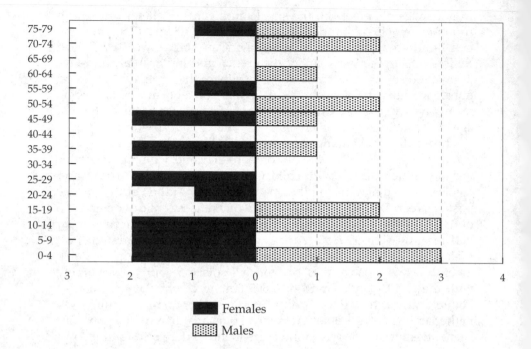

Figure 3. Slaves on the Lafrenière Estate by Age and Sex, 1769
SOURCE: Lafrenière to Lafrenière, March 18, 1769, in SJR, LHC.

recorded. Seven slaves had died in 1759, probably because of wartime shortages, and four had died between 1760 and 1769. Ten slaves under the age of eleven had been born since 1759. Six slaves were sold in 1760. Although the sex ratio was even, no children were inventoried apart from both parents, scrupulous attention was paid to the slave family, and the fertility rate was high (a child/woman ratio of 1.000), this population was at risk. Aside from the fact that there had been eleven deaths and ten births during the previous decade, and six slaves had been sold and none purchased, the skewed age structure among the inventoried slaves did not bode well for the plantation's future.[46] Deaths and sales had stripped the estate of mature

46. John Preston Moore, *Revolt in Louisiana: The Spanish Occupation, 1766–1770* (Baton Rouge, 1976), 40, 182, 208; Sale, Lafrenière to Lafrenière, March 18, 1769, in SJR, LHC.

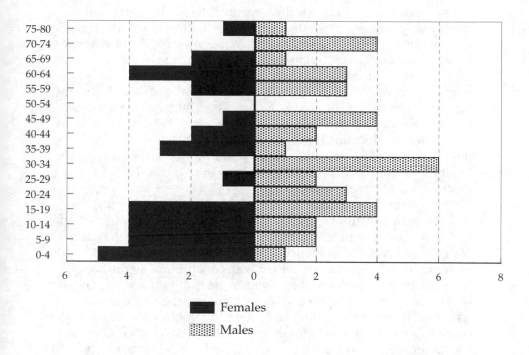

Figure 4. Slaves on the Prévost Estate by Age and Sex, 1769

Source: Calculated from Edith Dart Price and Heloise H. Cruzat, trans., "Inventory of the Estate of Jean Baptiste Prévost, Deceased Agent of the Company of the Indies, July 13, 1769," *LHQ,* IX (1926), 411–98.

adults. And while elderly men married to young women continued to father children, the life expectancy of the elderly slaves was not great, and deaths among the elderly could probably not be compensated for by births over the ensuing years.

The Prévost estate, an indigo plantation fronting Lake Borgne, south of New Orleans, was inventoried the same year. Jean Baptiste Prévost administered the affairs of the Company of the Indies in Louisiana. He was wealthy and secure. The Prévost estate contrasted sharply with the Lafrenière estate, though the age structure was also badly skewed. Rather than a normal, pyramid shape with large numbers of children at the bottom and a gradual decrease in numbers with advancing age, there were eighteen children under age fifteen, twenty-eight adults between the ages of fifteen and forty-four, and twenty-six over age forty-four.[47] Unlike the Lafrenière estate, the sex ratio on the Prévost estate was uneven: a sex ratio of 170, or 1.7 males for each female. Its age structure was a mirror image of the Lafrenière estate. Males outnumbered females, especially in the mature years. Mature men were undoubtedly purchased from planters in distress as well as from British slave traders. The child/woman ratio was 0.500—half that of the Lafrenière estate. The Prévost estate was geared for production, not procreation. It relied upon purchasing young men and did not stress fertility among women, a pattern that became generalized under Spanish rule when African slaves began to be imported in large numbers.

One of the most widespread, common organizing principles of West African societies is reverence for the elders stemming from ancestor worship—certainly a highly transportable cultural material. Many of the Africans in French Louisiana who survived the Atlantic slave trade and the deprivations of warfare and famine during their first few decades in the colony lived to be quite old. Both of these inventories reflect a high survival rate among the elderly, many of whom were married couples, all of them, with little doubt, old Africans. Evidently, only the strong survived the Atlantic crossing and the ravages of brutalizing labor, warfare, and hunger on the Louisiana frontier. These survivors lived long, productive lives. There were only three generations of slaves brought into Louisiana and born during the period of French rule. The presence of African parents and grandparents living on the same estate as their creole descendants throughout the French colonial period further Africanized Louisiana creole culture. African slaves had great power and influence over their children and grandchildren.

The strategic position of the old Africans is shown in these two slave inventories dating from 1769, six years after France abandoned Louisiana to Spain. In a population of thirty-one slaves on the Lafrenière estate, there were only six adults between the ages of fifteen and forty-five. Five of them were women, two of whom were married to much older men. There were twelve children under age fifteen and seven men and four women over age forty-five. A slave who was fifty years old in 1769 had been born in 1719, so we can safely assume that the eight slaves aged fifty and older were Africans. Barbier, the coach-

47. Edith Dart Price and Heloise H. Cruzat, trans., "Inventory of the Estate of Sieur Jean Baptiste Prévost, Deceased Agent of the Company of the Indies, July 13, 1769," *LHQ*, IX (1926), 411–98.

man, aged fifty, and his twenty-five-year-old wife were the parents of two children, aged two and ten. Grand Colas, aged fifty, and his wife, Diouguou, aged forty-five and probably also an African, were parents of five children, aged eighteen, ten, six, four, and two. Another daughter had died. Cesar, aged sixty, and his wife, Catherine, aged fifty-eight, had two daughters and six grandchildren on the estate. Monga, aged seventy-five, and Jelasie, his wife, aged seventy-five, had a thirty-five-year-old son who was single and lived on the estate. Boyau, aged seventy, and Fauchonette, his wife, aged twenty-five, had a ten-year-old son. But another of Boyau's sons, Yaco, was sold in 1759 along with Yaco's daughter, Marianne, and Marianne's daughter, Louise. Thus, Boyau married a fifteen-year-old girl and had a son by her the same year his son, granddaughter, and great-granddaughter were sold. All the fathers on this estate were Africans. Eight of the Lafrenière slaves lived on the same estate with both of their African parents, and six slaves with both of their African grandparents. Three small children had African fathers and much younger mothers, almost certainly creoles.[48]

The cultural impact of the Africans brought to Louisiana during the French slave trade is engraved upon the very structure of language as well as in the history of its use. The Louisiana creole language was created by the African slaves brought to Louisiana and by their creole children. It belongs to a special language group, the Atlantic Creoles, which are languages created by African slaves brought to the Americas. These languages are markedly similar in grammatical structure, in pronunciation, and in literal translations of African idioms, though the vocabulary is largely that of the language of the respective European colonizers. Morris F. Goodman's pioneering comparative study of French-based Creoles is historically oriented, suggesting that the study of the origin and development of these languages can best depart from a thorough investigation into the history of the slave trade, European colonization, and culture and language contacts. Such a study should give insight into how new languages develop and change. More recently, Derek Bickerton has minimized the importance of African language structures and forms of expression upon the creation of the Atlantic creole languages, claiming that the grammatical similarities found in these languages derive from universals, or linguistic bio-programs in the human brain. Bickerton's thesis has been effectively challenged by other specialists in sociolinguistics and

48. Lafrenière to Lafrenière, March 18, 1769, in SJR, LHC.

creolistics. John Holm has demonstrated the marked influence of African languages upon pronunciation and calquing—that is, the translation of idioms word for word from one language to another—as
well as upon grammatical structure that cannot be explained by
universals or bio-programs, concluding that these languages "arose
among speakers of partially similar African languages learning partially similar European languages under partially similar social conditions." The most convincing and exciting work in linguistics is coming from creolists who emphasize the importance of contact among
peoples who speak different languages, and therefore their studies of
the development of languages is rooted in the history of human contact, migration, and interaction.[49]

The vocabulary of Louisiana Creole is overwhelmingly French in
origin, but its grammatical structure is largely African. There has
been no systematic study of African words that survived in Louisiana
Creole, but some immediately come to mind. In the proverb *Bouki fait
Gombo, Lapin mangé li* (The stupid hyena makes the gumbo, the rabbit
eats it), *bouki* is a Wolof word meaning a loudmouthed, stupid hyena.
Bouki does not mean he-goat, though that is the way it has been translated from Louisiana creole folklore. *Gombo*, the word from which the
famous New Orleans seafood dish takes its name, means okra in
Bambara and in many other African languages. Although a number
of African words have survived in creole languages, this connection
has not been systematically studied, except in regard to Gullah and a
few other languages.[50]

Creolists believe that all creole languages were created during the
first two decades after the arrival of African slaves. The Suriname case
is instructive. Almost all the English had departed with their slaves
twenty years after they had founded the colony. Nevertheless, an
English-based creole language, Sranan, became the national language
of the Dutch colony of Suriname. It had to be created in those few
years during the first two decades of colonization when Dutch-owned
slaves overlapped English-owned slaves.[51]

---

49. Morris F. Goodman, *A Comparative Study of Creole French Dialects* (The Hague,
1964); Derek Bickerton, *The Roots of Language* (Ann Arbor, 1981); Holm, *Pidgins and
Creoles*, I, 217.

50. Daniel J. Crowley, *I Could Talk Old Story Good: Creativity in Bahamian Folklore*
(Berkeley, 1966), 29; Bickerton, *The Roots of Language*; Holm, *Pidgins and Creoles*, I,
61–68, 79–89, 218. For survival of African words in a creole language, see Lorenzo D.
Turner, *Africanisms in the Gullah Dialect* (1949; rpr. Ann Arbor, 1974).

51. Sidney W. Mintz and Richard Price, *An Anthropological Approach to the Afro-
American Past: A Caribbean Perspective* (Philadelphia, 1976), 25.

The Creole Slaves

The early creation of Louisiana Creole and its widespread use among whites as well as blacks up until World War II is strong evidence for the strength of the African ingredient in Louisiana creole culture. While the Sapir-Whorf hypothesis, which holds that there is no thought without language, that there is no limit to variability among languages, and that language absolutely determines thought, is now considered an exaggeration, there is no doubt that the impact of language upon thought is substantial. The widespread survival of Louisiana Creole until recent times and its use by whites of various social positions as well as by blacks and mixed-bloods had, no doubt, a great impact upon Africanizing Louisiana culture. The choice to speak a particular language and to adopt or retain speech patterns identified with a given social group is an act of cultural identity. Individuals both identify themselves and identify with others by the language they speak and their usage of speech patterns.[52] Members of language communities share grammar, the structure of language, and the symbols representing thought as well as objects. They share idioms, styles, and modes of communication, including rhythm, intonation, gestures, and vocabulary. The use of proverbs in speech, as well as their content, is crucial to socialization. Folk tales and song lyrics are, of course, communicated in a particular language, and their meanings cannot be adequately conveyed through translation. Louisiana Creole became a vital part of the identity not only of Afro-Creoles but also of many whites of all classes who, seduced by its rhythm, intonation, humor, and imagination, adopted it as their preferred means of communication. There are still a significant number of whites who are monolingual speakers of Louisiana Creole.

In most immigration situations, the children of the first generation help their parents communicate in the language of the new country. But the Atlantic creole languages were created partially by both generations, enhancing the power and influence of the Africans. Although sociolinguists have argued that slaves had to develop pidgin and creole languages in order to communicate among themselves as well as with the white dominant group, since "the slavers would break up tribal groups to minimize the risk of rebellion," the slave traders' and slave owners' ability and, at times, desire to fragment the African population is questionable.[53] Slave traders in Africa and slave

---

52. R. A. Hudson, *Sociolinguistics* (Cambridge, Eng., 1980), 96–105; R. B. Le Page and André Tabouret-Keller, *Acts of Identity: Creole-Based Approaches to Language and Ethnicity* (Cambridge, 1965), 5; Hudson, *Sociolinguistics*, 49, 74.

53. Hudson, *Sociolinguistics*, 64.

masters in the Americas were eager for slaves and could not always choose their nations. Furthermore, slave owners from various colonies had preferences for slaves of particular African nations.[54] It is probably fair to conclude that the primary purpose for creating Louisiana Creole was to enable the slaves to communicate with whites and the African slaves' children who spoke distinct African languages at home to communicate with each other, except for the relatively few African slaves who were torn away from their speech community in Africa and could not rediscover a significant number of speakers of their mother tongue in Louisiana. Once the language was created and widely spoken, the newly arriving African slaves were motivated to learn Louisiana Creole in order to communicate with the creole slaves, as well as with whites who spoke the language, though their motivation probably varied in accordance with whether or not there was a social and/or speech community in their mother tongue. Two people can constitute a speech community, but a social community implies large enough numbers to allow for at least a rudimentary social organization. An individual's motivation for learning a foreign language could vary sharply, depending upon the size and availability of a social community using his or her native language, the sociability of the person, the gifts the person had for learning languages, and his or her openness to people of other ethnic groups, languages, and cultures.

It has been established, through linguistic as well as historical evidence, that Louisiana Creole was created in Louisiana and was not derived from Haitian or other West Indian varieties of French-based Creoles. Ingrid Neumann, a German creolist, has recently argued, from linguistic evidence, that Louisiana Creole developed independently of the Creoles of the French West Indies. Neumann's interpretation coincides with the historical facts. We have seen that the slaves brought to Louisiana during the formative period of the language came directly from Africa, not from the French West Indies. For economic as well as legal reasons, the importation of slaves from the French islands was quite limited throughout the eighteenth century. And though there was probably smuggling and misrepresentation of the true origins of slaves, only 6 out of 2,632 slaves listed in Pointe Coupee slave inventories between 1771 and 1802 were creoles of the French West Indies.[55]

54. See Daniel C. Littlefield, *Rice and Slaves: Ethnicity and the Slave Trade in Colonial South Carolina* (Baton Rouge, 1981).
55. Ingrid Neumann, "Bemerkungen zur Genese des Kreolischen von Louisiana

Some creolists believe that the Atlantic Creoles derive from a Portuguese-based pidgin, or trading language, that developed in West Africa during the fifteenth and sixteenth centuries, when Portugal was the only European power engaged in the slave trade. A pidgin is a contact language with a limited vocabulary, allowing communication between two or more peoples speaking dissimilar languages. A pidgin is not the primary language spoken by any people. It becomes transformed into a Creole when a new generation expands its vocabulary and adopts it as its native tongue. According to this monogenesis theory, the original Portuguese-based pidgin was relexified—that is, English, French, and Dutch vocabularies were introduced into the existing pidgin at and around the trading posts and on the slave ships of the respective European nations. A number of facts lend credence to this theory. There is a substantial nautical vocabulary in the Atlantic Creoles, and some of the basic vocabulary of the Atlantic Creoles remains Portuguese. The mere existence of words of Portuguese origin does not prove that the Atlantic Creoles derive from a Portuguese-based pidgin, because contact, migration, and changes in control of colonies in and around the Caribbean could account for the introduction of Portuguese words or of Spanish words that are similar to Portuguese.[56] For the French-based Creoles in the West Indies, Spanish vocabulary that can be mistaken for Portuguese was no doubt introduced by the Island Carib, whose earliest contacts with Europeans were with the Spanish.

Louisiana Creole closely resembles Mauritius Creole, a French-based creole language created in Isle de France, an island in the Indian Ocean. Mauritius Creole exhibits "remarkable similarities shared by other varieties of American Creole French—notably that of Louisiana." A majority of West African slaves coming to Mauritius between December 31, 1730, and December 31, 1735, also came from Senegal/Gorée. Both of these creole languages probably derived from the same pidgin spoken in Senegal around the same time period. Little documentation of this pidgin has come to light. But we do have samples of the Louisiana Creole language at a very early stage of its formation that show survivals of a Portuguese pidgin. Du Pratz published several sentences in Louisiana Creole. Although he published

und seiner historischen Relation zum Kreolischen von Haiti," in *Akten des Essener Kolloquiums über "Kreolsprachen und Sprachkontakte,"* ed. Norbert Boretsky, Werner Enninger, and Thomas Stolz (26 vols.; Bochum, 1985), I. Information on creole slaves calculated from DB Inventories.

56. Holm, *Pidgins and Creoles*, I, 90–93.

his work in article form in 1751, 1752, and 1753 and in book form in 1758, he lived in Louisiana between 1718 and 1734. These quotations, therefore, had to date from before 1734 and are some of the earliest documented examples of any creole language. One sentence quoted from Samba Bambara was "*M. le Page li diable li sabai tout*" ("Mr. Le Page is a devil who knows everything"). The word *sabai* is core vocabulary pointing toward a Portuguese-based pidgin. It cannot be convincingly argued that there was Spanish or Portuguese influence upon the formation of the Louisiana Creole language during these early years. Samba Bambara had been an interpreter, a *maître de langue*, in both Senegal and Louisiana. The language he was quoted in was probably a Creole in formation from a Portuguese-based pidgin that had been relexified with French vocabulary in Senegal and then brought to Louisiana. Another quotation was "*Monsu, nègre Mian Mian boucou trabail boucou, quand Nègre tenire bon Maitre, Nègre veni bon.*" Du Pratz's translation into French was "*Monsieur, quand un Nègre est bien nourri, il travail bien; quand un Nègre a un bon Maître, le Nègre devient bon*" ("Sir, when a *Nègre* is fed well he works well; when *Nègre* has a good Master, *Nègre* becomes good").[57] *Nyam*, a word that means to eat, is found in many Niger-Congo languages and is believed to be derived from an early pidgin.[58] Maritime terms are found in the language: for example, *halé*, to haul, and *baille*, a large wooden bucket. Louisiana Creole evidently developed from a Portuguese-based pidgin that had been relexified with French vocabulary in Senegal. This pidgin was spoken by a number of African slaves brought to Louisiana between 1719 and 1731. The first generation of creole slaves adopted the language as its mother tongue, expanding and nativizing its vocabulary, including Indian terms for local fruits and plants. It was widely adopted by whites of all statuses.

Documentation exists of the widespread use of Louisiana Creole during the late eighteenth century. A trial of Mina slaves from the Pointe Coupee post, which began in 1792, shows that Creole was widely spoken by the slaves as well as by many whites, and that slaves recently arrived from Africa learned Louisiana Creole rather

57. Philip Baker and Chris Corne, *Isle de France Creole: Affinities and Origins* (Ann Arbor, 1982), 197, 198, 209; A. L. Boimare, "La Floride et l'ancienne Louisiane: Notes bibliographique et raisonnés," *LHQ,* I (1917), 42; Du Pratz, *Histoire de la Louisiane,* III, 304–17, published in article form in 1751–52 in *Journal Economique*. Du Pratz quoted another sentence spoken by Samba Bambara during his interrogation: "Who told you that?" (in Louisiana Creole, "*Qui cila qui dire cila à toi?*"). For Du Pratz's departure from Louisiana, see RSC, *LHQ,* V (1922), 255.

58. Holm, *Pidgins and Creoles,* I, 81.

than French or Spanish. The *comandante* of the post testified that the accused slaves had been interrogated in

> the Creole language which is a mixture of that of the blacks, and of French which is pronounced with great diversity. They do not understand either the real French language or English, but they all understand and can explain themselves perfectly well in Creole, which is a mixture . . . of the language of their nations and of French which is badly pronounced and even more badly conjugated, which language is not known by all the French and English settlers of the province, but I, the witnesses and the notary who assisted at the interrogation know it very well.[59]

This quotation clearly establishes that Louisiana Creole was well developed long before the massive immigration of Haitians to Louisiana after the outbreak of the Haitian Revolution, that newly arriving Africans learned Louisiana Creole rather than other languages, and that many whites, especially in the rural areas, spoke the language.

Louisiana Creole was widely spoken by all classes of whites in lower Louisiana up until World War II. Dr. Alfred Mercier, a native of New Orleans and a physician and writer, published in 1880 one of the earliest studies of any French-based creole language—a work that is still respected. He also published an enlightened novel containing much dialogue in Louisiana Creole. *Le Carillon*, organ of the White League of Louisiana, published satirical verse in Louisiana Creole in 1884 and 1885. Alcée Fortier published six Compair Bouki and Compair Lapin tales, as well as a most remarkable creation myth including the original, Louisiana Creole version of the famous Tar Baby folktale, *Piti Bonhomme Godron.*[60]

Although Fortier went to great lengths to trace these stories to medieval France, their Senegambian origins are clear. The creation myth conveys a reverence for all forms of life. God had ordered the animals not to destroy or eat each other but to eat only grass and fruits. "That was better, because they were all his creatures and it pained him when they killed each other; but as quickly as they would eat the grass and fruits, He, God, would take pleasure to make them grow

59. Testimony of Valentin Leblanc, *comandante* of the Pointe Coupee post, April 30, 1792, in Leg. 169-A, fols. 401–502, PC, AGI. Leblanc's testimony was recorded in Spanish, though he must have spoken in French.

60. Alfred Mercier, *Etude sur la langue créole en Louisiane*, Comptes rendus de l'Athenée louisianais, I (New Orleans, 1880); Alfred Mercier, *l'Habitation Saint-Ibars ou maîtres et esclaves en Louisiane: Récit Social* (New Orleans, 1881); Domínguez, *White by Definition*, 139; Alcée Fortier, "Bits of Louisiana Folklore," *Transactions of the Modern Language Association of America*, III (1887), 100–68.

again to please them." But the animals refused to obey. The lions ate the sheep, the dogs ate the rabbits, the serpents ate the little birds, the cats ate rats, the owls ate the chickens. To stop them from destroying themselves and to punish their cruelty, God sent a great drought. Although drought was a severe problem in Senegambia, which bordered the Sahara Desert, drought was never a problem in Louisiana. On the contrary, the biblical flood would have been more appropriate. The Bouki and Lapin tales are populated by lions and elephants. Mande folk literature includes the rabbit and the hyena stories.[61] Stories about the astute, resourceful rabbit who triumphs over the stronger but loudmouthed and stupid hyena, who retained his Wolof name, were no doubt brought by slaves coming from Senegambia. The Brer Rabbit tales collected by Joel Chandler Harris were Anglicized versions of these Louisiana Creole folktales of Senegambian origin.

Louisiana Creole, the language of the blacks, and the folklore in this language were widely known and cherished by creoles of all colors and classes. Louisiana Creole became the preferred means of communication among Louisiana's elite white creoles. It came to be looked upon by many of them as their true native language. Lyle Saxon and Robert Tallant wrote, "Mammy's influence was so great and so much of her time was spent with her children that most young [white] Creoles grew up speaking the language." But the language was by no means confined to blacks and elite whites. James F. Broussard, writing in 1942, reported that Louisiana Creole was spoken by a large black population in South Louisiana, by many whites who learned it in childhood from their nurses, and "by others who have adopted it as the language of their community." He had heard it spoken by groups of whites on the streets of St. Martinville, Breaux Bridge, New Roads, and other towns in southern Louisiana. "It is not uncommon . . . for the older educated Louisianians to return to the language of their childhood when in reminiscent moods." Broussard had learned the language from his nurse as a child and spoke it exclusively until he was seven years old. "Because of its naive simplicity, its inherent melody, its soothing rhythm, this dialect has expressed the sweetest memories of my childhood. It is particularly dear to me. It should prove of interest to scholars who like to see what a simple,

61. Fortier, "Bits of Louisiana Folklore," 138; Charles S. Bird, "The Development of Mandekan (Manding): A Study of the Role of Extra-linguistic Factors in Linguistic Change," in *Language and History in Africa*, ed. David Dalby (New York, 1970), 155.

emotional, and highly imaginative race can fabricate out of a cultured language to serve as a medium for their thoughts."[62]

It was customary for elite whites to speak Louisiana Creole even in the drawing rooms at times, for it was "far more native to Louisiana than French could ever be, and more flexible, being capable of turns and twists impossible in French." Until the late nineteenth century, upper-class white creoles spoke it exclusively until they were ten or twelve years old. Children had to be weaned from speaking the language with bribes and punishments. Louisiana Creole is still spoken by tens of thousands of people, white as well as black, in some parts of the state. Sometimes called "black French," "broken-down French," "Gumbo French," or "mo kuri mo vini," it is presently spoken by about sixty thousand to eighty thousand persons: by fifty thousand to sixty thousand blacks and by ten thousand to twenty thousand whites. It is impossible to arrive at more exact figures, because many whites are bilingual speakers of Creole and Cajun and are reluctant to admit to an investigator that they speak "nigger French." It is the native language of many whites, several thousand of whom are still monolingual speakers of Louisiana Creole.[63] In contrast, the Gullah dialect, an English-based creole language, survived in the isolated Sea Islands off the coast of South Carolina and Georgia and probably was never spoken by significant numbers of blacks or whites on the mainland.

Broussard concluded that Louisiana Creole was created by Senegalese blacks. He wrote that the plantation owners of the Bayou Teche country—St. Martin Parish in South Louisiana—"possessed a large number of slaves of dominant Senegalese blood. The Senegalese negroes were preferred to those from the Congo because of their tractability and superior intelligence." Broussard traced the master class of the Bayou Teche country to the "better class from Martinique and Guadeloupe and Creoles from New Orleans." Although his history was flawed, Broussard's linguistic conclusions are correct. Few Senegalese slaves could have come from the French islands. Gabriel Debien and his colleagues studied inventory lists of slaves from the

62. Fortier, "Bits of Louisiana Folklore"; James F. Broussard, *Louisiana Creole Dialect* (Baton Rouge, 1942), viii–ix.

63. Lyle Saxon, Edward Dreyer, and Robert Tallant, *Gumbo Ya-Ya* (Boston, 1945), 147; Henry Edward Krehbiel, *Afro-American Folksongs: A Study in Racial and National Music* (1913; rpr. New York, 1962), 38, 39, 71; Broussard, *Louisiana Creole Dialect*, viii–x; Ingrid Neumann, *Le créole de Breaux Bridge, Louisiane: Etude morphosyntaxique* (Hamburg, 1985), 20–22.

French West Indies. These lists, dating mainly from the late eighteenth century, show few slaves from Senegal. Debien wrote: "In the Antilles, where the 'Senegalese,' and particularly the Wolofs were never numerous, the Bambara were considered the best of the Africans. They were rare, no doubt because they were already half Islamized and they came from regions very far from the coast, the middle Niger. They were highly prized."[64]

Bambara and other Mande languages, as well as most West African languages, are tonal.[65] Rhythm as well as tonality not only determine the meaning of individual words but also play an important role in grammar. Functional tonality has been identified in a few creole languages. It is possible that the musicality of Louisiana Creole, which seduced generations of Louisianians and probably affected their own speech in Cajun and English as well as in French, is a nonfunctional survival of tonality in African languages. One of the ways in which musicality is expressed in Louisiana Creole is through onomatopoeia—through words that imitate sound. For example, in Louisiana Creole, a bullfrog is called a *ouaouaron;* the gabbling of birds is *zabotter;* a violin player is a *trouloulou;* a bird is a *zozo,* from the French word *oiseau,* but *zozo* also imitates the sound of the bird. Patterns of rhythm and tonality in Louisiana Creole might be linked to patterns of musical expression, including syncopation and jazz. It is surprising that linguists have paid relatively little attention to the study of rhythm and intonation in creole languages. Louisiana, which has been part of the United States for almost two hundred years, remains a trilingual state, where Louisiana Creole, Cajun, and English are all spoken. There is a linguistic continuum, in which Creole blends into Cajun, which in turn is becoming Anglicized.[66]

Some songs have survived in African languages. Slave hunters were common in eighteenth-century Louisiana. Aside from those slaves who had an official role as hunter, many slaves had to supplement their meager rations with game. The maroons, of course, had to

64. Broussard, *Louisiana Creole Dialect,* viii–x; Gabriel Debien, "Les origines des esclaves aux Antilles," *Bulletin de l'Institut français d'Afrique Noir,* Series B, XXIII (1961), 376, and Debien, "Les origines des esclaves aux Antilles: Conclusion," *Bulletin de l'Institut français d'Afrique Noir,* Series B, XXIX (1967), 548–49.

65. Charles S. Bird, John Hutchinson, and Mamadou Kanté, *An Ka Bamanankan Kalan: Beginning Bambara* (Bloomington, Ind., 1977); Charles Bailleul dit Nco Kulubali, *Cours pratique de Bambara* (Bobo-Dioulasso, Burkina Faso, 1977); Mervyn C. Alleyne, *Comparative Afro-American* (Ann Arbor, 1980). Wolof, however, is not a tonal language.

66. Holm, *Pidgins and Creoles,* I, 137–43; Neumann, *Créole de Breaux Bridge.* For a recent, detailed bibliography of Louisiana Creole, see Larbi Oukado, *Louisiana French: An Annotated Linguistic Bibliography* (Lafayette, La., 1979).

survive to a great extent through hunting and fishing. During the late nineteenth century, a hunting song in an unidentified African language was still being sung by freedmen in Louisiana. The song was possibly a ritual to control the *nyama* from the slain animals. These former slaves supplied the music and lyrics as well as a translation.

> Day zab, day zab, day koo-noo wi wi,
> Day zab, day zab, day koo-noo wi wi,
> Koo-noo wi wi wi wi Koo-noo wi wi wi wi mom-zah.
> Mom-zah, mom-zah, mom-zah, mom-zah,
> Rozah ro-zah, ro zah a-a mom-zah.

> Out from under the trees,
> Our boat moves into the open water,
> Bring us large game and small game.[67]

Proverbs often play a decisive role in preserving culture and tradition among mobile peoples. Such is the case in Senegambia, for example, among the Fulbe, who are nomadic herdsmen.[68] In Louisiana, the proverbs were, of course, creolized in language and content. Lafcadio Hearn collected proverbs in several French-based creole languages, including Louisiana Creole, but since his work was done during Victorian times, he left out "some . . . because of their naive indecency." The considerable body of folktales collected in Louisiana Creole suffers from the same prudish distortion. Louisiana Creole slave songs were secular, not religious. Love was a favorite theme.

> Ah! Suzette, Suzette to veux pas chère?
> Ah, Suzette, Chère amie, to pas l'aimin moin.
> M'allé dans montagne, zamie,
> M'allé coupé canne, chère amie,
> M'allé fait l'argent, mo trésor,
> Pour porter donné toi.

> Ah! Suzette, Suzette, to veux pas chère?
> Ah, Suzette, Chère aime, to pas l'aimin moin.
> Mo couri dans bois, zamie,
> Mo toué zozo, chère amie,
> Mo fé plain l'argent, mo trésor,
> Pou porter donné toi.

> Suzette, you do not love me,
> Ah! Suzette, why do you not love me?
> I will go to the bush, dear one,

67. Krehbiel, *Afro-American Folksongs*, 151–53.
68. Adamou Issa and Roger Labutut, *Sagesse de Peuls nomades* (Yaoundé, Camaroon, 1973). The Fulbe were called Poulard in Louisiana.

I will go cut cane, dear friend,
I will make money, beloved,
And bring it all to you.

Suzette, you do not love me,
Ah! Suzette, why do you not love me?
I went to the woods, dear one,
I killed some birds, beloved,
I made much money, sweetheart,
And brought it all to you.[69]

The Creole songs were bitingly satirical, taking particular pleasure in cutting down the high and the mighty. The pretentiousness of the mulattoes was a favorite theme. One song was directed against the Toucoutou family, which was attempting to pass for white.

Tou-cou-tou,
Yé con-nin vous,
Vous est ein Morico!
Na pas sa-von,
Qui as-sez blanc,
Pou blan-chez to la-po.
Au thé-atre mêm,
Quand vous prends loge,
Comme tou Blancs-comme yé fait,
Yé va fait vous prend Jac-de-loge,
N'a pas pas-sé tanto.
Tou-cou-tou,
Yé con-nin vous,
Vous est ein Morico!
Na pas sa-von,
Qui as-sez blanc,
Pou blan-chez to la-po.

Tou-cou-tou,
They know you,
You are a black-a-moor!
There is no soap,
White enough,
To bleach your skin.
Even at the theatre,
When you take a loge,
As white as you look,
They will make you go to the balcony,

69. Lafcadio Hearn, *Gombo Zhêbes: Little Dictionary of Creole Proverb* (1885; rpr. New York, 1960), 4; Emilie Le Jeune, "Creole Folk Songs," *LHQ*, II (1919), 454–62.

You haven't passed that much.
Tou-cou-tou,
They know you,
You are a black-a-moor!
There is no soap,
White enough,
To bleach your skin.[70]

As in other traditionalist Afro-American societies—for example, the descendants of the maroons of Suriname—the collective historical memory was communicated and passed down in song. Historical events were a crucial theme in Creole slave songs. In Louisiana, too, the Creole slave songs commented upon real events, and song was the vehicle through which the historical memory was transmitted from generation to generation. Hearn explained, "However artless and childish these Creole songs seem, they are invariably originated by some real incident." George Washington Cable commented on "the clownish flippancy with which the great events are sung, upon whose issue from time to time the fate of the whole land—society, government, the fireside, the lives of thousands—hung in agonies of suspense."[71]

The creole slaves were not enthused about being used for cannon fodder in wars in which they felt that they had no stake. Their loyalty was severely tested by the British invasion of Louisiana in 1815, since the British had promised the slaves freedom in return for their support. A Creole slave song about the Battle of New Orleans well expresses this sentiment:

Fizi z'Anglé yé fé bim! bim!
Carabin Kaintock yé fé zim! zim!
Mo di moin, sauvé to la peau!
Mo zété corps au bord de l'eau;
Quand mo rivé li té fé clair.
Madam' li prend' ein coup d'colère;
Li fé donn' moin ein quat' piquié
Passequé mo pas sivi mouchié;
Mais moin, mo vo mié quat' piquié
Passé ein coup d'fizi z'Anglé.

70. This song was composed by Joseph Beaumont, a free colored composer born in New Orleans in 1820. Roussève, *The Negro in Louisiana*, 66. The song and its translation can be found in Nickerson, "Afro-Creole Music in Louisiana," Supplement.

71. Richard Price, *First Time: The Historical Vision of an Afro-American People* (Baltimore, 1983); Krehbiel, *Afro-American Folksongs*, 24n, 25n, 135; Cable quoted in Christian, "For a Black History of Louisiana."

The English muskets went bim! bim!
Kentucky rifles went zim! zim!
I said to myself, save your skin!
I scampered along the water's edge;
When I got back it was daybreak.
Mistress flew into a rage;
She had me whipped at the "four stakes"
Because I did not follow my master;
But for me, the "four stakes" is better than
A musket shot from an Englishman.[72]

How do we account for the great resiliency of the Afro-Creole culture of Louisiana and its broad impact upon people of all classes and colors? Its creativity, intelligence, biting wit, joyfulness, musicality, poetic strain, and reverence for beauty make this culture inherently attractive. But what is most important is its powerful, universalist trend. Senegambia had long been a crossroads of the world, where peoples and cultures were amalgamated in the crucible of warfare and in the rise and fall of far-flung, trading empires. An essential feature of the cultural materials brought from Senegambia, as well as from other parts of Africa, was a willingness to add and incorporate useful aspects of new cultures encountered. This attitude was highly functional in a dangerous and chaotic world. New Orleans became another crossroads where the river, the bayous, and the sea were open roads, where various nations ruled but the folk continued to reign. They turned inhospitable swamplands into a refuge for the independent, the defiant, and the creative "unimportant" people who tore down barriers of language and culture among peoples throughout the world and continue to sing to them of joy and the triumph of the human spirit.

72. George Washington Cable, *Creoles and Cajuns: Stories of Old Louisiana*, ed. Arlin Turner (New York, 1959), 420–21.

Bas du Fleuve: The Creole Slaves Adapt to the Cypress Swamp

Pitis sans popa, pitis sans moman,
Qui ça 'ou' zut' fé pou' gagnein l'a'zanc,
No courri l'aut' bord pou' cercé patt c'at'
No tournein bayou pou' péç'é patassa;
Et v'là comm ça no té fé nou' l'a'zanc.

Pitis sans popa, pitis sans moman,
Qui 'ça 'ou' zaut' fé pou' gagnein l'a'zanc,
No courri dans bois fouillé latanié
No vend' so racin' pou' fou"bi' planç'é;
Et v'lá comm ça no té fe'nou' l'a'zanc.

Pitis sans popa, pitis sans moman,
Qui ça 'ou' zut' fé pou' gagnein l'a'zanc,
Pou' fé di thé n'a fouillé sassaf'as,
Pou' fé di l'enc' no po'té grain sougras;
Et v'lá comm ça no té fe'nou' l'a'zanc.

Pitis sans popa, pitis sans moman,
Qui ça 'ou' zut' fé pou' gagnein l'a'zanc,
No courri dans bois ramassé cancos;
Avé nou' la caze no trappé zozos;
Et v'lá comm ça no té fe'nou' l'a'zanc.

Pitis sans popa, pitis sans moman,
Qui ça 'ou' zut' fé pou' gagnein l'a'zanc,
No courri à soir c'ez Mom'selle Maroto,
Dans la rie St. Ann ou no té zoue' loto;
Et v'lá comm ça no té fe'nou' l'a'zanc.

Little ones without father,
Little ones without mother,
What do you do to earn money?
The river we cross for wild berries to search;
We follow the bayou a'fishing for perch
And that's how we earn money.

Little ones without father,
Little ones without mother,
What do you do to earn money?
Palmetto we dig from the swamp's bristling
   stores
And sell its stout roots for scrubbing the floors;
And that's how we earn money.

Little ones without father,
Little ones without mother,
What do you do to earn money?
For making tea we collect sassafras,
For making ink, we collect pokeberries,
And that's how we earn money.

Little ones without father,
Little ones without mother,
What do you do to earn money?
We go to the woods cancos berries to fetch;
And in our trap cages the birds we catch;
And that's how we earn money.

Little ones without father,
Little ones without mother,
What do you do to earn money?
At evening we visit Mom'selle Maroto,
In St. Ann's Street to gamble at keno;
And that's how we earn money.

—from George Washington Cable, *Creoles and Cajuns:
Stories of Old Louisiana*

Notes: In stanza 1, l. 2, *l'a'zanc* means money in Creole, from *l'argent* in French. I have altered Cable's translation from "How do you keep body and soul together?" to the literal meaning, "What do you do to earn money?" Cable was under the false impression that the creole slaves did not operate in a money economy and therefore changed the literal meaning of the song to conform with his mistaken impression. On l. 3, *patt c'at'* means, literally, "cat paws," a delicious little blue swamp berry. On l. 4, *patassa* is Creole for *perch*. In stanza 2, l. 3, *latanié* refers to dwarf palmetto, the roots of which were used as a scrubbing brush. In stanza 3, l. 4, *grain sougras* is Creole for pokeberries. In stanza 4, *cancos* is the Indian name for a wild purple berry, and *zozos* is from *oiseaux* in French.

The French settlements of lower Louisiana were located along the Mississippi River and some of the larger bayous that empty into it. The slave owners' lands stretched back from the waterways indeterminate distances, trailing off into cypress swamps and woodlands. Back from the waterfront, within and beyond the property lines of the French settlers, were the cypress swamps—*la ciprière*—often the most reliable source of wealth. The lands on and behind the estates afforded excellent, nearby refuge to runaway slaves. The geographic environment of lower Louisiana made it possible for slaves to move freely along its luxuriant waterways and to hide out in the cypress swamps. Much plantation activity centered on the *ciprière*, where slaves went largely unsupervised. Neither masters nor overseers were eager to follow the slaves into the swamps. Laws and regulations passed to keep slaves on their owners' plantations, isolate them from contact with slaves from other plantations, and keep them disarmed were futile. Slaves and maroons from various plantations met regularly in the *ciprière*. Huts were built, with secret paths leading to them. A network of cabins of runaway slaves arose behind plantations all along the rivers and bayous. Arms and ammunition were stored in the cabins.

Cypress does not rot under even the most humid conditions. With the revival of indigo production at mid-century, there was a demand for cypress logs for constructing buildings, for making masts and planking for ships and large vats and troughs for indigo production, and for exporting to the French West Indies. During the interval of peace between 1748 and 1756, the cypress industry flourished. In 1753, a visitor from Martinique wrote, "There are valuable cypress forests from which immense revenues are derived. Some plantations have a sawmill which once started with ten or twelve slaves will result in a net revenue of ten to twelve thousand livres per year. . . . Some of the cypress logs are monstrous and have to be hauled overland by the strength of arms, three or four pair of horses dragging them."[1]

The growth of the cypress industry led to a new form of *marronage*. Families of creole slaves adapted to the ecology of the swamp by founding permanent settlements. These slaves were usually well

1. [Clement Rondes] to [?], Martinique, *ca.* April 11, 1753, signature blurred and torn, in RSC, LHC.

armed, as were most runaway slaves in Louisiana. Although some of the maroons continued to raid plantations and kill cattle, there was a move toward production and trade for economic survival. They cultivated corn, squash, and rice and gathered and ground herbs for food. They made baskets, sifters, and other articles woven from willow and reeds. They carved indigo vats and troughs from cypress wood. And, as the above Creole slave song tells us, they gathered berries, dwarf palmetto roots, and sassafras, trapped birds, hunted and fished, and went to New Orleans to trade and to gamble. Although the maroons were denounced as brigands and murderers, their violence was almost entirely defensive. The danger they posed to the colony was more profound. They surrounded the plantations. Slaves remaining with their masters were in constant contact with them. Slaves would leave, or threaten to leave, if their masters or overseers tried to impose discipline on them. They did not have far to go, and they found old, familiar faces: family and friends who preceded them. The maroon communities that developed during the last half of the eighteenth century consisted almost entirely of creole slaves, though large numbers of Africans were brought in under Spanish rule. The runaways left in families, and there were a substantial number of women and children among them. They did not distance themselves from the plantations and towns; they surrounded them.

Runaway slaves hid out for weeks, months, and even years on or behind their masters' estates without being detected or apprehended. M. Macarty of Cannes Bruleés charged that fourteen of his *nègres* were guilty of running away, conspiracy, and rebellion. Each slave was interrogated separately in an effort to pinpoint an instigator. Eleven other slaves had left the plantation without permission of Joseph Verret, Macarty's overseer. Verret testified that on December 16, 1763, the slaves appeared late for work. He had warned them previously about their "laziness," and hence on this particular morning, he ordered them to be flogged. The next morning when they were called for work they refused to respond, and all of them were flogged again. Once outside their cabins they continued their mutiny, and they were flogged again. The next day they ran away and returned on January 10, nearly a month later. The overseer did not know who had been the instigator, but both Laurent Samba and Dautat were suspected.[2]

2. Testimony of Macarty's slaves in the following paragraphs is taken from January 1–28, 1764, RSC, LHC.

In their testimony, the slaves exhibited a strong sense of justice and solidarity as well as an awareness of their rights under the Code Noir, which prohibited the whipping of slaves with a stick or any hard object. Several of the creole slaves denied they were runaways, because they remained on their master's property, in his *ciprière*. None of the twelve slaves interrogated tried to throw the blame on any one of his fellow slaves. Samba, forty years old and a Catholic who had been accused of being the instigator, testified that they "ran away because we had been unjustly beaten. Bois Gras was the first to suggest flight when we returned from work, saying, 'What have we done for someone to beat us like that? We should not put up with such bad treatment,' and when he said that, all of us, truly, decided to run away."

Gabriel, a forty-year-old Mina, testified that one morning there was a heavy freeze. Breakfast was not ready, and they had to go to work without eating. "When we arrived at the fence, [the overseer] made us cut a whip made from a branch of a *goyou*, and beat all of us with it until we were nearly dead. We went on working until all of us determined truly to run away without any one of us proposing it first. We ate corn and potatoes which we brought with us, and alligators. We had no weapons."

Mathurin, a twenty-three-year-old creole, testified that they all received ten blows, not with a switch, but with a branch cut from a tree. When they returned from work, they all decided to run away. According to Antoine, a thirty-year-old creole, they were beaten because they wanted to make a fire to warm themselves, and the overseer "fell upon us with great blows of a branch which he cut from a tree with an ax. We all decided together to go maroon without any one of us having made the proposition." Nicolas, a twenty-year-old creole, testified, "All agreed together to go maroon." François, a twenty-five-year-old creole, said in his testimony that they were not maroons because they stayed in their master's *ciprière*. They had all decided to leave together. Appolon, a thirty-year-old creole, said they were hit with a big tree branch (*une grande perche*). Cézard, a fifty-year-old slave "from Guinea" told the same story. They all denied that they had killed a cow that was missing, establishing that a slave from another estate had killed it. They said they lived on potatoes, corn, and alligators. Runaways could often count upon help from the slaves remaining on the estates. For example, Luis, an escaped mulatto slave, had maintained himself on his master's plantation with the help of "the other *nègres* with whom he was in communication. No one feared M. Laveau who managed the place, and the whereabouts of Luis was known to all the *nègres* who hide him and protect him and because of this luck he has been able to live during the ten months that he has been away from his Madame."[3] This testimony reveals the slaves' adaptation to the cypress swamp, their awareness of their rights under the Code Noir, and solidarity among slaves who were blacks and mulattoes, creoles and Africans.

By the time the American Revolution was drawing to a close, the maroons of Louisiana had asserted their control over a strategically vital part of Louisiana: Bas du Fleuve, the area between the mouth of the Mississippi River and New Orleans. New Orleans is located between the Mississippi River and Lake Pontchartrain. Lake Pontchartrain leads past Lake Borgne into the Gulf of Mexico. Although oceangoing vessels came up the Mississippi River, the voyage past the ever-shifting sandbars at its mouth and then up the river was long and uncertain. The route through Lake Pontchartrain to the Gulf of Mexico was a vital alternate shipping route. Lake Borgne empties into the Rigolets, a narrow body of water between Lake Pontchartrain and the Gulf of Mexico. Lake Borgne means one-eyed lake. The reason for its name is clear: The rear of the lake trailed off into trackless swamps, marshes, and bayous. The Mississippi River swings eastward at English Turn, leaving a fairly narrow area consisting almost entirely of tidal wetlands between Lake Borgne and the Mississippi River. During the French period, a canal had been built connecting Bayou Barataria to the Mississippi River near English Turn. This point on the Mississippi River was always fortified, because any military force that controlled the territory between Lake Borgne and the Mississippi River could cut off all shipping to and from New Orleans.

Bas du Fleuve had an old, deeply rooted, heavily creole slave population. From the earliest years of African presence in Louisiana, there was a heavy concentration of black slaves along the east bank of the Mississippi River below New Orleans. The 1731 census counted 838 black slaves in Bas du Fleuve, including 237 children. There were 66 white men, 36 white women, 75 white children, 17 engagés (indentured servants), and 19 Indian slaves, or 4.32 blacks to each white and, including Indian slaves, 4.42 slaves to each free person. When Spain took over Louisiana and carried out a census in 1763, Bas du Fleuve contained 1,476 slaves: 32.1 percent of the slaves of lower Louisiana, and the largest number of slaves by far at any post. There were 4.56 slaves for every free person. By 1777, there were 2,484 slaves in Bas du Fleuve. Bas du Fleuve had the fastest-growing slave population of any post and had greatly outstripped Chapitoulas in propor-

3. October 30, 1777, in SJR, LHQ, XII (1929), 694.

Table 9. Slave Distribution and Proportion of Slave to Free at Posts in Lower Louisiana in 1763

Post	Number of Slaves	Percent of All Slaves	Proportion of Slave/Free
Bas du Fleuve	1,476	32.1	4.56
New Orleans	1,135	24.6	0.88
Chapitoulas	939	20.4	5.33
Pointe Coupee	610	13.2	1.40
German Coast	438	9.5	0.54

SOURCE: Antonio Acosta Rodríguez, *La poblacion de la Luisiana española (1763–1803)* (Madrid, 1979), 110, 112, 117.

Table 10. Changes in Slave Populations and Proportion of Slave to Free at Two Posts

Post	Year	Number of Slaves	Proportion of Slave/Free
Bas du Fleuve	1763	1,476	4.56
	1766	1,607	3.04
	1777	2,484	4.46
Chapitoulas	1763	939	5.33
	1766	962	5.37
	1777	1,259	2.58

SOURCE: See source for Table 9.

tion of slave to free. It had a much lower sex ratio among the adult slaves than did Chapitoulas, the post with the next largest number and concentration of slaves, indicating a higher level of creolization in Bas du Fleuve.[4] Thus, Bas du Fleuve had the largest, the oldest, and the most creolized slave population in Louisiana, and it was located very strategically.

4. Population figures for Bas du Fleuve in 1731 calculated from Charles R. Maduell, Jr., *The Census Tables for the French Colony of Louisiana from 1699 Through 1732* (Baltimore, 1972), 114, 115; Antonio Acosta Rodríguez, *La población de la Luisiana española (1763–1803)* (Madrid, 1979), 110, 112, 117.

Table 11. Sex Ratio Among Slaves of Different Age Groups in Bas du Fleuve and Chapitoulas in 1777

Age	At Bas du Fleuve	At Chapitoulas
0–14	106[1]	101
15–49	132	167
50 and over	149	181
TOTAL	127	216

SOURCE: See source for Table 9, but pages 55, 124.

1. These numbers represent sex ratios—that is, there were 106 males per 100 females in this age group at Bas du Fleuve.

By the early 1780s, the Spanish authorities were made aware of a higher level of organization among the maroons of Bas du Fleuve. The maroons living in the *ciprière* maintained a symbiotic relationship with sawmill owners. They cut and squared cypress logs, dragged them to the sawmills, and were paid for each log delivered. In April, 1781, Pedro de San Martin arrived at the plantation of his neighbor, Macarty, at the invitation of the latter. Macarty had captured and arrested a runaway slave belonging to San Martin. San Martin and Macarty took the prisoner back to the place where Macarty had caught him. They followed a path that led to a cabin of an old *nègre*, whom they described as a slave or free *nègre* of their neighbor, Bonne. There they found a number of maroons' huts near the canal that brought water to Bonne's mill, and a field planted with squash. They found a small, hidden pathway made of dried, woven palmetto leaves that crackled underfoot when stepped on. After following this pathway a short distance, they heard several voices. Since there were only two of them and there were many escaped slaves, they decided to ask Bonne for help. Bonne and his overseer each took a musket and returned with them to the hidden path, but the noise of their footsteps alerted the maroons. It was already dark, and all the maroons easily escaped.[5]

The next morning, the slave owners returned, accompanied by one of San Martin's slaves, by Alejandro, a schoolteacher, and by Cazelar,

5. Information in subsequent paragraphs about San Martin, Bonne, and the maroons is taken from May 26–27, 1781, in SJR, LHC.

a neighbor who was missing several of his slaves. Following farther along the same path, they found another cabin, which the *nègres* had deserted and burned, leaving behind some dishes and skins that they could not carry away with them. The search party returned to Bonne's sawmill, and in the presence of Bonne's brother, they remarked that Bonne's slaves must be keeping the maroons informed.

"What!" said Bonne's brother. "How dare you accuse me of having connection with *nègres marons!*" The schoolteacher Alejandro replied that he had not accused him, but he thought that Bonne's slaves must have known the maroons were there, because there was a field of squash planted near the cabin inhabited by the old Bonne *nègre*, and the maroons' huts were nearby. Bonne's brother replied that he himself had planted the squash, to which Alejandro replied, "If you planted them, you must have had your eyes closed if you did not see the maroons' cabins nearby."

Bonne threatened to go to New Orleans to charge San Martin with slander but instead sent San Martin a message to meet him on the levee in front of his house. San Martin asked Bonne why he was insulting him and threatening him, and Bonne replied that it was true that he had "let fly some words of contempt" because he was told that San Martin was declaring publicly that Bonne was employing *nègres marons* in his lumber operations. San Martin said he did not start the rumor but was only repeating what he had heard others say. He agreed to say no more about it, and the dispute was settled.

A few weeks later, Juan Bienvenu, captain of the urban militia of New Orleans, was missing a cow. He sent a party of his slaves armed with three guns and sticks to search the wilderness (*a batir el monte*).[6] According to Bienvenu, his slaves encountered two *nègres*, whom they knew to be maroons, behind the plantation of the king near Bienvenu's property. The slaves asked the *nègres* if they had seen Captain Bienvenu's cow. Although the *nègres* claimed that they knew nothing about the cow and that they had no meat, they were seized and brought to Bienvenu's house.

One of these maroons was named Juan Bautista, a slave of St. Amant. He had run away to the woods behind the Duparc plantation with two other slaves of his master, the *nègre* Tham and the *négresse* Margarita. They took from their master a barrel of rice, a musket with "enough powder," and a knife for hunting. They were joined by Pedro and Zéphir, slaves of the merchant Tournoir of Pointe Coupee.

6. *El monte*, or *the bush*, means any inaccessible place.

Zéphir had a knife but no other arms. They had a fish hook with which they caught fish and turtles.

Juan Bautista and Pedro had left the others five weeks earlier because, they claimed, they could not stand the company of the other maroons. Pedro explained that they had departed after seeing the damage the maroons did to the inhabitants of the neighborhood by robbing them. The Bienvenu slaves who had captured them "knew their whereabouts" and would probably have continued to leave them undisturbed if it had not been for the theft of Bienvenu's cow. They denied that they had seen the cow or that they had any meat, stating that it must have been some other maroons who took the cow. They were taken to Bienvenu's house, and after being questioned further, they said that the maroons who had their huts in the marsh behind Sieur Raquet's land must have taken the cow. Juan Bautista was put into irons, and Pedro was enlisted to lead the way to the huts they had referred to.

The search party consisted of San Martin and his son, Bienvenu and six of his armed slaves, two white overseers, and Pedro, the maroon who had been captured the night before. On Sunday, May 27, 1781, at nine o'clock in the morning, they approached a cabin, trying not to make noise, but their footsteps on the dried reeds and palmetto branches on the pathway alerted the maroons. There were three *nègres* and three *négresses* in the cabin. All the *nègres* fled. San Martin told them to halt, but they continued to run. He told them to halt again, and then fired at one of them, hitting him in the back, but he continued to flee. San Martin explained that he could not pursue the *nègres* because he had a bad knee from falling down among the thick reeds in which the maroons hid.

An ax, a knife, a file, and a German bayonet like those of Waldec's soldiers disarmed by Quesada during Bernardo de Gálvez' recent campaign against the British, were found in the cabin. No guns were found. Nancy, Margarita, and María Juana, the three *négresses*, were captured. Smoked beef and a cowhide from the cow that had been stolen from Bienvenu were found in the cabin. The captives informed the raiding party that other maroons' cabins were located near Raquet's *ciprière*.

Margarita, escaped slave of St. Amant, was asked if a cow skin and the remains of a cow were found in her hut. She said those things were found, but not in her hut. They were found in the cabin of Nancy and María Juana; her hut was elsewhere. Two or three days before her capture, Margarita had come to stay with the two other *négresses* after insisting to her *galan* Tham that she could not stand being so alone way back in the woods.[7] Nancy had told her then that the cow belonged to Bienvenu.

Nancy, a thirty-six-year-old escaped slave of De Kernion, spoke only English, and an interpreter had to be used for her interrogation. She claimed that not three but four *nègres* made their escape: Tham of St. Amant, Samba of Duparc, Zéphir of Tournoir, and another named Nicolas or Colas, the name of whose master she did not know. She admitted the cow belonged to Bienvenu and claimed that Zéphir killed it with an ax. She denied hearing anything about cutting or squaring wood, but she said that Tham and Pedro had money. The *nègres* left in the morning and returned in the evening. She never saw any guns, but they had knives. She knew nothing about the rest of the maroons.

María Juana, slave of San Martin, said that Samba and Zéphir brought the cow, killed it, and divided it up among them. While on Raquet's plantation, they lived on a little corn that Samba went to look for at a nearby plantation, but while they were behind Bonne's plantation, they lived and maintained themselves with the money that Bonne gave them for the work the *nègres* did in *el monte* for him—that is, squaring pieces of wood for his sawmill and dragging the logs out of *el monte*. After the logs were in Bonne's canal, the *nègres marons* brought them to dry land, where they were met by a cart that brought the logs to Bonne's sawmill. María Juana said she heard he paid Pedro, Tham, and Zéphir two reales for each piece. One day, she heard the other *nègres* say that they were going to Bonne's plantation. She became frightened and said, "How can you who are maroons go to the plantations of the whites?" They replied, "We are going there because we work for M. Bonne."

Captain Bienvenu questioned Pedro and Juan Bautista to find out if they worked in the woods preparing lumber for Bonne's mill and were paid by Bonne for their work, saying that he heard a rumor that Bonne procured, brought, and retained maroons to be used at his own place. Both maroons affirmed the rumor, saying that they received one and a half reales for each piece of squared timber. San Martin testified that it had been generally known that Bonne employed fugitive slaves around his sawmill and that he had been told this by a runaway slave of De Reggio, the alcalde of New Orleans. However, when Bienvenu testified and was asked if he had heard

7. *Galan* means a spruce, well-made man who is a wooer or lover.

that Bonne was using maroons to profit from their labor, he replied that this was the general belief, but he did "not wish to inquire about the details of a matter which might reflect upon the conduct of a good and reputable man."

Zéphir, a twenty-five-year-old slave of Tournoir, had been a maroon for a year. He had been captured in the slave cabins of De Reggio, where he had sought "a few ears of corn" after escaping from the patrol. Zéphir identified eighteen maroons belonging to twelve different masters in two separate camps behind Bonne's plantation, all of them apparently Louisiana creoles except for Nancy, who spoke English, and one Congo slave. There were four women and one fifteen-year-old girl.

Zéphir tried to throw the blame for killing Bienvenu's cow on Joseph, slave of De Reggio, whom he also tried to blame for a massive theft that had taken place on March 20 at the plantation of M. Canöe. This was no mere pilferage of supplies. Missing were half a case of sugar, a barrel of salt, a large earthenware jar of bacon, about a hundred bottles of wine, two large soup dishes, twenty sifters, a large churn for making lard, two oxen, and six pregnant cows. Zéphir claimed he knew that Joseph broke into the storehouse of his master's next-door neighbor and took all those items except for the animals, which he did not know anything about but which he thought Joseph might have killed during the time he was a maroon. Asked what he and his maroon comrades did for a living while they were behind Bonne's plantation, Zéphir testified:

> Like the rest of the *nègres* maroons, my comrades, I occupied myself in *el monte* making pieces of wood and bringing them down M. Bonne's canal to his water mill. After we received from him the agreed stipend, we divided it up in accordance with the work which each of us performed. We also cultivated a piece of land which he indicated, sowing it with some corn and vegetables during our leisure time, with the knowledge and consent of M. Bonne. We were also in touch with M. Bonne's slaves, giving them baskets, sifters and other items which we wove from willow which they brought to the city to sell, and in return for their value and price, they brought us the provisions we ordered. We stayed in the rear of Bonne's plantation for about three months, until we were pursued by several expeditions led by Cavalier Macarty. M. Bonne advised us through his slaves that we should take refuge behind the plantation of M. Raquet in the passage called the Bayou of the Canes.

When asked if there was a *pasaje* behind De Reggio's plantation, he replied that he did not know, since he had not been there except when he went to find something to eat and was captured. *Pasaje* meant an escape route or maroon settlement behind the various plantations. They were named after the plantation owner: for example, the *pasaje* of Bonne, or the *pasaje* of Raquet. The term was appropriate, because these maroon "passages" linked plantation slaves and maroons in a network of mutual intelligence and support. The plantations of lower Louisiana were encircled by an autonomous base of operations where runaway slaves acted as independent contractors for their labor and their agricultural and craft products. The maroon communities in the swamps of lower Louisiana, especially those near New Orleans, had become an extension of creole slave society, where the creole slaves openly asserted their control over their lives, their families, their property, and their territory.

The Spanish authorities were concerned that the maroons had formed several bands of considerable numbers in various places in *el monte*, especially in Bas du Fleuve at a place the maroons called Gaillardeland, far from the settlers' cultivated lands. Gaillardeland was a vast, uncharted territory in what is now St. Bernard Parish.[8] The paths to Gaillardeland were unknown and almost impracticable and inaccessible. Both the syndic of the Cabildo of New Orleans and Governor Miró feared the establishment of a permanent settlement of maroons, as had occurred in Jamaica. Miró explained that the land the maroons had settled could be defended by five hundred men against any number. It could only be entered through Lake Borgne, which had so many narrow branches that only one pirogue at a time could pass. These branches led to high ground, called Terre aux Boeufs, where the runaway slaves planted corn. Miró wrote, "It is a most propitious land for the maintenance of human life because of sweet potatoes, because of the great abundance of forest products, of much fish and shell fish, and abundant wildlife."[9]

The maroons of Bas du Fleuve were led by St. Maló, a charismatic leader from the German Coast. He was known as Juan Maló when he was a d'Arensbourg slave.[10] He and his followers controlled the swamps below New Orleans between the Mississippi River and Lake Borgne, moving freely along the bayous connecting the lake with higher ground to the south. St. Maló had established several permanent settlements. One was named Ville Gaillarde; another, Chef

8. *Gaillard* means strong, healthy, free, adept, and clever.
9. Miró to Gálvez, July 31, 1784, Miró to Espeleta, July 1, 1784, both in Leg. 3A, Docs. 638, 639, PC, AGI.
10. D'Arensbourg was the leader of the German community located several miles above New Orleans.

Menteur.[11] Runaway slaves were attracted to St. Maló's settlements from the various maroon *pasajes* behind the plantations. A spy sent to infiltrate these maroons reported that as St. Maló returned to Gaillardeland at the beginning of April, 1784, he buried his ax into the first tree he encountered, saying, "'*Malheur au blanc qui passera ces bornes*' ['Woe to the white who would pass this boundary'], to which his companions gave a shout of approbation."[12]

The name St. Maló is interesting. *Malo* means bad in Spanish. It could also derive from the name of the French port St. Malo. However, in the Spanish documents, the accent is placed on the last syllable. *Malo* means shame in Bambara and refers to the charismatic leader who defies the social order, whose special powers and means to act may have beneficial consequences for all his people when social conventions paralyze others. St. Maló had a wide following. He attracted and won the loyalty of creole slaves who remained with their masters, as well as that of the maroons from the various *pasajes* behind the plantations. Spanish officials believed, with good reason, that there were few slaves in the colony who were not directly or indirectly accomplices of St. Maló. The prosecutor reported that masters were obliged to suffer in silence because at the slightest reproof, slaves would threaten to join the runaways. He also reported that their lands were being left uncultivated because of lack of labor. St. Maló's hiding place, which had to be approached by wading through reeds and water up to the chest, defied entry by the smallest canoe.[13]

In 1782, as the war with England was drawing to a close, Spain authorized any nation to import slaves into Louisiana duty free, and African slaves began to pour into the colony in large numbers. Slave control became a high priority. The authorities began to raid the maroon settlements in Bas du Fleuve. The colored militia was ordered to root out the maroons, but their raids were fruitless. In 1782, Captain Bautista Hugon and a detachment of twenty native-born troops were sent in search of the maroons. They were led into an ambush by four

11. According to Charles Gayarré, Chef Menteur was named for a Choctaw chief who was exiled from the tribe for lying and who retired there with his family and a few adherents (Charles Gayarré, *History of Louisiana* [4 vols.; 1854–66; rpr. Baton Rouge, 1974], I, 351).

12. Miró to Gálvez, July 31, 1784, Miró to Espeleta, July 1, 1784, both in Leg. 3A, Docs. 638, 639, PC, AGI.

13. Charles S. Bird and Martha B. Kendall, "The Mande Hero," in *Explorations in African Systems of Thought*, ed. Ivan Karp and Charles S. Bird (Bloomington, Ind., 1980), 13–26; Maude Caroline Burson, *The Stewardship of Don Esteban Miró, 1782–1792* (New Orleans, 1940), 114, 115, 155n.

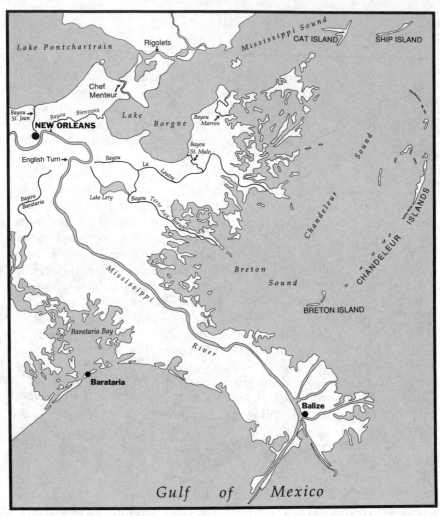

Location of St. Maló Maroon Communities, 1780s

Map by John Snead

maroons who had offered to guide them to St. Maló's hiding place. One of the militiamen was killed, and several were wounded. White troops were no more successful. The maroons captured Don Carlos de Villiers, lieutenant of the Company of the 1st Battalion.[14]

In early 1783, Chacala, a slave of Madame Mandeville, guided a military expedition to Ville Gaillarde in return for his freedom and two hundred pesos. On March 1, 1783, Don Guido Dufossat, second lieutenant of the Fixed Infantry Regiment of Louisiana, informed acting governor Miró that he left the capital commanding a number of blacks and free mulattoes to search for some fugitive slaves. They killed one maroon and captured twenty-three. The raiding party used seven pirogues, some commanded by whites with crews of free blacks, mulattoes, and some slaves. The party arrived at Lake Borgne. They landed and walked into the woods, where they found groups of blacks who began to move their baggage as soon as they saw the expedition. The raiding party tried to surround the blacks, but they fled. The order was given to fire. The discharge killed one black. Twelve maroons were captured, including Juan Luis, slave of de Reggio. Ten escaped and could not be overtaken. Chacala guided the expedition to Ville Gaillarde, where they found eight more maroons. One was seized and the rest surrendered. The captives were bound and placed in the pirogues.[15]

Patricio Macnamara testified that he commanded a pirogue in which there were seven men, blacks and mulattoes, three of whom were free, three of whom were his slaves, and one of whom was a slave belonging to another person. They headed back to New Orleans with some of the captured maroons. They were about three-quarters of a league away from the other pirogues when a small pirogue with four maroons drew up about ten paces from them. Two gunshots were discharged from the little pirogue. The first shot killed de Reggio's Juan Luis, one of the prisoners. Scipion, another captured maroon, was wounded in a finger on his right hand. Macnamara fired upon his pursuers, wounding Jasmin, one of the four attacking maroons. Jasmin fell into the water, overturning the little pirogue. The other three maroons fell into the bayou, losing their guns. All four swam toward Macnamara's pirogue. Macnamara assumed that the

14. Roland C. McConnell, *Negro Troops of Antebellum Louisiana: A History of the Battalion of Free Men of Color* (Baton Rouge, 1968), 22, 23; September 27, 1782, in Acts, Vol. II, 136–37; May 28, 1784, in Acts, Vol. II, 209.

15. Information and testimony about St. Maló, the raiding party, and Ville Gaillarde in this and subsequent paragraphs are taken from March 1, December 23, 1783, August 7, October 25, November 10, 1784, all in SJR, LHC, unless otherwise indicated.

maroons intended to get into his pirogue and surrender, but they all grabbed Macnamara's pirogue on the same side. One of them shouted to the rest, "Use force." They tried to capsize Macnamara's pirogue but failed. The crew members rained blows on the maroons, and they were obliged to let go. One fled. The rest of them tried to capsize the pirogue again, without success. One of the attacking maroons, Esteban, was drowned when his skull was smashed with the butt end of a gun. The rest headed for the shore, and the raiding party pursued them. Two were captured, and one escaped. The one who escaped was St. Maló.

Alejandro, a fifteen-year-old fugitive who had been gone for a year and had surrendered voluntarily, testified that he had seen St. Maló and the three other maroons in the boat. They said they were going to free the prisoners. The two captives, Carlos and Jasmin, testified that they had both been fugitives for about two months. A curator was named for Carlos because he was under age twenty-five. He was a twenty-two-year-old native of Guinea who had been living in one of the maroon cabins in the *ciprière* behind M. Chabert's plantation. When asked about his occupation, Jasmin, the other captive, replied that he squared timber for a sawmill. He had been with ten or twelve other maroons behind Madame Bienvenu's plantation. The night before the encounter with Macnamara's pirogue, St. Maló returned from New Orleans with the news that the free mulattoes were forming an expedition to search for them. The maroons were heading for Ville Gaillarde to look for their wives and their baggage when they met the pirogue commanded by Macnamara. They all had guns and other weapons in the pirogue. St. Maló and Esteban fired simultaneously.

Jasmin was asked where he got his ammunition. He replied that he had brought some of it with him from his master's plantation. The rest he had bought on the plaza in New Orleans, but he did not remember the name of the person who had sold it to him. When asked why the maroons walk about armed with gun, hatchet, and knife, he replied, "We maroons never walk about without arms, in case we should pass some house on the road, and besides, since we are fugitives, we have no other way to live except by eating the things we kill. Then, too, we cannot leave our guns exposed in the *ciprière*, because they would be stolen."

The widow of Domingo St. Amant petitioned that Carlos and Jasmin, her slaves, be declared free of the crime imputed to them. She claimed that only St. Maló fired on Macnamara's pirogue; the others had grasped the boat to stop from drowning. If we can judge by the two thousand pesos paid de Reggio for the appraised value of his slave Juan Luis killed in Macnamara's pirogue, the two hundred pesos normally due the masters of executed slaves was only a small fraction of their value. Madame St. Amant's slaves were found guilty and sentenced to three hundred lashes and sent into exile thirty-three leagues from the city. St. Amant and Belleville each got the usual two hundred pesos for their dead slaves, and Chacala got two hundred pesos for "risking his life by telling where the *pasaje* was." Chacala was freed.[16]

The most detailed picture we have of St. Maló is contained in the testimony of Juan Pedro, one of the maroons arrested at Ville Gaillarde during the March 1, 1783, raid. Juan Pedro had been a fugitive for three years and had associated with St. Maló for about a year and a half. He identified several slaves who sold him ammunition and a free mulatto who sold him a musket. Other slaves gave him ammunition, but he claimed he never used it. He testified that Bernoudy's slave Alejandro supplied St. Maló many times with the munitions he needed in exchange for large tubs, troughs, and other merchandise that St. Maló made. St. Maló always went out to get the powder they needed.

On one occasion, Juan Pedro, his wife, María, their son Joli Coeur, and St. Maló went by boat to Bay St. Louis on the coast of the Gulf of Mexico. Each of them had a gun. They encountered a party of Americans who tricked them into coming ashore by offering to meet them to exchange guns. When they met, the Americans shot Juan Pedro in the neck, seized all of them except St. Maló, and took all their guns. The Americans bound them, put them in a pirogue, and headed toward New Orleans. When the Americans stopped and went on shore, leaving one person to guard their prisoners, St. Maló appeared and untied their bonds. He gave them the guns, which were unloaded, and took a hatchet and a carbine belonging to one of the Americans who had gone ashore. Joli Coeur snatched the hatchet and broke the American's head with it, killing him. They fled with the pirogues and baggage of their captors and went to Chef Menteur, where they stayed three months while Juan Pedro's wound healed. After he had recovered somewhat, St. Maló left him, but he returned many times to his cabin to visit him.

St. Maló moved around freely. He lived at Chef Menteur, but he frequently visited Ville Gaillarde, where he had built a cabin. He had gone to the German Coast to look for someone and apparently re-

16. March 14, 1783, in Acts, Vol. II, 163–64.

turned too late to stop the impending raid (on March 1, 1783), after he received news of it. Juan Pedro said St. Maló told him they had killed four Englishmen who had left the Conoy plantation loaded with provisions for Pensacola and Mobile, taking possession of a gun, which he gave to Michel, another major maroon leader.

The testimony of the maroons captured on the March 1, 1783, raid reveals strong family ties among them. Entire families fled together. Apparently, Ville Gaillarde was the haven for the wives and children of the maroons. Goton testified that she ran away because her master punished her. She was a fugitive for about two months. No one induced her to run away. She left of her own free will with her husband, Huberto, her son Cupidon, her daughter, Catiche, and her little son Bautista, all Henrique Desprez' slaves. They hid behind their master's plantation for two months, eating rice and meat. They had taken the rice with them, but the meat was supplied by other fugitives her husband met in the woods. She identified these other fugitives as four slaves belonging to three different masters.

They left the bayou and went to Ville Gaillarde, where there already were houses in which to live.[17] Goton said she met several other fugitives along the way, all heading for Ville Gaillarde, and they joined her. Two of them were women. One was La Violette, who was killed by a gunshot when Ville Gaillarde was attacked. Goton testified that there were eleven people living in Ville Gaillarde, and she identified Joli Coeur and Juan Pedro as the leaders. There were many new and old cabins that were occupied in common. The maroons ate the root of an herb called China-smilax, which they pounded into flour and cooked.

The strength of family ties was revealed in the testimony of Theresa. She was Goton's daughter-in-law. Theresa ran away because she wished to go to her husband, Cupidon. Both of them belonged to Henrique Desprez. Before they went to Ville Gaillarde, they lived in the fields and woods of their master's plantation, eating rice and corn they received or had carried away with them. She testified that there were about six of her master's slaves and many others living at Ville Gaillarde. Theresa gave herself up when she saw a fugitive, who she thought was her husband, being killed by the whites.

17. Porteus mistranslated this passage. Her version reads, "It is true they left the Bayou to go to the said land because it was there that they had built their cabins to house themselves." The Spanish version says, "en ella tenían ya sus cabañas fabricadas para alojarse," which means that the houses were *already* built and waiting for them to occupy. The significance is, of course, that Ville Gaillarde was a permanent settlement to which maroons were invited to come (SJR, *LHQ*, XX [1937], 846).

Catiche, daughter of Goton, was captured at Ville Gaillarde. She testified that she ran away because her mother and stepfather were running away. They stayed in the woods behind their master's plantation, eating what they brought with them, as well as some ducks and birds they caught. At Ville Gaillarde, they ate roots and herbs, powdered and cooked. Here we have one family, all Desprez slaves, consisting of mother, stepfather, son, daughter-in-law, daughter, and small child, who either ran away together or followed each other. They were six out of eleven or twelve slaves the witnesses claimed were living at Ville Gaillarde.

The testimony of María reveals another family network involved in flight, all of them living at Ville Gaillarde. Again, the flight was precipitated by the master punishing the wife. She was accompanied by her husband, Juan Pedro, and her son, Joli Coeur, both of them leaders of the maroons, and Pelagie, her daughter. Juan Pedro testified that he had been gone for three years. It is unclear whether he left first and came back for his family or if they all left together. Before going to Ville Gaillarde, they wandered about in the woods, living by stealing provisions from the plantations in the surrounding neighborhood. After they moved to Ville Gaillarde, Juan Pedro went to the city at night with fish to sell, and he used the money to buy powder and balls and other things they needed. When arrested, María was with Juan Pedro and her children, fishing in the bayou near Ville Gaillarde.

Juan Pedro testified that he ran away because his master punished his wife and threatened to do the same to him. The first year he went to the lakeshore and ate four barrels of corn that he raised himself, supplemented by whatever he could steal from the plantations. The second year was passed raising provisions at Ville Gaillarde, and the third year he worked on Madame Mandeville's land for a *nègre* slave named Colas who was the son of Chacala, the Mandeville slave who had led the raiding party to Ville Gaillarde. Perhaps Chacala was able to discover the location of Ville Gaillarde because Juan Pedro worked for his son, and Chacala profited from this information to gain his freedom and a monetary reward. Juan Pedro testified that when he left his master's plantation, he took a horn full of powder and that when he was working with Madame Mandeville's slave Colas, the latter supplied him with half a pound of powder, a pound of munitions, and five or six balls.

Here was another family of four living at Ville Gaillarde. Since the maroons who attacked the Macnamara pirogue were going to Ville Gaillarde to look for their wives, a woman maroon named La Violette was killed there, and Goton testified that she was joined by a group of maroons heading for Ville Gaillarde whose names she could not remember except for the woman who was killed, the witnesses were obviously protecting the maroons still at large by undercounting the population there. The existence of many houses, old and new, that were occupied in common lends further credence to the conclusion that Ville Gaillarde was more populated than the captured maroons indicated. It was an established settlement in 1783, and a growing one.

The strength of the family ties among Afro-Creoles, slave and free, black and mixed-blood, was recognized by the syndic of the Cabildo of New Orleans. Their experience with the militia of free blacks and mixed-bloods made officials reluctant to use them against the maroons. He pointed out that both blacks and mixed-bloods of free status, including members of the militia, not only engaged in commerce with the maroons "but even favor them and supply them all they need for their defense." The Spanish officials also discovered from "criminals whom we have apprehended that most of the maroons are creoles of this province" whose kinship networks extended into New Orleans and other settlements. Their family ties were so strong and their kinship groupings so numerous that free blacks and coloreds were afraid that the relatives of the maroons they might capture or kill would seek vengeance and retaliate against them. Thus, the expeditions by the free black and colored militia had proved to be useless.

The syndic, distrusting the blacks and mulattoes, suggested that as many soldiers of the regular army as possible be sent against the maroons to accompany the militia and the free blacks. In an ordinance dated May 1, 1784, Governor Miró proclaimed that the free blacks and mulattoes of the colony would be held especially responsible for all damages that the public suffered if they had information about the maroons and had not communicated it to the authorities, or if they did not assist in rooting out the maroons when asked to do so.[18] Clearly, then, we see a powerful family network uniting maroons and plantation slaves and including free blacks and mulattoes, most of whom, it was claimed, actively aided the maroons, or at least feared them and their relatives enough to discourage them from informing on them or pursuing them.

The raid on Ville Gaillarde was a serious blow to St. Maló and the maroons of Bas du Fleuve. But the authorities were unable to follow up their victory. In May, 1784, Miró wrote to Captain General Gálvez

18. June 4, 1784, in Acts, Vol. II, 215–17; Miró to Gálvez, Cartas y Ordenanza, July 31, 1784, in Leg. 2549, Doc. 127, fol. 550, SD, AGI.

that while the previous year an expedition against the maroons resulted in the capture of forty-three of them, their main leaders had
escaped, and the maroons were attacking the white settlements. Every day they were finding the remains of dead cattle in the fields. The
settlers feared for their lives because six *voyageurs* had been killed by
the maroons on two separate occasions. It was difficult to find the
whereabouts of the maroons. Miró had sent a black spy to join the
maroons, hoping to get information about St. Maló's whereabouts.
The spy brought back vague news on two occasions, and Miró concluded that the "spy" was deceiving him and stopped using him.
Meanwhile, winter arrived, the coldest winter ever known in the
colony. It was impossible to organize an expedition against the maroons, because the expedition members would have had to remain
outdoors for two weeks, crossing various frozen swamps, and they
would have died of cold. At the beginning of April, Don Carlos Hono-
rato Olivier, a leading planter, was approached by his slave Bastien,
a maroon who was a member of St. Maló's band. Attracted by an offer
of a reward, Bastien offered to guide a military expedition to the *pasaje*
where the maroons lived.[19]

Miró had to go to Pensacola to negotiate a treaty with the Indian
nations. Lieutenant Colonel Francisco Bouligny was appointed acting
commander of the province in the absence of Miró, and Captain Don
Gilberto Guillemard was put in charge of the expedition against the
maroons.[20] Bouligny wrote regularly to Miró, giving details of the ups
and downs of his efforts to destroy the maroon settlements.

Before Miró left, he promulgated a special ordinance, on May 1,
1784, aimed at preventing slaves, free blacks, and mulattoes from
helping the maroons. The ordinance was prefaced with the statement
that since all the efforts made during his rule to convince the maroons
to return to their masters had failed, officials were faced with the hard
necessity of taking more serious measures to prevent the frequent
robberies and incidents for which the maroons were responsible. This
ordinance went to great lengths to restrict the movement of slaves. It
authorized any settler to give twenty-five lashes on the spot to, and
then return to the master, any slave who was off the master's plantation without a written permit, whether by day or by night, on foot or
on horseback, armed or unarmed. If a maroon was apprehended, the
settler was to bring him or her to the prison to be punished. Trade
with slaves was outlawed, particularly the sale of alcohol, powder, or

19. *Ibid.*
20. Miró to Gálvez, July 31, 1784, in Leg. 3A, Doc. 638, PC, AGI.

munitions. The ordinance prohibited masters from leaving horses or firearms in the possession of slaves except for hunters, whose guns were to be marked with the name of the master. Masters were forbidden to send their slaves hunting during May and June of 1784, and they were ordered to inspect their slave quarters regularly for fugitive slaves and to imprison any of their slaves who aided the fugitives by giving them food or shelter. Only skilled slaves such as blacksmiths and carpenters were to be allowed to work for themselves. Free blacks and mulattoes were required to carry at all times a document proving their status.[21]

During the spring of 1784, a dispute broke out between members of St. Maló's band and the slaves of the Prévost plantation over the attentions of a woman slave. Before this conflict, there was a close, symbiotic relationship between the maroons and the Prévost slaves. The maroons always received all the help they needed from the Prévost slaves, including arms and ammunition. In return, the maroons did all the work in the woods that Prévost demanded of his slaves, cutting lumber, collecting firewood, and making stakes. The maroons cultivated all the *conucos,* the vegetable gardens, of Prévost's slaves. The Prévost slaves stole cattle and drove them to the edge of the woods, and the maroons killed and butchered the cattle. The maroons and the Prévost slaves ate together in the woods every day. Many of the maroons of St. Maló's band had their wives among the Prévost slaves, and the Prévost slaves had wives among the maroons.[22]

On May 19, 1784, the Prévost slaves brought to Bouligny a maroon they had wounded after he had defended himself with a gun. Bouligny praised the Prévost slaves. He wrote to Miró, "If all the blacks were as vigilant and exact as those of Prévost, in a short time there would be no more maroons." The next day, he changed his mind about the Prévost slaves. Another maroon, this one a slave belonging to Chabert, was brought in by Dufossat's slaves. He had been living in the cabins behind the Prévost plantation with St. Maló's band for six months. Bouligny described him as a *"negro criollo y muy ladino."*[23]

21. Miró to Gálvez, Cartas y Ordenanza, July 31, 1784, and Ordenanza de Estevan Miró, May 1, 1784, both in Leg. 2549, Doc. 127, fols. 550–53, SD, AGI.
22. Information in this and subsequent paragraphs about the dispute between St. Maló's band and the Prévost slaves comes from Bouligny to Miró, May 18, 1784, in Leg. 10, fols. 128–32, PC, AGI.
23. The phrase means a creole slave who was well socialized into the Spanish language, religion, and culture.

Angered with the Prévost slaves and intimidated by Bouligny, he revealed the support the Prévost slaves had given St. Maló and the
maroons.

The dispute with the Prévost slaves cut off St. Maló and his band
from vital supplies and information and exposed them to attack.
Abandoning their settlements behind the Prévost plantation in late
April, almost all of them went to Gaillardeland. Before leaving, St.
Maló told all those who did not want to follow him that they should
return to their masters. Some of the maroons, who had committed no
other crime than to run away and who did not want to enter forever
into the wilderness of Gaillardeland, separated from St. Maló. Chabert's slave and several other maroons returned to the cabins behind
the Prévost plantation. None of them knew exactly where St. Maló
and his band were going. But Michel, one of the principal maroon
leaders, remained behind, probably to gather information and supplies. Chabert's slave was sure that Michel knew the exact location
where St. Maló intended to reestablish his settlement, because he was
supposed to join him. Chabert's slave reported that St. Maló's band
consisted of twenty to twenty-five men and five women. Some of the
maroons who had remained behind the Prévost plantation had been
captured by the Prévost slaves; the others were scattered. Four slaves
belonging to Madame Doriocourt were special favorites of the Prévost
slaves, and they had hidden them in the woods. The informant offered to show Bouligny their exact location.

To test the reliability of this informant, Bouligny ordered Guillemard to lead twelve mulattoes and six grenadiers to attack the settlement of the four Doriocourt maroons behind the Prévost plantation.
Bouligny was optimistic about the results of this attack, but his hopes
were dashed. Guillemard and his troops left at sunset and did not
arrive at the settlement until 2 A.M., after following the worst imaginable trail through mud up to their waists. Upon their arrival, they
found the settlement destroyed. Bouligny assumed his "informant"
had tipped off the Prévost slaves that he planned to reveal the location of the settlement. Bouligny was pessimistic. He wrote,

> We have wasted 14 pesos in this expedition, and I am afraid that it will
> always be the same. All these swamps are so terrible and so vast that it is
> impossible to attack all the maroon settlements which are spread out in
> the swamps without having a sure guide for every shack, where there are
> never more than three or four blacks. Besides, the noise which many men
> must make in order to go along such passages serves as a warning and
> facilitates the escape which they are sure to find within ten paces of their

huts, throwing themselves into water up to their necks. A single gunshot alarms all of them. . . . The situation of this country is fatal, above all when the maroons find shelter in all the plantations.

In spite of the thousand difficulties of the terrain of Gaillardeland, Bouligny was still confident that he could wipe out St. Maló's band, because they were no longer in a position to receive aid from the plantations. As we shall see, Bouligny was right.

Bouligny's confidence in Chabert's slave was further shaken when a maroon, who belonged to Madame Le Compte and who had given himself up, told him that many of the maroons who, according to Chabert's slave, were with St. Maló in Gaillardeland were actually in settlements behind the Bienvenu plantation. When Chabert's slave offered to bring in Michel's head within three days if Bouligny released him, Bouligny did not accept the proposition because he feared his informant would stay with the maroons, enlightening them about Bouligny's plans based upon the questions he had asked. But Bouligny was taken with the idea of putting prices on the heads of the maroon leaders. He suggested a price of two hundred pesos and freedom to any slave who brought in the head of St. Maló, and freedom to any slave bringing in the head of Michel, Philipe, or Etienne, the three most daring and fearless maroons. Bouligny had been assured by the *regidores* that Miró would approve such an offer, but since he had not heard it directly from Miró, he urged Miró to approve. Bouligny assured Miró, "There is no doubt that they would soon be destroyed. . . . It seems to me that this method is the surest and least costly and I do not believe that it is in any way against the Laws which are always intended to assure public tranquility." Miró disapproved of the suggestion that a price be placed on St. Maló's head, and Bouligny explained that he made the suggestion only out of frustration.[24]

A list of maroons remaining in the St. Maló band was dated June 3, 1784, the day that Bastien, their most reliable spy, reappeared:

> San Maló of Mr. Daresbourg
> Cecilia of Mr. Canuet, St. Maló's wife
> Michel of Madame Le Compte
> Bautista of Madame Le Compte
> Caton of Madame Le Compte
> Jason of Madame Le Compte
> Francisca of Madame Le Compte

24. Bouligny to Miró, June 3, 1784, *ibid.*, fols. 160–64.

Juan, English black, master unknown
Telemac of M. Macarty
Cesar of M. Maxent
Theresa, black woman belonging to the hospital
[illegible] of M. Belleville
Janneton, of M. Piernas
His wife
Meli of M. St. Amant
Naneta de M. Aerenque
Bastien of M. Olivier
Marguerita of M. Chabert
Jean St. Louis of M. Reur
Prestan of M. Mersier
Ismael of M. Thomasein
Charlota of M. Thomasein
Colas of M. Thomasein
Genoveva of M. Lomer
Phelipe of M. Trenoner [Philipe of Trénonay]
Julie of Madame Doriocourt
Bacus of Madame Lecompte
Francisco of M. Prevost
Guis of M. Larchet
A black woman of Don Joseph Fides
Margarita of M. Dufosat
Bonus of Madame Pollock
Rosete of M. Thomasen

Dupard's maroons, three of Verret's maroons, and two of Canuet's maroons had just given themselves up. There was also a band of five maroons in Barataria. One had been captured, and the other four, described as *famosos pícaros* (notorious rogues), were still at large. On May 28, Miró wrote to Bouligny approving a military expedition against the maroons. Fifty men were to pursue St. Maló's band in Gaillardeland; forty more men were to be stationed in Lake Borgne and at the entrances to the bayous leading into the lake to prevent the escape of maroons pursued by soldiers. Members of the expedition were to be upright people with known talents and experience. The fund to compensate masters was exhausted, and the Cabildo of New Orleans was to pay for the expedition and to advance money to compensate masters whose slaves were killed or sentenced to death as a result of the expedition.[25]

The big slave owners controlled the Cabildo. They had the most to

25. Lista de los Negros Cimarrones que se hallan en la Banda de San Maló, June 3, 1784, *ibid.*, fol. 164; Miró to Bouligny, May 28, 1784, in Leg. 3A, Doc. 609, *ibid.*

lose if the maroons were allowed to continue to undermine slavery. If escape through the *pasajes* continued and increased and the slaves feared no retribution, the slave system could have dissolved, resulting in a redistribution of wealth in favor of the slaves and of the sectors of society that were relating economically to the maroons as free workers, at the expense of the large slaveholders. Masters with a heavy investment in slaves and an authoritarian approach to controlling them probably were incapable of adjusting to a free-labor system. They stood to lose their capital investment in slaves and to become economically irrelevant. Acting through the Cabildo, the big slave owners manipulated the fears of the white population, trying to create hysteria about a mythical "revolt" of the maroons to take over the colony. The danger the maroons posed was the destruction, not of the colony, in which they had an important stake, but of slavery, at least for the creole slaves of the colony. Miró, in his letter to Captain General Gálvez, explained that the masters dared not make their slaves fulfill their obligations to them; that the maroons were hard to capture; and that they were afraid the maroons would grow to the point where they would openly attack the plantations.[26] But there was no hint of an open revolt of the slaves to take over the colony.

The syndic of the Cabildo of New Orleans described St. Maló as "audacious, daring, and active" (*"atrevido, osado, y activo"*), which was fair enough, but he also portrayed him as ruthless and bloodthirsty. He claimed that St. Maló killed a woman maroon, whom he had chosen to be his wife, because she wanted to return to her master, and that he killed a maroon for refusing to carry out his orders to kill a calf. He presented the killing of the Americans at Bay St. Louis and the killing of the Englishmen and the seizure of their pirogues as if these incidents had just happened and as if the Americans at Bay St. Louis were innocent travelers returning home who were assaulted and robbed along the way. He failed to add that the maroons had been tricked, that Juan Pedro had been shot in the throat and the rest captured and bound, and that they had killed their captors while escaping. He dealt with Joli Coeur's ax attack against the American as if it were a separate incident from the Bay St. Louis killings.[27] Juan Pedro had testified about all these events after he was captured on March 1, 1783. The maroons were never accused of attacking any

26. May 28, 1784, in Acts, II, 209–15; June 4, 1784, *ibid.*, 215–17; Miró to Gálvez, July 31, 1784, in Leg. 3A, Doc. 638, PC, AGI.

27. Claims by the syndic of the Cabildo in this and subsequent paragraphs come from May 28, 1784, in Acts, II, 209–15, and June 4, 1784, *ibid.*, 215–17.

colonists of Louisiana except when they were defending themselves against raids into what they considered to be their territory. The maroons' violence was almost entirely defensive.

The syndic of the Cabildo claimed that "until now the blacks of this colony have had neither the temerity nor the cruelty to soil their hands in the blood of whites." This was clearly absurd. St. Maló and his band had only attacked Englishmen or Americans—the distinction between them was not very clear in 1783. These attacks took place when Spain was still at war with England, and blacks and mulattoes, slave and free, had been eagerly recruited into the Spanish Army to, indeed, soil their hands in the blood of whites. The syndic reported that masters were obliged to suffer in silence because at the slightest reproof slaves would threaten to join the runaways, and that "several plantations have remained uncultivated because of the flight of said blacks." He complained of "the daring of the blacks who . . . are presently no longer under the power of their masters, but proclaim openly their intention of going to join the maroons."

It is clear from the language of the syndic that it was the independent attitude of the slaves that concerned the slave owners—language like "they have dared to go beyond the limits of the submission which they owe," references to their "roots of independence," and his call for "uprooting this kind of sedition." He couched his demands for blood in touching words of concern for the welfare of widows and orphans crying for the tribunal to protect their lives and property.

The syndic claimed that the maroons had become more bold and had stepped up their assaults, robberies, and murders. They were stealing corn, rice, and flour. The syndic claimed that these thefts proved that the maroons were preparing for a general uprising since, according to him, they already had plenty of food in their retreats. A list of all the militiamen in the district was made, signaling out all men who were used to going out on the lakes to hunt. Those unaccustomed to *el monte* were to stay behind and replace those sent to pursue the maroons.

Members of the St. Maló band, cut off from supplies and intelligence, had to take chances. They sent raiding parties to obtain food. On May 18, it was reported that they stole a large pirogue and broke into a storehouse on the German Coast, taking twenty barrels of corn, eight of rice, and one of flour. It was a well-planned operation, carried out with the support of slaves who signaled to each other along the river. At the end of May, the maroons broke into Madame Mandeville's food storehouse. The black guard posted at the storehouse was found shot, his body thrown into the mud. Bouligny organized an expedition of one hundred men to pursue the maroons into Gaillarde-land. Cut off from information about the expedition being organized against them, the maroons sent four spies in two small pirogues to steal food and to spy on the expedition. Among them was Bastien, slave of Olivier, who had been recruited by Bouligny to spy on the maroons and then to lead the expedition to the headquarters of St. Maló in Gaillardeland. On June 3 at three o'clock in the morning, Bastien sought out Marigny, a militia officer who had remained at his plantation for a day longer than anticipated. Bastien led Marigny to his three companions. All three were captured and imprisoned, in-cluding the famous Michel, who was badly wounded. Privy to the first information about the exact location of St. Maló's headquarters, Marigny proceeded on his own to seek out the St. Maló band. Al-though his orders were to guard the mouth of the Río de los Perros, he hoped to win all the glory of capturing St. Maló by himself. Ma-rigny led his detachment onto Lake Borgne at two o'clock in the after-noon. Instead of joining Guillemard as he had been ordered to do, he kept to himself the information supplied by Bastien. Guillemard saw that Marigny was moving away from him and sent a canoe to ask Marigny what he was doing. Marigny informed Guillemard that he was going to take the mouth of the Río de los Perros. Instead, in broad daylight and without taking the least precaution, Marigny en-tered the bayou where the maroons were located and began to fire. He wounded Isidore, slave of Don Basilio, and all the rest escaped. He burned their huts and then rejoined Guillemard after having carried out what Bouligny called sarcastically "this heroic action." Bouligny wrote that Marigny's conduct undermined their hopes of destroying the maroons with one blow. "Almost all of the most dan-gerous maroons were there together. There are only 10 or 12 others wandering around Barataria, Chapitoulas and La Concepción."[28]

Bouligny tried to relieve Marigny of his command, but his fellow officers successfully defended him. The expedition, reinforced with sixteen militiamen commanded by Olivier, received orders to map out all the hiding places of Gaillardeland. Bouligny was confident that it was a matter of time before the maroons were destroyed. He had taken measures to make sure that the maroons would receive no aid from the plantations. He reported that the St. Maló band was bottled up in Gaillardeland and could not escape. But the expedition no

28. Bouligny to Miró, May 18, June 3, June 9, 1784, all in Leg. 10, fols. 128–32, 160–64, and 173–76, respectively, PC, AGI.

longer had a spy to lead them to the maroons' settlement. Chabert's slave, whom Bouligny had sent back once more as a spy, and two black women maroons had surrendered to Marigny, destroying any hopes they had in this spy.[29]

The expedition returned to Gaillardeland with little hope of finding the maroons. They searched for three days without finding a trace of them. Marigny's party withdrew; Guillemard and his men remained, joined by Olivier and his sixteen militiamen. They sent several little pirogues along the labyrinths of bayous, seeking out traces of the maroons. Bautista Hugon, an officer of the colored militia, evidently a tracker, found traces of the path of the maroons. Guillemard sent well-armed men in five pirogues to follow their tracks, with instructions to take every precaution and to maintain silence. After following the maroons' tracks for two hours, they came so close to the maroons that they heard their voices. Shielded by rushes, the troops ran forward and discovered the maroons spread out along the banks of the bayou within gunshot of the expedition. They opened fire, and the maroons fled across a prairie full of holes and impenetrable rushes, water up to their waists. Guillemard could not follow them because of a bad leg. He climbed a live-oak tree, from which he could see all the maroons "running like deer over the rushes." He showed his men where the maroons were running to, sometimes by voice, sometimes with his hat or his handkerchief. Almost all the maroons were captured. St. Maló was wounded by Olivier, who fired upon him from a great distance without knowing who he was. "Seeing him fall, he approached him and discovered that he was St. Maló, who begged him to finish him off because he knew that his crimes merited death."[30]

Seventeen maroons were captured. Philipe, slave of Trénonay and one of the principal leaders of the maroons, fell wounded on the other side of a lagoon where they could not follow him. He was evidently finally captured, because Trénonay turned him over to a ship's captain to be sold to an unsuspecting slave owner in St. Domingue. Three maroons—Printens of Mersiers, described as the least valuable of the band, Etienne of Meder, and Colas of Thomasein—were fishing in a little pirogue and fled when they heard the shots. The expedition returned to New Orleans on June 12. All the captives were imprisoned and put at the disposition of de Reggio, to be tried. Seven

29. *Ibid.*
30. *Ibid.*

more slaves were arrested at the Prévost and Bienvenu plantations. By June 14, there were forty men and twenty women in prison, and more arrests followed. Ten or twelve maroons remained scattered in the depths of Gaillardeland and Barataria. St. Malô's wound was so serious that the surgeon did not expect him to live through the trial. Gangrene had set in.[31]

The *procurador general* clamored for swift and exemplary punishment of the captured maroons, as well as of those who had given them supplies and who had hidden them, claiming that an uprising had been planned "under the protection of the maroon leaders and the large numbers of blacks who it is said were to unite with them." Otherwise, he claimed, new disorders would take place that could be even more dangerous and that could result in the loss of the colony. The Cabildo of New Orleans voted unanimously for swift and exemplary punishment of the prisoners in the hands of the alcalde, as well as of those who had helped them, in accordance with the Laws of the Indies on maroons.[32]

How large was St. Malô's band? The list dated June 3, 1784, was most likely supplied by their most reliable spy, Bastien of Olivier, who reappeared on that same date. This list counted 37 or 38 maroons, almost all of whom were named, and it included at least 12 women, only 2 of whom were listed as wives of maroons.[33] On July 1, 1784, Miró reported that a total of 103 maroons had been captured, which no doubt included those captured in the raid on Ville Gaillarde on March 1, 1783. Some of the maroons were not captured or even identified. It is clear that an impressive number of slaves, especially creole slaves, were maroons. If we compare the size of St. Malô's band with that of the most famous maroon band in St. Domingue, a colony with half a million slaves, we find that when the Maniel band left their mountain retreat after making a treaty with France and Spain, they numbered only 133 persons. It has been esti-

31. Trénonay to [?], October 28, 1784, in Leg. 216A, fol. 767, *ibid.*; Bouligny to Miró, June 14, June 19, 1784, both in Leg. 10, Doc. 103, fols. 182–89, 192–95, *ibid.*

32. June 11, 1784, in Acts, Vol. II, 217–19.

33. See Gilbert C. Din, "*Cimarrones* and the San Malo Band in Spanish Louisiana," *LH*, XXI (1980), 237–62, for a lower estimate of the size and overall significance of St. Malô's band. The size quoted by Din came from an estimate made by Bouligny based upon information obtained from other, unnamed sources and from Chabert's slave, who reported that St. Malô's band consisted of twenty to twenty-five men and five women, though he could only name fifteen men (Bouligny to Miró, May 18, 1784, in Leg. 10, fols. 128–32, PC, AGI).

mated that only about 500 maroons ever occupied the entire wooded, mountainous area separating French St. Domingue from Spanish Santo Domingo.[34]

If there was evidence of a general uprising planned by the maroons, no trace of it has been found. In contrast to the March 1, 1783, raid, there is no written record of testimony of the accused. There was no trial. De Reggio made a personal investigation and pronounced sentence. Although Bouligny wrote to Miró that St. Maló confessed and vigorously implicated his companions, there are several cogent reasons to doubt this confession.[35] First of all, in the same letter in which he described St. Maló's "confession" and implication of his comrades, Bouligny was defending his conduct in the eyes of Miró. Bouligny had received a letter from Miró stating that he expected to take charge of the trial and the sentencing of the maroons himself after he returned from Pensacola. Miró had evidently asked Bouligny to respond to the charges made against him by Cirilo de Barcelona, auxiliary bishop–elect of Cuba, who knew Louisiana well, having served as chaplain with the Gálvez expeditions of 1780 to 1781. Cirilo de Barcelona accused Bouligny of cooperating with de Reggio in his tyrannical conduct and in the illegal trial and punishment of the maroons. Baptiste, one of the condemned, belonged to the Capuchin Order and was evidently a skilled and trusted slave. He had not been captured in the raid. When he was arrested, he was rented to himself, working on a plantation. Cirilo de Barcelona was in New Orleans on June 19, 1784, the date the executions were carried out. He wrote an indignant letter to the king and presented it to the Cabildo of New Orleans, protesting that he could not "tolerate the inhumanity of seeing a manservant of this House [Capuchins] suffer without the formalities of justice and criminal trial to which he is entitled, and I ask that his case be handled by the prosecutor of the province so that he may be judged in conformity with law, and I protest as master of the said manservant of the nullity of so many being

34. Miró to Espeleta, July 1, 1784, in Leg. 3A, Doc. 639, PC, AGI; David Geggus, "Marronage, Voodoo, and the St. Domingue Slave Revolt of 1791," *Proceedings of the International Congress of the French Colonial Historical Society,* ed. Philip Boucher (in press, University Press of the Americas); Anne Pérotin-Dumon, *Etre patriote sous les tropiques: La Guadeloupe, la colonisation et la révolution (1789–1794)* (Basse-Terre, Guadeloupe, 1985), 104.

35. Bouligny to Miró, June 19, 1784, in Leg. 10, Doc. 103, fols. 192–95, PC, AGI. For an uncritical acceptance of St. Maló's alleged confession, see Din, "*Cimarrones* and the San Malo Band in Spanish Louisiana."

executed precipitously and irregularly, because the natural right of self-defense is allowed to all, and the law applies to the greatest crime."[36]

From Bouligny's description, the questioning of the maroons was a private, one-man show. Bouligny's letter clearly implies that he himself had not witnessed St. Maló's "confession." He explained that one day, out of curiosity, he went to hear the depositions and reflections of St. Maló and found de Reggio bathed in perspiration in a small and poorly ventilated room, complaining of the excessive heat and fatigue he suffered from remaining there ten to twelve hours every day. Bouligny suggested that he move to the *sala del crimen*, which was inside the prison, in order to be more comfortable while taking the depositions, and that he ask the chief marshal to let him use that room for eight to fifteen days.[37] Evidently, de Reggio did not feel that it was necessary to prolong the depositions. The maroons were "tried" personally by de Reggio and executed within a week of their capture.

According to de Reggio, St. Maló implicated Joli Coeur, Henri, Prince, and Baptiste in the killings at Bay St. Louis. However, Juan Pedro's recorded testimony taken the previous year placed only himself, his wife, María, and his son, Joli Coeur, at this incident. If Juan Pedro did not lie to protect himself, his wife, or his son, it seems unlikely that he lied to protect maroons who were not related to him. On June 19, 1784, as St. Maló was taken from the prison on his way to be hanged, and again when he was at the top of the gallows, he told the people around him that Prince and Baptiste were innocent of the crime for which they were being punished. Several people told Bouligny that they heard St. Maló say this, but Bouligny claimed he only heard Baptiste tell St. Maló, "It would have been better for you to say that before, when there was still time." Prince and Baptiste were tied to the foot of the gallows and flogged two hundred times by the public executioner for their alleged participation in the Bay St. Louis killings. St. Maló, Joli Coeur, Michel, Henri, and Cecilia Canuet, St. Maló's wife, were all sentenced to be hanged, Cecilia as St. Maló's "inseparable companion in all his exploits." Cecilia was not hanged, because she claimed to be pregnant. She was not really pregnant, or else she miscarried, because on October 25, 1784, her execu-

36. Bouligny to Miró, July 9, 1784, in Leg. 10, fols. 232–33, PC, AGI; Cirilo de Barcelona to de Reggio, June 19, 1784, in Minutes, meeting of June 18, 1784, in Acts, II, 220.

37. Bouligny to Miró, July 9, 1784, in Leg. 10, fols. 232–33, PC, AGI.

tion was suspended when she claimed again to be in the early stages of pregnancy.[38]

Cirilo de Barcelona and all the Capuchins protested the executions and floggings by refusing to accompany the condemned prisoners to the gallows. They stood on a balcony overlooking the public square while the executions were taking place, shouting that they could not stand to see an innocent member of their house suffer. All of them refused to give last rites in protest against the procedure. De Reggio reviewed the situation that he claimed the colony faced and wrote of the jubilation of the population on seeing St. Maló dragged in chains from the *ciprière*. He quoted settlers expressing satisfaction that they no longer needed to sleep with their guns to protect their wives and children. They could sleep soundly at night, confident that their provisions and their cows would not be stolen. He emphasized the value of avoiding the delay of punishment by a long, drawn-out trial. He wrote of the approbation of public opinion (*la vox pública*) to the summary executions, but not one word about the so-called revolt to take over the colony and kill the whites.[39] This very *vox pública*, these fears that led settlers to sleep fitfully with their guns beside them, were created and manipulated by these gentlemen of the Cabildo in an attempt to regain control over their slaves.

Bouligny believed that the Capuchins had done a great deal of damage to the cause of public order and tranquillity among the slaves. He wrote, "All of the slaves were, or showed themselves to be, happy with the imprisonment and punishment of St. Maló and his companions. They viewed it as just and indispensable. God only knows what their dispositions will be now. It is reasonable to believe that this same punishment is now regarded as unjust and tyrannical because our Bishop and the rest of the Capuchins have disapproved of it with so much notoriety."[40]

In August, four more maroons were sentenced to be hanged. Three maroons received three hundred lashes and were exiled from the colony. Seventeen received two hundred lashes and were shackled with a twelve-pound chain for thirteen months. Six women received two hundred lashes and were branded on the right cheek with an *M*. Ten women received three hundred lashes and were shackled with a twelve-pound weight for three months. Two maroons who helped

38. Bouligny to Miró, June 14, 1784, in Leg. 10, Doc. 103, fols. 192–95, PC, AGI; Bouligny to Miró, July 9, 1784, *ibid.*, fols. 232–33; October 25, 1784, in SJR, *LHQ*, XX (1937), 863.

39. De Reggio, Address to the Cabildo, June 25, 1784, in Acts, II, 221–25.

40. Bouligny to Miró, June 14, 1784, in Leg. 10, Doc. 103, fols. 192–95, PC, AGI.

the expedition were pardoned. Five slaves belonging to Captain Bien-venu were convicted of assisting and trading with fugitives, and an-other of his slaves was convicted of running away without robbing or assisting in committing any crime. They were not sentenced to death, "which they merit because the principal leaders no longer exist and that would perhaps ruin an innocent and poor master." They were branded on the cheek with an *M* and returned to their master. In April of 1785, Gálvez at last responded to Miró's letter written the summer before. Gálvez expressed his gratitude for, and his approval of, the capture and exemplary punishment of the maroon leaders.[41]

After the Civil War was over and the slaves were freed, an old woman in St. Bernard Parish, the home of Gaillardeland, sang the following Creole slave song describing the execution of St. Maló:

> Alas, young men, come make lament,
> For poor St. Maló in distress!
> They chased, they hunted him with dogs,
> They fired a rifle at him.
> They dragged him from the cypress swamp,
> His arms they tied behind his back.
> They tied his hands in front of him,
> They tied him to a horse's tail.
> They dragged him up into the town,
> Before those grand Cabildo men.
> They charged that he had made a plot
> To cut the throats of all the whites.
> They asked him who his comrades were.
> Poor St. Maló said not a word!
> The judge his sentence read to him,
> And then they raised the gallows tree.
> They drew the horse—the cart moved off
> And left St. Maló hanging there!
> The sun was up an hour high.
> They left his body swinging there
> For carrion crows to feed upon.
>
> Aïe! zein zens vini fé ouarrâ,
> Pou Pôv St. Maló dans l'embas!
> Yé çassé li avec yé chien,
> Yé tiré li ein coup d'fizi.
> Yé halé li la cyprière,
> So bras yé 'tassé par derrier.

41. August 7, October 25, November 10, 1784, all in SJR, *LHQ*, XX (1937), 861–65; Gálvez to Miró, April 16, 1785, in Leg. 11, Doc. 144, fol. 196, PC, AGI.

Yé tassé so la main divant,
Yé marré li apé queue choual.
Yé trainein li zouqu'à la ville,
Divant michés là dans cabil'e.
Yé quisé li li fé complot
Pou' coupé cou à tout yé blancs.
Yé 'mandé li qui so compères.
Pôv St. Maló pas di' a-rien!
Zize là li lir' so la sentence,
Et pis li fé dressé potence.
Yé halé choual—çarette parti—
Pôv St. Maló resté pendi!
Eine hèr soleil deza levée.
Yé laissé so corps balancé
Pou carencro gagnein manzé.[42]

The destruction of St. Maló and the maroons did not change the indomitable character of the creole slaves of Louisiana or their creative adaption to the topography of the country. But between 1777 and 1788, the slave population of Bas du Fleuve decreased by 24.8 percent, to 1,883. The drop in the slave population of Bas du Fleuve was sharper than that of the white population (down from 4.46 in 1777 to 3.72 slaves to each white in 1788) at a time when the slave population was increasing much faster than the white population in the rest of Louisiana. Acosta Rodríguez finds the population drop in Bas du Fleuve "difficult to explain because it was located near New Orleans and Chapitoulas."[43] Evidently, there was a policy of population removal because of the strategic nature of the area and the adaptation of the slaves to the bayous and swamps of Gaillardeland.

According to the Creole slave song, St. Maló's body was left hanging from the gallows to be consumed by birds of prey. The manner of St. Maló's death had a transcendent significance that no doubt escaped the Cabildo men. In earlier times, the corpses of Bambara were hung on trees until they rotted, and their bones were preserved for making charms. The more violent the death, the stronger the charms. Special charms were created to preserve the souls of individuals who died violently through murder, warfare, or justice. These charms were believed to contain the souls of all those who had died in com-

42. Cited and translated in George Washington Cable, *Creoles and Cajuns: Stories of Old Louisiana*, ed. Arlin Turner (New York, 1959), 418–19. Cable might have mistranslated the first line of the song. *Zinzin* means a charm or amulet of support in both Bambara and Louisiana Creole.

43. Acosta Rodríguez, *Población de la Luisiana española*, 219, 225, 456.

bat, and they were kept in a separate sack and carried to the battle-field in wartime to lend the spiritual support of the warrior ancestors to their descendants.[44]

The debt that poor whites of Louisiana owe to the maroon communities of the eighteenth century is engraved on the language they still speak today. The Cajuns and the Canary Islanders, poverty-stricken immigrants who came to Louisiana during the last half of the eighteenth century, had to learn to adapt to the swamps, an environment that was totally foreign to them. The ancestors of the fiercely defiant and independent people who live in the swamps of Louisiana learned to survive, physically and economically, from the runaway slaves who first sought refuge there. Variants of Louisiana Creole are still spoken by about ten thousand whites living along the Atchafalaya Basin. They are farmers, trappers, and fishermen living in small, isolated communities in the countryside and in the swamps. They themselves, not without some shame, characterize their language as *français nègre*. According to Ingrid Neumann, "It is not surprising to find, at times, young white boys at ease in speaking creole when they accompany their fathers on hunting expeditions. . . . It seems to have the status of a secret language used by men. The traditional male occupations like fishing and hunting . . . are often linked to the usage of the vernacular." Men recruited into the primary resource economy move quickly from being passive bilingual into being active speakers of the vernacular.[45] Neumann does not explain how poor whites have come to adopt the language of the blacks, but the explanation seems quite clear. It is the language of the economy of the swamps, derived from slave hunters and maroon settlements during the eighteenth century, and retained and regenerated by the white men who fish, trap, and hunt. Some poor whites of Louisiana call themselves coonasses, meaning the behind of the racoon, identifying themselves in a defiant manner with the animal who survives in the swamps through independent and self-sufficient occupations. Identification with this quick and cunning animal, as well as the language used to describe the occupations pursued in the swamps, derives from Louisiana's Afro-Creole traditions.

44. Germaine Dieterlen, *Essai sur la religion Bambara* (Paris, 1951), 87, 94, 147. It is possible that charms were created from the blood, hair, nails, and bones of St. Maló, many of them no doubt fakes, and distributed and sold throughout the colony. Perhaps the first line of the song is calling for the preservation of St. Maló's soul in *zinzin*, fetishes of support, for his help in future combat.

45. Ingrid Neumann, *Le créole de Breaux Bridge, Louisiane: Etude morphosyntaxique* (Hamburg, 1985), 40–43, 43*n*.

The Pointe Coupee Post: Race Mixture and Freedom at a Frontier Settlement

Neg' pas ca-pa' marché sans mais dans poche,
C'est pou vo-lé poule,
Milâtre pas ca-pa' marché sans la corde dans poche,
C'est pou volé choual,
Blanc pas ca-pa' marché sans la'-zen dans poche,
C'est pou volé filles.

The black cannot walk without corn in his pocket,
To steal chickens,
The mulatto cannot walk without rope in his pocket,
To steal horses,
The white cannot walk without money in his pocket,
To steal girls.

—Louisiana Creole proverb from George Washington Cable, *Creoles and Cajuns: Stories of Old Louisiana*

Gardé milé la, Miché Bainjo,
Com li insolent!
Chapo en ho coté, Miché Bainjo,
Dicanne dan so lamain, Miché Bainjo,
Botte kapé fé "crin-crin," Miché Bainjo,
Gardé milé la, Miché Bainjo,
Com li insolent!

Look at that mule there, Mister Banjo,
Isn't he insolent!
Hat cocked on one side, Mister Banjo,
Walking stick in hand, Mr. Banjo,
Boots that go "crank-crank," Mister Banjo,
Look at that mule there, Mister Banjo,
Isn't he insolent!

—Creole song from Alcée Fortier, "Bits of Louisiana Folklore"

Note: The Creole version of "Miché Bainjo" was published in *Transactions of the Modern Language Association of America*, III (1887), 101–68, correcting an earlier version published by George Washington Cable that was actually in French. The English translation was by Cable.

As the mighty Mississippi River reaches Louisiana, it loses its straight course, meandering and spiraling through the delta where no natural obstacles impose order upon its path. About fifty lieus north of New Orleans along the winding river, the river changed its course and left behind a branch cut off from the new course. Looking every bit like the Mississippi, it leads nowhere. This body of water is called, appropriately, False River, and the post there was named Pointe Coupee, meaning cut-off point. It is here that one can closely observe the incubation of new, hybrid cultural forms in response to the human and ecological environment. Red, white, and black met under crisis conditions. The insecurity of this frontier world created a society in which the three races were deeply dependent upon each other and physical survival was often more important than accumulation of wealth. Racial lines were blurred, and intimate relations among peoples of all three races flourished. The population of this face-to-face community, living in danger and isolation much of the time, adapted by creating a flexible, permeable world where human talents and abilities were at a premium. Hybrid race, culture, and language were created. Louisiana Creole was the only language spoken by most whites of the district, as well as by blacks, well into the twentieth century. When folktales were collected from both black and white monolingual speakers of Louisiana Creole in 1931, the white storytellers used more archaic forms of the language than did the black.[1]

At Pointe Coupee, as at many French settlements in lower Louisiana, the French and Canadian colonists were socialized to Indian ways of dress, housing, cultivation, and preparation of food. During the French period, the whites were almost entirely small owners holding few slaves. They participated in an acculturation process that was a mutual exchange of knowledge, perceptions, and techniques—an exchange in which Africans, as well as Indians, were often more influential than whites. Some Pointe Coupee planters came to believe in the magical powers of their slaves. They brought a lawsuit against Sieur Le Doux for using one of his slaves to bewitch the

---

1. Lafayette Jarreau, "Creole Folklore of Pointe Coupée Parish" (M.A. thesis, Louisiana State University, 1931); Ulysses S. Ricard, Jr., conversation with the author, June, 1988.

son of Nicolas de La Cour. The Superior Council found that the whole affair stemmed from a rumor started by a slave. Several imprisoned slaves belonging to various masters were ordered released.[2]

Race mixture at Pointe Coupee was extensive. A rigid socioracial hierarchy was absent. A close study of the Pointe Coupee post during the eighteenth century supports the claim of Charles Roussève, an Afro-Creole historian, that the French and Spanish colonists of Louisiana were more considerate of their mixed-blood children than were settlers in other parts of America, "accepted them as members of their families, freed them, and educated them. Eventually, the descendants of many were totally absorbed into the white Creole group." Roussève's interpretation, indicating widespread passing of mixed-bloods into the white population, not only is accurate but also is pivotal to understanding race relations in colonial Louisiana. A recent study by anthropologist Virginia Dominguez clearly shows awareness of racial passing at the vital statistics office in New Orleans.[3] Additionally, this writer has been informed by archivists in Louisiana that white genealogists tracing their ancestry sometimes turn up ancestors of African descent about whom they knew nothing. Although race mixture and social fluidity were perhaps more pronounced at Pointe Coupee than elsewhere in Louisiana because of the relative remoteness of the settlement and its insecure beginnings, a similar process of acculturation took place throughout lower Louisiana during the eighteenth century.

The extent of race mixture and emancipation in French Louisiana has been minimized by excessive reliance upon Spanish censuses, which overlooked the passing of mixed-bloods into the "white" race. The census taken by the Spanish in 1769 reported a total of 200 mulattoes, slave and free, in the entire colony, and only 165 free people of African descent, 80 percent of whom were mulattoes.[4] These figures are not convincing. French creole settlers took local censuses and sent in their reports to Spanish officials, who tabulated the results. The local census-takers often counted free people of African descent as whites. The impact of Spanish law obligating the master to ap-

2. James T. McGowan, "Planters Without Slaves: Origins of a New World Labor System," *Southern Studies*, XVI (1977), 5–26; July 29, 1756, in RSC, LHC.

3. Charles Barthelemy Roussève, *The Negro in Louisiana: Aspects of His History and His Literature* (New Orleans, 1937), 25; Virginia R. Domínguez, *White By Definition: Social Classification in Creole Louisiana* (New Brunswick, N.J., 1986).

4. James T. McGowan, "Creation of a Slave Society: Louisiana Plantations in the Eighteenth Century" (Ph.D. dissertation, University of Rochester, 1976), 176, 177.

praise and free the slave for purchase or self-purchase can only partially account for the growth of the free population of African descent under Spanish rule. Another important factor was one of definition. The French colonists tended to absorb free people of African descent, especially concubines and descendants of French men, into the white population. The Spanish corporatist concept of racial hierarchy sought to create separate social groupings based upon varying degrees of race mixture, promoting the emergence of separate groups among the free population of African descent: blacks, mulattoes, quadroons, pardos. These concepts were foreign to the French creoles and created an awkward dilemma for local census-takers, a dilemma that was resolved by including many free people of African descent among the whites. This early pattern of race relations was quite resilient. When this writer was growing up in New Orleans during the 1930s and 1940s, there were families known to be of mixed-blood ancestry who were accepted as white, by consensus of the white community.

The racial openness that prevailed in colonial Louisiana can be explained at least partially by frontier conditions. The Indian population remained pivotal throughout the eighteenth century, both in numbers and in military importance. In view of constant attacks and threats from Indian nations allied with the British, it is not surprising that rigid racial definitions hardly arose among the thinly populated and militarily weak French and Canadian colonists of Louisiana. African and Indian slaves often lived on the same estates, and there was extensive race mixture among them. Their descendants were designated *grif*. Concubinage between white men and slave women was extensive and was openly accepted by white women as well as by white men. There was a strong social consensus shared by white women that the concubines and children of white men should be free. Race mixture between white male settlers and nonwhite women can sometimes, but by no means always, be explained by a shortage of white women. At the Pointe Coupee post, free women of marriageable age who were counted as white often substantially outnumbered men. Nevertheless, white men who were well off economically and had the means to marry white women often preferred dark women, sometimes their own slaves. They freed them, maintained lifelong conjugal relationships with them, provided for their children, and sometimes openly acknowledged them. These women were listed as white in the censuses regardless of their color, and their white mates remained among the most respected members in the community, holding positions of trust in the judiciary and the militia. It is, indeed, hard to find prominent families in eighteenth-century Pointe Coupee who do not have descendants of partially African ancestry.

Conditions prevailing in French Louisiana produced one of the most racially flexible societies in the Americas, regardless of the colonizing power. Racial attitudes among all social groups in Louisiana were quite open, compared not only with attitudes in Anglo North America but also with attitudes in the French Caribbean. During the last half of the eighteenth century, a rigid racial hierarchy was most pronounced in St. Domingue but was also very strong in Martinique and Guadeloupe. Attitudes toward race mixture in Louisiana contrast sharply with the pattern in Anglo North America. According to Allan Kulikoff, "A man's reputation [in the Chesapeake] could be ruined by fathering a mulatto child; 'he would be scorned, dishonored; every house would be closed to him.' And although white women might tolerate casual affairs between their sons and husbands and slave women, serious love affairs and stable unions would have raised the status of black women to a level approaching that of free white women and were therefore strongly, and effectively opposed." The situation in South Carolina was a little more fluid, at least during the early years of colonization. Peter H. Wood wrote that concubinage during the late seventeenth and early eighteenth centuries was "more openly, and perhaps more frequently interracial than in later years." He cites several examples of white men who freed and provided for black, mulatto, and Indian women and their offspring in their wills. There was enough race mixture between black slaves and white women, both servant and free, to inspire an act passed in 1717 that imposed a seven-year term of servitude upon any white woman who gave birth to a child by a black father, whether slave or free. Some black-Indian mixtures were called "mustee." One documented case exists of a mixed-blood family passing into the white population. Before 1720, there may have been a slightly higher proportion of legally free blacks, but their status was close to that of slaves. But the freed population in prerevolutionary South Carolina was scarce: never as many as two hundred freed blacks lived in the entire region during the 1760s, nor was more than 1 percent of the black population free during the fifty years that South Carolina was a royal colony. Eugene D. Genovese presents a much more nuanced picture of interracial sexual unions in Anglo-America, indicating that truly familial bonds between masters and slave-women concubines and their offspring were not uncommon and that sexual relationships between black men and white women were more accepted during slavery than in the New South.[5]

While the Indian population continued to be the most effective military force in Louisiana throughout the eighteenth century, the Indian population in the English colonies along the Atlantic coast declined sharply at a much earlier stage of colonization. Between 1670 and 1730, the area stretching westward from the Carolina coast to East Texas witnessed a drastic decline in the Indian population and a sharp rise in the combined white and black population, which outnumbered the Indians by 1730. Although blacks began to outnumber whites in Carolina by 1910, blacks were confined largely to the coastal areas before 1760. By 1759, the population in South Carolina was 55,000 black and 36,000 white, but whites overwhelmingly outnumbered blacks in the townships and in the middle and back country. Thus, the frontier areas were overwhelmingly white. After 1760, large numbers of slaves were imported into the South Carolina back country from Africa as well as from other North American states. While less than one-tenth of South Carolina's slaves lived in the back country in 1760, half the slaves were there by 1810.[6] By the time blacks began to populate the back country in large numbers, there was a relatively large, local white population capable of defending itself, and the frontier was reasonably secure. In contrast, the white settlers of Louisiana depended heavily upon both reds and blacks for their military, as well as their economic, survival.

Like most French rural settlements in Louisiana, the Pointe Coupee post was born in an Indian village: the Tunica village located five leagues north of the post. Two French missionaries from Quebec, Fathers Davion and Montigny, found an English trader at the Tunica

5. Nicole Vanony-Frisch, *Les esclaves de la Guadeloupe à la fin de l'ancien régime d'après les sources notariales (1770–1789),* extrait du *Bulletin de la Société d'Histoire de la Guadeloupe,* Nos. 63–64 (1985), 153–55; Alan Kulikoff, *Tobacco and Slaves: The Development of Southern Cultures in the Chesapeake, 1680–1800* (Chapel Hill, 1986), 395–96, quoting Bayard, *Travels of a Frenchman,* 20; Peter H. Wood, *Black Majority: Negroes in Colonial South Carolina from 1670 Through the Stono Rebellion* (New York, 1974), 131; 98–103, 161n; Eugene D. Genovese, *Roll, Jordan, Roll* (New York, 1974), 413–30. Genovese has since encountered additional documents that support this point of view (Eugene D. Genovese to Gwendolyn Midlo Hall, September 9, 1990, in Gwendolyn Midlo Hall Collection, Bentley Historical Library, University of Michigan).

6. Peter H. Wood, Introduction to Verner W. Crane's *Southern Frontier, 1670–1732* (1928; rpr. New York, 1981), xiv, xv; W. Stit Robinson, *The Southern Colonial Frontier, 1607–1763* (Albuquerque, 1979), 171; Philip D. Morgan, "Black Society in the Low Country, 1760–1810," in *Slavery and Freedom in the Age of the American Revolution,* ed. Ira Berlin and Ronald Hoffman (Charlottesville, Va., 1983), 84.

village in 1699, the first year of colonization in Louisiana. They accompanied the trader to the Chickasaw, learning of the flourishing Indian fur trade carried out by packhorse from Charlestown in South Carolina. The first permanent French mission in the lower Mississippi basin was established among the Tunica. By 1705, the Tunica's alliance with the French exposed them to destructive raids from the Chickasaw allies of the English.[7]

The French settlement at Pointe Coupee was established in 1717 and grew slowly. A 1722 census lists two land concessions: Terre Blanche, the de Mezières concession, with thirteen men and six women, and the St. Reyne concession, with fifteen men, five women, and two children. There were ten Frenchmen living at the Tunica village, four of whom were living with their wives, one with a wife and a child, and two others with women who were not described as their wives. Thus, seven out of the ten Frenchmen living in the Tunica village had mates. By 1726, the Pointe Coupee settlement contained only four households, three with wives, three with children. The French population was only twenty-one, eight of whom were children and four of whom were *engagés*. The French population in the Tunica village had expanded sharply. There were fifteen households, fourteen with wives, eleven with children. The total French population living in the Tunica village was fifty-two, including seventeen children and five *engagés*.[8] It is likely that some, if not most, of the wives of whites in the Tunica village were Tunica Indians.

A fertile settlement located halfway between Natchez and New Orleans, Pointe Coupee was considered an important way station as the Natchez settlement developed. Before the Natchez rebellion, plans were in motion to establish missions at Pointe Coupee and at the Tunica village and to station twenty-five soldiers drawn from the Natchez post under the command of a prudent captain who understood the disputes among the settlers, who would see that they did their duty, and who would keep the officials informed. After the Natchez settlement was destroyed in 1729, the Pointe Coupee post

7. Crane, *The Southern Frontier*, 67, 86; Charles Edward O'Neill, *Church and State in French Colonial Louisiana: Policy and Politics to 1732* (New Haven, 1966), 17. In other documents, the Tunica village was reported to be located eight or nine leagues above the Pointe Coupee settlement.

8. Census of Habitants of the Concessions Along the Mississippi River dated May 13, 1722 as Reported by Sieur Diron, in Charles R. Maduell, Jr., *The Census Tables for the French Colony of Louisiana from 1699 Through 1732* (Baltimore, 1972), 29; General Census of All the Inhabitants of the Colony of Louisiana dated January 1, 1726, etc., *ibid.*, 52–53. *Tunica* was spelled *Tominea* in the transcription.

became the front line of defense against the Natchez and the Chickasaw, serving as headquarters for assembling a militia and for obtaining information about developments among the Indian nations. The
French settlers' precarious relations with the Indian nations had been
aggravated by Governor Périer's extraordinary insensitivity. He alienated the Illinois by burning alive three Chickasaw who had been sent
to him as envoys by the Illinois with the understanding that their lives
would be spared.[9] While Périer stereotyped the Indians, considering
all of them treacherous, the Pointe Coupee settlers tried to avoid ex-
asperating them, obtained information from them, and strove to win
their loyalty. The Pointe Coupee settlers' intimate knowledge of, and
close ties with, the Indians made them an invaluable asset to the
colony during the decades following the Natchez massacre. For the
thin French population in Pointe Coupee, it was a matter of survival.
The Tunica village was, with few lapses, a source of information, material, and police and military support for the Pointe Coupee post
throughout the eighteenth century.

When the Natchez abandoned their village and crossed the Mississippi River, Périer put Captain Delahaye of the Pointe Coupee militia
in charge of the defense of the area and of all the troops, including
volunteer militia and Indians. Delahaye claimed that he led Tunica
and other Indian detachments "with the greatest possible success,"
discovered the Natchez retreat, which even the Indians did not know
of, and led the army to attack them via the Black River. Captain Delahaye's version of the cowardice of the regular troops and the effec-
tiveness of the militia was confirmed in reports by Périer. In 1731,
the Tunica nation, as well as some of the French settlers living in
their village, was nearly wiped out by the Natchez whom the Tunica
had invited with the intention of negotiating peace between them and
the French.[10] Thereafter, the Pointe Coupee settlement grew independently of the Tunica village.

9. Father Raphael to Abbe Raguet, April 18, 1727, in Ser. C13A (10), fol. 324, ANC;
Mémoire pour servir a l'établissement de la Louisiane et pour rendre cette colonie flo-
rissante, n.d. [before the Natchez rebellion of November 28, 1729], in Ser. C13C 1,
fol. 113, ANC; Salmon to the Ministry of the Colonies, June 20, 1732, in Ser. C13A 15,
fols. 149–50, ANC.

10. Lettre en forme de rélation du Deslayes au sujet de massacre des françois fait
par des sauvages le 28 novembre 1729, New Orleans, March 15, 1730 (received in
Balize, April 16, 1731), in Ser. C13C 4, fols. 179–80, ibid.; Périer to the Ministry of the
Colonies, New Orleans, March 18, 1730, in Ser. C13A 12, fol. 43, ibid.; Diron d'Arta-
guette to Maurepas, June 24, 1731, in MPA, IV, 76–78; Beauchamp to Maurepas,
November 5, 1731, in MPA, IV, 78–79.

Between the Natchez uprising of 1729 and the end of the Chickasaw Wars in 1741, Pointe Coupee was constantly exposed to Indian raids. M. Paillart, a resident of Pointe Coupee who leased the de Mezières concession, had petitioned for the cancellation of his lease because frequent attacks by Indians made it impossible to cultivate the land. It had to be guarded at all times. Périer claimed that Paillart was having panic attacks and that he was the only one to complain. In February, 1732, forty to fifty Indians attacked the de Mezières estate in broad daylight, burning all of the buildings except for the pigeon house, killing two mother cows and four calves, and stealing everything they pleased, and either kidnapped or ran off one black man, two black women, and six black children. They left behind two tomahawks, the war insignia of the Natchez and the Chickasaw. Paillart was allowed to rent the remaining slaves to other settlers in more secure locations. Several settlers at Pointe Coupee retreated to New Orleans, and the seven or eight who had been on the east bank of the river moved to the west bank, where most of the settlers were located, the better to protect themselves from attacks by the Indians. Périer believed that these attacks had been carried out, not by the Natchez or Chickasaw, but by the small nations in the area, allies of the French who were "getting even with our French who cheat them when they trade with them. . . . If this is so, it would be even more dangerous for the colony because we would have serpents in our midst." Périer sent fifteen Swiss soldiers commanded by an ensign to reinforce the two soldiers at Pointe Coupee. Attacks continued at Pointe Coupee and at the Tunica village. The Tunica Indians were said to be very attached to the French. A stone fort was built, garrisoned by twelve soldiers and an ensign. In October, 1731, three Frenchmen and a French woman were hacked to death in a *ciprière* at Pointe Coupee. Périer became convinced that they were victims of the Chitimachas, by then a small nation of about forty warriors located south of Pointe Coupee. Périer did not dare reveal the identity of the attackers, because he believed that they were also responsible for the attack upon the de Mezières plantation, and panic had already seized the colony.[11]

It soon became clear that there was still a substantial Natchez presence in the area. On June 4, 1732, a contingent of 10 soldiers and 40

11. Salmon to the Ministry of the Colonies, March 24, 1732, in Ser. C13A 15, fols. 50–52, ANC; Bienville and Salmon to the Ministry of the Colonies, May 12, 1733, in Ser. C13A 16, fol. 73, *ibid.*; October 16, 1731, entry for Chronologie des mouvements des nations sauvages du 28 avril au 22 octubre 1731, in Ser. C13A 13, fols. 85–93, *ibid.*; Périer to the Ministry of the Colonies, April 6, 1732, in Ser. C13A 14, fols. 59, 60, *ibid.*

Indians commanded by Sieur Jurant went in pursuit of a party of Natchez Indians who had seized cattle and several blacks at Pointe Coupee. Their pursuit was fruitless, but on their way back they encountered 4 Ofougoula Indians, French allies, who reported that on May 18, ten pirogues of Natchez Indians returning from their attack upon Pointe Coupee had camped out overnight at Petite Rivière near the French fort at Natchez. They killed 2 Ofougoulas and wounded 2 others, but some managed to escape. The Natchez had told them that they would return to attack the Tunica village and then Pointe Coupee, and thereafter descend upon the German Coast slightly north of New Orleans, where they would camp out and await the English who would come by the big lake (Lake Pontchartrain) to seize Périer. Jurant reported that the Natchez had begun to carry out this plan. During the night of June 13 to 14, 1732, the Natchez built a camp surrounded by trenches near Pointe Coupee and left two tomahawks as a declaration of war. Thereafter there were reports of Natchez parties roaming the area. A contingent of 25 to 30 Tunicas sent in pursuit found 14 Natchez camps near the post. The Tunicas destroyed the camps, killed 4 Natchez, wounded 2, and ran off the rest. It had been thought that all the Natchez had taken refuge with the Chickasaw, but Jurant reported that most of them, 180 warriors without counting the young people, were wandering about with no other idea than to seize the blacks and sell them to the English for merchandise. By July, 1732, it became clear that it was, indeed, the Natchez, not the small nations along the river, who had destroyed the de Mezières concession and seized the slaves. One of the black women escaped from the Natchez and fled to the Tunicas. She reported that within the month, the Natchez would organize a party of 200 men to attack Pointe Coupee. The settlers built two small forts at each extremity of the settlement, with 15 French soldiers at one end and 20 Swiss soldiers at the other. An Ofougoula Indian and a black slave who were out hunting together in a pirogue to obtain food for the settlers were attacked by a party of Natchez Indians. The slave was killed, and the Ofougoula was wounded by several arrows. The Natchez cut up the pirogue and left it on the shore with broken arrows and tomahawks as a war signal. Travelers often found paths and fires in the Red River area, which convinced the authorities that this region had not been completely abandoned by the Natchez.[12]

By June of 1733, Bienville, back in command, had uncovered the retreat of a party of Natchez established near their old settlement. He

12. [Salmon?] to X., July 25, 1732, in Ser. C13A 15, fol. 183, *ibid.*

ordered the Tunica to force the Natchez out of their retreat and destroy their village. The Tunica were armed and marched off at once, under the command of Jurant. They found the village abandoned except for five or six families who were expecting an abundant harvest, but they were so much on their guard that the Tunica could not surprise them. They ran away, leaving behind only one old woman. The attackers destroyed the crops and burned the cabins. The old woman, who had been taken prisoner, informed Bienville that there had been about twenty warriors in the group when Bienville began to pursue them. Realizing that their retreat had been discovered, they had accepted the invitation of the Chickasaw, who had been urging them to take refuge among them and had been promising all kinds of advantages from the English. The woman informed Bienville that the other Natchez party that had been along the Ouachita River the previous year had also taken refuge among the Chickasaw. No more than forty warriors and as many young women remained near the Mississippi, and they were dispersed and hiding in the mountains not far from the village where she had been captured.[13]

In 1732, it was reported that there were nearly forty settlers in Pointe Coupee occupying nearly two lieus of land. They were described as good men, almost all of whom were Walloons.[14] The first black slaves appeared in the 1731 census. There were as many adult blacks as adult whites: sixty-three black adults and seven black children, all slaves, three Indian slaves, thirty-seven white men, twenty-five white women, seven *engagés*, and twenty-six white children. Among the thirty-three households, only six had no slaves. Pierre Germain, who began his career in the Tunica village, held one Indian and nine black slaves. The rest of the households held between one and five slaves. The even distribution of slaves in small households, and their common danger, encouraged intimate ties among masters and slaves. Between 1735 and 1739, French settlers stood as godparents for their own and each others' slaves during baptism. In twenty-two out of twenty-seven baptisms that took place during those years, the baptized slave was given the first name of the godparent. These were probably adult baptisms, since neither date of birth nor mother or father is given. There were twenty female baptisms and only seven male, indicating a greater resistance to Chris-

13. Bienville to the Ministry of the Colonies, July 26, 1733, in Ser. C13A 16, fols. 277–78, *ibid.*
14. [Salmon?] to X., July 25, 1732, in Ser. C13A 15, fol. 183, *ibid. Walloon* means Franco-Belge.

tianization among the men. All the baptized slaves were identified as black, except for one mulatto, one Indian, and two whose race was not indicated. All the godparents were white except for one woman listed as *griffe*. The godfather in this baptism was Joseph Decuir, a white slave owner. This dual relationship, godparent and namesake, had profound significance for both godchild and godparent.[15]

It is easy to understand the closeness and intimacy that developed among red, white, and black during the early years of settlement at Pointe Coupee. When the settlement was attacked by the Natchez, the Chickasaw, and, at times, individuals of the smaller nations allied to the French, the Chitimachas and the Tunicas, the white and Indian victims were murdered and scalped. The blacks, perhaps a little more fortunate, were a prized commodity. They relived their own, or their parents', experience in Africa. They were kidnapped and sold, this time to the Chickasaw, who exchanged them for trade goods with the English in South Carolina. Throughout the 1730s and early 1740s, the Pointe Coupee post suffered raids from hostile Indians, aggravated by the Chickasaw Wars. A Frenchman and an Ofougoula Indian were killed in a pirogue above Pointe Coupee. Bienville made inquiries among all the nations along the Mississippi and was informed that the killers were five Tunica Indians who were returning from smoking the calumet with the Chitimachas. Bienville hastened to point out that the Tunica, a nation of fifty warriors, had not been responsible for these deaths. These killers were only a few rebels whose heads he would demand when the chiefs came to the capital in the spring. Bienville explained that he would proceed as gently as possible in order to avoid war with this nation. Meanwhile, he removed the garrison from the Tunica village and reinforced the garrison at Pointe Coupee. In November of 1738, two settlers from Pointe Coupee arrived in the capital to report that an Indian informant told them about a widespread conspiracy among the Chitimachas, the Avoyelles, the Tunicas, the Natchitoches, and nations along the upper reaches of the Red River to destroy the French settlements at Natchitoches and Pointe Coupee. Ten soldiers were sent to Pointe Coupee to reassure the settlers there and to stop them from abandoning their houses and belongings, which would have precipitated the flight of settlers along the whole length of the river. The commanders at Natchitoches and Natchez were warned and were ordered not to let any armed Indians

15. Census of Inhabitants Along the River Mississippi dated 1731, in Maduell, *Census Tables*, 118, 199; Registre de Baptismes, enterrement et marriages, 1728–1765, of St. Francis Church of Pointe Coupee, Book 1, Catholic Life Center, Baton Rouge, La.

enter their forts under any pretext whatsoever. No arms, powder, or balls were to be given to the Tunica until further orders.[16]

Indian raids continued into the 1740s. In 1741, a bold party of seven Chickasaw Indians camped out for two days on the land of Sieur Ricard at the center of the settlement at Pointe Coupee. They were only a pistol shot away from the main road. During the religious holiday of Fête Dieu, fifty or sixty settlers passed along the road on their way to church, unaware of the presence of the Chickasaw. Luckily, they were not fired upon. Before the Chickasaw left, they seized three little black girls and a white orphan boy who had been collecting reeds. A party of fifty French and Indian men pursued them, concluding from their abandoned camps that there were fifteen Chickasaw. The Chickasaw eluded their pursuers, taking their captives with them. Although the initial reports indicated that the orphan was still alive, he was eventually killed. An eyewitness reported that the three black girls were sold to the English. A local official wrote, "It is to be feared that we will be visited by [the Chickasaw] frequently . . . which would upset the settlers very much, especially since we are about to have an abundant harvest, the best I have ever seen." When a pirogue of Chickasaw Indians tried to make a descent into the middle of Pointe Coupee in 1741, the settlers assembled and armed their black slaves, and the Chickasaw fled.[17] Clearly, the primary concern of whites, blacks, and friendly Indians was mutual protection. The common danger they faced cemented ties among them.

In spite of its insecure beginnings, the Pointe Coupee settlement grew. By 1739, there were forty-eight farms occupying about two and a half lieus along the Mississippi River. The land was described as very good and high enough not to require levees. *Ordonnateur* Salmon obliged the settlers to pay fifteen hundred livres to build a church and ordered their lands surveyed. By 1741, Salmon wrote that the post had at least one hundred settlers, probably meaning male heads of family, and more than five hundred blacks of all sexes and ages. The east bank of the Mississippi River opposite the Pointe Coupee post was not settled because of fear of the Indians who wandered about there from time to time. These lands were too low for cultivation, and

16. Bienville to the Ministry of the Colonies, December 20, 1737, in Ser. C13A 22, fols. 115–16, ANC; Louboey to the Ministry of the Colonies, November 28, 1738, in Ser. C13A 23, fol. 173, *ibid.*

17. Louboey to the Ministry of the Colonies, October 2, 1741, in Ser. C13A 26, fol. 200, *ibid.*; Extrait d'une lettre de Trénonay, subdélégué de commissaire ordonnateur à la Pointe Coupée, à Salmon, Pointe Coupée, June 5, 1741, *ibid.*, fols. 154–55; Salmon to the Ministry of the Colonies, New Orleans, October 4, 1741, *ibid.*, fol. 171.

paths there led to the Chickasaw Indians and to "New England." The inhabited part of Pointe Coupee fronted the river and ran twenty to sixty arpents deep, beyond which were cypress swamps full of water, lakes, and flooded prairies. Indigo, corn, and tobacco were cultivated. At times, the river rose fifty pieds and flooded the lands, obliging the settlers to build levees to protect themselves. Few fish could be found in the area, but there were many alligators and reptiles and an abundance of many varieties of insects, which reduced the settlers to despair. There were many birds, some transitory, including ducks, Canadian geese, cranes, and other aquatic varieties, as well as Amazonian parrots, cardinals, and woodcocks, which were hunted at night by torch. Deer and bear had become rare since the post was settled, obliging the Indians to live elsewhere. There were no more wild cattle, and wildcats had become rare as well. Cypress was the most common tree but was neither of the size nor the quality of the cypress in and around New Orleans.[18]

By 1746, Pointe Coupee reportedly contained about two hundred settlers and four hundred blacks. Their principal occupation was the cultivation of tobacco on small farms and of subsistence crops. Warfare, lack of shipping, and low prices for tobacco stunted the growth of the post. By 1747, tobacco had been piling up for two years because of lack of shipping. Of four hundred boucauts (casks) ready to ship, there was room to load only one hundred. Aside from shipping problems, the price of tobacco had fallen so low that the settlers were ready to abandon its cultivation. Vaudreuil urged them to continue to grow the crop. He requested that the king's ships load it in preference to any foreign staple and that the king purchase it at six sols per pound, promising to send only tobacco of good quality. The governor pointed out that tobacco grew well in the colony and was the only resource of the small planters, who had few slaves or none at all. He claimed that some small planters had started out planting tobacco and within a few years' time had become big planters. By 1749, the end of King George's War allowed for the revival of shipping. Tobacco cultivation began to thrive at the post, and pelts and indigo were also being shipped. With an assured market and available shipping, tobacco cultivation expanded during the early 1750s, and by 1752, colonial officials were calling for more peasants and black slaves, for

18. Salmon to the Ministry of the Colonies, January 12, 1739, in Ser. C13A 24, fols. 117–18, ibid.; Salmon to the Ministry of the Colonies, October 4, 1741, C13A 26, fol. 171, ibid.; Idée historique du Poste de la Pointe Coupée (fragment), n.d., in Leg. 196, fol. 708, PC, AGI.

police, and for discipline among the troops to assure the future of the colony. Although markets and shipping became available during the few years between the end of King George's War in 1748 and the beginning of the French and Indian War in 1754, new problems arose that stemmed from regressive, exploitative, and corrupt political practices. *Ordonnateur* Salmon accused Vaudreuil of appointing local officials who gave him kickbacks. Many of them were his relatives. Vaudreuil accused *Ordonnateur* Michel of protecting Trénonay de Chanfret, his subdelegate at Pointe Coupee, who was preying upon the settlers by imposing confiscatory fines arising from disputes that he himself had stirred up.[19] It appears that both of these officials were right.

Trénonay de Chanfret forced Pierre Germain, the most active, prosperous, and generous settler of the district, to leave the colony. Trénonay had established his authority in 1741 over the objections of Sieur Delahoussay, the hero of the Natchez Wars and military commander of the post. By 1750, Trénonay was well established, enjoying the protection of *Ordonnateur* Michel, who praised him highly to the government, asking for perquisites and expenses to encourage him to continue to carry out his duties at the post. Germain, who had begun his career in the Tunica village, was accused of using his own brand on some cattle belonging to his neighbors. The branding was carried out by Germain's slaves; according to Vaudreuil, it was an honest mistake. However, Trénonay imposed confiscatory fines on Germain. Although Germain had agreed to all his demands, Trénonay convinced a number of settlers to leave their work and descend to New Orleans to protest against Germain. The harassed Germain sold his estate, along with all his slaves, at a very low price, and he and six other families—his wife's relatives whom he had generously established at the post—were planning to leave. Vaudreuil pointed out that since Germain had no children, his departure would deprive settlers at the post of his rich inheritance, as well as that of those he had helped establish and others he planned to establish in the future. Other settlers were planning to leave because Trénonay tyrannized over the

19. Mémoire sur l'etat de la Colonie de la Louisiane en 1746, in Ser. C13A 30, fols. 248–49, ANC; Vaudreuil to the Ministry of the Colonies, October 5, 1747, in Ser. F3 24, fol. 448, AN (duplicate of letter in Ser. C13A 31, fols. 74–75, ANC); Vaudreuil to the Ministry of the Colonies, March 8, 1749, in Ser. C13A 33, fol. 26, August 28, 1749, in Ser. C13A 33, fol. 66, January 31, 1750, in Ser. C13A 34, fol. 250, all in ANC; Michel to the Ministry of the Colonies, January 18, 1752, in Ser. C13A 36, fol. 229, ANC; Michel to Rouillé, July 20, 1751, in *MPA*, V, 97–105; Vaudreuil to the Ministry of the Colonies, January 28, 1752, in Ser. C13A 36, fols. 32–35, ANC.

settlers, abusing his authority by inflaming the least conflict that arose and profiting from the least incident. Vaudreuil asked the government to eliminate the post of subdelegate and have only a commanding officer, a system that he claimed worked smoothly at the German Coast.[20]

The French and Indian War reduced the Pointe Coupee settlement to desperate straits. Shipping was cut off, markets were eliminated, supplies were extremely scarce, and Indian raids resumed. Two settlers were murdered during an Indian raid. Nature added to manmade miseries. In 1758, there was a bad harvest, and famine struck. The settlers were reduced to hunting in order to survive. Flour and gunpowder were distributed to them. In 1760, a new fort was completed at Pointe Coupee—one of the last, feeble gestures to protect French Louisiana.[21]

The Pointe Coupee post prospered greatly after Spain took possession of Louisiana. Claude Trénonay, nephew and heir of Trénonay de Chanfret, became one of the handful of big slave owners who emerged during the late eighteenth century. In 1785, during the indigo boom, he had purchased 40 *nègres bruts* right off the slave-trade ship from Africa. He was assured by the slave traders from whom he bought the slaves that they were of good nations (*de bonne nations*), aged between sixteen and twenty-two. They were to be delivered on his plantation by March 1, 1786, and each was to arrive clothed with a good woolen blanket, a shirt and a hat. By 1791, Trénonay owned 111 slaves, 52 of whom were Africans.[22]

On July 9, 1791, at about 8 P.M., Trénonay was seated at his dining room table with Joseph Etienne Blanc, his personal physician and surgeon, François Mayeux, his manager (*econome*), and André Gariot, his

20. Copies des lettres de M. Delahoussay au Trenanay écrits à la Pointe Coupée, January 23, 1741, and Réponse de M. Trenaunay à la Lettre de M. Delahoussay du 24 janvier 1741, January 29, 1741, both in Ser. C13A 26, fols. 247–49, ANC; Michel to the Government, January 29, 1750, and Michel to [?], May 22, 1751, both in Ser. C13A 35, fols. 211–13, 305, *ibid.*; Vaudreuil to the Ministry of the Colonies, January 28, 1752, in Ser. C13A 36, fols. 32–35, *ibid.*

21. Rocheblave to Rochemore, Pointe Coupee, October 24, November 22, 1758, in Ser. C13A 40, fols. 249, 251, respectively, *ibid.*; Rochemore to the Ministry of the Colonies, June 23, 1760, in Ser. C13A 42, fol. 118, *ibid.*

22. The total price for the 40 slaves was 12,400 piasters. He paid 8,000 piasters and 1,933 pounds of good indigo down. The balance was to be payable the next December at the latest in indigo (vente d'esclaves, October 17, 1785, Doc. 1451, in OAPC). The slave traders were George Profit, David Ross, and Jerome Lachapelle. Figures for Trénonay slaves in 1791 are from July 10, 1791, Doc. 1761, in OAPC.

"man of confidence." Trénonay and his retainers were being served by three of his domestic slaves: Jeanne Mulâtresse, Zénon Mulâtre, and Esther, a *négresse* of the Fon nation. The soup course had been served, and the three domestic slaves were in the kitchen eating their own dinner. Suddenly, a shot rang out. Gariot ran to the door of the dining room, but when he heard a profound sigh coming from Trénonay, he ran back to help him, calling for Blanc to come and attend to the wounded man. Blanc, however, was hiding. He claimed that the bullet had grazed his right ear and that he had crumpled and fallen under his chair before running to hide under the porch steps. Jeanne Mulâtresse came running into the dining room, where she found her master in the hands of Gariot. Trénonay was bleeding from the nose and mouth. After examining the site of the wound and Trénonay's condition, Blanc concluded that the wound was fatal. Trénonay's companions left him where he had fallen. They went for Valentin Leblanc, *comandante* of the post, who arrived to find Trénonay's body slumped at the dinner table. François and Auguste Allain, both militiamen, were already there when the *comandante* arrived.[23]

Magloire Mulâtre Créole, Julien Mulâtre Créole, and André Nègre Créole all testified that they saw the assailant. He was Trénonay's slave Latulipe Ibo, a maroon for the past three weeks. Latulipe had shot his master with a small musket, firing through the dining-room window while standing near the porch. Three of Trénonay's slaves, one of whom was a hunter, identified Latulipe Ibo's footprints near the porch steps. Latulipe had small feet and toes that spread out. André Nègre Créole added that he knew that Latulipe "had bad intentions towards his master." Several slaves working at the infirmary witnessed Latulipe's flight from the scene of the crime. Marie Thérèse ran out of the infirmary when she heard the shot and recognized Latulipe as he fled. Madelaine Grive, the cook, Fauchon Nègresse, the nurse, and her daughter Marie Thérèse all testified that they recognized Latulipe's voice. He said: "It is I! It is I myself! Latulipe! You are done for today, and so am I" (*"C'est moi! C'est moi moi-même, La-*

---

23. Testimony of François Mayeux, July 11, 1792, Testimony of André Gariot, July 12, 1792, Testimony of Joseph Étienne Blanc, July 12, 1792, Testimony of Jeanne Mulâtresse Créole, July 12, 1792, Testimony of Zénon Mulâtre Créole, July 12, 1792, Testimony of Esther Nègresse Fond, July 12, 1792, untitled document, July 11, 1792, all in Doc. 1880, Procès criminel au sujet de l'assassinat commis en la Personne de Sieur Claude Trénonay le 10 juillet 1792, (bound after Doc. 1761), in OAPC.

tulipe! Toi fini, moi aussi. C'est ton dernier jour aujourd'hui, mon tienne aussi").[24]

Jeanne Mulâtresse explained Latulipe's motives for killing his master. Trénonay had accused Latulipe of stealing, and had him flogged and put into a wooden stock (*cep*) located in the infirmary. Both Jeanne Mulâtresse and Fauchon, the nurse, reported that the day Latulipe was put in the stocks he said to his master, "I believe you do not need me anymore" (in Louisiana Creole, *"Moi crois toi pas besoin moi encore"*). The master replied that he needed him, but not a rogue who was always involved in thefts (*"qu'il avoit besoin de lui, mais non d'un coquin, qui se trouvoit toujours compliqué dans les vols"*). After five days, Latulipe succeeded in breaking the hinge of the stocks and escaped. He was gone for three weeks before he returned and killed his master.[25]

Comandante Leblanc declared a full alert to find the killer. A militia patrol searched the Trénonay slave quarters for firearms but found nothing. Leblanc sent for Panarois, chief of the Tunica Indians, and showed him Latulipe's footprint. Panarois and four of his men were sent to look for Latulipe. They were offered big rewards if they found him, but they found neither Latulipe nor his footprints. Three militia patrols were sent to all the slave quarters every night for an indefinite period.[26]

On July 12, Magloire Mulâtre came forward to report that he had seen Latulipe the day before at about 3:30 P.M. Latulipe had been walking through the Trénonay slave quarters carrying a little musket. Magloire was not sure it was Latulipe until he spoke, saying simply, "Bonjour, Magloire." Latulipe then headed for the woods. Magloire Mulâtre said he had not reported the incident sooner because he was afraid.[27]

At 4:00 A.M. on July 14, Narcisse Bacoco was on his way to the fields when he hit his foot on a small musket lying along a path leading to the slave quarters. He brought the gun to Mayeux, Trénonay's manager. At 5:00 A.M. the same day, Simon Nègre, second *comman-*

---

24. Testimony of Magloire Mulâtre Créole, July 11, 1792, Testimony of Julien Mulâtre Créole, chasseur, July 11, 1792, Testimony of André Nègre Créole, indigotier, July 11, 1792, Testimony of Marie Thérèse, fille de Fauchon, July 12, 1792, Testimony of Marie Thérèse, July 13, 1792, Testimony of Madelaine Grive, cuisinière, July 13, 1792, Testimony of Fauchon Nègresse, hospitalière, July 12, 1792, all *ibid.*

25. Testimony of Jeanne Mulâtresse, July 12, 1792, Testimony of Fauchon Nègresse, July 13, 1792, both *ibid.*

26. Report of July 12, 1792, Testimony of Panarois, July 13, 1792, both *ibid.*

27. Testimony of Magloire Mulâtre, July 12, 1792, *ibid.*

deur, was returning from the fields. As he passed Latulipe's cabin, he noticed that the door, which had been left open since Latulipe ran away, was closed. He opened the door and found Latulipe hanging. He yelled out, "There's Latulipe!"[28]

Mayeux entered Latulipe's cabin and found he had hanged himself with his shirt. They cut him down. Near the body they found a fabric bag containing ten grains of lead (*plomb mayeu*) wrapped in a cloth, a ball that seemed to have been already fired, a bad musket stone, and several little pieces of torchwood.[29]

Leblanc ordered all the Trénonay slaves to Latulipe's cabin and said to them, "There is the one who killed your master. And he who wants to show his regret will prove it by cutting off his head." Charlot Nègre Créole, first *commandeur*, did so. André Nègre Créole, indigo maker, then cut off a hand. Segué Mulâtre, gardener, cut off the other hand. Magloire Mulâtre cut off one foot, and César Nègre the other foot. Mayeux ordered all these body parts to be exposed at the top of a post in view of the slave quarters of the plantation, and the remains of the body buried at the foot of the post.[30]

Was Latulipe Ibo among the forty *nègres bruts* "of good nation" purchased by Trénonay? If so, Trénonay was cheated. At the Pointe Coupee post, the Ibo were reputed to be a "bad" nation. For example, a *nègre brut* of unknown nation was sold, but the seller guaranteed that the slave was not an Ibo. Throughout the Americas, Ibo slaves were reputed to be suicidal. It was thought that their tendency to hang themselves stemmed from their belief in the transmigration of souls: that after death, they would return body and soul to their home in Africa. In Cuba during the nineteenth century, entire plantations of Ibos hanged themselves from trees simultaneously. They were mutilated to discourage other slaves from following their example, but other Ibos hung themselves from the same trees. Although there were a considerable number of Ibo slaves at Pointe Coupee, they were mainly women. Thirty-five Ibo women and only twenty-three Ibo men were found in the Pointe Coupee inventories from 1771 to 1802.[31]

---

28. Testimony of Narcise Nègre Bacoco, July 14, 1792, Testimony of Simon Nègre, July 14, 1792, both *ibid*.

29. Testimony of François Mayeux, July 14, 1792, *ibid*.

30. Document dated July 14, 1792, signed by attending witnesses Augustin Allain, Ricard de Rieutord, and Valentin Leblanc, *ibid*. These documents were ordered sent to the superior tribunal on July 15, 1792, and were sent on July 18, 1792.

31. Vente d'esclave, Monsanto à LeDoux, May, 1787, Doc. 1571, in OAPC; Gwendolyn Midlo Hall, *Social Control in Slave Plantation Societies: A Comparison of St. Domingue and Cuba* (Baltimore, 1971), 20, 21; number of Ibo slaves calculated from DB Inventories.

Three years after the murder-suicide of Trénonay and Latulipe Ibo, Jeanne Mulâtresse Créole petitioned *Comandante* Duparc for freedom for herself and for her three-year-old quadroon son, Honoré. They had been estimated in the Trénonay estate inventory at 450 piasters for both of them. She must have been dark, because Trénonay's manager, who appraised the estate, listed her as black and the race of her son as unknown. Honoré's baptismal record lists his mother as Jeanne Mulâtresse of Sieur Trénonay and gives no race for the child. The godparents were free mulattoes.[32]

In elegant language, Jeanne Mulâtresse wrote that her master, Claude Trénonay,

> intended to free me and my quadroon son Honoré, about 3 years old. He always repeated to me during his lifetime that I should be confident of my future, that I would never serve another master except him, in recognition of the good and agreeable services which I rendered to him daily, and above all, the attachment to him which I have demonstrated during all his illnesses, and because of the attention and assiduous care which I gave him. The intention of the said deceased is well known. M. Decuir who was defender of the absent heirs, and M. Armand Duplantier, the nephew of the deceased, have written to France to the brothers and sisters of my master to explain to them the reasons why they should agree to the well-known truth of their brother in relation to me. I therefore ask that you show regard for my just representations, and agree to suspend my sale and that of my son Honoré, addressing my humble request to the Superior Court.[33]

Comandante Duparc ordered Ricard de Rieutord, defender of the interests of the absent heirs, as well as the deceased's nephew, Armand Duplantier, and the deceased's mother, to appear to respond to Jeanne Mulâtresse's petition and to clarify the matter. Ricard de Rieutord declared under oath, "The intentions of Sieur Claude Trénonay towards the said Jeanne are perfectly well known to me, as well as her attentions and affection for her deceased master, and consequently I believe that justice would be badly served if I opposed the least obstacle to her claim for freedom." Armand Duplantier was then sworn in and declared under oath that Jeanne Mulâtresse's petition "conforms to the most exact truth." Trénonay's mother made no objections. Jeanne and her son, Honoré, were separated from the slaves

---

32. Honoré was born on October 11, 1790, and baptized on November 25 the same year (Registre baptistaire et mortuaire des nègres, 1786–1838, of St. Francis Church of Pointe Coupee, p. 25, Catholic Life Center, Baton Rouge).

33. January 17, 1794, Doc. 1799, in OAPC.

inventoried for sale and freed the following year. A few months later, her little girl, Eulalie Mulâtresse, father unknown, was baptized. Armand Duplantier was the godfather. Duplantier freed his three-year-old mulatto slave Robers.[34] There was an adult *mulâtre* named Duplantier at the post in 1795.

All of the prominent and respected men involved in these proceedings had concubines and children of African descent. Two of them, both bachelors, maintained lifetime relationships with their concubines, one of whom was black and the other mulatto. Both of them fathered several children by their concubines. In 1786, Ricard de Rieutord lived with Marianne, a free black woman, and her four mixed-blood children in the same household as François Allain and Marie Ricard, his wife, probably Ricard de Rieutord's sister, and their seven children. The Ricards and the Allains were involved in eleven emancipations of slaves, most of them gratuitous. Ricard de Rieutord helped several free mulattoes establish themselves with land, slaves, and merchandise. He mortgaged his own belongings and, by power of attorney, an estate belonging to Louis Ricard, *mulâtre libre*, so that the merchant Julien Poydras would furnish goods to the free mulatto. Joseph Decuir, who wrote to Trénonay's siblings in France asking them to free Jeanne Mulâtresse and Honoré, made a donation to the four quadroon children of Françoise Beaulieu Mulâtresse Libre "in recognition of the good services which the said Françoise Beaulieu Mulâtresse Libre has lent me, and for the good friendship which I feel towards the children of the said Françoise." He gave each child one of his slaves, providing that in case of the death of one of the children, the survivors would divide the donation among them. Antoine Decuir and Jean Baptiste Decuir were godfathers at the baptism of two of Françoise Beaulieu's children. Joseph Decuir appeared as grandfather at the baptism of Françoise Beaulieu's grandchild. These men were among the handful of large slave owners at the settlement. If the most prominent men of Pointe Coupee chose women of African descent, this was not because of a shortage of white women. In 1786, the sex ratio among "whites" aged fifteen to forty-nine was 0.77, or seventy-seven men to one hundred women. Only 54 percent of the white women aged fifteen to forty-nine at the post were married. It was only after 1795 that there was an influx of single white male im-

34. Décret du Tribunal de la Cour Supérieur, March 17, 1795, Doc. 1884, in OAPC; August 22, 1794, Registre baptistaire et mortuaire des nègres, 1786–1838, p. 53; Lettre de Liberté, Armand Duplantier à Robers Mulâtre, September 23, 1794, Doc. 1819, in OAPC.

migrants to the post, creating a sex ratio of 1.67 among "whites."[35]

At Pointe Coupee, remote from the center of Spanish government in New Orleans and its corporatist, hierarchical concepts of race, the separate category "free mulatto" did not clearly emerge until the census of 1803. Before 1803, few free people of African descent were listed as such. The census of 1763 listed no *affranchis*, either black or mulatto. In order to cut through the complexities of the Pointe Coupee population, the 1786 census lumped together all free people who were heads of families, regardless of race or gender, under the listing Whites and Free People of Both Sexes Who Are Heads of Families (*Blancs et Libres des 2 sexes Chefs de famille*). There was only one adult woman among the eight free people of African descent listed separately, and she was black. There were five mixed-blood children, one mixed-blood adult male, and one elderly black male. The 1790 census put all free people in the category Names of Heads of Families, Foreigners, and Free Persons (*Noms des Chefs de Famille, étrangers et Libres*) and totaled them under the category Whites. There was no separate category for free people of African descent. The categories for the totals were black slaves, mixed-blood slaves, and whites. All free people of African descent, regardless of race, were counted with the whites. The black concubine of Ricard de Rieutord, Libre Marianne, five children, and six other adults in her household were counted among the whites. Louis Ricard, described in notarial records as a free mulatto, his wife, and two children were counted with the whites. That the 1790 census did not enumerate free people of African descent as a separate category is clear from a 1792 report that listed three free mulatto men—Luis Claudio el Claire, Juan Bautista Grande

---

35. Censo de Punta Cortada, 1786, in Leg. 2361, PC, AGI. For information on the emancipations, see the following documents in OAPC: May 12, 1780, Doc. 1004; March 13, 1781, Doc. 1199; January 31, 1782, Doc. 1161; August 30, 1783, Doc. 1295; September 9, 1799, Doc. 2054; December 1, 1786, Doc. 2093; February 1, 1802, Doc. 2154; January 1, 1797, Doc. 1918; May 3, 1797, Doc. 1939. The following documents, also in OAPC, concern Ricard de Rieutord and the mulattoes: March 20, 1771, Doc. 418; November 9, 1782, Doc. 1216; April 8, 1786, Doc. 1488. March 22, 1797, Doc. 1925, in OAPC; Baptism of Antoine Mulâtre, born October 27, 1788, of Françoise Beaulieu Mulâtresse Libre and an unknown father, baptized December 7, 1788, godparents, Antoine Decuir and Marie Tournoir, and Baptism of Celeste Mulâtresse, daughter of Françoise Mulâtresse Libre, June 5, 1791, godfather, Jean Baptiste Decuir, in Registre baptistre et mortuaire des nègres, 1786–1838; information on the baptism of Françoise Beaulieu's grandchild in Ricard Family Papers, Amistad Research Center, New Orleans; 1786 Pointe Coupee sex ratio calculated from Antonio Acosta Rodríguez, *La población de la Luisiana española (1763–1803)* (Madrid, 1979), 175, 208; 1795 sex ratio calculated from *ibid.*, 239, 274, 474.

Megon, and Juan Fara—and four free black men—Pedro Dumas, Juan Bautista Disbregenon, Pedro Juin, and Gime—who resided in the district. A church census dating from 1795 listed thirty-seven free mulatto children under age fourteen—fifteen boys and twenty-two girls—eleven adult free mulatto men, and no free mulatto women. All free people of African descent were listed as mulattoes, and all slaves were listed as blacks. The free mulattoes jumped from six in 1786 to forty-seven in 1795 and fifty-five in 1803. Persons listed as free blacks declined from two in 1786 to none in 1795 and in 1803. Evidently, once the Pointe Coupee community was forced to acknowledge free people of African descent as a separate category, they listed all of them as mulattoes, regardless of race. The 1803 census of Pointe Coupee and False River counted twelve male and twenty-three female free mulatto children (under age fifteen), eight free male and eight free female mulatto adults, and no elderly people (over age forty-nine), pointing to a recent emergence of free people of African descent as a separate category. Yet only 38.5 percent of the slaves who were emancipated were males. This discrepancy in sex ratio between the "free mulatto" population and that of emancipated slaves is accountable only partially by the migration to New Orleans of more freed women than freed men. It is likely that by 1803, women *affranchis* and their children were counted as mulatto when they were married to *affranchis* men and white when they were married to, or concubines of, white men. Françoise Beaulieu, for example, was listed under Names of Whites in the 1803 census.[36]

While free blacks and mixed-bloods did not show up in the censuses, they did appear in the notarial records. At the Pointe Coupee post, the *lettres de liberté* stated that a former slave can "negotiate, contract, sell, appear in justice, present documents, and do all that free and nonsubject persons can do, enjoying in all things full and free will." In 1771, Jean Baptiste Mulâtre Libre bought an estate and a Nago slave from M. Olivo. In 1779, Jeannot Mulâtre Libre bought a Senegal slave. In 1782, Jean Baptiste Bienville Mulâtre Libre and his wife, Marie, purchased six slaves from Ricard de Rieutord: an Ibo

36. Recensement de la Pointe Coupée et la Fausse Rivière, Année 1786, January 20, 1786, in Leg. 2361, PC, AGI; Recensement de la Pointe Coupée et Fausse Rivière, March 29, 1790, in Leg. 227A, Carpeta 21, Doc. 2, *ibid.*; Report of Valentin Leblanc, May 16, 1792, in Leg. 206, fol. 627, *ibid.*; Thomas Marc Fiehrer, "The Baron de Carondelet as Agent of Bourbon Reform: A Study of Spanish Colonial Administration in the Years of the French Revolution" (Ph.D. dissertation, Tulane University, 1977), 410, 412; Recensement général de la Pointe Coupée, Fausse Rivière et Isles au Chata, May 28, 1803, in Leg. 212A, Carpeta 14, PC, AGI.

couple, their three creole children, aged six years, four years, and eighteen months, and a young Ibo man, aged twenty-three. In 1784, Pierre Avare, a white of Canadian origin, wrote in his will "that all my aforesaid goods or those which remain after my death should be put at the disposition of my neighbor named Jean Baptiste Mulâtre, of whom I have proof of his friendship and sage conduct." Avare left him his buildings, tools, and furniture as an outright legacy, and left him the use of his land and slaves and 10 percent of the value of their sale. In 1785, Venus Négresse Libre bought a Mina slave. In 1787, Henri Mulâtre Libre bought some land.[37]

The extent of concubinage and racial passing in Pointe Coupee is difficult to determine with great precision, but it was undoubtedly substantial. During the French period, emancipation of slaves was quite informal. For example, in 1745, Vincent Le Porche of Pointe Coupee filed a statement with the Superior Council that one Marie Louise was not a slave but should enjoy complete liberty, since she was the daughter of a Frenchman. It was only as late as November 9, 1770, that all acts relating to slaves had to be in notarial form, and thereafter a formal document, a *carta de libertad*, was issued when slaves were freed. It was the biggest slave owners and most prominent people who were most likely to leave traces in the documents, including in the emancipation papers. It was only the rich settlers who could easily afford to emancipate their concubines, redeem their mixed-blood children from slavery, and pass property on to them. At Pointe Coupee a sex ratio of 1.28 among creole slaves aged fifteen through thirty-four between 1771 and 1794 points toward formal and informal emancipations of female creole slaves. After 1794, the sex ratio among creole slaves of this age group dropped to 1.07, reflecting the substantial number of male creole slaves who were executed or exiled following the 1795 slave conspiracy trial.[38]

The high sex ratio among mature creole slaves cannot be accounted for entirely by export of female slaves, nor by excess deaths among

37. Lettre de Liberté, Euphrasie Négresse, April 15, 1799, Doc. 2033, in OAPC; Vente de Terre et d'esclave, Simon Négre, Nation Nago, Olivo à Jean Baptiste Mulâtre Libre, March 20, 1771, Doc. 418, *ibid.*; Inventaire et Vente des Biens de la Succession Taylor, December 1, 1779, Doc. 1018, *ibid.*; Vente des esclaves, November 9, 1782, Doc. 1216, *ibid.*; Testament de Pierre Avare, March 14, 1784, Doc. 1369, *ibid.*; Vente d'esclave Marianne Négresse Mina, Charles Lachapell à Venus n.l. [*négresse libre*] de ce poste, October 15, 1785, Doc. 1442, *ibid.*; Vente de Terre, François David à Henri Mulâtre Libre, November 1, 1787, Doc. 1591, *ibid.*

38. November 14, 1745, in RSC, *LHQ*, XIV (1931), 598; Hans S. Baade, "The Law of Slavery in Spanish Louisiana," in *Louisiana's Legal Heritage*, ed. Edward F. Haas (New Orleans, 1983), 67; information on sex ratios calculated from DB Inventories.

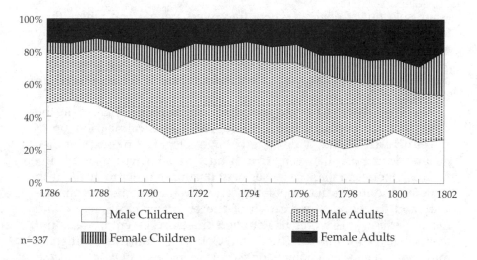

n=337

Male Children   Male Adults

Female Children   Female Adults

Figure 5. Burials of People of African Descent at Pointe Coupee, 1786–1802

SOURCE: Calculated from Registre baptistaire et mortuaire des nègres, 1786–1838, of St. Francis Church of Pointe Coupee, Catholic Life Center, Baton Rouge, La.

females. On the contrary, the death rate among female slaves of all ages was substantially lower than among male slaves. The sex ratio among slaves buried in the Catholic Church between 1786 and 1795 was 2.84, though the sex ratio among all slaves found in the Pointe Coupee inventories was 1.40. The slaves executed for involvement in the 1795 slave conspiracy were not buried in the Church. There is little evidence of export of slaves from the post, especially of females. The estate and sales inventories clearly reflect a strong tendency to keep slaves, especially female creole slaves, in the district when slaves had to be sold. The 2,680 slaves listed in the Pointe Coupee inventories, almost all of whom were sold, either through estate and other types of plantations sales or as individuals or small groups, revealed only 13 slaves sold out of the district, and only 2 of them were women: one an African and one of an unidentified nation. Eight of the 11 men sold out of the district were either of unidentified nations or they were foreign slaves; the other three, two of whom were sold out in 1795, were probably suspected of involvement with the slave conspiracy. A few female creole slaves were probably exported to New Orleans, where the sex ratio favored women, and some male creole slaves were probably purchased outside the district. But creole slaves during the eighteenth century managed to effectively oppose being sold out of districts where they were known and where their families lived. The males imported into Pointe Coupee were probably almost entirely Africans. The fact that there were 28 percent more adult male than adult female slaves of marriageable age among creoles before 1795 points toward the passing of creole slave women into the white population.[39]

The Spanish censuses are useful for determining changes in the slave and free populations over time, the numerical distribution of slaves on estates, and, at times, gross age categories by sex. But they do not distinguish between African and creole slaves. Nor are the racial categories in these censuses very useful. In order to distinguish between the local slave population and the imported slave population, and to get some indication of the extent of race mixture and racial passing, this writer has studied the slave inventory lists and emancipation documents. The Pointe Coupee documents distinguish four racial categories among people of African descent: *nègre, mulâtre, grif,* and *quarteron. Nègre* meant entirely black; *mulâtre* meant half white and half black; *grif* meant a mixture of black and Indian; *quarteron* meant three-quarters white and one-quarter black.

The use of the term *grif* reflects legal concerns as well as problems of definition. A significant number of creole slaves, especially the first generation, had Indian mothers. Slaves who were descendants of Indians were rarely acknowledged as such in the lists of slaves, for a practical reason: Indian slavery was prohibited under Spanish law, and therefore, slaves descended from Indian women were legally entitled to their freedom. One can safely conclude that those slaves listed in the Pointe Coupee inventories as *grif* were only a fraction of the slaves who were mixtures of blacks and Indians. By the early 1790s, *grif* slaves disappeared entirely from the Pointe Coupee lists and mulatto slaves increased, indicating a redefinition to prevent slaves descended from Indian mothers from claiming their freedom under Spanish law.

Aside from legal considerations, the racial designations in the lists of slaves were based partially upon physical appearance and partially upon knowledge of ancestry. In the absence of knowledge of ancestry, much confusion could arise. For example, Denis Macarti, a free man of color from New Orleans who was unknown in the district, was stabbed by a mulatto slave at a party held in the Poydras slave cabins at Pointe Coupee. Although his wound was slight, he unex-

39. Sex ratios calculated from Registre baptistaire et mortuaire des nègres, 1786–1836, and from DB Inventories.

The Pointe Coupee Post

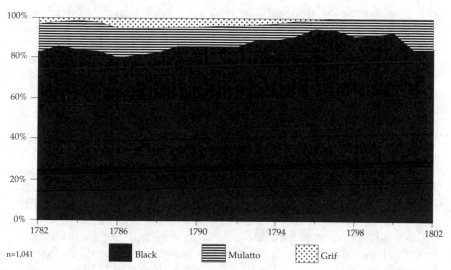

n=1,041 | ■ Black | ☰ Mulatto | ▦ Grif

Figure 6. Racial Designations of Creole Slaves at Pointe Coupee, in Five-Year Moving Averages
SOURCE: Calculated from Pointe Coupee Notarial Records, 1771–1802, Pointe Coupee Parish Courthouse, New Roads, La., entered into DB Inventories.
NOTE: There are no extant records for 1772–1777 or for 1780–1781.

pectedly died within a few days. When he was first stabbed, he was a *nègre libre*. While being treated, he was a *grif*. When he was buried, he was a *mulâtre*.[40]

While the designation *quarteron* has fairly clear meaning in the emancipation documents, there are only 4 *quarterons* among the 2,680 slaves inventoried at Pointe Coupee between 1771 and 1802. All of them involve Nanette and her 3 children. When Nanette appeared in the inventory of the estate of Jean Decuir in 1771, she was listed as one of 3 mulatto children of a *grif* mother. When she was inventoried again upon the death of the widow Decuir in 1779, she was a quadroon (*quarteronne*) mother of Antoine and Lezarie, 2 young mulatto boys. When she and her children were inventoried again in 1798, her race was unidentified and her children had become red quadroons (*quarterons rouges*). After her aunt purchased her in order to free her after years of litigation, she became a mulatto.[41] There was one clear-

40. Requêtes faites au sujet du meurtre commis par le mulâtre Lambert, May 5, 1802, Doc. 2161, in OAPC.
41. February 18, 1771, Doc. 393, March 2, 1778, Doc. 912, October 12, 1779, Doc. 1014, May 12, 1798, Doc. 1984, all in OAPC.

cut case of socioracial promotion upon emancipation. We have seen that Jeanne was listed as black and her son's race unidentified when they were inventoried for sale after the death of her master, Claude Trénonay. When they were both freed after she established with little doubt that Honoré was fathered by Trénonay, she became a mulatto and her son became a quadroon.[42]

There is evidence of fairly widespread socioracial promotion of black to mulatto among concubines of white men. The total census for Louisiana in 1777 counts 166 free and 286 mixed-blood slave females but only 107 free and 259 mixed-blood slave males, or a total of 452 mixed-blood females and 366 mixed-blood males, giving a male/female ratio of 0.81 (that is, 81 males to each 100 females), which is not convincing for a locally born population.[43] Since these figures include all of Louisiana, migration among districts is not a factor.

It is difficult to compare the extent of race mixture in Louisiana with that in other colonies. Among the slaves inventoried at Pointe Coupee between 1771 and 1802, approximately 6 percent were listed as mixed-bloods. The absolute numbers are 157: 85 males, 70 females, and 2 whose sex was not indicated. There were 2,396 blacks, 91 percent of the sample. The race of 126 slaves, or 4.8 percent, was not identified. In Guadeloupe between 1770 and 1789, 14.3 percent of the slave population was racially mixed. These crude percentages do not help us compare the extent of race mixture with other regions if all the slaves are lumped together, including Africans and other imported slaves. Furthermore, the length of time that slaves of African descent had been in the region is an important factor, since the descendants of any racially mixed slave are necessarily racially mixed. By 1664, slaves began to be brought to Guadeloupe in large numbers, whereas slaves first appeared in the census at Pointe Coupee in 1731.[44] The Pointe Coupee post had a much higher percentage of adult Africans than the South Carolina and Georgia low country, Martinique, or Guadeloupe. While the problem of lumping together locally born and imported slaves can be solved by making calculations based upon local creoles only, the impact of the length of time slaves had been in the region is difficult to quantify. Furthermore, we have established that in Louisiana, significant numbers of racially mixed slaves were freed and passed into the white population.

42. March 20, 1794, Doc. 1800, in OAPC.

43. Padron General de todos los individuos de la provincia de Luisiana, May 12, 1777, in Leg. 2351, fol. 216, PC, AGI.

44. Vanony-Frisch, *Esclaves de la Guadeloupe*, 6, 37.

The earliest lists of slaves in Pointe Coupee date from 1771, when 20 percent of the creole slaves were racially mixed. There was a fairly steady proportion of racially mixed slaves among the creoles, with a slight decrease after the 1795 conspiracy, when nine male mulatto slaves were executed or exiled. After 1800, the numbers of mulatto slaves increased, equaling the proportions found in the earliest lists of slaves, though this increase must be partially explained by a re-definition of some of the *grifs* as mulattoes. Although the racial definitions in these documents are at times imprecise, the evidence points overwhelmingly toward matings between white men and black women as the main source of mulatto children. It is less likely that mulatto slaves were born of two mulatto parents. Relatively few mulatto women remained enslaved for long, and those defined as such were often black-Indian women who were particularly defiant and rarely mated with white men. There were few quadroon slaves on the lists. Out of the sixty-eight racially mixed children whose race and the race of whose mother can be reasonably determined, black creole women gave birth to forty-one mulatto children and four *grif* children; mulatto women gave birth to two mulatto children and eight *grif* children; *grif* women gave birth to three mulatto children and one *grif* child; and African women gave birth to five mulatto and two *grif* children. It seems clear that the mulatto children were overwhelmingly first-generation racial mixtures whose mothers were black and whose fathers were white. Slave women designated as mulattoes rarely mated with white men, and African women whose children were racially mixed mated more often with white than with mulatto men. These patterns contrast sharply with those in Guadeloupe, where there was a steady drop in mixed-blood slaves, especially mulattoes between 1778 and 1786, and a rise in the proportion of second generation racially mixed slaves: quadroons (*métis*) and slaves who were three-quarters black, deriving from matings between mulatto and black slaves (*câpres*).[45] In Louisiana, matings between white men and black slave women continued apace.

Pointe Coupee slave inventories from 1771 to 1802 show that the percentage of mixed-bloods in the creole slave population diminished sharply with age. While 17.7 percent of the creole slaves under age fifteen were mixed-bloods, only 10.8 percent aged fifteen and older were racially mixed. It is unlikely that mixed-blood slaves had a higher mortality rate than black slaves, or that significant numbers of

45. Information on racially mixed children calculated from Databases Free and Inventories; Vanony-Frisch, *Esclaves de la Guadeloupe*, figures on p. 39.

them were sold out of the district. Sales and estate sales documents from Pointe Coupee reveal that no mixed-blood slaves were sold out of the district, and that seven were sold into the district. While some could have been removed from the district and sold elsewhere, mulatto slaves, especially men, were highly valued and trained to play police and management roles on the estates. Their reduced numbers in higher age groups were due almost entirely to emancipations.

The Pointe Coupee post documents dating between 1771 and 1802 contain sixty-one examples of emancipation of slaves, even though documents for the years 1772, 1773, 1774, 1775, 1776, 1777, 1780, and 1781 are entirely missing and there are large gaps in later years. In Spain, there is a list of emancipation documents of seventeen other slaves from Pointe Coupee.[46] These numbers are probably only a fraction of the emancipations that actually took place, since there has been a systematic destruction of emancipation records in Louisiana. The price of having an African ancestor has been extremely high. Emancipation documents, *lettres de liberté*, have been largely neglected in parish courthouses, and access to these records has gone unsupervised. But even these minimal figures indicate a comparatively high emancipation rate.

These seventy-eight emancipations are the minimum that actually took place. This writer is inclined to consider those records for 1780 found in Spain—that is, eight per one thousand—as probably the most reliable. Only one of those eight could conceivably have been freed for military service during the war against the British. This emancipation rate is much higher than that in the British West Indies during the early nineteenth century, exceeded only by St. Vincent and the Bahamas in 1834 after general emancipation had already become law, and substantially higher than the emancipation rate in nineteenth-century Cuba.[47]

In a district where the slaves, whose race and sex were identified, were 91 percent black and 58.4 percent male, it is striking that those seventy-eight emancipated slaves were, in contrast, 38.5 percent black and 38.5 percent male. The other emancipated slaves were 48.7 percent mulatto, 1.3 percent *grif*, and 5.1 percent quadroon, and the race of 6.4 percent was not indicated. Clearly, then, black male slaves were least likely to be freed, followed by black females, mixed-blood

46. Pointe Coupee emancipation figures calculated from DB Free; Leg. 206, fols. 57–116, PC, AGI.

47. Barry W. Higman, *Slave Populations of the British Caribbean, 1807–1834* (Baltimore, 1984), 381; Robert L. Paquette, *Sugar Is Made with Blood: The Conspiracy of La Escalera and the Conflict Between Empires over Slavery in Cuba* (Middletown, Conn., 1988), 64.

Table 12. Slave Populations and Emancipations at Pointe Coupee, 1763–1803

Emancipations		Populations	
Year	Number Freed	Year	Number of Slaves
		1763	610
1771	1	1766	680
		1776	826
		1777	999
1778	1		
1779	2		
1780	8		
1781	4		
1782	4		
1783	6		
1784	4		
1785	2		
1786	3	1786	1,311
1787	1		
1788	7	1790	1,533
1793	4		
1794	4		
1795	4		
1796	3		
1797	3		
1798	2		
1799	4		
1800	2		
1801	7		
1802	2		
		1803	1,904

SOURCES: DB Free. Emancipation figure for 1780 from Leg. 206, fols. 57–166, PC, AGI.

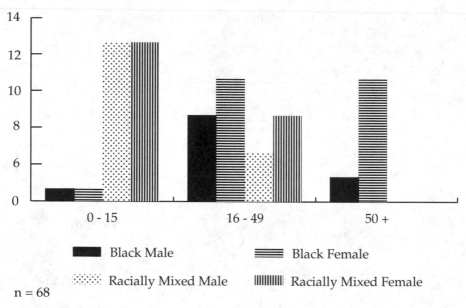

Figure 7. Age, Sex, and Racial Designation of Slaves Emancipated at Pointe Coupee, 1771–1802
SOURCE: Calculated from Pointe Coupee Notarial Records, Pointe Coupee Parish Courthouse, New Roads, La., entered into DB Free.

males, and mixed-blood females. The black men about whom we know the circumstances of emancipation bought themselves, two after litigation. There were two elderly African men, one Bambara and one Congo, freed through self-purchase. One black adult male slave was freed conditionally as a reward for his services. In 1784, Arnaud Dubertrand, master surgeon of the post, returned to France. He sold his entire estate, including fifty-eight slaves, to Julien Poydras. Included in the sale were the services of Pierre Nègre Créole, *commandeur*, for a period of five years, "after which the said Sr. Dubertrand, seller, wishes and understands that his freedom will be given to him and the buyer, Poydras, obligates himself to free him in the proper form."[48] Pierre seemed to fit the category of management-level slaves on the estates whose loyalty was sought by the promise of eventual freedom. Although Pierre was black, many of them were mixed-blood men.

48. Emancipation information calculated from DB Free; Inventaire et Vente, Dubertrand à Poydras, March 26, 1784, Doc. 1355, in OAPC.

Among the seventeen mixed-blood males found in the emancipation records, thirteen were between one month and fifteen years of age. Three of these children were bought by white men for the purpose of freeing them. Four were freed gratuitously by their owner during his lifetime. One was recognized as the natural child of the owner and freed under his will. One was the eight-year-old mulatto son of a Congo woman, and both mother and son were freed under their owner's will. Another child and his mother were freed under their owner's will. A mulatto of undetermined age was freed gratuitously by the heirs, in the absence of a will, because his deceased master had promised to free him.[49]

Three adult mulatto men, aged twenty-eight to thirty-four, bought themselves, and they paid dearly. Isidor Mulâtre, aged thirty-four, paid 875 piastres, a good price, but in addition, he obliged himself to give five more years of free service, working as before but not cultivating the land. Honoré Mulâtre paid his master 753 piastres and agreed to provide him with six years of free service. A twenty-eight-year-old mulatto bought his freedom unconditionally but paid 1,000 piastres, a high price. Many male mulatto slaves were highly valued. They played the role of armed guards on the estates. In a case involving the shooting of a slave who was found stealing from his neighbor's cornfield, M. Bourgeat explained that his black creole slave was given a gun with which to guard the cornfield, because his mulatto was not home.[50]

Although the relatively large numbers of mixed-blood females who were freed appears, at first glance, to involve freedom for concubines of white men, a closer look at the data does not bear this out. Emancipation did not come easily for any adult woman. Among the twenty-four mixed-blood females freed, ten children and only five adults were freed gratuitously by whites. Three mixed-blood females were purchased by nonwhite female relatives, including a quadroon child freed by her slave mother. Five mixed-blood women bought themselves, three of them after initiating litigation to force their masters to sell them. Eleven black women bought themselves, four after litigation. Augustine Négresse petitioned to be estimated and sold by her master, but three years after the decree of the court, she and her master, Joseph Aguiar, arrived at a compromise. He promised not to

49. DB Free.
50. Lettre de Liberté, Felicité Langlois, veuve de Pierre Langlois à Isidor Mulâtre Créole, fils de son esclave Thérèse, February 1, 1798, Doc. 1978, in OAPC; February 12, 1795, Doc. 1833, *ibid.*; December 12, 1788, Doc. 1632, *ibid.*; Procès entre Joseph Bourgeat et Colin Lacour au sujet du nègre nommé Paul, October 7, 1785, Doc. 1445, *ibid.*

mistreat her and to treat her like a good domestic servant, and she promised to serve him faithfully and well for nine years, after which he would free her. Marie dit Mariquine successfully sued Pierre Méthode to confirm the freedom he had already granted to her and to her mixed-blood son when he denied he had freed them and tried to sell them. Most of the black women who bought themselves were elderly. Among the twenty-two black women freed, ten were aged fifty and over. Even at this advanced age, the women paid handsomely for their freedom, which was, besides, sometimes conditional. Some of them remained obligated to perform services for their masters for various time periods. Augustine, aged fifty, paid 360 piastres for herself, but she did not have the right to enjoy her freedom until after the death of her master, who explained that he was happy with her faithfulness and her services. Marie Négresse, aged sixty, was freed by the Widow Le Jeune, provided she continued to "faithfully serve the two demoiselles Brigitte and Pélagie." Augustine, aged sixty, was freed by her daughter, who paid 438 piastres, a very high price for a slave her age. Genneviève, aged fifty-four, paid 240 piastres for her freedom. Manon, aged seventy, paid 100 piastres for herself and was mortgaged to Dame Allain. Thérèse, aged sixty-five, paid 120 piastres and Françoise, aged fifty, paid 230 piastres respectively for their freedom. Catherine, aged sixty-five, paid 64 piastres in the form of eight oxen and cows. Only two of these elderly black women, probably "mammies" of white children, were freed unconditionally. Françoise Négresse Créole, aged fifty, was freed by François Allain and Marie Ricard, his wife, gratuitously and unconditionally. Euphrasie, a black woman aged sixty, was freed in 1799 unconditionally by her living master.[51] It is questionable whether freedom granted to all old slaves was a favor. It could have been a means of abandoning responsibility for an elderly and no longer useful slave.

Prices paid for freedom for young slaves and for, or by, elderly slaves were quite high. In 1785, Thérèse Négresse Libre paid 300 piastres for her two-year-old grandson, after forcing his master to al-

51. December 3, 1793, Doc. 1791, *ibid.*; November 8, 1780, in SJR, *LHQ,* XV (1932), 165–66; Lettre de Liberté, Martin Porche à Augustine Négresse, August 2, 1787, Doc. 1578, in OAPC; Inventaire des Biens, Succession Michel Lejeune, May 5, 1788, Doc. 1621, in OAPC; Lettre de Liberté, Ternant à Augustine Négresse, payé par Heosty, fille de Augustine, February 2, 1797, Doc. 1916, in OAPC; January 31, 1782, Doc. 1161, in OAPC; December 31, 1788, Doc. 1632, in OAPC; February 4, 1799, Doc. 2022, in OAPC; October 8, 1786, Doc. 2089, in OAPC; Lettre de Liberté, Marguerite Bourgeat Vve. à Catherine Négresse, October 25, 1793, Doc. 1788, in OAPC; Lettre de Liberté, August 30, 1783, Doc. 1295, in OAPC; April 15, 1799, Doc. 2033, in OAPC.

low her to purchase him through litigation. In 1793, a forty-year-old mulatto woman was freed for 1,050 piastres; in 1796, a two-year-old mulatto male for 280 piastres and a six-year-old quadroon female for 350 piastres. In 1800, a eight-year-old quadroon male was freed for 700 piastres, and in 1802, a ten-year-old *griffe* female for 1,050 piastres. A thirty-six-year-old black woman was freed for 1,225 piastres in 1801. In 1794, according to Governor Carondelet, a black man recently arrived from Africa was worth about 250 piastres.[52]

There were few cases of slaves freed gratuitously by whites who were not their lovers or their fathers. Among the eight black women freed gratuitously by whites, four were clearly concubines, some of them mothers of mulatto children. One of them was identified as African: Louise Congo, mother of a mulatto child, both of whom were freed under the will of their master. Some white men were reluctant to totally abandon their property rights in their concubines. This pattern is documented as early as 1746, when Antoine Meuillon, surgeon of the Pointe Coupee post, granted freedom to his female slave Charlotte of the Senegal (Wolof) nation and to her two-year-old child, Louis. She was to serve him as a slave as long as he remained in the colony and was to enjoy her liberty only if he returned to France or died. George Olivo, *fils*, freed the five mulatto children born to his *négresse* Magdelaine. Their ages were eight, seven, six, three, and ten months. Two days later, he freed their mother, "provided she continues to serve me until the day of my death, as she has until now." Cecille's white lover purchased her freedom, but he tried to have her reenslaved after she left him, so that she could become his love slave in law as well as in fact. Simon Croisset freed a black woman and her two mulatto children from the estate of Louis Renard Duval, but the woman was obligated to serve him for a year after Duval's death. Croisset compensated the estate for the price of these three slaves, though two of them had been freed under the will of the deceased and the third was born after the will was written. Half their value was deducted from the price Croisset paid, since he was an heir entitled to half the estate.[53]

52. Lettre de Liberté, October 6, 1785, Doc. 1459, in OAPC; November 1, 1793, Doc. 1790, *ibid.*; February 1, 1796, Docs. 1899, 1898, *ibid.*; December 1, 1786, Doc. 2093, *ibid.*; February 1, 1802, Doc. 2154, *ibid.*; April 30, 1801, Doc. 2109, *ibid.*; Governor Carondelet to Eugenio Llaguno de Amirola, May 17, 1794, in Leg. 2563, fols. 964–66, SD, AGI.

53. January 1, 1782, Doc. 1152, in OAPC; February 1, 1746, in RSC, *LHQ*, XV (1932), 134; Lettres de Liberté, January 20, 23, 1801, Docs. 2096, 2097, in OAPC; Inventaire et Vente des Biens, Succession Louis Renard Duval, January 7, 1784, Doc. 1337, in OAPC.

A few white men were openhanded. Jean Baptiste Balquet freed his *négresse* Genneviève for "good service, fidelity, and in remuneration of other services which this *négresse* has rendered me." He also freed her two children, aged two and three years, whose race was not indicated, "for having been born in my house." Jean Baptiste Nicollet, a merchant born in Rochefort, wrote in his will that he was a bachelor, had no children, and wanted to free his slave Roze and her son. To protect them from his heirs residing in France, he left 2,000 piasters, a handsome sum, to Ricard de Rieutord to take charge of his affairs after his death. In his will, Simon Lacour recognized two mulatto children as his natural children. This was unusual, because most documents hinted broadly at, but did not openly avow, the relationship. Lacour asked his brother to protect his mulatto children, to make sure their rights were defended, and to free them. In this case, the widow opposed the emancipation of her husband's mulatto children, but without success. This was the only instance encountered in which an heir tried to prevent the emancipation of either a concubine or a natural child of the deceased. The widow and heirs of Jean Decuir freed Louis Mulâtre even in the absence of a will, because the deceased had promised him his freedom.[54]

These records reveal two patterns of emancipation. Almost all the mulattoes freed gratuitously were children purchased by white men, or freed under the will, or by the heirs, of the master. In eleven cases, slaves were purchased by white men in order to free them. Nine of them were mulatto children between two and ten years of age. Emancipation of mulatto children, very likely by their white fathers, accounts for the high percentage of mixed-bloods among the emancipated and for half of the males freed. Male adults were only 19.1 percent of those freed whose age could be determined, and they all had to purchase themselves at a high price and/or continue to provide free service. The adult black women were most likely the concubines and were usually mothers of mulatto children. The mixed-blood women were more often redeemed by their nonwhite female relatives or bought themselves. We know that some of these women were not mulattoes but black-Indian mixtures and very defiant individuals. A few elderly black women were freed gratuitously, but most of them either bought themselves, or were bought by their female relatives, at high prices; and even then, their freedom was sometimes conditional.

54. Lettre de Liberté, February 6, 1786, Doc. 1480, in OAPC; Testament de Jean Baptiste Nicollet, June 1, 1788, Doc. 1627, *ibid.*; Inventaire des Biens de la Succession Simon Lacour, July 26, 1779, Doc. 1004, *ibid.*; Inventaire des Biens de la Succession Jean Decuir, February 18, 1771, Doc. 393, *ibid.*

The patterns that emerge from the emancipation records explain the evolution of the mixed-blood slave population over time, and by advancing age groups. Mulatto children sired by white fathers of means tended to be freed as children. Mixed-blood adults, perhaps children of white soldiers or others without the means to free them, second-generation mixtures, or descendants of Indians were freed more gradually, either through self-purchase or purchase by non-white relatives. New mulattoes continued to be born at a steady pace through matings of white men and black women slaves.

It is clear from this study of the Pointe Coupee post that race mixture and the emancipation of nonwhite concubines and mixed-blood children of white men was extensive in eighteenth-century Louisiana. Many emancipation documents have, no doubt, been destroyed. There is strong evidence that significant numbers of women of African and Indian descent and their children passed informally into the white population. While no systematic study of other districts has been thus far carried out, the most casual search turns up similar patterns throughout the colony. In one estate sale that took place in St. Charles Parish in 1790, André Mackernie bought two quadroon children, Joseph, age eight, and Felicité, age three and a half, "recognizing her as his natural daughter" and obligating himself to free them. Emancipation of slave children, often, no doubt, by their white fathers, was common enough to be a major reason why, in 1807, the First Legislature of the Territory of Orleans passed a law that banned the emancipation of slaves under the age of thirty.[55] If the motivation had been simply to limit the growth of the free population of African descent, the age limit would have been higher. The mere fragments of emancipation documents found for the Pointe Coupee post indicate a high emancipation rate compared with Anglo North America before the American Revolution as well as with the British West Indies and Cuba during the nineteenth century.

Although the emancipation of white men's concubines and mixed-blood offspring was widely practiced and socially sanctioned, if not demanded, in Pointe Coupee, a substantial number of black and mixed-blood women obtained their freedom through litigation and self-purchase. There were three women, Marie Jeanne, Thérèse Négresse Libre, and Cecilia India Libre, whose struggle to obtain their own freedom and freedom for their relatives is documented in some

---

55. Sale of Goods, March 15, 1790, in Unmarked Book of French Records, fols. 94–95, Succession of Pierre Lorea, OAOP; Joe Gray Taylor, *Negro Slavery in Louisiana* (Baton Rouge, 1963), 154.

detail. Although all three had evidently had sexual relations with white men, the relationships were apparently brief. The male relatives of these women were deeply involved in the struggle against slavery and played leading roles in the 1795 conspiracy.

Slaves worked, saved, and litigated to free themselves and their families. The network among women was particularly strong. Women played a leading role in winning freedom for themselves and for their kin through litigation, purchase, and self-purchase. The elderly black women freed through sacrifices made by their daughters, or through their own labor and savings, is touching. Nevertheless, sexual relations with white men was a major road out of slavery for slave women and their children. The creole slave proverb at the beginning of this chapter explained the priorities among men. The black man stole chickens. His first priority was food. The mulatto stole horses. His first priority was wealth. The white man used his money to steal girls. The Afro-Creole women of Pointe Coupee exploited the white men's taste for dark women in order to obtain freedom for themselves and for their kin. It was a strategy that often worked. As hard and bitter as their struggle was, some of these women succeeded in transforming themselves and members of their families from slaves into free people.

CHAPTER 9

Re-Africanization Under Spanish Rule

An-a-qué, an'o'bia,
Bia'tail-la, Qué-re-qué,
Nal-le oua, Au-Mondé,
Au-tap-o-té, Aupé-to-té,
Au-qué-ré-qué, Bo.

—Work song from George Washington Cable,
The Grandissimes

[This work song, in an unidentified African language, was sung by workers counting sugarcane as they cut it in late nineteenth-century Louisiana.]

After its defeat in the French and Indian War, France abandoned the North American continent. Britain had occupied Guadeloupe during the war, and in order to get this valuable sugar island back, France gave up Canada. With the loss of Canada, France's interest in keeping its expensive and troublesome Louisiana venture disappeared. Canada and the east bank of the Mississippi River, except for New Orleans, were ceded to Britain; New Orleans and the west bank of the Mississippi River, to Spain. Britain returned Havana to Spain in exchange for Florida. Thus, Louisiana became part of the old, wealthy, well-established Spanish empire in the Americas.

The transition process was slow and painful. Although the transfer became official in 1763, Antonio de Ulloa, the first Spanish governor, did not arrive until 1766, and he brought few troops and little money with him. Prominent Louisiana creoles, frustrated by Ulloa's attempts to restrict commerce, organized a revolt that expelled the new governor. Governor Alejandro O'Reilly arrived in 1769 with a large contingent of troops, reestablished Spanish rule, and hanged several prominent white creoles for their instigation of the revolt against Spain.[1]

Spain actually ruled Louisiana between 1769 and 1803, a little over three decades. Spanish rule was a vast improvement over French rule. Brutality and corruption in the French regime had been extreme. To France, both Louisiana and Canada were useless wastelands compared with the wealthy French Caribbean islands. Merchants from the French islands were allowed to exploit Louisiana without mercy, and Louisiana's economic potential was not developed.

While France placed little value upon Louisiana, the colony held great strategic importance for Spain. With Britain occupying the east bank of the Mississippi River and all of Florida, Spain's control of Louisiana was vital in order to forestall British expansion into the Spanish Caribbean and New Spain (Mexico). Spain took control of Louisiana during the rule of Charles III, the great Bourbon reform emperor. This enlightened ruler loosened trade restrictions to encourage population growth and economic development. Louisiana was given privileged status within Spain's vast empire in the Americas. During the period of Spanish rule, Louisiana was Spain's most heavily subsidized colony, developed at the expense of other parts of

1. John Preston Moore, *Revolt in Louisiana: The Spanish Occupation, 1766–1770* (Baton Rouge, 1976).

the empire in the Americas. Louisiana tobacco enjoyed a monopoly of the Mexican market. Louisiana was given a monopoly of the production of wooden boxes in which sugar was exported throughout the Spanish empire. Only Louisiana sugar boxes could be used in the Spanish empire ports touching the Gulf of Mexico. Cypress became an important export item, and the industry thrived. Most ships leaving Louisiana were involved in the cypress trade. By the late eighteenth century, Havana alone imported 200,000 Louisiana sugar boxes a year, accounting for 50 ships' cargoes. More than 30 sawmills were constructed near New Orleans.[2]

Immigration was encouraged and subsidized. It is estimated that between 2,600 and 3,000 Acadians immigrated to colonial Louisiana, about 1,000 of whom arrived by 1770. About 2,000 Canary Islanders, the only important contingent of Spanish-speaking immigrants brought to Louisiana by Spain, were brought into the colony. Mortality among them was high, and the survivors lived in isolation in a few rural areas, exerting little cultural influence upon the more numerous French, Acadian, and Creole-speaking inhabitants. Many of these poverty-stricken immigrants survived only where they could build upon the economy of the swamps that had been developed by runaway slave communities—along Bayou Terre aux Boeufs, formerly Gaillardeland, in St. Bernard Parish, for example. Canary Islanders were settled near the swamps south and east of New Orleans, where St. Maló had reigned, and in Barataria, where remnants of his band had fled. But maroons continued to occupy these regions, as well as the swamps and woodlands all along the Mississippi River from Plaquemines to Natchez. By the 1790s, settlers were offering rewards for the capture and return of maroons, but these measures failed to reduce the maroon population.[3]

There is no doubt that Africans were, by far, the largest group of people introduced into Spanish Louisiana. Total population figures for Spanish Louisiana are difficult to calculate because of shifts in territory and incomplete and unreliable censuses after 1788. During the American Revolution, Spain seized all of Florida and the east bank of the Mississippi River, adding Pensacola, Mobile, Baton Rouge, and Natchez to lower Louisiana. In 1795, Natchez was handed over to the

2. *Ibid.*, 219; Maude Caroline Burson, *The Stewardship of Don Esteban Miró, 1782–1792* (New Orleans, 1940), 122, 123; Pontalba's Memoir, September 15, 1800, quoted in Charles Gayarré, *History of Louisiana* (4 vols.; 1854–66; rpr. Baton Rouge, 1974), II, 439.

3. Carl A. Brasseaux, *The Founding of New Acadia: The Beginnings of Acadian Life in Louisiana, 1765–1803* (Baton Rouge, 1987), 73, 91; Gilbert C. Din, *The Canary Islanders of Louisiana* (Baton Rouge, 1988), xi, 52, 59, 60.

United States. The 1788 census counted 20,673 slaves and 18,737 free people in lower Louisiana, or a total of 39,410 people, including Natchez. After the outbreak of the French Revolution in 1789, the population, both slave and free, appears to have declined. The economy went into a tailspin because of disruption of markets and shipping. Guaranteed crown purchases of tobacco ended in 1792. The indigo crop was devastated by blight, vermin, and floods in 1793, 1794, and 1796. Few slaves could be imported or purchased. In February, 1796, Governor Carondelet banned the importation of slaves of any origin. In November, 1800, the African slave trade was reopened, but slaves from the French Caribbean islands were still banned. After the general census of 1788, the population data became spotty. Extant records are not very reliable: Many are ecclesiastical censuses, some of which excluded Protestants and their slaves as well as other residents who avoided costly Catholic church membership and rituals. According to the 1795 census, the total population of lower Louisiana, including Natchez, Pensacola, and Mobile, was 36,230. In 1797, the population, free and slave, excluding Natchez, Arkansas, and Illinois, was estimated at 43,087, and in 1800, it was estimated to be 44,116, including West Florida. Between 1770 and 1795, the free population officially designated as of African descent increased from 165 to 1,500. Although this increase probably involved redefinition to some extent, James T. McGowan counted 788 acts of manumission recorded in New Orleans notarial records between 1770 and 1803. Despite manumissions and successful flights, the slave population increased from 5,600 in 1766 to 9,649 in 1777 and 20,673 in 1788.[4] There is no doubt that the slave population grew sharply between 1763 and 1790 and remained about 55 percent of the total population of lower Louisiana for the balance of the Spanish regime. Neither natural increase nor the importation of slaves from other parts of the Americas can begin to account for this rapid growth of the slave population.

4. 1788 population figures calculated from Antonio Acosta Rodríguez, *La población de la Luisiana española (1763–1803)* (Madrid, 1979), 440, 458; Thomas Marc Fiehrer, "The Baron de Carondelet as Agent of Bourbon Reform: A Study of Spanish Colonial Administration in the Years of the French Revolution" (Ph.D. dissertation, Tulane University, 1977), 436; 1795 population figures calculated from Derek Noel Kerr, "Petty Felony, Slave Defiance and Frontier Villainy: Crime and Criminal Justice in Spanish Louisiana, 1770–1803" (Ph.D. dissertation, Tulane University, 1983), 97; 1797 and 1800 population figures from Acosta Rodríguez, *Población de la Luisiana*, 242; James T. McGowan, "Creation of a Slave Society: Louisiana Plantations in the Eighteenth Century" (Ph.D. dissertation, University of Rochester, 1976), 196, 201.

Re-Africanization Under Spanish Rule

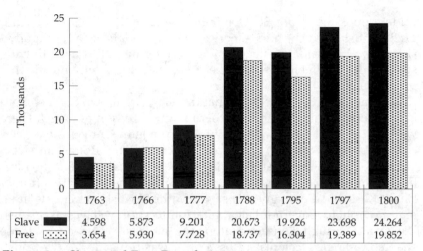

	1763	1766	1777	1788	1795	1797	1800
Slave	4.598	5.873	9.201	20.673	19.926	23.698	24.264
Free	3.654	5.930	7.728	18.737	16.304	19.389	19.852

Figure 8. Slave and Free Populations of Lower Louisiana During Spanish Rule, 1763–1800

SOURCES: Figures for 1795 calculated from Derek Noel Kerr, "Petty Felony, Slave Defiance and Frontier Villainy: Crime and Criminal Justice in Spanish Louisiana, 1770–1803" (Ph.D. dissertation, Tulane University, 1983), 97. All other figures calculated from Antonio Acosta Rodríguez, *La población de la Luisiana española (1763–1803)* (**Madrid**, 1979), 31, 110, 413, 438, 440, 458, 460, 474.

NOTE: The 1763 census covers settlements from the mouth of the Mississippi River through Pointe Coupee. The 1795 census includes Natchez, Pensacola, and Mobile. The 1797 census excludes Natchez and Arkansas. The 1800 census includes West Florida.

It is obvious that large numbers of slaves were imported into Spanish Louisiana. The origins of these imported slaves has not thus far been studied. Documents generated by the African slave trade to Spanish Louisiana do not help. While the French slave trade to Louisiana was highly centralized and well documented, the Spanish slave trade was neither. There was little direct involvement by the Spanish government. In 1777, a royal decree authorized the slave trade between Spanish Louisiana and the French West Indies, and in 1782, another decree allowed duty-free importation of slaves from friendly or neutral countries.[5] Slave traders from various nations were involved. No customs records were kept by Spain. Smugglers and interlopers operating from Jamaica and the British Atlantic colonies began introducing slaves into Louisiana in 1758. After Spain took control of the colony, some Cubans were also involved. French slave

5. Paul F. Lachance, "The Politics of Fear: French Louisianians and the Slave Trade, 1786–1809," *Plantation Society*, I (1979), 195.

traders operating from St. Domingue were active after 1777. After 1782, British, Scotch, and American slave traders legally imported slaves into Louisiana. It is impossible to determine, through studying slave-trade documents, where these slaves came from and in what proportions.

Acosta Rodríguez concluded that the slave traders in Spanish Louisiana were mainly British, and there is good reason to agree. There was a substantial slave trade organized from Jamaica by Scottish merchants operating through Pensacola, Natchez, Baton Rouge, and New Orleans. They were most likely interlopers and smugglers. In 1767, Robert Ross, a Scot living in Natchez representing the British firm of David Ross and Company and several other British merchants in Jamaica, wrote to Governor Ulloa, offering to supply slaves to Spanish Louisiana through Pensacola at prices at least as cheap as those charged to English colonists. Ross's offer was refused. But the British established along the east bank of the Mississippi River north of New Orleans were heavily involved in contraband trade. British and Scotch slave traders living in Natchez and Baton Rouge, including George Profit, sought Spanish protection and citizenship when American boats came down the Mississippi River in 1778. After the slave trade was opened to friendly and neutral nations in 1782, Scotch slave traders with headquarters in Jamaica were deeply involved. David Ross of Baton Rouge appeared frequently among the slave traders in the Pointe Coupee documents. The forty Africans bought by Trénonay in 1785 were sold by George Profit, David Ross, and Jerome Lachapelle. Several slave-trade ships that brought Africans to Pointe Coupee were probably operating from St. Domingue. In 1783, a Yoruba and a Maninga slave were sold by Charles La Chapell. They came from a slave ship whose captain was Joseph Ratty. In 1784, *la Thètes* arrived from Angola, and the slaves were sold by McKenzie of New Orleans. *Nôtre Dame des Carmes* arrived under Captain Robin in 1785. Two Chamba, a Mina, a Coromanti, and one Maninga from its "cargo" were sold by Charles La Chapell. The only other slave ship recorded in Pointe Coupee listing slaves arrived in late 1795, probably to replace the male slaves executed and exiled after the 1795 conspiracy. The ship was *la Paloma*, and Gaspard Aranda was its captain. This sounds like a Spanish or, more likely, a Cuban ship. All of its slaves were Congo, and they were sold by Jean Raymond et Cie., merchant of New Orleans. In 1784, Dr. Benjamin Farar, an American from South Carolina who settled in Pointe Coupee, asked the Spanish crown for permission to introduce 200 slaves from the coast of Africa in his own ship, which he proposed to buy in France or in England. His request was officially received in Spain six years later, the same year Farar died.[6]

Although slave-trade documents are lacking for Spanish Louisiana, the lists and inventories of slaves, especially in rural areas, are quite useful. This writer has made a detailed study of the Pointe Coupee post between 1771 and 1802, a time period that coincides with Spanish rule. Throughout most of this period, the slave population increased sharply while the white population declined. The 1763 census counted 610 slaves at Pointe Coupee, 13.2 percent of the 4,598 slaves in the colony. There were 1.40 slaves for each free person at the post in 1763, 1.57 slaves to free in 1777. By 1786, there were 3.06 slaves to each free person. There were only 88 free men and 114 free women aged fifteen to forty-nine. The proportion of slave to free remained stable through 1790. Between 1790 and 1803, the year the United States acquired Louisiana, the free population grew faster than the slave population. The economy collapsed in 1790 because of disruptions of markets and shipping with the outbreak of the French Revolution. Over forty seizures for debt of land, slaves, and goods took place that year. The indigo crop was devastated by bad weather and caterpillars in 1793 to 1794. The foreign slave trade was illegal most of the time after 1795. This cutoff in the African slave trade is reflected in an aging African slave population during the 1790s. In 1795, over 50 male slaves were executed or exiled in connection with the slave conspiracy. However, the free population increased sharply after 1795, largely because of the immigration of young, single men, resulting in a ratio of 2.09 slaves to each white by 1803.[7]

A knowledge of the origins of the slaves, their distribution on estates, and their role as parents, both biological and fictive, is essential to an understanding of cultural influences in Spanish Louisiana. The Pointe Coupee slave lists contain detailed information about the num-

6. Acosta Rodríguez, *Población de la Luisiana*, 216; October 8, 1784, Doc. 1374, in OAPC; October 15, 1785, Doc. 1442, and October 1, 1785, Doc. 1462, both in OAPC; Vente d'esclaves, October 17, 1785, Doc. 1451, in OAPC; December 1, 1795, Doc. 1892, in OAPC; May 12, 1784, in Leg. 2609, Doc. 226, SD, AGI; April 30, 1790, in Leg. 2555, Doc. 294, SD, AGI.

7. Acosta Rodríguez, *Población de la Luisiana*, 110, 112, 117, 136, 159, 175, 208, 239, 274, 474; Lachance, "Politics of Fear," 162–97; Recensement de la Pointe Coupée et la Fausse Rivière, Année 1786, January 20, 1786, in Leg. 2361, PC, AGI; Recensement de la Pointe Coupée et Fausse Rivière, March 29, 1790, 227A, Carpeta 21, Doc. 2, PC, AGI; Recensement général de la Pointe Coupée, Fausse Rivière et Isles au Chata, May 28, 1803, in Leg. 212A, Carpeta 14, PC, AGI.

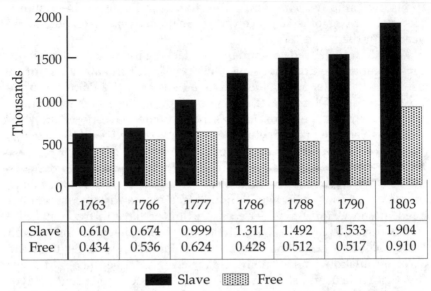

	1763	1766	1777	1786	1788	1790	1803
Slave	0.610	0.674	0.999	1.311	1.492	1.533	1.904
Free	0.434	0.536	0.624	0.428	0.512	0.517	0.910

■ Slave ▧ Free

Figure 9. Slave and Free Populations at Pointe Coupee, 1763–1803
SOURCE: Calculated from Antonio Acosta Rodríguez. *La población de la Luisiana española (1763–1803)* (Madrid, 1979), 31, 110, 413, 438, 440, 458.

bers, ages, gender, and nations of the slaves and changes over time.[8] Out of the 2,632 slaves inventoried, only 242 slaves had no nations indicated in the documents. More than fifty different African nations were listed, and local creoles and creoles born elsewhere in the Americas were also indicated. Such detailed information about the origins of slaves is unique, not only for the United States, but for all of the Americas.[9]

It is not possible to study vital rates of slave populations in the Americas using the techniques of classical historical demography developed for studying static populations in Europe.[10] However, the Pointe Coupee inventories allow us to answer some questions vital to

8. The term *nation* is used because that is the term found in the documents and because the more commonly used *ethnic group* becomes awkward with constant repetition.

9. See Note on Sources for a discussion of studies of slave lists in other countries in the Americas.

10. Dennis D. Cordell, Joel W. Gregory, and Victor Piché, "African Historical Demography: The Search for a Theoretical Framework," in *African Population and Capitalism: Historical Perspectives,* ed. Dennis D. Cordell and Joel W. Gregory (Boulder, 1987), 14–34.

the study of culture formation by establishing the numbers of local creoles, imported creoles, and Africans of various nations—questions about their age structure, their distribution on estates, and their role as parents who socialized the younger generation—and enable us to analyze changes over time. While definitive conclusions about the slave population of Spanish Louisiana will have to await a systematic study of slave inventories throughout lower Louisiana, the Pointe Coupee documents reveal an enormous African presence.

Although some of the increase in the slave population can be accounted for by American settlers who arrived in Louisiana accompanied by their slaves born in Virginia and South Carolina as well as in Africa, the Pointe Coupee inventories indicate that almost all the slaves brought in by traders from St. Domingue, Jamaica, the United States, and Cuba came directly from Africa. Almost all the English slaves encountered in the inventories had accompanied their master, Dr. Benjamin Farar. He was an immigrant from South Carolina who had settled in False River, accompanied by his slave force. His plantation, valued at 39,956 piastres, was inventoried in 1783 after the death of his wife. He held 153 slaves, by far the largest number of slaves on any plantation at the post. All the adult slaves on his estate were creoles of South Carolina (43) or creoles of Virginia (29), except for one woman who was a creole of Pennsylvania; or they were Africans who had also been brought in from South Carolina. The young children were listed as creoles, the older children as creoles of South Carolina. This estate reflected the composition of estates in South Carolina. Africans were about 45 percent of the adults. Eighteen were Angolan, 4 were Coromanti (Gold Coast), 18 were described as being from Guinea, a vague term. There was 1 Maninga male, 1 Chamba female, and 4 Ibo women. These slaves remained on his estate and were not sold to other planters. The child/woman ratio among these English creole and African women was very close: 0.519 for the creoles and 0.444 for the Africans. However, among children under the age of fifteen, 20 had been born to African mothers and 22 to creole mothers, though creole women of childbearing age outnumbered African women 27 to 18, pointing toward a surprisingly high fertility rate among African women in South Carolina.[11] At the time of Farar's death in 1790, his slave force had increased to 225. Unfortunately, this last inventory is useless for our purposes. Because of the size of the estate, a Spanish notary came from New Orleans to appraise it, and he categorized all the nations of the slaves as *bozal*, meaning a slave

11. May 10, 1783, Doc. 1275, in OAPC.

recently arrived from Africa, creole (*criollo*), probably meaning Creole-speaking, which included Africans who had arrived earlier, or else he did not indicate the nation at all.[12] Farar's daughter sold her share of her inheritance to Julien Poydras in 1800. Her brother had stripped their inheritance of skilled slaves, and those remaining were grouped in families and not deeply involved in staple production. Her 106 slaves had a high child/woman ratio of 1.524. With a sharp rise in the price of slaves after 1795, the value of her share of the estate increased substantially.[13]

Aside from the English slaves brought in by Farar, there were few imported creoles at the post. Although importation of slaves from the French Caribbean islands was legalized in 1777, few slaves from the Caribbean, either French or British, were found in the Pointe Coupee documents. Only 7 slaves from the French Caribbean were listed, including 2 from "Des Isles," 2 from Martinique, and 3 from St. Domingue. One of those from St. Domingue was freed. Another ran away and was sold to a man in Opelousas in exchange for cows, with no guarantees and no promise to deliver him. Few individual English slaves were brought into the district, and the reason seems clear enough. When the estate of Isaac Monsanto was inventoried in 1778, his 5 slaves—an English man and an English woman, a Congo man and a Congo woman, and a ten-year-old Wolof boy—had all run away. Their value was list as *pour memoire* only, because runaway slaves were rarely captured in Louisiana. Among the other 4 English creoles listed before 1780, 1 creole of Jamaica had been a maroon for a year and estimated *pour memoire* on another estate inventory. Another English slave had drowned himself in the river in the presence of George Baron, his master, even though he had not been threatened with punishment.[14] César, a creole of Jamaica, was accused of instigating a revolt of the Mina slaves at Pointe Coupee in 1791. This handful of slaves coming in from the Caribbean were probably those whom their masters, or their government, were trying to get rid of because they were uncontrollable. Only a handful of individual English-speaking slaves began to trickle into Pointe Coupee from the United States after 1800.

The Africans brought to Louisiana under Spanish rule came from four main areas: Senegambia, the Bight of Benin, the Bight of Biafra,

12. October 3, 1790, Doc. 1732, in OAPC.
13. Farar, wife of Butler, to Julien Poydras, January 26, 1800, Doc. 2099, in OAPC.
14. December 21, 1786, Doc. 1605, *ibid.*; Estate of Isaac Monsanto, May 7, 1778, Doc. 918, *ibid.*; June 7, 1771, Doc. 432, *ibid.*; February 26, 1779, Doc. 982, *ibid.*

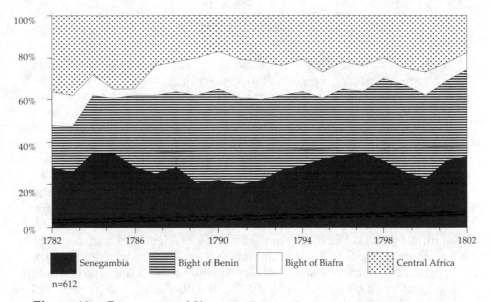

Figure 10. Percentage of Slaves at Pointe Coupee from Major Regions of Africa, 1782–1802, in Five-Year Moving Averages
Source: See source for Figure 6.
Note: See note for Figure 6.

Data Table for Figure 10.

	Senegambia	Bight of Benin	Bight of Biafra	Central Africa
1771	10	5	1	5
1778	9	10	6	15
1779	23	12	7	12
1782	8	5	7	7
1783	7	5	6	25
1784	14	13	5	7
1785	7	6	5	7
1786	4	1	0	3
1787	3	6	1	10
1788	17	12	0	11
1789	1	0	0	0
1790	9	17	3	14
1791	7	20	14	2
1792	2	1	0	1
1793	3	2	1	3
1794	21	42	17	7
1795	4	4	3	20
1796	1	3	2	1
1797	30	21	6	20
1798	17	18	4	6
1799	5	7	0	2
1800	0	6	1	5
1801	1	0	0	3
1802	12	13	3	5

and Central Africa. The ethnic makeup of the African slaves at Pointe Coupee, especially the comparatively small numbers of slaves from Central Africa and the large numbers from Senegambia, makes it unlikely that many of them came from the French slave trade. David Geggus calculated that the Congo were the largest African group in St. Domingue during the late eighteenth century, constituting one-third of the slave population in the plains and well over half in the mountains.[15]

From the Pointe Coupee inventories of slaves, it appears that the slave population of Spanish Louisiana was heavily Africanized. African slaves turned up on inventories quite early. On the first lists, dating from 1771, 29.7 percent of slaves of identified nations were Africans. Since the 1771 lists do not give ages, we cannot tell the proportion of Africans among adults. Although the foreign slave trade was outlawed between 1770 and 1777, the next lists, dating from 1778 and 1779, showed a greatly expanded African presence. Out of 208 slaves of identified nations, 101 were creoles and 107 were Africans. Africans totaled over 60 percent of the adults on slave inventory lists throughout the Spanish period, peaking at over 75 percent for a few years after 1782 when Spain allowed slavers of all nations to introduce their "merchandise" free of duty.[16]

This was a high percentage of Africans indeed. Philip D. Morgan found that Africans in South Carolina were 45.0 percent of the adult slave population in 1760, peaked at 49.1 percent in 1775, dropped to 40.3 percent in 1782, plummeted to 7.8 percent in 1800, and then rose to 20 percent in 1810. While confident assertions about the proportion of adult Africans in the slave population of Spanish Louisiana will have to await studies of inventories of slaves in other parishes, the evidence from Pointe Coupee calls for a reconsideration of Morgan's conclusion that the proportion of Africans among slaves in South Carolina was higher than in any other region of mainland North America.[17]

The contrast with the English Atlantic-coast colonies is not confined to the percentage of Africans in the slave population. There is also a sharp contrast between the African nations of origin of slaves brought to the Chesapeake, Carolina, and Georgia and those of slaves

15. David Geggus, "The Haitian Revolution," in *The Modern Caribbean*, ed. Franklin W. Knight and Colin A. Palmer (Chapel Hill, 1989), 23.

16. DB Inventories.

17. Philip D. Morgan, "Black Society in the Low Country, 1760–1810," in *Slavery and Freedom in the Age of the American Revolution*, ed. Ira Berlin and Ronald Hoffman (Charlottesville, 1983), 92, 129.

Re-Africanization Under Spanish Rule

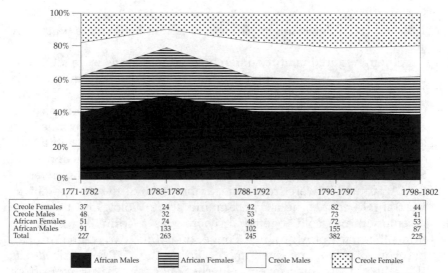

	1771-1782	1783-1787	1788-1792	1793-1797	1798-1802
Creole Females	37	24	42	82	44
Creole Males	48	32	53	73	41
African Females	51	74	48	72	53
African Males	91	133	102	155	87
Total	227	263	245	382	225

African Males   African Females   Creole Males   Creole Females

Figure 11. Percentage of African and Creole Slaves over Age 14 by Sex at Pointe Coupee, 1771–1802

SOURCE: See source for Figure 6.

NOTE: See note for Figure 6.

brought to Louisiana. The African slaves brought to the Chesapeake during the eighteenth century came mainly from the Bight of Biafra and were heavily Ibo, Ibibio, Efik, and Moko, with a significant minority coming from Angola.[18] Between 1735 and 1740, 70 percent of the Africans brought to South Carolina came from Angola. Between 1717 and 1767, 22 percent of the slave-trade ships came from Angola, while only 5 percent came from Gambia, though these figures are unclear because the origin of 61 percent of these voyages was listed simply as "Africa" and 8 percent as "Guinea." Margaret Washington Creel concludes that Senegambia and the Windward Coast provided 61 percent of the slaves entering Charleston from Africa from 1749 to 1787, with the percentage of slaves coming from Angola dropping to 11.1 percent. Slaves coming from Angola rose once again to 37.7 percent between 1804 and 1807, with those coming from the Windward Coast rising to 28.6 percent and those from Senegambia dropping to 7.5 percent. Slaves from the Gold Coast remained a substantial mi-

18. Alan Kulikoff, *Tobacco and Slaves: The Development of Southern Cultures in the Chesapeake, 1680–1800* (Chapel Hill, 1986), 321. See Philip D. Morgan, "Slave Life in Piedmont Virginia, 1720–1800," in *Colonial Chesapeake Society*, ed. Lois Green Carr, Philip D. Morgan, and Jean B. Russo (Chapel Hill, 1988), 433–84.

nority, fluctuating between 13.3 percent and 17.2 percent between 1749 and 1807. Slaves coming from the Bight of Benin were practically absent.[19]

Although more than fifty different African nations were identified in the Pointe Coupee inventories, most of them came from relatively few, and/or closely related, nations. In sharp contrast with South Carolina, Spanish Louisiana saw no dramatic shift in the origins of its African slaves. Most of the nations found in significant numbers on later lists were already present in 1771. The lists for 1771 had a total of eighty-five slaves, eleven of unidentified nations. Thirty percent of the slaves of identified nations were Africans. Among these twenty-two Africans, ten were from Senegambia. Two of the Senegambians were an old couple, he a Bambara and she a Wolof, and they were inventoried and sold together.[20] There was a sprinkling of slaves from other parts of Africa: five Congo, one Mina, two Nago (Yoruba), two Fon, one Ibo, and one Timbo. During the 1770s, the slave lists still reflected, to some extent, elderly Senegambian survivors from the French slave trade, but there were already many newly arrived Africans among them. The next extant inventories from the Pointe Coupee post date from 1778 and 1779, and by then, 51 percent of the slaves of identified nations were Africans. Thirty-six percent of the Africans whose region of origin could be identified were from Senegambia.

The continued importance of Senegambian slaves in Louisiana requires an explanation. Although Senegambia was an early source for the Atlantic slave trade, by the eighteenth century it played a relatively minor role. Nevertheless, because of timing, as well as preference among slave owners, slaves from Senegambia were brought to Louisiana in large numbers.[21] As we have seen, two-thirds of the slaves brought to Louisiana under French rule came from Senegambia. There was a substantial, well-organized Bambara language community in early Louisiana. This writer has argued, from evidence from Senegambia as well as from Louisiana, that the slaves

19. Peter H. Wood, *Black Majority: Negroes in Colonial South Carolina from 1670 through the Stono Rebellion* (New York, 1974), 335; Daniel C. Littlefield, *Rice and Slaves: Ethnicity and the Slave Trade in Colonial South Carolina* (Baton Rouge, 1981), 111; Margaret Washington Creel, *"A Peculiar People": Slave Religion and Community-Culture Among the Gullahs* (New York, 1988), Appendix A, 329–34.

20. February 18, 1771, Doc. 393, OAPC.

21. For an interesting discussion of preference for particular African nations among slave owners of South Carolina, see Littlefield, *Rice and Slaves.*

described as Bambara during this early, formative period actually were Bambara. Most of them were probably warriors captured in battle during the rise of the empire of Mamari Kulubali, founder of the Kingdom of Segu. The next surge in the slave trade in Senegambia took place as a result of the consolidation of another empire: that of Ngolo Jarra, a former slave soldier who founded a new dynasty and greatly expanded the Kingdom of Segu. This expansion in the export of slaves from Senegambia coincided with a resurgence in the African slave trade to Louisiana under Spanish rule. It is less clear whether the new African slaves listed on inventories in Spanish Louisiana as Bambara were all actually Bambara. By the late eighteenth century, *Bambara* had taken on a generic meaning and was widely applied to peoples coming through St. Louis from the interior of the continent. The vagueness of Bambara identity resulted from the incorporation of many different ethnic communities into the Bambara warrior group. On the other hand, the old Bambara, as well as the old colonists in Louisiana, must have been able to tell who was a Bambara and who was not. Among the slaves from Senegambia, 25 percent were Bambara, 29 percent were Maninga (Mandinga), 22 percent were Wolof, and 10 percent were Fulbe. The Bambara, if such they were, and the Maninga spoke mutually intelligible Mande languages, creating a substantial language community throughout the post. There were 123 Bambara and Maninga slaves, constituting 15.6 percent of the Africans of identified nations. They tended to be clustered on the same estates. There were 12 Mande slaves on the estate of Colin Lacour, 7 on the estate of Jean Baptiste Tournoir, 6 on the estate of Baptiste Lacour, 6 on the estate of Trénonay, and 5 on the estate of Louis Renard Duval.[22] The rest of the Mande slaves were clustered in groups of 4 or less. Only 13, or 10.6 percent, were on estates without other Mande slaves. More Mande slaves retained African-sounding names on the inventory lists than did slaves of other African nations. The high retention of African names among Mande slaves points toward a greater sense of cultural identity. Another possible explanation was that these names were familiar to the

---

22. Philip D. Curtin, *Economic Change in Precolonial Africa: Senegambia in the Era of the Slave Trade* (2 vols.; Madison, Wis., 1975), I, 179, 180, 182, 183; Lamiral, *L'Affrique et le Peuple Afriquain consideérés sous leurs rapports* (Paris, 1789), 184, cited in Gabriel Debien, "Les origines des esclaves aux Antilles," *Bulletin de l'Institut Français d'Afrique Noir,* Series B, XXIII (1961), 376; Richard L. Roberts, *Warriors, Merchants, and Slaves: The State and the Economy in the Middle Niger Valley, 1700–1914* (Stanford, 1987), 7; DB Inventories.

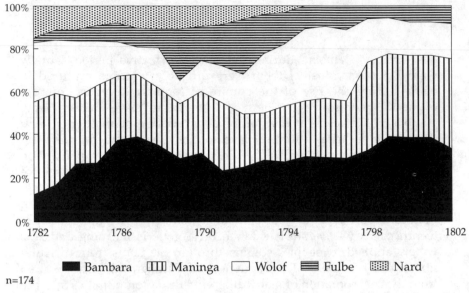

■ Bambara　ⅢⅢ Maninga　▢ Wolof　≣ Fulbe　▨ Nard

n=174

Figure 12.　Slaves from Senegambia at Pointe Coupee, 1782–1802, in Five-Year Moving Averages

SOURCE: See Source for Figure 6.

NOTE: See note for Figure 6. For exact numbers by nation and sex, see Appendix C.

Data Table for Figure 12.

	Bambara	Maninga	Wolof	Fulbe	Nard
1771	2	2	6	0	0
1778	3	3	3	0	0
1779	1	8	12	1	1
1782	1	3	2	0	2
1783	0	6	1	0	0
1784	3	3	5	0	3
1785	1	2	2	1	1
1786	0	3	1	0	0
1787	2	1	0	0	0
1788	6	5	4	1	1
1789	0	1	0	1	1
1790	6	1	1	0	1
1791	1	3	0	2	1
1792	0	0	2	0	0
1793	1	2	0	0	0
1794	5	6	3	5	2
1795	1	0	1	1	0
1796	1	0	0	0	0
1797	6	3	10	4	0
1798	4	7	4	1	0
1799	2	2	1	0	0
1800	0	0	0	0	0
1801	1	0	0	0	0
1802	4	5	2	1	0

colonists from the old Mande slaves surviving from the French slave trade who, as we have seen, tended to keep their African names.[23]

The largest number of slaves, 28.7 percent, came from the Bight of Benin. The Mina and the Fon maintained their numbers throughout the time period studied. The Yoruba (Nago) were present in largest numbers before 1783, tapering off at the end of the century. There was a steady increase of Chamba. The Adó bulged during the 1790s and disappeared thereafter. A handful of Hausa appeared, beginning in 1791. Significant numbers of Fon (Dahomean) and Yoruba women were clustered on the same estates. Because of a long history of contact in Africa through empire building, as well as cultural and religious interpenetration, slaves from the Bight of Benin constituted language, religious, and cultural clusters on estates. The Yoruba and the Fon claimed common descent from Odua. The Kingdom of Dahomey had been a tributary state of the Yoruba kingdom of Oyo since 1712. Yoruba *orisha* (gods) had long been syncretized with Arada (Dahomean) gods in Africa. At least one Yoruba slave at Pointe Coupee demonstrated that he was resistant to Christianization. When Aboidau, a Yoruba slave, was accused of being involved in a theft and was asked to take an oath and testify in his own defense, he denied any involvement in the theft but explained that he could not swear an oath that his testimony was true because he did not understand what was being asked of him. He only knew the god of his own country, or the Yoruba, which was his nation. Several large estates in Pointe Coupee had slaves who came overwhelmingly from the Bight of Benin. For example, the inventory of Claude Trénonay's slaves taken after his murder in 1791 showed that among 41 African slaves whose region of origin can be identified, 56 percent (twenty-three) were from the Bight of Benin. Seven were from Senegambia, six from the Bight of Biafra, and only two from Central Africa.[24]

All of the 24.8 percent of identified Africans coming from Central Africa were described in the Pointe Coupee inventories as Congo, except for one Sango and eighteen Angola, all of whom had been brought from South Carolina by Farar. The Congo all spoke closely related, though mutually unintelligible, Bantu languages.[25] It is likely

23. See Appendix D.

24. Eric R. Wolf, *Europe and the People Without History* (Berkeley, 1982), 213; Albert J. Raboteau, *Slave Religion: The "Invisible Institution" in the Antebellum South* (New York, 1978), 18; Procès entre Joseph Bourgeat et Colin Lacour au sujet du nègre nommé Paul, October 7, 1785, Doc. 1445, in OAPC; July 10, 1791, Doc. 1761, in OAPC.

25. Joseph C. Miller, *Way of Death: Merchant Capitalism and the Angolan Slave Trade 1730–1830* (Madison, Wis., 1988), 8.

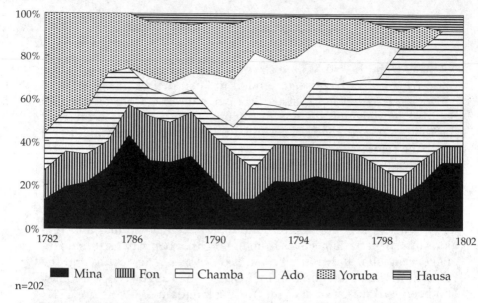

Figure 13. Slaves from Bight of Benin at Pointe Coupee, by Nation, 1782–1802, in Five-Year Moving Averages

SOURCE: See source for Figure 6.

NOTE: See notes for Figures 6 and 12.

Data Table for Figure 13.

	Mina	Fon	Adó	Chamba	Nago	Hausa
1771	1	2	0	0	2	0
1778	4	3	0	1	3	0
1779	4	3	1	1	3	0
1782	0	1	0	1	3	0
1783	1	1	0	1	2	0
1784	1	2	0	0	10	0
1785	2	0	0	3	1	0
1786	0	0	0	0	1	0
1787	2	2	0	2	0	0
1788	3	1	0	3	5	0
1789	0	0	0	0	0	0
1790	10	2	0	1	3	0
1791	2	6	3	1	6	2
1792	0	0	0	1	0	0
1793	1	0	0	1	0	0
1794	6	8	12	4	11	1
1795	0	0	0	1	0	0
1796	2	1	3	0	0	0
1797	7	3	0	7	4	0
1798	4	3	7	2	2	0
1799	0	0	0	6	0	1
1800	0	1	0	3	2	0
1801	0	0	0	0	0	0
1802	4	1	0	7	0	1

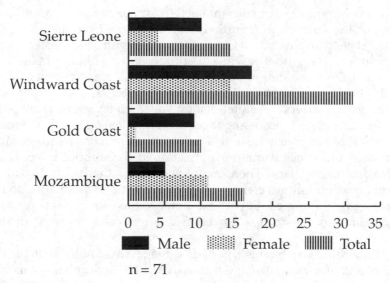

n = 71

Figure 14. Slaves at Pointe Coupee from Minor Regions of Africa, 1771–1802
SOURCE: See source for Figure 6.
NOTE: See note for Figure 6.

that the Congo (Bantu) impact upon Louisiana folklore has been exaggerated to the neglect of the Senegambian, and particularly the Mande, influence upon folktales and proverbs, though Congo names for folk dances were common.[26]

Other nations and regions of origin should be mentioned. A few Kissy slaves from Sierra Leone and Canga slaves from the Windward Coast began appearing in the inventories in 1779. Makwa slaves, mainly young women, were first listed in 1787. They were from East Africa, from the immediate hinterland of Mozambique City.[27] Only a handful of slaves came from the Gold Coast, almost all men, several of whom were brought in from South Carolina by Farar.

The cultural impact of the Africans introduced into Spanish Louisiana was magnified by conditions prevailing in the colony. While it has become a truism that masters separated slaves who were from the same African nations, in Pointe Coupee, slaves from the same nations

26. See, for example, Roger Bastide, *African Civilizations in the New World*, trans. Peter Green (New York, 1971), 173–74.
27. Philip D. Curtin, *The Atlantic Slave Trade: A Census* (Madison, Wis., 1969), 189–90.

and/or who spoke mutually intelligible languages were often clustered on the same estates. Furthermore, as we see from the testimony in the slave conspiracy trials and other documents, the master's right to stop his slaves from leaving his property was highly theoretical. Slaves of the same nation belonging to various masters met and socialized on a regular basis. They met in the *ciprière*, and parties held in the slave quarters were attended by slaves from various estates and by free people. African-language communities operated as social groups regardless of which masters the slaves belonged to. A Mina language and social community functioned throughout lower Louisiana for many years. There may have been other African nation-language communities centered in New Orleans and radiating to the rural areas, though confident assertions of the role of organized African communities in Spanish Louisiana will have to await further research.

Throughout the Spanish period, the age and family structure of the population facilitated the influence of the African slaves as biological, as well as fictive, kin. The vast majority of adults, male and female, were Africans. Many of the creole slaves had an African parent or parents, as well as living African grandparents or great-grandparents. Because of the high sex ratio among the Bambara, the oldest African grandfathers were reasonably likely to be Bambara, the grandmothers Wolof. There were some old African couples who no doubt came from the French slave trade. An old Bambara male/creole female couple was sold in 1771. An old Wolof couple was inventoried together in 1778. In 1779, an old Bambara male/Wolof female couple was sold. An old Congo couple was sold from the estate of Emond in 1786. On this estate, the median age of creoles over age fourteen was twenty-two, and of Africans, fifty, indicating that the creoles were likely to have been born of African parents.[28]

Which African nations supplied the mothers and which the fathers? The lists dating from the 1770s indicate that couples were often from the same African nation. On one estate inventoried in 1779, there was a Congo couple, an old Maninga couple, a Yoruba couple, and a Senegal (Wolof) couple and their child. Several Wolof couples and their children were inventoried together; two of these couples were on the same estate. One of these couples turned up again, with a new child. In 1782, a young Ibo couple, their three creole children, aged six, four, and one and a half, and a twenty-three-year-old Ibo man

28. January 3, 1771, Doc. 386, in OAPC; February 18, 1771, Doc. 393, *ibid.*; October 12, 1779, Doc. 1014, *ibid.*; December 14, 1786, Doc. 1522, *ibid.*

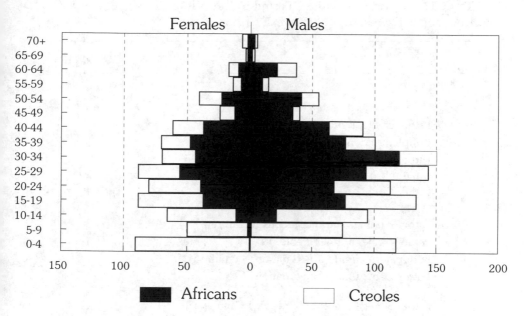

Figure 15. African and Creole Slaves by Age and Sex at Pointe Coupee, 1771–1802
SOURCE: See source for Figure 6.
NOTE: See note for Figure 6.

were sold to a free mulatto couple. Among the slaves from Senegambia, the Bambara had 9.8 men to each woman, the highest proportion; next came the Fulbe, with 8.5; then the Maninga with 2.4. Women were the majority among the Wolof: 0.76 man to each woman. Although there were few Bambara women in Louisiana, one was inventoried with her four children in 1798. Because of the high male sex ratio among the Bambara, we find, not surprisingly, Bambara men married to Wolof and creole women. A Bambara male/creole female couple and their two children were inventoried in 1778.[29]

What were the nations of the African fathers? The information about fathers of slave children in Spanish Louisiana is sketchy, especially after the 1770s. Nevertheless, Africans are well repre-

29. November 5, 1779, Doc. 1015, *ibid.*; January 7, 1784, Doc. 1337, *ibid.*; Sale of Slaves, Ricard de Rieutord to Bienville, *mulâtre libre,* and his wife, Marie, November 9, 1782, Doc. 1216, *ibid.*; January 18, 1798, Doc. 1968, *ibid.*; February 17, 1778, Doc. 908, *ibid.*

Table 13.   Nations of Fathers Found in the Pointe Coupee Slave
Inventories by Year and Number of Children

Year	Children
1771	
Couple unidentified nations, 3 children	3
Father creole, mother Ibo, 5 children	5
Couple, unidentified nations, 3 children	3
Father creole of Curaçao, mother unidentified nation, 2 children	2
Father Congo, mother Maninga, 1 child	1
1778	
Father Bambara, mother creole, 3 children	3
Father creole, mother creole, 1 child	1
Both parents unidentified nation, 4 children	4
Both parents unidentified nation, 1 child	1
1779	
Father Senegal, mother Senegal, 1 child	1
Father Senegal, mother Senegal, 1 child	1
1782	
Father Ibo, mother Ibo, 3 children	3
1783	
Father creole, mother creole, 1 child	1
Both parents unidentified nation, 2 children	2
1784	
Father Maninga, mother Wolof, 1 child	1
Father creole, no mother, 1 child	1
Father Kissy, mother unidentified nation, 4 children	4
1796	
Father creole, mother creole, 2 children[1]	2
1797	
Father Ibo, no mother, one fifteen-year-old child	1
1800[2]	
Father creole named Harry, mother creole named Rose, 3 children: Moly, Charity, Jack	3
Father Simon, creole, mother Dolly, creole, 3 children: Jesse, Payy, Humphrey	3
Father July, Guinea, mother Guinea, 3 children: Arehy, Tichemond, Sampson	3

(continued)

Table 13. (*continued*)

Year	Children
Father Moussa, brut, mother Sally, creole, 2 children: Prince and Bob	2
Father Robin, creole, mother Bety, creole, 2 children: Clarinda, Nancy	2
Father Louis, creole, mother Betty, creole, 3 children: Cesar, Mary, Sara (f.)	3
1802	
Father Mingo, Hausa, no mother, son Biron, age 7, sold together	1

SOURCE: DB Inventories.

1. This was a three-generation family from the estate of Père Bernard.
2. Slaves listed for 1800 were those inherited by the daughter of Dr. Benjamin Farar. They were all later sold to Julien Poydras. Many were English creoles.

sented among the relatively few fathers found in the Pointe Coupee inventories.

Among 26 fathers identified, 11 were Africans and fathered a total of 21 children. Ten of the fathers were creoles, including one from Curaçao and four English creoles, and they fathered 23 children. The 5 fathers whose nations were unidentified fathered 12 children. From these figures, admittedly scanty, it appears that African men were a slight majority of the fathers of identified nations and that they fathered nearly half the creole children.

Our information about the nations of the mothers is, of course, much more complete. A useful basis for comparison is the child/woman ratio, calculated by dividing the number of children under age five by females fifteen to forty-four years old. This is probably the most accurate gauge of fertility, since no African children under age five are listed in the records, and children were usually, but by no means always, inventoried with their mothers at this age. In the inventories, there were 259 African women and 203 creole women aged fifteen to forty-four. But the African women gave birth to only 132 children, 81 under age five, giving a slave child/woman ratio of 0.313 for African women. The creole women gave birth to 195 children, 135 under age five, giving a slave child/woman ratio of 0.665. All the women of this age group, including those of unidentified nations, totaled 557, and all the children under age fifteen totaled 636, with children under five totaling 262, giving a slave child/woman ratio of 0.470. The slave child/woman ratios for the British West Indies between 1817 and 1832 range from a low of 0.352 in Grenada in 1817 to a high of 0.738 in the Bahamas in 1834.[30] No transcendent conclusions should be drawn from these figures about the fertility of African women compared with creole women, because many of the African women had been torn away from their children when they were captured and sold in Africa. The main concern here is to gauge the percentage of creole children who were born to, and socialized by, African mothers. These figures reveal that 40.4 percent of children whose mothers' nations were identified were born to African mothers.

Thirty-three African children aged between five and fourteen had no mothers indicated on the slave lists. They had probably been shipped from Africa separately from their mothers or fathers. The largest number of them, 13, were Congo.[31] As we have seen, creole children were often separated from their mothers at an early age, and lack of recognition of biological fathers under the Spanish regime left many children living on estates without either parent and few with fathers present. The vast majority of adult slaves were Africans, and many of them had been separated from their own children in Africa. Because of the high sex ratio among slaves in Louisiana and the competition of white men for women of African descent, the chances for men to form new families were limited. African men tended to informally adopt the large numbers of creole children, as well as the sprinkling of African children, living on estates without their parents. Traces of the phenomenon of informal adoption can be seen in slave testimony in the conspiracy trials. The parental role assumed by African men toward creole and African children surely contributed toward re-Africanizing the culture and creating and extending a fictive kinship network.

Families were broken up by estate sales, but slaves were rarely sold out of the district; and the last thing Pointe Coupee slaves did was to remain on their respective estates. The separate sale of family members, far from breaking up the slave family, extended family networks throughout the area. Fictive kin, as well as blood kin, were involved. The godparents of newborn, and newly Christianized, slaves were usually slaves, *affranchis*, or masters from estates throughout the dis-

30. Barry W. Higman, *Slave Populations of the British Caribbean 1807–1834* (Baltimore, 1984), Table 9.9, p. 356.
31. Calculated from DB Inventories.

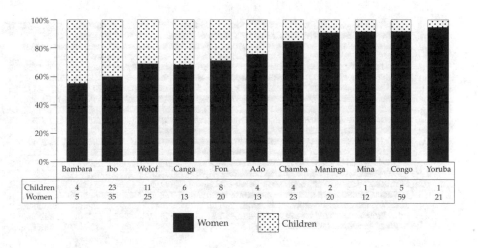

Figure 16. African Women and Their Children Under Age 14 at Pointe Coupee, 1771–1802
SOURCE: See source for Figure 6.
NOTE: See note for Figure 6.

trict. Slaves were very much aware of their maternal, and sometimes their paternal, descent.

Although African women gave birth to fewer creole children than did creole women, there was an enormous differential in birth rates among women of various African nations, as well as a sharp difference in the sex ratio among them. Ibo women were the most fertile, followed by Wolof and Canga women, though there were only thirteen Canga women found in the inventories. Fon women were the next most fertile. These same nations had the lowest sex ratios. The women of other African nations had few children. Only five children were identified on the lists as having been born to fifty-nine Congo women. Because women outnumbered or nearly equaled men among certain African nations brought to Louisiana, and the women of these same nations appeared to be substantially more fertile than other African women, the mothers of creole children born of African mothers during the Spanish period were likely to be Ibo, Wolof, or Fon. The higher fertility among these nations can perhaps be accounted for by the fact that they lived along the Atlantic coast and had not been as physically damaged as women brought from the interior.

We cannot draw any conclusions about the vital rates of the slave

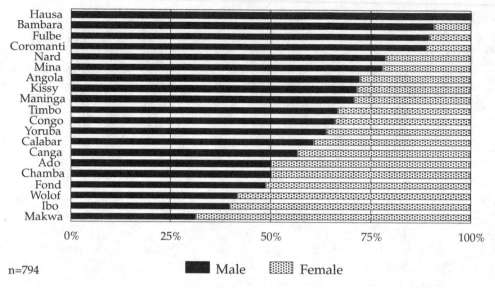

Hausa
Bambara
Fulbe
Coromanti
Nard
Mina
Angola
Kissy
Maninga
Timbo
Congo
Yoruba
Calabar
Canga
Ado
Chamba
Fond
Wolof
Ibo
Makwa

0%   25%   50%   75%   100%

n=794   ■ Male   ▦ Female

Figure 17. Percentage Male to Female Among African Nations at Pointe Coupee, 1771–1802
SOURCE: See source for Figure 6.
NOTE: See note for Figure 6. For absolute numbers, see Appendix C.

population from the data available. We are dealing with a mobile population. Even if we confine ourselves to studying the creole slaves, no conclusions can be drawn from the population at this one settlement. Many slaves, especially those of Protestant masters, were neither baptized nor buried in the Church, where vital records were kept. Except for a very few years, the baptismal records are confusing. There are gaps, sometimes large ones, between age of birth and baptism. Many of these records do not give age or date of birth at all, indicating perhaps baptisms of adult Africans, but it is impossible to tell from the records. Church records do not give the nation of the slaves. The burial records of St. Francis Church of Pointe Coupee dating between 1786 and 1802 are a bit clearer, but they only distinguish between male and female, child and adult without giving specific ages or nations. These burials should not be used to calculate crude death rates, because burying a slave in the Church cost money, and many masters, Catholic as well as Protestant, buried slaves on their estates when they could get away with it. They do show a clear pattern of disproportionate deaths of male slaves, especially of male children. While the sex index among all slaves at the post was 1.40, the

Re-Africanization Under Spanish Rule

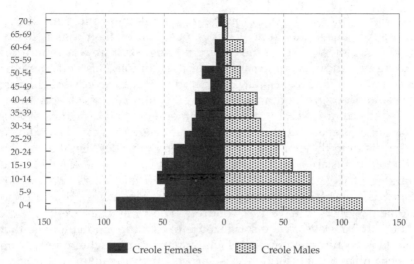

Figure 18. Creole Slaves by Age and Sex at Pointe Coupee, 1771–1802

SOURCE: See source for Figure 6.
NOTE: See note for Figure 6.

sex index among slaves buried in the Church was 2.03 for adults and 4.40 for children, though it appears that more males than females were born (see Figure 5). This same pattern of a disproportionate rate of births, as well as deaths, among male children can be seen in Guadeloupe. The sex ratio among creole slaves declined with age and evened out after age thirty-four.[32] It is possible that higher mortality among young males resulted from processing indigo, which is a toxic substance.

Clearly, then, the slave population at the Pointe Coupee post was heavily Africanized during the Spanish period. It is probable that most creole slaves had at least one African parent, and some of them had African grandparents and great-grandparents living at the post. The cultural influence of the new Africans was particularly great because of the breakup of the slave family under Spanish rule that began simultaneously with re-Africanization. Many of the children lived on estates without either parent and with adults who were overwhelmingly Africans who became fictive, as well as biological, kin. The two largest contingents of slaves arrived from Senegambia and

32. Calculated from DB Inventories; Nicole Vanonay-Frisch, *Les esclaves de la Guadeloupe à la fin de l'ancien régime d'après les sources notariales (1770–1789),* extrait du *Bulletin de la Société d'Histoire de la Guadeloupe,* Nos. 63–64 (1985), 63.

the Bight of Benin. If we can judge by the numbers and distribution of the Africans at the Pointe Coupee post and by their role as fictive as well as biological kin of the children, Mande culture was reinforced during re-Africanization, manifesting itself in folktales and proverbs of Mande origin in Louisiana Creole and in Mande words for charms: *zinzin* and *grisgris*. Fon and Yoruba religious practices deeply influenced the culture, accounting for the emergence and resilience of voodoo in Louisiana. Fon and Yoruba women were present in significant numbers, and they tended to be clustered on estates. Unlike Haitian voodoo, Louisiana voodoo was dominated by women. A substantial number of Congo slaves were brought in from Central Africa, but they did not speak mutually intelligible languages, and Congo women seemed to have few children. The Congo, as well as most other African slaves, were socialized into a culture and language that had long been formed by slaves who had come overwhelmingly from Senegambia. Congo influence is, however, discernible in the bamboula, a folk dance, and in the use of the term *wanga* (*ouanga*) for a magical charm.

Although the settlers at Pointe Coupee hastened to declare their loyalty to Spain when O'Reilly reestablished Spanish rule in 1769, the Pointe Coupee post remained French.[33] French and/or Louisiana Creole were spoken. All the reports from the post *comandantes* to Spanish officials were written in French. Almost all the documents at the post were in French. Spanish remained almost unknown at the post. The Louisiana creole language and culture had long been formed. Outside the capital, Spanish Louisiana remained French, Acadian, and Creole in language and culture.

The Indian frontier was more secure during the Spanish period. The important Indian fur trade along the Red River was monopolized by the merchant Tournoir, whose agent among them was described as a Great Haranguer. Fear of Indian attacks persisted, especially during wartime. At the outbreak of the American Revolution, there was a severe food shortage that no doubt affected the delivery of corn and other gifts normally provided to the Indians. Nevertheless, all the small nations, including the Tunica, who were described as very attached to the settlers, came to the fort to sing, dance, and smoke the calumet, renewing their allegiance to the king of Spain, promising to

33. Oath of Allegiance to the Spanish Government by the Inhabitants of Pointe Coupée and "Fausse Rivière," September 10, 1769, *LHQ,* IV (1921), 208–15.

make themselves worthy of his royal protection through their fidelity. Several chiefs asked for uniforms, medals, and flags. The *comandante* believed, however, that it was impossible to unite these small nations under a chief whom they would elect because of the divisions of interests and conduct among them.[34] When seven American boats commanded by James Willing descended the Mississippi River, arriving at the Pointe Coupee post on February 26, 1778, peace with the Indians was seriously threatened.[35] The post *comandante* reported that they "left nothing behind them except for the American settlers whom they did not touch." According to the *comandante*, the detachment, when commissioned at Philadelphia, consisted of twenty-eight men. By the time it reached Pointe Coupee, it comprised about two hundred men of all nations, motivated by the desire for loot. Willing had promised his men that all the fugitive slaves, as well as the slaves of all British subjects in the area, would be given up to them. They sought refuge at Pointe Coupee from a storm. The *comandante* refused to allow them to land with their arms, pointing out that the British subjects in the area were under the protection of the king of Spain. After leaving Pointe Coupee, they broke into the house of Jean Baptiste Mulâtre Libre at Baton Rouge, seizing thirty-two slaves belonging to two British merchants who had sought refuge there. They seized a British *engagé* off the ship of a settler who was heading for Natchitoches. British slave traders, including George Profit, and several other British subjects asked to become citizens of Spain, placing themselves and their property under the protection of the Spanish crown. They brought sixty or seventy slaves with them, as well as their belongings.[36]

As soon as the Americans arrived, Tunica and Ossot (Ofougoula?) Indians came to the fort in alarm. They were reassured by the *comandante* that the whites were fighting among themselves, not against the red men, who had nothing to fear. But after leaving Pointe Coupee for Manchac, the Americans shot five or six unarmed Choctaw warriors they encountered along the river, killing one of them. The *comandante* was alarmed by the reaction of the Indian nations, writing, "I

34. *Comandante* Delassize to Governor [Miró], August 17, 1783, in Leg. 196, fols. 734–35, PC, AGI; *Comandante* Grandpré to Governor Luis de Unzaga, August 17, 1776, in Leg. 189B, fols. 515–16, 513, *ibid*.

35. For a fuller discussion of Willing's raid, see John Caughey, "Willing's Expedition Down the Mississippi, 1778," *LHQ*, XV (1932), 5–36.

36. Charles de Grandpré to Bernardo de Gálvez, March 1, 3, 1778, in Leg. 189A, fols. 538–41, 544–46, respectively, PC, AGI.

am taking all necessary precautions here to avoid being attacked by the savages, of whom more than 80 from different nations have already arrived for a harangue."[37]

Willing was well received in New Orleans by Governor Bernardo de Gálvez and was allowed to sell most of his loot there. After the American Revolution, Spain became an important bulwark against the expansion of the United States at the expense of the Indian nations, strengthening Indian loyalty to Spain. The Tunica remained consistently loyal to the officials at Pointe Coupee. The Tunica village contained only thirty-three people in 1766, but individual, free Tunica Indians lived on several estates as well.[38]

Spain had an important legal impact upon Louisiana. The best-informed scholars have praised the Spanish judicial system as it was applied in Louisiana for its thoroughness, fairness, and economy, arguing that it was, in many ways, superior to what came before and after. There was a significant extension of rights to slaves, except in the vital area of protection for the slave family. Although O'Reilly directed the observance of the Code Noir when he took control of Louisiana in 1769, Spanish law and practice quickly superceded that of the French. While Spanish law extended certain formal rights to slaves, including the right to complain to the authorities about mistreatment and the right to force masters to estimate their price so they or others could purchase and free them, the protection of the slave family evaporated within a few years after Spain took control of Louisiana.[39] The French Code Noir had prohibited the separate sale of mother, father, and children under fourteen years of age. While the earliest slave lists from the Spanish period still reflect concern about inventorying and selling slave families together, including husbands and fathers, wives and children, there was a sharp deterioration in protection of the slave family within a few years after Spain took over Louisiana.

In 1773, the *comandante* at Pointe Coupee complained that two slaves inventoried on the estate of Dame Descour, one named Gasu and the other a *négresse* named Françoise dit Ponpon, claimed the

37. *Ibid.*

38. Light Townsend Cummins, "By the Stroke of a Pen: Louisiana Becomes Spanish," in *Louisiana: A History,* ed. Bennett H. Wall (2nd ed.; Arlington Heights, Ill., 1990), 65, 66; Jacqueline K. Voorhies, *Some Late Eighteenth-Century Louisianians: Census Records, 1758–1796* (Lafayette, La., 1973), 164.

39. Hans W. Baade, "The Law of Slavery in Spanish Louisiana," in *Louisiana's Legal Heritage,* ed. Edward F. Haas (Pensacola, 1983), 43–86.

right to choose their own master. They had left for New Orleans to insist that Françoise's mulatto children, aged six or seven, not be separated from her. The *comandante* wrote: "I was good enough not to take away the youngest from her, but she is not satisfied. . . . I beg you to state your intentions in this matter to serve me as a rule for the sale of *nègres* in the future.[40]

Thereafter, the practice was to inventory and sell slaves above the age of six or seven separately from their mothers. Sometimes, the filial relationship between mother and child was stated, but they were priced, and often sold, separately. Among the 636 children identified in the Pointe Coupee lists, 250, or 39.3 percent, were inventoried without any indication of who their mothers were. Eighty-nine of these children were under eight years of age, and 155 were between eight and thirteen. Three whose mothers had perhaps died were inventoried with their fathers alone. The baptismal records from the church of St. Francis of Pointe Coupee do not indicate the name of the father of newborn slaves. The baptismal records give the name of the mother, of her master, and of the godparents and describe the infant as a natural child born of an unknown father. Church marriages among slaves were rare indeed.

The *comandantes* at Pointe Coupee quickly discovered that the slaves were bold and independent-minded, very much aware of their rights, and ready to travel to New Orleans to complain if these rights were violated. During the summer of 1774, the *comandante* seized and sold the horses belonging to slaves, raising eleven hundred livres. He used this money to repair the fort, which was falling in ruins, and explained that he had taken this measure because it was illegal for slaves to own horses. The slaves had been traveling around freely at night, and their masters had closed their eyes to their slaves' activities, claiming that they had no way to stop them. The *comandante* wrote, "I thought it useless to inform you of this police action applauded by the settlers which is appropriate for repressing the disorder which has reigned here for a long time."[41]

Three *nègres*, described by the *comandante* as "the most notorious rogues of this coast," left for New Orleans without the permission of their masters to ask that the money obtained from the sale of their

40. Two letters from Villiers [to Unzaga?], Pointe Coupee, both dated April 6, 1773, in Leg. 189A, Doc. 918, PC, AGI.
41. Balthazard de Villiers to [?], Pointe Coupee, March 7, 1775, in Leg. 189B, Carpeta 28, fol. 390, PC, AGI.

horses be returned to them. The *comandante* wrote, "I hope that you will pay them no mind, and that they be punished as they deserve." The three *nègres* were put in jail for traveling to the capital without a passport or permission from their masters, "so that neither they nor other *nègre* will dare commit a similar action" until a decision was made about their complaints.[42]

The three *nègres* were back at the post within two weeks, boasting to all their friends that they had prevailed in the capital, that they had not been punished, that their complaints were heeded, and that the *comandante* would be relieved of his post because of their actions. Evidently, some of the masters backed up their slaves, questioning the amount of money the *comandante* had raised from the sale of the horses and what had become of it. He explained that the proceeds from the sale were placed in the hands of a depository named by him, as well as the fines "imposed in accordance with your orders and rulings," which evidently cut sharply into the receipts. He assured his superior that "the majority of the most sensible settlers came to beg me to repress this insolence which, if remaining unpunished, can only incite others to bring complaints to you about the least, deserved punishments."[43]

By 1776, there was a new *comandante* at the post. He found that all the *nègres* of the coast were armed and that some estates had fifty slaves with firearms, most of the guns given to them by their masters. He made a rule prohibiting masters from giving guns to their slaves, except for hunters using them with a permit that had to be returned at the end of each day. The rule also imposed a fine of six piasters and allowed for the confiscation of the guns for the benefit of those who seized them.[44]

The defiant spirit of the slaves increased with the outbreak of the American Revolution. Slaves escaped into nearby British territory, and English slaves escaped into Spanish territory. A slave belonging to Trénonay was working for an English settler who hid him when Trénonay's manager tried to bring him back. The *comandante*, complaining that the settlers suffered a great deal because of the loss of their slaves, as well as the loss of time spent in trying to apprehend them, tried to work out an agreement for the mutual exchange of runaway slaves between settlers in British territory and those at Pointe Coupee. After Spain entered the war against Britain, runa-

42. *Ibid.*; [?] to Villiers, March 21, 1775, *ibid.*, fol. 393.
43. Villiers to [?], April 2, 1775, *ibid.*, fol. 395.
44. Grandpré to Unzaga, August 17, 1776, *ibid.*, fol. 516.

ways increased. In 1779, eighty settlers lodged a complaint with the Cabildo, demanding the apprehension of thieves on the highways, especially runaway slaves. In October, 1783, an expedition went out to hunt runaway slaves in Pointe Coupee. The expedition cost ninety pesos, and two masters demanded compensation for maroons killed.[45] As we have seen, many maroons from Pointe Coupee headed south toward New Orleans, where economic opportunities were greater and maroon communities were better established.

The masters of Pointe Coupee were forced to make fairly drastic concessions to the slaves to convince them to stay. A slave named Michel was about to be leased for a year in the absence of his owner. The document explained that Michel was "very willful and capable of running away if he is leased to a master against his will." The slave was ordered to appear and state to whom he chose to be leased. He chose Charles Duflour, who agreed to lease him for a year. Nicolas Nègre Créole, who had been born on the estate of Louis Renard Duval in 1764 and sold to Pierre Le Doux in 1784 after Duval's death, did not like his new master.[46] Le Doux appeared in court and explained that for the past seven months, his *nègre maron* Nicolas had been causing damage to the settlers; and in spite of all his efforts, he had been unable to detain and arrest him. He explained that he was determined to sell Nicolas *maron* "because this *nègre* will return only on condition that he will no longer belong to the same master." Le Doux petitioned the court for an order demanding that Nicolas Nègre Créole return in order to be sold. The notice of sale was posted on the church door, and on September 27, 1785, Nicolas Créole was adjudged to Pierre Bergeron for the sum of seven hundred piastres.[47]

45. *Ibid.*, fol. 515; Syndico Procurador General, April 9, 1779, Doc. 984, in OAPC, listed in Kerr, "Petty Felony, Slave Defiance and Frontier Villainy," 363; Gilbert C. Din, "*Cimarrones* and the San Malo Band in Spanish Louisiana," *LH*, XXI (1980), 237–62.

46. Lease of slave Michel, December 21, 1786, Doc. 1535, in OAPC; Baptism of Nicolas *négrillon*, slave of Sieur Duval, born November, 1764, of Jeanne *négresse* of the same master and an unknown father, godparents Maurice Mulâtre Libre and Marie Louise, slave of Sieur Ricard, December 2, 1764, in Registre de Baptismes, enterrement et marriages, 1728–1762, of St. Francis Church of Pointe Coupee, Book II, Baptisms, 1742–1784, p. 272, item 1, Catholic Life Center, Baton Rouge, La.; Succession of Louis Renard Duval, November 5, 1779, Doc. 1015, in OAPC; Inventaire et Vente Biens, Succession Luis Renard Duval, January 7, 1784, Doc. 1337, in OAPC.

47. Vente Judiciare d'un Négre Nicolas appartenant à Pierre Le Doux adjugé à Bergeron, August 21, 1785, September 27, 1785, October 26, 1785, Doc. 1439, Vente d'esclave, Bergeron à Roy, September 10, 1786, Doc. 1490, both in OAPC. Details about Nicolas and Le Doux in subsequent paragraphs come from these sources.

After his judicial sale, Nicolas Créole was at the home of his new master. His former master became rancorous about the affair and convinced a militia officer to pick up Nicolas from Bergeron's home and return Nicolas to Le Doux. Nicolas was shackled, and a mulatto was placed over him to stand guard. In spite of these handicaps, Nicolas escaped again. Instead of running away to the swamps, he presented himself to the court, saying that he did not want to run away again. He had come to seek justice so that he could be returned to Bergeron, who had bought him legally—or in case Bergeron did not want to keep him, he should be placed with any other master except for Le Doux. He explained that he had been publicly promised that he would not be returned to his old master; he had given himself up only on the basis of this promise. The court records indicate that the militiaman had not been authorized to seize Nicolas from his new master. Nicolas was held at the fort and Bergeron was sent for to come get him.

In an agonized petition, Le Doux complained:

> I agree, and I am determined to follow the will of my *nègre* and give him a master of his choice, even though it is a poor example to set for my other slaves who wish to exercise the same privilege at the least disagreement which might occur. Nor do I wish to keep him after the most atrocious and horrible threats which could be made against a master which he has made against me, although I have never given him any reason whatsoever to run away. And the proof is that one cannot see any marks whatsoever on the bodies of my slaves, which proves that it is not a matter of a master who is too harsh.

Le Doux claimed that he only wanted the price he had paid for Nicolas from the estate of Renard Duval. In fact, he had already made a one hundred piastre profit on him. Bergeron sold Nicolas the following year at a profit, guaranteeing the buyer against any defects in Nicolas.

Louisiana's economy expanded sharply under Spanish rule. At the Pointe Coupee post, several large estates developed producing tobacco, indigo, corn, cattle, and lumber. In 1786, the post produced 7,900 pounds of tobacco, all at False River, 30,230 barrels of corn, and 61,926 pounds of indigo—nearly one-third of which was produced by Farar. Between 1777 and 1786, the slave population expanded while the white population stagnated and dropped. At the end of the war against Britain, the Pointe Coupee post was more bereft of young men than any other post, though it was an important way station for all watercraft plying the Mississippi River and for the Choctaw Indians

Re-Africanization Under Spanish Rule

Number of Estates

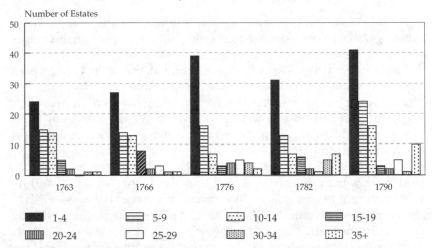

Figure 19. Changes in Distribution of Slaves on Estates at Pointe Coupee, 1763–1790

Sources: Figures for 1763 and 1766 calculated from Jacqueline K. Voorhies, *Some Late Eighteenth Century Census Records, 1758–1796* (Lafayette, La., 1973). Figures for 1776 calculated from Census of Slaves, March 22, 1776, Pointe Coupee, in Leg. 189B, fols. 462–66, PC, AGI. Figures for 1782 calculated from Head Tax Imposed on Slaves, Pointe Coupee, May 6, 1782, In Leg. 196, fol. 710, PC, AGI. Figures for 1790 calculated from Recensement de la Pointe Coupée et Fausse Rivière, March 29, 1790, in Leg. 227A, Carpeta 14, PC, AGI.

coming by land from east of the river.[48] By 1786, slaves outnumbered free people three to one.

In 1763 and 1766, only one planter owned more than thirty-four slaves (see Figure 19). In 1776, only two slave owners owned more than thirty slaves. By 1782, eight slave owners owned more than thirty-four slaves, and by 1790, ten slave owners did. The numbers of estates with more than thirty-five slaves increased steadily, but small owners also increased sharply between 1763 and 1790, dipping in 1782 because of the ravages of war on the free male population of military age. Although Pointe Coupee evolved into a community with a few large slave owners, its situation differed from that on some Caribbean islands with limited arable land. There, small holders were driven out by the rise of staple crops requiring extensive holdings of land and slaves. Substantial numbers of small farmers in Pointe Cou-

48. Recensement de la Pointe Coupée et la Fausse Rivière, Année 1786, January 20, 1786, in Leg. 2361, PC, AGI; *Comandante* Delassize to Governor, August 12, 1783, 196, in Leg. fols. 730–31, *ibid.*

pee held no slaves, or very few, and worked alongside their slaves growing tobacco and subsistence crops. Most of the small farmers were concentrated at False River.

There were distinctive patterns of crime at the post. Crimes committed by slaves usually involved theft of food and clothing. Free black women were sometimes accused of being involved in provoking thefts and receiving stolen goods. Nanette, a free *négresse* living at the house of the English commissioner Boukguard, was accused of stealing cloth from him and selling it to two male slaves in exchange for eight bottles of tafia and four barrels of corn. One of the men gave the cloth to a woman slave with which to make a shirt for him. Clothing was important to *affranchis* and to slaves. When the free *négresse* Marie dit Armand died, she left her effects—almost all clothing—in the slave cabin of Jean, slave of Madame Maure. It was estimated to be worth 506 piastres. Julien Poydras complained bitterly about the free *négresse* Charlotte who lived on the estate of his neighbor Simon Croisset. Poydras claimed that his slaves were always in her cabin performing services for her without his consent. One of them was injured while working for her and was sick for a month and a half and unable to work. Poydras claimed that she incited his slaves to steal fruits from his orchard, stakes from his courtyard, and chickens from his slave quarters. Poydras believed that she was brought into the district by two white men, Malard and Vitrac, who were profiting from her activities. Poydras sent his slave Marie to deliver his letter to the *comandante*, demanding the imprisonment of Charlotte and reparations for the chickens Charlotte had stolen from Marie. Vitrac was interrogated about his activities in relation to Charlotte.[49]

Most violent crime among people of African descent involved sexual jealousy. Since adult male slaves substantially outnumbered adult females, and since white men had the advantages of wealth and power when they competed for the sexual favors of slave women, it is not surprising that battles over the attentions of women surface occasionally in the documents. One case involved a love triangle among slaves on the estate of George Olivo, in which an uncle played a fatherly role in relation to his nephew. Augustin, nephew of Martin, became romantically involved with Angelique, wife of Etienne dit Amadou, a forty-five-year-old slave of the Fon nation. Martin testified

49. February 3, 1778, Doc. 912, in OAPC; April 26, 1785, Doc. 1429, *ibid.*; Poydras to Delassize, September 2, 1794, in Leg. 197, fols. 661–62, PC, AGI; Delassize to [?], October 7, 1794, in Leg. 197, fol. 665, PC, AGI; François Allain to Carondelet, February 20, 1793, in Leg. 208A, fol. 391, PC, AGI.

that he had scolded and once beat Augustin for being involved with Amadou's wife. Martin explained that Augustin was a young *nègre* of about twenty and had no cabin except his father's. As a result, he slept in all the cabins of his relatives. Amadou found his wife in bed with Augustin, murdered both of them with an ax, and then drowned himself in the Mississippi River.[50]

A group of slaves and free persons of all colors were having a party at the cabin of Marie dit Demba, a Poydras slave. All of them had contributed money for dinner and drinks, which they bought from neighboring merchants. Lambert, mulatto slave of Dame Bourgeat, got drunk and stabbed the free *nègre* Denis Macarti. Marie dit Demba's hand was cut trying to disarm Lambert. She was evidently too confident about how broadminded Lambert was about sharing her favors. When asked if Lambert was jealous of Macarti, she replied that "whatever gave her pleasure gave him pleasure too." Although the wound was slight, Macarti died unexpectedly within a few days.[51]

One case of violence among whites involved conflict over a slave woman. Le Doux, former master of the unhappy maroon Nicolas, was accused of severely beating a Spanish soldier who was sleeping with his slave Manon in her cabin. She testified that she had bought the drinks and that the soldier had given her some cloth, which she gave to her master. Le Doux's slave Bernardo testified that his master was very drunk at the time of the beating.[52]

Women slaves were mistreated, and sometimes tortured, by women as well as by men. Pierre Méthode beat his slave Hélène, then put gunpowder in her bleeding wounds and set her on fire. He was notified judicially to stop torturing his slave, but he started beating her again. Hélène was seized, nursed back to health by the post surgeon, and then sold judicially. Thereafter, Méthode acquired only foreign women slaves, probably in the hope that they could not as easily communicate his behavior to others.[53] In 1779, Bara dit Leblond brutally tortured his slave Genneviève, leaving her crippled. After Bara dit Leblond died, his son and his widow continued to maintain a charnel house. The cook, Perinne Négresse, a twenty-year-old creole, testified that she was being punished because she refused to mate with a *nègre* of the estate. She was kept in the kitchen on a long chain so that

50. Déclaration sur les Négres tués au George Olivo, April 5, 1798, Doc. 1992, in OAPC.
51. Requêtes faites au sujet du meurtre commis par le mulâtre Lambert, May 5, 1802, Doc. 2161, *ibid.*
52. May 31, 1779, Doc. 990, *ibid.*
53. Vente judiciale d'esclave négresse Hélène, September 10, 1783, Doc. 1299, *ibid.*

she would not run away but could continue to cook. They took her off the chain only so she could go to the fort to testify. She had no complaints about food or clothes, but her mistress choked her all the time, and it was hard to work always on a chain. Her mistress beat her often. She gave her too much work to do and she could not work as fast as her mistress wanted. Another domestic testified that after working all day she had to shuck corn for the turkeys at night. She was not allowed to sleep in a cabin but was locked up in a storeroom at night to prevent her from running off to the woods. She had many children, but God had been merciful and taken all but two of them. Her mistress did not allow her to see them or bring them food, because her mistress claimed she wanted to poison them. These notorious masters, all of them large slave owners, were evidently neither punished nor prevented from holding and buying more women slaves. However, the Spanish legal system allowed slaves the recourse of fleeing to New Orleans to complain against their masters, and there is evidence that sometimes discreet steps were taken to protect the slaves when they returned. For example, when Governor Gálvez returned two slaves who had run away from Trénonay, he instructed the *comandante* of the post to make sure they would not be mistreated. The *comandante* wrote, "I will neglect nothing in order to keep informed of the way the said Trénonay will treat these two slaves without arousing his least suspicion, in accordance with your orders."[54]

Frontier conditions created a deeply rooted tradition of violence and brutality that transcended race. Another example of extreme cruelty toward females is found in an investigation arising out of the slow torture and murder of a white indentured servant girl, named Emilia, by a mulatto woman, Marie Glass, who was married to a German miller. A white woman employee and a seven-year-old free mulatto boy had also been horribly tortured by her. Although several neighbors testified that they knew about the torture of Emilia, none of them had reported it to the authorities. Marie Glass was convicted of Emilia's murder and hanged. But neither Méthode nor the Baras were ever punished for torturing and maiming their slaves.[55]

While violence among slaves seemed to erupt mainly in connection

54. May 31, 1779, Doc. 991, *ibid.*; Procès pour justifier les Traitements de la Dame Bara dit Leblond en ses Esclaves, July 31, 1792, Doc. 1762, *ibid.*; Grandpré to Gálvez, March 1, 1778, 189A, fol. 541, PC, AGI.

55. For a discussion of this case based upon Henry P. Dart, "Trial of Mary Glass for Murder, February 7, 1780, through July 26, 1781," *LHQ*, VI (1923), 594–654, see McGowan, "Creation of a Slave Society," 247–51.

with struggles over women, violence among whites was broader in motivation. Jacques Landerneau complained before a judge that while visiting Sieur Bara, he was assaulted and severely injured by Nicolas de La Cour in a dispute over a small debt. Landerneau demanded damages and adequate compensation for his sufferings and expenses. Subdelegate Trénonay de Chanfret reported that La Cour had attacked six or seven persons and had been subjected to several small fines, and suggested a more severe punishment, since he was full of pride and could not be punished through his purse.[56]

Beaulayice Boisdoré was horsewhipped by his brother-in-law, André Plauché. Boisdoré hid in his cornfield, and as Plauché and his wife rode down the road on their horses, Boisdoré emptied his shotgun into Plauché, killing him and his horse. The neighboring whites, all of whom were related to both assassin and victim, denied knowledge of either the horsewhipping or the murder. The matter was clarified through the testimony of slaves, all of whom had better memories than their masters. Boisdoré and his slave Louis disappeared together, and all his possessions, including a ninety-year-old slave named Dinba, were seized. Jonathan Master, a sailor, filed a complaint against Martin Tournoir for putting out his eye with a firebrand.[57]

This tradition of violence and brutality did not, however, include hysteria about the purity of white womanhood and paranoic fears about the rape of white women by black men. The one case encountered in the Pointe Coupee documents involving alleged attempted rape dates from 1779. Jean Baptiste Nègre was accused of attempting to rape Dame Olivier, his master's neighbor. She complained that Jean Baptiste had passed under her window and made impertinent remarks to her. She claimed that the following night, he broke into her house, came into her bedroom, hit her on the head, grabbed her by the throat and the breasts, and tried to rape her. There was physical evidence of break-in, the bed was in disorder, and there were bruises on Dame Olivier's breast. Jean Baptiste was arrested and interrogated. He testified that he knew Dame Olivier but denied that he ever went to her house. She had asked him to work for her several times, but he always refused. He had passed near her house the day before

56. March 26, 1749, signed by Trenaunay Chanfret, in RSC, LHC; March 29–31, 1749, in RSC, *LHQ*, XX (1937), 496–99.

57. Copie d'enquête, mort de André Plauché, August 2, 1801, Doc. 2126, and Saisie des biens de Sr. Beaulayice Boisdoré, August 7, 1801, Doc. 2125, both in OAPC; G. Duparc, January 18, 1802, Doc. 2147, *ibid.*, listed in Kerr, "Petty Felony, Slave Defiance and Frontier Villainy," 366.

while going to dinner at a neighbor's house. His master was walking behind him. Dame Olivier asked him why he passed under her window instead of taking the road, saying it was no doubt to steal from her. He replied that he was far from her window and had absolutely no intention of stealing from her. He claimed that the night of the alleged attempted rape, he was sick and spent the night in a slave cabin of Dame Dauphine with two other *nègres* and one *négresse*, and that in the morning he moved cattle from one place to another. Marie Anne, *négresse* of Dame Dauphine, testified that Jean Baptiste had spent the entire night in her cabin and had not gone out. Jean Baptiste's statement was read to Dame Olivier. She was asked if she persisted in her version of what happened, and she said yes. Jean Baptiste was given thirty lashes. He continued to deny his guilt. He was given thirty more lashes, with the same result. After thirty more lashes, he still maintained his innocence. There were no other suspects. Dame Olivier, when told he denied his guilt under torture, reaffirmed that she was certain he was her attacker. Although she had not been able to see him because it was dark, she recognized his voice. She asked that he be held in prison because she feared for her life, since Jean Baptiste's master lived next door to her. The decision was that there was insufficient proof that Jean Baptiste was guilty of attempted rape, since he continued to deny his guilt under torture; that there was only sufficient proof of the impertinences (*injures*) that he had addressed to the complainant. The case was sent to the superior tribunal to be judged by Gálvez.[58] If these incidents had taken place during the enlightened twentieth century, Jean Baptiste would have surely been lynched with no questions asked.

Indifference to human life and suffering cannot be explained simply by projecting later attitudes toward race backward in time. Frontier conditions encouraged open attitudes toward race in Louisiana during the eighteenth century. Savage violence and brutality toward people of African descent motivated by race hatred came later. If we can judge by a conversation between this writer and a man at Pointe Coupee, the area remains a savage, violent place. On leaving the courthouse at New Roads in 1984, the writer met an old white man who was picking up trash in a park at the boat landing of False River, complaining about the smelly catfish heads, thrown in the

58. Procédure faite à la Requete de Dame Olivier contre le Nègre Jean Baptiste, esclave de Sr. Benon, May 27, 28, 31, 1779, Doc. 987, and Procédure Suite à la Requete de Dame Olivier contre le Nègre Jean Baptiste, May 22, June 2, 12, 1779, Doc. 988, both in OAPC.

trash cans, that he had to pick up. He spoke with a heavy French accent, and the writer switched to Parisian French, which was not exactly what he was speaking, but we managed to understand each other. He said he was the sole survivor of an old Pointe Coupee family, whose name appears in the eighteenth-century manuscripts. His grandfather, he said, had killed thirteen men. When asked why, he replied, "Because they were *nègres,* and they did not tip their hats to him when they passed him in the street. My grandfather was murdered by a boy he had raised, and my father was murdered too." When asked if it was still so violent at Pointe Coupee, he replied, "Oui!"

Unrest During the Early 1790s

Quand patate la cuite na va mangé li.

When that potato is cooked, it must be eaten.

—Refrain of Louisiana Creole dance from Alcée
Fortier, "Bits of Louisiana Folklore"

The eruption of the French Revolution in 1789 precipitated great unrest in Louisiana. Louisiana was a Spanish colony with a French population and a merchant class with close ties to France. National and cultural identity and the desire for the spoils of office, the major source of wealth as well as power, motivated Louisiana's white creole elite to seek reunification with France. When trade with France and the French West Indies ceased, merchants led revolutionary demonstrations. Merchants of Bordeaux and New Orleans sent petitions to Paris asking for the return of Louisiana to France. Merchants of New Orleans took up a subscription to offer a gift to the French Convention. In early 1793, 150 subjects signed a petition asking for the province to be reunited with France.

When the Baron de Carondelet became governor general on December 30, 1791, he found aphorisms and philosophies of the French Revolution repeated on the streets of New Orleans. Many short-lived Jacobin clubs distributed revolutionary literature in the capital. The "Marseillaise," "Ca ira," "Carmagnolle," and "Les aristocrats à la lanterne" were sung in the streets. The opposition to the Spanish regime was called Jacobin, Vagabond, Sans-Culottes, and American, terms meaning, vaguely, rebellious person. Governor Carondelet resorted to mass deportations. All persons who had come to the colony since 1790, as well as those who did not own property or have other permanent interests, were required to take an oath of allegiance to Spain. Those who refused had to go to the United States or to the Danish West Indies. A considerable group left. By July, 1793, sixty-eight suspected persons had been expelled from the capital.[1]

The outbreak of war between France and Spain in the spring of 1793 was a devastating blow to the security and the prosperity of the colony. By early 1795, disorder reigned in New Orleans. Houses were ignited, and dangerous mobs were attracted to the fires. The authorities did not have the forces to deal with these disorders, and officials stayed away from the scene to avoid precipitating a crisis or being assassinated. American royalist militia were brought from Natchez to restore order. The province was faced with an invasion threat by land and sea. Edmond Gênet, the French ambassador to the United States, conspired with United States general George Rogers Clark to seize

---

1. Ernest R. Liljegren, "Jacobinism in Spanish Louisiana, 1792–1797," *LHQ*, XXII (1939), 47–97.

the colony for France, promising free navigation of the Mississippi River to the United States. Clark recruited American frontiersmen from the upper Mississippi who were to descend upon New Orleans while a French squadron organized in New York blockaded the Mississippi River from the south. The conspirators organized a mass uprising in support of the invasion. Carondelet exiled those suspected of disloyalty to Havana. The Gènet-Clark scheme went awry. Spain's alliance with the Indians held up, and they spied on the American frontiersmen for Spain. President Washington published a proclamation prohibiting recruitment on United States soil for the invasion planned by Gênet and Clark. The fleet organized in New York to blockade New Orleans by sea never arrived. Its crew revolted.[2]

The French Revolution had an immediate, drastic impact upon Louisiana's economy. The colony's indigo crop was marketed in France via the French West Indies. Planters had sunk deeply into debt during the 1780s, obtaining slaves on credit against future indigo crops. Maritime trade was disrupted, and the market for indigo evaporated. Spain canceled Louisiana's monopoly of the Mexican tobacco market and stopped buying Louisiana tobacco. The Pointe Coupee post was hard hit because its two major export crops could no longer be sold. Planters defaulted on their debts. There were numerous seizures for debt at the Pointe Coupee post during 1790. Hunger and famine gripped the district.[3]

Slave control, never easy in colonial Louisiana, became increasingly difficult during the 1790s. Masters in Pointe Coupee built upon several themes in order to divide and rule their slaves. They created and tried to maintain a hierarchy of status, placing mixed-blood creole slaves over black creole slaves and all creole slaves in a privileged position over Africans. While the ideal of the masters resembled the pattern discerned by Vanony-Frisch in Guadeloupe, where mixed-blood slaves were at the top, black creoles in the middle, and Africans on the bottom, the hierarchy in Louisiana was bent at the edges. The *commandeurs*, both black and mixed-blood, were at the top, though a disproportionate number of *commandeurs* were mulattoes. Conflicts among African slaves were encouraged on the estates by tolerating organized language-ethnic communities, creating clusters of slaves from the same nation and culture region. Slaves from Senegambia continued to arrive in large numbers throughout the Spanish period.

2. *Ibid.*
3. Debt seizures calculated from OAPC; Goudeau contra Divers Habitans, April 6, 1790, Doc. 1712, in OAPC.

The Senegambian slaves, especially the Bambara, were close to the creoles, probably because of common ancestral ties dating from the French slave trade.[4] The proportion of slaves from the Bight of Benin rose sharply after 1782, when free trade in slaves was allowed. Slaves from Central Africa, almost all listed as Congo, were third in numerical importance, with their proportion among Africans diminishing over time (see Figure 7).

The advantages and disadvantages of allowing organized African ethnic communities to function became clear on the night of July 9, 1791, the same night that Claude Trénonay was assasinated by his Ibo slave, Latulipe. Valentin Leblanc, *comandante* of the Pointe Coupee post, was officially informed that the Mina slaves were about to rise up and kill their masters.[5] George Olivo, *père*, sent word to Leblanc that the slaves of the Mina and Bambara nations planned to rise up against all the whites of the district and that both nations planned to meet at New Roads in False River on July 6 to discuss plans to attack the French. The uprising did not take place, however, because of bad weather and because the slaves from outside False River were not adequately notified of where the meeting would be held. The Mina conspiracy was revealed a month before the first major slave revolt erupted in St. Domingue. The plan was to kill the masters, beginning with the merchant Tournoir, take arms and ammunitions from his store, and free themselves from slavery.[6]

Who were the Mina slaves of Louisiana? Although historians of the Atlantic slave trade sometimes include Mina slaves with Gold Coast slaves, assuming that their name indicates that they came through the slave-trade post of El Mina, this writer has included Mina slaves with slaves coming from the Bight of Benin, assuming that they came from the Mina coast and were probably Ewe and closely related to the Adó and the Fon (Dahomean).[7] In the Pointe Coupee lists, Fon slaves were

4. Nicole Vanony-Frisch, *Les esclaves de la Guadeloupe à la fin de l'ancien régime d'après les sources notariales (1770–1789)*, extrait du *Bulletin de la Sociétè d'Histoire de la Guadeloupe* Nos. 63–64 (1985), 151. For an interesting discussion of ancestral links between creole and African slaves as a factor in a slave conspiracy, see David Barry Gaspar, *Bondmen and Rebels: A Study of Master-Slave Relations in Antigua with Implications for Colonial British America* (Baltimore, 1985).

5. Ulysses S. Ricard, Jr., "The Pointe Coupee Slave Conspiracy of 1791," in *Proceedings of the International Congress of the French Colonial Historical Society*, ed. Philip Boucher (in press, University Press of the Americas).

6. Testimony of Antonio Decuir, July 9, 1791, fols. 1v–2v, in Mina, OAPC; Testimony of Cofi, Mina slave of Jacinto, July 12, 1791, fol. 51v, *ibid.*

7. The Adó could have been people from Otta, or southwestern Yoruba (Philip D. Curtin, *The Atlantic Slave Trade: A Census* [Madison, Wis., 1969], 187).

enumerated separately from Mina slaves, and neither the designations *Ewe* nor *Gege*, the Brazilian term for Dahomean, were used, leading to the strong possibility that the Mina slaves of Louisiana were Ewe. Pierre Verger explained that the Mina coast, or the coast east of Mina, was so named after the Dutch seized the slave trade post of El Mina from the Portuguese. They allowed the Portuguese to trade through four ports: Grand Popo, Whydah, Jaquin, and Apa to the east along the present coast of Dahomey. In Louisiana, the Mina were a well-organized language community, and therefore, the term *Mina* referred to a nation, not a slave-trade post. The Mina language in Brazil has been identified as a dialect of Ewe closely related to Fon.[8]

The Mina slaves of Pointe Coupee met and socialized as a group, maintaining a language and social community that had ties with an organized Mina community in New Orleans. The 1791 Pointe Coupee Conspiracy was an African ethnic movement organized from the estate of Widow Provillar by her Mina slaves and those belonging to a number of different masters. The Provillar estate was inventoried in 1790. Its slave force consisted of a sixty-year-old Mina woman, three Mina men, an Ibo woman, and a creole child. The accused conspirators held regular balls in the cabin of Juan Luis, Mina slave of the Widow Provillar, because her estate, located at New Roads of False River, allowed for easy communications between Pointe Coupee and False River. Only Mina men were invited. The king of each ball was responsible for providing the refreshments. Their conspiracy was betrayed because of ethnic conflicts among Africans and ties of fictive kinship between a creole and an African woman, both Olivo slaves. Venus, a slave of the Adó nation, was the godchild and namesake of a creole slave. Venus' baptismal name was Francisca, the name of her creole godmother. According to Venus, she was approached by Digue, Adó slave of Ternan, who informed her about the Mina conspiracy. She told him, "You are not a Mina. You are an Adó like me. Do not join them." Digue agreed not to join them and told her of the date and time of the uprising. According to Digue's version of this conversation, he warned Venus about Santiago Fabre's Mina slave Jacó, who had entered her cabin armed. Digue said, "Be careful with that *nègre* because he is a Mina and that nation is very bad." Venus,

---

8. Pierre Verger, *Flux et reflux de la traite des nègres entre le Golfe de Benin et Bahia de Todos os Santos du 17ième au 19ième siècles* (Paris, 1968), 7, 10; Antonio da Costa Peixoto, *Obra nova de lingua geral de mina,* ed. Luis Silveira (Lisbon, 1945); John Holm, conversation with the author.

her godmother, Francisca, Francisca's father, George Creole, and Pedro Chamba, all Olivo slaves, went to their master's house to warn him about the plot and then hid in his house to avoid retribution from the Mina slaves.[9]

The African slaves on the Olivo estate whose nations have been identified all came from the Bight of Benin, though there were no Mina slaves among them. Three of the Olivo slaves died in 1798 as the result of a murder-suicide love triangle involving a slave husband of the Fon nation. Olivo operated an old-style estate, where family ties among slaves were respected. He owned twenty-eight slaves in 1790, all of them black, with an even sex ratio among the fourteen mature adults. There were ten slave children on the estate.[10] Olivo testified for Marie Jeanne, mother of Antoine Sarrasin, the main leader of the 1795 conspiracy, in her efforts to have herself and her children emancipated on the grounds that they descended from an Indian woman. Olivo testified that he knew Marie Jeanne's mother and that she was, indeed, a full-blooded Indian. In 1801, Olivo's son freed his slave concubine and their five children.[11]

Although Venus' original testimony indicated that Digue said Bambara slaves were also involved in the plot, Digue's testimony did not indicate any such involvement. On the contrary, he quoted Jacó, one of the three leaders of the plot, as saying that if there were not enough Mina in False River, they would join up with those of Pointe Coupee. They did not need other nations. It seems likely that the Bambara had been approached by the Mina and refused to join, and Venus had prior knowledge of plans for both groups to rise up. Digue claimed that he knew nothing about the plot until Venus informed him of it and that Venus was a neighbor of Jacó and saw him regularly. Venus insisted that she was informed of the plot by Digue. Although some Bambara slaves were brought in and questioned, there is no record of

9. July 7, 1790, Doc. 1719, in OAPC; Testimony of Juan Luis, slave of Widow Provillar, July 12, 1791, fols. 42r, 42v, in Mina, OAPC; Testimony of Francisco Allain, January 19, 1793, fol. 522 (477), in Mina, AGI; Testimony of Venus, Adó slave of Olivo, July 9, 1791, fol. 9r, in Mina, OAPC; Testimony of Digue, Adó slave of Ternan, July 9, 1791, fol. 12v, in Mina, OAPC; Testimony of Venus, July 9, 1791, fols. 10r, 10v, in Mina, OAPC.

10. Déclaration sur les Nègres tués au George Olivo, April 5, 1798, Doc. 1992, in OAPC; Recensement de la Pointe Coupée et Fausse Rivière, March 29, 1790, in Leg. 227A, Carpeta 21, Doc. 2, PC, AGI. Spanish censuses defined mature adults as aged fifteen to forty-nine. Antonio Acosta Rodríguez, La población de la Luisiana española (1763–1803) (Madrid, 1979), 110, 313.

11. Lettre de Liberté, January 20, 1801, Doc. 2096, in OAPC.

interrogations or declarations of Bambara slaves, and no Bambara were detained or accused.[12] It seems likely that the Bambara slaves were too close to the creole slaves to act without them and were therefore reluctant to become involved in a purely African movement.

Although the Olivo slaves reported the Mina plot to their master on the night of Friday, July 8, it was not until the following night, July 9, 1791, at about 8 P.M., that Antoine Decuir reported it to the *comandante*. Patrols were sent out to arrest all the Mina and Bambara slaves of the district. A patrol reported that it found Cofi Mina knocking on the door of the Mina slave of Gabriel Roufat. According to the *comandante*, this slave had a knife and attacked a member of the patrol. The patrol searched the cabins but found nothing. After their initial interrogation, some of the Mina slaves were sent back to their masters. One of them, when called back to the fort for further interrogation, threw himself into the river and drowned.[13]

There is a written record of the initial interrogation of sixteen slaves at Pointe Coupee. The accused were all single laborers, and among those whose ages were given, three were in their forties, eight were in their thirties, two were in their twenties, and one was nineteen. According to this testimony, there were only Mina at the ball, except for César, a creole slave from Jamaica of Emable Couvillon, and Pedro, a nineteen-year-old Chamba slave who was raised by the Mina. Pedro Chamba acted as a courier among the leaders of the plot.[14] César, Juan Luis, and Jacó were the leaders. César was the main leader.

On August 1, 1791, the original testimony was forwarded to the superior tribunal and the prisoners were sent to New Orleans for trial. The accused slaves and the testimony arrived at a time when Governor Miró's attention was distracted by a series of arson incidents in New Orleans attributed to runaway slaves who had been frequenting cabarets outside the city, buying drinks and ammunition at very low prices. When the *ayuntamiento* ordered these cabarets

12. Testimony of Venus, July 9, 1791, fol. 8v, in Mina, OAPC; Testimony of Digue, July 9, 1791, fols. 13v, 14r, *ibid.;* Testimony of Digue, September 11, 1792, fol. 411 (366), and Testimony of Venus, September 11, 1792, fol. 409 (364), both in Mina, AGI; Testimony of Eustaquio Bedel, January 18, 1793, fols. 515–16 (470–71), Testimony of Juan Bautista Bara, December 17, 1792, fols. 484–86 (439–45), both in Mina, AGI.

13. Declarations of Luis Estevan, Guillermo Recuron, Pedro Oleinde, Joseph Porche, and Huber David, July 15, 1791, fols. 93r–103v, in Mina, OAPC; Testimony of Fernando Rodríguez, *escribano real*, September 20, 1792, fol. 417 (372), in Mina, AGI.

14. Testimony of Thomas, Mina slave of the Widow Latendresse, July 12, 1791, fols. 71r, 71v, in Mina, OAPC.

closed, a series of fires was set in several places in the city in order "to destroy whatever had been saved or rebuilt after the disaster of 1788." New Orleans had been burned down twice over the past few years. Arson trials began in New Orleans during the first week of July, 1791. Miró also suspected escaped *presidarios*, criminals sentenced to forced labor in Louisiana. He maintained two patrols of fifty men each to try to prevent and/or extinguish fires set in the capital. The *comandante* complained that the military needs of the Pointe Coupee post had been neglected; they had to go from house to house to assemble the militia because they had no drummer, the fort was in ruins, and there no cannon were mounted. Miró rejected this complaint, writing that Pointe Coupee was no longer considered a military post, since the British had evacuated the east bank of the Mississippi River. With great reluctance, the governor sent a drummer, two corporals, eighteen soldiers armed with twenty-one cartridges each, and thirty muskets for the local militia to reinforce the post, instructing the *comandante* to ask for six more men from Baton Rouge if necessary. He insisted that these reinforcements be sent back as soon as possible because they were needed elsewhere. He went on to berate the settlers for allowing their slaves to have arms and to move about freely among the plantations in violation of the laws promulgated.[15]

Carondelet inherited the problem of the Mina conspiracy from outgoing governor Miró. Carondelet assumed office a few months after the first major slave uprising in St. Domingue. The Spanish authorities were convinced that the slave revolt in St. Domingue was provoked by the mistreatment of slaves by their masters. Carondelet was instructed to see to it that Louisiana slaves were not similarly provoked into rebellion. He kept himself informed of conditions on the plantations and did, on a few occasions, intervene to protect mistreated slaves. He promulgated a protective slave code. In April, 1792, an overseer and a slave were sentenced to be hanged for beating a slave to death. Carondelet's reform policies provoked growing hostility from the slave owners. The new governor responded by cultivating the support of the slaves and the free colored population to prevent unrest and to serve as a counterweight to disloyalty among white creoles. He increased the colored militia, commissioning 29 free

15. Decree of July 21, 1791, fol. 103v, Original testimony sent to the governor general, August 1, 1791, fol. 105r, both *ibid.*; Maude Caroline Burson, *The Stewardship of Don Esteban Miró* (New Orleans, 1940), 122; Arson trial, July 5 to November 14, 1791, in SJR, LHC; Governor Miró to Captain General Luis de las Casas, July 2, 1791, in Leg. 2556, fol. 238, SD, AGI; Miró to Leblanc, July 14, 1791, in Leg. 2556, fols. 240–42, SD, AGI.

colored officers, and relied heavily upon the people of African descent for intelligence of all kinds. There was some hesitation among militiamen of African descent about which side to support during the threatened French invasion, but Carondelet attested to their loyalty to Spain. He strongly supported a petition by officers of the three companies of free people of African descent for the same pay and privileges as their counterparts in Havana, specifically, the enjoyment of the military *fuero*. These companies comprised two of pardos (mixed bloods) of 120 men each, one larger company of blacks, and 16 officers. They were all skilled workers earning considerably more than what they were paid when on militia duty. Carondelet praised them for their constant loyalty, especially during the war against France. They were always ready to march and publicly demonstrate their loyalty to Spain. They remained for over a month at the Plaquemine post, defending the entrance to the Mississippi River against the expedition organized in New York by Gênet, working arduously to strengthen the defenses of the fort.[16] We will never know which side they would have chosen if the French invasion had materialized.

The Mina trial began in New Orleans in March, 1792, while St. Domingue (Haiti) was up in flames. Carondelet presided personally over an extensive reinterrogation of the Mina slaves. All of the accused denied the truth of the documents that emerged from their original interrogations in Pointe Coupee. They claimed that they had been beaten when they refused to admit their guilt, and that they could neither understand nor properly answer the questions asked to them because of their limited knowledge of Louisiana Creole, the language in which they were interrogated. Their answers were not written down and read back to them. The persons who signed their interrogations as attending witnesses had not been present.

Comandante Leblanc explained that the accused slaves had been interrogated in the French creole language, which he described as "a mixture of the language of their nations and of French pronounced

16. April 19, 1792, in LHC, Doc. 2904, listed in Derek Noel Kerr, "Petty Felony, Slave Defiance and Frontier Villainy: Crime and Criminal Justice in Spanish Louisiana, 1770–1803" (Ph.D. dissertation, Tulane University, 1983), 337; James T. McGowan, "Creation of a Slave Society: Louisiana Plantations in the Eighteenth Century" (Ph.D. dissertation, University of Rochester, 1976), 350–56; Francisco Dorville and Noel Carrière, Captains of the Black and Pardo Militia, to Carondelet, February 1, 1797, and Memorandum from *Comandante* General Carondelet, February 20, 1797, in Leg. 6919, fol. 24, GM, AS. For a detailed study of the militia under Spanish rule in Louisiana, including the black and colored militia, see Jack D. L. Holmes, *Honor and Fidelity: The Louisiana Infantry Regiment and the Louisiana Militia Companies, 1766–1821* (Birmingham, Ala., 1965), especially pages 54–59.

with great diversity." And though not all the settlers knew the language, he, the witnesses, and the notary who presided at their interrogation knew French Creole very well. Leblanc expressed misgivings about the ability of the French interpreters in New Orleans to understand, or be understood by, the slaves, who did not know legitimate French. There had been a long delay before the accused slaves were reinterrogated because of the illness of the *auditor de guerra*. The jail was not set up to keep the prisoners separate from each other. They could have agreed among themselves to present false testimony.[17]

A notary was sent from New Orleans to Pointe Coupee to take sworn statements from all who had signed the documents as attending witnesses. It came out during the Mina trial in New Orleans that several solid citizens of Pointe Coupee perjured themselves, swearing falsely under oath that they had witnessed these interrogations. They all had to finally admit that they were pressured into signing these documents by Leblanc, who wrote them all in his own handwriting, many of them after the interrogations were over, even though Fernando Rodriguez, *escribano real*, was present at all of the interrogations. Isaac Fastiau, who signed all the interrogations taken at Pointe Coupee as official interpreter into Spanish, had not attended even one interrogation, and his grasp of Spanish was so poor that he himself needed an official interpreter into Spanish when he testified in New Orleans. Manuel Monsanto had to sign a bond for him so he could return to Pointe Coupee.[18]

Carondelet ordered the prisoners questioned again under oath and with proper interpreters, since he had serious doubts that the slaves had understood, and had been understood by, their interrogators. Antonio Cofi Mina and Juan Bautista Cupidon, both free Minas of New Orleans, were named as interpreters from the Mina language into Spanish, and two other interpreters from Louisiana Creole to Spanish were named.[19]

The wheels of justice ground slowly. While Carondelet personally presided, each accused slave was asked again each original question of his interrogation through the Louisiana Creole interpreters and was also asked to respond in the same language. Then each question was asked once more in the Mina language by the Mina interpreters.

17. Testimony of Valentin Leblanc, *comandante* of the Pointe Coupee post, March 30, 1792, fols. 399–403 (354–58), in Mina, AGI.

18. Testimony of Fernando Rodriguez, September 20, 1792, fol. 415 (370), *ibid.*; Testimony of Isaac Fastiau, November 26, 1792, fols. 455–58 (410–13), and Testimony of Manuel Monsanto, December 20, 1792, fols. 498–99 (453–54), both *ibid.*

19. September 20, 1792, fols. 421–22 (376–77), *ibid.*

During the reinterrogation of Jacó, slave of Santiago Fabre, the conclusion was, "While the accused understood many words, he did not understand the real meaning of the questions, because when the Mina interpreters explained them, he answered well and elaborated upon his answers." The linguistic capability of the Mina slaves in Louisiana Creole was generally poor, and they explained that their knowledge of the language had improved while they had been working in the city with the French during the past year. Evidently, Louisiana Creole was widely spoken in New Orleans at the time. One of the accused was fluent in Louisiana Creole, but he testified that no one had read to him what was written down and that he had not said what was in his original interrogation. It was claimed that Leblanc used his own Mina slave Rigodon to interpret from Mina when necessary, though the slaves denied that Rigodon was present.[20]

Although this trial took place during the height of the Haitian Revolution and though their slaves had been accused of plotting to kill them, most of the masters were eager to establish their slaves' innocence and take them home. They wished to avoid the cost of their slaves' imprisonment and to regain the benefit of their labor, which was a matter of economic survival, especially for the many small slave owners involved. Some of them seemed to sincerely believe that their slaves would not do such a thing to them. Their pride and self image were at stake. They referred to their slaves as "their own" ("*los suyos*"). Some of them seemed to be emotionally attached to their slaves. In May, 1792, Gabriel Rufat petitioned the court that Pedro, his imprisoned slave, was innocent and that he would answer for him "with his own body." He asked that Pedro be returned to him because he was a poor man and he needed his slave to do his work. Before Pedro was taken from Pointe Coupee, Rufat had been told he had to await the arrival of the proper documents before they would release his slave. Instead, Pedro was sent to New Orleans, and Rufat said he was ruined for having lost his labor. His slave had denied to him that

20. Interrogation of Jacó, slave of Santiago Fabre, September 22, 1792, fol. 423 (378), *ibid.;* Interrogation of Francisco, slave of Jorge Bergeron, September 22, 1792, fol. 429 (384), *ibid.;* Interrogation of Cofi of Juan Paul, September 22, 1792, fol. 430 (385), *ibid.;* Interrogation of Joseph of J. B. Tournoir, September 22, 1792, fol. 432 (387), *ibid.;* Interrogation of Jacó of the Widow Leblond, September 25, 1792, fol. 437 (392), *ibid.;* Interrogation of Thomas of the Widow Latendresse, September 25, 1792, fol. 438 (393), *ibid.;* Interrogation of Joseph of Pequeño Jorge, September 25, 1792, fol. 440 (395), *ibid.;* Interrogation of Cuyo of Francisco Porche, September 25, 1792, fol. 443 (398), *ibid.;* Testimony of Santiago of Miguel el Joven, September 25, 1792, fol. 442 (327), *ibid.;* Confrontation between Fernando Rodríguez and Jacó, slave of Fabre, September 22, 1792, fol. 426 (381), *ibid.*

he wanted to kill him. And when asked about the Mina ball, Pedro had replied: "There was a ball that lasted about 24 hours, in which a lot of liquor [*aguardiente*] was drunk. Several of them decided to steal from their masters and go off to become maroons to free themselves from mistreatment by their masters." Rufat denied that the slave who had been arrested by the patrol while knocking at the cabin door of his Mina slave had a knife or made any resistance, adding that he submitted very humbly. Rufat's slave was not released until July 12, 1793, after Rufat petitioned that his imprisoned slave was incurably ill and that he feared that Pedro might die unless he was released to him so Rufat could care for him.[21]

Jorge Bergeron denied Leblanc's statement that he had helped to obtain and had witnessed a confession from his slave Petit François. Bergeron doubted his slave's guilt and denied Leblanc's statement that was read to him.

> This citation is false in all its parts. And it is also false that I gave Petit François the declaration that was just read. What happened was that I went to get a loaf of bread for Petit François while he was being interrogated on the porch by the *comandante*. . . . The *comandante* called out to me saying that he understood Petit François better than I did, and that he was questioning him about the details of the so-called uprising of the Mina *nègres*. When I asked Petit François if he had gone to the ball, and for what reason, he replied that he had gone to enjoy himself. His violin got broken, and not liking the party, he left. I did not hear him say anything else, much less what was put in the declaration which was just read.[22]

Julien Poydras denied the *comandante*'s claim that he had witnessed Petit François' confession. He testified that though he was present when Bergeron brought Petit François to the *comandante* to be questioned, he "did not hear nor understand the questions of the one nor the answers of the other, because I was on guard at the fort and did not pay attention to any of that."[23]

Many prominent settlers of Pointe Coupee denied ever hearing any of the Mina slaves say that they had plotted to rise up against the whites, whether during interrogation or under any other circumstances, contradicting Leblanc's claims that they had reported such information to him. Joseph Decuir said that the militia patrol he com-

21. Testimony of Juan Bautista Bara, December 17, 1792, fols. 484–86 (439–45), *ibid.*; Testimony of Gabriel Rufat, May 22, 1792, fols. 403–406 (358–61), *ibid.*; Petition of Rufat, July 9, 1793, and Order of Release, July 12, 1793, fols. 539–40 (494–95), *ibid.*

22. Testimony of Jorge Bergeron, December 9, 1792, fols. 481–83 (436–38), *ibid.*

23. Testimony of Julien Poydras, November 26, 1792, fols. 459–60 (414–15), *ibid.*

manded never reported to him that the Mina slave who was knocking on the door of another Mina slave belonging to Rufat resisted with a knife when he was apprehended.[24]

It is clear that Leblanc put down whatever he pleased in the original interrogations. He intimidated the settlers into signing false documents and lying under oath when they were questioned at Pointe Coupee about the documents they had signed.[25] But it is also clear that the conspiracy was real. The Allain brothers, Auguste and François, did hear and understand the statements of some of the Mina slaves who were being interrogated, and it is their testimony that is most reliable. Auguste Allain testified that he was in the fort by chance while the *comandante* was interrogating Jacó, slave of Santiago Fabre. He heard Jacó say that his intention was only to go maroon. He also heard Juan Luis say, "Jacó had been talking like an old cow, because whatever he had said once he had to stick to." Juan Luis said that Jacó had incited him to rise up and kill the whites and that he had replied, "How can we do that when we have no arms?" According to Juan Luis, Jacó had said that they had pigs and other things and that they could sell them and buy whatever was necessary. Auguste Allain testified that the interrogations took place in French, "although corrupted and badly pronounced, which they call French *nègre* Creole." He understood them very well because he was accustomed to hearing the language, and he could tell that they could understand it, too.[26]

The tribunal had Allain ask Cofi a question in French Creole. Cofi did not understand him. When questioned through the Mina interpreter, Cofi denied that he had implicated César and that the Minas wanted to rise up and kill all the whites, adding that when he denied during the earlier interrogation that he was guilty, they had struck him.[27]

24. *Ibid.*, Testimony of Simon Croisset, December 9, 1792, fols. 475–79 (430–34), *ibid.*; Testimony of Juan Bautista Bara, December 17, 1792, fols. 484–86 (439–45), *ibid.*; Testimony of Luis Guillo alias Lajeunesse, December 17, 1792, fol. 487 (442), *ibid.*; Testimony of Eustaquio Bedel, January 18, 1793, fols. 514–18 (469–73), *ibid.*; Testimony of Joseph Decuir, January 21, 1793, fols. 526–29 (481–84), *ibid.*; Testimony of Domingo Seizan, April 6, 1793, fols. 536–37 (491–92), *ibid.*

25. See, for example, Testimony of Diego Ortiz, December 22, 1792, fols. 502–503 (457–58), *ibid.*

26. Testimony of Augustin Allain, captain of militia, December 17, 1792, fols. 488–92 (443–47), *ibid.*

27. Confrontation between Augustin Allain and Cofi, slave of Jacinto Chistes, December 22, 1792, fols. 506–509 (461–64), *ibid.*

Allain was confronted by Juan Luis, who spoke good French Creole. Juan Luis denied that he called Jacó an old cow, and said he had denied that there was a conspiracy to rise up and kill the whites. Allain was confronted with Jacó, and Jacó testified that he told the *comandante,* "We had no such intentions, because in Guinea, our land, we do not kill whites, and what recourse would we have here if we killed them, because they have done nothing harmful to the *nègres.* Nor did I tell the *comandante* that I intended to go maroon, because although on other occasions someone has made the proposition to me, I never consented because my master does not mistreat me, and that is why I never ran away before this event." [28]

François Allain testified that while he was on patrol on the night of July 9, 1791, to prevent communication between the *nègres* of the post and those of False River, there were no *nègres* congregated either in their cabins or in the countryside, and he made no arrests. But he did attend the interrogations of several slaves. He testified that Juan Luis admitted that various meetings had taken place in his cabin and that César had proposed the uprising. Although Juan Luis resisted, he was finally persuaded by César to become involved in the plot. He and the others asked César how they could succeed without arms. César replied, laughing, "Don't be like stupid cows. We have pigs and chickens, and we can sell them and buy guns, powder, and balls. And furthermore, we don't really need arms, because we can go around from one plantation to the other cutting off the heads of the whites with our axes, beginning with Tournoir who has guns, powder, and balls in his store. And if we fail, I can lead you to a country where we can be secure." [29]

François Allain had also been at the interrogation of Cofi, who spoke French very badly, but Allain thought he said: "If the French kill the Minas and not the *nègre* César, that would be bad, but if they kill César too, that would be good, because during the past year since the beginning of the planting of the indigo crop, he has been trying to persuade us to rise up and kill the whites." In the original testimony recorded at Pointe Coupee, Francisco Mina testified that the Jamaican César said to him in the presence of Jacó, "'How is it possible that we are always working? If you want to join us, we will kill

28. Confrontation between Augustin Allain and Juan Luis, slave of Widow Provillar, and between Augustin Allain and Jacó, December 24, 1792, fols. 509–12 (464–67), *ibid.*

29. Testimony of Francisco [François] Allain, January 19, 1793, fols. 518–24 (473–79), *ibid.*

all the whites of False River and Pointe Coupee.' To which I replied, 'How can the whites be killed?' César replied, 'I will show you what the English blacks do to kill the whites.'"[30]

Clearly, César, the Jamaican, was the main instigator of the plot.

François Allain testified that a slave belonging to Miguel Lejeune said that there was a meeting of the Minas, but it was to enjoy themselves at a ball; and though the proposition was made to him to rise up against the whites, he did not want to consent. The Minas sent Petit François, slave of Jorge Bergeron, several times to try to convince Lejeune's slave, but he never agreed. Lejeune's slave said: "I preferred to go warn the creole slaves at the ball they were having somewhere else. If I did not warn my master, it was because I did not think they could carry it out, and also, I was afraid of the *nègres* of my nation. I had asked them if the creole *nègres* were involved in the uprising or had consented to it, and they answered no. They had told them nothing about it because they considered the creoles great lovers of the whites [*muy amantes de los blancos*]."[31]

It is clear from the testimony that this conspiracy was real. The *comandante* did, in fact, find arms loaded with lead shot made by the Mina slaves, a bag containing one hundred cartridges, some with enough powder for one shot, and another bag containing two cartridges and some lead shot, which he sent to Miró. The Mina slaves' main defense was that they did not understand Louisiana Creole, the language in which they were interrogated. They coordinated their testimony and feigned ignorance of the language. Diego Ortiz, a Spanish soldier, claimed that the accused Mina slaves spoke better French during their interrogation at Pointe Coupee than during the reinterrogation. When asked to explain how their French could have deteriorated instead of improving after spending a year in New Orleans with people who spoke only French, Ortiz replied, "If the black does not speak well now it is because he does not want to."[32]

The Mina slaves broke down Ortiz' testimony when he persisted in his claims that he was at all the interrogations and understood what was being said. Four of the accused slaves gave an identical answer: that Diego Ortiz came in only to bring meals. Ortiz finally

30. *Ibid.;* Testimony of Francisco Mina, slave of Jorge Bergeron, July 11, 1791, fols. 37v, 38r, in Mina, OAPC.

31. Testimony of Francisco [François] Allain, January 19, 1793, fols. 518–24, Mina, AGI.

32. Valentin Leblanc to Governor Esteban Miró, July 11, 1791, in Leg. 6928, fols. 240–42, GM, AS; Testimony of Diego Ortiz, December 5, 1792, fol. 470 (425), in Mina, AGI.

had to admit that he had lied, that he had not remained at the inter-rogations but had gone in and out. When he had objected to signing the documents on the grounds that as a soldier he could not play such a role in a nonmilitary trial and he did not understand the questions or the answers, he was pressured into signing and did so "out of respect for the *comandante* who was his superior." François Allain tes-tified that the questions were asked in the French creole language, which the blacks spoke only fairly well (*regularamente*), and that they answered in the same language. He insisted that he understood very well what they were saying, and they understood perfectly well what was being asked.[33]

Pleading ignorance has always been a useful defense of the weak, appealing to the disdain of the powerful. But the Mina slaves had advice and help from an expert. Antonio Cofi Mina was one of the two official interpreters from the Mina language at the trial. He had been free since 1778, lived in New Orleans, was single, a Catholic, a shoemaker by trade, and a member of the black militia. Antonio Cofi Mina was recognized by the Mina as the leader of their community. His name figured prominently in the 1795 Pointe Coupee Conspiracy. During his trial in 1795, he testified that for over twenty years, all the Mina of the colony, even those he did not know, called him "*capitain*." The title was given to him by the *nègres* of the balls. Evidently, Mina balls had been held since 1775. He was recognized as a conduit to the Spanish establishment because of his close relationship with his for-mer master, Don Andrés Almonaster y Rojas, a Catalonian who was chief magistrate (*alférez mayor* and *regidor perpetuo*) of New Orleans and a colonel in the militia. A talented financier and noted philan-thropist, Almonaster was reputed to be the richest man in Louisiana and both Floridas. Three of Antonio Cofi Mina's sons were slaves of Almonaster, and they stayed at Cofi's house regularly. Cofi's influ-ence was widely recognized, not only by Mina, but by people of Af-rican descent of all races and status. During his trial he explained that he was stopped in the street by a little mulatto and given a letter from an English mulatto who was in jail and who asked for his help, and Cofi agreed to stop by the jail to see him. It came out during his trial that Cofi was illiterate, though he was a court interpreter from the Mina language and he testified in elegant French during his own trial.

33. Confrontation of Diego Ortiz with Jacob, Cofi, Jacó, and Juan Luis, December 5, 1792, fols. 469–72 (424–27), in Mina, AGI; Testimony of Diego Ortiz, December 22, 1792, fol. 502 (457), *ibid.*; Testimony of Francisco [François] Allain, January 19, 1793, fols. 518–24 (473–79), *ibid.*

He spoke Spanish and Louisiana Creole, and possibly Catalonian as well. A carbine, a musket, six hunting muskets, two lances, a sword, and a large arched pistol were found in his house. He claimed that several of these weapons belonged to a slave of Almonaster and two others to two free *nègres*, and that two of the other guns were old and out of service. Cofi's three sons testified that some of the other weapons belonged to them.[34]

The last testimony in the Mina trial was taken on January 21, 1793, the day King Louis XVI was executed in France. Within weeks, the French Republic went to war against Britain, Holland, and Spain. The Mina trial was suspended while the government attended to the more pressing matter of the threatened French invasion of Louisiana. The accused slaves languished in jail. Two and a half years after their arrest, their existence was called to the attention of the authorities when Cofi, slave of Jacinto Chistes, became ill. He was sent to the hospital, where he died after running up a bill. There were several exchanges of documents to determine who was responsible for paying this bill, and in April, 1794, his master was ordered to pay up at once. The next day, the masters of the three alleged leaders of the conspiracy petitioned the court to sell their slaves as advantageously as possible in order to pay for their imprisonment. They could not pay the expenses of their incarceration, since they were without means (*étant hors de situation et de moyens*). In June, 1794, these last three slaves still in prison were sent back to their masters. Jean Baptiste Nicollet paid the back bill for their imprisonment and accepted financial responsibility for returning them to the tribunal when needed. The explanation for their release was the poverty of their masters, who were described as "unfortunate settlers, fathers of families, in the most poverty stricken of circumstances" ("*unos infelices habitantes, padres de Familias, sumamente miserables*").[35]

The Spanish authorities went to great lengths to enforce proper judicial norms in dealing with the accused Mina slaves, clashing with the brutal, arbitrary tradition of Louisiana's white creoles. Spain was eager to project an image as a protector of the slaves because of the fragility of its control of Louisiana and its reliance upon the people of

34. Province of Louisiana vs. Coffy [*sic*], June 16, 1795, in Notarial Acts of Francisco Broutin, 1790–98, Vol. XXXVI, Doc. 21, pp. 944–84, OAOP.

35. February 25, 26, and April 8, 1794, fols. 541–43 (496–98), in Mina, AGI; Petition of Aimable Couvillon, Jacques Fabre, Bathélemy Olinde, owners of César, Jacó, and Juan Luis, April 9, 1794, Bond by Juan Bautista Nicollet, June 4, 1794, Order to Release Prisoners, June 6, 1794, fols. 544–46 (499–501), all *ibid*.

African descent for loyalty, intelligence, and defense. In truth, the Mina conspiracy posed no serious threat. It was a narrowly focused ethnic conspiracy involving slaves who belonged to small slave owners. Many of their masters were not listed in the 1790 census, indicating that they did not own land and lived in the households of other persons. The only slave from a large estate was Joseph from the Tournoir estate, which had forty-five slaves in 1790. The Mina slaves' distrust of the creole slaves alienated them from the most powerful and best-informed slaves and undermined the possibility of an alliance with the slaves from Senegambia, who were close to the creoles because of ancestral ties. There is no evidence of hysteria on the part of the masters of Pointe Coupee. On the contrary, the masters of these accused slaves, reluctant to lose their services and to be obliged to pay for their incarceration, defended them and took them home as soon as possible. The Mina conspiracy took place before the eruption of the slave insurrection in St. Domingue, when the French and Caribbean revolutions had an economic, and not yet an ideological, impact. By the time the Mina slaves came to trial, St. Domingue was in flames. Shortly after their trial was suspended, war broke out between France and Spain. While they remained in jail in New Orleans, they were put to work, no doubt loading and unloading ships and building fortifications. They mingled with Louisiana's multinational, multiracial underclass of deported convict laborers (*presidarios*) and soldiers whose character and social origins differed little from the rejects and deserters sent to Louisiana under French rule, though their treatment was considerably less brutal.[36] No doubt they established ties with the underclass of New Orleans and brought exciting news back to Pointe Coupee when they returned shortly after slavery was abolished in all French colonies and a French invasion was imminent.

Meanwhile, at Pointe Coupee, the structure of conflict among slaves, which had been established and promoted by the masters, was coming unglued. The close relationship between Bambara and creole slaves, as well as a growing identification between creoles and recently arrived Africans, is evident in testimony taken on the estate of Colin Lacour in 1792. Lacour was a large planter, owning eighty-eight slaves in 1790. His slave force was heavily Senegambian: They comprised 38.6 percent of the Africans. There were six Bambara

36. Recensement de la Pointe Coupée et Fausse Rivière, March 29, 1790, 227A, Carpeta 21, Doc. 2, PC, AGI; Kerr, "Petty Felony, Slave Defiance and Frontier Villainy," 192–221.

slaves, five Maninga, nine Wolof, four Poulard, and one Nard on his estate when it was inventoried in 1797.[37] An investigation arose out of charges against Lacour by his creole *nègre* André, who had run away to New Orleans and was working for the government. The testimony taken during this investigation reveals the master's inability to maintain divisions between creole and African slaves.

Lacour took André's desertion as a betrayal. He was not only a creole slave, but a privileged one. Lacour testified that André had run away under the pretext of "two or three blows with a cane which he received because he did not return promptly to work on the levee where his presence was very necessary to carry out the work." Lacour testified that he had taught André several trades. He was kindly treated and never beaten. He claimed that he had helped André's mother, a *négresse libre*, to purchase and free André's son born to a *négresse* of an estate in False River, in return for André's promise not to run away. He bought the *négresse* to please André, and she rendered him little service because of frequent illnesses.[38]

André ran away because his master attacked him and threatened to kill him for siding with the African slaves. All the slaves who were questioned, creole and African, including both creole *commandeurs*, confirmed André's story. It was a time of hunger. Fassou, a Bambara, and Fauchonnette, a Senegalese (Wolof) *négresse*, testified that the *nègres bruts* were only getting a pint of corn a day, which was not enough, and that they had gone three days without corn. When they asked their master for corn, he beat them with the fireplace tongs, demanding to know if it was André who told them to ask for their rations. Although they denied this, their master ran out into the fields to look for André.

Joseph Mulâtre Creole quoted his master as saying to André, "Why did you let the *nègres bruts* come ask for rations ahead of you, who are a creole *nègre*? You should have come before them, and not allowed these *bruts* to go ahead of you."

André replied that they were all hungry.

Lacour shouted, "It is you, you rogue (*coquin*), who put the *nègres* up to coming to ask for rations."

37. Recensement de la Pointe Coupée et Fausse Rivière, March 29, 1790, 227A, Carpeta 21, Doc. 2, PC, AGI; Inventory of Estate of Colin Lacour, May 25, 1797, Doc. 1941, in OAPC.

38. Information and quotations in the account regarding André and Lacour are taken from Procès entre Colin Lacour et Son Nègre André, July 5, 1792, and Testimony of Joseph Mulâtre Creole, Marie Barbe, Magdelaine, Françoise and Pierre, slaves of Colin Lacour, July 29, 1791, all Doc. 1760, in OAPC.

André replied, "We were all hungry, that's why we all asked for corn. I was hungry just like the rest."

The master shouted, "You are lying!" Then he hit André with his cane, breaking it. The master tried to take André's pickax away from him, but André threw it out of the master's reach and ran away. Lacour grabbed André's pickax, threw it after André, and missed him. The master then tried to take a pickax away from Fassou, but he would not let it go. Then the master shouted, "I am going home to get my gun to burn out your brains, and if you are a man you will wait here for me." André did not wait. He ran off to New Orleans and filed a complaint against his master for threatening his life. On August 1, 1792, the investigators, satisfied that there was sufficient proof of the threats made against André by his master, sent the case to Carondelet and to the superior tribunal for further action. André and other Lacour slaves, including their *commandeur*, were deeply involved in the 1795 conspiracy to abolish slavery at the post.

Both André of Colin Lacour and Antoine Sarrasin, the main leader of the 1795 conspiracy, were children of a network of women slaves who saved, fought, and litigated for their own freedom and that of their relatives. Thérèse Négresse Libre, André's mother, had obtained her own freedom through litigation in 1780. In 1784, she was the sole heir of Joseph Le Pire, a man born in Canada. He was not a rich man. He left her one old slave and a little property. The relationship between them is unclear. She might have simply nursed him during his final illness. In 1785, she was a key witness in a case involving the theft of corn from a cornfield by a slave. The same year, she sued to force the master of her grandson, André Nègre, son of her son, André Nègre of Colin Lacour, to have him estimated so she could purchase and free him. She paid three hundred piastres for this two-year-old child.[39]

The black-Indian mixtures of Pointe Coupee played a special role within the slave population, creating a "mulatto" slave population that was very independent-minded. The women spearheaded movements to free their relatives from slavery through legal action and purchase. While the cultural factors explaining the defiant stance of the black-Indian population are difficult to analyze, the social factors are clear. We have seen that mulattoes who had white fathers tended

39. Emancipation document, March 14, 1780, in Leg. 206, fol. 62, PC, AGI; October 1, 1784, Doc. 1371, in OAPC; Procès entre Joseph Bourgeat et Colin Lacour au sujet du nègre nommé Paul, October 7, 1785, Doc. 1445, in OAPC; Lettre de Liberté, October 6, 1785, Doc. 1459, in OAPC.

to be freed as children, either passing into the white population or becoming part of a separate grouping of free people of color called "free mulattoes" that emerged by 1803. Because of the shortage of women among the slaves brought from Africa, black-Indian mixtures had most likely descended from Indian mothers and black fathers, and their fathers were normally not in a position to free them. Some of the slaves listed as mulatto were black-Indian mixtures designated as such to avoid the Spanish prohibition of Indian slavery.

Since Indian slavery was prohibited under Spanish law, slaves who descended from Indian women were legally entitled to their freedom. When O'Reilly repossessed Louisiana for Spain in 1769 after Ulloa was expelled by the colonists, he found that there were Indian slaves in the colony. He published a decree on December 7, 1769, that proclaimed that no vassal of the king, nor even transients in the colony, could acquire, purchase, or appropriate any Indian slave. Those owning such slaves could not dispose of them in any manner except to free them. While awaiting further orders from the king, the *comandantes* of all the posts were to take a census of all Indian slaves, giving their name, sex, age, and ancestry, as well as their estimated price and the name of their owners.[40]

Although this order was sent to and published at all the posts, no such censuses have been found for lower Louisiana, nor is there any record of a decision made by the king. However, between 1790 and 1794, when Carondelet suspended such suits, there were at least thirteen lawsuits involving families of slaves descended from Indian women petitioning to be freed. Carondelet claimed that freeing the descendants of female Indian slaves in Louisiana would "ruin a number of families who have no other slaves but them" and would cause "a complete reversal of the fortune of many inhabitants." Carondelet supported the recommendation made by twenty spokesmen for Louisiana slave owners that slaves who could prove maternal descent from the Natchez would have the right to redeem themselves at their estimated price, while those descended from other nations who had been "saved by their masters from the violent death which their cruel enemies had in store for them" would be allowed to redeem themselves for 250 piastres, the price of a slave newly arrived from Africa (*bozal*). They would be freed a year after paying their purchase price, to give their masters time to replace them. The matter got lost in the bureaucratic maze of the Spanish Empire. No report of the O'Reilly

40. A copy of the O'Reilly order of December 7, 1769, concerning Indian slaves can be found in Leg. 2563, fol. 967, SD, AGI.

order could be found in the files. On September 11, 1794, it was referred to the Council of the Indies for prompt action in view of the seriousness of the matter. On December 18, 1795, the council asked for further information about what measures the king of Spain had taken in response to O'Reilly's order of 1769 about Indian slavery in Louisiana. No evidence of further action has been found. The status of slaves establishing maternal descent from Indians ground slowly through legal process. The lawsuits demanding freedom for families of black-Indian slaves were only the tip of the iceberg. There may have been other lawsuits that have not yet been found in these little-explored documents. There were no doubt many slaves who were descendants of Indian women who did not know their descent, did not know they could sue for freedom, did not choose to do so because they feared reprisals, or did not feel confident that they would succeed, especially after such suits were suspended. Furthermore, descendants of black women and Indian men had no right to their freedom, even in theory. Many of the black-Indian slaves were in Pointe Coupee. Over half of the twenty-nine slave owners who signed a petition protesting the freeing of slaves descending from Indian women were from Pointe Coupee.[41]

Cecilia India Libre and her family demonstrate the tireless energy and independent spirit of Afro-Indian creoles in Louisiana. Cecille, listed as a *négresse*, was a slave on the estate of Leonard and Marguerite Bordelon. According to Marguerite Bordelon, they got along well until Sieur Louis Patus, a white man from New Orleans, fell in love with Cecille and offered to force her masters to sell her to him so he could free her. Marguerite Bordelon believed they were lovers. Cecille was freed in 1780, but she refused to live with Patus. Patus tried to convince the Bordelons to destroy Cecille's emancipation papers and then sell her to him. They refused, and Cecille was free of Patus as well as of her masters.[42]

Cecille learned her lesson well. She took the name Cecilia India Libre and made various petitions to the superior tribunal of New Or-

41. Stephen Webre, "The Problem of Indian Slavery in Spanish Louisiana, 1769–1803," *LH*, XXV (1984), 125–26; February 2, 1794, in Leg. 2563, fols. 964–66, SD, AGI; Governor Carondelet to Eugenio Llaguno de Amirola, May 17, 1794, in Leg. 2563, fols. 964–66, SD, AGI; Francisco Cerda to Llaguno, December 18, 1795, in Leg. 2532, fols. 616–17, SD, AGI; Petition dated February 28, 1794, in Leg. 2563, fols. 968–69, SD, AGI.

42. List of emancipation papers beginning August 14, 1780, in Leg. 206, fol. 65, PC, AGI; Interview with Antoine Bordelon and Marguerite Bordelon, his wife, July 17, 1792, Doc. 1194, in OAPC.

leans to free her entire family from slavery. She established that they were descendants of an Indian woman at the Pointe Coupee post and argued that Spanish law did not permit Indian slavery. Cecilia India Libre claimed that her sister, María Juana (Marie Jeanne), then a slave of Edmond of the Opelousas district, was the daughter of an Indian woman of the Patucas nation who had been a slave of Germain and then of Jean Decuir. María Juana had given birth to several children: Carlata (Charlotte), slave of Edmond; Melania (Melanie), who had two sons who were slaves of François Decuir of Pointe Coupee; Santiago (Jacques), who belonged to Don Santiago Ozenne of Pointe Coupee; Babet, whose own daughter also belonged to Ozenne; and Nanette, slave of Jean Baptiste Tournoir of Pointe Coupee. Marie Jeanne and three of her children, Nanette, Babet, and Jacques, were indeed listed on the inventory of Jean Decuir in 1771. She was described as the *griffe* mother of these three mulatto children, and was ill at the time of the inventory. Her daughter Nanette was twenty-two in 1779 and was the mother of two sons, aged five and two.[43]

Cecilia, represented by Felipe Guinault, subpoenaed a number of free black women from the district to testify in her behalf. Françoise Négresse Libre, Marianne Négresse Libre, and Thérèse Négresse Libre all testified under oath that they knew Marie Jeanne's mother. Her name was Marie, and she was indeed a pure Patucas Indian. Marie was a slave of Germain, then Normand, and then Jean Decuir. They traced the lineage of Marie's descendants and indicated their owners, confirming all Cecilia's allegations. Melanie had two children, and Nanette, slave of Tournoir, had three. Jacques Ozanne defended his rights over his slaves Jacques (Santiago) and Jacques' niece, the daughter of Babet, deceased.[44]

In January, 1795, Cecilia India Libre petitioned Carondelet, pointing out that he had issued an order that no Indian be mistreated by those who suppose themselves to be their master and that Tournoir had had her niece Nanette and Nanette's son flogged three times by his brother-in-law. Nanette's other son had also been mistreated, according to Cecilia's petition. She asked, in the name of justice, that those who had mistreated her relatives be punished in accordance

43. February 18, 1771, Doc. 393, in OAPC; February 17, 1778, Doc. 908, *ibid.*; March 2, 1778, Doc. 912, *ibid.*; May 16, 1778, Doc. 919, *ibid.*; October 12, 1779, Doc. 1014, *ibid.* The first discussion of Cecilia India Libre was in McGowan, "Creation of a Slave Society," 343.

44. Cecilia, free Indian woman, *vs.* Edmond, *et al.*, Testimony of December 16, 1793, in Notarial Acts of Francisco Broutin, 1790–1798, Vol. XXII, Doc. 2, File 49, fols. 27–31, OAOP; At Post of Attakapas, March 16, 1794, fol. 50, *ibid.*

Table 14. The Afro-Indian Network at Pointe Coupee

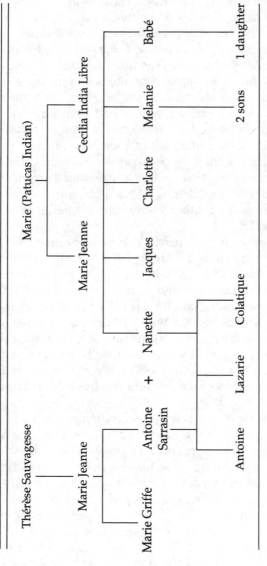

SOURCES: Cecilia, free Indian woman, vs. Edmond, *et al.*, October 17, 1793, in Notarial Acts of Francisco Broutin, 1790–1798, Vol. XXII, Doc. 2, File 49, fols. 21–81, OAOP; Diligencias practicadas por María Juana, hija de una India, y de un Negro, perteneciente a Don Manuel Monsanto, sobre pretender su Libertad, September 4, 1793, *ibid.*, fol. 303; Testimony of George Oliveau, Pointe Coupee, October 24, 1793, *ibid.*, fol. 309; Testimony of Gremillion, Pointe Coupee, October 25, 1793, *ibid.*, fol. 310; Testimony of Mme. Guillaume André, signed by Marguerite Mayeux, and of Marie Françoise Négresse, Pointe Coupee, October 29, 1793, *ibid.*, fol. 311; DB Inventories.

with law and that her relatives be freed right away. Otherwise, they would be exposed daily to many atrocities, "even worse than those imposed upon the blacks." They would not, for example, be given any clothes. Hearings were held among Tournoir's neighbors and his slaves. Simon Croisset said that he was often in Tournoir's house and had never seen Nanette mistreated; that she was, not worse, but better dressed than the other slaves; that she and her son were the best dressed of the slaves. He denied that she had been flogged. *Comandante* Duparc testified that he had not seen Nanette being daily mistreated; but he said that the previous summer, Madame Tournoir gave her two or three slaps in the face because she had not come to help the other slaves remove water from the house after a storm. He said he had no knowledge of the flogging of Nanette or of her son by Jean Baptiste Decuir, Tournoir's brother-in-law. He testified that he always saw her well dressed.[45]

Alexandre, *commandeur* of Tournoir's slaves, testified that he had not seen Nanette being daily mistreated by Tournoir or by Decuir. When asked if Nanette and her son had been flogged three times, he replied that he had been sick but had heard that her son Zari [Lazarie] had been flogged. Alexandre said he did not know the reason for the flogging. He affirmed that Nanette was well dressed, and her son was as well dressed as the other *nègres*. Louison Négresse, the cook, denied that Nanette was flogged by Jean Baptiste Decuir and stated that she and her son were as well dressed as the other slaves. But she added that since she worked in the house, she did not know what went on in the field.[46]

Another Marie Jeanne, daughter of an Indian woman and a black man, appeared in court in September of 1793, claiming her freedom as a daughter of Thérèse, a pure Indian woman who had belonged to Jean Rondeau. She also claimed freedom for her two natural children held in slavery by Julien Poydras. One was Antoine Sarrasin, *métis*, and the other was Marie Griffe. A number of whites from Pointe Coupee testified in support of freedom for Marie Jeanne and her two children. George Olivo, aged fifty-seven, Louis Gremillion, aged eighty-three, Madame Guillaume André, and Marie Françoise Négresse all affirmed that Marie Jeanne was the daughter of Thérèse Sauvagesse *pûre*, former slave of Jean Rondeau, and that Antoine Sarrasin and Marie Griffe were her two "so-called natural children." Antoine Sar-

45. New Orleans, January 18, 1795, fols. 65–66, *ibid.*; Pointe Coupee, March 27, 1795, fols. 68–70, *ibid.*
46. Pointe Coupee, March 28, 1795, fols. 71, 72, *ibid.*

rasin was the main leader of the 1795 conspiracy. Sarrasin had been, according to Poydras, condemned to perpetual slavery under Governor Unzaga. Sarrasin had lost his suit against the estate of Deshôtel for his freedom on the grounds that his deceased master had promised to free him. Poydras added that Sarrasin and his sister were priceless to him because of the time and the effort he had put into giving them "all the qualities one can demand from people in their situation."[47]

These two lineages of Afro-Indian slaves were linked through Antoine Sarrasin and Nanette, niece of Cecilia India Libre. They had apparently been a couple for many years. Nanette's oldest son, born around 1774, was named Antoine. After Sarrasin was arrested and held prisoner in the fort at Pointe Coupee, his mother, Marie Jeanne, described as a slave of the Benjamin Monsanto estate, arrived at the post with a decree of the superior tribunal, probably freeing her, and left at night with Maturin Boisseau, a white *engagé voyageur* who was interrogated during the trial. Nanette, described as a quadroon slave of Tournoir, disappeared the same night, along with her three children. *Comandante* Duparc was convinced that Marie Jeanne had instigated her grandchildren and their mother's flight. Nanette was finally freed from the estate of Jean Baptiste Tournoir after his death in 1798. Cecilia India Libre petitioned that Nanette either be freed gratuitously as a descendant of Indians, or that she be estimated so she, Cecilia, could purchase and free her. Nanette was listed as Nanette Bordelon on the Tournoir inventory—a tribute, evidently, to Marguerite Bordelon for refusing to cooperate with Louis Patus, Cecilia's white lover, in his efforts to reenslave her. Nanette's age was estimated at forty-eight. She was suffering from a hernia. Her estimated price was two hundred piastres. Cecilia India Libre paid six hundred piastres for her.[48]

47. Diligencias practicadas por María Juana, hija de una India, y de un Negro, perteneciente a Don Manuel Monsanto, sobre pretender su Libertad, September 4, 1793, in Notarial Acts of Francisco Broutin, 1790–1798, Vol. XXII, fol. 303, OAOP; Testimony of George Oliveau [Olivo], Pointe Coupee, October 24, 1793, *ibid.*, fol. 309; Testimony of [Louis] Gremillion, Pointe Coupee, October 25, 1793, *ibid.*, fol. 310; Testimony of Mme. Guillaume André, signed by Marguerite Mayeux, and of Marie Françoise Négresse, Pointe Coupee, October 29, 1793, *ibid.*, fol. 311; March 7, 1774, in SJR, LHC, cited in Webre, "Indian Slavery," 128; Letter of Julien Poydras, in Diligencias practicadas por Maria Juana . . . , New Orleans, December 23, 1793, in Notarial Acts of Francisco Broutin, 1790–1798, Vol. XXII, fols. 324–28, OAOP.

48. October 12, 1779, Doc. 1014, OAPC; *Comandante* Duparc to Carondelet, Pointe Coupee, March 24, 1795, in Leg. 31, Carpeta 23, Doc. 88, fol. 817, PC, AGI; June 25, 1798, Doc. 2002, in OAPC.

Antoine Sarrasin, *commandeur* of the Poydras estate, was the main leader of the 1795 conspiracy. He was the son of a white settler of Pointe Coupee and bore his father's full name. He had one Indian grandmother and one African grandfather, and his other grandmother and grandfather were French. Antoine Sarrasin was a true creole.

The 1795 Conspiracy in Pointe Coupee

Tremblant' terr' vini 'bralé moulin,	An earthquake came and shook the mill,
Tonner' chiel tombé bourlé moulin.	The heavens thunders fell and burned it.
Tou' moun dans moulin lá péri.	Every soul in the mill perished.
Temoins vini qui vend Libin.	Witnesses came who betrayed Lubin.
Yé dit Libin metté di fé.	They said he set the mill on fire.
Yé hissé saffaud pou' so la tête.	They raised a scaffold to take off his head.
Saïda! m'allé mourri, Saïda!	Saïda! I am going to die!
Mo zamis di comm' ça: "Libin,	My friends speak in this way: "Lubin,
Fout to donn' Zilié to bitin."	You ought to give Julia your plunder."
Cofaire mo sré donnein Zilié?	Why should I give it to Julia?
Pou moin Zilié zamein lavé.	For me Julia never washed clothes.
Zilié zamain passé pou moin.	Julia never ironed for me.
Saïda! m'allé mourri, Saïda!	Saïda! I am going to die!

—George Washington Cable, *Creoles and Cajuns: Stories of Old Louisiana*

[Bitin (*butin* in French) literally means plunder, but it was used by creole slaves as the word for personal property.]

In April, 1795, a number of slaves were arrested at Pointe Coupee for plotting to rise up and kill their masters in order to abolish slavery. The conspiracy was organized from the estate of Julien Poydras. The plan was to set fire to a building on the Poydras estate, and when masters from neighboring estates rushed to put out the fire, they would be slaughtered. The slaves would then take arms and ammunition from Poydras' store and wipe out the remaining masters, as well as the creole slaves who refused to become involved in the plot. Although Poydras' slaves were the most numerous among the accused, slaves throughout Pointe Coupee and False River and several local whites were also involved. The plot had ramifications throughout lower Louisiana: to Natchitoches, Opelousas, the German Coast, and New Orleans. There were military as well as ideological links with international Jacobinism.

The trial began at Pointe Coupee on May 4, 1795. Fifty-seven slaves and three local whites were convicted. By June 2, twenty-three slaves were hung, their heads cut off and nailed on posts at several places along the Mississippi River from New Orleans to Pointe Coupee. Thirty-one slaves were sentenced to floggings and to hard labor in Spanish fortresses in Mexico, Florida, Puerto Rico, and Cuba. All three whites were deported, and two of them were sentenced to six years of forced labor in Havana.[1]

Historical myths about the Pointe Coupee Conspiracy of 1795 were deeply implanted into the consciousness of white Louisianians. They became the cornerstone of ideology justifying racist violence and oppression of Afro-Louisianians and of whites who opposed slavery and racism. White schoolchildren were taught that this conspiracy proved that Afro-Louisianians were only awaiting an opportunity to rise up and massacre all whites, except for the young white women who were to serve them as love slaves; that it was only fear instilled by racist terror that ensured the survival of the white race

1. Carondelet to Marques del Campo, June 19, 1795, in Leg. 8137, Atado 2, Doc. 105, Estado, AS. Informe Rendon to Gadoqui, June 15, 1795, in Leg. 2612, Doc. 54, fols. 498–501, SD, AGI, reported twenty-one hangings and thirty-one floggings. Noticia de las sumas que reclama el executor of Justicia Antonio Sousa, New Orleans, June 10, 1795, in Leg. 1, Doc. 31, PC, AGI, cited in Juan José Andreu Ocariz, *Movimientos rebeldes de los esclavos negros durante el dominio español en Luisiana* (Zaragoza, 1977), 55n, 171–72, shows an executioner's bill dated June 10, 1795, for hanging twenty-three and flogging twenty-three.

and protected white womanhood from a fate worse than death. Nineteenth-century white creole historian Charles Gayarré explained the involvement of whites in this conspiracy against slavery as a cynical manipulation of the ignorant, naïve slaves who would have been incapable of rising up against slavery on their own. This historical myth functioned well in controlling Louisiana's defiant, multiracial, multinational underclass, as well as its people of African descent. It pinpointed whites who opposed slavery and racism as the greatest danger to the survival of the white race, mobilizing the violent heritage of the frontier against Louisiana's long, deep tradition of racial openness.[2] It was used to enlist white Louisianians, regardless of class, to defend a racist system that was against the interests of the vast majority of the population. The basest instincts among whites, especially men, were manipulated. Louisiana's deeply rooted universalist tradition was brutally repressed. This historical myth continued well into the twentieth century. It was taught to this writer in public schools in New Orleans during the early 1940s.

What is the truth about this conspiracy? It was a complex movement, the causes of which cannot be reduced to any one factor. It was not an isolated movement that simply sought to take advantage of control mechanisms weakened by warfare resulting from the French Revolution.[3] There were economic, ideological, and military reasons why this particular conspiracy developed at this particular time and place. It was not a movement of blacks against whites. It was part of a multiracial abolitionist movement supported by a large segment of the dispossessed of all races in Louisiana and throughout the Caribbean: a manifestation of the most radical phase of the French Revolution, which had spilled over from Europe to the Americas.

By the 1790s, Louisiana still resembled Anne Pérotin-Dumon's model of the "open islands" like Guadeloupe and Puerto Rico. These colonies were economically marginal to the metropolis. St. Domingue and Martinique in the French empire and Cuba in the Spanish empire were geared toward the production and export of staple crops. They imported directly from the metropolis and sent the inferior leftovers to the marginal colonies at greatly marked-up prices. The marginal colonies remained faithful to the earliest stages of colonization when the sea was the open road, and when coastwise trade, smuggling,

2. Charles Gayarré, *History of Louisiana* (4 vols.; 1854–66; rpr. Baton Rouge, 1974), II, 355.

3. For a discussion that emphasizes the military factor in slave revolts, see David Geggus, "The Enigma of Jamaica in the 1790s: New Light on the Causes of Slave Rebellions," *William and Mary Quaterly*, 3rd ser., XLIV (1987), 274–99.

and piracy were the most vital economic activities. The marginal colonies incubated a bold, egalitarian, cosmopolitan, mobile, seafaring population that moved easily from legitimate trade to smuggling, piracy, and, during periods of open warfare, privateering.[4] A large, tough breed of French privateers functioned as a counterweight to British naval supremacy during the prolonged naval warfare that began with the American and French revolutions and ended with the Napoleonic Wars. Sailing under the flag of the French Revolution and then of the French empire, the privateers financed themselves through legitimized piracy. Operating from Charleston and from Guadeloupe during the French Revolution, they dispersed when Britain conquered Guadeloupe in 1810. The privateers reemerged as the insurgent corsairs, playing a major role in the maritime dimensions of the Latin American independence wars, which began in 1810.[5] Some of these privateers, under the leadership of Jean Lafitte, came to Louisiana. They settled at Barataria, the last refuge of the remnants of St. Maló's maroons.

The 1795 conspiracy in Pointe Coupee took place during the most radical phase of the French Revolution, when France and Spain were at war, when the lower classes throughout Europe and the Americas had risen up in an international movement against social tyranny. The slogan *Liberté, Egalité, Fraternité* was legally extended to the free people of African descent in the French Caribbean by the law of April 4, 1792, that gave them full civil and political rights. In January, 1793, King Louis XVI was executed, and in February and March of the same year, France declared war against the crowned heads of Europe in Britain, Holland, and Spain. On February 4, 1794 (16 pluviôse), the French National Convention abolished slavery in all French colonies, "decreeing that all men, without distinction of color living in the colonies are French citizens enjoying all rights assured by the Constitution." This decree was published in English and in French and was widely distributed throughout the Caribbean.[6] As the French Revolution became radicalized, the French slave owners became royalists. Losing their enthusiasm for France, as well as for the French Revolu-

4. For an interesting study of the culture of Anglo-American maritime workers during the first half of the eighteenth century, see Marcus Rediker, *Between the Devil and the Deep Blue Sea: Merchant Seamen, Pirates, and the Anglo-American Maritime World, 1700–1750* (Cambridge, Eng., 1987).

5. Anne Pérotin-Dumon, *Être Patriote sous les tropiques: La Guadeloupe, la colonisation et la révolution (1789–1794)* (Basse-Terre, Guadeloupe, 1985), 68–69, 205–23.

6. Las Casas to Carondelet, June 12, 1795 (copy), in Leg. 6929, GM, AS.

tion, they went into exile in the British and Spanish islands. Slave owners sided with Britain when it invaded St. Domingue.

The cause of France and the French Revolution was left in the capable hands of soldiers stationed in the colonies and of port workers and seafarers: an internationalist, multiracial population that spread the latest news about the revolution throughout the ports of the Americas. Some merchants, local officials, clergy, shopkeepers, and small planters were also involved. Many of these white Jacobins had recently arrived from France and were still culturally very attached to the motherland. In July, 1794, Commissioner Victor Hughes arrived in Guadeloupe and retook the island from the royalists. Between January and June, 1795, he occupied the Dutch islands of St. Martin and St. Eustache, conquered St. Lucia from the British, and launched campaigns against St. Vincent and Grenada. Hughes's success was due to a great extent to his informing slaves throughout the Caribbean that France had abolished slavery in all its colonies. Slave revolts mushroomed throughout the Caribbean during 1795. In 1796, after the most radical phase of the French Revolution ended, Hughes was kept in power under the new title of agent of the directorate.[7]

The French Revolution became Americanized in its purest and most dramatic form in St. Domingue, where the free people of African descent rose up for equality, and in August, 1791, the slaves revolted en masse. After many years of civil and international war, slavery was definitively abolished and Haiti established herself as the second independent nation in the Americas.[8] When the large slave owners and merchants abandoned France as well as the French Revolution, the white Jacobins in the Americas were mainly the dispossessed: merchant seamen, dock workers, *voyageurs*, indentured servants, and soldiers. They were eager to ally themselves with slaves and free people of African descent, supporting full equality for peoples of all races and the abolition of slavery by any means necessary.

This internationalist, revolutionary effervescence among the lower classes led by seafarers, the *gens de mer*, washed up on the shores of Louisiana, radiating to New Orleans and along her major waterways. Louisiana was "blanketed with partisans of the revolution who came

7. Pérotin-Dumon, *Guadeloupe et la révolution (1789–1794)*, 19, 227, 232, 323–30.
8. The best account of the Haitian Revolution remains C. L. R. James, *The Black Jacobins* (2nd ed.; New York, 1963). For an interesting recent study based upon some new research, see Carolyn E. Fick, *The Making of Haiti: The Saint Domingue Revolution from Below* (Knoxville, 1990).

in many guises and colors. They appeared in the smallest outposts, among the clergy, in all the city's taverns, and among the immigrant merchant community. They were French, Saint-Domingan, and locally bred. They were white, brown, and black. Their precise contact with and influence among the slaves, though unknown, was a source of numerous nightmares."[9]

The ideology of the Rights of Man reverberated throughout lower Louisiana. France had abolished slavery in all its colonies a little over a year before the conspirators were arrested. The Pointe Coupee conspiracy was widely supported by lower-class whites in Louisiana. It was directed, not against whites, but against slavery.

The Spanish authorities were concerned that the free people of African descent and the slaves of Louisiana and of the Hispanic Caribbean would follow the Haitian example. They tried to quarantine the revolutionary contagion coming from France and from St. Domingue. Their fear of the international ramifications of the egalitarian ideology of the French Revolution is well illustrated by their response to the Louisiana mulatto Beauré, who arrived in late 1791 at Balize at the mouth of the Mississippi River aboard a ship coming from Bordeaux. Beauré had lived in France since childhood and was returning to Louisiana, his native land, where his mother and siblings still resided. According to the captain and passengers aboard the ship, Beauré was well informed and talkative, discussing the "operations of the National Assembly, the Rights of Man, and the class of active citizen." The commander at Balize sent Governor Miró a document, in Beauré's handwriting, entitled "Plan for a Society among Mulattoes and Mulatress." The society was to hold a ball every week at which each man would "take care of his *compañera* in terms which would indicate disorder of customs." Miró, citing royal orders calling for great care in dealing with affairs of France and prohibiting the introduction of any free black or mulatto from the French colonies into Louisiana, arrested Beauré and seized his passport. The governor argued that though Beauré was born in Louisiana, he could be considered a foreigner because he had been an expatriate since childhood. On June 1, 1792, Carondelet, the new governor, agreed to Beauré's request to be sent to Havana in order to go elsewhere from there. But municipal officials in Havana refused to allow him to reside in Cuba and put him in jail, telling him he could embark for any foreign colony he

9. Thomas Marc Fiehrer, "The Baron de Carondelet as Agent of Bourbon Reform: A Study of Spanish Colonial Administration in the Years of the French Revolution" (Ph.D. dissertation, Tulane University, 1977), 473.

chose. He chose to go to Guarico (St. Domingue), but he was not allowed to land there and was returned to Havana. The Cuban governor feared that Beauré, expelled from his native land, could become another Ogé, the free mulatto whom he considered the principal instigator of the slave revolution that was destroying St. Domingue. Beauré was kept in prison until he was embarked for Cádiz. The governor of Cádiz found that the governor of Louisiana did not have grounds to deprive Beauré of the right to return to his native land "to live with his Mother, brothers and sisters." The law applied to free blacks and mulattoes of the French colonies, not to natives of Louisiana. But if it was inconvenient for him to return to his native land under the prevailing circumstances, he should reside temporarily in Spain. On December 24, 1794, Beauré was sent to Córdoba, where he worked as a hairdresser. He was threatened with forced labor and other punishments if he did not modify his "conduct, conversations, and obscene ideas."[10]

The Pointe Coupee slaves were well informed about the war between France and Spain, the French Convention's abolition of slavery in all French colonies, and the revolutionary advances throughout the world. While there were local reasons for discontent, including deprivations suffered as the result of economic collapse, the main reason the slaves acted is that they had realistic hopes for freedom if France took over Louisiana. The trial summary indicates that the conspiracy was inspired by the Haitian Revolution and that whites, as well as slaves, were deeply involved: "It is evident that these slaves proposed to put their depraved subversions into execution under the barbarous tyranny of those of Guarico, and no one can doubt . . . from the malicious conversations and false news spread that there were various whites as well as blacks who instigated and animated the scheme to attract supporters to this frightful enterprise which if successful would have spread throughout the Province."[11]

It is clear from the extensive testimony of slaves involved in the 1795 conspiracy that the ideology of the Rights of Man, given new impetus by the French Revolution and its impact throughout the world, and the slave revolt in Haiti were well known among slaves in Pointe Coupee. Joseph Bouyavel, a Waloon teacher from St. Omer en Artoil who lived on the Goudeau estate, read paragraphs to the *nègres*

10. Captain General of Louisiana re mulatto Beauré, June 1, 1792, July 28, 1794, December 24, 1794, in Leg. 6917, Doc. 190, GM, AS, and Conde del Campo de Alange, San Lorenzo, November 20, 1794, *ibid.*, Doc. 448.

11. Trial summary by Don Manuel Serrano, May 22, 1795, fols. 254–59, in Trial, OAPC.

of the district about the revolution in France, at Le Cap (in St. Domingue), and *partout* (everywhere). A copy of the book *Théorie de l'impôt*, containing the Declaration of the Rights of Man advocating freedom for the slaves, was found in his possession. Bouyavel admitted that the book belonged to him and that he knew its contents. Bouyaval had been telling the slaves that slavery would soon be abolished, but the slaves did not take him too seriously because he was a drunk. One slave testified that his master's schoolteacher Bouyavel "came into my cabin one night a little drunk [*un peu souil*] and told me in the presence of my wife that all the slaves were free in the Capital and that undoubtedly they would soon be free here. I told the mulatto François what he said without positively believing it." Several Goudeau slaves tried to protect Bouyavel. Petit Pierre testified that Bouyavel had told them that all the slaves in the capital were free, but he also told them "to be patient because slavery would not last very long. Bouyavel also said that the whites wanted us to be free. This is what he told us when he was in his right mind [*dans son bon sense*]." [12]

A meeting had taken place in Antoine Sarrasin's cabin. Slaves from several estates were present, as well as three Louisiana whites who were *engagés* from New Orleans and the tailor George Rockenbourg, a local white who described himself as a German born in Philadelphia. One *engagé* was quoted as saying: " 'Why make petitions? There are letters asking if it would not be better for you to do like the *nègres du* Cap.' And at that moment, Noël Capitaine [a Fulbe Poydras slave] began to jump with joy. I saw Rockenbourg writing a petition. Noël took it, saying he would bring it to town when he went with his master, and if that failed they would kill all the whites." [13]

Jean Baptiste, slave of Widow Lacour, testified that Rockenbourg had told him and other *nègres* several times that the *nègres* of the post were all free but that the *comandante* did not want to give them their freedom, and if they wished, he would make a petition to send to the

12. Testimony of Jean Baptiste, *commandeur* of Poydras, May 10, 1795, fol. 73, *ibid.*; Final statement of Joseph Bouyavel, May 16, 1795, fol. 232, *ibid.*; Testimony of Louis, slave of Goudeau, May 9, 1795, fols. 35–38, *ibid.*; Testimony of Petit Pierre, slave of Goudeau, May 9, 1795, fols. 46–48, and Testimony of Philbis dit Félicité, slave of Goudeau, May 9, 1795, fol. 41, both *ibid.*

13. Testimony of Philipe Jumeau, slave of Widow Lacour, May 12, 1795, fols. 117–19, *ibid.* The *engagé* was later identified by Philipe as Jean Sorgo, a native of the Republic of Raguse, a revolutionary state established in Yugoslavia during the height of the French Revolution (May 14, 1795, fols. 162–63, *ibid.*); Final statement of Jean Sorgo, May 16, 1795, fol. 236, *ibid.*

government. Timothée testified that Rockenbourg made a petition to send to town. Cecille, slave of Tournoir, was to bring it to their captain, Antonio Cofi Mina, the black militiaman who interpreted for the Mina slaves during their trial in New Orleans.[14]

Both Bouyavel and Rockenbourg denied the charges that they gave false news of liberty to encourage the *nègres* to revolt. Several Lacour slaves defended Rockenbourg, testifying that they never heard him speak of freedom or offer to make a petition.[15]

Another slave testified that some Indians had been taunting the *nègres,* saying they were cowards because one hundred *nègres* let themselves be ruled by a single white, to which Jean Baptiste, Poydras *commandeur* and one of the principal leaders of the conspiracy, replied, "You see that this man is right, because we could do the same here as at Le Cap."[16]

Reports that the slaves had already been freed came from all directions. Free coloreds and whites came upriver from New Orleans and informed slaves of Pointe Coupee that the king had freed all the slaves but that the masters and the *comandante* of the post were not telling them. Antoine, *commandeur* of Widow Lacour, was told by the *nègres* of his atelier that some *voyageurs* coming up the river from New Orleans said that if the French won the war they would all soon be free. Sarrasin testified that two or three months earlier, two free mulattoes passed by in a boat heading for Natchez and told them that all the slaves had been freed by the king.[17] Jeanne and Louison, two women slaves of Widow Lacour, were planting corn when they were approached by four whites who were coming from New Orleans in a pirogue. They were led by a heavy-set, five-foot-tall, brown-faced man named Charles. Jeanne thought he was "Spanish by the way he spoke French." He asked her what she was doing, and she replied that she was sowing corn. He said that was useless, because as soon as peace was published, they would all be free. A Poydras slave testified that Jean Baptiste, their *commandeur,* would not allow them to

14. Testimony of Jean Baptiste, slave of Widow Lacour, May 11, 1795, fols. 84–86, *ibid.;* Testimony of Timothée, slave of Widow Lacour, May 12, 1795, fol. 136, *ibid.*

15. Testimony of Jeanne and Eugene, slaves of Widow Lacour, May 12, 1795, fols. 94–95, *ibid.*

16. Testimony of Michel Mulâtre, slave of Charles Duflour, May 9, 1795, fols. 52–54, *ibid.*

17. Testimony of Antoine, *commandeur* of Widow Lacour, May 11, 1795, fols. 86–88, *ibid.;* Testimony of Antoine Sarrasin, May 11, 1795, fols. 88–91, *ibid.* Sarrasin identified the free mulattoes as George who lived at Bayou St. Jean and as Domingue.

plant corn, and no corn was planted on the Poydras estate. The Poydras slaves had not planted corn, though the season was far advanced, because they no longer wished to serve masters. A Poydras slave asked a Goudeau slave why they still planted corn. Pointe Coupee slaves who had been sent to pick up merchandise in New Orleans reportedly confirmed that the slaves were already free in the capital.[18]

The Pointe Coupee slaves became convinced that their masters were trying to force them to sign a petition renouncing their freedom. Jean Baptiste, *commandeur* of the Poydras estate, testified that about three months before the trial, he had met a *nègre* who was a creole of Curaçao on his way to the *ciprière* of his master, Ségu. The Curaçao slave told Jean Baptiste

> that they are awaiting at the Capital an Order of the King which declares all the slaves free, and to prove that this was true, he pointed out that Sieur Le Blanc and Sieur de Verbois wanted to sell all their slaves. Antoine Sarrasin, the other Poydras *commandeur*, told me that when this order of freedom had arrived, the *comandante* was at Avoyelles and they were awaiting his return to see if he would carry it out. A little later M. Duffief [administrator of the Poydras estate] had begged the *comandante* not to publish the order of freedom. Duffief made a petition for the slaves to sign [renouncing their freedom] without telling them what the petition said, and if all this was true, they must oppose it and kill the whites. I as well as the *nègres* of my master and of other masters were convinced.[19]

Louis Bordelon, Poydras slave, was quoted as saying, "The King had given us our freedom, but the masters made a petition to prevent it, making the *nègres* sign renouncing their freedom and saying that they wanted to end their days with their masters."[20]

The slaves' suspicions were reinforced by a trick played on them to force them to work. On Palm Sunday, Marie Neyou Griffe who was "in communication with" Sieur Duffief, began to swear at the *nègres* for refusing to plant corn, saying that she would send for the petition that Duffief had made for them to sign and that "when all the *nègres* will be free, you will never be free here." After this speech, all the

18. Testimony of Jeanne, May 9, 1795, fols. 48–49, and Testimony of Louison, May 10, 1795, fol. 55, slaves of Widow Lacour, both *ibid.*; Testimony of François, mulatto slave of Goudeau, May 8, 1795, fols. 24–27, and Testimony of Eveillé, Ibo slave of Poydras, May 10, 1795, fols. 58–60, both *ibid.*

19. Testimony of Cofi Mina, slave of Poydras, May 12, 1795, fols. 99–101, *ibid.*; Testimony of Jean Baptiste, *commandeur* of Poydras, May 10, 1795, fols. 65–73, *ibid.*

20. Testimony of Louis, slave of Charles Duflour, May 10, 1795, fol. 63, *ibid.*

nègres on the estate were convinced that if Duffief tried to force them to sign, they would massacre the whites rather than obey.[21]

Although the slaves of Pointe Coupee were bombarded with rumors coming from several directions that all the slaves of Louisiana had been freed by order of the king, but that the planters of Pointe Coupee were suppressing the order and pressuring the governor not to publish or enforce it, they maintained a reasonable amount of skepticism about this news. Stanislao Anis, Bara *commandeur*, testified that he told the slaves to await his return from the capital to see if the stories they heard about being free were true. He was asked, "Wait for what?" He replied, "The *Nègres* would go off to become maroons in case their liberty was refused, and that is why I told them to await my return."[22]

The conspiracy had been planned several months in advance. It was clearly well organized and remained a secret for a surprisingly long time, especially considering how openly and confidently the conspirators acted. The masters, no doubt aware of unrest among the slaves, were powerless to control them. Sarrasin was clearly the major leader of the conspiracy. When the slaves involved in the conspiracy were about to be hanged, all the condemned reproached Sarrasin. Although Sarrasin claimed that Jean Baptiste, the other Poydras *commandeur*, was the only leader, Jean Baptiste more accurately attributed the leading role to Sarrasin. Jean Baptiste pointed out that it was Sarrasin who gave the order to assemble at the bridge of New Roads and who traveled around to all the slave quarters solving the problems that came up. Several slaves testified that Sarrasin was the main leader and that he traveled widely. Lambert, mulatto slave of Bourgeat, testified that Sarrasin approached him about becoming involved in the plot, asking him if he was a man. He replied, "Why do you ask?" Sarrasin said, "We will find out at the fort when you are made to sign." Lambert replied, "I do not know how to sign, but my little master will sign for me." Sarrasin then threatened to have his throat

21. Testimony of Jean Baptiste, *commandeur* of Poydras, May 10, 1795, fols. 65–73, *ibid.*

22. Testimony of Antoine Sarrasin, May 11, 1795, fols. 88–91, *ibid.*; Testimony of Guillaume, slave of Widow Le Doux, May 9, 1795, fols. 38–40, *ibid.*; Testimony of Jeanne, slave of Widow Lacour, May 9, 1795, fols. 48–49, *ibid.*; Testimony of Louison, slave of Widow Lacour, May 10, 1795, fol. 55, *ibid.*; Testimony of Jean Baptiste, *commandeur* of Poydras, May 10, 1795, fols. 65–73, *ibid.*; Testimony of Cofi Mina, slave of Poydras, May 12, 1795, fols. 99–101, *ibid.*; Testimony of Stanislao Anis, *commandeur* of Bara, May 11, 1795, fols. 75–78, *ibid.*

cut, saying, "Don't you know we are free?" Lambert replied, "Do you believe that the French who have worked for so long to buy us would give us our freedom without any conflict?" Sarrasin replied, "I do not want to say any more, there will be time to tell you the rest."[23]

Lambert also testified that Sarrasin got on his horse two or three nights between nine and ten o'clock and traveled to the upper coast. Charles, a Poydras slave, believed that all the other *nègres* north of Pointe Coupee were also involved because Sarrasin "had gone up there to inform them." Jean Baptiste, the other Poydras *commandeur*, testified, "Sarrasin told me that the *nègres* of Natchez as well as all the *nègres* down the river only awaited the moment that the *nègres* of this post rose up to revolt themselves." The slave owners, as well as the slaves, of Natchez were largely English-speaking, and there were many English-speaking slaves in Opelousas as well. The Farar estate, by far the largest at the post, was English-speaking. Some slaves testified that all the *nègres* of Pointe Coupee, including all the Farar slaves, were involved in the plot. One Poydras slave was Jamaican and a Protestant. But the major link with the English-speaking slaves was no doubt Capitain, a sixty-year-old Mande slave of Farar. He needed an English interpreter during his interrogation. One slave testified that Capitain's real name was Antoine Bambara dit Capitain, but he identified his nation as Mandinga when he was sentenced. He was able to communicate with the Mande slaves on various estates, as well as with the English-speaking slaves. Capitain was sentenced to five years at hard labor in Havana. He and three other Pointe Coupee slaves survived the sentence.[24]

The Spanish officials believed that the Pointe Coupee Conspiracy had wide ramifications among the slaves in the colony. Carondelet

23. Andreu Ocariz, *Movimientos rebeldes*, 159; Testimony of Antoine Sarrasin, May 11, 1795, fol. 89, in Trial, OAPC; Testimony of Jean Baptiste, *commandeur* of Poydras, May 10, 1795, fols. 65–74, OAPC; Testimony of Martin Bourgeat, May 4, 1795, fols. 6–7, and Testimony of Lambert Mulâtre, slave of Widow Bourgeat, May 8, 1795, fol. 23, both in OAPC.

24. Testimony of Lambert Mulâtre, slave of Widow Bourgeat, May 8, 1795, fol. 23, *ibid.*; Testimony of Louis Bordelon, slave of Poydras, May 9, 1795, fols. 49–51, *ibid.*; Testimony of Antoine Sarrasin Mulâtre, May 11, 1795, fols. 88–91, *ibid.*; Testimony of Jean Baptiste, *commandeur* of Poydras, May 10, 12, 1795, fols. 65–73, 114, *ibid.*; Testimony of Grand Charles, slave of Poydras, May 12, 1795, fols. 95–99, *ibid.*; Testimony of Auguste Mulâtre, slave of Bergeron, May 11, 1795, fols. 78–80, *ibid.*; Testimony of Tham, slave of Poydras, May 10, 1795, fols. 60–62, *ibid.*; Testimony of Jean Baptiste Forgeron, slave of Widow Lacour, May 8, 1795, fols. 27–30, and Final statement of Capitain, slave of Farar, May 16, 1795, fol. 212, both *ibid.*; Andreu Ocariz, *Movimientos rebeldes*, 228.

wrote, "All appearances indicate that all the slaves from Pointe Coupee to the capital, which is a distance of more than 50 leagues, had knowledge of what was going on there."[25]

There was coordination with the Opelousas post, where a slave revolt had taken place in February, 1795.[26] An English settler wrote to the *comandante* that in late April seven *nègres* had visited his slave cabins after the family had gone to bed and had informed his slaves that they were "only three days from Pointe Coupee where the slaves were all in arms against the whites, and they had been assigned to make lead, and if possible to drive the whites out of the country. Then all would be their own masters and they should be free. They asked if there was any ammunitions in the house, and particularly where it was kept, what number of fuses I had." The slaves from Pointe Coupee said that they were well supplied with fuses but needed powder and balls. Before they left, they promised to return soon to see their new acquaintances. A thirteen-year-old slave boy informed his master about the visit and the conversation.[27]

Bringier, an influential merchant-planter from the German Coast, reported that the night of April 22, 1795, he heard a wild cry answered by another wild cry from the opposite bank of the Mississippi River. Hiding behind a hedge on the levee, he listened in on a conversation between two *nègres*, hearing some alarming phrases about arms. Another *nègre* arrived in a pirogue from the opposite bank, reporting that all was well, they were all one, and they discussed the availability of arms and ammunition.[28]

The conflict with the slave owners intensified during Holy Week. The night before Easter, Sarrasin returned from the estate of the merchant Tournoir, reporting that they had flogged several *nègres* and that the whites had agreed that if they found only two *nègres* together who were not of the same estate, they would be flogged. The conspirators organized a show of force at the entrance to the church on Easter Sunday. They agreed to assemble there in groups of ten, fifteen, twenty, and thirty, daring the whites to flog them. If the whites flogged them, they planned to kill all the whites to get even

25. Carondelet to Luis de las Casas, New Orleans, July 30, 1795, in Leg. 2564, Doc. 556, fols. 661–69, SD, AGI.

26. Slaves tried for theft of rice during the slave rebellion, February 20, 1795 (illegible), in SJR, LHC, listed in Kerr, "Petty Felony, Slave Defiance, Frontier Villainy," 344.

27. Theodore Collins to Martin Duralde, captain of militia, *comandante* of Opelousas post, May 5, 1795, in Leg. 31, Carpeta 21, Doc. 187, fol. 772, PC, AGI.

28. James T. McGowan, "Creation of a Slave Society: Louisiana Plantations in the Eighteenth Century" (Ph.D. dissertation, University of Rochester, 1976), 363–64.

with them for trying to deprive them of the freedom the king had granted them.[29]

Slaves were vigorously, widely, and openly recruited for this assembly at the church on Easter Sunday. More than self-confident, they were intoxicated. Jean Baptiste, Poydras *commandeur*, said of a slave who denied that he was involved, "He was not only involved in the plot, but he even said that if he had seven balls in his body, that would not be enough to make him surrender. He tried to recruit several others." One slave testified that when he was told they would kill Duffief when he was on the road on his way to town, he said that he saw many difficulties. They replied that it would be a small matter; that it would take only a moment to destroy all the whites; and that they expected the *nègre* Stanislao Anis from the capital with other *nègres* of Dame Bara "who were all *gens gaillards*."[30]

Lucas, a Goudeau slave, testified, "The *nègre* Guillaume of Madame Le Doux entered my cabin and told me, in the presence of François and Louis, that he was coming from the upper coast from the slave quarters of Dame Lacour on business. Louis asked him, 'What business?' To which he replied, 'Don't you know that we are going to attack the whites?' To which Louis answered, 'With what, our teeth?' Guillaume replied, 'I have my knife, my ax, and a lance, and that will be enough.'" Another Goudeau slave testified, "He was all worked up, holding a dagger in one hand and a stick in the other, and he told us he had a lance and 46 arms in his cabin, and he would surely 'find the way to make a path among the whites'" ("*trouveroit bien le moyen de se faire un chemin parmi les blancs*"). The Goudeau slaves claimed that when they refused to join, Guillaume said they were nothing but women, adding, "We do not need you. The slaves of Poydras, Lacour, and Bara are brave enough to destroy all the whites and the slaves who do not wish to join us."[31]

Frederick Riché testified that while listening outside a Poydras slave cabin, he heard Guillaume say that they knew very well not all of them could have guns, but that there were knives; that a good stick

29. Testimony of Jean Baptiste, *commandeur* of Poydras, May 10, 1795, fols. 65–74, and Testimony of Grand Charles, slave of Poydras, May 12, 1795, fols. 95–99, both in Trial, OAPC.

30. Confrontation between Jean Baptiste of Poydras and Honoré of Simon Croisset, May 14, 1795, fol. 165, *ibid.*; Testimony of Eveillé, Ibo slave of Poydras, May 10, 1795, fols. 58–60, *ibid.*

31. Testimony of Lucas, Françoise Mulâtre, and Louis, slaves of Goudeau, May 8, 1795, fols. 24–38, *ibid.*

would do, and he hoped that thunder would crush him if he was afraid. Guillaume, who described himself as a creole of the post, was asked before being sentenced why he lent himself to the crime of revolution to kill the whites, knowing that he deserved to be hanged. He replied, "Because I was not afraid." [32]

Evidently, the masters did not accept the slaves' challenge on Easter Sunday. Petit Pierre, slave of Goudeau, testified that the revolt did not occur on Easter because "our leaders said that we should first allow the voyage of Sieur Duffief to take place. Brise Feu told me this, saying that their leaders had decided to suspend the affair until the return of Nöel, Cossi, Charles Nègre and Baptiste Mulâtre, all Poydras slaves who were to bring provisions and munitions from the city." [33]

After the show of force at the church on Easter Sunday, Sarrasin called a meeting behind the Vigne estate at the bridge of New Roads at False River to decide when the revolt should begin. On April 9, before the meeting could take place, Charles Duflour and Martin Bourgeat informed Alejandro de Blanc, militia officer of Pointe Coupee, about the plot. Duflour testified:

> I learned from one of my *nègres* named Pierre that Jean Baptiste, slave of Dame Lacour, had come between seven and eight o'clock at night and called him to the road, telling him that they were free but the whites did not want to give them their freedom, and they must take it. Pierre asked him how, and he replied that they must kill all the whites. Pierre told him in the presence of Charlot Nègre, slave of Sieur Riché who had come along and entered into the conversation, "I do not want that kind of freedom. You can keep it for yourself. My father and my mother were born slaves and so was I. I do not pretend to be free in this way. Since I have no money with which to buy my freedom, I do not want this kind of freedom. Besides, it is not possible that the whites would give freedom to all the slaves."
>
> Jean Baptiste left, and Charlot Nègre, slave of Sieur Riché, advised Pierre, "Go on to your cabin, my son, the words of this *Nègre* are not good at all."

Duflour went to Riché's to check Pierre's story with Charlot. Charlot confirmed the story word for word. That evening, about ten or eleven o'clock, Riché left his house to look around. He heard a *nègre* say to his companion, "We are free, but the settlers do not want to give us

---

32. Testimony of Frederick Riché, May 5, 1795, fols. 9–10, *ibid.;* Final statement of Guillaume, slave of Widow Le Doux, May 16, 1795, fol. 170, *ibid.*

33. Testimony of Petit Pierre, slave of Goudeau, May 9, 1795, fols. 46–48, *ibid.*

our freedom. We must wipe them all out. We have enough axes and sticks to kill them. We missed once, but I do not think this coup will miss, because it is led by *des gens gaillards.*"[34]

Madelaine and Françoise, two Tunica women who lived on the Riché estate, informed Riché about the slave conspiracy the same day. They had first heard about it in the *ciprière* of Widow Lacour. There some slaves had told them that they had sent Philip Mancot, slave of David Lacour, to the capital to find out if it was true that the *comandante* had received a letter from the government giving the slaves their freedom. But since Mancot had not returned, the slaves had "decided to take their freedom by destroying the whites, beginning by setting fire to a Poydras cabin to attract the whites, kill them, and seize the arms in the Poydras storehouse where the powder, balls, and rifles were kept." Even though the whites did not want to give them their freedom, "they were going to take it themselves, destroying all the whites, including the old women and the children, keeping only the young women and girls to make use of." L'Eveillé, Ibo slave of Poydras, confirmed the slaves' intentions to keep the young women and girls. According to Françoise and Madelaine, Chika, another Tunica woman who lived in the slave quarters of Widow Lacour, reported that Marie Jeanne, the wife of the *commandeur* of Colin Lacour's slaves, insulted and threatened her, saying that the blacks were ready to finish off the whites and that they (the Tunica women) had caused their coup to fail by warning the whites. The Tunica women felt they were in danger from the blacks, and they had nothing further to report because they were afraid of leaving their cabins.[35]

The revolt was planned in the *ciprière*, where slaves from various estates could meet freely. The slaves were well aware that they outnumbered the whites three to one. They held a meeting in the slave quarters of Widow Bourgeat after they left the mass at the church on Easter. Sarrasin called another meeting for the Saturday after Easter at sunset at the bridge at False River to decide upon how and when

34. Declaration of Martin Bourgeat, Louis Riché, Frederick Riché, Jean Baptiste Riché, April 24, 1795 (pretrial statements), unnumbered, in OAPC; Testimony of Charles Duflour, May 4, 1795, fols. 5, 6, and Testimony of Petit Pierre, slave of Charles Duflour, May 8, 1795, fol. 20, both in Trial, OAPC.

35. Declaration of Jean Baptiste Riché, April 24, 1795, unnumbered, in OAPC; Testimony of Jean Baptiste Riché, May 5, 1795, fols. 10–11, in Trial, OAPC; Declarations of Françoise and Madelaine, Tunica Indian women questioned through an interpreter, April 27, 1795 (pretrial statements), unnumbered, in OAPC; Testimony of Louis, slave of Goudeau, May 8, 1795, fols. 35–38, verified in testimony of l'Eveillé, Ibo slave of Poydras, May 10, 1795, fols. 58–60, both in Trial, OAPC; Testimony of Françoise and Madelaine, Sauvagesses, May 6, 1795, fols. 13–18, in Trial, OAPC.

to carry out the coup against the whites. Jean Baptiste assured them that they should not be afraid: After they had killed the whites, he was capable of presenting himself to the government to explain their reasons for carrying out this massacre; and, he reminded them, they had arms. Nöel, a Poydras slave, said that he would furnish all the ammunition. It was said that all the blacks were involved in the plot, as well as all the Poydras slaves. Eight bars of iron were found in Marcos Dick's pirogue. He and his crew all testified that the iron had been furnished by La Pique, jailer of the New Orleans prison, and sent with his black, who was traveling in the pirogue and who said the iron belonged to him. A Poydras slave claimed that the 33½ piasters found in his strongbox in New Orleans came from poultry and pigs that he had sold for himself and other slaves, and that the three guns found on Duffief's boat belonged to him, Nöel, and Petit François. The guns had been put in the boat before they left Pointe Coupee without telling Duffief.[36]

Before the meeting could take place at the bridge of False River, Sarrasin and several other slaves were arrested. There was a second plot, this time to free the arrested slaves from the patrol before they could be removed from the district. Jean Baptiste claimed that Joseph Mina took the initiative in the second plot, testifying that a few days after the first arrests were made,

> Joseph Mina came to see me and told me he could not sleep since they arrested Antoine Sarrasin, and he had decided to attack the patrol. I asked him if he was capable of doing it, and how he expected to attack the patrol without arms. He replied, "Don't you know that in the place where one writes, there are four guns, and two others in the bedroom of Sieur Gaunce?" Since Joseph Mina was determined, I told him to go see the *nègres* of Monsieur Goudeau, and if they were convinced to come back and tell me.[37]

The Goudeau slaves were a bad choice. Although three Goudeau slaves were convicted during the trial, this was an old-style estate

36. Testimony of Jean Baptiste Forgeron, slave of Widow Lacour, May 8, 1795, fols. 27–30, in Trial, OAPC; Testimony of Auguste Mulâtre, slave of George Bergeron, May 11, 1795, fols. 78–80, and Testimony of Jean Baptiste, slave of Widow Lacour, May 11, 1795, fols. 84–86, both *ibid.*; Testimony of Marcos Dick, Jean Aubert, Jean Sorga, and Maturin Boisseau, May 14, 1795, fols. 158–61, *ibid.*; Testimony of Baptiste Mulâtre, slave of Poydras, May 11, 1795, fols. 81–83, *ibid.*

37. The two conflicting versions of the second plot, which are recounted in subsequent paragraphs, are drawn from Testimony of Jean Baptiste, *commandeur* of Poydras, May 10, 1795, fols. 65–74, and in Testimony of Joseph Mina, May 9, 1795, fols. 42–46, both *ibid.*

with close emotional ties between masters and slaves. The estate had eighteen slaves with an even sex ratio among them in 1790. In 1798, Femme Goudeau agreed to mortgage her separate property in a vain effort to save her husband from economic ruin. She excluded a creole slave woman and her children from the mortgage, but they were all eventually seized and sold by Poydras. The teacher Bouyavel lived on the estate and no doubt influenced the slaves, but the Goudeau slaves were not ready to kill their master. Instead, they informed him immediately about Joseph Mina's proposition.[38]

According to Jean Baptiste, Joseph Mina reported that he did approach the Goudeau slaves, and they agreed to kill their master and then join the Poydras slaves at their slave quarters. Jean Baptiste sent Louis Bordelon to tell the Goudeau *nègres* not to act until he notified them. Jean Baptiste said he told the Poydras slaves, "It would be better to do this after all of us agree to it, and you should not believe that it is fear which makes me say this, because I am just as determined as the rest of you." Grand François Poulard said, "I see that this affair will never have an end." Jean Louis Mina said, "Any man who wants to get himself killed does not need company."

Jean Baptiste said he persuaded Joseph Mina not to act. That night, Petit Pierre, a fifteen-year-old Goudeau slave, came and told them that a *négresse* told Goudeau about the plot. Joseph Mina said, "We are lost!" They heard three gunshots from the fort, which they interpreted as a signal to the whites to assemble and to arrest the blacks of the Poydras estate. That evening, Jean Baptiste said, Joseph Mina came looking for him at the slave quarters and said, "They are going to arrest us tonight. We should run away." He replied, "Where do you expect to go?" Joseph Mina answered, "We should try to reach the Choctaws." Jean Baptiste asked, "Do you know the way?" Joseph Mina said, "Yes." Jean Baptiste told him, "It is useless. It is better to stay."

But Joseph Mina claimed that it was Jean Baptiste who took the initiative for the second plot: "At noon, Jean Baptiste, *commandeur* of the Poydras slaves, told me he thought the *comandante* was going to send my godfather Sarrasin Mulâtre, *commandeur* of the said estate, to town, and Jean Baptiste ordered me to go to the fields of M. Goudeau and ask the *nègres* of this estate if they would join them to attack the patrol and kill the whites, to which the *nègres* Hector, Lucas, Jean

38. Docs. 1968, 1976, in OAPC; Duparc to Carondelet, April 22, 1795, in Leg. 31, Carpeta 23, Doc. 84, fols. 812–14, PC, AGI.

Antoine did not reply, only asking him what time, saying, 'Hé! Hé!' which made me believe that they consented."

Joseph Mina explained the second plot in some detail:

> The plan was to go to the master's house that evening, kill the whites who were there, force the storehouse to get arms and then join the other *nègres* of the plot and attack the guard at the fort, free Antoine Sarrasin and the other prisoners, and at that time kill all the whites and the other slaves of the plot who did not want to join us. Charles, slave of Poydras, told me that the *nègres* named Stanislao Anis, Jean Louis, and François of Widow Bara and many others had returned and were waiting in the *ciprière* to kill the whites and the *nègres* who did not want to be part of the plot. And when someone asked how this could be done because there were a lot of people at Natchez, and did they think themselves capable of resisting cannon, Charles and Jean Baptiste replied that it did not matter, if they had to die, they would die.

After he returned from talking to the Goudeau slaves, Joseph Mina said, he was told that the plot had been discovered. He told Jean Baptiste that he was afraid and wanted to run away. Jean Baptiste advised him not to run away, because in case he was arrested, he, Jean Baptiste, would not name him. Joseph Mina and Louis Bordelon ran away when they heard that Tournoir's *mulâtresse* had left for town. They were captured two miles beyond the east bank of the Mississippi River by Frederick Riché. On May 29, fifteen slaves were hanged in Pointe Coupee before ten o'clock in the morning. Joseph Mina, at the age of eighteen, mounted the scaffold, laughing and saying good-bye to his friends.[39]

Although the slave cabins were thoroughly searched for arms, none were found. *Comandante* Duparc feared that the slaves kept arms hidden in the woods. Widow Lacour made the mistake of sending Timothée Mulâtre for two guns. Instead of bringing them to her, he left with the guns to become a maroon. When recaptured, Timothée claimed that he had given the guns to her slave Bambara. Both Timothée and Bambara were severely lashed, but neither revealed the whereabouts of the firearms.[40] They were both found guilty during the trial.

39. Testimony of Joseph Mina, May 9, 1795, fols. 42–46, and Testimony of Louis Bordelon, slave of Poydras, May 9, 1795, fols. 49–51, both in Trial, OAPC; Duparc to Carondelet, April 24, May 31, 1795, in Leg. 31, Carpeta 23, fols. 812–14, 847–48, PC, AGI.

40. Duparc to Carondelet, Pointe Coupée, May 1, 1795, in Leg. 31, Carpeta 23, Doc. 95, fols. 829–31, *ibid.*

Estates with the largest numbers of slaves and with imbalanced sex ratios were most deeply involved in the conspiracy. Most of the slaves convicted were from large, heavily Africanized estates. The Colin Lacour estate, for example, was heavily Senegambian. An inventory, dating from 1782, of the Bara dit Leblond estate shows that its slave force was more heavily African than that of the average Pointe Coupee estate. Twenty-one out of the twenty-eight slaves inventoried were Africans. Two of the seven creoles were children. There were three African children, aged five, ten, and twelve. This estate was 78.3 percent adult African, and even the majority of children were Africans, though the African nations were unidentified. The vague term *Guinea* was used.

The 1795 conspiracy was organized from the estate of Julien Poydras, a native of Nantes, France, who played an important role in Louisiana history. Poydras began publishing poetry in 1779 and is considered the first literary figure of Louisiana. He became one of the wealthiest merchants and planters and an important political figure after the United States acquired Louisiana. He held several offices and chaired the statehood convention. By 1822, when Poydras made his will, he owned four plantations in Pointe Coupee and two in West Baton Rouge Parish. His will provided that the slaves he owned at his death be attached to their respective plantations and not sold. After twenty-five years of service they were to be freed. A retirement pension of twenty-five dollars a year was provided for slaves or former slaves reaching age sixty. The Poydras will gave rise to endless litigation and was never fully executed.[41]

During its formation, the Poydras estate was heavily populated by slaves from the Bight of Benin, and it was heavily Africanized because of its unusual gender, family, age, and ethnic structure. The men were forced to develop sexual relationships and family ties off the estate, and family networks radiated from the Poydras estate to various other plantations. Although an inventory of the Poydras estate around the time of the 1795 conspiracy does not exist, the development of its slave population can be traced through notarial records, including acts of sale and two early inventories. Poydras began purchasing individual slaves during the early 1780s.[42] Normally, after the death of the master, the slaves were dispersed through sale to various

41. Light Townsend Cummins, "The Final Years of Colonial Louisiana," in *Louisiana: A History*, ed. Bennett H. Wall (2nd ed., Arlington Heights, Ill., 1990), 75, 76; Joe Gray Taylor, *Negro Slavery in Louisiana* (Baton Rouge, 1963), 164–65.

42. Poydras purchased three slaves in 1782 and four in 1783. There are no extant documents for 1780 and 1781 (from DB Inventories).

local slave owners. But in 1778, Dr. Armand Dubertrand bought the entire estate of Meuillon, including all his slaves. There were twenty-four Africans among the forty-seven slaves, two of them children, and twenty-three creoles, four of them children. Thus, 53.7 percent were adult Africans. Five of the Africans were from Senegambia, eight from the Bight of Benin, four were Ibo, and seven were Congo. Among the slaves from the Bight of Benin, two were Yoruba women and three were Mina men. In 1784, Dubertrand returned to France and sold his estate, including all his slaves, to Poydras. There were fifty-eight slaves, twenty-nine of whom were adult Africans. There were eleven creole children and eighteen creole adults. Africans were 61.7 percent of the adults. The ethnic composition and sex ratio among Africans had shifted sharply. The Congo had dropped from seven to two. The Ibo had dropped from four to two. Among the seven slaves from Senegambia, Wolof women had increased from one to four. Among the twelve slaves from the Bight of Benin, Yoruba women had risen from two to seven. The gender structure was unusual among both creoles and Africans. There were only six adult creole women and twelve adult creole men, giving a sex ratio of 2.0, or two men for every woman, among the creoles, while the average sex ratio among creole slaves at Pointe Coupee was 1.24. But the African sex ratio favored women. There were thirteen male and sixteen female Africans, a sex ratio of 0.81, while the average sex ratio among Africans at Pointe Coupee was 1.92. This estate was heavily weighted toward the Bight of Benin, especially toward Yoruba women, with African women outnumbering creole women sixteen to five. The parents of the children were not indicated. Between 1785 and 1790, there is a record of nine slaves purchased by Poydras. Five of them were Africans, two males and three females, including an eleven-year-old girl and children aged four, seven, and thirteen. Only one adult creole, a seventeen-year-old male, was purchased.[43]

The 1790 census listed Poydras as a bachelor who lived alone on his estate with his seventy-two slaves. There were six elderly women, almost certainly overwhelmingly Africans, some of them very likely Yoruba. There were only four women of childbearing age, including one mixed-blood. Nevertheless, there were twenty children on the estate: eight girls and twelve boys. There were no elderly men and forty-two mature men, two of whom were mixed-bloods. Poydras purchased six slaves, all Africans, three men and three women, from the Claude Trénonay estate sale in 1794. Mature, single men outnum-

43. Calculated from DB Inventories.

bered women of childbearing age by more than ten to one. The sex ratio was 10.5, while the average sex ratio among all slaves at Pointe Coupee was 1.41. Evidently, Poydras did not like young women, especially young creole women. His inclination to purchase children without their mothers and his strong preference for Africans possibly stemmed from his desire to mold his slave force to his liking. It appears from the 1790 census and Poydras' pattern of purchasing slaves that the Poydras estate was a matriarchy of elderly African women, likely Yoruba women. The extremely unbalanced gender and age structure on this estate surely enhanced the power and influence of elderly African women and contributed to restlessness and discontent among the men, forcing them to travel widely to find sexual gratification as well as to form families. There were a significant number of children on the plantation without either parent. Those mothers who were present were most likely mainly African.[44] Children, especially male children, were acculturated to a great extent by African men who became fictive kin.

The impact of the distorted gender, age, ethnic, and family structure on the Poydras estate is reflected in the brief career of Joseph Mina. Joseph was only three years old when Dubertrand acquired the Meuillon estate and was listed without a parent.[45] He must have been deeply influenced by the Mina men on the estate. After he grew up, he was called Joseph Mina, though he was a creole.

Fifteen Poydras slaves were convicted for the 1795 conspiracy, including seven Africans, only one of whom was a Mina. His other African slaves convicted were one Ibo, two Chamba, and three Fulbe. One creole of Jamaica was convicted from the Poydras estate. Both creoles of New Orleans convicted were Poydras slaves who no doubt had relatives in the capital. Only five of the Poydras slaves convicted were local creoles, including Joseph Mina.

The Mina influence on the 1795 conspiracy obviously transcended the two Mina slaves convicted. It was manifested through the role of Antonio Cofi Mina, the free black leader of the Mina community who served as interpreter in the Mina trial. His prestige was high because he was credited with saving, and eventually freeing, the Mina slaves. Cofi Mina was viewed as a key figure in the 1795 conspiracy, at least by the slaves involved. His role in this conspiracy earned him depor-

44. Recensement de la Pointe Coupée et Fausse Rivière, March 29, 1790, in Leg. 227A, Carpete 21, Doc. 2, PC, AGI; Sale of Trénonay Estate, January 17, 1794, Doc. 1799, in OAPC.
45. Doc. 919, in OAPC.

tation to Havana. Several slaves testified that various slaves were sent to approach Cofi in order to coordinate their uprising with one planned for New Orleans. Although Cofi testified that he knew few slaves of Pointe Coupee and had not seen them for years, this was clearly untrue. He claimed that he knew the accused Mina slaves for whom he interpreted only slightly, and not by name. He admitted that he knew Jean Baptiste Forgeron (blacksmith), slave of Lacour, but had not seen him since the 1788 fire in New Orleans. Evidently, skilled slaves from rural areas were sent to help rebuild New Orleans after this fire. Antonio Cofi Mina testified that he was approached by a Chamba slave who could speak "a little Mina." Tham, Mina slave of Bara, testified, "It is true that I was charged to ask Cofi if it was true that all the slaves were free, but it is false that I wanted to attack the whites in case it was not true because in case the French took the country, we should fight against them to the death to defend the whites." Stanislao Anis testified that Tham had spoken of defending the country against the French earlier, but later he had agreed with the rest of them to attack the whites.[46]

Although Cofi Mina denied knowing André Nègre, slave of Colin Lacour, André testified that Cofi knew him well. Cofi must have become acquainted with André when he was working for the king in New Orleans, after André ran away when his master threatened to kill him. André testified that he cautiously approached Cofi and said, "The blacks of Pointe Coupee are acting like fools up there, and there are mulattoes mixed up in it. They want to be free by force" ("*Les Nègres de la Pointe Coupée font des bétises par la haut, il y a des mulâtres fourrés la dedans, et qu'ils vouloient être libre par force*"). Cofi claimed that he replied that he did not want to hear about it, saying, "Why do you tell me that? You should take care of your own affairs among yourselves. That is none of my business" ("*Pourquoi me dites voùs ça? Arrangez-vous, vous autres, ce ne sont pas mes affaires*"). André testified that Cofi Mina added, "The number of slaves is not great and if the free blacks and mulattoes fall on the whites using the *nègres*, then effectively, the Indians will also fall on the said *nègres*."[47]

Cofi Mina's observation was astute. Indians were still the principal military force in the colony. Their loyalty to the Spanish regime intensified because of pressure from the new, vigorous, expanding United

46. Andreu Ocariz, *Movimientos rebeldes*, 161; Confrontation between [Stanislao] Anis and Tham Mina, both slaves of Widow Bara, May 14, 1795, fol. 145, in Trial, OAPC.
47. Province of Louisiana *vs.* Coffy [*sic*], June 16, 1795, in Notarial Acts of Francisco Broutin, 1790–1798, Vol. XXXVI, Doc. 21, fols. 944–84, OAOP.

States. In 1785, the Houma Indians were used to put down an anticipated imminent slave insurrection along Bayou Lafourche. They hunted down Philippe, a free black who had organized the slaves to strip the Bayou Lafourche area of arms, putting them in the hands of a company of fugitive slaves. Three blacks and one white sympathizer were arrested and punished. There is no evidence of cooperation between the conspirators and Indians during the Pointe Coupee conspiracy. A creole slave expressed contempt for them, saying, "The Indians are all barbarians because they do not know the good Lord, and a child would take up his gun to kill his father."[48]

Tunica Indians betrayed the 1795 conspiracy and chased runaway slaves for the masters. Indians hunted slaves who ran away after the conspiracy was exposed. The Tunica Indians of Pointe Coupee were a mere remnant of their former selves. The Tunica village contained only thirty-three people in 1766.[49] But Tunica Indians lived on estates in Pointe Coupee, and if we can judge by their role in the 1795 conspiracy, they were there to spy on the slaves.

There were clearly tensions between slaves on subsistence farms, where the old, intimate, familial tradition between masters and slaves remained, and those on estates involved in large-scale production of export staples. There was considerable reluctance among slaves on the old-style farms to join the plot, some of which clearly stemmed from their affection for their masters and their unwillingness to harm them. Some slaves did not want to take risks when the outcome was unclear. One slave testified that he said, "I will not be the first, but I will not be the last." A Bambara slave testified that he said to a creole, "It's up to you to begin, because you are free, and I will follow."[50]

There was widespread intimidation of those who might betray the plot and of those who refused to join. A number of slaves, especially the creoles, were intimidated by the conspirators, fearing retribution not only from them but also from their families if the conspirators were arrested and condemned. Louis Bordelon testified that the leaders of the plot threatened to burn up the first one who informed the whites and throw his ashes on the others. Several slaves finally

48. Carl A. Brasseaux, *The Founding of New Acadia: The Beginnings of Acadian Life in Louisiana, 1765–1803* (Baton Rouge, 1987), 193–94; Testimony of Michel Mulâtre, slave of Charles Duflour, May 9, 1795, fols. 52–54, in Trial, OAPC.

49. Jacqueline K. Voorhies, *Some Late Eighteenth-Century Louisianians: Census Records, 1758–1796* (Lafayette, La., 1973), 164.

50. Testimony of Jacob, slave of Jean Pierre Decuir, May 14, 1795, fol. 140, in Trial, OAPC; Confrontation between Jean Baptiste and Bambara, slaves of Widow Lacour, May 14, 1795, fol. 148, *ibid.*

confessed, claiming that they were intimated into joining the plot. Timothée admitted, "I really was involved in the plot, because I was warned that all the creoles who refused to get involved would have their throats cut, and I was obliged to do like the others." Before being sentenced, he said, "I consented out of fear, and because I believed that if the plot were uncovered before the revolt broke out, they would hang only the captains."[51]

Jean Baptiste, another Lacour slave, made the following statement before being sentenced: "I was intimidated, being told that the creole slaves who refused to enter the plot would be killed like the whites." Several other slaves, in their final statements, also claimed that they had been intimidated. One slave testified that he knew all about the plot to kill the whites and that those refusing to participate "would have their throats cut." He claimed he never consented to join. Five other slaves stated, before sentencing, that they entered the plot because "I believed the threat of Jean Baptiste"; "I consented through fear"; "I entered the plot through fear"; "I consented out of fear that the other slaves might kill me"; "I consented out of fear of the crowd [*Grand monde*] who told me that the same thing would happen to me as to the whites."[52]

While the condemned slaves can be suspected of making a plea for leniency on the grounds that they had been intimidated into joining the plot, it is clear from testimony of slaves who admitted involvement in, and leadership of, the plot that the conspirators did indeed intend to kill the slaves who refused to join the revolt.[53]

The creole slaves, though a minority among adults, were a tightly woven community reinforced by both blood and fictive kinship ties ramifying throughout the district. Stanislao Anis, *commandeur* of the Bara estate, testified that he met his brothers François and Jean Louis, both Bara slaves, in the *ciprière*.[54]

Three brothers and a son of one of them, all slaves of Widow Lacour, were convicted. Two of them, Philipe and Jacob, were identical

51. Testimony of Louis Bordelon, May 9, 1795, fols. 49–51, *ibid.*; Confrontation between Jean Baptiste and Timothée Mulâtre, both slaves of Widow Lacour, May 14, 1795, fol. 151, *ibid.*; Final statement of Timothée Mulâtre, slave of Widow Lacour, May 16, 1795, fols. 186–87, *ibid.*

52. Final statements of Baptiste, slave of Poydras, fol. 175, of Jean Baptiste, slave of Widow Lacour, fol. 177, of Rokelaure, slave of Widow Lacour, fol. 182, of Philipe Bambara, slave of Widow Lacour, fol. 185, of Petit Pierre, slave of Goudeau, and of Baptiste, slave of Décuir, fols. 242–43, all May 16, 1795, *ibid.*

53. See, for example, Testimony of Joseph Mina, May 9, 1795, fols. 42–46, *ibid.*

54. Testimony of Stanislao Anis, slave of Bara, May 11, 1795, fols. 75–78, *ibid.*

twins. Jacob testified, "I was not involved in any plot. I stayed in the *ciprière*. Jean Baptiste Forgeron told me that the slaves wanted to kill the whites to have their freedom and asked me to join but I refused and said I would warn my mistress, and he told me they would kill me if I did. I was sick and I stayed in my cabin. I think it was my twin brother Philipe who was at the Church on Easter Day." Philipe confirmed that it was he, not his twin, who had gone to the show of force at the church on Easter Sunday. He testified that he tried to stop his brother Jean Baptiste from getting involved in the plot, without success. Other slaves claimed that they tried to stop their family members from getting involved. One father testified that he went to look for his son to stop him. Grand Joseph, *commandeur* of the Colin Lacour estate, went to look for his son at the Riché estate "to forbid him from going to the Poydras estate," but he could not find him. Although Grand Joseph was sixty-nine years old, he was convicted and flogged.[55]

Family ties among the slaves of the district were so strong that the slaves and the free Indians who denounced the conspirators feared vengeance from their relatives. Only after it was clear which way the wind was blowing did Marie Louise, a Riché slave, ask to speak. She testified, "Up to this time, I was reluctant to admit that it was I who revealed the secret of the plot to the authorities because I was afraid that the relatives of the criminals would try to kill me, but now having thought it over, I did in fact tell my master." She did not show up to ratify her declaration, claiming to be sick. Marie Louise, slave of Riché, the two Tunica women, Françoise and Madelaine, and Jean Baptiste Forgeron, slave of Widow Lacour who had informed Marie Louise about the plot and told her to tell her master, were all given rewards. Jean Baptiste Forgeron was freed and sent to New Orleans, evidently in the hope of anonymity.[56]

Mulatto slaves were involved far out of proportion to their numbers in the slave population, but other black-Indian mixtures besides Sarrasin might have been designated mulattoes. Among those found

55. Testimony of Jacob Jumeau, Philipe Jumeau, and Timothée, slaves of Widow Lacour, May 12, 1795, fols. 115–19, 136, *ibid.*; Testimony of André, slave of Charles Duflour, May 12, 1795, fols. 106–107, *ibid.*; Testimony of Michel Mulâtre, slave of Charles Duflour, May 9, 1795, fols. 52–55, *ibid.*; Testimony of Grand Joseph, *commandeur* of Colin Lacour, May 12, 1795, fols. 92–93, *ibid.*; Execution of sentences, May 29, 1795, fol. 262, *ibid.*

56. Act of May 18, 1795, fol. 243, *ibid.*; Testimony of Marie Louise, slave of Louis Riché, April 10, 1795, fol. 74, *ibid.*; Testimony of Jean Baptiste Forgeron, slave of Widow Lacour, May 9, 1795, fols. 27–30, *ibid.*; Gratificacions, May 22, 1795, fol. 258, *ibid.*

guilty and sentenced during the trial were nine mulatto and twenty-six creole blacks and nineteen Africans. The Africans from Senegambia were five Bambara, one Maninga, and four Fulbe (Poulard). The one Maninga was Capitain from the Farar estate. There were two Mina, two Congo, two Chamba, one Ibo, one Caraba, and one Thoma.

There is strong evidence to support the belief that the conspiracy was linked to a broader plan, very likely the aborted Gênet-Clark invasion. The slaves discussed which side to support if France invaded Louisiana, and they chose France for the sake of liberty and abolition. The final statements made by the leaders before being sentenced point toward a broader plan. When asked why they lent themselves to the crime of revolution to kill the whites, of which they were charged, knowing that they deserved to be hanged, Jean Baptiste, *commandeur* of Poydras, replied, "I know the crime and the penalty, but I was surprised and fooled." To the same question, Antoine Sarrasin replied, "I consented through bad advice." Stanislao Anis, *commandeur* of Bara, replied, "I only consented through bad advice."[57]

The vast majority of the accused refused to admit any knowledge of the conspiracy. When asked the foregoing question before being sentenced, forty-one of the accused slaves and all three of the accused whites denied all the charges against them.

The Spanish authorities believed that the conspiracy was linked to the projected French invasion of Louisiana, and that plans were coordinated through soldiers and through boatmen plying the Mississippi River. Governor Carondelet asked that French soldiers stationed in the Spanish army in Louisiana be exchanged for Spanish soldiers stationed in Havana, because French soldiers were involved in the slave conspiracies; but he could not prove it. In order to discover the broader ramifications of the conspiracy, Carondelet ordered the investigation to continue after the trial and sentencing. He had no doubt that there were many white provocateurs spreading false rumors of freedom among the slaves, especially among the Lacour and Poydras slaves, but their names were never revealed. The night before his execution, Sarrasin asked to speak to *Comandante* Duparc. The contents of this conversation are not known, but Sarrasin did not reveal any names of others involved. Duparc spoke to several other

57. Confrontation between Anis and Tham Mina, both slaves of Widow Bara, May 14, 1795, fols. 145–47, *ibid.*; Final statements of Antoine Sarrasin, fol. 178, of Jean Baptiste, *commandeur* of Poydras, fol. 173, of Stanislao Anis, *commandeur* of Widow Bara, fol. 179, all May 16, 1795, *ibid.*

condemned slaves, without results. Attempts to get the condemned leaders to reveal the names of their contacts failed. According to the Spanish official who questioned them the night before their execution, the condemned slaves refused to talk and "took their secret to their graves, with firm courage."[58]

Spanish officials feared a renewal of the slaves' insurrectionary plots because of the "resentful and vengeful character of the people of color." They pointed out the inherent danger of the physical setting. If the plot had not been discovered in time, "the fire would have gone from plantation to plantation throughout the length of the Province, and the settlers would not have had the time to assemble for their respective defense because all the plantations are spread out and distant from each other on both banks of the river by at least a quarter league. Four or five whites surprised by 20, 50, or 100 of their blacks could neither defend themselves nor could they expect help from their neighbors."[59]

Carondelet asked permission to expel all freedmen from Pointe Coupee, because they had no other place of refuge except the slave cabins. A captain of the Mixed Legion of Mississippi was sent to look for a free black named Lexime who had arrived at night at a plantation in Pointe Coupee and had remained in the slave quarters for two days "under the pretext that he was repairing a tool in the blacksmith shop of the district." A free black named Jimi was suspected of being involved in the slave conspiracy. Arms and munitions belonging to him had been found in a slave cabin. He was given a passport to go to the capital and told not to return to Pointe Coupee, but he returned anyway to make tools for a blacksmith. He was arrested and held at the fort.[60]

The arrival in New Orleans of the convicted prisoners created alarm among Spanish authorities, because the condemned slaves had

58. Copia del oficio reservado no. 140 y sus documentos del Gobernador de la Luisiana al Capitan General, and Carondelet to Luis de las Casas, New Orleans, July 30, 1795, in Leg. 2564, Doc. 556, fols. 661–69, SD, AGI; Duparc to Carondelet, Pointe Coupee, May 31, 1795, in Leg. 31, Carpeta 23, fols. 847–48, PC, AGI. For a fuller discussion of the involvement of French soldiers and free people of African descent in slave conspiracies, see McGowan, "Creation of a Slave Society," 349–55.

59. Rendon to Gardoqui, June 15, 1795, in Leg. 2612, Doc. 54, fols. 498–501, SD, AGI; Carondelet to Las Casas, New Orleans, July 30, 1795, in Leg. 2564, Doc. 556, fols. 661–69, ibid.

60. Duparc to Carondelet, Pointe Coupee, May 5, 1795, in Leg. 31, Carpeta 23, Doc. 95, fols. 829–31, PC, AGI; Duparc to Carondelet, Pointe Coupee, May 1, 1795, ibid.

kinship ties with slaves there. Both Jean Baptiste and Grand Charles, Poydras slaves who were leaders of the insurrection, were born in New Orleans. Sarrasin's mother, Marie Jeanne, and his spouse, Nanette, as well as their two adolescent boys, were also most likely in the capital, hosted by Cecilia India Libre, who had lived in New Orleans for many years. According to Carondelet, the presence of these prisoners in New Orleans, where they had many relatives, would increase unrest among the slaves in the capital. New Orleans had been burnt to the ground again in December, 1794. Over two hundred of the best houses were destroyed. Three or four arson attempts were made in the city to enable the prisoners to escape during the confusion. Prisoners were secretly embarked on the *Mississippi*, which was about to leave for Havana. They were guarded by soldiers and officers of the Fixed Infantry Regiment of Louisiana, who had orders to separate the slaves and watch them closely to prevent any escape plot. Antonio Cofi Mina was deported to Havana on the same ship, along with a free black named Louis Benoit, a native of St. Domingue who was accused of being "very imbued with the revolutionary maxims which have devastated the said colony." Luis de las Casas, captain general of Cuba, wrote to Carondelet, complaining that if these free blacks were prejudicial in Louisiana, they could be even more harmful in Cuba. Furthermore, he wrote, the captains of merchant ships refused to take them to any other colony. He concluded, "In the future, send such individuals to some foreign country, which is easier to do directly from New Orleans than from Cuba, because we have nowhere to send them and no funds to maintain them."[61]

The Pointe Coupee Conspiracy developed a core of leaders who operated collectively. Meetings were held, and plans were discussed and agreed upon. Jean Baptiste, Poydras *commandeur*, believed that the revolt failed because the conspirators disagreed among themselves: "Some time before last Easter, we disputed among ourselves about the most propitious hour to carry out our coup in case we did carry it out. One said at midnight; another said at 4 A.M., and I said at suppertime, and our differences remained undecided. When I proposed something, some of them accepted it and others rejected it, depending upon what they saw in each slave quarters."[62]

Unlike some slave conspiracies in Anglo North America, the Pointe

---

61. Andreu Ocariz, *Movimientos rebeldes*, 160–62.
62. Testimony of Jean Baptiste, *commandeur* of Poydras, May 10, 1795, fols. 65–74, in Trial, OAPC.

Coupee Conspiracy was a secular, not a religious, movement.[63] It was therefore more dangerous. Millenarian movements tend to focus upon the one, charismatic leader, encouraging blind loyalty. They are vulnerable to destruction if the leader is killed and discourage both participatory democracy and continuity. When Toussaint l'Ouverture was removed from St. Domingue in chains, he said that he was only the trunk of the revolution: It would spring up again by its roots, because they were many and deep. The abolitionist movement in Louisiana sprang up again, too. Despite the hangings and the brutal display of bodies along the Mississippi River, despite moves for massive deportation of slaves considered dangerous, the blacks were not intimidated. Festivals for the dead, honoring the executed slaves, were held in the homes of free blacks. In March, 1796, Carondelet sent forty troops by riverboat and thirty others overland to suppress a plot on the German Coast. In 1797, the government offered an amnesty to maroons who returned to their masters voluntarily. But maroons increased instead of diminished. More slave conspiracies were discovered in February, March, and April of 1796 in Pointe Coupee and on the German Coast. There were some complaints that some blacks and mulattoes who were, or claimed to be, free were armed with swords and acting insolent. When anyone tried to clarify their status, they did not respond except to place their hands on their swords. The militia of Baton Rouge was ordered to kill any dog belonging to a slave at the slightest sign of unrest. Armed maroons moved about freely. In spite of the patrols, maroons could cross the district from one end to the other without being seen. Ledoux, a Pointe Coupee settler, informed the *comandante* that when an Indian spotted a group of seven armed *nègres*, two of them chased the Indian. They were believed to be heading for Natchitoches.[64]

In the 1795 conspiracy, the desires of all the slaves at Pointe Coupee for freedom were fused. There is no doubt about its reality. The slaves were very well informed about the conflicts between France and Spain. Inspired by the ideals of the French Revolution and its successes throughout the world, they had realistic hopes for freedom and found slavery intolerable. Aside from the intoxication with demo-

63. For a discussion of the religious roots of the Denmark Vesey conspiracy in South Carolina, see Margaret Washington Creel, *"A Peculiar People": Slave Religion and Community-Culture Among the Gullahs* (New York, 1988), 161.

64. Eugene D. Genovese, *From Rebellion to Revolution: Afro-American Slave Revolts in the Making of the Modern World* (Baton Rouge, 1979), 122–23; Andreu Ocariz, *Movimientos rebeldes*, 125–28, 203, 204, 207, 211, 223; Durale to Carondelet, Opelousas, May 10, 1795, in Leg. 31, Carpeta 21, fols. 773–74, PC, AGI.

cratic and antislavery ideals, there was direct instigation of revolt by Jacobin agents laying the groundwork for the French invasion of Louisiana.

The 1791 conspiracy of the Mina slaves was an early stage of the agitation for freedom that gripped the slave population of the Pointe Coupee post. It was an African ethnic conspiracy; therefore, it was doomed to failure and was much less frightening. Masters defended their slaves and doubted their guilt during the Mina conspiracy trials in 1792. But the 1795 conspiracy was another matter. It was broadly based and included slaves of all colors and nations, free people of African descent, and poor whites: *voyageurs*, indentured servants, and soldiers. The leaders of the conspiracy claimed that there would be no lack of whites to help them.[65] The slaves of Pointe Coupee were well informed about revolutionary developments in France, in Haiti, and throughout the world. The Declaration of the Rights of Man was read to them by Joseph Bouyavel, an abolitionist white schoolteacher and tailor who worked on the Goudeau estate. He admitted that he had burned two other books that he had bought in New Orleans. The leaders of the conspiracy traveled widely and sent couriers throughout lower Louisiana. Jacobins of all colors traveled through Pointe Coupee, informing the slaves that they had already been freed but that their masters were not telling them. Slaves were aware that slavery had been abolished in all French colonies and that if France won the war, they would all be free.[66] Their revolt was to be coordinated with slave uprisings in Natchez, Opelousas, the German Coast, and New Orleans, probably linked to the anticipated French invasion.

The 1795 conspiracy of Pointe Coupee was not a race war. Jacobins of Louisiana of all races and nationalities fought against slavery and social tyranny. It was a sophisticated, well-organized movement. It involved mulatto and black creole slaves born in Pointe Coupee, a creole of Jamaica, two creoles of New Orleans, one slave from New York, African slaves of eight different nations, free blacks and mulattoes, and white Jacobins who hated slavery, including a Waloon schoolteacher, a German tailor born in New York, and an indentured servant *voyageur* plowing the Mississippi River who described himself as a native of the Republic of Raguse. Soldiers stationed throughout

---

65. Testimony of Grand Charles, slave of Poydras, quoting Jean Baptiste, *commandeur* of Poydras, May 12, 1795, fols. 95–98, in Trial, OAPC.

66. Testimony of Joseph Bouyavel, May 15, 1795, fols. 167–68, *ibid.*; Testimony of Antoine, *commandeur* of Widow Lacour, May 11, 1795, fols. 86–88, *ibid.*

lower Louisiana were involved in the plot. It was led by the most skilled and trusted slaves: by the *commandeurs*, by mulatto slaves, who often played the role of police on the larger estates, and by the creole slaves. The African thrust came from the Mina and the Mande slaves, who historically were the leaders among the African slaves of Louisiana. There was widespread support among the white Jacobins of Louisiana who, by 1795, were no longer white creole merchants and planters but the international, maritime working class and soldiers. Inspired by the ideals and successes of the French and Haitian revolutions, the longings for freedom of slaves of all races and nations and of the despised and mistreated soldiers, sailors, and indentured servants were fused. The 1795 conspiracy took place because the slaves of the remote Pointe Coupee post became deeply involved in the international revolutionary ferment of the 1790s.

Conclusion

The Pointe Coupee Conspiracy of 1795 was a turning point in the attitude toward slave control in Louisiana. This conspiracy demonstrated that the slaves of lower Louisiana were not a fractionalized, immobilized, ignorant, isolated people who were incapable of organizing to overthrow the slave system. On the contrary, the slaves proved themselves to be both competent and indomitable. The semi-egalitarian tradition among masters and slaves born on the insecure frontier gave way to systematic, preventative terror. Although the ideology supporting this terror evolved into contempt for people of African descent, presenting them as incompetent, irrational savages whose base instincts had to be controlled through terror, it was their competence that was feared.

The new philosophy of slave control was enunciated in a letter sent to the Cabildo of New Orleans. The letter expressed the belief that the slave conspiracy at Pointe Coupee would be contained by arresting the leaders, by making an example of them that would control the other slaves, and by encouraging the vigilance and activity of the inhabitants. But it was a warning that they should take every imaginable precaution, even more than necessary, in order

> to wake up those among us who sleep in a security which is too profound. The spark has appeared at Pointe Coupee, but it is possible that the source was here [in New Orleans]. The effervescence of mind, the licentious tone which has been unknown before this, the insubordination which reigns, the impact of the freedom which they flatter themselves with, are reasons enough to induce us to believe that they can become involved in grand movements. The insurrection of St. Domingue did not have a more violent beginning. . . . We should not await the strength of the evil, if it exists, to remedy it, because it can become incurable. And if it does not exist, sagacious precautions should prevent it.[1]

Although the Spanish crown continued to provide a weak, formal, and distant brake upon the systematic, racist terror promoted by Louisiana's creole slave owners, by 1795, Spain had lost interest in Louisiana. Governor Carondelet began his term of office by showing great concern that slaves not be mistreated by their masters, intervening to protect them. When the 1795 conspiracy was revealed, Carondelet believed that the white creoles were plotting to assassinate him

---

1. Fleuriau to Dapen, April 22, 1795 (duplicate), in Leg. 6929, GM, AS.

and seize control of the colony. He claimed that the Cabildo of New Orleans was trying to take control of the conspiracy trial and then extend their control to other aspects of government that were beyond their powers. He also said that the white creoles were spreading rumors among "the principal inhabitants, the city population, the troops, and even among the secular clergy" that he sided with the slaves and backed their insurrectionary plans in order to wipe out the white French creoles. Carondelet asked that the principal conspirators be deported to Havana and their families held as hostages in Louisiana, and that troops be sent from Havana secretly, otherwise the conspirators would seize New Orleans and Plaquemine before their arrival.[2]

But Carondelet's conflict with the Cabildo quickly evaporated. The Cabildo voted full confidence in Carondelet's handling of the conspiracy trial. There was an agreement that Manuel Serrano, a Spanish legal expert, should preside over the trial. He arrived in Pointe Coupee on May 7.[3] Although the Cabildo had initially voted to send attending witnesses chosen by them, only attending witnesses from Pointe Coupee were used.

Luis de las Casas, captain general of Cuba who held jurisdiction over Louisiana, made it clear that Spain's priorities had changed. Spain no longer feared a revolt by the white creoles, especially the slave owners, in support of a French invasion. The war with France was drawing to a close, formally ending on July 25, 1795. Nor was Spain still concerned about an invasion of the American frontiersmen down the Mississippi River to enforce free trade and navigation. The dispute with the United States was settled. Under the Treaty of San Lorenzo, signed October 27, 1795, Spain gave the United States Natchez and all territory to its north located east of the Mississippi River, as well as free navigation of the river. Las Casas enclosed a clipping from the *Courier* of London, dated March 13, 1795, reporting that a treaty had just been signed between Spain and the United States allowing free navigation of the Mississippi River. He urged Carondelet to make friendly overtures to the Kentuckians. Las Casas did not believe there was any danger of revolt by the wealthy slave owners of Louisiana in spite of loose talk among them. He refused to allow the deportation of prominent white creoles who Carondelet be-

2. Carondelet to Cabildo of New Orleans, May 1, 1795, and Carondelet to Las Casas, May 3, 1795 (duplicates), both in Leg. 6926, *ibid.*

3. Meeting of Cabildo of New Orleans with various Spanish officials, in Carondelet to Cabildo of New Orleans, May 2, 1795 (copy no. 3), in Leg. 6929, GM, AS; Act of May 7, 1795, fol. 20, in Trial, OAPC.

lieved were plotting against Spanish rule. He enclosed a copy of the decree, of February 4, 1794, abolishing slavery in all French colonies and giving full citizenship rights to all people of African descent. He pointed out that if France took back the colony, Louisiana's slave owners stood to lose their slaves, their greatest source of wealth. Las Casas urged Carondelet to be more concerned about unrest among the people of African descent than among the whites, because men act out of self-interest, not by what they believe to be just. Therefore, wrote Las Casas, the greatest danger came from the free men of color and the slaves, who knew that the state of abjection in which they saw themselves among the Spanish would change. They would obtain equal citizenship rights under the French, and the slaves would have what they most desired: their freedom. He sent a battalion of Mexican troops and two ships, urging Carondelet to return them as soon as possible because they were sorely needed to defend the coast near Havana from the multitude of corsairs infesting the waters.[4] Spain was moving toward extricating herself from this expensive and troublesome colony. In 1800, she agreed to return Louisiana to France, though the transfer did not formally take place until a month before the United States took control in 1803.

The protective policies of the Spanish crown were still being enunciated in 1800, the year Spain abandoned Louisiana. The civil governor, addressing the Cabildo of New Orleans, stated:

> The petition is asking that the slaves not be heard when they complain of the cruelties inflicted upon them by their masters, that the masters be authorized to oppress and inflict injury on the blacks at their own whims, and even to shoot and kill them if they attempt to run away and fail to halt, as was done in the past; that this be also applicable to the free black people, and that those persons be tolerated who inflict ill-treatment and trample under foot those black people without any investigation or justification of the truth of their disrespect, because they are white. The Spanish government is far from lending its assistance to this chicanery, for it is diametrically opposed by the Sovereign.[5]

Nevertheless, pressure from the slave owners made itself felt among Spanish officials in Louisiana. Carondelet's conversion to the big slave

4. Ernest R. Liljegren, "Jacobinism in Spanish Louisiana, 1792–1797," *LHQ*, XXII (1939), 47–97; Las Casas to Carondelet, two letters dated June 12, 1795 (copy), in Leg. 6929, GM, AS.

5. Nicolas María Vidal, Civil Governor, to the Cabildo of New Orleans, October 21, 1800, in Ronald Rafael Morazan, ed. and trans., "Letters, Petitions, and Decrees of the Cabildo of New Orleans, 1800–1803" (2 vols.; Ph.D. dissertation, Louisiana State University, 1972), II, 203.

owners' point of view is clear from his handling of the case of Don Guido Dreux, a militia captain accused of killing his slave Agata. Dreux claimed that he killed her accidentally. He got up early one morning and found her at an open cabinet from which silver had been missing several times. When he began to scold her, she answered him disrespectfully, walked away from him, and descended the stairs. Dreux flew into a rage and threw "a little sword which he only used for cutting tree branches" after her and, unfortunately, killed her. Zenon Nègre, Agata's fifteen-year-old son, reported the murder. Agata's mulatto daughter Isabel witnessed the murder and took the sword out of her mother's body. Isabel testified that Dreux complained that the cabinet smelled of cockroaches and had reproached her mother for not cleaning it. She denied that her mother was insolent or that her master accused her of lying. Emilia Negra, a nineteen-year-old slave, testified that Agata was always well behaved, fulfilled her duties, and had never been shameless or insolent with her owners. Dreux appealed for leniency, pointing out that he lived in the city with his wife and five children, from whom he had already been separated for two months. If he was punished arbitrarily, no slave would obey his orders when he returned to his house, and this bad example would infest the entire province. Carondelet asked for a pardon for Dreux for this "accident" in return for his freeing Agata's two children, explaining that this would amount to a fine of at least one thousand pesos. He argued that if this honorable citizen was punished for the "accidental" death of his slave Agata, "we will see the disagreeable consequences of the insubordination of his slaves which would quickly ruin him: an example which would extend from one plantation to another, spreading throughout the entire province, putting most of the slaves in a position to attack their masters to obtain by these means what they cannot obtain for themselves." To the credit of the crown of Spain, the king refused to pardon Dreux.[6]

In spite of the wave of repression unleashed by the large slave owners, poor whites, slaves, and free people of African descent continued to socialize freely. The attorney general tried to outlaw dances organized for free people of African descent, despite the strong support for these dances by the officers of the militia units of African descent, on the grounds that "the numbers of slaves of both sexes attending the dances is the same as or larger than the number of free

6. Testimonios, Petition of Don Guido Dreux, December 30, 1796, in Leg. 6820, No. 21, GM, AS; Carondelet to Laguno de Amirola, February 20, 1797, *ibid.*, No. 27; Decision of King, Aranguez, March 25, 1798, *ibid.*, No. 18.

people; that the soldiers, failing in their duties, attend the dances dressed as civilians to disguise themselves and mingle with sailors from galleys and vessels, some of these sailors probably being criminals. To hide this terrible situation, the guards do not permit decent citizens to enter the premises."[7]

The repression unleashed against the people of African descent only strengthened the ties among them. The naturalist C. C. Robin, who visited Louisiana during the first few years of the nineteenth century, described the solidarity among people of African descent of all colors, both slave and free.

> The free men of color participate in these assemblages of slaves as the slaves are admitted to theirs. . . . Thus, free or slave, black or mulatto, they seem to form a single family united in their abjection. Among themselves they display a touching affection. They never approach each other without displaying signs of affection and interest, without asking each other news of their relations, their friends, or their acquaintances. To the best of their ability they try to do each other as much good as they can. They are usually discreet, particularly in those matters that concern white people. When a slave is surprised in a misdemeanor it is rare that he implicates his accomplices. Even the most rigorous punishments do not obtain a confession from him. This mutual affection renders him capable of honorable traits. Those who have earned or found the means to obtain a portion of the sum necessary to buy their precious freedom will be able to borrow the remainder from among those of their color. In buying, they always favor merchants of their own color. I have noticed especially in the city that while the funerals of white people are only attended by a few, those of colored people are attended by a crowd, and mulattoes, quadroons married to white people, do not disdain attending the funeral of a black.[8]

Systematic, racist terror lost its formal, legal limits after Spain abandoned Louisiana. But Louisiana's tradition of racial openness did not die spontaneously. Nor could it ever be completely destroyed. A heavy-handed repression of whites as well as blacks who opposed racism and racist terror was essential to the survival of slavery and subsequent forms of exploitation and repression in Louisiana.

7. Letter from Don Pablo Lanusse, attorney general of the Cabildo, August 14, 1801, in Morazon, "Letters, Petitions, and Decrees," II, 39. See Petition from officers of the Battalions of Octoroons and Quadroons, October 24, 1800, Doc. 367, *ibid.*, 204–10.

8. C. C. Robin, *Voyage to Louisiana, 1803–1805*, trans. Stuart O. Landry, Jr. (New Orleans, 1966), 248.

Basic Facts About All Slave-Trade Voyages from Africa to Louisiana During the French Regime

Ship Name	Num-ber [1]	Ton-nage	Departures	Arrivals
l'Aurore	3115	200	St. Malo 7/1718	
				Cap Lahou 8/28/1718
				Juda 10/18/1718
			Juda 11/30/1718	
				Grenada 3/20/1719
				Louisiana 6/1719
le Duc du Maine	3116	350	St. Malo 8/1718	
				Juda 3/1719
				Grenada 5/8/1719
				Louisiana 6/1719
le Ruby	2468	—	Le Havre 12/1719	
				Senegal 3/19/1720
				Gorée 7/16/1720
				Louisiana 7/16/1720
l'Afriquain	3121	180	La Rochelle 2/3/1720	
				Côte Maniguette 5/12/1720
				Cap Apollonie 5/19/1720
				Juda 7/3/1720
			Juda 8/9/1720	
				Xavier (Juda) 8/11/1720
			Xavier (Juda) 8/26/1720	
				Grenada 12/15/1720
				Biloxi 3/17/1721
le Maréchal d'Estrées	2473	100	Le Havre Senegal 4/9/1721	
				Louisiana 8/11/1721

Basic Facts About Slave-Trade Voyages

No. Slaves Embarked					No. Slaves Landed					Comments
M	W	G	B	Total	M	W	G	B	Total	
				200[2]					201	
									250	
				130[3]					127	
					65	53	35	29	182	15 deaths among crew
				200					196	

(*continued*)

Ship Name	Number[1]	Tonnage	Departures	Arrivals
le Duc du Maine	2851	350	Juda	
				Grenada 12/20/1720
				Biloxi 3/23/1721
le Néréide	2041	250	La Rochelle 4/1720	
				Cabinda 10/1720
				Grenada 2/6/1721
				Biloxi 4/20/or 22/1721
le Fortuné	2853	—	[Lorient?]	
				Juda
				Grenada 3/18/1721
				Biloxi 6/10/1721
l'Expédition	2478	100	Le Havre 10/10/1722	
			Gorée 6/13/1723	
				Biloxi 9/23/1723
				New Orleans 10/12/1723
le Courrier de Bourbon	2859	130	Lorient	
				Senegal 5/1/1723
			Senegal 5/9/1723	
				Gambia 5/30/1723
			Gambia 6/29/1723	
				Gorée 7/5/1723
			Gorée 7/28/1723	
				Grenada 9/17/1723
			Grenada 10/4/1723	
				Balize 11/1/1723

Basic Facts About Slave-Trade Voyages

No. Slaves Embarked					No. Slaves Landed					Comments
M	W	G	B	Total	M	W	G	B	Total	
					181	121	37	37	349[4]	11 deaths among crew
					116	66	26	86	294	11 deaths among crew
					205	64	11	23	303	
				100		67	20	1	91	5 slaves left sick in Biloxi; 2 died
60	40			100, plus 4 or 5 infants[3]					87	Left Gambia with 55 adults, plus 4 or 5 infants; sold 2 adults and 1 infant in Grenada. 13 dead of illnesses; 1 executed

(continued)

Ship Name	Number [1]	Tonnage	Departures	Arrivals
la Mutine	2890	260	Lorient 5/30/1725	
				Senegal 9/5/1725
				Gorée 10/8/1725
			Gorée 10/12/1725	
				Bissau 10/17/1725
			Bissau 11/26/1725	
				Grenada
				Biloxi 1726
l'Aurore	2883	200	Lorient 4/3/1725	
				Gorée 8/24/1725
				Joal 10/1725
			Joal 12/16/1725	
				Grenada 1/13/1726
				Louisiana 3/29/1726
l'Annibal	2897	218	Lorient 1/30/1726	
				Senegal 2/26/1726
			Senegal 6/10/1726	
				Le Cap 12/26/1726
			Le Cap 2/27/1727	
				Balize 4/1727
le Prince de Conti	2900	300	Lorient 10/20/1726	
				Senegal 11/17/1726
			Senegal 1/31/1727	
				Gorée 1/31/1727
			Gorée 2/5/1727	
				Albreda (Gambia) 2/25/1727
			Gambia 5/29/1727	
			Gorée 6/3/1727	
				Martinique 7/11/1727

Basic Facts About Slave-Trade Voyages

No. Slaves Embarked					No. Slaves Landed					Comments
M	W	G	B	Total	M	W	G	B	Total	
95	94	2	46	235[5]	91	79		43	213	8 slaves died en route to Grenada, 5 at Grenada, 5 to Louisiana. 2 men, 2 women sold at Grenada. 1 sailor died at Bissau, 10/27/1725, 6 died at sea. Crew of 66. Captain: La Clisse
				350					290	22 slaves died en route to Grenada. 4 deaths among crew of 54 or 55. 4 desertions at Grenada Captain: Sicard
										12 deaths among crew of 70. Captain: Du Moulin
				300[3]					266	Left Martinique with 296 blacks. 3 deaths among crew of 70. Captain died of scurvy at Le Cap, 8/4/1727. 5 desertions. Captain: La Forte Maison, then Tredillac

(continued)

Ship Name	Number[1]	Tonnage	Departures	Arrivals
				Martinique 7/11/1727
			Martinique 7/12/1727	
				Le Cap 7/19/1727
			Le Cap 8/28/1727	
				Balize 9/21/1727
le Duc de Noaille	2901	250	Lorient 5/5/1727	
				Senegal 6/6/1727
				Gorée 7/27/1727
			Gorée 10/15/1727	
				Senegal 10/21/1727
			Senegal 11/15/1727	
				Caye St. Louis 12/25/1727
			Caye St. Louis 1/27/1728	
				Balize 2/12/1728
la Diane	2902	300	Lorient 10/27/1727	
			Juda 5/1728	
				St. Domingue Balize 10/11/1728
la Venus	2903	300	Lorient 2/9/1728	
				Senegal 3/1/1728
			Senegal 3/27/1728	
				Gorée 3/28/1728
			Gorée 4/21/1728	
				Balize 6/15/1728

No. Slaves Embarked					No. Slaves Landed					Comments
M	W	G	B	Total	M	W	G	B	Total	
				350					262	Left Senegal with 347 blacks; 3 embarked at St. Domingue. Left 18 sick at Caye St. Louis. 5 deaths among crew of 63; 1 passenger died. Captain: Dupuis
				516					464	10 deaths among 63 crew. Captain: Chevalier de Tourneville, then Cochart de Boissy
				350[3]					341	5 black women, 1 black man, and 14 infants died at sea. 3 deaths among 60 crew. Captain: La Renaudais

(continued)

Ship Name	Number [1]	Tonnage	Departures	Arrivals
la Flore	2904	280	Lorient 3/18/1728	
				Cap Sainte-Anne 4/13/1728
			Cap Sainte-Anne 5/6/1728	
				Senegal 5/10/1728
			Senegal 6/13/1728	
			Gorée 6/18/1728	
la Galathée	2905	300	Lorient 5/27/1728	
				Senegal 6/27/1728
			Senegal 9/26/1728	
				Gorée 10/4/1728
			Gorée 10/21/1728	
				St. Louis 11/29/1728
			St. Louis 12/13/1728	
				Balize 1/18/1729
			Balize 2/1/1729	
				New Orleans 2/23/1729
la Venus	2909	300	Lorient 2/4/1729	
				Senegal 2/26/1729
			Senegal 3/20/1729	
				Gorée 3/21/1729
			Gorée 4/16/1729	
				Balize 6/17/1729

Basic Facts About Slave-Trade Voyages

No. Slaves Embarked					No. Slaves Landed					Comments
M	W	G	B	Total	M	W	G	B	Total	
350	40	10		400[3]					356	Went up Mississippi River to just below Natchez. 4 deaths among 58–60 crew. Captain: Butler
				400[3]					273[6]	Left 45 sick blacks in St. Louis; arrived at New Orleans with 260 blacks. Left New Orleans for Leogane, 9/1729. 11 deaths, 2 desertions among 56-57 crew. Captain: Preville Quinette
				450[3]					363[6]	Left Senegal with at least 101 blacks, all landed at Gorée. Landed 320 blacks at New Orleans. 2 deaths among 57 or 61 crew. Captain: La Renaudais

(continued)

Ship Name	Number[1]	Tonnage	Departures	Arrivals
l'Annibal[7]	2908	200	Lorient 2/4/1729	
				Senegal 2/28/1729
			Senegal 4/12/1729	
				Gorée 4/14/1729
			Gorée 4/23/1729	
				Gambia 4/28/1729
			Gambia 5/24/1729 Revolt 5/26/1729 Gambia 5/27/1729	
				Caye St. Louis 7/9/1729
le Duc de Bourbon	2910	200	Lorient 5/21/1729	
				Senegal 6/26/1729
			Senegal 7/27/1729	
				Gorée 7/31/1729
			Gorée 8/30/1729	
				Caye St. Louis 10/16/1729
			Caye St. Louis 11/7/1729	
				Louisiana
le St. Louis	2911	250	Lorient 7/10/1729	
				Senegal 8/10/1729
			Senegal 10/7/1729	
				Gorée 10/13/1729
			Gorée 11/7/1729	
				Portendic (Senegal) 12/18/1729
			Portendic 1/11/1730	
				Gorée 1/12/1730
			Gorée 4/18/1730	

Basic Facts About Slave-Trade Voyages

No. Slaves Embarked					No. Slaves Landed					Comments
M	W	G	B	Total	M	W	G	B	Total	
				300, then 249[8]						Left Gorée with 200 blacks, Gambia (5/24) with 300. Left Gambia (5/27) with 249 blacks. 7 deaths among 45 crew, 4 in slave revolt. Captain: de Kerguenel
				400[3]					319	Arrived in Caye St. Louis with 383 blacks. 1 death among 48 or 53 crew. Captain: La Salle
279	71			350, plus 11 infants					291[6]	102 blacks landed at Martinique, 45 or 48 at Caye St. Louis. 111 blacks, survivors of *la Néréide*, embarked at Caye St. Louis. 6 deaths among crew of 50 or 52. Captain: Breban

(*continued*)

Ship Name	Num-ber [1]	Ton-nage	Departures	Arrivals
				Senegal 4/29/1730
			Senegal 8/12/1730	
				Gorée 8/20/1730
			Gorée 9/14/1730	
				Martinique 10/20/1730
			Martinique 11/14/1730	
				Caye St. Louis 11/30/1730
			Caye St. Louis 12/13/1730	
				Balize 1/21/1731
la Néréide	2913	200 or 250	Lorient	
				Senegal 12/19/1729
			Portendic (Senegal) 7/6/1730	
				Gorée 7/9/1730
			Gorée 7/12/1730	
				Gambia 7/15/1730
			Gambia 7/28/1730	
				Gorée 8/1/1730
			Gorée 9/28/1730	
				Senegal 9/28/1730
			Senegal 10/10 or 15/1730	
				Caye St. Louis 11/20/1730
			Caye St. Louis 12/23/1730	

No. Slaves Embarked					No. Slaves Landed					Comments
M	W	G	B	Total	M	W	G	B	Total	
				200, plus 3 in- fants[9]					72 (or 50)[10]	Left Gambia (7/28/1730) with 200 blacks plus a little boy. Left Gorée (9/28/1730) with 94 blacks. Embarked 111 blacks at Caye St. Louis to take to Louisiana, then returned to France. 11 or 17 deaths among 39 or 42 crew. Captain: Dentuly, then Alexandre de Billy

(continued)

Ship Name	Num- ber [1]	Ton- nage	Departures	Arrivals
le St. Ursin	2170	80	La Rochelle 3/2/1743	Gorée 5/7/1743
			Gorée 6/5/1743	
				Louisiana 8/23/1743

SOURCE: Jean Mettas, *Autres Ports* (Paris, 1984), Vol. II of *Répertoire des expéditions négrières françaises au XVIIIième siècle,* ed. Serge and Michelle Daget.

1. Ship numbers are all from Mettas, *Autres Ports.*
2. From Juda.
3. From Gorée.
4. Since the sex of nursing infants was not recorded, discrepancies sometimes occur between the breakdown for men, women, girls, and boys and the total number landed.
5. From Bissau.
6. At Balize.
7. Incorrectly listed by Taillemite as *l'Amiral.*
8. From Gambia.
9. From Senegal.
10. At St. Domingue.

Basic Facts About Slave-Trade Voyages

No. Slaves Embarked					No. Slaves Landed					Comments
M	W	G	B	Total	M	W	G	B	Total	
				220					190	Voyage sponsored by Dalcourt and Dubreuil. Captain: Gaultier

African Nations of Slaves Accused of Crimes in Records of the Superior Council of Louisiana

July 8, 1729: One Bambara

Biron, a Bambara slave coming off *l'Aurore*, was accused of running away and grabbing the gun of his master after having been recaptured. Samba Bambara served as interpreter.

Heloise H. Cruzat, "Trial and Sentence of Biron, Runaway Negro Slave, Before the Superior Council of Louisiana, 1728," RSC, *LHQ*, VIII (1925), 23–27.

September 5, 1729: Three Bambara

Nègre Changereau, Bambara by nation, aged about twenty, ran away with three fellow slaves because he was underfed. Manade's *nègre* killed a heifer, and Changereau ate some of the meat. Pierot, Bambara by nation, aged about twenty-seven or twenty-eight, slave of Dalby, ran away because he was too sick to work and was afraid of punishment. He helped kill "young beast" and stole some corn. Sabany, Bambara, about thirty years old, slave of Vielanille, had not run away, but the others gave him meat.

Henry P. Dart, ed., "Criminal Procedure for Killing Cattle," RSC, *LHQ*, IV (1921), 348.

September 27, 1729: One Bambara

Bambara Malama, belonging to Trudeau, was accused of persistent violent threats against his master and mistress.

RSC, LHC.

December 15, 1738: One Bambara

Delalande Dalcour reported the disappearance of a Bambara slave, belonging to the Delachaise estate, who had been missing for three weeks. The slave could be recognized by a gunshot in his right thigh, which he had received about six months earlier.

RSC, *LHQ*, VI (1923), 284.

December 29, 1739: One Bambara

Report of the now-suspicious absence of Bambara T—, sent in pursuit of another black who had since returned.

RSC, *LHQ*, VII (1924), 522.

January 16, 1741: One Biefada

Pierrot, of the Biefada nation, about thirty years old and baptized, ran away because he was put in irons and wrongly accused of stealing.

RSC, *LHQ*, X (1927), 567.

January 16, 1741: Two Bambara, three Samba
Report of runaways: Denny of Samba nation, aged fifty; Sans Peur, Bambara nation, aged thirty; La Richer, Bambara nation, aged twenty-five; l'Eveillé, Samba nation, aged thirty; Bambara of Samba nation, aged twenty-seven.
RSC, *LHQ*, X (1927), 567.

January 4, 1742: One Sango
Jasmin, twenty-five-year-old slave of the Sango nation, was accused of attacking a French soldier at Natchez.
RSC, *LHQ*, XI (1928), 288–92.

September 10, 1743: One Wolof (Senegal)
Interrogation of Pantalon, Free Senegal [Wolof] *nègre* aged thirty-five, accused of stealing.
RSC, *LHQ*, XII (1929), 145–47.

December 7, 1743: Two Bambara, one Fon
Report by Jacques Larche of four runaway slaves: Malborough, of the Bambara nation, about thirty years old; another Bambara, about twenty-eight years old; Michel, of Fonda [Fon] nation, about forty-five years old.
RSC, *LHQ*, XII (1929), 489.

March 13, 1744: One Wolof (Senegal)
Interrogation of Alexandre, a Senegal *nègre* owned by Leoteau, accused of theft.
RSC, *LHQ*, XII (1929), 674.

August 3, 1746: One Bambara
Master reported flight of a Bambara named Sans Peur [without fear] from New Orleans.
RSC, LHC.

January 5, 1748: One Bambara
Pierrot was accused of being an accomplice in a murder.
RSC, LHC.

February 7, May 4, 1748: One Fulbe
A slave named Baraca, of the Poulard nation, murdered his wife, Tacó, by hitting her on the head with a log.
RSC, LHC.

June 9, 1748: One Bambara
Joseph, aged about thirty and a Dubreuil slave, was accused of theft. The charge was vigorously denied by him and by his master.
RSC, *LHQ*, XIX (1936), 1091–94.

June 9, 1748: Two Bambara
Two Bambara, Mamourou and Bayou, neither baptized, both in their forties, were runaways from the Illinois country, heading downriver for New Orleans.

RSC, *LHQ*, XIX (1936), 1094–96.

March 26, 1752: One Bambara
Thomas, Bambara, aged twenty-five, was accused of stealing. He had been in Martinique and was arrested in New Orleans.

RSC, LHC.

Slaves Found in Pointe Coupee Inventories Between 1771 and 1802: Breakdown by Origin, Nation, Sex, and Percentage in Population

Table 1. Grand Totals

	% of Total	M	F	Total	Sex Index
Africans	39.4	684	353	1,037	1.94
Local Creoles	43.8	644	509	1,153	1.27
Imported Creoles	5.3	75	64	139	1.17
Unidentified Nations	11.5	132	171	303	0.77
TOTAL		1,535	1,097		1.40

SOURCE: DB Inventories.

Table 2. Nations of 798 Slaves Whose Region of Origin in Africa Has Been Identified

	M	F	Total	% of Slaves from Region	Sex Index
Senegambia (27.1% of total) *Nations*					
Bambara	49	5	54	25.0	9.80
Maninga	49	20	69	31.9	2.50
Poulard (Fulbe)	17	2	19	8.8	8.50
Senegal (Wolof)	25	35	60	27.8	0.71
Nard	11	3	15	6.9	3.70
Total	151	65	216		2.32
Sierra Leone (1.8% of total) *Nations*					
Kissy	5	2	7	50.0	2.50
Thoma	1	0	1	7.1	—
Timbo	4	2	6	42.9	2.00
Total	10	4	14		2.50

(*continued*)

	M	F	Total	% of Slaves from Region	Sex Index
Windward Coast (3.9% of total) *Nations*					
Canga	17	13	30	96.8	1.31
Gola	0	1	1	3.25	—
Total	17	14	31		1.21
Gold Coast (1.3% of total) *Nations*					
Coromanti	8	1	9	90.0	8.00
Cote d'Or	1	0	1	10.0	—
Total	9	1	10		9.00
Bight of Benin (28.7% of total) *Nations*					
Adó	13	13	26	11.4	1.00
Chamba	23	23	46	20.1	1.00
Fon	19	20	39	17.0	0.95
Hausa	6	0	6	0.7	—
Mina	42	12	54	23.6	3.50
Yoruba (Nago)	37	21	58	25.3	1.80
Total	140	89	229		1.57
Bight of Biafra (11.5% of total) *Nations*					
Caraba	21	13	34	37.4	1.62
Ibo	23	35	58	63.7	0.66
Moko	0	1	1	1.1	—
Total	44	48	92		0.92
Central Africa (23.8% of total) *Nations*					
Congo	114	59	173	91.1	1.93
Angola	13	5	18	9.5	2.60
Sango	1	0	1	0.5	—
Total	126	64	190		1.97
Mozambique (2.0% of total) *Nation*					
Makwa	5	11	16	2.0	0.45

SOURCE: DB Inventories.

Table 3.   Slaves of African Nations Listed but Unidentified

	Male	Female
Augta		1
Aya		1
Barary		1
Bioco	1	
Boco	1	
Bococo	2	
Bougy	1	
Bouqui	1	
Canare	1	
Cenare	1	
Colangua	1	
Corri	1	
Delus	1	
Fongy	1	
Gabon	1	
Gibon	2	
Gusi	1	
Hanga	1	
Hisucon	1	
Heriqui	3	
Hotango	2	
Macona		1
Malaba	1	
Manat		1
Noion	1	
Nolo	1	
Oucis	1	
Tipida	1	
Worre	1	
Yoco	1	
Zobo	10	
Zoucou	2	

SOURCE: DB Inventories.
NOTE: The rest of the Africans in the inventories were identified simply as coming from Africa or Guinea, or as *brut* or *bruto*.

Table 4. Breakdown of Imported Creoles By Place of Birth

	Male	Female	Total	Sex Index
Bermuda	1		1	
Carolina	24	21	45	1.14
Curaçao	1		1	
Dalia	1		1	
Des Isles		1	1	
English	9	4	13	2.25
Georgia	1	2	3	0.50
Illinois	1	1	2	1.00
Jamaica	9	4	13	2.25
Kentucky	1		1	
Martinique	2		2	
New Orleans	1	1	2	1.00
N. America		1	1	
N. Carolina	5	2	7	2.50
Opelousas		1	1	
St. Domingue	3		3	
St. Augustine	1		1	
Virginia	14	23	37	0.61
Pennsylvania		1	1	
U.S.A.	1	2	3	0.50

SOURCE: DB Inventories.

Evidence of Widespread Survival of African Names in Colonial Louisiana

A few slaves retained African names in pure, but usually reinterpreted, form on the Anglo–North American continent. But in colonial Louisiana, African names in their pure form were used extensively. Listed here are samples of African names encountered in documents throughout the colonial period. Both African and French names found in the inventory of the Nègres du Roy, dating from 1760, are included to illustrate the high proportion of African names on this inventory from very late in the French period. The highest proportion of French names was at Mobile. Many of the names from Louisiana are Islamic, and some of the French names, including women's names, have the suffix *Baraca*, an Islamic religious title. Islamic names do not necessarily mean that these slaves were Muslims, because Islamic names had been widespread in Senegambia since the rise of the Almoravides Empire during the eleventh century. But the use of the Islamic religious title Baraca is harder to explain. It might have simply meant someone who was recognized as a spiritual leader. It is common to encounter slaves whose official names were French but whose nicknames were African. They and other slaves who testified in court referred to them by their African, not their French, names.

1727

Choucoura (m).
July 20, 1727, in RSC, *LHQ*, IV (1921), 224.

1729

Combasla (f).
May 28, 1729, in RSC, *LHQ*, IV (1921), 334.
Changereau, Bambara by nation.
September 5, 1729, in RSC, *LHQ*, IV (1921), 348.
Sabany Bambara, Bambara by nation, aged twenty-seven or twenty-eight, ate fresh meat but was not marooning.
September 5, 1729, in RSC, *LHQ*, IV (1921), 348.

1736

Amadit, Poulard (Fulbe) nation.
August 10, 1736, in RSC, *LHQ*, V (1922), 383.
Sandigue.
September 17, 1736, in RSC, *LHQ*, VIII (1925), 497.

1737

Guela, aged about thirty, not baptized, "speaks good French," ran away to the cypress swamp.
January 4, 10, 12, 1737, in RSC, *LHQ*, V (1922), 386–88.
Diocou, a free black.

June 28, 1737, in RSC, *LHQ*, V (1922), 401.
Pierre Almansor, a free black, contracted with physician of the king for treatment of venereal disease in return for service as cook or other work, except for wielding an ax or working the ground, to begin after he was cured.
March 2, 1737, in RSC, *LHQ*, IX (1926), 115.

1737–38

Male names, from Inventory of Slaves:
Aqua, Boress, Gouyat (twelve years old), Niat, Gollias, Nea Bambara, Charcola, Fadiguy, Bocary, Papa, Quatio, Atchoupa, Gaza, Houlou, Kiflo, Sivry, Duban, Mary Couellon, Congo, Gribouille, Anat, Baye, Samba, Dozon, Nonion Payemain, Falgure, Chocola, Dayee, Gampé.
Female names, from Inventory of Slaves:
Pinda, Acria, Bayoc, Comba Nea, Naninne, Comba Fadiguy, Ragoude, Fatima, Aguimita, Adigune, Calot, Cosqoage, Ouyet, Jeccabane, Comba Guy, Soudo, Prinda Sivry, Quiame, Gomba Duban, Anat, Medioza, Comba.
Heloise H. Cruzat, trans., Inventory of Slaves, in "Documents Concerning Slave of Chaouaches Plantation in Louisiana, 1727–1738," *LHQ*, VIII (1925), 628–31.

1738

Sangarot, a male slave on a lease of four slaves, including one couple.
March 4, 1738, in RSC, *LHQ*, IX (1926), 729.

1739

Death of slave Fatima, wife of Samba, "from the effects of a burn, occasioned by her falling into the fire, whilst in one of her usual attacks."
March 22, 1739, in RSC, *LHQ*, VI (1923), 310.
Death of black named Sambaya, while under treatment for smallpox.
May 15, 1739, in RSC, *LHQ*, VI (1923), 505.

1740

Bradiguine (f). Sold from the plantation of the king.
March 23, 1740, in RSC, *LHQ*, X (1927), 272.

1744

Declaration of death of Goujon (m).
April 15, 1744, in RSC, *LHQ*, XIII (1930), 131.
The slave Jupiter dit Gamelle was convicted of breaking in and burglary and was sentenced to ordinary torture and hanging.
March 21, 1744, in RSC, *LHQ*, XIII (1930), 120–23.

1745

Yacine (f) ran away.
March 8, 1745, in RSC, *LHQ*, XIII (1930), 95.

1747

Tertaguet and Sambas ran away.
February 18, 1747, in RSC, *LHQ*, XVII (1934), 381.
Guibela, Gagnin and his wife, Habeny, Daoueys, Nianga, Zenon (a boy), and Souman.
Complete list of names of slaves on a lease. April 5, 1747, in RSC, *LHQ*, XVIII (1935), 162.

1748

Kakaracou, a creole slave, not baptized, described himself as a member of the Coneda nation. Doffy, Gengrou, Moussa, and Caffou mentioned by a Bambara slave during his interrogation.
January 4–12, 1748, in RSC, LHC.
Baraca, Poulard (Fulbe) nation, murdered his wife, Tacó. They were both slaves of the king. Their *commandeur* was named Flatagué. The slave who witnessed the murder was named Laourfa. Although all the documents described the murderer as simply Baraca, he identified himself as François dit Baraca.
February 7, May 4, 1748, in RSC, LHC.

1758

Names from Inventory of Estate of Joseph Dubreuil: Holo Dalcoro, an old *nègre*; Comba, wife of François; Mangaye, a *nègre*; Akia, an old *négresse*; Ongué, wife of Joly Coeur; Jarry, a *nègre*; Marie Gaolo, a *négresse*; Phady, a *nègre*; Mamouzou [Mamarou, Mohammed?], a *nègre*; Choucanne, wife of Scipion; Louis Guiguia and Déla, his wife; Sénégal, a *nègre*; Mozongué, an old *nègre*; Zongué, a *nègre*; Tauitar, an old *nègre*, and his wife, Adoux [Adó?]; Bobo, a *nègre*; Vitout, wife of Pierrot; Boguio, wife of François, who was sold with her husband and her mother-in-law; Yoyo, a *nègre*; Dolé and Bossi, his blind wife; Gottet, a *nègre*; Guesó, a *nègre*; Nata, sold with his wife and daughter; Holococo, old *nègre*; Chamba La Forge [the blacksmith]; Guiodou, a *nègre*; Kiakia, a *négresse*; Rosumé Kiabé, an old *négresse*; Malva, a *nègre*; Carithon, a *nègre*; Boffa, sold with his wife; Nomaque and Bouqui, his wife, sold with their son; Azada, sold with her husband and son; Nago and Mahon, his wife; Fatterma [Fatima, daughter of Mohammed?], a *négresse*; Doua, a *nègre*; Yaounou, a *nègre*; Sambas, a *nègre*; Jacob Tolli, a *nègre*; Nionion Françoise, sold with her son; Fanchon, sold with her two children; Tolly, an old *nègre*; Troutouby, sold with his wife; Faguio, sold with his wife, Coüda, and his daughter; Paugio, a little boy; Gueba, sold with her two children; Pha, a *nègre*; Dede, a *négresse*; Sercandier, sold with his wife; Guinauk, sold with her husband; Tenay, sold with her two children; Boulanguier, sold with his wife and two children; Jean Gauza and his wife Fanchon.
Succession Sale of the Estate of Dubreuil, in Henry P. Dart, "The Career of Dubreuil in French Louisiana," *LHQ*, XVIII (1935), 291–331.

1760

Complete List of Names of the *Nègres du Roy:*
at the estate of the king—Lataguay *commandeur* (m); Dianguenet (m); Beimba (m); Salanguay (m); Quiquo (m); Mamary (m); Pierrot (m).

at the storehouse—Jacques; Niaman (m); Goldron (m); Pierrot Patey (m); Deimba (m).

at the hospital—Baptiste; Nicolas, for the record; Jacques; Louison; Jeanneton, for the record; Marie Joseph.

at the workshop—Guillaume; Barrilo (m); Quebled (m).

at the prison—Gros Jean; Etienne.

at the commissary—Jean Baptiste Baraca; St. Pierre Baraca; Baptiste Patey (m); Jean fils de Jeannot; Joseph Gou; Louis fils de Bernard; Izalle Goldron (f); Thérèse; Marie Baraca; Genneviève.

at the government—Louis fils de Jeannot; Cathine fille.

at M. Belisle's—Michel, for the record; Joseph, for the record; Mamaroux, the executioner (m).

at M. Goudon's—Marie Thérèse; Magdelaine Negritte.

at Balize—Sara Boulanger (m); Moreau (m); Dombe, his wife; Moquet (m); La Moquet, his wife.

at Mobile—Ceriba; Marie Joseph; Jeanneton; Jeannette; Jeanne; Boucary; Genneviève; François Baraca; Marguerite; Françoise; Jacqueline; Luy; Marie.

négrillons—Pierre; Augustin; Jean Baptiste.

female slaves—Codou, Faiment Dianguenet; Grande Catherine; Comba; Jassongol; Fatiment Bonneayu; Bougoument; Lisette; Acouba; Marianne Motrille; Fanchon Patey; Suzon; Marie Falangay; Suzanne Congo; Angelique.

sick—Molon Gonis (m); Laourseau (m); Noton Natchez (m); Charles.
Etat des nègres, négresses, négrillons et négrittes du Roy, January 1760, in Ser. C13A 42, fols. 66–67, ANC.

1762

Soumat (m); Daouin (m); Boucary Le Grand; Sabary (m); Momu (f).
January 21, 1762, Judicial Sale, Gregoire Volant Succession, in RSC, *LHQ,* XXII (1940), 597–602.

1769

Sembas the blacksmith, aged 70, shepherd; Gnia-Ouy, crippled, aged 60; Jacquine, his wife, aged 75; Senegal, a digger, aged 60; Combas (f), aged 58; Sambas, aged 70; Langue, wife of Sambas, aged 68; Cossa (m), aged 75; Sarcandier (m), aged 70; wife Marie Anne, aged 60; Bossa, blacksmith, aged 56; Guems (m), aged 45; Almensor (m), aged 30; Malva (m), aged 65.
Inventory of the Estate of Jean Baptiste Prévost, Deceased Agent of the Company of the Indies, July 13, 1769, *LHQ* IX (1926), 411–98.

1771–1802

African names of Mande slaves (Bambara and Maninga) at the Pointe Coupee post:

males—Seniba, Bara, Dimba, Semba, Chatigni, Farrar, Samba, Atis, Sarra, Bara, Bambara, Bambara, Coffy, Agi, Dorguer, Maga, Saguoin, Botta, Timba, Raizno, Ocole, Soinquatie, Guerey, Nequi, Sambo, Keloi, Barra, Bucary, Roque.

female—Demba.

Note on Sources

During the past two decades, American historians have begun to pay serious attention to the crucial, formative period of slavery and race relations in the English colonies that became part of the United States. Beginning with Peter H. Wood's *Black Majority: Negroes in Colonial South Carolina from 1670 Through the Stono Rebellion* (New York, 1974), a study of colonial South Carolina, there has been a shift toward treating slavery within the context of time, place, and circumstance. In "Time, Space, and the Evolution of Afro-American Society on British Mainland North America," *American Historical Review*, LXXXV (1980), 44–78, Ira Berlin has criticized historical scholarship since World War II for focusing upon the mature phase of slavery in the antebellum South, promoting an essentially static vision. He discussed diverse development in three regions—the north, the Chesapeake, and the Carolina and Georgia low country—during the seventeenth and eighteenth centuries, identifying varying patterns of the slave trade, proportions between whites and blacks, and the labor demands of particular export crops as crucial factors shaping the formation of the particular slave culture of each region. Those readers familiar with this writer's first book, *Social Control in Slave Plantation Societies: A Comparison of St. Domingue and Cuba* (Baltimore, 1971), will be aware that she treats slavery, not as the same institution in all times and places, but as a dynamic system that responded to changes in the population and the economy as well as in the *raison d'être* of the colony.

Although Louisiana has been and is a vital stream feeding the formation of American society and culture, its history during the eighteenth century has been badly neglected. Africans and Afro-Creoles of eighteenth-century Louisiana have largely been ignored. There are practical reasons for this neglect. The documentation is scattered throughout archives in France, Spain, and Louisiana and is sometimes quite hard to read. The documents are hand written, the handwriting changes often, the spelling is only approximate, and the documents are often faded and torn. While the amount of existing documentation for the French period is almost manageable, some of it is extremely difficult to read. The documentation for the Spanish period is massive and little explored. Administrative documents for the Spanish period are, of course, mainly in Spanish, though many notarial and rural administrative documents are in French. For the American period throughout most of the nineteenth century and into the early twentieth century, many of the documents are still in French.

Note on Sources

Published and translated documents cannot be relied upon. There are several collections of published documents for Louisiana history during the eighteenth century. Pierre Margry, *Découvertes et établissements des Français dans l'ouest et dans le sud de l'Amérique septentrionale (1614–1754): Mémoires et documents originaux* (6 vols.; Paris, 1876–86), deals mainly with discovery and early colonization. Two volumes focus on Louisiana, but Africans, slavery, and Afro-Creoles are hardly mentioned. The location of the original documents is omitted, and accuracy in transcription has been challenged. Benjamin French published five volumes of documents translated into English: *Historical Collections of Louisiana and Florida* (5 vols.; New York, 1846–53). A few of these documents discuss slaves and slavery, but they are quite inaccurate. In *The Jesuit Relations and Allied Documents: Travels and Explorations of the Jesuit Missionaries in New France, 1610–1791* (Cleveland, 1896–1901), Vols. LIX and LXVII of 73 vols., Reuben Gold Thwaites, ed., published an extensive set of English translations of French Jesuit documents, but the volumes dealing with colonial Louisiana contain little about Africans, Afro-Creoles, or black slavery. Le Page du Pratz, *Histoire de la Louisiane* (3 vols.; Paris, 1758), is very useful in the original French edition. The English translation, Le Page du Pratz, *The History of Louisiana*, facsimile reproduction of the 1774 British edition, ed. Joseph Tregle, Jr. (Baton Rouge, 1975), is condensed and leaves out some of the most precious material. The first three volumes of Dunbar Rowland and A. G. Sanders, eds. and trans., *Mississippi Provincial Archives* (3 vols.; Jackson, Miss., 1919–32), are useful, but many of the documents are not complete but fragmentary. The material is, of course, filtered through the eyes of the editors not only by their selection of documents and fragments of documents to be translated but also by the translation itself. There is an improvement in both the completeness and the quality of the documents selected in Patricia Kay Galloway, ed., and Dunbar Rowland and A. G. Sanders, eds. and trans., *Mississippi Provincial Archives* (Baton Rouge, 1984), Vols. IV and V. All the documents in *Mississippi Provincial Archives* come from the Archives Nationales in Paris, Series C13, Correspondence à l'arrivée en provenance de la Louisiane, a series that has long been available on microfilm in several depositories in the United States. The documents are in good condition and quite legible. It is important to consult the original documents—a task greatly facilitated by the excellent inventory published by the Archives Nationales in Paris, Marie-Antoinette Menier, Etienne Taillemite, and Gilberte de Forges, *Correspondance à l'arrivée en provenance de la Louisiane* (2 vols.; Paris, 1976, 1983). The staff was kind enough to allow me to consult the original documents.

The *Louisiana Historical Quaterly*, I–XXXIII (January, 1917–October, 1950), has published extensive translations of French and Spanish documents and fragments of documents into English. See Heloise H. Cruzat, trans., "Records of the Superior Council of Louisiana," *Louisiana Historical Quarterly*, II–XXII (1918–39), and Laura L. Porteus, trans., "Index to the Spanish Judicial Records of Louisiana," *Louisiana Historical Quarterly*, VI–XXXI (1923–48).

These are useful for the study of Africans and Afro-Creoles in colonial Louisiana. Several longer documents have been translated and published in full in this excellent journal. A useful index has been published. See Boyd Cruise, *Index to the "Louisiana Historical Quarterly"* (New Orleans, 1956). The scope of these indices and translations is broad ranging and can serve as a guide to a careful study of these sometimes extremely difficult documents. But they should not be heavily relied upon because of omissions and inaccuracies, especially in the most sensitive and the least legible documents. There has been an all-too-human tendency to omit what the translator does not expect and to read into them what the translator expects. The index to the Spanish judicial records does not go beyond March, 1785. All of these translations, except for volumes IV and V of the *Mississippi Provincial Archives*, were published many years ago, when the interests of historians focused upon discovery, conquest, politics, warfare, administration, biography, and genealogy. The original documents are a treasure for contemporary scholars, containing rich material for social history, family history, ethnic history, women's history, demographic history, maritime history, and creole linguistics. The original documents are housed at the Louisiana Historical Center of the Louisiana State Museum in New Orleans, but they have become nearly inaccessible. Although many of the documents have been microfilmed, even the originals are extremely hard to read, and microfilm copies are daunting for even the most dedicated researcher. Unfortunately, there are very serious problems at this collection. These unique, irreplaceable documents, housed in the old mint, are not kept in a climate-controlled environment but are subjected to the 80 percent humidity prevailing in the building. The collection is open three days a week, by appointment only. The staff has been deprofessionalized. A calendaring project funded by the National Endowment for the Humanities during the 1970s created more problems than it solved. The documents were microfilmed before calendaring began. For the French period, documents referring to the same case are scattered under the date generated by the particular document. The French documents were only calendared through 1734, and the Spanish through 1789. The Spanish documents were better organized to begin with, but the Louisiana Historical Center has not had a copy of the Spanish calendar, that has been partially completed under the National Endowment for the Humanities project since 1982. They only have old finding guides that do not conform with the dating system under which the documents were refiled by the National Endowment for the Humanities project. Many, if not most, of the documents are either unfindable or missing. There are no finding guides, either old or new, after 1789. A project to calendar the map collection was not completed either. No one seems to know what the total collection actually contains. Original Audubon prints were not missed after they were stolen by a volunteer. The theft was discovered only after the police returned the prints. Conditions prevailing at this collection are clearly the greatest obstacle to the possibility of future historical research on colonial Louisiana.

Note on Sources

Since the publication of Philip D. Curtin's pioneering book *The Atlantic Slave Trade. A Census* (Madison, Wis., 1969), a great deal of attention has been paid to quantitative studies of this trade. For the French slave trade of the eighteenth century, American scholars, including Curtin, have relied upon the works of Gaston Martin, *Nantes au XVIIIième siècle: l'ere des négriers* (Paris, 1931), and of Dieudonné Rinchon, *La Traite des congolais par les Européens* (Brussels, 1929), *Les armements négrier au XVIIIième siècle* (Brussels, 1956), *Pierre-Ignace-Liéven van Alstein, capitaine négrier* (Dakar, 1964), who studied only voyages from Nantes, and by no means all of them. The French slave trade during the eighteenth century has long been associated almost exclusively with Nantes. But generalizations based upon the African slave trade from Nantes can be misleading. Most slave-trade voyages left from other ports. Any study of the French slave trade during the eighteenth century must begin with the two-volume, posthumous work of Jean Mettas, *Nantes* (Paris, 1978) and *Autres Ports* (Paris, 1984), Vols. I and II of Mettas, *Répertoire des expéditions négrières françaises au XVIIIième siècle*, ed. Serge and Michelle Daget. This work lists basic facts about every slave-trade voyage leaving from every French port during this century, gives important, well-organized, and uniform data, and is, in general, more accurate than Rinchon. David Eltis has computerized the Mettas study. Studies based upon Mettas might significantly alter the conclusions thus far drawn about the eighteenth-century French slave trade.

Not one slave-trade voyage to Louisiana left from Nantes. The voluminous studies based upon Martin and Rinchon hold somewhat limited relevance for Louisiana except to suggest questions of general interest to historians of the slave trade. But these questions can best be answered by a close, multifaceted study utilizing a much broader range of documents than quantitatively oriented historians tend to use. Studies of mortality during the Atlantic slave trade, which have been based upon almost purely quantitative data, have been thoroughly superceded by the rich approach of Joseph C. Miller, *Way of Death: Merchant Capitalism and the Angolan Slave Trade, 1730–1830* (Madison, Wis., 1988). Almost all the slave-trade voyages from Africa to Louisiana left from and returned to Lorient, the port of the Company of the Indies. The archives of the Port of Lorient contains documents about each voyage. The documents of *armement* and *désarmement* contain passenger lists as well as lists of merchandise brought back to France. N. M. Miller Surrey's study, *The Commerce of Louisiana During the French Regime, 1699–1763* (1916; New York, 1968), is still very useful, though there are mistakes about the first few years of the African slave trade to Louisiana, and in general, her sources could have been broadened. John G. Clark's *New Orleans, 1718–1812: An Economic History* (Baton Rouge, 1970), is interesting but, unfortunately, undocumented. Any study of trade and commerce to French Louisiana should not neglect the ports or the documents of Section Marine, including Series B3, Correspondance à l'arrivée, in the Archives Nationales in Paris, especially Series 4JJ, Journaux du bord (pilot's logs). The Archives Nationales, Paris, is by far the most important depository for French Louisiana. Section Coloniales, Series C13A, C13B, and C13C, Louisiana, is essential. Section Coloniales, Series C6, Sénégal et côtes occidentales d'Afrique, Boxes 5 through 12, is most relevant for the slave trade from Senegal to Louisiana.

There are vast amounts of little-explored documentation about Africans and Afro-Creoles of Spanish Louisiana in the Archivo General de Indias in Seville, Spain. The best discussions of documents in Spanish archives important for the history of Louisiana are by Light Townsend Cummins, "Spanish Louisiana," and Gilbert C. Din, "Sources for Spanish Louisiana," in *A Guide to the History of Louisiana*, ed. Light T. Cummins and Glen Jeansonne (Westport, Conn., 1982). The Historic New Orleans Collection has an ambitious project to microfilm documents relating to Louisiana from the Papeles de Cuba and the Papeles de Santo Domingo at the Archivo General de Indias in Seville, and it has already received a significant part of these documents. The Center for Louisiana Studies at the University of Southwestern Louisiana, established in 1967 by Glenn R. Conrad, its present director, has accumulated an extraordinary microfilm collection of documents in French, including reports of the post *comandantes* during the Spanish period. For a full discussion of the holdings of this remarkable collection, see Carl A. Brasseaux, "The Colonial Records Collection of the Center for Louisiana Studies," *Louisiana History*, XXV (1984), 181–88.

The New Orleans Public Library houses the Acts and Deliberations and Letters, Petitions, and Decrees of the Cabildo of New Orleans. The originals are extremely hard to read. The English translation is almost incoherent. The Spanish transcription is best to work with and can be purchased on microfilm. Church records, especially vital statistics records—births, deaths, and marriages—are valuable sources, but their availability varies from one diocese to the other in Louisiana. Those for New Orleans are now quite inaccessible. The records controlled by the Archdiocese of Baton Rouge are housed at the Catholic Life Center in that city and are well organized, maintained, and accessible. While some of these records have been published, those about people of African descent have been neither thoroughly analyzed nor published. Before 1786, vital statistics maintained at St. Francis Church of Pointe Coupee were entered into the same book, regardless of race. From 1786, vital statistics relating to people of African descent were kept in a separate book, Registre baptistaire et mortuaire des nègres, 1786–1838. Baptismal records dating between 1814 and 1834 are missing, very likely to conceal the African descent of people reputed to be "pure" white.

The volatile and often contradictory relationships among blacks and Indians on mainland North America during the eighteenth century has only begun to be studied with some depth and sophistication with the publication of Gary B. Nash's exciting work, *Red, White and Black: The Peoples of Early America* (Englewood Cliffs, N.J., 1974). The earlier work of Kenneth Porter, "Negroes on the Southern Colonial Frontier, 1670–1673," *Journal of Negro History*, XXXIII (1948), 53–78, relied heavily upon secondary sources without consulting many unpublished manuscripts in English, much less in French or Spanish. William S. Willis, Jr., in "Divide and Rule: Red, White, and Black in the Southeast," *Journal of Negro History*, XLVII (July 1963), 157–76, erred in assuming that the colonizers' divide-and-rule policy was always a reality. Jane Landers' exciting work, "Black Society in Spanish St. Augustine, 1784–1821" (Ph.D. dissertation, University of Florida, 1988), uses unpublished Spanish, as well as English, documents. This work is being revised for publication by the University of Illinois Press.

Much has been published about maroons throughout the Americas. For recent bibliographies, see Richard Price, ed., *Maroon Societies: Rebel Slave Communities in the Americas* (2nd ed.; Baltimore, 1979), 399–416, Gad Heuman, ed., *Out of the House of Bondage* (London, 1986), 185–96, and Joseph C. Miller, *Slavery: A Worldwide Bibliography, 1900–1982* (White Plains, N.Y., 1985), 438–39, regularly updated in *Slavery and Abolition*. Recent studies of maroons on the Anglo–North American continent focus upon quantitative studies of advertisements for runaway slaves: their disappearance and recapture. See Daniel C. Littlefield, *Rice and Slaves: Ethnicity and the Slave Trade in Colonial South Carolina* (Baton Rouge, 1981), Gerald W. Mullin, *Flight and Rebellion: Slave Resistance in Eighteenth-Century Virginia* (New York, 1972), and Philip D. Morgan, "Colonial South Carolina Runaways: Their Significance for Slave Culture," in *Out of the House of Bondage*, ed. Heuman, 57–78. In these advertisements, particular attention was paid to stating the African nations of the runaways, the better to identify them. Advertisements for runaway slaves seem to be one of the best sources for studying African nations brought to the Anglo–North American continent, where Africans ran away far out of proportion to their numbers in the slave population. We do not have such sources for eighteenth-century Louisiana. There was no newspaper in the colony before 1796, and runaway slaves were rarely recaptured during the eighteenth century. But we do have rich, extensive administrative records about runaways and, even more important, a considerable amount of court testimony by and about runaway slaves. In Spanish Louisiana, the vast majority of runaways were creoles, though there was a high percentage of African slaves in the colony.

The most rewarding and least explored documents are the extensive parish archives dating from the Spanish period. Those for New Orleans are housed at the Notarial Archives at the Civil Courts Building of that city. Some of these documents are available on microfilm through the Mormon Genealogy Branch Libraries. A most useful bibliographic guide to unpublished documents located in Louisiana from the French and Spanish period can be found in Henry Putney Beers, *French and Spanish Records of Louisiana: A Bibliographic Guide to Archive and Manuscript Sources* (Baton Rouge, 1989).

The list of secondary works that deal with Africans and Afro-Creoles in Louisiana during the eighteenth century, both published and unpublished, is short. Charles Gayarré's *History of Louisiana* (4 vols.; 1854–66; rpr. Baton Rouge, 1974), dates from the mid-nineteenth century. While an interesting and pioneering work, it touches only slightly upon people of African descent. It is, in general, not too accurate and, in places, tends to be more myth than history. Unfortunately, it has not been superceded because of the linguistic and other difficulties involved in researching and reinterpreting colonial Louisiana history. The most impressive modern work on colonial Louisiana was published by the French historian Marcel Giraud, *Histoire de la Louisiane française* (4 vols.; Paris, 1953–74). LSU Press has published Vol. 5: *A History of French Louisiana: The Company of the Indies, 1723–1731*, trans. Brian Pearce (Baton Rouge, 1991). He writes very little about Africans, Afro-Creoles, slavery, or the slave trade, however. Joe Gray Taylor's work *Negro Slavery in Louisiana* (Baton Rouge, 1963) touches briefly on the colonial period, relying upon a few published translations. Marcus Bruce Christian's interesting and as-yet-unpublished manuscript, "For a Black History of Louisiana," has been frequently cited in this book and can be consulted at the Earl K. Long Library of the University of New Orleans. There is an important Ph.D. dissertation written by James T. McGowan, "Creation of a Slave Society: Louisiana Plantations in the Eighteenth Century" (University of Rochester, 1976). McGowan discovered an impressive number of hitherto unknown documents located in Louisiana, including the testimony in the Pointe Coupee Conspiracy Trial of 1795. This was a pioneering work, especially for a dissertation. Although there are some inaccuracies, they could have been corrected and they are perfectly understandable in the light of the difficult nature of the study and the time pressures that beginning historians are subjected to in the profession. It is tragic that this scholar did not continue his work in history. Daniel H. Usner, Jr., is revising his dissertation, "Frontier Exchange in the Lower Mississippi Valley: Race Relations and Economic Life in Colonial Louisiana, 1699–1783" (Duke University, 1981), for publication. Derek Noel Kerr has written a useful dissertation, "Petty Felony, Slave Defiance and Frontier Villainy: Crime and Criminal Justice in Spanish Louisiana, 1770–1803" (Tulane University, 1983), which includes listings and discussions of criminal cases in Spanish Louisiana. Thomas Marc Fiehrer's dissertation, "The Baron de Carondelet as Agent of Bourbon Reform: A Study of Spanish Colonial Administration in the Years of the French Revolution" (Tulane University, 1977), is an administrative study dealing with a pivotal time in the history of Spanish Louisiana when slave unrest could not be ignored. A number of interesting new works about the free people of African descent in Colonial New Orleans are being prepared and published. Most notable among these are Kimberly S. Hanger, "Personas de varias clases y colores: Free People of Color in Spanish New Orleans, 1769–1803" (Ph.D. dissertation, University of Florida, 1991), Thomas N. Ingersoll, "Free Blacks in a Slave Society: New Orleans, 1718–1812," *William and Mary Quarterly*, XLVIII (April, 1991), 173–200, and Lois Virginia Meacham Gould, "In Full Enjoyment of their Liberty: The Free Women of Color of the Gulf Ports of New Orleans, Mobile, and Pensacola, 1769–1860" (Ph.D. dissertation, Emory University, 1991), a study that is partially sociological in approach and touches upon Spanish New Orleans. There

are two important books published in Spanish: Antonio Acosta Rodríguez'
La población de la Luisiana española (1763–1803) (Madrid, 1979) is a demographic study based upon Spanish censuses, and Juan José Andreu Ocariz'
Movimientos rebeldes de los esclavos negros durante el dominio español en Luisiana
(Zaragosa, 1977) is a well-researched book about slave unrest in Spanish Louisiana. Paul F. Lachance has published interesting articles about eighteenth-
century Louisiana, though his work now focuses on the early nineteenth century. See, for example, Lachance, "The Politics of Fear: French Louisianians
and the Slave Trade, 1786–1809," *Plantation Society*, I (1979), 162–97.

The normal sources used for studying slavery in the United States—
plantation records, planters' diaries, slave narratives, newspapers, maga-
zines, and parliamentary debates—are absent for eighteenth-century Louisiana. There are a few good memoirs of officials and accounts by travelers.
Nevertheless, the sources for eighteenth-century Louisiana are uniquely rich.
There is extensive testimony of slaves and free people of African descent in
court cases. Attention is paid to the African nations of origin of slaves who
testify, as well as of slaves listed in notarial documents dating from the Spanish period. It appears that this attention was characteristic of French slave
owners in the Americas. From the Pointe Coupee documents already thoroughly studied and analyzed, as well as from a sampling of documents from
other settlements in Spanish Louisiana, one can see that local appraisers' attention to identifying African nations is unusual, compared not only with
appraisers in eighteenth-century Anglo-America but also with appraisers in
the French Caribbean. Among the 1,836 Africans on lists of slaves from Guadeloupe between 1770 and 1789, 1,162, or 63 percent, were described as
nègres de Guinée, a vague term meaning, broadly, from the coast of West and
Central Africa. The nations of only 674 Africans were identified. See Nicole
Vanony-Frisch, *Les esclaves de la Guadeloupe a la fin de l'ancien régime d'après les
sources notariales (1770–1789),* extrait du *Bulletin de la Société d'Histoire de la
Guadeloupe,* Nos. 63–64 (1985), 21, 27, 33, 152. Only 19 percent of the Africans
at Pointe Coupee were listed by vague terms such as *slaves of Guinea, brut,
bozal,* or *African.* Attention to the African nations of the slaves would appear
to be more intense in Louisiana than in St. Domingue. During the 1960s,
Gabriel Debien and a team of French historians published a series of articles
based upon studies of lists of slaves made by notaries in the French West
Indies. These lists were relied upon by Curtin in his famous Atlantic slave
trade study. The most detailed lists came from various regions in St. Domingue, which Curtin broke down decade by decade, identifying the regional origin of the vast majority of the African slaves. From the slave lists
produced by Debien and his associates for St. Domingue, Curtin counted 188
Africans for the 1760s, 174 for the 1770s, 568 for the 1780s, and 570 for the
1790s—fairly small numbers coming from a colony with a huge slave population, estimated to be about half a million by 1790 (Curtin, 192–95). Roseline
Siguret, in her study of slave lists coming from the Jacmel region between
1757 and 1791, indicates that many of these lists did not specify the nations

of origin of the African slaves. See Siguret, "Esclaves d'indigoteries et de caféières au quartier de Jacmel (1757–1791)," *Revue française d'Outre-Mer*, LV (1968), 190. The sampling by Debien *et al.* from islands other than St. Domingue is sparse and scattered in time. David Geggus is doing a more detailed study of slave inventories from St. Domingue. For some recently published results, see Geggus, "Sex Ratio, Age, and Ethnicity in the Atlantic Slave Trade: Data from French Shipping and Plantation Records," *Journal of African History*, XXX (1989), 23–44.

The samplings used by Curtin for Peru and Mexico are small. Relying upon James Lockhart, *Spanish Peru, 1532–1560: A Colonial Society* (Madison, Wis., 1968), Curtin counted 207 African slaves on lists dating between 1548 and 1560 in Peru and identified their nations and regional origins. The sample Curtin used for Mexico derives from the work of Aguirre Beltran, *La población negra de México, 1519–1810* (Mexico, 1946), from one inventory dating from 1549: that of the property of Hernando Cortes, consisting of 123 African slaves, only 83 of whom could be identified by place of origin (Curtin, 96–98).

Barry W. Higman studied slave registration lists from the British West Indies compiled between 1812 and 1834 as part of the process leading up to abolition of slavery. The Higman study, *Slave Populations of the British Caribbean, 1807–1834* (Baltimore, 1984), contains quite complete information about the African origins of slaves in colonies that had been French or had a large French creole population: that is, St. Kitts, St. Lucia, Trinidad, Berbice, and Anguilla. These were the only British colonies that listed the particular African nations of the slaves. While these lists are practically complete, they are frozen in time. The most numerous and detailed information on African nations of the slaves came from Trinidad, which had been colonized to a great extent by free colored planters from Martinique (see Higman, Table 2.1, p. 8, and Appendix, Sec. 3, Birthplace, 442–59). A. Meredith John, *The Plantation Slaves of Trinidad, 1783–1816: A Mathematical and Demographic Enquiry* (Cambridge, Eng., 1988), a study of slave demography in Trinidad, pays extraordinarily little attention to African slaves and none to their nations or regions of origin, though such data are far from lacking in the sources consulted.

Stuart B. Schwartz, *Sugar Plantations in the Formation of Brazilian Society* (New York, 1985), paid slight attention to pinpointing the origins of the slaves in plantation records and parish registers in Brazil, no doubt because of lack of information in the sources. Pierre Verger, in *Flux et reflux de la traite des nègres entre le Golfe de Bénin et Bahia de Todas os Santos du 17ième au 19ième siècles* (Paris, 1968), made a study over time of the origins of the slaves inherited by minors in Bahia. His work was based upon inventories that had been previously published in *Anais de Archivo Publico da Bahia*, Vol. XXXVII. These lists date between 1737 and 1841. Only 18 particular African nations or places of origin are used in the lists, and these designations include the vague term *Guinea* (see Verger, Appendix III, pp. 672–83). Studies of the African origins of slaves are less developed for the English Atlantic colonies and for the thirteen original states of the early United States. The sources on African origins of the slave population in the Chesapeake appear to be thin. See Philip D. Morgan, "Slave Life in Piedmont Virginia, 1720–1800," in *Colonial Chesapeake Society*, ed. Lois Green Carr, Philip D. Morgan, and Jean B. Russo (Chapel Hill, 1988), 433–84. Discussions in the recent literature focus on the regions of origin, as defined by Curtin, of the slave trade ships, and on calculations from data published in Curtin's *Census*, by Roger Anstey in *The Atlantic Slave Trade and British Abolition, 1760–1810* (Atlantic Highlands, N.J., 1975), and by Elizabeth Donnan in Donnan, ed., *Documents Illustrative of the History of the Slave Trade to America* (4 vols.; Washington, D.C., 1935). Particular attention to African origins of slaves seems to have been characteristic of French slave owners, and those of Louisiana were the most scrupulous in recording this information.

Stuart Schwartz wrote the first systematic, computerized study of emancipation based upon emancipation records in Bahia, Brazil. See Schwartz, "The Manumission of Slaves in Colonial Brazil: Bahia, 1684–1745," *Hispanic American Historical Review*, LIV (1974), 603–35. Nicole Vanony-Frisch has published a computerized study of slaves from notarial records from Guadeloupe between 1770 and 1789. In *Les esclaves de la Guadeloupe à la fin de l'ancien régime d'après les sources notariales (1770–1789)*, she studies, among other important questions, race mixture among slaves, but she does not discuss emancipation at all, which leaves us in the dark about the extent to which race mixture led to emancipation and the extent to which emancipation reduced the numbers of racially mixed slaves. A study of changing patterns of emancipation can enlighten us about evolving attitudes and policies toward race mixture. Vanony-Frisch concludes that there was a rigid hierarchy of, and exclusive attitudes toward, race and color among slave and free in the French West Indies that was most intense in St. Domingue but was nevertheless strong in Martinique and Guadeloupe as well. Although our study involves French planters during a closely parallel time period, we find some striking differences between Louisiana and Guadeloupe. In Louisiana, attitudes toward race and color were much more flexible among all sectors of the population.

Professional historians are encouraged to emulate the values of the production line. It is speed and quantity that count, not quality, and certainly not originality. The study of colonial Louisiana offers penalties, not rewards. The historian must master both French and Spanish, not simply be able to count slaves on lists, or even read books and published documents. Documents from the Spanish period are often in French. Progress in researching and writing Louisiana history without neglecting its crucial African and Afro-Creole component will require a team of historians with language skills, open minds, and a high level of motivation.

Index